Second Edition

Misconceiving Canada

The Struggle for National Unity

Kenneth McRoberts

Oxford University Press is a department of the University of Oxford.
It furthers the University's objective of excellence in research, scholarship,
and education by publishing worldwide. Oxford is a registered trade mark of
Oxford University Press in the UK and in certain other countries.

Published in Canada by
Oxford University Press
8 Sampson Mews, Suite 204,
Don Mills, Ontario M3C 0H5 Canada

www.oupcanada.com

First Edition published in 1997

Library and Archives Canada Cataloguing in Publication

McRoberts, Kenneth, 1942-, author
Misconceiving Canada: the struggle for national unity / Kenneth
McRoberts. – Second edition.

Includes bibliographical references and index.
Issued in print and electronic formats.
ISBN 978-0-19-902581-7 (softcover).—ISBN 978-0-19-902582-4 (PDF)

1. Federal government–Canada. 2. Canada–English-French
relations. 3. Québec (Province)–History–Autonomy and independence
movements. 4. Canada–Politics and government–1963-1984. 5. Canada–
Politics and government–1984-1993. 6. Canada–Politics and government–
1993-2006. 7. Canada–Politics and government–2006-2015. I. Title.

FC98.M37 2018 971.064 C2018-903492-0
C2018-903493-9

Cover image: Steve Bly/Getty Images
Cover design: Laurie McGregor
Interior design: Sherill Chapman

Oxford University Press is committed to our environment.
Wherever possible, our books are printed on paper which comes from
responsible sources.

Printed and bound in Canada

1 2 3 4 — 21 20 19 18

Misconceiving Canada

Contents

Acknowledgements

Preparing a new edition of a book such as this, after the passage of 20 years, is a daunting, even foolhardy, task. More is required than a simple updating to take account of developments since the original edition was prepared. Over the last two decades, a great amount of scholarship has offered new and important insights into many of the issues that were treated in the original edition. In addition, of course, that edition provoked critical commentaries that need to be taken into account. Finally, the mere passage of time can produce new perspectives on the major issues of the past. For all these reasons, preparing this new edition has been akin to preparing a new book. Most of the original chapters have been extensively revised and rewritten; a new chapter seeks to take account of recent developments. While the basic argument remains the same, hopefully it has been strengthened in the process.

In the original edition, I acknowledged the contribution that a large number of colleagues, as well as graduate students, made to the preparation of that volume. I remain very much in their debt. As well, in preparing this new edition I have been able to draw upon commentaries on draft chapters provided by several individuals: Graham Fraser, Danielle Juteau, André Lecours, Marcel Martel, David Miller, Alain Noël, Roberto Perin, Peter Russell, Don Stevenson, and Reg Whitaker. I thank them for their collegial support. In addition, I would like to join Oxford University Press in thanking a number of reviewers: Julián Castro-Rea, Raffaele Iacovino, Sanjay Jeram, Stephen Kenny, and Brian Tanguay, along with four individuals who wish to remain anonymous. I deeply appreciate all these contributions to the project while bearing in mind that, as ever, final responsibility for the manuscript remains with me.

At Oxford University Press, Katherine Skene was quick to embrace the notion of a revised edition, as was Stephen Kotowych who helped bring it forward. Kerry O'Neill offered a rigorous and thorough, yet enthusiastic, reading of the various chapters as I drafted them. Heather Macdougall provided careful copy editing.

As was the case with the original version, this revised edition is dedicated to Susan Chapman, my wife. Neither edition would have been possible without her unwavering understanding and support.

Timeline of Main Events

5 July 1960	Jean Lesage becomes Quebec premier after his party, the Liberals, defeat the Union nationale in a general election.
10 September 1960	Formation of the Ralliement pour l'indépendance nationale, committed to Quebec independence.
22 April 1963	Lester Pearson becomes prime minister of Canada after Liberals defeat Progressive Conservatives, led by John Diefenbaker, in a general election.
1 February 1965	Royal Commission on Bilingualism and Biculturalism releases its *Preliminary Report*.
16 June 1966	Daniel Johnson, Sr, becomes premier after the Union nationale defeats the Liberals in a general election. In that election, parties committed to Quebec independence, the Ralliement pour l'indépendance nationale and the Ralliement national, win no seats but together receive close to 9 per cent of the popular vote.
14 October 1967	René Lévesque leaves Quebec Liberal Party over rejection of his proposal for sovereignty-association.
6 April 1968	Pierre Elliott Trudeau selected as leader by Liberal Party convention.
20 April 1968	Pierre Trudeau becomes prime minister of Canada.
2 October 1968	Jean-Jacques Bertrand becomes Quebec premier.
13 October 1968	Parti québécois is formed with René Lévesque as leader.
June 1969	Trudeau government releases white paper: "Statement of the Government of Canada on Indian Policy."
9 September 1969	Official Languages Act receives royal assent.
12 May 1970	Robert Bourassa becomes Quebec premier after the Liberals win a general election in which the Parti québécois wins seven seats but 23.5 per cent of the popular vote.
17 June 1971	First ministers agree to Victoria Charter for a patriated and revised Canadian constitution. However, Quebec premier Bourassa rescinds his conditional agreement five days later.
8 October 1971	Pierre Trudeau presents policy on multiculturalism to House of Commons.
25 November 1976	René Lévesque becomes premier after Parti québécois wins Quebec provincial election.
4 June 1979	Joe Clark becomes prime minister after Progressive Conservatives defeat Liberals in a general election.
3 March 1980	Pierre Trudeau becomes prime minister once again after Liberals win a general election.

20 May 1980	In Quebec, 60 per cent vote No in referendum on sovereignty-association.
28 September 1981	Supreme Court declares that the Trudeau government's plan to seek constitutional patriation and revision would be legal but would violate convention unless it had a "substantial degree" of consent among the provinces.
5 November 1981	All first ministers but René Lévesque agree to terms of patriation and revision of the Canadian constitution. Lévesque declares Quebec's opposition to the agreement.
17 April 1982	Queen Elizabeth, in person at Ottawa, gives royal assent to Constitution Act, 1982.
30 June 1984	Pierre Trudeau steps down as Liberal leader; John Turner becomes prime minister.
17 September 1984	Brian Mulroney becomes prime minister after Progressive Conservatives win a general election.
3 October 1985	René Lévesque steps down as Parti québécois leader; Pierre-Marc Johnson becomes Quebec premier.
12 December 1985	Robert Bourassa becomes premier once again after Liberals defeat Parti québécois in a general election.
21 July 1988	Canadian Multiculturalism Act receives royal assent.
28 July 1988	Revised Official Languages Act receives royal assent.
30 April 1987	First ministers agree to Meech Lake Accord.
23 June 1990	Meech Lake Accord fails because time limit for ratification has been reached.
15 June 1991	Creation of Bloc québécois, with Lucien Bouchard as leader.
25 June 1993	Brian Mulroney steps down as prime minister to be replaced by Kim Campbell.
4 November 1993	Jean Chrétien becomes prime minister after Liberals win a general election.
11 January 1994	Daniel Johnson, Jr, replaces Robert Bourassa as premier.
26 September 1994	Jacques Parizeau becomes Quebec premier after Parti québécois wins a general election.
30 October 1995	In Quebec, 50.58 per cent vote No in referendum on Quebec sovereignty.
29 January 1996	Lucien Bouchard replaces Jacques Parizeau as premier of Quebec, while Parti québécois remains Quebec government party.
20 August 1998	Supreme Court of Canada presents judgement on Quebec secession.
29 June 2000	Clarity Act receives royal assent.
8 March 2001	Lucien Bouchard steps down as premier to be replaced by Bernard Landry.

29 April 2003	Jean Charest becomes Quebec premier after Liberals defeat Parti québécois in a general election.
12 December 2003	Paul Martin becomes prime minister after Liberals win a general election.
6 February 2006	Stephen Harper becomes prime minister after Progressive Conservatives win a general election.
27 November 2006	House of Commons adopts resolution declaring that "the Québécois form a nation within a united Canada."
19 September 2012	Pauline Marois becomes Quebec premier after Parti québécois wins a general election.
23 April 2014	Philippe Couillard becomes Quebec premier after Liberals win a general election.
4 November 2015	Justin Trudeau becomes prime minister after Liberals win a general election.

Introduction to the Second Edition

When the original edition of this book was published, back in 1997, Canada was still recovering from the 1995 referendum on Quebec sovereignty. Clearly, with a result so razor-thin—a No vote of 50.6 per cent and a Yes vote of 49.4 per cent—it could have gone either way. Fewer than 55,000 voters had made the difference, preventing the breakup of Canada.

The book sought to explain how the country could have reached such a state of affairs. Simply put, it placed primary responsibility on a national unity strategy that had been conceived by Pierre Elliott Trudeau and implemented during the 1970s and 1980s under his leadership as prime minister. At the heart of the strategy was rejection of the dualist notions, which had long enjoyed public support in Quebec, that Canada is based on two founding peoples and that the Quebec government has the privileged role of speaking for the Francophone people, since most of Canada's French-speaking population is located in that province. Instead, through the new strategy Quebec Francophones would be led to identify with all of Canada, rather than just their province. This would be accomplished primarily by raising the status of French, both in Ottawa and across the country. Entrenching language rights would be the essential purpose of a charter that would come about with the patriation of Canada's constitution. In this way, the Quebec government would hold the same status as the other provinces and, as a result of these reforms and their impact on Quebeckers, would no longer be able to draw upon the premise of two "founding peoples."

Yet, the book argued, these measures were not sufficient to lead Quebec Francophones to drop their historical attachment to Quebec, let alone their belief in Canadian dualism. To compound matters, the new charter was adopted without the agreement of the Quebec government. A subsequent effort to get that agreement failed due primarily to Trudeau's personal campaign against it, defending his vision of Canada. In the wake of this failure, support for Quebec independence surged dramatically, leading to the near victory of Yes forces in the 1995 referendum.

All this, the book contended, stemmed directly from a conception of Canada, articulated by Trudeau, that clashed with Quebeckers' historical understanding of the country and was largely rejected by them. At the same time, this conception of Canada had a strong appeal to Canadians outside Quebec where, responding to the English-Canadian search for a new national identity, it became the basis of a new Canadian nationalism that, by definition, precluded recognition of Quebec's specificity or Francophones' status as a "founding people."

As a result, after decades of federal "national unity" efforts, Quebec Francophones and Canadians in the rest of the country were further apart than they had ever been before. A strategy intended to create national unity had produced precisely the opposite effect and had helped to make the breakup of the country a very real possibility.

Now, 20 years later, Canada seems to be in a very different state. National unity is no longer at the forefront of public debate. In Quebec, support for independence has fallen dramatically, securing only a minority of Quebeckers, and the standard-bearer of sovereignty, the Parti québécois, is in difficult straits. The PQ's federal-level counterpart, the Bloc québécois, is no longer a significant political force. Indeed, Canada has just completed a year-long celebration of its 150th anniversary. It's as if the crisis of 1995 never happened—or never could happen again. One might even conclude that Pierre Trudeau's national unity strategy has succeeded at last. Indeed, outside Quebec there has been a certain revival of interest, if not nostalgia, in Pierre Trudeau himself. The year 2016 alone saw the publication of no less than three English-language books about him, two explicitly focused on the "Trudeaumania" of the late 1960s; another two books appeared in 2017.[1] To top it off, another Trudeau, the son of Pierre, has become prime minister.

Yet appearances can be deceiving. In its new edition, this book continues to argue that Canada has survived not *because* of the national unity strategy but *despite* it. It's due to the strategy and its consequences that federalist forces came so close to losing the 1995 referendum. In fact, they had to break from the Trudeau vision to secure the support they did get, professing sympathy for a measure ("the distinct-society clause") that Trudeau had vigorously opposed. Trudeau himself was kept out of the referendum campaign.

Moreover, present-day Canada remains profoundly affected by the prolonged national unity crisis—and by the strategy that produced it. The most glaring consequence of the pursuit of that strategy is that Canada's constitution remains incomplete. Thirty-five years after patriation Quebec is still not a signatory to Canada's constitution, even if during most of those years it has been led by governments committed to the federal order. The main effort to remedy the situation, the Meech Lake Accord, ended in a debacle. Since then, no serious discussions have taken place. Justin Trudeau rejected out of hand a plea by the Quebec government for a new conversation among Canadians that might lead to Quebec's constitutional signature, declaring that such an effort would be an exercise in semantics and would distract attention from important matters. Yet the constitution is a matter of fundamental importance in *any* country, and a federal system in particular must rest on the formal consent of all its components. Beyond that, in the case of Canada the continuing failure to secure Quebec's consent to the constitution precludes resolution of other constitutional issues for which there is widespread public concern.

The continuing influence of the Trudeau vision also hampers deliberations on the question that has displaced Quebec as the central focus of public debate in Canada: the status of Indigenous Peoples. As with the Quebec question, the fate of Indigenous Peoples cannot even be comprehended within the vision of national unity that Pierre Trudeau conceived. His White Paper on Indian Policy, with its individualist assumptions, made that very clear, as did Trudeau's opposition to the recognition of Indigenous Peoples in the ill-fated Charlottetown Accord of 1992. As in its original edition, this book argues that both questions, relating to Indigenous Peoples and to Quebec, can be addressed only by retrieving the conception of Canada that had informed most of its history. This historical conception is of a Canada that is based upon compacts among communities, whether they be the provinces, linguistic collectivities, or even Indigenous Peoples. Within this conception, Canada is neither just a collection of individuals, nor a single nation. Indeed, as with Quebec, the first step in addressing the status of Indigenous Peoples is to reconfigure Canada as a multinational federation.

Finally, while support for independence may be currently low in Quebec the contemporary importance of secession movements in such settings as Scotland and Catalonia suggests that even in Quebec new circumstances could put independence back on the political agenda. Only the recognition of Canada's multinational character can accommodate the Quebec identity and thus prevent yet another escalation in support for independence.

In sum, as when this book was first published, there are compelling contemporary reasons to assess critically the vision of national unity that dominated the federal government during the 1970s and much of the 1980s, and to weigh the consequences of the strategy that sought to put it in place. At the same time, the work of scholars and observers over the last two decades has produced a wealth of new material that bears directly on the book's argument. In addition, the political life of the last two decades must be taken into account. Finally, the act of reflecting on the past should itself produce new thoughts and insights.

For all these reasons, a new edition of the book seems to be in order. However, more is needed than simply an update to cover the years since the book was originally published. Accordingly, for this edition most of the chapters of the original text have been extensively revised and even rewritten. The argument, however, remains very much the same.

As with the original edition, the book begins by exploring the deep historical roots of the conception of Canada that Trudeau and his colleagues attempted to change. In particular, Chapter 1 shows how Francophones have long seen themselves not only as a distinct collectivity but, for over two centuries, as a collectivity rooted in Quebec. Inevitably, that has meant seeing Confederation on a dualist basis, as the creation of two founding peoples, with Quebec as the centre of the Francophone people. Historically, English Canadians saw Confederation very differently, starting from the premise that they were part of a British nationality that transcended Canada. At the same time, English-Canadian leaders came to see Canada itself as a "compact" among the colonies that formed it. To that extent, there was the basis of a common framework through which English Canadians and French Canadians could understand Canada. They might disagree over precisely who the parties to the compact were—whether colonies and provinces, or nations and "races"—but at least Confederation itself was a compact among collectivities, however defined.

In the 1960s, the rise of a new nationalism in Quebec forced the federal political leadership to re-examine the relationship between Quebec and the rest of the country. At first, as Chapter 2 shows, it searched for formulas to accommodate the nationalist demands for a new relationship. The Liberal government of Lester Pearson led the way. Not only did Pearson himself openly recognize Canada's dualist foundations and the central place of Quebec within them, but he appointed a royal commission to determine how Canada might become an "equal partnership between the two founding races." He and his colleagues also developed an "asymmetrical" view of Canadian federalism, by which the Quebec government was able to assume responsibilities that in the rest of the country remained with the federal government. Both the Progressive Conservative (PC) Party and the New Democratic Party (NDP) formulated similar policies on Quebec, in the process radically departing from their own traditions. Within the NDP, the "Waffle Movement" took the process of reimagining Canada one step further by declaring *English Canada* to be a nation, along with Quebec. Prominent English-Canadian intellectuals were closely involved in all these endeavours. One could even talk of a consensus among English-Canadian élites on the need to accommodate Quebec nationalism.

Yet, as Chapter 3 shows, by the late 1960s this general consensus had been replaced by a new national unity strategy, formulated by Pierre Elliott Trudeau. The strategy was itself rooted in a world view, distinctive to Trudeau, that was based on his particular experiences and trajectory. After being committed until his mid-twenties to the creation of an independent Quebec state, Catholic and Francophone, Trudeau turned against Quebec nationalism, indeed all forms of nationalism, and embraced the primacy of the individual and freedom of choice. Steadfastly attached to these new beliefs the rest of his life, Trudeau was especially fervent in his antipathy to *Quebec* nationalism and, for this reason, constructed his strategy to defeat it by implanting a new vision of Canada centred on constitutional entrenchment of official bilingualism. Given his hostility to Quebec nationalism, Trudeau could not count on the automatic support of his Quebec colleagues during his campaign for the leadership of the Liberal Party. Nevertheless, with his selection as party leader and his subsequent election as prime minister, Trudeau was able to persuade English Canadians that his vision of Canada and his strategy for achieving it were in fact "what Quebec wanted."

His vision became the basis of a new Canadian nationalism, tied to the Canadian state. The effort to put that vision in place was to dominate the next 16 years of Canadian political life and to leave a lasting imprint on Canada's institutions.

The centrepiece of the national unity strategy was official bilingualism, the subject of Chapter 4. After examining the recommendations of the Royal Commission on Bilingualism and Biculturalism, we see how federal language policy was shaped by Trudeau's own individualism and conception of national unity. Significant recommendations of the B&B Commission were ignored in the process. The effort to create a truly bilingual public service was undermined. Moreover, by calling for official bilingualism not just at the federal level but at the provincial level as well, the Trudeau government's language policy clashed with the Quebec government's attempts to support the French language in Quebec, which was clearly the priority of most Quebec Francophones. Moreover, it provoked resistance among Anglophones in other parts of the country. Over time the individualist assumptions of Trudeau's approach to language were overridden by the demand of Francophone minorities that support of the French language be focused on the Francophone *communities* rather than individuals. But, even then, the demographic decline of the Francophone minorities has not be reversed. Finally, Trudeau's emphasis on personal bilingualism provoked a rise in bilingualism among Canada's Anglophones. However, that phenomenon is also in decline. More than ever, despite the vigorous language measures of the Trudeau years, Francophones, and bilingualism, are concentrated primarily in Quebec.

Chapter 5 deals with another component of what became the Trudeau vision of Canada: multiculturalism. Unlike official bilingualism, Trudeau never displayed much interest in multiculturalism. Indeed, it did not sit easily in his personal world view, which was all about the primacy of the individual and freedom of choice. Nonetheless, as a vision of Canada, multiculturalism did serve the purpose of supplanting biculturalism, to which Trudeau was very much opposed. As policy, however, multiculturalism strayed from Trudeau's individualism to embrace the preservation and enhancement of groups—leading even to apologies to groups for past state transgressions. More to the point, multiculturalism did not dissolve the underlying cultural duality of the country. Over the years, Quebec not only developed an alternative policy framework, interculturalism, but conducted its own debate about cultural accommodation and secularization.

Finally, the Trudeau government tried to reform Canada's political institutions to make them accord better with its vision of the country. Beyond strengthening the symbols and practices of Canadian sovereignty, this meant asserting the role and visibility of the federal government as the "national" government of all Canadians. In particular, it meant giving Canada a constitution that would better embody the Trudeau vision. Chapter 6 shows how the Trudeau government was remarkably successful in achieving this objective. Indeed, the Constitution Act, 1982, conforms precisely to the priorities that Trudeau had enunciated in 1967, not only patriating the constitution but inserting a bill of rights with language rights as its centrepiece. At the same time, this fundamental constitutional change was secured without the consent of the Quebec government or the National Assembly and was opposed by a broad range of federalists in Quebec, including the leader of the Liberal Party. In effect, this crowning measure of the national unity strategy directly violated the basic view of Canada, including the notion of a "double compact," held by generations of Francophones. The two principal attempts to remedy this major failing, the Meech Lake Accord and the Charlottetown Accord, both ran up against the deep loyalty among Canadians outside Quebec to the Trudeau vision—and were defeated by it.

As Chapter 7 argues, the 1995 Quebec referendum with its near victory of the Yes vote can only be seen as proof of the failure of the Trudeau strategy. The several years before the referendum had seen a remarkable surge in support for independence, precipitated by the collapse of the Meech Lake Accord—itself the result primarily of Pierre Trudeau's dramatic intervention. At the same time, the referendum demonstrated that, for most Quebeckers, support for independence was conditioned on a continuing economic, and even political, partnership with the rest of Canada. Neither the Trudeau vision of Canada nor full Quebec independence could secure majority support. For its part, the Supreme Court helped to attenuate this impasse with a pioneering judgement on Quebec secession that demonstrated the richness of Canada's constitutional tradition. While overly rigid, the Clarity Act gave form to the Court's basic contention that secession could be accomplished under the rule of law.

Chapter 8 traces political developments over the two decades since the Quebec referendum. In particular, it shows how each of several federal governments and two federalist Quebec governments sought to break with the Trudeau orthodoxy. Asymmetrical arrangements have become the norm in federal–provincial relations. In the House of Commons, the federalist parties even contrived a recognition of the *Québécois* nation. Yet no government has felt itself able to address the fundamental weakness of the 1982 constitutional revision: the absence of Quebec from the signatories. There could not be a clearer demonstration of the enduring impact of the national unity strategy or of the Canadian nationalism to which it gave rise.

The concluding chapter reviews the remarkable success with which Pierre Trudeau was able to put in place the elements of his strategy. But it also analyzes how that strategy failed to secure its essential objective: transforming how Quebec Francophones see Canada and their place within it. Finally, it shows how Canada's future can be assured only by escaping the premises of the Trudeau strategy, and the Canadian nationalism which they spawned, and recognizing directly Canada's essence as a multinational federation.

Note

1. The books alluded to in this paragraph are: Allen Mills, *Citizen Trudeau, 1944–1965: An Intellectual Biography* (Toronto: Oxford University Press, 2016); Paul Litt, *Trudeaumania* (Vancouver: UBC Press, 2016); Robert Wright, *Trudeaumania: The Rise to Power of Pierre Elliott Trudeau* (Toronto: Harper Collins, 2016); Darryl Raymaker, *Trudeau's Tango: Alberta Meets Pierre Elliott Trudeau, 1968–1972* (Edmonton: University of Alberta Press, 2017); and Robert Bothwell and J.L. Granatstein, *Trudeau's World: Insiders Reflect on Foreign Policy, Trade, and Defence, 1968–84* (Vancouver: UBC Press, 2017).

Part I

Two Visions of Canada

Chapter 1

The First Century

Separate Nationalities

From the beginning, English-speakers and French-speakers have seen Canada in fundamentally different ways. At the time of Confederation, most Anglophones saw themselves as members of a British nationality that transcended the boundaries of the new Dominion, whereas most Francophones identified with a *canadien* nationality that fell considerably short of these boundaries. By the same token, the ways in which they understood the basic terms of Confederation were fundamentally contradictory, and continued to be so. To this day most Anglophones and Francophones have different, indeed incompatible, visions of Canada.

The attachment that most Francophones feel to Canada has been mediated through their continued primary attachment to a more immediate, distinctly Francophone society, itself a national community. Moreover, they have tended to see this collectivity as rooted in Quebec. Indeed, the link between Francophones and the territory of Quebec was formalized in 1791, through the Constitution Act that established Lower Canada as a distinct colony. Historically, Francophones have been divided over the precise boundaries of their national community. Whereas many have limited it to Quebec, others have extolled the idea of a *nation canadienne* that extends throughout Canada wherever Francophones are present. Some have even gone further, imagining an *Amérique française* that includes parts of the United States inhabited by Franco-Americans. Few, though, have seen their nation as the whole of Canada.

For that matter, the very term *Canadien* emerged long before Confederation. With the transformation of New France into a British colony, *Canadien* was appropriated to designate all residents of the colony, Francophone and Anglophone alike. Francophones then began to call themselves *Canadiens français*. Yet the ambiguity persisted: for many Francophones, *Canadien* continued to designate their own distinctly Francophone society.

Historically, Anglophone Canadians have seen themselves, and Canada, very differently. Initially, most of them saw themselves first and foremost as members of a larger collectivity that subsumed Canada: the British Empire. Indeed, this was the primary basis of a sense of nationality. Sir John A. Macdonald captured a strong popular sentiment when he declared in 1891, "A British subject I was born and a British subject I will die."[1] Confederation was itself quite consistent with that imperial sentiment since it had been encouraged by the British Colonial Office. The Confederation project did imply an incipient Canadian nationalism, but this new nation was to be an integral part of the Empire. To quote Sir John A. again, the new Canada was to be "a British nation under the British flag and under British institutions."[2]

Some Anglophones, of course, also identified strongly with their historic colonies. In particular, Maritimers hesitated to link their futures with Canada, fearing that their economic interests would be subordinated to those of the other provinces. For that matter, the residents of Upper Canada (modern-day Ontario) had themselves functioned as a separate entity from 1791 until the creation of the United Canadas in 1840.[3] For them, a primary purpose of Confederation was to escape "domination" by Lower Canada. But there was an important difference between these colonial identities and the *canadien* identity: they were not based on a sense of nationality. For most Anglophones, nationality remained British.

With time, and the decline of Britain, the sense of a British nationality atrophied. By and large, it was replaced with a new conception of a Canadian nationality, directly attached to the Canadian state and unmediated by any previous identity. Few Anglophones have felt any attachment to a distinctly English-Canadian nationality.

To be sure, the involvement of Indigenous Peoples with Canada has also stemmed from their membership in a prior collectivity, but until quite recently Indigenous Peoples were not in a position to force their claims upon the Canadian political scene. If only because of their much larger numbers, Francophones (at least in Quebec) have always been able to do so.

The Roots of Nationality

The sense of distinct nationality that Francophones brought to Confederation had taken form decades before, borne of the struggles between Francophones and Anglophones in Lower Canada. It was based on a collective identity as *Canadiens* that had been firmly established during the French regime.

The *canadien* identity seems to have emerged quite spontaneously. The various French regional identities that colonists brought to New France gradually merged into a common *canadien* identity, just as their various vernaculars merged into a common French dialect.

This process was fostered not only by palpable cultural differences from, and open conflict with, the Indigenous population and the rival English-speaking colonists, but also by simple isolation from metropolitan France. It was further strengthened by struggles for power and status between the permanent residents of the colony (or *habitants*) and the metropolitan French who monopolized the positions of authority—ecclesiastical, political, and military—in the colony. Certainly, this process of "identity formation" was not fostered or even sanctioned by the colonial authorities.

At the same time, of course, New France did not produce a nationalist movement seeking autonomy from France in the name of the *Canadiens*.[4] That was precluded not only by the colony's economic dependence on France, but also by the absolutist ethos that reigned in the colony. Nor did the mere fact of conquest produce a nationalist movement.[5] That was not to come until several decades later.

Nevertheless, the sense of collective identity among the *Canadiens* and their attachment to their cultural distinctiveness were sufficient to frustrate the British plans for the new colony. Under the Royal Proclamation of 1763, the Catholic Church would have lost its legal status and privileges, the seigneurial system would have been eliminated, and the common law would have replaced the civil law of the *ancien régime*. The first colonial governor quickly concluded that this assimilationist strategy could not succeed, and these provisions of Proclamation were never enforced.

The Origins of Dualism

Twelve years later, the colonial authorities switched to the opposite policy of formally recognizing and legally entrenching the distinctive *canadien* institutions. Under the Quebec Act, the Church's legal privileges (including the right to collect tithes) were restored, the seigneurial system was re-established, and the civil law was adopted for the colony. In this way, the Quebec Act laid the basis for Canadian dualism. Even today, supporters of Canadian dualism begin with the Quebec Act as they construct their cases.

At the same time, the dualism of the Quebec Act was purely traditional: at the urging of clerical leaders, an elected representative assembly was not established in the colony. More fundamentally, this cultural dualism was profoundly conservative, restoring as it did the quasi-feudal privileges of the Church and seigneurs. But that situation did not last long, for the clamouring of a growing Anglophone merchant class and an emerging *canadienne* petite bourgeoisie of liberal professionals resulted in the Constitution Act of 1791.

Linking Culture and Territory

The Constitution Act granted representative institutions to the British colony and divided it into Lower Canada and Upper Canada. Although, strictly speaking, the division was territorial, the rationale was to accommodate cultural dualism. In the words of the British colonial secretary, its main purpose was to reduce "dissensions and animosities" among two "classes of men, differing in their prejudices, and perhaps in their interests."[6] The measure served to link Francophones with a specific territory. In the words of the historian George F.C. Stanley, the act "was to give renewed vigour to the idea of French Canadian separateness. It provided the French fact with a geographical as well as a political buttress."[7] Once established, this buttress was to prove unmovable.

At the same time, the separation of the "two classes of men" was not complete, and in Lower Canada, the Francophone majority and Anglophone minority were soon embroiled in a dispute over control of the colony's political institutions. In the new legislative assembly the *canadien* majority, led by an increasingly assertive petite bourgeoisie composed largely of liberal professionals, challenged the predominance of executive bodies in which Anglophones were in the majority. Fuelling the steadily growing struggle was a conflict of economic interests between the Anglophone colonial bourgeoisie and the predominantly agrarian *Canadiens*, with their liberal professional leaders. But the struggle was also due to periodic attempts by Anglophone leaders to advance the old dream of assimilation by eliminating separate Francophone schools or reuniting Upper and Lower Canada.

By the early 1800s, these conditions had produced a full-fledged nationalist movement that claimed the status of nation for the *Canadiens* and demanded more power for Lower Canada's representative assembly and greater autonomy for the colony itself from Britain.[8] Although, during the 1830s, this struggle for democracy enlisted some members of Lower Canada's Anglophone population, it remained quite distinct from a comparable popular movement developing in Upper Canada. The armed insurrections that broke out in both colonies in 1837 were themselves dualist, functioning separately under two very different leaders: Louis-Joseph Papineau and William Lyon Mackenzie.

With the defeat of the rebellions, the British authorities gave Lord Durham the task of determining the cause of the insurrection and devising prescriptions to ensure it would not happen again. In his report, which he wrote in 1838, Durham saw French–English dualism as the heart of the problem. In an oft-quoted passage Durham declared, "I expected to find a contest between a government and a people; I found two nations warring in the bosom of a single state: I found a struggle not of principles but of races."[9] Accordingly, while recommending that responsible government be granted, he proposed that the two colonies should be merged into one—the United Canadas.

The purpose of the second recommendation was to eliminate the cultural underpinning of dualism. Citing the assimilation of Louisiana's French-speakers as a model, Durham declared, "The only power that can be effectual at once in coercing the present disaffection, and hereafter obliterating the nationality of the French Canadians, is that of a numerical majority of a loyal and English population."[10] Expressing the belief in the superiority of British civilization that pervaded the British ruling class and that perhaps followed logically from his own liberalism,[11] Durham insisted that in any event such an assimilation would be to the benefit of the *Canadiens*: "There can hardly be conceived a nationality more destitute of all that can invigorate and elevate a people, than that which is exhibited by the descendants of the French in Lower Canada, owing to their retaining their peculiar language and manners. They are a people with no history, and no literature."[12]

The United Canadas: Formalizing Dualism

In one of the greatest ironies of Canadian history, not only did cultural dualism survive union, but the political institutions of the new United Canadas soon evolved into a most elaborate scheme of political dualism. Indeed, the French-Canadian attachment to the United Canadas, with its cultural and political security, was to complicate greatly the subsequent transition to Confederation, and the memory of this dualism was to affect how French Canadians evaluated the development of Confederation.

In fact, the new assimilationist strategy had little chance of success. As William Ormsby noted, "The assimilation of French Canada would have been difficult, if not impossible, in 1791—fifty years later it was an entirely unrealistic objective."[13] The colonial governors soon realized this; their masters in London took much longer to do so.

Unfortunately, from the point of view of the assimilation policy, the link between French Canadians and a specific territory could not be completely eliminated. If the two Canadas had been fully merged and seats in the new common legislature awarded according to representation by population, Lower Canada would have had considerably more seats than Upper Canada. Accordingly, Upper and Lower Canada were maintained, under new names—Canada West and Canada East.[14] They were assigned equal numbers of seats. Only English was to have official status in the new legislature.

Durham and the British colonial authorities had incorrectly assumed that the English Canadians in the new legislature would be sufficiently cohesive to exploit their numerical preponderance and form a reliable government. But divisions soon developed among the English Canadians over responsible government, which the British refused to grant. As a result, the initial Conservative government was soon defeated by defections to Robert Baldwin's Reform caucus. In the name of responsible government, it formed a coalition with French Canadians under Louis-Hippolyte Lafontaine, who had been briefly involved in the 1837 insurrection. Although the colonial secretary in London was furious, he finally had no choice but to accept a government formed of this Baldwin–Lafontaine coalition.

Beyond the issue of responsible government, the English Canadians of Canada West and Canada East were also separated by the inevitable economic rivalry between Toronto and Montreal. And Canada West was divided by a host of internal issues.[15]

Finally, as Douglas Verney has shown, the British colonial authorities apparently felt obliged to allow Quebec's public service, with its predominantly French-Canadian clientele, to continue providing services in French. Nor did they eliminate the Quebec civil law or the Church's responsibility for education. Thus, the United Canadas maintained separate senior administrative positions, such as provincial secretaries, commissioners of Crown lands, and deputy superintendents of education.[16]

Given this intractable social reality, the United Canadas developed an elaborate set of practices.[17] First, thanks in part to the dualism in administrative structures, the ministries were themselves dual. There were separate superintendents of instruction and ministers of public works for Canada East and Canada West. There were even dual prime ministers.

Second, the capital actually shifted between Canada East and Canada West. During its first session, in 1841, the new legislature decided that the capital should alternate between Quebec City and Toronto,[18] but after that, repeated efforts to agree on a permanent site failed. During the 1840s, Kingston and Montreal were also used as capitals. In 1849 the legislative assembly decided that the capital should alternate between Quebec City and Toronto every four years. Although this arrangement must have produced major administrative costs and delays,[19] a contemporary did allow that the "perambulating system" also brought benefits: "It had undoubtedly the effect of making not only the public men but all men of large affairs in either province very much better acquainted with the state of things and the temper of the people in Quebec and Ontario, respectively, than they were ever before or since."[20]

Third, the provision that all records of the United Canadas legislature should be in English alone was eliminated in 1848. Fearful of rising French-Canadian discontent, the Canadian governor had already called for such a move in 1845. But his recommendation provoked the extreme displeasure of Prime Minister Sir Robert Peel. Three years passed before the British Parliament finally repealed the offensive provision. In 1849 the governor, Lord Elgin, began the practice of reading the Throne Speech in both English and French.[21]

Finally, within the Union legislature a certain presumption developed that a measure affecting one of the sections would not be adopted unless a majority of the members of that section were in favour. During the Confederation debates, Sir John A. Macdonald was to claim this had been a rigorous practice of the legislature: "We have had a Federal Union in fact, though a Legislative Union in name."[22] However, over the years there were a good many occasions when this presumed "double-majority" convention was not followed.[23] In the mid-1840s leaders of the

French-Canadian caucus had tried, unsuccessfully, to establish the principle that the government should itself be constructed on the double-majority principle.[24] Lower Canadian and Upper Canadian seats in the Executive Council would be controlled by whatever party had the legislative majority in that section. Nevertheless, at least among the French-Canadian members there was a belief that the affairs of the United Canadas should be guided by the notion of double majority.

It is striking to see how far dualistic practices were extended, given not only the assimilationist intent that lay behind the United Canadas but also the requirements of parliamentary procedure. For instance, according to established practice only one minister could be appointed prime minister. Thus, as Verney recounts, the leaders of the Upper Canadian and Lower Canadian partners in the government, who usually held the position of attorney general, would simply decide which one of them the governor should appoint first (prime) minister (later, they assigned the title to a third member).[25] In practice, however, they functioned as co-leaders.

Nevertheless, by the 1850s the very dualism that endeared the United Canadas to the French Canadians of Canada East became intolerable to much of the Canada West political leadership. Changes in population had a lot to do with it. Just as the population statistics had commended to the British and Upper Canadians the premise that Lower Canada should have no more seats than Upper Canada, so the population statistics undid the premise. The 1851 census demonstrated that Canada West's population had become substantially larger than Canada East's. Canada West's Reform leaders were rapidly converted to the logic of "rep by pop," and their old alliance with the French Canadians of Canada East fell apart. Indeed, in their effort to preserve the existing structure, French-Canadian leaders found themselves allied with Canada West's Tories. The new alliance was able to form governments during the 1850s, but in Canada West pressure for a new regime built steadily. The demands by Canada West for rep by pop and French-Canadian resistance led to frequent deadlocks, and a series of governments failed to maintain confidence.

In a fierce denunciation of dualism, Reform leader George Brown declared in 1864, "We have two races, two languages, two systems of religious belief, two systems of everything, so that it has become almost impossible that, without sacrificing their principles, the public men of both sections could come together in the same government. The difficulties have gone on increasing every year."[26] At the time, Brown was advocating a new federalism for the United Canadas in which power would be almost totally devolved to separate legislatures. Shortly after, he joined his long-standing political rivals to embrace a new strategy for escaping the structures of dualism: the incorporation of the United Canadas in an enlarged British North America.

As the forces for Confederation gathered, French-Canadian leaders viewed the prospect of change with alarm. Despite the original intent of union, it had served the French Canadians well. They had been able to force the British authorities to abandon the goal of assimilation and even to accept the formal recognition of French in the United Canadas legislature. Rather than dissolving Quebec in a larger system, the United Canadas had afforded Quebec considerable administrative and even legislative autonomy. Finally, with its far-reaching application of the principle of duality, "union" had given the French-Canadian nation a semblance of equality with English Canada. In fact, between 1848 and 1864, the dual ministries had always had a French Canadian as one of their heads.[27] It would prove difficult to abandon such a practice. Indeed, the experience of the United Canadas and its example of dualism continued to shape French-Canadian political ambitions and notions of justice long after the new regime of Confederation was in place.

For English Canadians, however, the very idea of duality had been thoroughly discredited by the final years of the United Canadas. Not only was a serious application of dualism rendered irrelevant by the changes in population, but the United Canadas had been proven to be unworkable.

The issues were to be joined in 1864 at two conferences. First, in Charlottetown, delegates from the United Canadas joined delegates of the three Maritime colonies. Then at a conference in Quebec delegates of the same colonies, plus Newfoundland, adopted 72 resolutions. The Quebec Resolutions were approved by the legislatures of the United Canadas, New Brunswick, and Nova Scotia. (Approval came only in 1873 in PEI and not at all in Newfoundland.) In December 1866 and early 1867, delegates in London approved the resolutions and put them into the form of a statute. From this process emerged the British North America (BNA) Act, passed by the British Parliament, given assent by Queen Victoria, and placed in effect on 1 July 1867.

Confederation: From Dualism to Federalism

The leaders of the movement for Confederation had no interest in applying the principle of dualism. In the new Canada, French Canadians and Quebec would be very much in the minority. Indeed, for many English Canadians the very reason for Confederation was to escape the stalemates and the alleged subordination to French-Canadian interests that had come to characterize the United Canadas.

By the same token, in his famous proclamation of the new "political nationality" to be created through Confederation, the leader of French-Canadian supporters, George-Étienne Cartier, avoided any forthright evocation of dualism. He insisted that this nationality would be purely political and thus would be fully compatible with the "diversity of the races." In describing this racial diversity, he declared, "In our own Federation we should have Catholic and Protestant, English, French, Irish and Scotch, and each by his efforts and his success would increase the prosperity and glory of the new Confederacy."[28]

Yet such was the sense of nationality and fear of English-Canadian domination among the French-Canadian leaders that they were not prepared to abandon dualism unless another formula, namely federalism, was applied in its place. In fact, as we have seen, a form of federalism had already emerged during the United Canadas. Not only had Lower Canada retained its distinctiveness, as Canada East, but on some occasions the double-majority principle had been observed, giving Lower Canada effective autonomy in matters that affected it alone.

It was clear that federalism would be the price of Confederation, given French-Canadian attitudes, although even then the liberal *rouges* were likely to remain opposed. And the Maritime leaders, fearful of dominance by Upper and Lower Canada, were seizing on federalism as a way to protect their own autonomy.

Indispensable as federalism may have been to securing the necessary support for Confederation, however, the major English-Canadian promoters of the new Canada were most reluctant to embrace it. They wanted a strong government. After all, the leading force for Confederation was the English-Canadian bourgeoisie, which wanted a government with the capacity to underwrite its ambitious engineering projects, such as the construction of railways.[29] And for many English Canadians the threat of military invasion from the United States seemed to warrant the strongest possible government.

Thus, for Upper Canadians in particular, federalism would be at best a regrettable concession imposed by Quebec and, to a lesser degree, the Maritimes. In 1865 Sir John A. reiterated his oft-stated preference for a "legislative union":

> [But] we found that such a system was impracticable. In the first place, it would not meet the assent of the people of Lower Canada, because they felt that in their peculiar position—being in a minority, with a different language, nationality and religion from the majority . . . their institutions and their laws might be assailed, and their ancestral associations . . . attacked and prejudiced.

Second, he noted: "We found too, that . . . there was as great a disinclination on the part of the various Maritime provinces to lose their individuality, as separate political organizations, as we observed in the case of Lower Canada herself."[30]

Nevertheless, he confidently predicted in a famous private letter that within a lifetime the provinces would be absorbed into the federal domain.[31] Indeed, according to some sources, at the final round of constitutional negotiations in London, Macdonald tried once again to secure a unitary system. In this, he had the support not only of most of his Anglophone colleagues but of the British colonial authorities as well. Only a threat by George-Étienne Cartier to return to Canada and mobilize support against this last-minute change prevented it from being carried through.[32]

Not surprisingly, given their desire for a strong central government, many of the English-Canadian participants in the Confederation debates betrayed a quite confused idea of what federalism represented. P.B. Waite says of the authors of the Quebec Resolutions:

> The word "federal" was used to describe the Quebec plan, not because it defined the proposed relations between the central and the provincial governments, but because it was the word the public was most familiar with. . . . The French Canadians and the Prince Edward Islanders insisted that the constitution be federal, and the constitution was certainly called federal; what it was really intended to be was another matter.[33]

Indeed, when Macdonald declared at one point in the debates that the new regime would be based on "the well understood principles of federal government," the ensuing elaborations by his supporters showed that most members of his coalition thought that federalism had to do with different bases of representation in the Senate and the House of Commons![34]

The terms of the BNA Act closely reflect this balance of forces and attitudes. There was little trace of dualism. To be sure, the French language was given equal status with English in the federal Parliament and courts, as well as in the legislature and courts of Quebec. But there was no provision for the hyphenated ministries of the United Canadas. And Quebec representation in the House of Commons was to be based on its population.[35] In the Senate it was fixed at one-third.

The new regime did give Quebec a government of its own, restoring what had been lost in 1840. Once again, French Canadians would have a legislature in which they would form the clear majority. But this concession to French-Canadian demands was heavily circumscribed.

First, over the fierce objections of many French-Canadian supporters of Confederation, measures were included to protect the interests of Quebec's English-speakers.[36] That is why the BNA Act guaranteed the status of English in Quebec's legislature and courts.[37] There is no comparable measure protecting the French-Canadian minorities of the other provinces. Similarly, protection of Quebec's English Canadians was also the primary reason why the act protects denominational schools in both Quebec and Ontario.[38] In addition, the act has special provisions to protect the representation of Quebec's English-Canadian districts in the Senate and the Quebec legislature.[39]

Second, the division of powers outlined in the act is heavily weighted in favour of the federal government. To be sure, the provinces were assigned jurisdictions that bore directly upon Quebec's distinctive cultural institutions: education, civil law, solemnization of marriage, health, and so on. Thus, in areas crucial to their cultural survival, French Canadians would not have to rely on a government responsible to a primarily English-Canadian electorate. However, owing to the predominance of the English-Canadian bourgeoisie in the Confederation movement, the federal government was given the critical jurisdictions affecting Canada's economic life, as well as exclusive access to the primary source of revenue, indirect taxes. Moreover, a provision giving Ottawa broad responsibility for "peace, order and good government" and possession of all jurisdictions not exclusively assigned to the provinces was clearly intended to ensure that the federal government would play the pre-eminent role.

Indeed, Ottawa was granted prerogatives that are directly at odds with the federal principle. In particular, it was given the right to "disallow" legislation already passed by provinces and to instruct a lieutenant governor to "reserve" legislation passed by a provincial legislature until such time as federal cabinet should consent. By some readings, the system is not federal at all.[40]

All this did not stop the proponents of Confederation in Quebec from promoting the new regime as a decidedly federal one that would give Quebec a strong government of its own. Indeed, some of the rhetoric has a familiar ring to it. To quote one leading *bleu* newspaper, "In giving ourselves a complete government we affirm the fact of our existence as a separate nationality, as a complete society, endowed with a perfect system of organisation."[41] On the day of Confederation's birth, the same newspaper declared: "As a distinct and separate nationality, we form a state within the state. We enjoy the full exercise of our rights and the formal recognition of our national independence."[42]

In fact, it was apparently the need to make the new regime acceptable in Quebec that led its authors to dub it a "confederation." To quote one authority: "'Federation' and 'confederation' seem to have been deliberately used to confuse the issue. It is clear that there was a certain amount of camouflage. . . . The object was to carry the proposals."[43] By any reasonable standard the system was definitely not a confederation, which would imply that the provinces possess exclusive sovereignty and Ottawa's authority be delegated to it by them. Even its credentials as a federation were far from clear.

Nevertheless, it was on the basis of its promise of federalism that the new regime was accepted in Quebec. Even at that, among the 49 French-Canadian members of the United Canadas legislature, only 27 voted in favour of the proposal. The rest voted against.[44]

Their reason for doing so had been expressed well during the debates by the *rouge* leader, Jean-Baptiste-Éric Dorion:

> I am opposed to the scheme of Confederation, because the first resolution is nonsense and repugnant to truth; it is not a Federal union which is offered to us, but a Legislative union in disguise. Federalism is completely eliminated from this scheme, which centres everything in the General Government. . . . In the scheme we are now examining, all is strength and power, in the Federal Government; all is weakness, insignificance, annihilation in the Local Government![45]

It appears that many English Canadians also saw Confederation in those terms. As Waite observes,

> the French Bleus thought it was [a federation], but for a powerful majority of others Confederation was an attempt to put aside the insidious federal contrivances that had grown up within the Union of Canada, to relegate the questions that had caused them to the care of *subordinate, local* legislatures, and to establish at Ottawa a strong, cohesive, sovereign, central government [emphasis added].[46]

In short, federalism may have been the only basis upon which French Canadians were prepared to give up the dualism of the United Canadas, but its status in the new Confederation was precarious indeed. Over the following decades, political leaders and commentators, especially Francophone, frequently called for a return to the "spirit of Confederation." But it is clear that more than one spirit presided at the deliberations that led to Confederation. From the outset, Anglophones and Francophones had very different understandings of the political order that had been created.

The First Few Decades

As was to be expected, there was virtually no application of the duality principle in the new federal government beyond the provisions of the BNA Act for the use of English and French in Parliament and federal courts. First, the United Canadas' practice of two first ministers was definitively abandoned: in inviting Sir John A. Macdonald to become first minister, the governor general was careful to specify that Sir John A. alone would be prime minister. Indeed, Lord Monck declared, "I desire to express my strong opinion that in future . . . the system of dual First Ministers which has hitherto prevailed, shall be put an end to."[47] Apparently this statement provoked no protest among French-Canadian politicians.[48]

The question of titles was quite a different matter. When Monck recommended that Macdonald be knighted, George-Étienne Cartier refused to accept the lesser title recommended for him, calling it a slight to French Canadians.[49] Eventually, Cartier got his wish. Dualism may have been relegated to the margins of Canadian politics, but French Canadians were not prepared to see it dismissed from the symbolic realm as well.[50] (Of course, Cartier's personal vanity was also a factor.[51])

Second, none of the other cabinet positions was dual. In fact, of the thirteen places in Sir John A.'s first cabinet, only four were held by Quebeckers (three of whom were French Canadian). As W.L. Morton has noted, this was significantly fewer than what the French-Canadian proportion of the Canadian population would have warranted. For that matter, the United Canadas cabinets had always contained *four* French Canadians.[52] Although Cartier was a senior member of the cabinet, as was in keeping with his personal status and long-standing relationship with Macdonald, the other two French Canadians received relatively minor positions.[53]

Third, in Parliament, Quebec's new diminished status followed the terms of the BNA Act. In the House of Commons, where rep by pop was to prevail, Quebec was given 65 of 181 seats. In the Senate, Quebec held 24, or one-third, of the seats.

Finally, the capital no longer alternated between English and French Canada. It was established permanently in Ottawa, overlooking the Ottawa River from the Ontario side.

The organization of the new federal government clearly showed that for Quebec, and its French Canadians, the price of gaining its own provincial government was to lose any claim to dualism in the organization of the common government, beyond the BNA Act's section 133 obligations for the use of French in Parliament and the federal courts.

With time, however, some trappings of dualism appeared in federal institutions. Since the selection of Wilfrid Laurier, the federal Liberal Party has always alternated between English-Canadian and French-Canadian leaders, though without declaring openly that it is bound to do so.[54] Similarly, the first Canadian governor general, Vincent Massey, was succeeded by a French Canadian, Georges Vanier; subsequent federal governments have followed this alternation principle. However, these various office holders were not expected to act as representatives of their linguistic group.

Moreover, there was never any suggestion that dualism should be applied to decision making as it was in the United Canadas. The proportion of Francophones and Quebeckers in the cabinet was roughly equal to their proportions of the Canadian population, and, in particular, there is no evidence that Francophone ministers or Quebec ministers were able to exercise a veto. Perhaps the most significant concession to dualism lies in the provision of the Supreme Court Act, 1875, that two of the six Supreme Court justices should be from the bench or bar of Quebec and in the practice of reserving appeals from Quebec for panels in which Quebec justices are in a majority.[55]

As it happened, the new Quebec provincial government paid greater deference to the principle of dualism, owing to the economic and political strength of its English-Canadian minority. Not only were the provisions of section 133 duly observed in Quebec, but English was used, along with French, as a language of service to the public. Indeed, some documents were routinely published in English only.

Beyond that, English Canadians enjoyed a numerical presence in provincial cabinets that greatly exceeded their share of the population. From 1867 to 1897, three of the six or seven cabinet members were usually Anglophones. In fact, two Anglophones were premier for a short time. The Speaker of the Legislative Council (the appointed upper body) was usually an Anglophone.[56] Moreover, Anglophones were well represented in senior portfolios. In fact, the minister of finance was almost always an English Canadian, who reportedly was usually selected by the Bank of Montreal.[57]

Dualism was also the rule in the new province of Manitoba created in 1870. Here it was due to the fact that Anglophones and Francophones (largely Métis) were almost equal in numbers. This dualism was to be short-lived. By the 1890s the Francophone proportion (including Métis) had fallen to about 10 per cent of the population and English was made the sole language of the Manitoba legislature.[58]

In short, with Confederation dualism persisted primarily in Quebec itself rather than in federal institutions. Rather than a complement to federalism, dualism was a way of blunting federalism, preventing the domination of provincial institutions that would have followed from French Canadians' overwhelming demographic preponderance in the new province. Moreover, it seemed, dualism was acceptable only to protect Anglophone minorities, not Francophone ones.

On the other hand, as Confederation took form, federalism became quite robust—far more so than many of the Fathers of Confederation, especially Upper Canadian ones, had anticipated or would have wanted. It was to be expected that French-Canadian élites in Quebec would value Quebec's full autonomy as a province. For them, federalism was the great compensation for the loss of dualism in Canadian institutions. At first, however, the expression of provincialism was muted by the dominance of the Quebec provincial legislature by *bleu* allies of the Conservative government in Ottawa.[59]

The wariness about Canadian domination with which the Maritimes had viewed Confederation ensured that they would be strongly attached to their provincial governments. Indeed, a year after Confederation the Nova Scotia legislature passed a resolution calling for the repeal of the new arrangement.[60]

It was perhaps less predictable that Ontario's provincial government would become a leading champion of provincial autonomy, given the aversion that many Upper Canadians participating in the Confederation debates seemed to have had for federalism. Nevertheless, some Upper Canadians had in fact developed a strong loyalty to their region before Confederation.[61] Beyond that, Ontario's autonomism was fuelled by class conflict between Ontario farmers and lumbermen, on the one hand, and financial interests allied with Ottawa, on the other.[62] All this was reinforced by partisan conflict between Liberal administrations in Ontario and the Conservative federal government[63] and by the normal self-interest of political élites in the importance of their governments. These factors all combined to make the Ontario government, especially under Oliver Mowat, a leader in defending provincial jurisdiction and powers.[64]

Indeed, Oliver Mowat joined forces with Quebec premier Honoré Mercier to convene the first interprovincial conference in 1887, which five of the seven provinces attended (Conservative-controlled British Columbia and Prince Edward Island declined). Held in Quebec City, the conference approved 22 resolutions calling either for constitutional changes to limit federal powers, such as abolition of its "quasi-unitary" powers, or for increased federal subsidies and access to sources of revenue.[65]

The ultimate evidence of the extent to which the federal principle had taken hold was the celebration by provincial leaders of a new doctrine to justify provincial autonomy: the compact theory of Confederation. The theory was first elaborated in the early 1880s by a Quebec judge, T.J.J. Loranger, who expressed alarm at the threat to specifically French-Canadian interests posed by federal encroachments on Quebec's provincial autonomy. Loranger declared, "The confederation of the British Provinces was the result of a compact entered into by the Provinces and the Imperial Parliament which, in enacting the British North America Act, simply ratified it."[66] From this it followed that there could be no enhancement of federal powers without the consent of all the provincial governments.[67] The theory was quickly embraced by Quebec premier Honoré Mercier, strong advocate of Quebec nationalism, who elaborated it at the 1887 interprovincial conference. In fact, it became a basic tenet of the political leadership of most provinces. By the end of the century, "It would be difficult to find a prominent politician who was not willing to pay at least lip-service to the principle of provincial rights and its theoretical underpinning, the compact theory."[68]

The Revival of Dualism

In embracing the concept of federalism, Mowat and other English-Canadian provincial leaders did not, however, embrace the spirit in which French Canadians viewed it. For most French Canadians the ultimate purpose of Quebec's provincial autonomy was to protect their cultural distinctiveness. For English-Canadian leaders the purpose of provincial autonomy was quite different. Indeed, time would show that they were quite prepared to use provincial autonomy against the distinctiveness of French-Canadian minorities in their own provinces.

At the time of Confederation, French-Canadian leaders from Quebec had expressed little concern about any French-Canadian communities in other parts of the Dominion. Ever since the Constitution Act created a distinct Lower Canada in 1791, it was in Quebec that French Canadians sought to maintain their nationality.[69] The union of Lower Canada with Upper Canada had not led Quebec's French Canadians to extend their notion of a *canadien* nation. To be sure a certain number of Quebec French Canadians did emigrate to Ontario, and the diocese of Ottawa was part of the Church's Quebec province.[70] But the focus *of* Quebec's French-Canadian leaders remained centred on Quebec. Thus, the main virtue of the United Canadas for Quebec lay in the extent to which, through the development of dual ministries and a certain application of the double-majority principle to legislative decision making, Lower Canadians (and the *canadien* majority) were able to exercise some autonomy.

During the Confederation debates there had been no French-speaking participants from Canada West or the Maritime colonies. And of course, no provisions were adopted to protect French language rights in the other provinces. Only denominational rights were protected, and that was essentially the indirect result of the campaign of English Canadians in Quebec to protect their position. The French-Canadian delegates were preoccupied with Quebec's status since protecting the *canadien* nation meant securing the autonomy of Quebec.

Nevertheless, as Arthur Silver has demonstrated, a series of events forced French Canadians in Quebec to take account of the fate and tribulations of French-Canadian communities beyond their borders. In 1871 the New Brunswick legislature passed a statute preventing local school boards from supporting denominational schools. Although the act did not specifically refer to the province's *Acadiens*, Quebec's French-Canadian leaders did become concerned about this treatment of fellow Catholics. Then, in 1885 Ontario forced its unilingual French schools to become bilingual. As members of these minorities took their complaints to Ottawa for redress, Quebec's French Canadians became more aware of their fate.[71]

Events in Manitoba were to have the most powerful impact on Quebec. In 1870 the Métis leader Louis Riel led a rebellion against the terms under which the Red River settlement had become British territory, subject to transfer to Canada. In the process, Riel was responsible for the execution of an English-Canadian opponent. In the 1880s, Riel was at the centre of a new Métis uprising, which was finally put down in 1885. Riel was sentenced to hang and, after the mobilization of Ontario opinion in favour of execution and of Quebec opinion against it, he was indeed executed.

As Silver carefully details,[72] immediately after Confederation French Canadians still had no particular interest in the Canadian North West and were largely opposed to annexation of its territory. However, they developed a certain sympathy for Riel in 1870, especially after they began to see the Ontario campaign against Riel as a campaign against French Catholics. Even then, Riel and his followers were still seen as "savages."[73] Their success in obtaining French language rights under the Manitoba Act of 1870 made them useful allies, but they were not fellow French Canadians. During the 1870s, a debate over whether Ottawa should grant amnesty to the participants in the Red River Rebellion aroused French Canadians to a clearer identification with the Métis cause.

However, when in 1885 Riel was sentenced to hang, emotions in Quebec reached a fever pitch. Believing that Riel was basically insane and that, in addition, the conditions of the Métis constituted extenuating circumstances, French

Canadians tended to see the sentence as an expression of English-Canadian hatred for all French-speaking Catholics. With the hanging, emotions exploded. French-Canadian newspapers declared, "The death of Riel is an impious declaration of war, an audacious defiance hurled at the French-Canadian race" and "We all know that they'd have liked to slit all our throats, to kill all of us French Canadians."[74]

By allowing the execution to take place, the Macdonald government had confirmed that, under Confederation, Quebec French Canadians could not count upon the federal government to protect their interests. In a confrontation between the two linguistic groups, the English-Canadian majority was bound to prevail at the federal level. French Canadians could rely only on the Quebec government to embrace their interests.[75]

Coupled with these developments beyond Quebec's borders, a series of events in Canada's external relations underscored further the inability of French Canadians to make their positions prevail in the federal government. Canada was being called upon to participate in imperial military ventures, and many English Canadians welcomed these opportunities to express their identity as British North Americans. French Canadians, however, tended to reject such ventures, seeing themselves as members of a distinct *canadien* nationality.

First, at the turn of the century Britain called upon Canada to commit Canadian troops to fight in the Boer War. English Canadians were favourable; French Canadians were strongly opposed. Although he first relied on volunteers, Prime Minister Wilfrid Laurier did send a contingent of regular Canadian troops in 1899.

Second, in response to British pressure, Laurier created a small Canadian navy in 1910. While English-Canadian Conservative politicians denounced it as too small, French-Canadian nationalists called it a dangerous move that would make participation in imperial wars inevitable.

Most important of all, during the First World War the federal Union government of Robert L. Borden imposed conscription for overseas service, evoking a tidal wave of protest in Quebec. After imposing the measure, Borden called a federal election, in which his government won only three seats in Quebec.

As if that were not enough, the question of French-Canadian minority rights outside Quebec emerged once again. In 1912, just before the war, Ontario passed Regulation 17, which restricted French-language education, and in 1916 Manitoba abolished bilingual schools.

A "Double Compact"

It was clear that the established version of the compact theory was no longer an adequate protection for French-Canadian interests, since the provinces could evoke it to fend off criticism of their treatment of French-Canadian minorities or federal intervention to force a remedy. And it was no defence against untoward actions of the federal government in its own jurisdictions, whether it be the hanging of Riel or the commitment of Canadians to imperial military adventures.

It fell to Henri Bourassa, the leading French-Canadian nationalist at the turn of the century, to reformulate the theory. This new version was to become deeply rooted in Quebec and to shape fundamentally how its Francophones view Canada.

In 1902 Bourassa presented the notion of a "double compact." Reaching back to the United Canadas, he seized upon its dualism, arguing that it constituted a moral premise of Confederation:

> The imperial statute which the current government has given us is only the force of a double contract. One was concluded between the French and the English of the old province of Canada, while the aim of the other was to bring together the scattered colonies of British North America. We are thus party to two contracts—one national and one political. We must keep a careful eye on the integrity of these treaties.[76]

Thus, beyond a "political" contract, to which all the provinces were party, there was a "national" contract, which was the exclusive product of the United Canadas. The substance of the two contracts differed. Apparently, the national contract guaranteed French–English duality whereas the political contract protected French Canadians from the imposition of imperial military obligations by their English-Canadian compatriots.[77]

There is in fact a certain plausibility to the notion of a dualistic contract that was distinctive to the United Canadas and its successors. Historian George C.P. Stanley has shown how statements by leading Upper Canadian politicians demonstrate that, for many of them, "the mutual acceptance of equality of status was a vital and fundamental principle of the constitution; that it constituted, if not an unbreakable pact, at least a gentleman's agreement between the two racial groups which went to make up the population."[78] Not surprising is Lafontaine's 1849 declaration of support of "the principle of looking upon the Act of Union as a confederation of two provinces." More striking is Sir John A. Macdonald's 1861 claim that "the Union was a distinct bargain, a solemn contract" and his reference in 1865 to the "Treaty of Union" between Lower and Upper Canada.[79] (Considering that the creation of the United Canadas was imposed by the British authorities in an effort to assimilate the Francophones, this was a remarkable reinterpretation of the arrangement.)

To be sure, as they entered into discussions with Maritime leaders about a new Confederation, the leaders of the United Canadas began to refer to a pact between territorial units as opposed to "races."[80] But even then, the notion of compact remained a primarily "Canadian" one, which did not have the same resonance for the Maritime participants. And for the Canadians it retained its "bi-racial" connotations since it was "in its origin, a racial concept." In short, there was a certain basis to Henri Bourassa's claim that there existed a national compact formed in the United Canadas that guaranteed cultural duality.[81]

Of course, Bourassa did not claim that the terms of the compact could be directly derived from the British North America Act, the formal text of Confederation. Neither did Stanley, for that matter. Rather Bourassa (and Stanley) pointed to "the spirit of the constitution." For Bourassa it would be foolish to rely exclusively on a detailed exegesis of the Act's provisions without considering the origins of British constitutionalism and "the particular circumstances that preceded and surrounded the signing of the federal pact."[82] As Ramsay Cook argues, "Bourassa's cultural compact was, in the last analysis, a moral compact."[83]

Yet how could such a cultural compact be applicable throughout the whole of Canada? Bourassa had offered a second line of reasoning in 1905, during a debate over whether minority rights should be recognized in the creation of Alberta and Saskatchewan. Referring to section 93 of the BNA Act, which guarantees denominational schools, Bourassa said it was intended to guarantee that "a man, in whatever province of Canada he may choose to be his abode, can rest assured that justice and equality will reign and that no matter what the majority may attempt they cannot persecute the minority."[84] He acknowledged that this contract was unwritten but argued that it dated as far back as the Quebec Act of 1774. He pointed out, moreover, that the territory upon which the two provinces were to be established had been bought with the money of all Canadians, Catholic and Protestant, English Canadian and French Canadian.[85]

Two additional points about Bourassa's vision of dualism must be stressed. First, if the notion of a cultural compact was developed largely in response to the use that some governments had made of their provincial autonomy at the expense of their French-Canadian minorities, it was not to diminish, let alone replace, the long-standing notion of a compact among all the provinces.[86] After all, Quebec still remained the heart of French Canada, and Quebec's provincial autonomy was the indispensable first defence of French Canada's interests. In Bourassa's words, Quebec was the "particular inheritance of French Canada."[87] Thus, the two ideas remained together in an uneasy co-existence.[88] The contract was a double contract.

In fact, within one formulation of the double contract, the cultural compact was derived from Quebec's provincial autonomy. In 1912 Bourassa argued that, since the main purpose of federalism was to preserve French Quebeckers' nationality as French Canadians, then the possessors of that nationality should have a "right to equality throughout the whole of this confederation."[89]

Second, while strongly committed to the extension of French language rights throughout Canada, Bourassa insisted that the two cultures must remain separate and distinct. His opposition to Canada's participation in imperial military ventures had made him a strong Canadian nationalist, but his nationalism rested on a particular conception of Canada. He did not see it as a single undifferentiated nation. Rather, as his reformulation of the compact theory suggests, he saw Canada as composed of two distinct collectivities. As Bourassa declared in 1912, he was seeking not "some bastard fusion of the two races, in which they would lose their distinctive qualities and characteristics, but a fruitful alliance of the two races, each one remaining distinctly itself, but finding within the Canadian confederation enough room and liberty to live together side by side."[90]

In fact, partly because he saw Canada in such rigorously dualist terms, Bourassa was not prepared to support Canadian independence from Britain. Despite his fierce opposition to British imperialism, he had to recognize that Canada was not ready for independence because "a more open and clear agreement" did not exist between the "races."[91]

In the course of a famous response to Jules-Paul Tardivel, a turn-of-the-century French-Canadian separatist, Bourassa declared:

> The nation which we wish to see developed is the Canadian nation, composed of French Canadians and English Canadians, that is to say a nation of two elements separated by language and religion and by the legal arrangements necessary for the preservation of their respective traditions, but united by a sentiment of brotherhood in a common attachment to a common country.[92]

Thus, Bourassa was careful to stress that the two "elements" were "separated" by language and religion, as well as by the "legal arrangements" necessary to preserve them.

However sincere may have been Bourassa's attachment to Canada, his vision had little resonance with English Canadians, most of whom were unsympathetic to his fierce rejection of imperial military obligations. At the time few English Canadians embraced his notion of a cultural compact.[93] The compact theory had become deeply rooted within English-Canadian politics, but only as a compact among provinces.

In Quebec, however, the notion of a double contract, in which an interprovincial compact was coupled with a national compact between the two founding peoples, became firmly entrenched. Most French-Canadian constitutional scholars were convinced of its existence and vigorously defended it in exchanges with their English-Canadian colleagues.[94] It was invoked regularly by Quebec's political élites. When the Quebec provincial government of Maurice Duplessis passed a law in 1953 authorizing the creation of a royal commission (the Tremblay Commission) on constitutional questions, it began the law with this statement: "Whereas the Canadian Confederation, born of an agreement between the four pioneer provinces, is first and above all a pact of honour between the two great races which founded it."[95] By the same token, in its report the commission duly affirmed the notion of a double compact.[96]

By some accounts, the notion of dualistic compact had by then become a basic premise of all Francophones in Quebec. In 1958 the dean of Francophone sociologists, Jean-Charles Falardeau, declared that however much English Canadians might dismiss such a notion, "the sociologically significant and important fact" is that since the end of the nineteenth century French Canadians have understood Canada in those terms:

> It became a persistent theme, articulated in various forms by French Canada's religious and political leaders right up to the present day. Whether or not English-Canadian commentators and legal scholars find it acceptable, it will persist as one of the most tenacious elements of the way in which French Canadians understand the history of their Canada.[97]

It is clear that during the first century of Confederation English Canadians and French Canadians became rooted in fundamentally different conceptions of the country they shared. For many English Canadians, Canada was simply the North American expression of a British nationality. After all, the institutions created through Confederation had been carefully fashioned on that assumption. As Confederation developed, it took on much more of a federal form than had been expected. Indeed, by the late 1800s, the English-Canadian political élites generally agreed that Confederation itself was based on a compact among the provinces. But the predominant sense of nationality was British, and the symbols of the Canadian political order remained resolutely so.

For their part, the Francophones of Quebec continued to view Canada in terms of their own nationality as French Canadians or *Canadiens*. And this nationality was firmly anchored in the territory and political institutions of Quebec. Formally established in 1791, through the Constitution Act, this link between French Canadians and Quebec had persisted without interruption. Even the forced merger of Quebec with present-day Ontario had not shaken the bond; indeed, union had reinforced it. Involvement in Confederation, and concern with issues beyond Quebec's borders, had not broken this link either: Quebec remained "the particular inheritance" of French Canadians. Instead, Francophone leaders had been led to portray Quebec as central to a dualistic racial compact, supplementing the notion of a provincial compact now firmly established in English Canada.

With the turn of the century, Henri Bourassa and other French-Canadian leaders had started to contest openly Canada's identification with Britain and British nationality and to champion a Canadian nationhood. In this, they matched an emerging sense among English Canadians of a distinctly

Canadian nationality. Yet these two conceptions of Canadian nationhood were fundamentally different. For the French-Canadian political and intellectual élites, any idea of a Canadian nationality was rigorously rooted in cultural dualism. Canada was a "bicultural pact" and Quebec was a partner to that pact. The emerging sense of Canadian nationalism in English Canada had no room for such notions. Indeed, it had little patience for compacts of any kind, whether between races or among provinces.

After the Second World War: Competing Nationalisms

During the Second World War, these competing notions of nationality led to a bitter struggle over the issue of conscription for overseas military service. As a 1942 Canada-wide referendum clearly established, Anglophones were overwhelmingly in favour while Francophones were opposed, claiming that they had no obligation to fight Britain's wars. Nevertheless, the federal government did send some conscripted soldiers overseas. After the war, the contradiction in definitions of nationality gave rise to a new struggle, between Ottawa and Quebec City.

Ottawa as the "National" Government

There were a variety of reasons why the federal government began to assert its new role as the "national" government of Canada. Among many English Canadians, if not French Canadians, pride in the exploits of Canadians in the Second World War heightened the sense of Canadian nationality, as did Britain's postwar decline. During the war, Ottawa had already assumed unprecedented predominance over the provinces. Citing the demands of war, it had deployed emergency powers and persuaded the provinces to allow it to monopolize personal and corporate tax. As the war came to an end, federal officials naturally wished to preserve their new power. Finally, the Keynesian doctrines of economic management and elaboration of a welfare state provided a tailor-made rationale for Ottawa to remain the primary government. Both the depression that followed the First World War and the Great Depression of the 1930s were cited as examples of what might happen if the federal government were to relinquish its new-found ability to steer the Canadian economy and society.

In the postwar years Ottawa took a series of steps to formalize Canadian nationhood. In 1946, the Canadian Citizenship Act was passed, making Canadian citizenship distinct from the status of British subject. In 1949, the Supreme Court was made the final court of appeal in all matters, and the right of Canadians to take cases to the Judicial Committee of the Privy Council was abolished. In 1952, a Canadian was appointed governor general for the first time. The term

"Dominion" was quietly discarded,[98] and the federal government increasingly referred to itself as the "national" government.

By the same token, Ottawa elaborated a complex of social programs, based on the notion that all Canadians were entitled to certain minimum public benefits wherever they might live. As the 1944 Speech from the Throne declared:

> Plans for the establishment of a national minimum of social security and human welfare should be advanced as rapidly as possible. Such a national minimum contemplates useful employment for all who are willing to work; standards for nutrition and housing adequate to ensure the health of the whole population; and social insurance against privation resulting from unemployment, from accident, from the death of the bread-winner, from ill-health and from old age.[99]

This agenda amounted to no less than a "new National Policy," to use Donald Smiley's evocative phase.[100]

At the same time, the federal government became more active in supporting distinctively Canadian cultural production, as a way of reinforcing the national identity of Canadians. In 1949, it established a Royal Commission on National Development in the Arts, Letters and Sciences, declaring in an order-in-council, "It is in the national interest to give encouragement to institutions which express national feeling, promote common understanding, and add to the variety and richness of Canadian life."[101] The commission had a single chair, Vincent Massey, even though in Quebec it was often dubbed "the Massey–Lévesque Commission," suggesting that commissioner Georges-Henri Lévesque was co-chair. The commission called upon the federal government to undertake two major new initiatives to support national cultural life: to create a Canada Council to foster cultural activity and to establish a program of federal grants to universities. Both were adopted during what was, in Claude Bissell's words, "a period of intense nationalism and pride."[102]

This new conception of Ottawa as a national government meant a very different relationship with the provincial governments. If Ottawa was to meet new responsibilities to maintain national standards in such areas as social policy and post-secondary education, it would have to act in jurisdictions that had been assigned to the provinces under the BNA Act and from which, up to that point, Ottawa had been largely absent. In part, this was accomplished through conditional grants that Ottawa made available to the provincial governments on condition that they be devoted to designated programs and abide by conditions set by Ottawa. But it also meant that the federal government was providing funds directly in areas of provincial jurisdiction to individuals, as in the case of family allowances, and to institutions, as in the case of grants to universities. To do all this Ottawa tried to maintain its wartime role as exclusive collector of income tax, a source of revenue that, under the BNA Act, it shared with the provinces. In short, the provinces were to be assigned a subordinate place in "the new National Policy."[103]

As the federal government pursued these goals, sometimes in the face of fierce opposition from some provinces, it was quite prepared to challenge long-standing notions about the prerogatives of the provincial governments. The compact theory had long been rejected by federal officials. Accordingly, during the 1940s Ottawa began to call upon the British Parliament to make amendments to the BNA Act, which remained a British statute, without first obtaining the approval of the provincial governments. In each case, it argued that, since the changes did not affect provincial responsibilities, prior approval by the provincial governments was not necessary. Each of the requests was granted. Two of them, including the amendment governing Newfoundland's union with Canada, were made over Quebec's objections. Finally, in 1949 Ottawa obtained an amendment to the BNA Act giving it the power to alter unilaterally certain parts of the act that, it contended, did not affect the provinces.[104] In effect, Ottawa rendered moot the essential premise of the compact theory: that the constitution was, in its entirety, a pact among the provinces that could not be altered without their consent.

Despite Quebec's consistent opposition to Ottawa's initiatives, the later ones in fact had been the work of a French-Canadian prime minister, Louis St. Laurent. Fully bilingual and bicultural,[105] St. Laurent saw Canada in resolutely individualist terms, dismissing any notion of a dualist Canada composed of distinct collectivities:

> He saw the relationship between French and English Canadians not on a group, but on an individual basis, as citizens of the same state, with equal rights. He described his concept of Canadian citizenship as "a situation of absolute equality, equality not only in the text of our constitutional laws but practical equality in the daily application of these texts, in the real situation of each individual . . . in his everyday relations with his fellow citizens."[106]

From the outset of his career in federal politics, St. Laurent had explicitly rejected the compact theory of Canada, flatly declaring in 1943, as justice minister, "Confederation was not really a pact among the provinces."[107] Hence, he regularly insisted that Ottawa had the right to change unilaterally parts of the constitution that did not directly involve the provinces. Once he even appeared to confirm that Parliament had the power to eliminate application of section 133 regarding the use of English and French, although he was clearly opposed to such a measure.[108] In a famous 1954 Quebec City speech in which he denounced Quebec separatism and proclaimed that Francophones were fully able to compete with other

Canadians, St. Laurent scandalized Quebec nationalists by declaring that "the province of Quebec can be a province like the others."[109]

With St. Laurent as prime minister, appealing to an incipient Canadian nationalism, asserting Ottawa's pre-eminence as the national government, and proclaiming Ottawa's constitutional powers, the federal government's challenge to the predominant French-Canadian view of Canada could not have been clearer.

Quebec Government: The National Government of French Canada

The concerted postwar effort of Ottawa to assume the mantle of Canada's national government reinforced the Quebec provincial government in its historical role as government of the French-Canadian nationality, a role which had become well established during the first few decades of the twentieth century.

The dualism of post-Confederation Quebec had begun to decline as the government became a more clearly Francophone institution. The economic predominance of Quebec's Anglophone minority remained very much intact, but its political élites gravitated to Ottawa. After 1920, Anglophone representation in the provincial cabinet was limited to two members, and after 1944 all finance ministers were Francophones.[110]

Moreover, the various crises over the status of Francophones outside Quebec and Canada's imperial military obligations had a marked effect on Quebec's provincial politics. Reaction against the hanging of Louis Riel had resulted in the election of Honoré Mercier's Parti national, born from an infusion of the provincial Liberal Party with French-Canadian nationalists. Anger at the imposition of conscription during the First World War had in 1918 led to a resolution in the provincial legislative assembly proposing that Quebec leave Canada if this should be the wish of the rest of the country.[111] More important, it had sealed the fate of the provincial Conservative Party.

Having failed to win power in 1931, despite the onset of the Depression and the best efforts of a populist party leader to exploit resentment against the English-Canadian "trusts," the Conservatives joined with French-Canadian nationalist forces. In 1935, Conservative leader Maurice Duplessis entered into a formal alliance with Action libérale nationale, a group of nationalists and discontented Liberals. Consolidated under Duplessis's firm leadership, and dubbed the Union nationale, this coalition won control of the Quebec government in 1936. After losing power in 1939, the Union nationale was re-elected in 1944, partly by exploiting the French Canadians' anger at conscription during the Second World War. Confirmed in his nationalist vocation, Duplessis found plenty of ammunition in the need to respond to Ottawa's postwar campaign to become a national government and to intervene in areas hitherto left for the provinces.

The most important elaboration of Quebec's role as the national government of French Canada was in fact a direct response to a federal initiative. The report of the Massey Commission provoked the Duplessis government to appoint a royal commission on constitutional problems, commonly known as the Tremblay Commission. After years of deliberation, the Tremblay Commission produced a voluminous report offering not only a diagnosis of the conflicts within Canadian federalism and an outline of the responsibilities which rightly belong to Quebec, but a statement of the underlying nature of French-Canadian society.[112]

The Tremblay Commission's deeply conservative view of French-Canadian society set the tone of the report as a whole, which was based on the assumption that French Canada was by nature a Catholic society in which the role of government should be limited by the historical reliance upon private institutions. Thus, the recommendations concentrated on limiting the power of the federal government rather than expanding that of the Quebec government. On this basis, the constitutional framework established in 1867 was quite satisfactory, as long as Ottawa retreated from the many intrusions into provincial jurisdictions that had begun in the postwar years.

Although its constitutional position may have been conservative, as was its view of French-Canadian society, the commission offered a strong challenge to Ottawa's claim to be a national government. If "nation" was to be understood in sociological terms, then Ottawa's claim was a clear threat to the French-Canadian nation, which was centred in Quebec. If "nation" was to be understood politically, then the Quebec government had as much claim to national status as Ottawa.[113] Moreover, the commission's demand that the federal government should defer to the provinces in social and cultural policy[114] threatened much of the edifice of programs and services that Ottawa was developing in the name of the Canadian nation.

The Duplessis government demonstrated in quite concrete terms how Ottawa's efforts to establish national programs could be undermined by Quebec's own claims to national status. During the 1950s, the Quebec government simply refused to participate in a number of conditional-grant programs that Ottawa offered to the provinces. These included grants regarding hospital insurance, vocational training, forestry, civil defence, and the Trans-Canada Highway.[115] In addition, the Duplessis government ordered Quebec universities to refuse the direct grants that the federal government established in 1951. The funds that the universities would have received simply accumulated in Ottawa until 1960, when Ottawa and Quebec City agreed to allow Quebec to recover through a federal tax abatement the money intended for universities.

To be sure, this tactic was highly effective in blunting Ottawa's plans, but it was a costly one for the Quebec government. By one estimate, Quebec's non-participation in conditional-grant programs cost it $82,031,000 in federal funds, or $15.60 per capita of the Quebec population, in the fiscal year 1959–60 alone.[116] Only a government that was not itself committed to rapid expansion of the role of the state could contemplate using it. During the 1960s, Quebec governments were to use other strategies, which were even more threatening to Ottawa's plans.

The Duplessis government's refusal to participate in federal programs demonstrated the potential for conflict that lay in the federal government's postwar assumption of the mantle of national government. It also dramatically revealed how the understanding of Canada held by French-Canadian élites differed from that of their English-Canadian counterparts. For, by and large, Quebec's Francophone élites supported the Duplessis government in its vigorous defence of provincial autonomy and in the claim to national status that underlay this defence.[117] In the rest of Canada, political and intellectual élites instead were quite favourable to Ottawa's new initiatives. For that matter, Quebec was the only provincial government that refused to take part in federal shared-cost programs.

In short, during the postwar years the federal government challenged in a way it never had before the established French-Canadian understanding of Canada. In the name of its new role as the seat of the Canadian nation, the federal government began to develop the symbols of a distinctly Canadian nation, to construct an edifice of social, economic, and even cultural programs designed to develop and strengthen the Canadian nation, and to establish national standards of social services that all Canadians, as Canadians, could expect as a basic right. Inevitably, this entailed involvement in provincial jurisdictions. By and large, English-Canadian élites and public opinion welcomed the new power that Ottawa was assuming and the nationalist discourse upon which it rested. Only in Quebec was there resistance, as Francophone élites defended the historical notion of a distinctly French-Canadian nation and of the Quebec government as protector of that nation. Clearly, the new Canadian nationalism which Ottawa was articulating had the potential to divide English Canadians and French Canadians more profoundly than ever before.

From the outset English-Canadian and French-Canadian élites viewed Confederation in very different ways, owing to the profound differences in historical experience, sense of nationality, and central preoccupations that they brought to the new arrangement. As a result, at the time of Confederation they held radically opposed understandings of the nature of the new regime. If they supported it, they did so for very different reasons.

The differences were to persist. The English-Canadian understandings of Canada were to change, as the notion of a British nationality gave way in the postwar years to that of a distinctly Canadian nationality. Despite the fierce determination of many English-Canadian Fathers of Confederation to establish a unitary system, as Confederation developed, most English-Canadian élites became clearly wedded to federalism and even to the notion that it rested upon a historical compact. Yet however much English-Canadian views of Canada may have changed, they remained fundamentally different from those of French Canadians, who continued to be firmly committed to a French-Canadian nationality. For them, federalism had a different purpose, the defence of culture as opposed to regional or economic interest, and the compact that underlay it had to be understood as a "double compact." Ultimately, Confederation could not erase the French-Canadian belief in dualism as a basic principle both of political organization and of justice.

Yet the notions of federalism and compacts at least provided French-Canadian and English-Canadian élites with a common discourse: they simply interpreted the concepts differently. The postwar years demonstrated the reaction that could arise in Quebec if these concepts should be challenged by a federal government that claimed for itself the title of "national" government.

Notes

1. P.B. Waite, *The Life and Times of Confederation, 1864–1867* (Toronto: University of Toronto Press, 1962), 22.
2. Ibid.
3. Robert C. Vipond, *Liberty and Community: Canadian Federalism and the Failure of the Constitution* (Albany: State University of New York Press, 1991), 32–3.
4. Michel Brunet, *La présence anglaise et les canadiens* (Montreal: Beauchemin, 1964), 58.
5. See ibid., 47.
6. As quoted in Peter H. Russell, *Constitutional Odyssey: Can Canadians Become a Sovereign People?*, 3rd edn (Toronto: University of Toronto Press, 2004), 13.
7. George F.C. Stanley, "Act or Pact: Another Look at Confederation," *Proceedings of the Canadian Historical Association*, 1956, 5.
8. Jean-Paul Bernard, *Les rouges* (Montreal: Presses de l'Université du Québec, 1971), 11–19.
9. Gerald M. Craig, ed., *Lord Durham's Report*, Carleton Library no. 1 (Toronto: McClelland & Stewart, 1963), 22–3.
10. Ibid., 154.
11. See William Ormsby, *The Emergence of the Federal Concept in Canada, 1839–1845* (Toronto: University of Toronto Press, 1969), 6; and Janet Ajzenstat, *The Political Thought of Lord Durham* (Montreal and Kingston: McGill-Queen's University Press, 1988).
12. Craig, *Lord Durham's Report*, 150.
13. Ormsby, *Emergence of the Federal Concept*, 123.
14. Stanley, "Act or Pact," 7.
15. Douglas V. Verney, *Three Civilizations, Two Cultures, One State: Canada's Political Traditions* (Durham: Duke University Press, 1986), 197.
16. See the discussion of these points in ibid., 199, and in Ormsby, *Emergence of the Federal Concept*.
17. See the discussion in Donald V. Smiley, *Canada in Question*, 3rd edn (Toronto: McGraw-Hill Ryerson, 1980), 214–17.
18. Ormsby, *Emergence of the Federal Concept*, 106.
19. J.E. Hodgetts, *Pioneer Public Service* (Toronto: University of Toronto Press, 1955), 59.
20. Sir Richard Cartwright, "Reminiscences: Toronto, 1912," 6, as quoted in Hodgetts, *Pioneer Public Service*, 59.
21. Ibid., 118–19.
22. Ormsby, *Emergence of the Federal Concept*, 124.
23. Ibid., 124–5, and Verney, *Three Civilizations*, 200–1.
24. Ormsby, *Emergence of the Federal Concept*, 120.

25. Verney, *Three Civilizations*, 200.
26. As quoted in Ramsay Cook et al., *Canada: A Modern Study* (Toronto: Clarke Irwin, 1963), 83.
27. W.L. Morton, "The Cabinet of 1867," in Frederick W. Gibson, ed., *Cabinet Formation and Bicultural Relations*, Studies of the Royal Commission on Bilingualism and Biculturalism, no. 6 (Ottawa: Queen's Printer, 1970), 4.
28. P.B. Waite, *The Confederation Debates in the Province of Canada, 1865*, Carleton Library, no. 2 (Toronto: McClelland & Stewart, 1963), 50–1. Ramsay Cook sees this passage as an example of the general absence "of anything that might be called 'racial' thinking in the statements of the Fathers"; see Cook, *Provincial Autonomy, Minority Rights and the Compact Theory, 1867–1921*, Studies of the Royal Commission on Bilingualism and Biculturalism, no. 4 (Ottawa: Queen's Printer, 1969), 52. To be sure, later in the same statement Cartier does say that French Canadians and English Canadians would be "placed like great families beside each other." See *The Confederation Debates*, 51. Peter Russell sees this as evidence of dualism; see Russell, *Constitutional Odyssey*, 33.
29. Stanley B. Ryerson, *Unequal Union* (Toronto: Progress Books, 1968), Chap. 18.
30. Waite, *The Confederation Debates*, 40.
31. Arthur Silver, *The French-Canadian Idea of Confederation, 1864–1900* (Toronto: University of Toronto Press, 1982), 36, n. 20.
32. Stéphane Kelly, "Les imaginaires canadiens du 19e siècle," Doctoral dissertation, Département de sociologie, Université de Montréal, 1995, 439. Ryerson calls this "an unconfirmed but plausible story." See Ryerson, *Unequal Union*, 371. See also Jean-Charles Bonenfant, *La naissance de la Confédération* (Montreal: Leméac, 1969), 18. Creighton makes no reference to such a possibility in his account of the London Conference in Donald Creighton, *The Road to Confederation* (Toronto: Macmillan, 1964), Chap. 14.
33. Waite, *Life and Times of Confederation*, 109.
34. Ibid., 110.
35. More precisely, Quebec's House representation was set at 65; representation of the rest of the new Dominion was to be in proportion to that. There was an additional accommodation of cultural dualism: a never-enacted provision of the BNA Act for standardization of law related to property and civil rights did not apply to Quebec, with its civil code (section 94). Finally, section 98 provides that judges of the Quebec courts must be members of the Quebec bar.
36. Silver, *The French-Canadian Idea of Confederation*, 55.
37. Under section 133 of the British North America Act, English and French can be used in the Quebec legislature, must be used in the journals, records, and statutes of the Quebec legislature, and may be used in Quebec courts. The provisions are discussed in Royal Commission on Bilingualism and Biculturalism, *Book I: The Official Languages* (Ottawa: Queen's Printer, 1967), 52–5.
38. As Silver documents, French-Canadian opinion leaders complained that the constitutional protection of Protestant schools demanded by Quebec's English Canadians would be an unacceptable restriction on their new province's autonomy. If such protection should be unavoidable, then fairness at least required that Ontario's Catholic minority should be similarly protected. See Silver, *The French-Canadian Idea of Confederation*, Chap. 3.
39. British North America Act, s. 22 and 80.
40. The British constitutional authority K.C. Wheare took this view. See Garth Stevenson, *Unfulfilled Union*, 3rd edn (Toronto: Gage, 1989), 30.
41. *La Minerve*, 17 July 1866, as translated and quoted in Silver, *The French-Canadian Idea of Confederation*, 41.
42. Ibid.
43. The statement is by W.P.M. Kennedy, as quoted in Ryerson, *Unequal Union*, 443. See also Stevenson, *Unfulfilled Union*, 6–7.
44. Bonenfant, *La naissance de la Confédération*, 11.
45. Waite, *Confederation Debates*, 147.
46. Waite, *Life and Times of Confederation*, 116.
47. Sir Joseph Pope, *Memoirs of the Right Honourable Sir John Alexander Macdonald* (Toronto: Musson, 1930), 339, as quoted in Donald V. Smiley, *The Canadian Political Nationality* (Toronto: Methuen, 1967), 10, n. 12. This reference is drawn from Verney, *Three Civilizations*, 231, who discusses the question at some length.

48. Morton, "The Cabinet of 1867," 4.
49. Ibid., 5. See also the discussion in Kelly, "Les imaginaires canadiens," 442.
50. Sir Charles Tupper, for one, recognized that French Canadians had justly felt slighted by the decision. See A. De Celles, *Cartier et son temps* (Montreal: Beauchemin, 1907), 36, as quoted in Kelly, "Les imaginaires canadiens," 443.
51. Kelly, "Les imaginaires canadiens," 442.
52. "It is possible to hold, therefore, that the French were in some respects under-represented in the cabinet, both in numbers and weight of portfolios." See Morton, "The Cabinet of 1867," 15.
53. Ibid.
54. Peter Regenstreif, "Note on the 'Alternation' of French and English Leaders in the Liberal Party of Canada," *Canadian Journal of Political Science* 2 (Mar. 1969): 118–22. The pattern of alternation has continued to the present day, although classification of Justin Trudeau as Francophone might be problematic. The terms commonly used to refer to two leading royal commissions suggest they had Anglophone and Francophone co-chairs, but that was not the case. With the Rowell–Sirois Commission, Sirois was a commissioner who replaced Rowell as chair upon the latter's resignation. With the Massey–Lévesque Commission, Massey was in fact the only chair.
55. Donald V. Smiley, "French–English Relations in Canada and Consociational Democracy," in *Ethnic Conflict in the Western World*, ed. Milton J. Esman (Ithaca: Cornell University Press, 1977), 193–6.
56. Paul-André Linteau, René Durocher, and Jean-Claude Robert, *Histoire du Québec contemporain: de la Confédération à la crise* (Montreal: Boréal, 1979), 265.
57. Jean Hamelin and Louise Beaudoin, "Les cabinets provinciaux, 1867-1967," in *Le personnel politique québécois*, ed. Richard Desrosiers (Montreal: Boréal, 1972), 99.
58. Janice Staples, "Consociationalism at Provincial Level: The Erosion of Dualism in Manitoba," in *Consociational Democracy*, ed. Kenneth McRae (Toronto: McClelland & Stewart, 1974), 288–302.
59. Cook, *Provincial Autonomy, Minority Rights and the Compact Theory*, 14.
60. Ibid., 10.
61. Robert Vipond presents compelling evidence that support for provincial rights for Ontario was an extension of a sentiment that was already present during the Confederation debates and formally endorsed by the Ontario Reform Party just before Confederation. See Vipond, *Liberty and Community*, 33.
62. Stevenson, *Unfulfilled Union*, 76.
63. Russell, *Constitutional Odyssey*, 35–6.
64. See Vipond, *Liberty and Community*, 33.
65. Cook, *Provincial Autonomy, Minority Rights and the Compact Theory*, 41–3.
66. T.J.J. Loranger, *Letters upon the Interpretation of the Federal Constitution known as the British North America Act (1867)* (Quebec City, 1884), 61, as quoted in Cook, *Provincial Autonomy, Minority Rights and the Compact Theory*, 30.
67. See the discussion in Cook, *Provincial Autonomy, Minority Rights and the Compact Theory*, 31; see also Stevenson, *Unfulfilled Union*, 100–1.
68. Cook, *Provincial Autonomy, Minority Rights and the Compact Theory*, 44. See also Edwin R. Black, *Divided Loyalties* (Montreal and Kingston: McGill-Queen's University Press, 1975), 151–8.
69. Silver, *The French-Canadian Idea of Confederation*, 15.
70. Ibid., 11.
71. Ibid., 23.
72. Ibid., Chap. 4.
73. Ibid., 75.
74. Ibid., 169.
75. To compound matters further, upon his election in 1896 (with strong Quebec support), Wilfrid Laurier entered into an agreement with the Manitoba government that fell far short of the full restoration of French-language Catholic schools that French-Canadian nationalist leaders had been seeking.
76. Henri Bourassa, *Le patriotisme canadien-français: ce qu'il est, ce qu'il doit être* (Montreal, 1902), 8, as translated and quoted in Cook, *Provincial Autonomy, Minority Rights and the Compact Theory*, 57.
77. Cook, *Provincial Autonomy, Minority Rights and the Compact Theory*, 57.
78. Stanley, "Act or Pact," 9.
79. Ibid.
80. Ibid., 13.

81. In 1915 Bourassa insisted that the more important purpose of Confederation was to resolve conflict within the United Canadas and that it took the form of a national contract:

    La Confédération, on ne saurait trop le rappeler, fut *la résultante d'un contrat national*. Ses auteurs avaient en vue deux objets principaux: grouper les diverses colonies anglaises de l'Amérique du Nord et mettre fin aux conflits séculaires des deux races. Le second de ces objets occupa une place plus importante que le premier dans l'esprit des hommes d'État du Haut et du Bas-Canada. (Henri Bourassa, *La langue française au Canada* [Montreal, 1915], 28, quoted in Richard Arès, *Dossier sur le pacte fédératif de 1867* [Montreal: Bellarmin, 1967], 70) (emphasis in original).

82. My translation of "Les circonstances particulières qui ont précédé et entouré la signature du pacte fédéral." (Ibid.)
83. Cook, *Provincial Autonomy, Minority Rights and the Compact Theory*, 62.
84. House of Commons, *Debates*, 1905, 3256, as quoted in ibid., 59.
85. Ibid.
86. Silver, *The French-Canadian Idea of Confederation*, 194.
87. Bourassa, *Le patriotisme canadien-français*, as quoted in Silver, *The French-Canadian Idea of Confederation*, 194.
88. Silver, *The French-Canadian Idea of Confederation*, 194.
89. Henri Bourassa, *Pour la justice* (Montreal, 1912), as quoted in Silver, *The French-Canadian Idea of Confederation*, 205. This construction of Bourassa's argument is Silver's.
90. Bourassa, *Pour la justice*, as quoted in Silver, *The French-Canadian Idea of Confederation*, 193.
91. My translation of "une entente plus franche et plus nette." As Michael Oliver observed in his analysis of Bourassa's political thought, "the plural conception of Canadian nationality was usually subordinate to the dual one." See Michael Oliver, *The Passionate Debate* (Montreal: Véhicule, 1991), 23. Henri Bourassa, *Grande Bretagne et Canada* (1901), as quoted in Jean Drolet, "Henri Bourassa: une analyse de sa pensée," in *Idéologies au Canada français, 1900-1929*, ed. Fernand Dumont et al. (Quebec City: Presses de l'Université Laval, 1974), 232.
92. Henri Bourassa, "Réponse amicale à la Vérité," *Le Nationaliste*, 3 Apr. 1904, as translated and reproduced in Joseph Levitt, ed., *Henri Bourassa on Imperialism and Biculturalism, 1900–1918* (Toronto: Copp Clark, 1970), 107. On Bourassa's rejection of Quebec independence, see Oliver, *Passionate Debate*, 28–30.
93. "It would be difficult to find a single English Canadian who supported the idea in the years before 1921 [the final year of study]—unless Macdonald's candidacy is accepted." See Cook, *Provincial Autonomy, Minority Rights and the Compact Theory*, 62. See also pp. 67–9.
94. Roger Brossard and H.F. Angus, "The Working of Confederation," *Canadian Journal of Economics and Political Science* 3, no. 3 (Aug. 1937): 355, as cited in Arès, *Dossier sur le pacte fédératif*, 84.
95. As reproduced in Quebec, *Rapport de la Commission royale d'enquête sur les problèmes constitutionnels* (Quebec City, 1956), vol. I, v.
96. Ibid., Chap. 5.
97. My translation of

    Elle est devenue un thème persistant, orchestré avec diverses variations par les chefs religieux et politiques du Canada français jusqu'à l'époque contemporaine. Que les publicistes et les juristes canadiens-anglais la trouvent acceptable ou non, elle persistera comme l'un des éléments les plus tenaces de la définition que le Canadien français donne de l'histoire de son Canada. (Jean-C. Falardeau, "Les Canadiens français et leur idéologie," in *Canadian Dualism*, ed. Mason Wade [Toronto: University of Toronto Press, 1960], 25.)

    In a book published in 1999 Stéphane Paquin argues that the notion of a dualist pact has no juridical or conventional standing. Instead, it is simply an "invented myth." (Stéphane Paquin, *L'invention d'un mythe: le pacte entre deux peuples fondateurs* [Montreal: VLB Éditeur, 1999]). Yet, as myth, the dual compact has become so deeply rooted in Quebec that any violation was bound to produce a strong reaction. These issues are examined in Paul Romney, *Getting It Wrong: How Canadians*

Forgot Their Past and Imperilled Confederation (Toronto: University of Toronto Press, 1999).

98. Philip Resnick, *The Masks of Proteus* (Montreal and Kingston: McGill-Queen's University Press, 1990), 57–8, and Donald Creighton, *Canada's First Century* (Toronto: Macmillan, 1970), 277.
99. House of Commons, *Debates*, I, 1944, 2, as quoted in Donald V. Smiley, *Constitutional Adaptation and Canadian Federalism since 1945*, Documents of the Royal Commission on Bilingualism and Biculturalism, no. 4 (Ottawa: Queen's Printer, 1970), 10.
100. Smiley, *Constitutional Adaptation and Canadian Federalism*, Chap. 2.
101. As quoted in Richard Simeon and Ian Robinson, *State, Society and the Development of Canadian Federalism*, Collected Research Studies of the Royal Commission on the Economic Union and Development Prospects for Canada, vol. 71 (Toronto: University of Toronto Press, 1990), 142. See also Joyce Zemans, "The Essential Role of National Cultural Institutions," in *Beyond Quebec: Taking Stock of Canada*, ed. Kenneth McRoberts (Montreal and Kingston: McGill-Queen's University Press, 1995), 138–62; and Paul Litt, "The Massey Commission, Americanization, and Canadian Nationalism," *Queen's Quarterly* 98, no. 2 (Summer 1991): 375–87. While insisting that French-Canadian reaction in general was "remarkably sympathetic" to the commission, Litt acknowledges that French-Canadian nationalists were alarmed at the new responsibilities it proposed for the federal government. See Litt, "The Massey Commission," n. 3. On the other hand, Michael Behiels states that only a "small proportion of French Canadians" supported the Massey Commission and Father Lévesque's position. He details widespread opposition among French-Canadian nationalists. See Michael Behiels, *Prelude to Quebec's Quiet Revolution* (Montreal and Kingston: McGill-Queen's University Press, 1985), 206–11. So too does William D. Coleman, *The Independence Movement in Quebec, 1945–1980* (Toronto: University of Toronto Press, 1984), 70–4.
102. Claude Bissell, *Massey Report and Canadian Culture*, 1982 John Porter Memorial Lecture (Ottawa: Carleton University, 1982), 21, as quoted in Zemans, "The Essential Role of National Cultural Institutions," 147.
103. Smiley, *Constitutional Adaptation and Canadian Federalism*, 18.
104. See the account in Russell, *Constitutional Odyssey*, 65–8.
105. Dale Thomson writes of St. Laurent: "Considered by the population as a whole, and by himself, a French-speaking Canadian, he spoke flawless English, thought in many matters like an English Canadian, and was better informed about English Canada as a whole than some of his English-speaking colleagues." See Dale Thomson, "The Cabinet of 1948," in Gibson, *Cabinet Formation and Bicultural Relations*, 144. St. Laurent was quite able to present Canada as being "a political partnership of two great races," but he did not draw the same conclusions from this as the French-Canadian nationalists and the compact theorists. See Thomson, *Louis St. Laurent: Canadian*, 528.
106. Thomson, "The Cabinet of 1948," 144.
107. My translation of "La Confédération n'a pas été vraiment un pacte entre les provinces." As quoted in Arès, *Dossier sur le pacte fédératif*, 92.
108. When asked whether Parliament had such a right, St. Laurent simply responded that "the principles of British freedom and British fair play" provide a surer protection of language rights than anything contained in section 133. See Thomson, *Louis St. Laurent: Canadian* (Toronto: Macmillan, 1967), 189.
109. My translation of "la province de Québec peut être une province comme les autres." As quoted in Jacques Lacoursière and Claude Bouchard, *Notre histoire Québec-Canada* (Montreal: Éditions Format, 1972), 1104. See also Thomson, *Louis St. Laurent: Canadian*, 378, and J.W. Pickersgill, *My Years with Louis St. Laurent: A Political Memoir* (Toronto: University of Toronto Press, 1975), 256.
110. Hamelin and Beaudoin, "Les cabinets provinciaux," 98–9.
111. The resolution, presented by J.-N. Francoeur, precipitated a widely publicized debate in which legislators denounced English-Canadian treatment of French Canadians and Quebec while declaring their continued belief in federalism and their attachment to Canada. After this debate, the resolution

was withdrawn before any vote was taken. See the account in Linteau, Durocher, and Robert, *Histoire du Québec contemporain: de la Confédération à la crise*, 583.

112. Quebec, *Rapport de la commission royale d'enquête sur les problèmes constitutionnels*, five vols, 1956.
113. Ibid., vol. II, 72.
114. Ibid., 73.
115. Smiley, *Constitutional Adaptation and Canadian Federalism*, 72. Smiley notes that Quebec did accept federal funds in some areas including public health (including hospital construction) and public assistance.
116. Ibid.
117. On the other hand, many Francophone élites were highly critical of the Duplessis government's conservative economic and social policies, and were frustrated by the extent to which Quebec's refusal of federal funds further limited the prospect that the Quebec state would intervene in Quebec's economy and society. See Behiels, *Prelude to Quebec's Quiet Revolution*, and Kenneth McRoberts, *Quebec: Social Change and Political Crisis* (Toronto: McClelland & Stewart, 1993), Chap. 4.

Chapter 2

The 1960s

Coming to Terms with Duality and Quebec Nationalism

The 1960s were marked by an open dialogue and debate about the nature of Canada that died with the end of the decade and would not be repeated in the many decades since. During the 1960s, Francophone and Anglophone Canadians confronted, in a way they never had before, their fundamentally divergent conceptions of Canada. That process was triggered, of course, by developments in Quebec.

Changes in Quebec: Forcing English Canada to Take Notice

As we have seen, most French-Canadian notions of Canadian dualism had always afforded a privileged status to Quebec as the centre of the Francophone collectivity. In the early 1960s, this pre-eminent status of Quebec was made much more explicit as nationalist thought and strategies were fundamentally recast.

The New Quebec Nationalism

The very definition of the nation began to change: in place of a "French Canada," defined in ethnic terms and present throughout Canada wherever people of French descent continued to speak French, intellectual and political leaders began to refer to the nation as "Quebec," a territorial entity consisting of the province of Quebec. Although the Quebec nation was to be predominantly French-speaking, it would not be based on ethnicity. This gradual shift to a territorial conception of nation was due, in turn, to the ascendancy of notions of social and political organization that were difficult to accommodate in the older idea of a French-Canadian nation: those of a modern, secular society.

However sanctified a rural agrarian society might have been in traditional nationalist thought, its fate had long been sealed. The modernization of French-Canadian society was already under way at the turn of the century.[1] By the 1930s, Quebec had become a predominantly urban, industrial society. If French Canada was to survive, it would be as such a society. Nationalists argued that only in Quebec, where French-speakers were the overwhelming majority, was it possible to imagine the full economic, social, and cultural institutions of a modern society functioning in the French language. Even in Quebec the construction of a fully modern Francophone society was a daunting task given both the limitations of the Church-controlled private institutions that continued to dominate education, health, and social services and the extent to which ownership and management of the Quebec economy remained largely in the hands of Anglophones. Only through intervention by the state could these constraints be overcome. By definition, the state that would modernize the Francophone nation had to be a state that was itself under the control of Francophones: the government of Quebec. In short, the Quebec government had to become the *moteur principal* of the new Quebec nation.

Sociologically, the conversion of nationalism to the goals of modernity was due to the multitude of changes in French Quebec society that had been under way during the first part of this century: urbanization, industrialization, the emergence of mass media, and, in particular, the rise of new social classes. The bearers of the ideology tended to be a new middle class of intellectuals, academics, administrators, and other salaried professionals.[2] In their campaigns to have the Quebec state assume more active roles, the new middle class could usually count on the strong support of organized labour.

In ideological terms, the transformation of nationalist discourse resulted from the long-delayed triumph of liberalism in French Quebec. In the early 1800s, liberal conceptions of political authority and the role of the Church had been proclaimed by French-Canadian liberal professionals. They had contributed to the abortive rebellions of the 1830s. But with the failure of the rebellions and the subsequent dominance of the Church in French Quebec, political and social liberalism was very much on the defensive. The twentieth-century modernizing processes fostered a resurgence of liberal forces. By the 1950s, Francophone intellectual and social leaders were decrying the anti-democratic tendencies of the Duplessis regime and calling for an expansion in the social and economic responsibilities of the Quebec state.[3] With the election in 1960 of the Liberal government of Jean Lesage, in which the Francophone new middle class was a major presence, liberal forces had a new foothold in the Quebec state and the period of the Quiet Revolution began.

Many of the greatest achievements of the Quiet Revolution can be seen only as expressions of liberal ideals of democracy and equality. Educational reform involved not only the creation of a ministry of education and construction of a complete public system, but also a concern with social equality in public institutions, as with the CEGEPs' combination of pre-university and vocational education. Electoral practices were fundamentally reformed by establishing the autonomy of the Director General of Elections, reducing disparities in the sizes of constituencies, and regulating party finances through measures—such as reimbursement of electoral expenses—that were then among the most progressive in Western democracies.[4] In the overhaul of labour relations, the right to strike was extended to the public sector, for the first time in North America.

At the same time, the discourse of the Lesage government was also resolutely nationalist. The government proclaimed that the Québécois had to become "maîtres chez nous"—"masters in our own house." The nationalization of private electrical firms to create a comprehensive public hydro utility was justified on a variety of grounds, but certainly one of them was the desire to reduce Anglophone dominance of the upper levels of the Quebec economy. It was primarily in this way that the nationalization would bring about the "libération économique" of Quebec.

In effect, the Quiet Revolution represented a new departure for Quebec: combining nationalism with liberalism. Most observers have interpreted the Quiet Revolution in precisely these terms.[5] Yet for one prominent observer, Pierre Elliott Trudeau, such a combination of nationalism and liberalism was logically impossible. Upon his rejection of the Quiet Revolution would hang much of the future of Canadian politics.

Once it had become predominant among French Quebec's intellectual and political leaders, the new liberal nationalism virtually dictated a radical re-examination of Canada's political structures. Within the new understanding of Quebec and its needs, old Canadian ways of doing things that had always been sore points for Quebec's leaders now became intolerable. And long-standing Francophone assumptions about Quebec and its place in Canada now had to be made explicit.

The Need to Restructure Canadian Federalism

Once the Francophone nationalist leadership had fully embraced modernity and could in fact claim that, at least in Quebec, their society already possessed the defining traits of modernity, the old ideals of dualism and equality with the rest of Canada took on a new urgency. As a modern society, Francophone society could settle for no less than full equality with its Anglophone partner. Moreover, since this modernity achieved its fullest expression in Quebec the demands for equality between Francophone Canada and its Anglophone equivalent tended to focus on Quebec's relationship with the rest of Canada.

The central place of the Quebec government in the project of a modern Francophone society gave a greatly expanded meaning to the long-standing claim that Quebec was not "a province like the others." As the fundamental institution of the Quebec nation, the Quebec government could not have the same status as the other provinces. Indeed, the Lesage government systemically replaced the term "la province de Québec" with "l'État du Québec." Not only did the project of a modern Quebec nation require that the Quebec government be confirmed in the status of a national government, but it meant that the Quebec government's powers and resources had to be greatly expanded so that it could assume its new responsibilities.

In short, the new liberal Quebec nationalism gave rise to demands that the Canadian political order be refashioned to conform better to the Canadian duality and the centrality of Quebec to it. In part, this involved symbolic recognition of these two premises, making explicit for all Canadians what had always been understood among Francophones. But it also entailed major structural changes in federal institutions and in the place of Quebec in the federal system. In both cases, however, the goal of most Quebec nationalists was to redefine the Canadian relationship, not to terminate it.

These objectives were embraced, in one form or another, by each of the three premiers of Quebec during the 1960s. For Jean Lesage, who led the Liberals to victory in 1960, the preferred formula was a *statut particulier.* In an address in Vancouver in 1965, Lesage insisted that however the status of French might be improved in federal institutions, French Canadians "feel that in Quebec there is a government that is able to play an irreplaceable role in the development of their collective identity, their way of living, their civilization, their values. . . . I believe there is nothing wrong, far from it, in recognizing this fact as one of the fundamental elements of Canada's future."

He noted, "We are already on the way . . . to establishing the beginnings of a particular status for Quebec" to which might be added new powers, such as relations with other countries. All this was necessary because the Quebec government, "for historical and demographic reasons, will assume, in addition to the responsibilities that normally belong to a provincial government these days, the special function of being the instrument through which the French-Canadian community affirms itself."[6]

For Daniel Johnson, the Union nationale leader who became premier in 1966, the focus initially was more on restructuring Confederation on a bi-national basis. In his 1965 best-selling book, *Égalité ou indépendance*, Johnson wrote, "This [new Canadian] constitution should, in my opinion, be conceived so that Canada is not only a federation of 10 provinces but a federation in which two nations are equal in law and in fact."[7] As premier, however, Johnson insisted upon additional powers for Quebec, declaring at the 1968 constitutional conference, "Given the insights of our history, the French Canadians of Quebec, who constitute 83 per cent of the Francophone population of Canada, cannot be expected to entrust the leadership of their social and cultural life to a government where their representatives are in the minority and, in addition, are bound by ministerial responsibility and party discipline."[8]

Similarly, at a constitutional conference in 1969, Jean-Jacques Bertrand, who had succeeded Johnson as Union nationale leader in 1968, insisted that Ottawa's proposals for official bilingualism missed the fundamental problem, that of equality between two nations, one of which was centred in Quebec:

> For the French Canadians of Quebec what is important is not the ability to speak, as individuals, their language in the regions of the country where it has little chance of being understood; it is the ability to live collectively in French, to work in French, to build a society in their image; it is the ability to organize their collective life according to their culture.[9]

None of these three premiers was separatist, nor were their political organizations, the Quebec Liberal Party and the Union nationale. But they were all committed to a major restructuring of Canadian federalism so as to accommodate the new Quebec.

By the same token, during the 1960s most of Quebec's Francophone intellectuals contended that the new Quebec nationalism required an extensive restructuring of the Canadian political order. André Laurendeau, the nationalist intellectual leader of his generation who, as we shall see, became co-chair of the Royal Commission on Bilingualism and Biculturalism, believed that the Canadian crisis could not be resolved without a major change in Quebec's constitutional position.[10] Claude Ryan, Laurendeau's successor as editor of *Le Devoir*, tirelessly promoted the same objective. In 1967, he produced a two-volume supplement to *Le Devoir* in which 40 experts assessed the concept of special status. Neither Laurendeau nor Ryan was a separatist. Laurendeau had definitively abandoned separatism in his youth, partly from apprehension over the excesses of nationalism.[11] Ryan was a lifelong federalist; indeed, as head of the Quebec Liberal Party he was official leader of the federalist forces in the 1980 referendum.

The Limited Strength of Separatism

To be sure, the social and political upheavals of the late 1950s and early 1960s did produce an authentically "separatist" movement calling for Quebec to become a fully sovereign state, with little or no economic links to the rest of Canada. Separatist leaders such as Pierre Bourgault, Marcel Chaput, and André d'Allemagne and their Rassemblement pour l'indépendance nationale, the first formally separatist political party since Confederation, captured the attention of the English-Canadian press, as did the mailbox bombings by members of the Front de libération du Québec. Moreover, their activities were often referred to by Quebec's political leaders who, seeking a refashioning of the Canadian political order, claimed that rejection of their demands would strengthen the hand of the separatists and lead to the end of Canada.

Nevertheless, while much of English Canada was shaken by this sudden and unprecedented appearance of separatism, it remained a minor force in Quebec throughout the 1960s. Opinion surveys indicated that public support for Quebec independence remained low, averaging 8 per cent in the early 1960s and 11 per cent from 1968 to 1972.[12] Two separatist parties, the Ralliement pour l'indépendance nationale (RIN) and the Ralliement national (RN), did run candidates in the 1966 provincial election, but none of them was successful; between them the two parties received only 9 per cent of the popular vote.[13]

In 1967, René Lévesque adopted the goal of Quebec sovereignty but in a way that assumed a comprehensive continuing relationship with the rest of Canada—indeed he called it a "new Canadian union."[14] For that reason, his option had considerably more public appeal than the independence of the RN and RIN.

In sum, during the 1960s, processes of economic and social change within French Quebec, dating back to the turn of the century, finally had their full impact and Quebec's political and intellectual leadership mobilized around the project of a modern society. The project was to be a liberal one, the construction of a secular, pluralist society, but it was also a national project, that of the Quebec nation.

For many Quebec Francophones, this new Quebec nationalism made intolerable several long-standing aspects of the Canadian political order, such as the under-representation of Francophones and the French language in Ottawa and the denial of French-language rights in all provinces but Quebec. Clearly, for Canadian dualism to have any meaning, these matters had to be addressed.

However, the new nationalism involved much more. After all, it was driven by the project of completing the construction of a modern Francophone society in Quebec. Of necessity it called for a change in the status and powers of Quebec. To most of Quebec's political leaders this was quite compatible with a continuing Canadian relationship. Indeed, they believed it could be accommodated within a federal order. But it did require that Quebec's specificity be recognized in a new way.

English Canada: Growth of Canadian National Feeling

For its part, English Canada was becoming increasingly confirmed in a new *Canadian* nationalism.[15] Unlike Quebec nationalism, this nationalism lacked a clearly defined notion of a people or a national society. And until the late 1960s, it lacked a thorough analysis of Canada's economic and cultural dependence on the United States. By and large, the new Canadian nationalism was limited to politics and, in particular, to the status and attributes of the Canadian state.

As we have seen, for most English-speaking Canadians political nationality had always been defined in terms of Great Britain. Many of them could trace their ancestry to one part or another of the United Kingdom; Canada had enjoyed the status of a key component of the British Empire and a leading "Dominion" within the Commonwealth. Moreover, much more may have been involved than simple attachment to the "mother country" or pride in being part of the world's largest empire. British values and traditions were seen as the core of Canada's political culture and institutions. Indeed, some Canadians had contended that their country was a superior expression of "Britishness": a "better Britain."[16] Thus, arguably, a sense of nationality rooted in Great Britain in fact constituted a form of Canadian nationalism.

In any event, by the mid-twentieth century international forces were working against such a conception of Canada's political nationality. Great Britain's steady economic and political decline, confirmed in the postwar years, meant that the British connection could no longer provide a viable basis for defining Canada's place in the world order. This was clearly demonstrated by John Diefenbaker's failure to renew trade relations with Great Britain.[17] In fact, by the 1960s, Britain was much more preoccupied with defining its relationship with Europe than with sustaining the remnants of a far-flung empire. Moreover, during the 1950s, Canada was assuming a certain status and prestige as an "honest broker" among nations, culminating in Lester Pearson's role in resolving the Suez crisis. Association with Britain was an inconvenience: Egyptian president Abdel Nasser had apparently objected to Canadian troops entering Egypt as peacekeepers, given the British cast of their uniforms.[18]

More fundamentally, during the 1950s Canada's southern neighbour had assumed unrivalled global power, triggering conflict on a number of fronts: the extraterritorial application of US trade laws, American desire to maintain nuclear armed missiles in Canada, Canada's reluctance to support the American intervention in Vietnam, and growing reaction against the predominance of US interests in the Canadian economy. Beyond new economic and political might, the United States constituted a cultural threat. American media and cultural industries had easy access to English-speaking Canada and were making steady inroads. All of this seemed to make the entrenchment of a purely Canadian national identity an urgent necessity.

The growth of Canadian nationalism among English Canadians was also the result of developments in the Canadian state. As we saw in the previous chapter, from the late 1940s onward the federal government had articulated a new Canadian nationalism to legitimize its actions in a wide range of areas. Acting upon the recommendations of the Massey Commission, Ottawa created the Canada Council, which was crucial to the emergence of a Canadian professional arts community.[19] Through a long series of post Second World War initiatives the federal government put in place a comprehensive welfare state, directed from Ottawa, on the rationale that all Canadians, as Canadians, were entitled to a minimum level of personal well-being wherever they might be in the country. By the same token, Ottawa undertook to give clear legal status to the notion of Canadian citizenship.

These various pressures to put in place a new distinctly Canadian national identity led the Pearson government to take on the arduous struggle to adopt a new Canadian flag, replacing the Red Ensign and its Union Jack. They also spurred the Pearson government's decision to unify Canada's armed forces, with the adoption of distinctively Canadian uniforms. In effect, to use C.P. Champion's terms, the flag was an "invented tradition" and the Pearson government was pursuing a "neo-nationalist" agenda. After all, the flag's focus on a maple leaf reflected a single, unified vision of Canada and avoided any reference to Canada's "two founding peoples," as could have been represented by such symbols as the Union Jack and the *fleur de lis*. Pearson declared in Parliament that the projected flag "will stand for one Canada: united, strong and independent and equal to her tasks."[20] Champion may be correct in his claim that opposition to the new flag, embodied by former prime minister John Diefenbaker, represented a more "traditionalist" form of Canadian nationalism, although José Igartua shows that the Conservative opposition was also "blatantly anti-French and anti-Quebec."[21] In any event, the neo-nationalist vision, with its resolute break from the past, definitively carried the day, marking "the last hurrah for English-Canadian believers in a British Canada."[22] In effect, for most English Canadians the understanding that they had held of their country well into the 1950s was no longer valid. It was a profound change in a short period of time.[23] For Pearson, the adoption of the flag was one of his most enduring achievements as prime minister; certainly, it was among the hardest won.[24]

While the Pearson government could defend its proposed flag by pointing to the need to respond to Quebec nationalism, this was not the only motivation. Pearson and his English-Canadian colleagues themselves felt a need to break with the formal symbolism of the British connection.[25] Nonetheless, the measure did address an old French-Canadian grievance against a Canada defined solely in British terms. At the same time, however, it expressed a new Canadian nationalism (or "neo-nationalism") rooted in the Canadian state.

The common emphasis of both Canadian and Quebec nationalisms upon the state, albeit different states, was to complicate greatly the possibility of any accommodation of Quebec within a continuing Canadian relationship. The older, French-Canadian, nationalism had been largely focused on private, Church-related institutions. Thus, the nation could be advanced in ways that did not impinge at all on the Canadian political order. With the new nationalism, focused on the Quebec state, a questioning of that order was inevitable. And with the growing Canadian nationalism, focused on the Canadian state, English Canadians were less disposed to enter into such a debate.

The contradiction might have been eased or even avoided if English-Canadian political and intellectual leaders had been prepared to embrace the idea of a distinctly English-Canadian nation, as many Quebec nationalists urged them to. Perhaps it could have been based on historical notions of "Britishness" or "High

Toryism."[26] But until the late 1960s, few English Canadians were prepared to recognize a distinct English-Canadian collectivity. Their nationalism remained an essentially political nationalism, centred on the Canadian state. From that perspective, the new Quebec nationalism was necessarily a problem and a threat. As the poet and academic Douglas LePan wrote in 1966: "We in Ontario have never thought of ourselves, or of English-speaking Canada, as a nation because we thought that there was one nation, Canada, to which both we and our compatriots in French Canada belonged."[27]

Nevertheless, a number of English-Canadian political and intellectual leaders saw that the adoption of new distinctly Canadian symbols was not a sufficient response to Quebec nationalism. During the early and mid-1960s they struggled earnestly to comprehend Quebec's new aspirations and find ways to accommodate them, however much these ambitions may have clashed with the new Canadian nationalism. Starting in 1961, the annual meetings of the Congrès des affaires canadiennes at Laval University provided English-Canadian leaders with the opportunity to learn first-hand of the concerns of their Quebec counterparts.[28] The results of these exchanges were themselves published in fully bilingual volumes. Quebec nationalists, such as René Lévesque, came to English Canada to make their case directly, as with a 1966 conference at Glendon College in Toronto. The spirit of the times was reflected in the book *Dear Enemies: A Dialogue on French and English Canada*, published in both English and French,[29] in which an Anglophone opinion leader and a Francophone counterpart exchanged their views on the challenges facing the country. According to historian Valérie Lapointe-Gagnon such initiatives "sought to find a specifically Canadian way to create the opportunity for a reconciliation between the two founding peoples." During the 1960s, an enormous effort was made "to give Canada a bicultural direction, to create an enduring dialogue."[30] In the process, all three federal parties adopted positions that, in one fashion or another, responded directly to Quebec's demands.

The Early Years: Looking for a Formula to Accommodate Quebec Nationalism

The Liberal Government of Lester Pearson

The Liberal Party, under Lester Pearson, led the way. The Liberals, of course, had been responsible for the massive postwar expansion of the federal government with its assumption of the mantle of national government. And we have seen how Prime Minister St. Laurent flatly rejected Quebec's claim to distinctiveness. In the early 1960s, however, Liberal Opposition leader Lester Pearson actively sought to fashion a means of accommodating Quebec's new demands. Though

Pearson had been a prominent member of the Liberal cabinets of the 1950s, he had been preoccupied with Canada's foreign relations. Thus, he was less imbued than other Liberals with the postwar centralist notions.[31] Moreover, his international experience had made him more disposed to recognize the need to respond to forces of social and political change, as did the perspective he acquired through his early years as a professor of history. And his successes in international diplomacy had strengthened his belief that conflict should be resolved through conciliation and accommodation. In short, he was singularly well equipped to initiate new approaches to the Quebec question.

In this enterprise, Pearson could draw upon Quebec Francophones in the party, such as Maurice Lamontagne, Jean-Luc Pepin, and Maurice Sauvé,[32] who, though deeply committed federalists, were in touch with the new nationalist currents in Quebec. Beyond that, two of Pearson's English-Canadian advisers had known Jean Lesage for many years. Tom Kent, Pearson's main political adviser, had become acquainted with Lesage in the 1950s through work on fiscal questions. And Gordon Robertson, who served as clerk of the Privy Council when Pearson became prime minister, had been Lesage's deputy minister when the latter was federal minister of natural resources. Together, Kent and Robertson not only gave Pearson a direct contact to Lesage but helped to fashion Pearson's attempts to find an accommodation with the Quebec government.[33]

Lester Pearson was obviously uneasy with the new Quebec nationalism and the ways in which Lesage was responding to it.[34] But as he related in his memoirs, he saw that only by directly accommodating this nationalism could Quebec separatism be undermined:

> The intensity of [national feeling in Quebec] made it clear that if we failed to contain and destroy separatism by coming to terms with the Quiet Revolution, that if we failed to treat Quebec as the heart of French culture and French language in Canada, as a province distinct in some respects from the others, we would have the gravest difficulty in holding our country together.[35]

Pearson had already made his concerns known while he was leader of the Official Opposition. In a major address to the House in December of 1962 he had observed that Canadians were "anxious, indeed uncertain, about our future" and "unable to agree on all the symbols of nationhood long after we have become a nation." He had gone on to contend that "Confederation may not have been technically a treaty or a compact between states, but it was an understanding or a settlement between the two founding races of Canada made on the basis of an acceptable and equal partnership" and that English-speaking Canadians had lost sight of that understanding. Dwelling at length on social and economic changes in Quebec, Pearson had stressed that French Canadians were no longer prepared to accept exclusion from direction of the province's economy by "capital, management and skilled personnel . . . largely imported from English speaking Canada or from the United States of America." Noting that "The world around us shows that nations, when reasonable and acceptable compromises are postponed or are offered too late, will resort to desperate solutions," Pearson had declared that

> we have now reached a stage when we should seriously and collectively in this country review the bicultural and bilingual situation in our country; our experiences in the teaching of English and French, and in the relations existing generally between our two founding racial groups.[36]

Upon assuming office in April 1963, Pearson lost little time in putting in place a Royal Commission on Bilingualism and Biculturalism. The idea of a commission had originally been suggested by André Laurendeau, a leading Quebec intellectual and editor of *Le Devoir,* whom Pearson named as co-chair and chief executive officer.[37] If only to persuade Laurendeau to accept the position, Pearson had given the Commission a mandate (in fact, prepared by Maurice Lamontagne) that far exceeded such nominal forms of dualism as language practices in the federal government. The Commission was

> to inquire into and report upon the existing state of bilingualism and biculturalism in Canada and to recommend what steps should be taken to *develop the Canadian Confederation on the basis of an equal partnership between the two founding races,* taking into account the contribution made by other ethnic groups to the cultural enrichment of Canada and the measures that should be taken to safeguard that contribution.[38]

Moreover, the Commission's inquiry should go beyond the federal government alone to examine the impact that "private organizations" had on bilingualism and biculturalism (at Laurendeau's insistence) and the extent to which the provincial systems of education enable students to become bilingual.[39]

Beyond the Commission's mandate, its very structure was deeply rooted in the ideal of dualism. The co-chairs were a Francophone and an Anglophone: Laurendeau and Davidson Dunton, president of Carleton University. Of the other original members, three were Francophone (two from Quebec) and three were Anglophone (two from central Canada). In addition to these eight members, there were two representatives of "the other ethnic groups" that were integrated into one or the other "official" cultures: a French-speaking Polish Canadian and an English-speaking Ukrainian Canadian.[40] Similarly, the bureaucracy of the Commission had Anglophone and Francophone co-secretaries along with an Anglophone director of research and a Francophone special consultant on research.[41]

Such a commission could draw upon a network of scholars and intellectuals, itself squarely bilingual and bicultural, that had emerged during the 1950s and early 1960s. For instance, a pilot project of the Canadian Social Sciences Research Council, promoting contact between Anglophone and Francophone scholars, had resulted in the 1960 publication of a major collaborative volume, *La dualité Canadienne: essais sur les relations entre Canadiens français et Canadiens anglais/Canadian Dualism: Studies of French–English Relations*, with contributions by 20 scholars.[42] As Valérie Lapointe-Gagnon demonstrates, there had already emerged an intellectual network marked by a "desire for dialogue and interest in the Commission's two key notions: bilingualism and biculturalism. The Commission did not come from nowhere."[43] The basis was in place for a far more ambitious research enterprise: the research program of the B&B Commission, drawing upon more than 400 academics. By the end of 1966–67, the Commission had spent close to $7 million,[44] greatly exceeding the expenditure of any previous royal commission.

At the same time, beyond reinforcing Canadian dualism, Pearson saw the need to respond directly to Quebec's demands for recognition of its specificity. He straightforwardly embraced the underlying claims of Quebec nationalists when, addressing a meeting of the Canadian French-language Weekly Newspapers Association at Murray Bay, Quebec in 1963, he declared, "While Quebec is a province in this national confederation, it is more than a province because it is the heartland of a people: in a very real sense it is a nation within a nation." Similarly, in a January 1964 interview, Pearson said on English-language CBC television that Quebec was "in some vital respects not a province like the others but the homeland of a people."[45] Both of those statements drew national attention and were subsequently referred to by leaders in the other federal parties, whether positively or negatively, as authoritative statements of the Liberal position.[46]

Pearson also elaborated the notion of a "co-operative federalism" in which Quebec would be able to assume a role different from the other provinces, provided that the same opportunity was made available to the other provinces. He explained in his memoirs:

> We might make provision for Quebec to develop *de facto* jurisdiction in certain areas where she desired it most. Although the federal government had to retain intact certain essential powers, there were many other functions of government exercised by Ottawa which could be left to the provinces. By forcing a centralism perhaps acceptable to some provinces but not to Quebec, and by insisting that Quebec must be like the others, we could destroy Canada. This became my doctrine of federalism. I wanted to decentralize up to a point as the way to strengthen, indeed to establish and maintain, unity.[47]

On this basis, the Pearson government entered into a wide variety of federal–provincial arrangements that enabled Quebec to take full responsibility for programs that in the rest of the country were managed jointly by the federal and provincial governments or even by Ottawa alone. Known as "contracting out," the arrangement had in fact been included in the Liberals' 1963 election platform at the instigation of Maurice Sauvé.[48] Each of the arrangements was made available to all the other provinces, but Quebec was the only one to use the opportunity. The formula was applied to a large number of programs where Ottawa and the provinces would share the cost.

The framework for the arrangement was spelled out in the Established Program (Interim Arrangements) Act of 1965, which was itself based on an agreement reached between Ottawa and Quebec City the previous year. Under the act, provinces choosing to opt out of a program would be able to recover the funds on their own, thanks to an extra abatement on the federal personal income tax. The provinces were required to undertake that during an interim period they would both maintain the programs and provide the federal government with audited accounts of the expenditures they were devoting to them. In fact, under the 1964 agreement Quebec even pledged that it would not dismantle the programs after the interim period had expired.[49] To that extent the arrangement amounted to a formality: the nature and scale of programs remained intact. Yet, as Tom Kent was to write many years later, "A federation . . . rests on getting its formalities right."[50]

The "contracting out" formula was even applied to exclusively federal programs, such as the youth allowance and student loan programs that Ottawa established in 1964.[51] The most prominent instance was, of course, the Canada Pension Plan. In 1964, Ottawa had declared its intention to establish a national contributory plan. At a stormy federal–provincial conference in Quebec City, the Quebec government presented its own plan for a pension scheme. Moreover, it threatened not to support the constitutional amendment that would be necessary for the federal government to operate its program. After protracted discussions, including secret bilateral negotiations between Ottawa and Quebec City, all governments agreed on a compromise by which provincial governments would be able to "opt out" of a federal pension program; the terms of the federal program were themselves modified so as to be more attractive to the provinces, lessening the likelihood that any province would withdraw. In turn, Quebec agreed to the necessary constitutional amendment. Under the legislation establishing the Canada Pension Plan, the plan would not operate in a province if, within a specific period of time, its government declared that it intended to establish a program of its own. Quebec was the only province to do so.[52]

Not surprisingly, Jean Lesage proclaimed the outcome of the pension plan issue to be a victory: "I used all means that Providence has given me so that Quebec, in the end, would be recognized as a province with special status in Confederation. And I have succeeded."[53] But it is striking how the arrangement also met with general approval outside Quebec. The *Globe and Mail* declared, "[Pearson] appears to have pulled a political triumph out of the teeth of disaster."[54] In the House, NDP leader Tommy Douglas was highly congratulatory; John Diefenbaker was generally approving, though he used the opportunity to deride the Pearson government for the inadequacies of its original scheme.[55] For the members of the Pearson government who had been involved in the negotiations, the agreement ended a crisis that they believed had threatened to destroy the country.[56] This view was shared by Stanley Knowles, a member of the Opposition and a close student of pension questions:

> I felt it was one of the best examples of co-operation between Canada and Quebec, between English and French Canada, or English Canada and French Quebec. . . . Negotiating that kind of an agreement so that face was saved on both sides and nobody lost anything [was a great achievement]. . . . I think Confederation was saved at that point. I think there was a risk of Confederation coming apart at the seams over that whole social security package, and that was avoided, and avoided successfully.[57]

In effect, the predominant English-Canadian reaction was one of relief, as this first confrontation with Quebec nationalism had been resolved.

A reaction against the accommodative strategy did begin to build in some areas of the federal government. In the spring of 1964, Al Johnson, the new assistant deputy minister of finance with responsibility for federal–provincial relations, began a concerted campaign to eliminate contracting out.[58] He enlisted the support of Mitchell Sharp, who became minister of finance after the election in November 1965.

Mitchell Sharp had opposed the concept of contracting out ever since it was adopted as party policy in 1963, believing that tax rates should be standard across the country.[59] Moreover, his opposition to contracting out was strengthened by the influence of a newcomer to the federal scene, Pierre Elliott Trudeau, who vigorously rejected contracting out or any other special arrangement with Quebec. Rather than the Pearsonian search for accommodation, Trudeau argued for a very different strategy for the Quebec question: confronting Quebec nationalism head on and avoiding special arrangements for the province. In his memoirs, Sharp relates that he was greatly impressed during a cabinet committee in 1966 when, for the first time, he heard Trudeau, who was attending as Pearson's parliamentary secretary, argue that policies that result in a special status for Quebec were but a slippery slope to separation.[60]

Still, according to some officials of the time, the contracting issue may not have been the main reason that Finance demanded a change in fiscal arrangements. For some key players, including deputy finance minister

R.B. Bryce, the opposition to shared-cost arrangements may have had much more to do with taking control of the federal government's finances by reducing the burden of federal transfer payments to the provinces. In effect, the presumed need to standardize fiscal arrangements could be a convenient argument for simply cutting back on the financial commitments.[61] In the case of post-secondary education, standardizing arrangements meant converting *all* the provinces to Quebec's special arrangement of tax abatements and ending the transfers that they had become used to.

Whatever its motives, Finance was well placed to make its arguments prevail since it had primary responsibility for defining the federal position on fiscal relations with the provinces. Thus, in September 1966 Finance Minister Mitchell Sharp announced that the federal government was moving away from shared-cost programs, in the process eliminating the very basis of contracting out. In return for taking over the largest of the programs, the provinces would receive additional income tax points. But otherwise, Sharp said, Ottawa would not continue its past practice of "making room" for the provinces through tax abatements. The provinces would have to raise the necessary funds themselves.[62]

Nevertheless, even though Finance had succeeded in its campaign against contracting out, it had not changed the minds of the architects of asymmetry, Tom Kent and Gordon Robertson.[63] Kent had already left the Prime Minister's Office at the end of 1965 to become deputy minister to Jean Marchand in the new Department of Manpower and Immigration. In 1967, Kent and Marchand ended job training grants to the provinces and introduced a new scheme by which Ottawa arranged for training services itself, by entering into contracts with the provinces or with private parties. The policy was not part of any new tough strategy with Quebec. In fact, Ontario was the most opposed to it.[64] At first, Ottawa and Quebec City struggled over control of employment policy in the province, but the dispute was resolved through the creation of a joint Quebec–Ottawa committee, which in turn established a *special role* for Quebec in employment programs.[65]

Gordon Robertson, who remained clerk of the Privy Council, had resisted Finance's campaign and argued in favour of contracting out. This is made clear in Al Johnson's account of an exchange with him in early 1966:

> Mr Robertson pointed out that our reasoning with respect to shared-cost programmes was based upon the assumption that contracting-out was "a bad thing"—that it would lead to an associate state. He said he was not inclined to accept this proposition: he thought contracting-out might well give Quebec the special status she seems to want, for symbolic reasons, and that, having accomplished this she might be deterred from asking for further measures which would make manifest, in Quebec, the special status which that province enjoyed.[66]

Despite this argument with Finance over contracting out, Robertson did not renounce the notion of asymmetry as a way of dealing with Quebec.[67]

Most important, it does not appear that Pearson himself abandoned his belief that Quebec needed to be accommodated through special arrangements.[68] As long as he was prime minister, that remained part of his approach to the Quebec question. Some commentators have claimed that Pearson had been disabused of these ideas by Pierre Elliott Trudeau. Not only did Trudeau's role as Pearson's parliamentary secretary give him an advantageous position from which to persuade Pearson to accept his views, but these views were being echoed by Marc Lalonde, who became Pearson's chief policy adviser in April 1967.[69] However, Pearson's close associates dismiss the notion that Trudeau had such influence with Pearson. They contend that as long as he was prime minister Pearson took his cue from Jean Marchand, whom he regarded as his Quebec leader, and whom he wanted to succeed him as prime minister. Of a more pragmatic bent than Trudeau, Marchand did not have the same objections as Trudeau to special arrangements for Quebec, nor did he share Trudeau's visceral antagonism to Quebec nationalism.[70]

By late 1967, Pearson and his close associates were becoming concerned that Quebec's demands were too great to be met through the ad hoc, non-constitutional arrangements they had been pursuing. They would have to tackle constitutional revision.[71] Trudeau's campaign against asymmetry and a distinct role for Quebec was beginning to have an influence on English-Canadian public opinion; Pearson's new policy adviser, Marc Lalonde, was arguing along the same lines. Nevertheless, Pearson continued to declare an openness to specific arrangements for Quebec. Thus, in October of 1967 he stated in a Montreal speech: "I believe that particular provisions for Quebec, as well as for other provinces where required to ensure the fulfilment of particular needs, can be recognized and secured in the constitution without destroying the essential unity of our Confederation."[72]

As justice minister, Trudeau had a crucial part in the preparations for the first federal–provincial constitutional conference, which Pearson convened in February 1968. In particular, the order of priorities which the federal government set, starting with entrenchment of a charter of rights, shows Trudeau's influence.[73] However, as prime minister, Pearson was still in charge. In opening the conference, he stated that he foresaw a "comprehensive constitutional review" of which an important part would be "the division of powers and jurisdiction between federal and provincial governments."[74] Indeed, by all reports he was quite uncomfortable with the highly abrasive style that Trudeau adopted at the conference. When Trudeau, as justice minister, engaged Quebec premier Daniel Johnson in a fierce debate, Pearson found Trudeau's behaviour inappropriate and brought the exchange to an end.[75] In sum, throughout his tenure as prime minister, Pearson instinctively considered accommodation, rather than confrontation, to be the proper way of handling the Quebec question.

Royal Commission on Bilingualism and Biculturalism

In February of 1965, the Commission released its *Preliminary Report*. The *Report* began with the forthright declaration "Canada, without being fully conscious of this fact, is passing through the greatest crisis in its history." Moreover, it insisted, the crisis had its source in Quebec "but, although a provincial crisis at the outset, it has become a Canadian crisis, because of the size and strategic importance of Quebec, and because it has inevitably set off a series of chain reactions elsewhere."[76]

The *Preliminary Report* also made it clear that the Commission was intending to interpret its mandate in the broadest possible terms, taking "in every aspect of life in the Canadian community" as they bear on the two languages and cultures. Moreover, as to the development of Canada, it saw an "equal partnership between the two founding races" to be the "dominating idea" of its terms of reference.[77]

To justify its contention that Canada was in "its greatest crisis," the *Report* summarized in detail the proceedings of a series of regional public meetings, 23 in number, that it had convened across the country, "thus helping to establish a great dialogue from coast to coast."[78] These regional meetings had been supplemented by sessions with various groups and associations as well as meetings with all 10 premiers, themselves occasions to meet with a number of provincial opinion leaders. The *Report* acknowledged that the commissioners did not yet have the findings of a massive research program that they had set in motion.

Front and centre in the regional public meetings, according to the *Report*, had been the gulf between Francophone and Anglophone reactions to the Commission's mandate to make Canada "an equal partnership." (Indeed, the *Report* acknowledged that the public meetings had taken the form of soliloquies rather than dialogues.[79]) For the most part, Francophone participants subscribed to the historical notion of Canada as a dualistic compact and contended that the terms of the compact had not been honoured. (Quebec separatists, for their part, dismissed "equal partnership" as a sheer impossibility.) On the other hand, Anglophones tended to be perplexed by the very idea of an "equal partnership" and to offer a very different understanding of their country.

By way of its own preliminary analysis of the Canadian "crisis," the *Report* argued that Quebec constituted "a distinct society"—the very term which, 25 years later, was to provoke so much dissension during the Meech Lake Accord debate. Quebec was not only "distinct" but, thanks to language, "separate" from the rest of Canada. Moreover, it was undergoing a profound social transformation which was causing all to be placed in question not only within Francophone Quebec but in Quebec's relations with Anglophone Canada. Quebec's decision about its future "will undoubtedly be made in light of attitudes adopted by English-speaking Canada." Thus, the importance of "the Commission's central concept of 'equal partnership.'"[80]

On the other hand, the Commission reported, most English-speaking Canadians saw little need for important changes in their relationships with Francophones. "Practically all appeared to us to be content with Confederation."[81] The *Report* concluded plaintively:

> It was plain to us . . . that . . . the great majority of English-speaking Canadians misunderstand the nature of the problems raised by contemporary French Canada. To very many Canada appears as essentially an English-speaking country with a French-speaking minority, to which certain limited rights have been given. So far most do not seem to have understood, or to be ready to meet the implications of "equal partnership."[82]

In short, as with the Liberal government that had created it, the B&B Commission urgently summoned English-speaking Canadians to come to terms with the new Quebec. Indeed, Canada was to become "an equal partnership" between Anglophones and Francophones and between Quebec and the rest of the country.

Beyond the Liberals, and the B&B Commission, the other two main federal parties also became committed to trying to find a way to accommodate the new Quebec nationalism. The processes that led the Progressive Conservatives and the NDP in these new directions were similar. Both parties were electorally weak in Quebec and needed to make themselves more attractive to Quebec voters. This meant overcoming the legacy of decades of estrangement from Quebec. In each case, the parties were pulled in this direction by Quebec nationalists who actively challenged them to recognize the new Quebec, provoking but overcoming considerable resistance. Their new receptiveness to Quebec nationalism was of course limited by the Canadian nationalism that most English Canadians shared. Nevertheless, it was a radical change from the traditional positions of each party. The two parties may have had their own reasons for adopting their new policies, but the intellectual and political climate of the early and mid-1960s allowed and even encouraged them to do so.

The Progressive Conservatives: Struggling with "Two Nations"

Until Diefenbaker's electoral victories, the Progressive Conservatives had been effectively excluded from Quebec for decades. After the conscription crisis during the First World War, the Conservatives had secured on average 7.8 per cent of Quebec's seats and 27.1 per cent of its popular vote. Diefenbaker's tenure as prime minister, from 1957 to 1963, did not really improve that state of affairs—even though in 1958 the Conservatives had won 50 seats in Quebec.

The Diefenbaker government undertook some not insignificant reforms to recognize dualism in federal institutions, such as simultaneous translation in the House of Commons and Senate and bilingual paycheques in the federal public service. With the appointment of Georges Vanier as governor general after Vincent Massey, Diefenbaker established the principle of alternating this office between Anglophones and Francophones.[83] And in 1959, Diefenbaker entered into an agreement with Quebec premier Paul Sauvé that ended the six-year stand-off precipitated by Maurice Duplessis's refusal to allow Quebec universities to accept federal grants.[84] That had been the first time that Quebec opted out of a federal spending program with compensation, and the arrangement laid the groundwork for the whole edifice of *de facto* special status for Quebec that the Pearson government created in the 1960s.

Nevertheless, as prime minister, Diefenbaker articulated a vision of Canada that rejected any notion of Canadian duality let alone the distinctiveness of Quebec. Throughout his political career, he championed the ideal of an "unhyphenated" Canadianism in which cultural differences were, by definition, immaterial. As he explained in his memoirs, the primary motive behind his long struggle to establish a Canadian bill of rights had been "to assure Canadians, whatever their racial origins or surnames, the right to full citizenship and an end to discrimination. This was basic to my philosophy of 'One Canada, One Nation.'"[85] In 1961, he even ordered the Dominion Bureau of Statistics to introduce the category "Canadian" as a possible response to the census question on ethnic origin. He reversed the order in light of protests from Francophone nationalist groups, which feared that it would threaten the idea of a distinct French-Canadian nationality and might cause the size of the French-Canadian population to be underestimated.[86]

Beyond that, Diefenbaker's discomfort with a specifically French-Canadian perspective affected relations with the French-Canadian members of his caucus.[87] Upon his election in 1957, Diefenbaker appointed only one Francophone to his cabinet; even after winning his majority in 1958, and having far more Francophones to choose from, he appointed only six, and largely to minor positions.[88] In the 1963 election, in which the Pearson Liberals were victorious, the Conservatives won only eight seats in Quebec. Two years later, the result was the same.

After Diefenbaker was defeated in 1963, forces within the PC Party embarked upon efforts to refashion the image and policies of the party so as to attract support in French Quebec. For many members, of course, that entailed replacing its leader. In April 1965, the party's ostensible Quebec lieutenant, Léon Balcer, left the party after failing to secure a leadership convention and declaring that Diefenbaker "is genuinely against French Canada."[89] Finally, in 1967, these efforts culminated in both an extended debate over the Quebec question and a leadership convention. The party emerged with general adherence to a new strategy regarding Quebec, premised on the notion that Canada is composed of "two nations," and a new leader prepared to put this strategy into effect.

In August 1967, the party held a "thinkers' conference" at the Maison Montmorency in Courville, Quebec.[90] Invited to give a "major address" on the constitution, Marcel Faribault, a prominent Quebec financier and legal expert, tried to confront the essentially English-Canadian conference participants with neo-nationalist trends in Quebec. He argued that, given the French-Canadian understanding of the term "nation," there is "nothing in the two-nation concept that is opposed to a federal political regime." And, reviewing Claude Ryan's proposals for a special status for Quebec, Faribault announced, "With the best will in the world it is impossible for me to find anything in this program that is revolutionary, anti-federalist or *a fortiori* separatist."[91]

Frustrated by the apparent intransigence that had greeted his address, Faribault spoke to the conference participants a second time, further underlining the strength of nationalist currents in Quebec and effectively demanding that the participants respond to them:

> Now, what about particular status? . . . Don't you realize that this is the evolution? Are you unable to realize that this is what is happening to the country? . . . The same way the question of the two nations is no longer debatable in the Province of Quebec. Admit that you will put . . . admit that you must put, at the preamble of a new Constitution, something which will be the recognition that there are in this country two founding peoples. *You put that down.* We might translate it in French "two nations." You will translate it, two "founding races or people" if you want. We cannot say "people" because "*people* in our case doesn't mean nation, the same way as "nation" in English doesn't mean "*nation*." [emphasis in original][92]

Faribault's second intervention had the desired effect: the participants of the constitution committee approved a summary statement that does indeed refer to Canadian duality in the terms he suggested. Calling for a national conference on the constitution, the statement declared that the constitutional change should take into account:

> That Canada is and should be a federal state.
>
> That Canada is composed of two founding peoples (deux nations), with historical rights who have been joined by people from many lands.
>
> That the constitution should be such as to permit and encourage their full and harmonious growth and development in equality throughout Canada.[93]

The French phrase "deux nations" was inserted into this English-language text for clarity.[94] The committee ignored Faribault's challenge to address the concept of special status. Indeed, others had issued the same challenge much more pointedly. In fact, York University historian Paul Stevens had proposed to the constitutional committee that Quebec be granted complete jurisdiction over housing, manpower, and social welfare, participate directly in the administration and programming of the CBC and have some responsibilities in external relations. Quebec MP Martial Asselin had enthusiastically supported Stevens's proposal.[95] But no hint of such arrangements appears in the final statement.

For that matter, the concrete proposals accompanying the statement's endorsement of "two founding peoples (deux nations)" treated duality in purely linguistic terms, calling for "complete equality of language rights for French and English throughout Canada, subject only to the practical necessary adjustments within the several provinces."[96] The statement did, however, embrace the conception of Canada that underlay the demands of Quebec nationalists, and that was enough to infuriate John Diefenbaker, who was still leader of the party and still a potential candidate at the party leadership convention scheduled for September. He proclaimed, "Montmorency was not representative of Conservative thinking in his country. . . . There's only one Canada. Only one nation, one national idea, and one national dream."[97]

The September convention was to demonstrate that a broad consensus had in fact developed in the party to the effect that Canada is composed of two nations, however defined and whatever the institutional implications. In the days preceding the convention, a study group approved the Montmorency report with hardly any dissent and the PC national policy committee gave its approval without difficulty.[98] So as to avoid a fight on the floor over the two-nations question, the convention organizers agreed that the policy committee would simply report its decisions to the convention; there would be no debate or vote.

Diefenbaker, however, tried to force the issue. He used his address as party leader to call upon the delegates to renounce the policy and, to that end, presented himself as a last-minute candidate for re-election. There were some expressions of support for Diefenbaker's position: the Saskatchewan delegates endorsed it and the Alberta premier and BC attorney general telegraphed their approval.[99] But the convention debate did not take place, though as a partial concession, the organizers agreed that the report would be tabled rather than presented without debate to the convention, as had been originally planned.[100] After coming a distant fifth on each of the first three ballots, Diefenbaker withdrew from the race. The notion of two nations was explicitly endorsed in the convention addresses of most of the leading candidates: Fleming, Fulton, Hees, McCutcheon, Roblin, and Stanfield.[101]

Clearly, there were limits to this new PC consensus on the notion of two nations. Its proponents were usually careful to rule out any notion of separate state structures. Faribault and others had placed great store in the increasingly tenuous argument that, unlike English Canadians, French Canadians saw the term "nation" in essentially cultural and social terms. As we have seen, during the 1960s, nationalist leaders in Quebec had come to give the state a central place in their idea of nation. English-Canadian proponents of two nations tended to see French Canada rather than Quebec as the "other" nation and to hedge about the existence of an English-Canadian nation. Nevertheless, the party had come far indeed from the "one Canada" of John Diefenbaker. It had embraced a dualist conception of Canada that had been proposed by leaders of Quebec itself and that offered the basis for a new relationship with Quebec nationalism.

The new party leader, Robert Stanfield, had repeatedly expressed sympathy for a distinctive place for the Quebec government in Canadian federalism. Just before the convention, an article by Stanfield containing the following passage had appeared in *Le Devoir*: "The Quebec situation presents certain distinctive aspects. Quebeckers feel that, in order to achieve their aims and ambitions, they must be given more authority over economic and social affairs in their province. I don't think any solutions that we will find for the problems of our federation will be able to ignore this feeling in Quebec."[102] And speaking before the convention's policy committee, Stanfield said he disliked the term "special status" but then outlined "some kind of different arrangement in the distribution of authority, in respect to social and economic matters" for Quebec.[103] On that basis, he obtained the endorsement of Claude Ryan, editor of *Le Devoir*, for leader of the party and, in the following year, for prime minister.[104]

The NDP: "Two Nations" and "Special Status"

Like the Progressive Conservatives, the NDP had a heavy legacy in Quebec to overcome. Its predecessor, the Co-operative Commonwealth Federation (CCF), had never been able to establish a base in French Quebec, where it faced the combined opposition of the clerics, who attacked its Protestant roots, and French-Canadian nationalists, who attacked its centralist predilections. Indeed, to the extent the CCF had any support in Quebec, it was in the English-Canadian community in Montreal. The prominence in the party of such figures as F.R. Scott, son of an Anglican priest and lifelong supporter of a strong federal government, only confirmed the claims of the party's French-Canadian detractors.[105] A primary reason for replacing the CCF with a new party had been to overcome this deficiency in Quebec. Beyond that, the prospect of a new social democratic party had attracted a good number of Quebec Francophone union leaders and social activists who were at the same time deeply involved in the new Quebec nationalism. They were determined to secure a place for themselves and their ideas within the new party.[106] Thus, from the outset the party was under strong pressure to try to come to terms with the new Quebec nationalism.

Before the party's founding convention in 1961, the Quebec NDP members and sympathizers held a colloquium to formulate common positions and reached agreement on three principles: the affirmation that Canada is composed of two nations, the need for a renewed and decentralized federalism, and recognition of Quebec's right to self-determination. It was agreed that for tactical reasons the last proposition would not be explicitly put to the convention. On this basis, the Quebec delegates submitted a resolution to the party's National Committee requiring that in all NDP official documents the term "federal" or "Canadian" should be used in place of "national" and that "Confederation," "country," or "Canada" should be used instead of "nation."

Initially, the National Committee rejected the proposition. In response to protests from Quebec, the leadership agreed to modify the party program, but not the party's constitution, along those lines. At the convention, the committee persisted in this refusal. Speaking for the Quebec delegation, Michel Chartrand insisted that, since French Canadians form a distinct nation, the application of "national" to the federal NDP would be incomplete, unacceptable, and assimilationist. The counter-attack was led on behalf of the party leadership by Eugene Forsey, who declared, "Canada is composed of two ethnic groups but not two nations."[107] Confronted with this open debate, the leadership relented; the party's statutes committee adopted the Quebec position.

The next day, the Quebec delegation succeeded in having the draft party program modified to its satisfaction. In particular, a revised section begins with the declaration: "The New Democratic Party declares its belief in federalism, the only system that can assure the joint development of the two nations which originally joined together to create Canadian society, as well as the development of other ethnic groups in Canada."[108] To be sure, this general statement of principle offered no indication of what types of institutional arrangements were warranted.[109]

During the 1960s, the NDP worked its way to a formal endorsement of a distinctive place for Quebec within the federal system. Once again, this came about largely at the prodding of the Quebec caucus. In 1965, the selection of a promising new Quebec leader, Robert Cliche, together with the acceleration of the constitutional debate, forced the party leadership to address the Quebec question in more concrete terms.

The initial formulation alluded to a special role for Quebec but also insisted that "certain basic matters had to be left to the jurisdiction of the federal government"; it drew up a list of such "matters" that effectively undercut any enhancement of Quebec's position.[110] When the proposal met with widespread criticism from Quebec nationalists and a Quebec NDP convention failed to adopt it,[111] a new, stronger version was presented, and approved, at the party's third federal convention, in July 1965. At the same time, the convention adopted a series of resolutions that would have entailed centralization of power in Ottawa.[112]

Nevertheless, the party leadership began to use the term "special status" to denote the party's position on Quebec. In addressing Parliament in 1966, NDP leader Tommy Douglas declared,

> We believe that a Canadian constitution must be sufficiently flexible to give the federal government the necessary power to provide for equality of treatment and equality of opportunity for all Canadians, while at the same time recognizing a special status for the province of Quebec in terms of language, culture and the civil code, in keeping with the principle of the equal partnership of the two founding races.[113]

Finally, at its fourth biennial convention in 1967, the party responded to prodding from the editor of *Le Devoir,* Claude Ryan, by overwhelmingly approving a description of special status, formulated by Charles Taylor:

> In fields of government which touch a community's way of life—fields such as social security, town planning, education and community development—Quebec must have the right and the fiscal resources to adopt its own programmes and policies in place of those designed and financed by the federal government. At the same time, the federal government must be able to play an increased role in these fields where this is desired by the people of other provinces.[114]

During the 1968 election campaign, Tommy Douglas vigorously defended this position:

> The NDP takes the position that we must have a strong federal government. It must have power it has never had before to grapple with modern problems that are conspicuously beyond the grasp of the provincial and municipal governments. . . . Thus, it may mean that in any area such as education and housing, where Quebec feels that a strong federal power may erode provincial rights, it may be necessary to have two programs—one for English-speaking Canada and one for Quebec.[115]

NDP campaigners argued that the federal government would not be able to extend its activities in ways that were urgently needed unless Quebec were permitted to exempt itself, at least to some degree, from such measures. By recognizing special status, they argued, "Canadians elsewhere can seek federal action in these fields without creating misunderstanding, frustration and intolerable strains to our confederation."[116] By the same token, party leaders blamed Trudeau's alternative of official bilingualism for the creation of "poisonous antagonisms," especially in western Canada.[117]

There is evidence that the party activists themselves supported these efforts to accommodate Quebec nationalism. According to Alan Whitehorn's survey of NDP convention delegates, 63.9 per cent supported a "special status" for Quebec in 1971. This support fell substantially during the 1970s.[118]

During the 1960s, all three major federal parties made a sustained effort to understand the new Quebec nationalism and to devise constitutional formulas and structures that would accommodate it. The Liberal Party, under Lester Pearson, took the lead in this process, launching a national inquiry into the conditions needed to create "an equal partnership between the two founding races" and building an asymmetrical federalism that in effect provided Quebec with a distinctive status. The PCs adopted a dualistic conception of Canada that repudiated the "one Canada" of John Diefenbaker. And the NDP formally adopted both a two-nations vision of Canada and a "special status" for Quebec.

To be sure, no party was fully united around these positions. John Diefenbaker had fought a bitter rearguard resistance to the PC's new position. The decision of the NDP founding convention that the party constitution recognize two nations precipitated Eugene Forsey's departure and alarmed Frank Scott and Pierre Trudeau;[119] the party's subsequent endorsement of special status for Quebec was denounced by Ramsay Cook and Kenneth McNaught.[120] Nevertheless, the leaders and many members of all three parties were committed to a new approach to the Quebec question, designed to accommodate nationalist demands.

English-Canadian Intellectuals

Parallel processes were taking place among English-Canadian intellectuals. Some actively promoted the new effort to find an accommodation of Quebec nationalism within Canadian federalism. English-Canadian academics had been prominent in such events as the Progressive Conservatives' Montmorency conference, where the historian, Paul Stevens, had presented a blueprint for Quebec special status. Charles Taylor and others had played similar roles in the NDP.

Other English-Canadian intellectuals went one step further, attempting to lay the basis for a new distinctly English-Canadian nationalism, centred on an English-Canadian nation.[121] Unlike the nationalism of the federal government, with its emphasis on Canada's political sovereignty vis-à-vis Great Britain, this new strand of nationalism saw the nation in much broader terms. Rather than a merely political entity, the nation was also a social and cultural collectivity. Moreover, the new nationalism bore a critical analysis of the United States and its impact on Canada and the globe in general. The primary goal of the new nationalism was not to keep intact the Canadian federal system but to emancipate the nation from American domination. From that perspective, the nation could be readily envisaged as English Canada, rather than Canada as a whole, and Quebec nationalism could be an ally, rather than a threat. On this basis, the logic of two nations would no longer be one-sided. The two nations could work together to combat their common domination by the United States. The catch phrase was "two nations, one struggle."

Gad Horowitz, for instance, regularly used the pages of *Canadian Dimension* to make the case for an English-Canadian nationalism. In 1965, he wrote in an article called "The Future of English Canada,"

> The greatest threat to the existence of Canada is not the autonomist drive of Quebec. It is the weakness of the will to nationhood in English Canada. . . . There is no way of avoiding an autonomous Quebec. Quebec demands and deserves autonomy. She will have autonomy within confederation, or there will be no more confederation. . . . The obvious solution to Canada's difficulties would appear to be a federal government which is weak in relation to Quebec, but strong in relation to the other provinces—in other words, a "special status" for Quebec within confederation.[122]

At the same time, such academics as George Grant, Kari Levitt, and Mel Watkins were developing a comprehensive critique of Canadian economic and cultural dependence on the United States.[123] Together with a reaction against the influx of Americans into Canadian universities in the 1960s, these writings were to be the basis for a more clearly defined form of Canadian nationalism, focused upon American imperialism. In sociological terms, this new Canadian nationalism was propelled by social forces in English Canada not unlike those that championed the new Quebec nationalism. As in Quebec, the clearest social base of the new Canadian nationalism was a rapidly growing class of salaried professionals, composed of intellectuals, teachers, artists, and administrators.[124]

With the late 1960s, the new English-Canadian nationalism spawned a political movement: "the Waffle." An informal grouping of leftists under the leadership of two academics, Mel Watkins and Jim Laxer, the Waffle published a manifesto, in August 1969, under the title "For an Independent Socialist Canada." The manifesto sought to enlist the New Democratic Party in its campaign against American imperialism. Given the Waffle's commitment to the idea of an English-Canadian nation it was only logical that it would recognize the existence of a Quebec nation: "there is no denying the existence of two nations within Canada, each with its own language, culture and aspirations."[125] By the same token, given the Waffle's commitment to the emancipation of the English-Canadian nation from American domination, it only followed that it would recognize the right of the Quebec nation to its own emancipation—or, more specifically, Quebec's right to self-determination. In Laxer's words, "Quebeckers must have the right to self-determination, up to and including the right to form an independent Quebec state."[126] In calling upon the NDP to commit to the principle of Quebec self-determination, recognizing that this could entail Quebec independence, the Waffle was forcing upon the party a debate which the Quebec wing of the party had long hesitated to open and which the party leadership had long sought to avoid. Yet it followed logically from the Waffle's premise that the nation was not Canada but English Canada.

During the 1960s, discussion about Canadian unity was marked by an extraordinary willingness to examine new and unconventional approaches. When the B&B Commission's *Preliminary Report* was released, 5000 copies were sold in the first day. The Liberal government of Lester Pearson may have provided the lead, but both opposition parties became involved in the effort to find a way to accommodate the new demands of Quebec nationalists, as did many English-Canadian intellectuals, some of whom went further to argue that English-speaking Canada should see itself as a nation, in tandem with the Quebec nation. In fact, one leading political observer, Anthony Westell, claimed that by 1967 the idea of particular status for Quebec had become fairly conventional within Quebec and that "it was accepted in some measure by many English Canadians in the political capital of Ottawa and the communications capital, Toronto."[127]

In a very few years that was no longer true.

Notes

1. Among other places, these processes are discussed in Kenneth McRoberts, "La thèse tradition-modernité: l'historique québécois," in *Les frontières de l'identité: modernité et postmodernisme au Québec*, ed. Mikhael Elbaz et al. (Sainte-Foy: Presses de l'Université Laval, 1996), 27–45.
2. See Hubert Guindon, *Quebec Society: Tradition, Modernity, and Nationhood* (Toronto: University of Toronto Press, 1988); William Coleman, *The Independence Movement in Quebec, 1945–1980* (Toronto: University of Toronto Press, 1984); and Kenneth McRoberts, *Quebec: Social Change and Political Crisis*, 3rd edn (Toronto: McClelland & Stewart, 1993).
3. See Michael D. Behiels, *Prelude to Quebec's Quiet Revolution* (Montreal and Kingston: McGill-Queen's University Press, 1985); and Jean-Louis Roy, *La marche des Québécois: le temps des ruptures, 1945-1960* (Montreal: Leméac, 1976).
4. See Dale Thomson, *Jean Lesage and the Quiet Revolution* (Toronto: Macmillan, 1984), 174–5.
5. See, for instance, Léon Dion, *Nationalismes et politique au Québec* (Montreal: Hurtubise HMH, 1975).
6. My translation of

   > sentent qu'il y a, au Québec, un gouvernement susceptible de jouer un rôle irremplaçable dans l'épanouissement de leur identité collective, leur mode de vie, leur civilisation, leur échelle de valeurs. . . . Je crois qu'il n'y aurait pas de mal, loin de là, à reconnaître ce fait comme un des fondements du Canada de l'avenir. . . . Nous sommes déjà en voie . . . d'instituer pour le Québec un embryon de statut particulier. . . . Pour des raisons historiques et démographiques, [le gouvernement du Québec] se verrait confier, en plus de toutes les responsabilités qui doivent à notre époque normalement appartenir à un gouvernement provincial, la tâche plus particulière d'être l'instrument de l'affirmation de la communauté canadienne-française. (Address to the Canadian Club, Vancouver, BC, 24 September 1965, as quoted in Gérard Boismenu, "La pensée

constitutionnelle de Jean Lesage," in *Jean Lesage et l'éveil d'une nation*, ed. Robert Comeau [Sillery, Quebec: Presses de l'Université du Québec, 1989], 97.)

7. "Cette constitution devrait, à mon sens, être conçue de telle façon que le Canada ne soit pas uniquement une fédération de dix provinces, mais une fédération de deux nations égales en droit et en fait." Daniel Johnson, *Égalité ou indépendance* (Montreal: Éditions de l'Homme, 1965), 116.
8. "On ne peut s'attendre, compte tenu des renseignements de notre histoire, à ce que les Canadiens français du Québec, qui forment 83 pour cent de la population francophone du Canada, confient la direction de leur vie sociale et culturelle à un gouvernement où leurs mandataires sont en minorité et soumis par surcroît au jeu de la responsabilité ministérielle et de la discipline de parti." As quoted in Jean-Louis Roy, *Le choix d'un pays: le débat constitutionnel Québec-Canada, 1960-1976* (Montreal: Leméac, 1978), 168.
9. "L'important pour les Canadiens français du Québec, ce n'est pas de pouvoir individuellement parler leur langue même dans les régions du pays où elle a très peu de chances d'être comprise; c'est de pouvoir collectivement vivre en français, travailler en français, se construire une société qui leur ressemble; c'est de pouvoir organiser leur vie communautaire en fonction de leur culture." Ibid., 185.
10. See Michael Oliver, "Laurendeau et Trudeau: leurs opinions sur le Canada," in *L'engagement intellectuel: mélanges en l'honneur de Léon Dion*, ed. Raymond Hudon and Réjean Pelletier (Sainte-Foy: Presses de l'Université Laval, 1991), 354–5.
11. Ibid.
12. From 1962 to 1965, 76 per cent were opposed and 17 per cent undecided; from 1968 to 1972, the figures were 73 per cent and 17 per cent. All these figures are drawn from a summary of survey results presented by Maurice Pinard, "The Dramatic Reemergence of the Quebec Independence Movement," *Journal of International Affairs* 45, no. 2 (Winter 1992): 480. For that matter, support for independence grew more during the early and mid-1970s, as the Trudeau strategy was being put into effect, reaching 18 per cent in 1976, when the Parti québécois was first elected.
13. In 1968, a new party, the Parti québécois, absorbed the RN and RIN. However, control within the new party was in the hands of Lévesque and his colleagues from the Mouvement Souveraineté-Association (MSA)—themselves largely dissidents from the Liberal Party. The RN was a founding member, but it played a marginal role. The RIN was not even invited into the PQ; it simply disbanded. Most of its members joined the PQ but tended to be marginalized by Lévesque and his moderate colleagues. By the same token, the PQ was clearly wedded to Lévesque's conception of a sovereignty-association, as opposed to outright independence which was supported by the RN and RIN.
14. In *An Option for Quebec*, Lévesque proposed that a sovereign Quebec and Canada would remain "associates and partners in a common enterprise"—a comprehensive association that "would best serve our common economic interests: monetary union, common tariffs, postal union, administration of the national debt, co-ordination of policies, etc." The collaboration could even extend to the treatment of minorities and to defence and foreign policy. René Lévesque, *An Option for Quebec* (Toronto: McClelland & Stewart, 1968), 27–9. Such an option, he insisted, cannot be described as "separatist" (ibid., 36).
15. J.L. Granatstein, *Canada, 1957–67: The Years of Uncertainty and Innovation* (Toronto: McClelland & Stewart, 1986), Chap. 8.
16. C.P. Champion, *The Strange Demise of British Canada: The Liberals and Canadian Nationalism, 1964–1968* (Montreal and Kingston: McGill-Queen's University Press, 2010), 10.
17. Granatstein, *Canada, 1957–67*, 45; and Philip Resnick, *The Land of Cain: Class and Nationalism in English Canada, 1945–1975* (Vancouver: New Star, 1977), 107–8, and José Igartua, *The Other Quiet Revolution: National Identities in English Canada, 1945–71* (Vancouver: UBC Press, 2006), 129–36.
18. J.L. Granatstein, *Canada 1957–1967*, 201; and Igartua, *The Other Quiet Revolution*, 173–4. For his part, Champion is dubious about this anecdote and contends that the uniforms worn by Nasser and

his colleagues were themselves of British design (Champion, *The Strange Demise of British Canada*, 200). Igartua shows that the English-Canadian press were divided as to whether the Canadian government should have remained steadfast in support of Britain rather than abstaining from a United Nations vote condemning the intervention of Britain and others in Suez (Igartua, *The Other Quiet Revolution*, 115–29).

19. Granatstein, *Canada, 1957–1967*, Chap. 6.
20. As quoted in Igartua, *The Other Quiet Revolution*, 182.
21. Igartua, *The Other Quiet Revolution*, 192.
22. Ibid., 173.
23. Ibid., 223.
24. Granatstein, *Canada, 1957–1967*, Chap. 6.
25. Champion describes the development of ambivalence about the British (and "othering" of Britishness) among Pearson and fellow Anglo-Canadians during their studies at Oxford (*The Strange Demise of British Canada*, Chap. 5). In analyzing the pressures that led to the unification of the armed forces, Champion acknowledges that accommodation of Francophones "was clearly a key factor" but also declares that "It is this internal English Canadian conflict that Hellyer brought to a head in the unification debate, even if it was sometimes cast in the name of fairness for French Canadians" (203).
26. Ibid., 178.
27. Douglas LePan, "The Old Ontario Strand in the Canada of Today," *Queen's Quarterly* 73 (1966): 487, as quoted in Resnick, *Land of Cain*, 15.
28. Valérie Lapointe-Gagnon, "Les origines intellectuelles de la commission Laurendeau-Dunton: de la présence d'une volonté de dialogue entre les deux peuple fondateurs du Canada au lendemain de la Seconde Guerre mondiale, 1945-1965," *Mens* 14, no. 2-11 (2014): 146–54.
29. Gwethalyn Graham and Solange Chaput-Rolland, *Dear Enemies: A Dialogue on French and English Canada* (New York: Devin-Adair Co., 1965).
30. My translation of "ont voulu trouver une voie spécifiquement Canadienne et ouvrir le chemin vers la réconciliation entre les deux peuples fondateurs" and "énergie déployée . . . pour donner un élan biculturel au Canada, pour créer un dialogue durable," Lapointe-Gagnon, "Les origines intellectuelles de la commission Laurendeau-Dunton," 173.
31. This point was made by Tom Kent in an interview with the author, 20 June 1996.
32. Pepin had sketched out his conception of Canada and "co-operative federalism" in September 1964. Among the premises of his co-operative federalism is that "in the *socio-political* field, *the theory of two nations*, whether true or false in the eyes of history, is now recognized by the best Canadian constitutionalists and political leaders in both nations. . . . Canadian society is bi-national; the Canadian state is the result of at least a moral agreement between the two founding nations." (Address to l'Institut canadien des affaires publiques, and published as Jean-Luc Pepin, "Co-operative Federalism," *Canadian Forum*, Dec. 1964, 207, emphasis in original.)

    One of the elements of co-operative federalism is "the right of the French Canadians, 'a minority not like the others,' the right of Quebec, 'a province not like the others,' to a particular status. All we have just set forth makes possible particular status for *Quebec* within Canadian federalism if, for example, it wants to take advantage of options, 'contracting out,' and withdrawal from joint plans." (Ibid., 209, emphasis in original.)

    On Maurice Sauvé's relationship with the Lesage government, see Tom Kent, *A Public Purpose: An Experience of Liberal Opposition and Canadian Government* (Montreal and Kingston: McGill-Queen's University Press, 1988), 278.
33. Indeed Lesage tended to deal with Pearson through Robertson and Kent, whom he found more compatible than Pearson. Kent, *A Public Purpose*, 229.
34. In March 1962, Pearson confided to a friend his "fear and uneasiness . . . about the direction Jean Lesage feels he must go in order to cope with some of the pressures to which he is subjected." See Granatstein, *Canada, 1957–1967*, 261.
35. Lester B. Pearson, *Mike: The Memoirs of the Right Honourable Lester B. Pearson*, ed. J.A. Munro and A.I. Inglis (Toronto: University of Toronto Press, 1975), 238–9.
36. Canada, House of Commons, *Debates*, 25th Parliament, 1st Session: Volume 3, 2722–6.

37. André Laurendeau, "Pour une enquête sur le bilinguisme," *Le Devoir*, 20 Jan. 1962.
38. Royal Commission on Bilingualism and Biculturalism, *Preliminary Report* (Ottawa: Queen's Printer, 1965), 151, emphasis added. The term "two founding races" seems to exceed the term "les deux peuples fondateurs" used in the French-language version. According to Lamontagne, it had been substituted for "two founding peoples" at the suggestion of Jack Pickersgill and over the heated objection of representatives of Canadian Jews but with Pearson's disclaimer that it referred to biological as opposed to ethnic characteristics. Peter Stursberg, *Lester Pearson and the Dream of Unity* (Toronto: Doubleday, 1978), 141.
39. B&B Commission, *Preliminary Report*, 151.
40. This contrasts dramatically with, for instance, the Citizens' Forum on Canada's Future (better known as the Spicer Committee), which the Mulroney government created in 1990. Among the 12 original members of the Citizens' Forum, there were only three Francophones, all from Quebec. Six of the nine original Anglophones appear to be of British origin. (Based on biographies in "Cross-Canada Checkup," *Maclean's*, 12 Nov. 1990, 18–19.)
41. This structural dualism and secondary status of non-Charter-group Canadians was denounced in various places, including the House, where John Diefenbaker and an NDP member from BC, Harold Winch, criticized it in commenting on Pearson's announcement of the Commission. See *Debates of the House of Commons*, 1st session, 26th Parliament, 1963, 2441, 2443. In his memoirs, Pearson acknowledged the validity of this criticism. See Pearson, *Mike*, 240.
42. Mason Wade (ed.), *La dualité Canadienne: essais sur les relations entre Canadiens français et Canadiens anglais/Canadian Dualism: Studies of French–English Relations* (Quebec: Presses de l'Université Laval, and Toronto: University of Toronto Press, 1960).
43. My translation of "cette volonté de dialogue et cet intérêt pour les deux notions clés de la Commission: le bilinguisme et le biculturalisme. La Commission n'a donc pas surgi de nulle part." Lapointe-Gagnon, "Les origines intellectuelles de la commission Laurendeau-Dunton," 172.
44. Granatstein, *Canada 1957–1967*, 254.
45. Both of these statements are quoted in Peter C. Newman, *The Distemper of Our Times* (Toronto: McClelland & Stewart, 1968), 320.
46. The Murray Bay statement was quoted, with disapproval, four years later by Eric Neilsen. See *Debates of the House of Commons*, 1967, 118. On the other statement see Stursberg, *Lester Pearson*, 197–8.
47. Pearson, *Mike*, 239. To be sure, Pearson preferred the term "co-operative federalism" over "special status" and saw institutional limits to the granting of a different role for Quebec. See the testimony of Pearson's adviser, Tom Kent, in Stursberg, *Lester Pearson*, 203, and Kent, *A Public Purpose*, 266–72.
48. Interview with Tom Kent, 20 June 1996.
49. Kent, *A Public Purpose*, 296. In addition, the agreement even contained the statement: "The government of Quebec has expressed its firm belief that the wishes of all Canadians can be best fulfilled within a federal structure, and its resolute determination that the rights of the provinces should be exercised not to the disruption but to the enhancement of the unity of Canada." See ibid.
50. Ibid.
51. See Donald V. Smiley, *Constitutional Adaptation and Canadian Federalism since 1945*, Document no. 4, Royal Commission on Bilingualism and Biculturalism (Ottawa: Queen's Printer), Chap. 6; and Kenneth McRoberts, "Unilateralism, Bilateralism and Multilateralism: Approaches to Canadian Federalism," in *Intergovernmental Relations*, Collected Research Studies of the Royal Commission on the Economic Union and Development Prospects for Canada, vol. 63, ed. Richard Simeon (Toronto: University of Toronto Press, 1985), 83–6.
52. See Richard Simeon, *Federal–Provincial Diplomacy: The Making of Recent Policy in Canada* (Toronto: University of Toronto Press, 1972), Chap. 3.
53. Stursberg, *Lester Pearson*, 197.
54. As quoted in Simeon, *Federal–Provincial Diplomacy*, 59.
55. Canada, *Debates of the House of Commons*, 2nd session, 26th Parliament, vol. II, 20 Apr. 1964, 2334–8.
56. See the testimonies in Stursberg, *Lester Pearson*, 189–97.
57. Ibid., 197.

58. Yves Vaillancourt, "Le régime d'assistance publique du Canada: perspective québécoise," Doctoral Thesis in Political Science, Université de Montréal, 1992, 181–218. See also Simeon, *Federal–Provincial Diplomacy*, 66–8; and Thomson, *Jean Lesage and the Quiet Revolution*, 401–4.
59. Mitchell Sharp, *Which Reminds Me . . . A Memoir* (Toronto: University of Toronto Press, 1994), 134–9.
60. Ibid., 137–9. Sharp maintains that his concern about Quebec MPs voting on bills, such as the Canada Pension Plan, that did not apply in their province was shared by "many of [his] colleagues" (139).
61. This interpretation was offered by Tom Kent, 20 June 1996, and confirmed by Gordon Robertson in an interview with the author, 22 Aug. 1996.
62. Simeon, *Federal–Provincial Diplomacy*, 76.
63. Clarkson and McCall say that in early 1966 "Lesage knew Trudeau's views were bolstered by enthusiastic allies in the PMO. Tom Kent, Pearson's policy adviser, and Gordon Robertson, his clerk of the Privy Council—as well as the new minister of finance, Mitchell Sharp—had insisted that Pearson summon up the courage to resist the apparently insatiable government of Quebec by rebuffing demands that the province be allowed to opt out of further federal programs, as it had with the Canada Pension Plan in 1964." See Christina Clarkson and Stephen McCall, *Trudeau and Our Times*, vol. 1, *The Magnificent Obsession* (Toronto: McClelland & Stewart, 1990) 100. But, although that describes accurately the views of the finance minister, Mitchell Sharp, and his deputy minister, Al Johnson, it apparently does not fully reflect the views that Kent and Robertson held at the time (interviews with Tom Kent, 20 June 1996, and Gordon Robertson, 22 Aug. 1996). Kent, who had in any event left the PMO by that point, offers a strong defence of the Pearson government's dealings with Quebec in his book, *A Public Purpose*: "I think it can now be said to be proven that the country is better served by Pearson-style diplomacy in federal–provincial relations than by Trudeau-style confrontation." See Kent, *A Public Purpose*, 414.
64. Interview with Tom Kent, 20 June 1996.
65. Anthony G.S. Careless, *Initiative and Response* (Montreal and Kingston: McGill-Queen's University Press, 1977), 68.
66. Johnson to Bryce, 12 Jan. 1966, as quoted in Vaillancourt, "Le régime d'assistance publique," 184.
67. Interview with Gordon Robertson, 22 Aug. 1996.
68. My reading differs from that of Vaillancourt, who, on the basis of his analysis of Ottawa–Quebec City dealings over social policy and of Finance's success in undermining contracting out, concludes that Pearson and Robertson had turned against asymmetrical federalism per se. See Yves Vaillancourt, "Quebec and the Federal Government: The Struggle Over Opting Out," in *Canadian Society: Understanding and Surviving in the 1990s*, ed. Dan Glenday and Ann Duffy, (Toronto: McClelland & Stewart, 1993), n. 22. John English believes that through 1965 federal officials, including Pearson, thought their approach to Quebec was the right one, that it was not a sign of weakness, and that they were not making undue concessions. (English himself describes the approach as "appeasement.") Lesage's rejection of the Fulton–Favreau formula in 1966 did, however, suggest the policy had been unsuccessful and led to a more negative retrospective view of it. See John English, *The Life of Lester Pearson*, vol. 2, *The Worldly Years* (Toronto: Knopf, 1992), 303.
69. Peter C. Newman suggests that Trudeau used his position as parliamentary secretary to Pearson to persuade Pearson to change his strategy: "The prime minister had appointed Trudeau his parliamentary assistant on January 9, 1966, at a time when he was coming around to the view that his own policy of co-operative federalism should be abandoned for a tougher, more defensible approach. During long evenings of discussion in the privacy of the study at 24 Sussex Drive, Trudeau provided the prime minister not just with a rationale for a practical new concept of Canadian federalism but with perceptive insights into Quebec society." See Newman, *Distemper of Our Times*, 442. See also p. 325. This is also the position of Andrew Cohen in *Lester B. Pearson* (Toronto: Penguin, 2008), 162–3. Yet the testimony of Kent and

Robertson, plus the 1967 Montreal speech, suggest otherwise.

70. Interviews with Tom Kent, 20 June 1996, and Gordon Robertson, 22 Aug. 1996. Writing in the summer of 1967, Donald Smiley noted, "the Honourable Jean Marchand has not, so far as I can discover, addressed himself directly to the constitutional question." See Smiley, *Constitutional Adaptation and Canadian Federalism*, 135. By the same token, Peacock notes that when Trudeau joined the cabinet and began to argue for a direct confrontation with Quebec nationalism, virtually all his fellow ministers apparently resisted his arguments. See Don Peacock, *Journey to Power: The Story of a Canadian Election* (Toronto: Ryerson, 1968), 210.
71. Robert Wright's quotations from a confidential memo that Pearson circulated in early December confirm Pearson's decision to proceed with constitutional discussions and to focus the discussions on a constitutional bill of rights, as proposed by Trudeau. It is less clear that Pearson actually had been converted to Trudeau's overall argument against any accommodation of Quebec. (Wright, *Trudeaumania: The Rise to Power of Pierre Elliott Trudeau* [Toronto: Harper Collins, 2016], 112)
72. Peacock, *Journey to Power*, 122. Though trying to show that Pearson was moving toward Trudeau's position, Peacock acknowledges that "Pearson was never entirely convinced that the uncompromising one nation–two languages approach was right." See ibid., 121. Indeed, in a speech to be read on his behalf in Banff, shortly before the Montreal speech, Pearson refused to incorporate passages that explicitly rejected special status. See ibid.
73. Gordon Robertson, 22 Aug. 1996.
74. Gordon Robertson, *Memoirs of a Very Civil Servant* (Toronto: University of Toronto Press, 2000) 239.
75. Kent, *A Public Purpose*, 414; and Peacock, *Journey to Power*, 212.
76. Royal Commission, *Preliminary Report*, 11.
77. Ibid., 21.
78. Ibid., 26.
79. Ibid., 129.
80. Ibid., 119.
81. Ibid., 124.
82. Ibid., 125.
83. In his memoirs, Diefenbaker takes great pride in Vanier's appointment, claiming it to have been entirely his own idea. See John G. Diefenbaker, *One Canada*, vol. 2: *The Years of Achievement, 1957–1962* (Toronto: Macmillan, 1976), 60–1. But Pierre Sévigny claims that it was his idea. See Peter Stursberg, *Diefenbaker: Leadership Gained, 1956–62* (Toronto: University of Toronto Press, 1975), 199.
84. In his memoirs, Diefenbaker cites this agreement as a major achievement, while refusing to recognize the principle of exclusive provincial jurisdiction over education. See Diefenbaker, *One Canada*, vol. 2, 291.
85. Ibid., 255. See also Peter C. Newman, *Renegade in Power: The Diefenbaker Years* (Toronto: McClelland & Stewart, 1963), 282–3.
86. André Lamoureux, *Le NPD et le Québec, 1958-1985* (Montreal: Les Éditions du Parc, 1985), 40.
87. See the comments of Quebec Conservatives in Stursberg, *Diefenbaker*, Chap. 12.
88. Marc La Terreur, *Les tribulations des conservateurs au Québec de Bennett à Diefenbaker* (Quebec City: Presses de l'Université Laval, 1973); André Lamoureux, *Le NPD et le Québec*, 38; and Newman, *Renegade in Power*, Chap. 20.
89. Newman, *Distemper of Our Times*, 120.
90. The discussion draws in part on Dalton Camp, "Reflections on the Montmorency Conference," *Queen's Quarterly* 76, no. 2 (Summer 1968): 185–99. See also the account of the Progressive Conservative debates over "two nations" in Edwin R. Black, *Divided Loyalties* (Montreal and Kingston: McGill-Queen's University Press, 1975), 201–8.
91. *Report on the Montmorency Conference, Courville, Quebec, August 7–10, 1967*, prepared by the Progressive Conservative Policy Advisory Conference of the Centennial Convention, undated, 98.
92. Ibid., 102–3.
93. Ibid., 104.
94. Camp, "Reflections," 199.
95. Frank Howard, "Davis Assures Quebec Areas of Agreement Remain Ontario's Goal," *Globe and Mail*, 8 Aug. 1967.
96. *Report on the Montmorency Conference*, 104–5.

97. Martin Sullivan, *Mandate '68* (Toronto: Doubleday, 1968), 183.
98. Anthony Westell, "Diefenbaker Won't Continue; Tories Back 2-Nation Plan," *Globe and Mail*, 8 Sept. 1967.
99. Michael Vineberg, "The Progressive Conservative Leadership Convention of 1967," M.A. thesis, Dept. of Economics and Political Science, McGill University, Aug. 1968, 110.
100. Sullivan, *Mandate '68*, 198.
101. See the accounts in the *Globe and Mail*, 9 Sept. 1967. Stanfield apparently was not as clear-cut in his speech, but he had already closely associated himself with the two-nations theme. Some speakers did insist that they would not support "two nations" if it were to imply separate states. Michael Starr was the only candidate to reject "two nations" explicitly.
102. Sullivan, *Mandate '68*, 177. By the same token, he approved the Canada/Quebec Pension Plan arrangement, saying that opting out "didn't bother [him] as long as it was available to all." See Stursberg, *Lester Pearson*, 200. At the same time, like most English-Canadian politicians, Stanfield eschewed the term "special status." See Sullivan, *Mandate '68*, 177; and "Stanfield: gare aux mots," *Le Devoir*, 1 Sept. 1967.
103. Peacock, *Journey to Power*, 81.
104. Claude Ryan, "Le congrès conservateur de Toronto," *Le Devoir*, 7 Sept. 1967.
105. On F.R. Scott and his vision of Quebec and Canada, see Guy Laforest, *Trudeau et la fin d'un rêve canadien* (Sillery, Quebec: Septentrion, 1992), Chap. 3.
106. This account of the convention draws primarily upon Lamoureux, *Le NPD et le Québec*, 85–129. The efforts of the NDP to address the Quebec question are traced in detail in Peter Graefe, "From Coherence to Confusion: The CCF–NDP Confronts Federalism," major research paper, M.A. Program in Political Science, York University, Sept. 1996.
107. Lamoureux, *Le NPD et le Québec*, 114, my translation.
108. My translation of "Le Nouveau Parti démocratique proclame formellement sa foi dans un régime fédéral, le seul qui puisse assurer l'épanouissement conjoint des deux nations qui se sont associées primitivement en vue de former la société canadienne, ainsi que l'épanouissement des autres groupes ethniques au Canada." See ibid., 116. In a 1990s overview of the NDP's relationship with Quebec, Michael Oliver and Charles Taylor trace these lobbying successes to "the euphoria of English Canadian delegates at the presence and participation of so many Francophone Quebeckers" (Michael Oliver and Charles Taylor, "Quebec," in *Our Canada*, ed. Leo Heaps (Toronto: James Lorimer, 1991), 145. Still, Lamoureux argues that even this modification fell far short of the full recognition of Quebec's nationhood that the Quebec caucus had wanted and that it reflected the leadership's refusal to recognize Quebec's right to self-determination (117, 126).
109. Indeed, party members did not agree on the significance of the wording. Michael Oliver, who was a prominent member of the party at the time, insists that the party did not formally endorse the two-nations formula. Though the program acknowledged that French Canadians might regard themselves as constituting a "nation," it did not claim that English Canadians saw themselves as a nation. (Private communication, 9 June 1996.)
110. Desmond Morton, *NDP: The Dream of Power* (Toronto: Hakkert, 1974), 59.
111. Lamoureux, *Le NPD et le Québec*, 148.
112. Morton, *NDP*, 61.
113. House of Commons, *Debates*, 1st session, 27th Parliament, vol. 1, 28 Jan. 1966, 411.
114. Desmond Morton, *The New Democrats, 1961–1986: The Politics of Change* (Toronto: Copp Clark Pitman, 1986), 77. *Canadian Dimension* maintained that the resolution fell far short of the type of special status that it had been regularly advocating:

    > The NDP repeated its support for "special status" for Quebec, though this now appears to have taken on a new meaning: Quebec would retain all of its present programs (whether it would take over some federal ones is not specified in the resolution), but the other provinces could, if they wanted to, transfer some of their programs to Ottawa. . . . Fearing to antagonize one side or the other, the framers of this policy have deliberately shorn the concept of "special status" of any substance. It is doubtful whether anyone will be fooled by a slogan without content.

    See "The NDP Federal Convention—1967," *Canadian Dimension*, Sept.–Oct. 1967, 4.

115. *Canadian Annual Review*, 1968, 60.
116. Ibid., 35.
117. Richard Simeon and Ian Robinson, *State, Society and the Development of Canadian Federalism*, 109.
118. In Whitehorn's presentation of results from three different conventions, it appears that this figure applies to 1971 as opposed to 1979. In 1983, support had slipped to 46.2 per cent. The results of another question are clearly identified with 1971: 66.6 per cent agreed "to provide some special recognition for Quebec 'within Confederation'." See Alan Whitehorn, *Canadian Socialism: Essays on the CCF–NDP* (Toronto: Oxford University Press, 1992), 126.
119. On Scott and Trudeau, see Christina McCall and Stephen Clarkson, *Trudeau and Our Times*, vol. 2, *The Heroic Delusion* (Toronto: McClelland & Stewart, 1994), 69; and Stephen Clarkson and Christina McCall, *Trudeau and Our Times*, vol. 1, 89.
120. Morton, *The New Democrats*, 77–8. See also Lamoureux, *Le NPD et le Québec*. Forsey's opposition is elaborated in his "Canada: Two Nations or One?" *Canadian Journal of Economics and Political Science* 28, no. 4 (Nov. 1962).
121. Resnick argues that the idea first appeared "in the student movement in the middle and late 1960s, which here, as on the issue of anti-imperialism, played a seminal role." See Resnick, *Land of Cain*, 192. He notes, "The Canadian Union of Students and the Union générale des étudiants du Québec began to put into practice the theory of two separate nations—English Canada and Quebec" (193).
122. Gad Horowitz, "The Future of English Canada," *Canadian Dimension*, July–Aug. 1965, 12.
123. See, for instance, George Grant, *Lament for a Nation* (Toronto: McClelland & Stewart, 1965); Kari Levitt, *Silent Surrender* (Toronto: Macmillan, 1970); and Ian Lumsden, ed., *Close the 49th Parallel* (Toronto: University of Toronto Press, 1970).
124. Resnick, *Land of Cain*, 167–78, 201.
125. Statement from the Waffle manifesto as quoted by Pat Smart, "The Waffle and Quebec," *Studies in Political Economy* 32 (Summer 1990): 198. Smart states that Jim Laxer prepared this passage as part of four paragraphs for inclusion in the manifesto. It should be noted that this passage does not actually appear in the manifesto, as reproduced by Socialist History Project. However this text does include the statement: "Quebec's history and aspirations must be allowed full expression and implementation in the conviction that new ties will emerge from the common perception of 'two nations, one struggle'." (Socialist History Project, *The Waffle Manifesto: For an Independent Socialist Canada* [1969], #17)
126. March 1970 statement by Jim Laxer as quoted by Smart, "The Waffle and Quebec," 199.
127. Anthony Westell, *Paradox: Trudeau as Prime Minister* (Scarborough, ON: Prentice-Hall, 1972), 7.

Chapter 3

Trudeau and the New Federal Orthodoxy

Denying the Quebec Question

As we have seen, not all English-Canadian political and intellectual élites supported the effort to accommodate Quebec neo-nationalism. By the mid-1960s, some federal officials were trying to reverse the Pearson government's experiments with asymmetry. Prominent members of both the Progressive Conservative and New Democratic parties had vigorously opposed the new directions their parties had embarked on. Still, through most of the 1960s these remained minority positions. By the end of the 1960s, these had become majority positions. The effort to accommodate Quebec nationalism was over and was to remain so for decades to come. Instead, all three parties were united around a strategy of confronting and undermining Quebec nationalism.

Such a complete and rapid reversal was made possible by a new political phenomenon: a Francophone from Quebec who insisted that accommodation of Quebec nationalism was unnecessary, wrong-headed, and, in fact, immoral. In its place, he proposed to incorporate Quebec Francophones into a new pan-Canadian identity. While resistance to accommodation may have been steadily growing in English Canada, this development "tipped the balance."

Pierre Elliott Trudeau's vision of Canada was not shared fully by most of his fellow Quebec Francophones. Nor did it correspond to the way in which most English Canadians understood their country. Yet ultimately it was to have a profound impact on Canadian politics. Indeed, it became so deeply incorporated into Canada's most important political institutions, especially the constitution, that the primary attempt to depart from it formally, the Meech Lake Accord, ended in debacle. And subsequent attempts by Quebec-based federalists to secure constitutional change have been simply ignored in the rest of the country.

The Trudeau Political Vision

A Unique Political World View

Never before had the world view that a Canadian prime minister brought to office been more clearly defined and publicly known. And never before had a prime minister's world view had such a profound and long-standing impact on Canada's political life. During the 1950s and early 1960s, Trudeau had tirelessly expounded his beliefs through essays in periodicals such as *Cité libre*, which he co-founded, through interviews and commentaries on radio and television, and by participation in a multitude of conferences and public events. When he entered federal politics, there could be no doubt where he stood.

Yet it has now become known that Pierre Trudeau did not always hold these views. Recent scholarship that draws upon his personal papers, available for the first time upon his death in 2000, enables a much more subtle understanding of the development of Trudeau's political thought than was previously possible. In particular, it demonstrates that until his mid-twenties he held a political world view that, in key respects, was the polar opposite of the one he professed during the 1950s and for the rest of his life. Indeed, the beliefs that he had expounded before his ascent into federal politics, and by which he defined his role and purpose as prime minister, came about as the result of a deep personal struggle. Moreover, this experience of internal struggle appears to have had a lasting effect, giving a particular urgency and even rigidity to the set of political beliefs upon which he had finally settled. Trudeau's intellectual development is more complex than previously understood and, for this reason, all the more fascinating.

Primacy of the Individual

At the centre of the political world view that Trudeau first articulated in the early 1950s was the primacy of the individual over any institution or collectivity. As he declared in a series of articles, published in 1958 in *Vrai* magazine, through which he sought to familiarize the Quebec public with the theory and practice of liberal democracy:

> Society is made for man: if it serves him badly he is entitled to overthrow it. The purpose of living in society is that every man may fulfil himself as far as possible. Authority has no justification except to allow the establishment and development of a system that encourages such fulfilment.[1]

Coupled with this focus on the individual was an abiding commitment to individual rights. If the individual is to be free, he or she must enjoy the political and legal capacity to exercise that freedom. By and large, as in the *Vrai* articles,

Trudeau presented rights in quite conventional terms. (To be sure, as we shall see, there were occasions when he did extend his analysis to economic and social rights.) Citizens, he presumed, could actually hold their government responsible through the simple act of voting. If they did not use that right properly, they simply got the governments they deserved.[2] The institutions of representative democracy were sufficient to hold governments to account as long as they functioned properly and were accompanied by such rights as free speech and assembly, equality before the law, and the right to a fair trial.[3]

In another respect, however, Trudeau's notion of rights was quite unconventional, for he insisted that, in the case of Canada, they must extend beyond conventional notions of legal, political, and even social rights, to incorporate *linguistic* rights: "In a country such as ours, with its two founding linguistic groups, the preservation of individual rights also must mean the guarantee of the linguistic rights of both groups."[4]

Moreover, Trudeau had very definite ideas as to how these various rights should be safeguarded. In the case of Canada, the traditional legal and conventional bases were insufficient. Nothing less than a formal charter of rights, entrenched in the constitution, would do. As early as 1955, Trudeau had advocated the constitutional entrenchment of a bill of rights,[5] of which a central purpose was the protection of language rights.[6] Indeed, in a 1968 CBC interview, Trudeau presented entrenchment of language rights as the virtual solution to Canada's national unity problems:

> I think the essential thing is to ensure that French-speaking Canadians are not locked into the Province of Quebec and that therefore no one Provincial Government can say I speak for the French and you other governments speak for the English. And I think that after we've solved this language problem and if we manage to make sure through Constitutional amendment or through Provincial act and Federal act, if we could ensure the rights of the French language outside of Quebec are spread across the Country then I think the so-called crisis is finished.[7]

Catholic Personalism

While rooted in liberal notions of the primacy of the individual, and the rights that follow, Trudeau's political world view was also informed by his private, and deeply spiritual, Catholicism. He was a practising Catholic throughout his lifetime, attending mass, meditating with the Benedictine Community in Montreal and participating in retreats at Saint-Benoît-du-Lac.[8] Indeed, until at least the age of 31, he even abided by the Church's Index, faithfully requesting the bishop's permission to read banned works.[9]

To be sure, determined as he was to inculcate the ideals and practice of liberal democracy in French Quebec, Trudeau was quite prepared to denounce the Quebec Church for propagating anti-democratic values, colluding with the Duplessis regime or intruding into secular matters. For this, he was attacked by conservative clerics and even summoned to a meeting with Cardinal Paul-Émile Léger.[10]

More to the point, Trudeau was closely familiar with developments in Catholic thought and was attracted to a particular school: French personalism. Originally developed by French theologian Emmanuel Mounier, and expounded by such Catholic thinkers as Jacques Maritain, personalism stressed the centrality of the human person, thus distinguishing itself from Marxism, while also stressing the individual's membership in a community, indeed a number of communities, thus distinguishing itself from liberalism. On the basis of their own freely adopted beliefs, individuals had a personal responsibility to contribute to the community's common good. By the same token, the community had an obligation to enable each of its members to pursue their unique vocations. It was only through the community that they could do so.[11] In Trudeau's own words, recalling his conversion to personalism several decades later, under personalism "The person . . . is the individual enriched with a social conscience, integrated into the life of the communities around him and the economic context of his time, both of which must in turn give persons the means to exercise their freedom of choice."[12]

With its emphasis on personal responsibility to the community and active engagement, French personalism had a great appeal to Quebec Francophones who perceived the need for social and economic transformation of their society. They found in personalism the justification, indeed obligation, for action on their part. Nonetheless, it was bound to challenge the traditional notions of authority and social order that prevailed through much of the Quebec clergy. During the 1950s, personalism inspired many young Quebec Catholics, including Trudeau, who found a way to pursue social and economic change through such formally Catholic organizations as Jeunesse étudiante catholique.[13] JÉC members, especially Gérard Pelletier, were the prime movers behind *Cité libre*, itself modelled on Mounier's *Esprit*.

Trudeau saw personalism as a central element of his belief system. Indeed, looking back decades later, Trudeau declared his conversion to personalism to have been his "epiphany," more exhilarating and important than any event in his personal or public life.[14] Yet, strictly speaking, there was a tension between the communitarian assumptions of personalism and the liberal emphasis on individual rights that informed so much of Trudeau's writings, and was central to his world view. André Burelle, an adherent to personalism who was a speech-writer and adviser to Trudeau in the late 1970s and early 1980s, contends that through most of his public life Trudeau was torn between the two, with individualist liberalism ultimately prevailing in the constitutional revision of the 1980s.[15]

Social and Economic Democracy

In accord with personalism's call for active engagement, Trudeau embraced a wide range of social and economic causes during the 1950s and early 1960s. In fact, this new engagement began in 1949, when Trudeau championed the cause of French-Canadian workers during an illegal strike at Asbestos and Thetford Mines. The employer, an American corporation, had the active support of the Quebec government, as well as its police. The dominant, traditionalist forces in the Church were very much opposed to the strike, despite the support of the workers by the Archbishop of Montreal and much of the clergy. For his part, Trudeau played a relatively minor role during the strike itself, consisting of speeches urging the miners on in their struggle.[16] Subsequently, however, he spearheaded the preparation of a book in which a number of intellectuals, academics, and labour leaders analyzed the strike as a critical moment in Quebec's history. Introducing the book was a lengthy, if polemical, essay by Trudeau himself which was unsparing in its attack on conservative, often clerical, social and political thinking in Quebec. When published in 1956, *La grève de l'amiante* touched off an explosion of reactions, both positive and negative, thus confirming Trudeau's stature as a leading voice for social and economic change in Quebec.

By the same token, in the early 1950s he became legal counsel to the Fédération des unions industrielles du Québec (FUIQ), a new entity designed to integrate Quebec's craft and industrial unions in response to unification movements in the United States and Canada. As such, Trudeau toured the province to educate the membership on political activism, gave a keynote address to the FUIQ's founding convention and drafted the FUIQ's statement to a provincial royal commission (the historic Tremblay Commission) on Quebec's constitutional position.[17]

At the same time, Trudeau became engaged with the primarily Anglophone milieu of the Quebec CCF, which had its own long-standing preoccupation with workers' conditions and commitment to social justice.[18] Indeed, *La grève de l'amiante* was spawned by a study group, *Recherches sociales*, drawn together by McGill law professor and CCF eminence Frank Scott. While somewhat diffident about the CCF given its centralizing bias and estrangement from Quebec,[19] Trudeau was a member, donor, and participant in party events and conferences.[20]

In a number of essays written during the 1950s, Trudeau outlined an essentially socialist critique of the workings of capitalism, calling upon the state to be freed from special interests and able to meet social needs and the common good. For instance, in an essay on "economic rights," presented to an Ottawa conference in 1958 and published in the *McGill Law Review* in 1962, Trudeau contended that conventional civil libertarian rights were insufficient. He argued for "consumer rights," understood as the right of a man to a share of society's production "sufficient to enable him to develop his personality to the fullest extent possible"[21] and for "producers rights," understood as the right of workers to safe and fairly paid jobs, to strong trade unions, and to strike (including protection from strike breakers). Documenting the extent to which Canada fell short in terms of either set of rights, Trudeau declared that "Industrial democracy will not be reached any more easily than political democracy was, but it must be reached."[22]

Beyond workers' rights and the struggle for social justice within Quebec and Canada, Trudeau also became preoccupied with international causes. He spent 1949 travelling throughout Europe and the Middle East. From that experience, he developed an abiding commitment to the advancement of colonized peoples, and a deep animosity toward Western imperialism. In the process, he acquired a certain respect if not sympathy for communist forces struggling to free colonized areas, as well as for Mao's China and even the Soviet Union. (Mills notes that, during the 1950s, Trudeau had a "soft spot for Russia and the Soviet Union," giving the Soviet regime the benefit of the doubt and muting his criticisms.[23]) By the same token, he was suspicious of the United States, itself an imperialist force, and had no sympathy for the American-led intervention in the Korean War.

From these assumptions, Trudeau favoured an independent foreign policy for Canada, freed from US dominance and oriented to the movement of non-aligned countries led by India and Indonesia. (This made him an early and vigorous critic of the artisan of Canada's foreign policy: Lester Pearson.) By the same token, Trudeau was greatly concerned about US–USSR tensions and the possibility of nuclear war. Thus, he was drawn into movements and organizations favouring "peaceful coexistence" and an end to the Cold War. He participated in a number of international conferences that were geared to these themes—and that were suspect in some quarters for linkage to the Soviet Union and international communism. On that basis, in 1952, he attended an International Economic Conference in Moscow. For this act, he was banned from travel to the United States and widely condemned in Quebec and elsewhere for being a "dupe" and fellow traveller.[24]

In sum, through active support of workers and unions, membership and involvement with the CCF, and his many international engagements, Trudeau clearly placed himself on "the left"—and earned a reputation as such. Indeed, in November 1962 he wrote in the pages of *Cité libre* that he was "a man of the left."[25] Needless to say, precisely where he should be situated on "the left" has been a matter of some dispute. Historian Ramsay Cook characterized Trudeau as "liberal, left liberal."[26] Another historian, Robert Wright, calls him "a near-classic liberal."[27] Nonetheless, Trudeau's writings and actions during the 1950s and early 1960s suggest a deeper commitment than that. Closer to the mark, at least for this period of time, is Mills's contention that Trudeau was a "social democrat" who saw the inadequacies of capitalism and favoured "social regulation and planning, wealth distribution, and cultural freedom and material sufficiency for all."[28] For their part, Max and Monique Nemni present Trudeau as a believer in "democratic and Christian socialism."[29]

Federalism

As well as championing the central role of the state, including the Quebec provincial government, in advancing equality and social justice, Trudeau fastened on a particular form of the state: federalism. There were strong reasons for him to do so.

As it happened, federalism was seen by the personalists as the ideal state form. They contended that federalism enables participation by citizens in their proximate communities, thus avoiding both the dissolution of communities into mass society and the construction of the nation-state, which equated the state with a single community, the national community. At the same time, federalism maintains a central state to promote the common good of communities and to participate in international developments.[30]

Federalism also was highly regarded in socialist circles, if not the CCF of Frank Scott and fellow centralizers. In particular, it was championed by Harold Laski, Britain's leading theoretician of socialism, democratic or otherwise. Given the deepening pluralism of contemporary society, Laski argued, only a federal state could govern civil society in a democratic and egalitarian fashion.[31]

Finally, the crucial argument for Trudeau, federalism could be seen as a means of taming ethnic nationalism. The nineteenth-century British writer Lord Acton had theorized that federalism is a superior form of political organization since it can enable the creation of a multinational state bringing together societies, even nationalities, that would not otherwise share the same political system and thus avoiding the nationalist excesses of the nation-state.[32] Trudeau was quick to make the argument his own. For Trudeau, federalism had the promise of replacing the emotion of nationalism with reason. By their very logic, he argued, federal systems must be based on accommodation and continual bargaining:

> Federalism is by its very essence a compromise and a pact. It is a compromise in the sense that when national consensus on *all* things is not desirable or cannot readily obtain, the area of consensus is reduced in order that consensus on *some* things be reached. It is a pact or quasi-treaty in the sense that the terms of that compromise cannot be changed unilaterally.[33]

Ultimately, Trudeau claimed, federalism must privilege reason over emotion as the basis for political action and decision making. The language of politics must be dispassionate and rational. There can be no role for nationalism.

Trudeau did acknowledge that in some instances reason might be insufficient to hold a federation together, leading to a temptation to resort to nationalism. To be sure, in a multinational federation this would not be a narrow ethnic nationalism but it would be nationalism nonetheless. However, he insisted, such a strategy would probably be counter-productive:

> If the heavy past of nationalism is relied upon to keep a unitary nation-state together, much more nationalism would appear to be required in the case of a federal nation-state. Yet if nationalism is encouraged as a rightful doctrine and noble passion, what is to prevent it from being used by some group, region, or province within the nation? If "nation algérienne" was a valid battle cry against France, how can the Algerian Arabs object to the cry of "nation kabyle" now being used against them?[34]

For these reasons, in preparing the FUIQ's submission to the Tremblay Commission on Quebec's constitutional future, Trudeau presented a most favourable view of the Canadian federal arrangement, stressing the need to respect provincial autonomy. Contending that there can never be a definitive interpretation of the division of powers, Trudeau declared, "Since co-operation is inevitable, it seems reasonable to try to make the most of it."[35]

Indeed, given his understanding of the nature and value of Canadian federalism, Trudeau subsequently took positions in defence of provincial autonomy that collided with the centralist sympathies of his CCF colleagues, such as Frank Scott. In 1954, he defended the action of the Duplessis government in imposing a personal income tax and insisting on deductibility from the federal tax.[36] By the same reasoning, in 1957 he defended the Duplessis government's decision to penalize Quebec universities that accept direct grants from the federal government.[37] Indeed, in a 1961 article, "The Practice and Theory of Federalism," Trudeau chastised CCF thinkers for not fully recognizing the political reality of federalism and for thinking that reform necessitates an expansion of federal power. In the process, he questioned the central tool of federal activism: the spending power by which Ottawa can "decide (at the taxpayers' expense!) . . . whether provincial governments are properly exercising any and every right they hold under the constitution."[38]

Anti-nationalism

At the heart of Trudeau's attachment to federalism was his opposition to nationalism. Indeed, anti-nationalism was the central element of the set of beliefs and principles that he had so tirelessly expounded over the 1950s and early 1960s. It was in accord with his other beliefs. Personalism's thinkers clearly rejected the principle that the state should be coterminous with the national community, since this would favour one community over all others and could lead to the horrors of Nazism.[39] Leading socialist theoreticians, such as Harold

Laski, saw nationalism as a regressive force.[40] But Trudeau's opposition to nationalism was also driven by personal antipathy to a particular form of nationalism: *Quebec* nationalism.

Trudeau was unremitting in his attacks on Quebec nationalism. Indeed, he assigned it primary responsibility for all the many manifestations of Quebec's "backwardness." Quebec nationalism was nothing less than the enemy of democracy, individual rights, and social and economic justice. In the caustic analysis of Quebec society that formed the first chapter of *La grève de l'amiante*, Trudeau argued that nationalism had corrupted the Church's social doctrine:

> As a result, the Church's social doctrine, which in other countries opened the door to the democratization of peoples, the emancipation of workers and social progress, in French Canada was invoked in support of authoritarianism and xenophobia. And, worse still, this doctrine made it impossible for us to resolve our problems. . . . It rejected any solution that worked for our "enemies": the English, Protestants, materialists, etc.[41]

By the same token, he saw ethnic nationalism as the root cause of Quebec's dismal political life. In an article called "Some Obstacles to Democracy in Quebec," he described a political culture that tolerated massive corruption and the arbitrary use of state power because it did not comprehend the basic premise of democracy: that sovereignty must reside with the people. The *ancien régime* heritage of New France, the anti-democratic manipulations of an authoritarian clergy, and the fundamental corrosiveness of nationalism had conspired to prevent French Canadians from realizing that sovereignty should reside with them and that governments should be accountable to them. They thought that

> government of the people by the people could not be *for* the people, but mainly for the English-speaking part of that people; such were the spoils of conquest. . . . They adhered to the "social contract" with mental reservations; they refused to be inwardly bound by a "general will" which overlooked the racial problem. Feeling unable to share as equals in the Canadian common weal, they secretly resolved to pursue only the French-Canadian weal, and to safeguard the latter they cheated against the former.[42]

On this basis, there was no need for any enhancement of Quebec's place within the Canadian federation:

> By the terms of the existing Canadian constitution, that of 1867, French Canadians have all the powers they need to make Quebec a political society affording due respect for nationalistic aspirations and at the same time giving unprecedented scope for human potential in the broadest sense.[43]

Preparing to Be a Great Leader

In short, Trudeau was no ordinary liberal. Nor was he an ordinary politician. By the time he came to Ottawa, in 1965, he was firmly and publicly linked to a set of beliefs that was very much his own, combining liberal individualism with Catholic personalism, democratic socialism, federalism, and an abiding anti-nationalism. Moreover, these beliefs reflected various stages in a unique personal itinerary by which he studied at leading universities in three different countries, after having first excelled at Quebec's elite Jesuit classical college, Collège Brébeuf, and then secured a law degree from the Unversité de Montréal. Trudeau had been introduced to liberal democratic thought and theories of the economic and social role of the state at Harvard, where he pursued doctoral studies from 1944 to 1946. He became familiar with French Catholic personalism through a year's study in Paris, over 1946–7. At the London School of Economics, over 1947–8, he studied with Harold Laski, theoretician of socialism and proponent of federalism. In addition, after a year of backpacking through Europe, the Middle East, and Asia, he had spent two years in Ottawa serving as an official in the Privy Council Office. Thus, when Trudeau became prime minister in 1968, he appeared to the Canadian public to be "all of a piece," guided by a long-held set of beliefs and possessing a remarkable preparation for the position.

To be sure, Trudeau did seem to have been a bit of dilettante, flitting from university to university, and then globe-trotting for a year, without ever completing his Harvard doctorate or receiving a degree anywhere else. During the 1950s, he could not always be counted upon to follow through on his various political initiatives. Thérèse Casgrain, grande dame of the CCF in Quebec, recalled that when Trudeau was president of the Rassemblement (a political action movement he had helped to found) in 1959 "he took a trip overseas and when he returned the *Rassemblement* no longer existed."[44]

Thus, when Trudeau entered federal politics in 1965, there was widespread speculation that this was just another of his adventures, and would be similarly short-lived. While he subsequently became prime minister, this was because he was the proverbial right person at the right time: Lester Pearson was determined to be succeeded by a Quebec Francophone, Jean Lesage and Jean Marchand were unavailable, thus Trudeau was persuaded to take on a position that he had never really contemplated, let alone sought. This adventure, too, would not last.

On that score, the speculation was clearly wrong! Trudeau was the third-longest-serving prime minister in Canadian history, for a total of 15 years. Moreover, many of the other assumptions about Trudeau turned out to be wrong as well. Since Trudeau's death, in 2000, scholars have had access for the first time to his remarkably comprehensive personal papers. Throughout his life, Trudeau had carefully retained copies of all his publications, speeches, and correspondence as well as his personal journals and, from his student days, lecture notes and book summaries. Thus, the Trudeau papers provide important, in some cases astonishing, new insights into Trudeau's character and thinking. They have already served as the primary source for three new major biographies.[45]

The papers show that, far from being a dilettante who drifted into federal politics and the office of prime minister almost by accident, Trudeau had been preparing all his life to become a major political leader. At the age of 19, he wrote in his diary that "I would like so much to be a great politician and to guide my nation."[46] At the age of 24, he exclaimed to his then fiancée, herself the daughter of a past Quebec premier, that he wanted to be premier of Quebec. Trudeau's application to do graduate studies at Harvard spelled out his intent to assume political leadership. He forthrightly declared that "my profession will be statesman."[47] All his studies were geared to that objective. Time demonstrated that these were not simply the ambitions of youth.[48]

By the same token, the papers demonstrate that Trudeau was a most assiduous student. From his early days at Brébeuf, he took copious lecture notes. He was a voracious reader who recorded in detail both the arguments and his evaluation of each of the many books he read. Throughout his studies, he saw himself as acquiring the knowledge he would need for political leadership and, most of all, defining the set of beliefs that would guide his career. In short, from his earliest years, Trudeau had a very strong sense of purpose.

Starting Out as a Right-Wing Separatist

Yet while Trudeau's commitment to public leadership may have been strong, papers demonstrate that until at least his mid-twenties he held beliefs about the purpose and nature of public life that were very different—the polar opposite—from the views that he elaborated so widely in the 1950s and during his long career in Ottawa. That world view was in fact the end result of an intense personal struggle through which he had rejected beliefs he had held, and publicly championed, in the past. Thus, he held this world view with a particular vehemence that shaped his adult life and his career as prime minister.

The papers show that while a student at Brébeuf, and then the Université de Montréal, Trudeau had had little use for democracy, believing instead in the need to entrust power and authority to an élite that could provide French Quebec with strong, Christian leadership. He adhered to the conservative Catholic model of a corporatist society in which the state would draw together and direct the various elements of society.[49] By the same token, viewing the nation as "a community of faith, mind, blood, and language,"[50] he embraced the racist views of Charles Maurras and the French Action française[51] and supported the fascist, or near-fascist, regimes of Philippe Pétain in France, Francisco Franco in Spain, António de Oliveira Salazar in Portugal, and Benito Mussolini in Italy. He saw the Jewish presence in Montreal as a threat to French Canada[52] and argued against allowing additional immigrants into Quebec.[53] Most important, and extraordinary in light of his subsequent career, Trudeau was devoted to a "Revolution" through which Quebec would separate from Canada and become a French, Catholic state: Laurentia.[54] During his early days at Brébeuf, he even fantasized of leading the forces that would, in 1976, establish a separate Quebec state.[55]

Beyond merely holding and proclaiming such beliefs, Trudeau actively sought to put them into effect. In the 1930s, he apparently participated in a protest against visiting speakers who were seeking to rally support for the Republican cause in the Spanish Civil War.[56] He allegedly participated in other anti-Semitic riots in the early 1940s.[57] In 1942, speaking on behalf of Jean Drapeau's candidacy for federal Parliament with the anti-conscription Bloc populaire, Trudeau branded as traitors French Canadians who supported conscription, decried contamination of the French-Canadian people by foreigners, effectively equated the King government with "savages" that had threatened French Canadians in the distant past, and concluded by proclaiming "bring on the revolution."[58] Most remarkable, Trudeau was a leading member of a secret group, Groupe LX, which plotted a separatist insurrection to create Laurentia.[59] Its draft manifesto declared that "The fatherland reborn of the Revolution will be Catholic, French, and Laurentian."[60] In fact, decades later, when asked in Parliament if he had ever been a member of a secret movement favouring Quebeç independence, Trudeau gestured affirmatively.[61]

In his later years, as he recounted his life in *Memoirs*, Trudeau did not acknowledge that he had ever held such views, let alone acted upon them. He does mention his speech on behalf of Jean Drapeau's Bloc candidacy, but does not enlarge on the content.[62] Nonetheless, the evidence of his early separatist views and actions is compelling. Moreover, it was first brought to light by two scholars, Max and Monique Nemni, who themselves view Trudeau and his career most favourably and in Trudeau's later years had become his personal friends.[63] Other scholars who are themselves sympathetic to Trudeau have accepted the Nemnis' revelations.[64]

To be sure, one might question the extent to which Trudeau had actually been ready to act on his right-wing separatist views. The members of Groupe LX may have been plotting an insurrection but were they really prepared to follow through on their plans, and would they have had any likelihood of success? For that matter, apparently at the time there was a good number of such putative cells among young Quebec Francophones.[65] Still, there is no question that Trudeau did hold right-wing separatist beliefs. One might be tempted to view the matter as no more than youthful fantasy and game-playing. Ramsay Cook refers to a "youthful dalliance with nationalism."[66] John English, in his biography of Trudeau acknowledges that "Trudeau did and said some foolish things. Yet perspective is needed." He notes that the activities of Groupe LX "seem strikingly immature"; at the time, Trudeau himself saw the group as badly disorganized.[67] However, whatever the limitations of

Groupe LX, the record does suggest that Trudeau was a separatist, with highly conservative views, over a good number of years, extending well into his early twenties. After all, he was already 23 when he made his speech on behalf of Jean Drapeau. Trudeau did seem less committed to political action during the following two years leading up to his departure, at age 25, to Harvard for graduate studies. But this seemed to spring more from disillusionment with the possibilities for political change, given the poor electoral performance of the anti-conscription Bloc populaire, than any abandonment of fundamental beliefs. In short, Trudeau's right-wing separatism cannot be dismissed as simply a teenage aberration. As such, it is in total contradiction with the raison d'être of Trudeau's later career as prime minister.

Accounting for Right-Wing Separatism

Before scholars' discovery of Trudeau's early right-wing separatism, the political world view he brought to Ottawa could be readily seen as the direct result of the uniquely bilingual, and bicultural, conditions of his early life. His anti-nationalism and strong individualism seemed to have come almost naturally from a life experience that transcended any division between linguistic communities. In effect, being a member of both the Anglophone and Francophone communities, he would not have been inclined to identify with either one. Not belonging exclusively to either community, it seemed that he would have seen himself almost by default in highly individualist terms.

In his *Memoirs*, Trudeau himself stresses how he lived his childhood in both English and French. His father spoke to him in French but "my mother spoke in either language, depending on the subject and on how she felt at the time."[68] The relatives on his father's side always spoke French; his mother's father spoke to her in English. His first three years of study were conducted in English but, with fourth grade, he was switched to the French side of the school.[69] He claims that the transition was not at all difficult. His later studies, at Collège Brébeuf, were pursued in French. Beyond that, he had pursued graduate studies in three different countries, using English in two and French in the other, and had spent a year travelling around the world.

Some observers suggest that, in fact, the young Trudeau was quite troubled by his inability to see himself as exclusively Francophone or Anglophone. John English suggests that, at age 21, Trudeau "had become a troubled young man" since "he had to make a choice: Would he be a French or an English Canadian?" His failure to win a Rhodes Scholarship precipitated the choice to be a Quebec Francophone.[70] Nino Ricci treats Trudeau's early separatism as a symptom of an identity confusion:

> The portrait of Trudeau that emerges from the war years is of someone living a divided identity, throwing himself full force into a lunatic

> revolutionary movement as if to prove he would never be the one to betray his race, as his anonymous accuser at Brébeuf had suggested, yet still winning his accolades at school, and still living out his Englishness at home.[71]

For their part, Stephen Clarkson and Christina McCall contend that, during his years at Brébeuf, Trudeau experienced a "mounting ambivalence about being a French Canadian."[72]

Yet the depth of the young Trudeau's separatism and involvement in the anti-conscription movement suggest that he was not at all uneasy with his identity as a French Canadian. His writings, both personal and public, and his activities at school and in the political arena demonstrate a deep engagement with French Quebec. Nor was he as able as some suggest to transcend linguistic duality. Apparently, the application he sent to Harvard in 1944 had sufficient stylistic awkwardness and spelling errors to demonstrate that, at least at that point, English was very much his second language.[73] In fact, according to the Nemnis, Trudeau was always more comfortable writing texts in French than English.[74]

It is now fully evident that, throughout his life, Trudeau saw himself as a Francophone and, as such, remained preoccupied with Quebec.[75] While his political world view may have undergone a radical transformation, repudiating Quebec nationalism and separatism, Trudeau remained a Quebec Francophone, whatever his nationalist adversaries may have claimed. It is in these terms that we can best understand the fierce opposition to Quebec nationalism that animated his political career.

Ostensibly, Trudeau's conversion from Quebec nationalist to fierce anti-nationalist began when he went to Harvard. There, beyond exposure to liberal democratic philosophy and theories of an interventionist state, Trudeau gained a much better understanding of the ongoing Second World War and the horrors of Nazism and its fascist allies elsewhere in Europe. All of this was further confirmed by his studies in France and Britain and his subsequent world travels. Frequently, this understanding of Trudeau's intellectual development is tied to the premise that French Quebec as a whole was a "closed society" bound up in a xenophobic, near-fascist view of the world. Within this interpretation, Trudeau had to leave Quebec physically in order to escape this world view. Such an understanding of French Quebec as a whole is at best highly questionable. In any event, the issue at hand is Trudeau's own early world view, however acquired, and its impact on his subsequent career as public intellectual and, then, prime minister.

Trudeau's transformation in fundamental values could not have happened easily.[76] It could not have been a purely intellectual exercise in which, through simple exposure to new ideas, one set of ideas is replaced by another. Rejecting his past world view would have involved a moral judgement about French Quebec, at least as he understood it, and about his own past actions as an emerging member of its élite. In letters to a friend in Quebec written while he was at Harvard, Trudeau anguished over the fact that he had not participated forthrightly in the war and had ignored its full meaning.[77]

Moreover, once he had become fully attached to his new set of beliefs, Trudeau could not view his own society in the same way. Indeed, he might come to see it in unduly negative and stereotypical terms. In his *Memoirs*, Trudeau speaks of his disappointment with the Quebec to which he returned in 1949: "Quebec had stayed provincial in every sense of the word, that is to say marginal, isolated, out of step with the evolution of the world."[78] He could no longer see that society as his own. For that matter, its conservative clerical leadership actively rejected him, given his new-found championship of social justice. Three different attempts to secure a permanent position at the Université de Montréal were unsuccessful, in part due to intervention by Premier Duplessis. Thus, it was by default that, in a move that greatly surprised his Quebecker friends,[79] he ended up going to Ottawa to take up a position with the Privy Council Office.[80]

By the same token, Trudeau may have felt more than mere frustration with French Quebec. The virulence of some of his subsequent essays, most notably the introduction to *La grève de l'amiante*, suggests a deeply rooted anger against his society. In a widely cited review of that essay, André Laurendeau suggested that Trudeau "is a French Canadian [who is] disappointed in his own kind." He may reject French Canada's "monolithic" conservatism intellectually, but it "hurts him in his very being." In fact, Laurendeau states, "I believe that he is ashamed to have such forebears." Thus, the need for a radical rupture with their ideas.[81]

To be sure, Trudeau was not the only one of his generation of Francophone intellectuals to reject the conservative nationalism in which they had been educated. Yet his reaction seems to have been quite distinctive. Most Francophone Quebec intellectuals who shared this discontent with their society, including some of Trudeau's friends and colleagues, didn't abandon Quebec nationalism. Instead, they embraced a new nationalist formulation, celebrating social and economic change, which became dominant with the Quiet Revolution.

Nevertheless, for his part, Trudeau became a fierce opponent of Quebec nationalism—and remained so for the rest of his life. In the words of Gérard Pelletier, friend and comrade in federal politics, "I'm afraid that Pierre's anti-nationalism has become dogmatic."[82] For his part, Trudeau's other comrade in federal politics, Jean Marchand, observed that "I am more in tune with Quebec nationalism than Pierre is. Of course I'm a Canadian. But in a certain sense I am more Québécois than Canadian."[83]

How, then, can Trudeau's particular evolution be best understood? Perhaps his reaction against Quebec nationalism, in all its forms, was all the greater because, as a member of Groupe LX, he had been so deeply committed to revolution and the creation of Laurentia. Perhaps his distinctive ability to participate in the English-speaking world made him especially sensitive to Anglophone criticism of Quebec's "backwardness" and failure to recognize the full meaning of the Second World War.

It may be that Trudeau can best be understood, not as an impressionable youth who toyed with ways to challenge (English-speaking) authority, but as a "true believer" who, forced to abandon deeply held beliefs, moves to the opposing set of beliefs and pursues them with the same zeal and rigidity he had displayed before. One faith replaced another. In effect, in his struggle against Quebec nationalism Trudeau was perhaps fighting not just ghosts of the past but ghosts within himself.[84]

This may be the key to understanding how, over his many years in federal politics, Trudeau was so quick to see Quebec nationalism as necessarily an *ethnic* nationalism, such as what he had known in the 1930s and 1940s, and was so convinced that any accommodation or formal recognition of Quebec's distinctiveness could only propel Quebec down a "slippery slope" to separation. As we shall see, when the Meech Lake Accord was negotiated to accomplish precisely that purpose, Trudeau had to respond, not just by opposing the Accord, but by attacking the Accord's authors themselves in the most personal of terms. In effect, they were violating what had become his life's purpose. Similarly, going back to the early 1960s, this mindset prevented him from embracing Quebec's Quiet Revolution.

Rejecting the Quiet Revolution

The 1960s presented Trudeau with a paradox: through the Quiet Revolution, Quebec was rapidly building the liberal, progressive society that he had been beseeching it to create, but nationalism, which he had seen as the abiding obstacle to such change, was stronger than ever. In fact, the leaders of the Quiet Revolution claimed to be guided by a *liberal* nationalism.

For Trudeau, this was an impossibility. As a general phenomenon, nationalism was hostile to liberal values. Nationalism in Quebec could never escape the fundamentally conservative social and political assumptions that had always governed French-Canadian nationalism. Given its intrinsic ethnic roots, it could never become a "territorial nationalism."[85] Trudeau was thus quick to claim that the Quiet Revolution had become a victim of counter-revolutionary sectarianism.[86]

His argument seemed forced, for the accomplishments of the Quiet Revolution were too substantial to be dismissed so easily. Certainly, he did not persuade many of his fellow Québécois, not even all his *Cité libre* collaborators. As Gérard Bergeron put it, Trudeau could never see what was "trudeauiste" in the Quiet Revolution.[87] In short, Trudeau remained marginal to Quebec, even as it was being transformed.

Trudeau was naturally troubled by the continuing attempts of Lester Pearson, Jean Lesage, and so many others to find an accommodation of Quebec nationalism within the Canadian federal system, believing that such an enterprise could only lead to disaster. The logic of nationalism was invariably one of secession and the construction of a separate nation-state.[88] Thus, the various schemes for *statut particulier* and similar arrangements were themselves either separatist or simply naive: by strengthening nationalism they would inevitably lead to separation.

Taking the Vision to Ottawa

By the early 1960s, Trudeau was pondering a new strategy: returning to Ottawa. Perhaps by establishing a strong presence in the federal government he and like-minded Francophones would be able to present Quebec Francophones with an alternative to the nationalism of the Quebec government and lead them out of their fixation upon Quebec. To do that, however, he and his colleagues would have to assume positions within the federal government; they would have to run for election.

To the extent Trudeau had been associated with any political party it had been the CCF and its successor, the NDP. But he had been repelled by the NDP's adoption of a bi-national vision of Canada. Moreover, it was obvious that the NDP was not going to form a government in the foreseeable future. The Liberals, on the other hand, who were the Official Opposition, could entertain such hopes, and the Pearson leadership was actively seeking prominent Francophone recruits. They were especially interested in Jean Marchand, former leader of the Confédération des syndicats nationaux and member of the B&B Commission. But Marchand insisted that he must be accompanied by others, namely his friend Pierre Trudeau and the journalist Gérard Pelletier.

There were complications, however. Trudeau, in particular, had been highly critical of Pearson's position that Canada should use American nuclear warheads and had expressed his views in bitter *Cité libre* articles. The issue was sufficient to preclude his running in the 1963 election.

By the 1965 election the warheads issue had receded. Moreover, the Pearson Liberals were in power. They were still keen on recruiting Marchand—but Trudeau was another matter. After all, in his denunciations of accommodation with the Lesage government and its neo-nationalism, he was directly attacking the very policy that the Pearson government had been pursuing. This was not lost on such architects of the policy as Maurice Lamontagne, who actually discouraged Trudeau from running.[89] Eventually, they bowed to Marchand's insistence that he would go to Ottawa only if Trudeau and Pelletier could accompany him. Even then, there was an embarrassingly long delay while Liberal Party organizers looked for a seat in which Trudeau might run. Finally, rather than a predominantly Francophone riding, as Trudeau had wanted, they settled on the heavily Anglophone, and affluent, riding of Town of Mount Royal.

Although Jean Marchand insisted that Trudeau (and Pelletier) should accompany him to Ottawa, even he did not fully share Trudeau's views on Quebec nationalism. After the election, in which all three were successful, Jean Marchand reportedly wrote to Pearson not to appoint Trudeau as his parliamentary secretary, warning that Trudeau was a poor guide to contemporary Quebec.[90]

The Trudeau Vision of Canada

As we have seen, Trudeau went to Ottawa with a coherent set of views not just on Quebec and its place in Canada, but on political life in general. He had developed a very distinctive understanding of the values that should animate the Canadian polity and of the ways in which its institutions should be organized. Thus, during the years leading up to his assumption of the prime ministership he was able to present Canadians with a radically new vision of their country.

If Pierre Trudeau's vision of the country was expressed far more clearly than that of most aspiring politicians, it was also far more personal than most. Rather than devices designed to attract supporters or ingratiate him with voters, Trudeau's writings were nothing less than an attempt to reconceive Canada on the basis of his own beliefs. As Gérard Bergeron has written, "from his own personal make-up, he extrapolated the model of the ideal Canadian citizen."[91]

In effect, his vision of Canada constituted the terms upon which he was prepared to accept Canada and Canadians. Trudeau made it clear on a variety of occasions that if Canadians would not conform to the model he had constructed, then they had no interest for him. In an interview with Anthony Westell of the *Toronto Star* in February 1969, he declared:

> If I don't think that we can create some form of a bilingual country, I am no longer interested in working in Ottawa. If I want to work as an English-speaking person I'll look for a job in another country or I'll go and work in Europe or I'll look for a job in Washington. . . . What attaches me to this country is the belief that the French language can have certain rights. I think it's true for many French Canadians who believe in federalism. . . . It's the only view that can make any sense.[92]

Clearly, the vision of Canada that Trudeau had so carefully and eloquently constructed differed radically from the way in which most Canadians saw their country. This was true even of French Canadians. Despite some superficial similarities, the Trudeau vision was in fact quite removed from mainstream French-Canadian thought. But most English Canadians did not know that.

The Trudeau Vision and French Canada

As Chapter 1 demonstrated, the established French-Canadian conception of Canada was rooted in a pervasive dualism. Most clearly delineated in the double-compact theory of Henri Bourassa, it saw Canada as composed of two distinct collectivities. In Bourassa's terms, Canada was "a fruitful alliance of the two races, each one remaining distinctly itself." At the same time, the province of Quebec had a special role as the centre of the Francophone collectivity as "the particular heritage of French Canadians."

This understanding of Canada had become firmly entrenched among French Quebec's political and intellectual élites. And it had been duly affirmed by Quebec provincial governments. In the process, it had come to be shared by most Quebec Francophones as a given of political life.

Trudeau's vigorous defence of language rights throughout Canada fell squarely within that tradition and was in perfect continuity with Henri Bourassa's campaigns against Ontario's Regulation 17. On this basis, Ramsay Cook could write in 1971, "Bourassa's position is best and most fully represented today by those French Canadians who follow Prime Minister Trudeau."[93]

Trudeau's dualism, however, went no further than individual language rights and in fact he rejected the underlying spirit of dualism as it was generally understood in Quebec, including Henri Bourassa's basic premises.[94] Indeed, despite the claim of some writers that in attacking Quebec neo-nationalism Trudeau was reiterating the pan-Canadian ideas that Henri Bourassa had first advocated,[95] Trudeau's main writings of the period, such as the pieces assembled in *Federalism and the French Canadians*, contain only cursory references to Bourassa.[96] Their intellectual inspiration lay elsewhere, most notably with the English political theorist, Lord Acton.

Trudeau's defence of language rights was based not upon the historical claims of collectivities, or races, but upon individual human rights. He was quite explicit that if there was a case for French language rights, which he strongly believed to be so, it was due to numbers. And other groups, with no pretense to historic claims, might make the same claim should numbers favour them as well: "Historical origins are less important than people generally think, the proof being that neither Eskimo nor Indian dialects have any kind of privileged position. On the other hand, if there were six million people living in Canada whose mother tongue was Ukrainian, it is likely that this language would establish itself as forcefully as French."[97]

In fact, Trudeau was explicitly opposed to granting legal recognition to a Francophone collectivity. He was strongly critical of the B&B Commission's notion of biculturalism, especially as it was developed under André Laurendeau. Biculturalism may have been in close continuity with Henri Bourassa's vision of Canada, but it was not part of his. According to Robert Wright, Trudeau demonstrated as much during preparations for the 1968 conference on constitutional revision. Viewing a text that had been drafted by his staff, Trudeau made some striking revisions: replacing the phrase "Canada is composed of two linguistic communities" with "all Canadians" and deleting outright a reference to "seeking to ensure an equal partnership in confederation," along with a reference to "all persons in Canada of whichever community."[98] Trudeau's individualism, and his vision of Canada, could not be clearer.

Finally, Trudeau was vehemently opposed to any enhanced recognition of Quebec as the primary base of Francophones, including the steps the Pearson government had taken in this direction. In 1966, he declared, "Federalism cannot work unless all the provinces are in basically the same relation to the central government,"[99] and in 1968, he proclaimed, "Particular status for Quebec is the biggest intellectual hoax ever foisted on the people of Quebec and the people of Canada."[100] Indeed, in 1967, he even used a vulgarism ("connerie" or "bullshit") to describe special status.[101]

In effect, Trudeau was attempting to redefine Canadian dualism, drastically reducing its meaning. Rather than a dualism of collectivities it was one of individuals who happen to speak one of two different languages. Nor was this dualism rooted in geography. It was to extend throughout Canada as a whole once language rights were recognized.

Trudeau's version of dualism offered a strategy for undermining the older notion of dualism, and the special significance it bestowed upon Quebec. Through his brand of linguistic dualism Quebec would be reduced to "a province like the others." If minority-language rights were protected throughout Canada, then the French-Canadian nation would stretch from Maillardville in British Columbia to the Acadian community on the Atlantic coast:

> Once you have done that, Quebec cannot say it alone speaks for French Canadians. . . . Mr Robarts will be speaking for French Canadians in Ontario, Mr Robichaud will be speaking for French Canadians in New Brunswick, Mr Thatcher will speak for French Canadians in Saskatchewan, and Mr Pearson will be speaking for all French Canadians. Nobody will be able to say, "I need more power because I speak for the French-Canadian nation."[102]

In effect, Trudeau was calling upon Quebec Francophones to change fundamentally the way in which they see Canada, to cease looking to the Quebec government as the protector of their distinctive interests, and to place their confidence in the federal government instead. As Jeremy Webber has observed, "As [Trudeau] would often tell Quebecers, they had to choose between two alternative—and not complementary—objects of allegiance: Quebec or Canada. Although Trudeau's administration preached respect for provincial jurisdiction, when it came to allegiance he used the language of a unitary state."[103]

The dominant Francophone view of Canada and of the central role of the Quebec government had deep historical roots. Indeed, the notion that Francophones had to place their confidence primarily in the Quebec government, with its largely French-Canadian electorate, had been established in 1791, with the creation of Lower Canada. And it had been reinforced time and again as Francophones struggled with their Anglophone compatriots over basic questions, including the very recognition of the French language. Now, thanks to the neo-nationalist leadership of the Lesage government, the notion of dualism, centred in Quebec, was more deeply rooted than ever. Trudeau could not simply wish away two centuries of history, however eloquent his vision of a linguistic equality that stretched from coast to coast. Besides, his vision simply lacked credibility, for most Francophones knew that their language and their collectivity could never have the strength in the rest of the country that it enjoyed in Quebec.

Thus, when Trudeau launched his bid for the leadership of the Liberal Party, he and his vision of Canada had limited appeal to Quebec Francophones; among the intellectual élites the rejection was massive and open. Symptomatic was the position taken by *Le Devoir* editor, Claude Ryan, whose commitment to federalism was beyond dispute but who had long insisted that there must be an accommodation of Quebec nationalism. Accusing Trudeau of being "dangerously rigid and haughty," he endorsed Paul Hellyer for the Liberal leadership, after Mitchell Sharp became unavailable.[104] At election time, Ryan noted that unlike the rigid and intransigent Pierre Trudeau, the Progressive Conservative leader Robert Stanfield had made a sustained and honest effort to comprehend the Quebec question. Moreover, in choosing Marcel Faribault as his Quebec leader, Stanfield demonstrated that he was prepared to risk displeasing English-Canadian opinion. Thus, Ryan declared his support, as a general rule, for Conservative rather than Liberal candidates.[105] Nonetheless, in February 1968 a petition in favour of Trudeau did appear in *Le Devoir* with the signatures of a very large number of prominent Quebeckers.[106]

The unease of many Francophone intellectuals about Trudeau and his diffidence toward Quebec was only confirmed in February 1968, when Trudeau, who was appearing on CBC English-language television, first attacked the nationalist intellectuals and then in effect ridiculed the whole of Quebec society by denouncing the quality of French spoken in Quebec: "I don't think Ottawa should give one single whit of power to the province of Quebec until it has shown the rest of Canada it can teach better language in its schools." Some Quebec nationalists, he said, spoke "awful French" and they wanted "to impose this lousy French on the whole of Canada."[107]

Among provincial political élites, there was open resistance. Not surprisingly, the Union nationale premier, Daniel Johnson, rejected Trudeau's position on many issues. Indeed, during the subsequent election campaign Trudeau directly attacked Johnson's claim, previously voiced by the Lesage government, that

Quebec was entitled to deal with foreign governments on matters that fell within provincial jurisdiction. The Union nationale organization actively supported the Conservative candidates in Quebec.[108]

Even Quebec's Liberal forces greeted Trudeau and his vision with great apprehension. A month before the convention most of the Liberal members of the Quebec legislature were actively campaigning against his candidacy.[109] Over the previous few years, the Quebec Liberal Party had embraced what was anathema to Trudeau: special status for Quebec. Jean Lesage had been propounding the idea since 1965.[110] The Quebec Liberals may have rejected René Lévesque's scheme of sovereignty-association at its 1967 convention, but, so pervasive was Quebec nationalism in the party that it had adopted an alternative scheme, defined in a lengthy report by Paul Gérin-Lajoie, that was nothing less than special status.[111] Jean Lesage had watched Trudeau's entry into federal politics with considerable alarm. He directly protested Pearson's appointment of Trudeau as his parliamentary secretary in 1965,[112] and was offended by Trudeau's "connerie" remark.[113] When the race began for Pearson's successor, he supported Robert Winters and despaired at the thought of Trudeau's being a candidate.[114] (Once it became clear that Trudeau was the front runner, some Quebec Liberals did come out in his support.[115])

Speaking for Quebec

In the end, fortune favoured Trudeau, allowing him to emerge as the leading Quebec voice in the federal arena. The Quebec leaders who had supported Pearson during his early years as prime minister, such as Maurice Lamontagne and Guy Favreau, were no longer there, for one reason or another. The three Quebec "doves"—Marchand, Pelletier, and Trudeau—had been brought in to fill the void. For his part, Pearson was determined that his successor be a Francophone. Indeed, the long-standing Liberal practice of alternance required as much. In fact, back in November of 1965, he had had an intermediary inquire of Jean Lesage as to his interest in being the successor.[116] Thus, on the day he announced his retirement, Pearson summoned Marchand and Trudeau to a meeting, apparently for this purpose.[117] He had presumed that Marchand would succeed him but, declaring that he would not run for the leadership, Marchand called upon Trudeau to take up the challenge. No other Quebec Francophone came forward.

Still the Quebec Liberals did not fall in line behind Trudeau, in part because of his views on Quebec. The Quebec wing was formally committed to a two-nations position.[118] During the months leading up to Trudeau's formal declaration of his candidacy, Senator Maurice Lamontagne, who had played such a critical role in developing the Pearson strategy for Quebec, had persisted in making the case for special status and arguing against Trudeau's views.[119] None of the leading Francophone cabinet members, other than Marchand, declared for Trudeau.

The senior Quebec cabinet minister, Maurice Sauvé, supported Paul Martin.[120] Jean-Luc Pepin, who had helped to elaborate Pearson's notions of "co-operative federalism," came out for Mitchell Sharp, shifting to Trudeau only with great reluctance after Sharp withdrew in favour of Trudeau.[121] Léo Cadieux declared himself firmly for Paul Hellyer.[122] Jean-Pierre Côté supported Robert Winters.[123] Newly minted cabinet member Jean Chrétien had no problem with Trudeau's vision—he had spoken out against special status for Quebec[124]—but he first supported his mentor, Mitchell Sharp, before following him to Trudeau.

Nor did the Quebec caucus rally behind Trudeau. Two months before the convention, only 20 of the 74 MPs and senators of the Quebec caucus showed up at a meeting to support Trudeau's candidacy.[125] Half of the caucus persisted in supporting other candidates during the whole leadership race.[126] Two weeks before the convention, Trudeau's organization claimed to have the support of half the Quebec backbenchers, but one of those named then declared for Robert Winters.[127] Indeed, the president of the caucus supported Paul Hellyer. According to a report prepared three days before the convention, the Quebec caucus was so badly divided that if the party as a whole had been in such shape it would have had difficulty surviving the convention.[128] Nonetheless, Jean Marchand and other power brokers had been pressing hard for Trudeau, incurring complaints in the process.[129] In the end, apparently the majority of Quebec MPs did vote for him.[130]

Trudeau's ascension as primary federal spokesman for Quebec was further aided in July 1968 by the death of André Laurendeau, at the age of 56. One of the leading Francophone intellectuals of his generation and the spiritual heir to Henri Bourassa, Laurendeau had gone to Ottawa as co-chair of the Royal Commission on Bilingualism and Biculturalism in order to represent the established French-Canadian view of dualism. As we shall see, that view pervaded the deliberations and reports of the Commission as long as he presided over them. No one else in the Commission, or in the federal arena, possessed Laurendeau's stature.

With Laurendeau's death, there was no one on the federal scene who could credibly dispute Trudeau's claim that his vision of Canada represented the aspirations of Quebec Francophones, and Trudeau had no difficulty disposing of those few English Canadians who tried to do so. Thus, Trudeau's vision of Canada, however widely it may have been rejected in Quebec, was accepted as the official definition of "what Quebec wants."

The Trudeau Vision and English Canada

Trudeau's vision of Canada had even less relationship to the predominant English-Canadian idea of Canada than it did to that of most Quebeckers. Certainly, English Canadians had never displayed much interest in dualism, even in Trudeau's highly attenuated linguistic form. And the predominantly English-Canadian provincial governments had all acted to reduce or eliminate French language rights, apparently with the support of most of their English-Canadian majorities. Nor had English Canadians ever shown much concern over the marginal status of French in federal institutions. English Canadians may have believed in human rights, to varying degrees, but they clearly did not see language rights as one of them.

By the same token, English-Canadian political and intellectual élites were far from united in support of a constitutional bill of rights. Thus, when Trudeau presented his proposal for a constitutionally entrenched bill of rights to the Canadian Bar Association, in September 1967, he met with widespread resistance from its leading members.[131] After all, Canada had always followed the British practice of relying upon convention and common law to protect basic rights. The notion of a charter collided with the British principle of parliamentary supremacy. John Diefenbaker had succeeded in securing a Canadian Bill of Rights, as a simple Act of Parliament, but of course it had nothing to do with protecting language rights. Indeed, when as prime minister, Trudeau presented his proposal for a bill of rights in February 1969, most provinces either rejected it outright or sought to restrict it to political rights alone.[132]

Nevertheless, even if Trudeau's vision of Canada had little similarity to the way most English-Canadians thought of their country, it still had something attractive to offer. Whereas Quebec Francophones were becoming more tied than ever in their historical notion of Canada, English Canadians were becoming increasingly uneasy with theirs. As we have seen, the notion of Canada that was rooted in the British connection and British political traditions was being threatened by the decline of Britain and the spread of American dominance throughout the world. Indeed, a distinctly Canadian nationalism had been steadily growing, thanks in part to a series of actions by the federal state itself.

Trudeau's vision provided some content to this emerging sense of Canadian nationhood. He offered Canada a new, compelling purpose that had significance for the world as a whole. Canada would show how different groups could live peaceably in the same country. Moreover, Canadians would not simply share the same country but they would come together to create a new society. In the process, Canada, and Canadians, would assume an importance that they had never had before. As H.D. Forbes has written:

> Trudeau's vision was a *moral* vision because it involved more than just good economic planning to increase the material wealth of Canadians. . . . It appealed to their moral sense, challenging them to rise above their irrational fears and traditional prejudices in order to do something important for mankind [emphasis in original].[133]

Much more was at stake than the mere survival of Canada. The real issue was the fundamental issue of politics everywhere: defence of reason, threatened by the forces of emotion. Trudeau's vision of Canada had a strong element of "rational messianism," to use Reg Whitaker's phrase.[134]

In short, Canada would be a different kind of nation because it would transcend conventional nationalism, and indeed emotions of any kind. Of course, such a sense of historic purpose can itself provide a powerful focus for nationalism, even if it should be in the name of a "non-nation." It might even support a sense of superiority to lesser countries.

Several years later, when the Canadian experiment seemed to be threatened by the unexpected election of René Lévesque's Parti québécois, Trudeau expressed this new Canadian messianism in especially dramatic terms:

> Times, circumstances and pure will cemented us together in a unique national enterprise, and that enterprise, by flying in the face of all expectations, of all experiences, of all conventional wisdom, that enterprise provides the world with a lesson in fraternity. This extraordinary undertaking is so advanced in the way of social justice and of prosperity, that to abandon it now would be to sin against the spirit, to sin against humanity.[135]

Even if English Canadians did not come to believe that the unity of the Canadian nation had such universal significance as Trudeau claimed, it was important for most of them. In these terms as well, Trudeau's vision had something to offer; namely a strategy for solving the Quebec problem. It was a strategy moreover that was far more congenial to most English Canadians than the effort to accommodate Quebec nationalism that Pearson and others had so laboriously pursued. Within Trudeau's strategy accommodation was no longer necessary; in fact, it was counterproductive. Instead, unity could be achieved simply through official bilingualism and a constitutional charter, measures applied throughout the country as a whole. There would be no more calls to make Canada "an equal partnership" between Francophones and Anglophones. Quebec could be treated as a province just like the others, and Quebec Francophones would become Canadians like everyone else.

For all these reasons, it is not surprising that many English Canadians should have seen Trudeau as the saviour, the embodiment of the Canadian nation—the perfect example of the new Canadian.[136] In Paul Litt's words, "Trudeaumania was the birth of a nation."[137] As well, Trudeau's iconoclastic and individualist personal style was well suited to the spirit of the sixties. He was "the mod candidate for a mod Canada."[138]

Moreover, Trudeau came on the public scene just as many English Canadians had become imbued as never before with the new Canadian nationalism. The 1967 Centennial celebrations had been a resounding success in much of the country.[139] As the year ended, concern grew over how this fervour might be sustained.[140] Trudeau, and his vision of Canada, provided the answer—and became central pillars of Canadian nationalism as a result. Two leading English-Canadian journalists captured this process well. Peter C. Newman described Trudeau's performance at the 1968 Liberal convention:

> It's as though Trudeau is performing what Norman Mailer once described as "the indispensable psychic act of a leader, who takes national anxieties so long buried and releases them to the surface where they belong". . . . He seems to hold out the promise that the process of discovering Canada has not come to an end, that Expo 67 wasn't just a momentary phenomenon, that this is a young nation with vast, unexploited possibilities. He personifies the hoped-for sophistication of the perfectly bicultural Canada of tomorrow.[141]

Remembering the mood of 1968, Richard Gwyn writes:

> The 1968 election and the Centennial and Expo were together the last time we were wholly confident of ourselves as a country. . . . In 1968, we invested a part of our national psyche in Trudeau. . . . We called it, in 1968, Trudeau-mania. Really, it was Canada-mania.[142]

From his different vantage point, Claude Ryan commented sardonically on the tendency of English Canada, ever since the fall of St. Laurent, to look to Quebec for a "political messiah" who will enable Canada to progress while at the same time avoiding discontent among French Canadians. Trudeau was simply the latest in a long line of candidates. To that point, no one had proved equal to the task.[143]

There is, of course, considerable irony in the possibility that English Canadians should have seen Trudeau as saviour of the Canadian nation. In his writings, he had gone to great pains to dissociate himself from Canadian nationalism, just as he so passionately rejected nationalism in general. "Manifeste pour une politique fonctionnelle," ("Manifesto for a Functional Politics") the 1964 manifesto of which he was a primary author, had declared:

> Making nationalism the decisive criterion for policies and priorities is a sterile and reactionary choice. . . . Whether it be the first budget, in June 1963, of the Honourable Walter Gordon, the regulations of the Board of Broadcast Governors on Canadian content, the current intolerance of "white, Anglo-Saxon Protestants," or the widespread notion that "the State of Quebec" should be the economic arm of French Canada, we are dealing with the same problem.[144]

As for Canada, it is simply a fact of history. To break it up would be to evade the real issues. To integrate it with the United States would be in conformity with world trends, but would be a mistake *at the present time*:

> First of all, there is this legal and geographic fact: Canada. To try to split it in two . . . strikes us as an escape from real and important tasks that need to be done. To try to integrate it with another geographic entity also strikes us as a futile undertaking at present, even though, in principle, that might seem more in accord with the way the world is evolving.[145]

Walter Gordon recognized that Trudeau was "not a nationalist" and hesitated to support him for the Liberal leadership.[146] (In the end, he did back Trudeau.[147]) By the same token, upon becoming prime minister, Trudeau had little patience for the concerns of English-Canadian nationalists about the economic and cultural domination by the United States. Walter Gordon abandoned the Liberal Party to found the Committee for an Independent Canada.[148] Of course, Trudeau's position evolved substantially during his tenure as prime minister.

At the same time, beyond offering English Canadians new hope and meaning for their country, whether as beacon to the world or a nation reunited by bilingualism, Trudeau had the more prosaic appeal of being a Quebec Francophone who seemed prepared to put Quebec in its place. He may not have proclaimed that intention himself, but his vehement opposition to special status may have seemed to promise as much, especially if his plans for official bilingualism should be ignored.

Finally, the fierceness of Trudeau's opposition to Quebec nationalism may have reassured English Canadians who were troubled by the continuing acts of violence by the Front de libération du Québec. Trudeau, it seemed, could be relied upon to restore order and respect for the law in Quebec.

Whatever the precise balance of factors at work, Pierre Trudeau's vision of Canada clearly did mobilize support among some English Canadians, both in his campaign for the Liberal leadership and in the subsequent federal election. And unlike their Quebec counterparts, leading English-Canadian intellectuals actively supported Trudeau's candidacy from the outset. Among them was Ramsay Cook, who had left the NDP in protest over the question of "two nations." For Cook, Trudeau was "straight" on Quebec.[149] Eventually 600 academics signed a petition in support of Trudeau's candidacy.[150]

Mobilizing English-Canadian Support: Intellectual and Cultural Élites

Similarly, a number of rising young Ontario MPs, such as Donald Macdonald and Robert Stanbury, formed an organization to rally support for Trudeau. Later, when Mitchell Sharp withdrew from the race, he threw his support to Trudeau. Indeed, Lester Pearson favoured Trudeau as his successor and let it be known in several ways.[151]

Still, to support Trudeau was not necessarily to endorse his approach to national unity, which in fact made some of his supporters quite uneasy. As we have seen, Pearson had serious reservations about Trudeau to the end. He found Trudeau to be too much of a centralist and was uncomfortable with Trudeau's confrontational style. He had wanted his successor be a Francophone, but had imagined it to be Jean Marchand and favoured Trudeau only after Marchand proved to be unavailable.[152] Even Mitchell Sharp, during his campaign for the Liberal leadership, made an effort to distinguish his position from Trudeau's, declaring that Ottawa should be flexible in its dealings with Quebec, because a confrontation between Ottawa and Quebec City would be "disastrous" for the country's future. After withdrawing in favour of Trudeau, Sharp still said he would prefer that Trudeau be less rigid in constitutional matters, although he did not expect any major disagreements with Trudeau.[153] For their part, Eric Kierans and John Turner both proposed a special status for Quebec. Indeed, all of Trudeau's opponents for the leadership professed a readiness to find an accommodation of Quebec, and distinguished themselves from Trudeau on that basis.[154]

Bringing Canada into Line

Winning the Liberal Leadership

Finally, at the Liberal convention on 6 April 1968, Trudeau won the leadership of the party and the right to become prime minister. The result had not been a foregone conclusion. Nonetheless, Trudeau won on the fourth ballot with 1203 votes, 249 more than his main rival, Robert Winters. Two weeks later, Trudeau became prime minister. However, on 23 April he announced to Parliament that, given the consent of the Governor General, Parliament was dissolved and a general election would take place on 25 June. As a consequence of dissolution, there was no opportunity for customary tributes to the outgoing prime minister, Lester Pearson.

During the election campaign Trudeau succeeded in making national unity the central issue. True to form, he railed against any notion of special status or arrangement with Quebec contending that he wanted a mandate to "put Quebec in its place," which meant being fully part of Canada. He attacked the Progressive Conservatives for their two-nations vision of Canada, portraying the party as hostage to Quebec nationalists. Stanfield, who by this point was moderating his support of two nations, accused Trudeau of misrepresenting the PC position.[155] Speaking in Saint John, Trudeau zeroed in on Marcel Faribault and other Quebec PCs who claimed that their conception of two nations was based on a "sociological" sense of nation. He argued that not only did this notion reject one-third of the country but that in any event it implied bi-national political institutions. He challenged Faribault and others to "say quite frankly that they are not talking of two nations in the sociological sense or any other—two nations which can lead into the kind of political consequences of special status." And he denounced special status as being not only unworkable but an insult to Quebeckers: "The people of Quebec don't want special status, treatment or privilege. They don't need a wheelchair or a crutch to get along."[156]

As it happened, his image as fierce defender of Canadian unity was cemented the evening before the election when, during a Montreal St. Jean Baptiste parade, he refused to abandon his place when separatist demonstrators began to hurl projectiles at the reviewing stand—and was the only dignitary to do so. On 25 June, the Liberals secured a majority of seats: 155 seats with 45 per cent of the popular vote, compared to the Progressive Conservatives' 72 seats (31 per cent), the NDP's 22 seats (17 per cent), and the Créditistes' 14 (4 per cent).

Getting a Majority

How should Trudeau's 1968 electoral victory be interpreted? Certainly, his personal appeal was a large part of the story. But how significant were his ideas on Quebec and its place in Canada? Even in Quebec, the Liberal support was not as great as it might have seemed. Although the Liberals' victory in 56 of Quebec's 74 ridings was interpreted by some observers as proof that Trudeau's vision expressed the aspirations of Francophones, it is not clear that the Liberals were supported by a majority of Quebec's Francophones. Although the Liberal popular vote in Quebec was the highest of all the provinces, it was still only 53.6 per cent; and Francophones in Quebec were considerably less likely than non-Francophones to support the Liberals.[157] Even then, the Liberal support may have been based as much on Trudeau's favourite-son status as on his vision of Canada. (Trudeaumania, of course, was a distinctly English-Canadian phenomenon.[158]) However receptive the PCs and NDP may have been to Quebec's demands for distinct status, the leaderships of both parties were effectively English Canadian. The PCs may have enlisted Marcel Faribault as their Quebec leader, and the NDP had the highly popular Robert Cliche, but neither of them even held seats; Trudeau was already prime minister. Still, the Liberal popular vote in Quebec was eight percentage points over their 1965 result.[159]

In any case, the 1968 electoral victory had the direct result that Trudeau's vision reigned supreme in the Liberal Party and in the federal government. The two other federal parties were still officially in favour of the 1960s strategy of developing openings to Quebec nationalism, but Trudeau's electoral victory took care of that too. The predominantly English-Canadian PC and NDP leaderships found their positions untenable when a Quebec Francophone prime minister, who had become the effective spokesperson for Quebec at the federal level, was claiming on the basis of deep personal knowledge of Quebec that such a strategy was both unnecessary and wrong-headed. Not surprisingly, many English-Canadian voters were finding his arguments very appealing. Indeed, during the 1968 election campaign Trudeau had been unsparing in his condemnation of the PCs and NDP for their Quebec strategies. Trudeau's comments on the NDP's support for special status provoked NDP leader Tommy Douglas to charge that Trudeau was dividing Canada as it had not been divided for a long time. "Anyone who talks about special status for Quebec or any negotiation is automatically called a separatist [by Trudeau]."[160]

The PCs and the NDP: Falling in Line

After the election, the PCs and the NDP soon fell in line with the new Trudeau orthodoxy. In the case of the PCs, the commitment to accommodate the demands of Quebec nationalists had in any event been qualified. Moreover, the architect of the opening, Marcel Faribault, went down to ignominious defeat. Thus, the PCs simply abandoned their strategy; no formal debate was necessary.

With the NDP things were more complicated. There, the commitment to an accommodation of Quebec nationalism was more deeply rooted. In fact, there had been pressure in the party in the late 1960s for a stronger position. Many of the members of the Quebec NDP had never been satisfied with the party's positions, which did not allow for as thorough a change in Quebec's constitutional position as they wanted. And the party had not granted their long-held wish for a formal recognition of Quebec's right to self-determination. In fact, the Quebec members had not even dared to present the proposition to the party, knowing it would be rejected.

By the late 1960s, however, pressure from Quebec was joined by radicalized forces within the English-Canadian membership, grouped around the Waffle. At the 1971 NDP convention, the Waffle and the Quebec NDP combined to support a resolution calling for formal recognition of Quebec's right to self-determination. For the party leadership this was unacceptable. Though it was prepared to support renunciation of the use of force to prevent separation, it feared that the notion of a right to self-determination conveyed an openness to Quebec independence that would offend the Canadian nationalism of most English Canadians. The resolution on Quebec's right to self-determination was defeated, receiving the vote of a third of the convention delegates. For its part, the leadership presented an alternative resolution, "Towards a New Canada," which, though it declared that "The unity of this country cannot be based on force," eschewed the language of self-determination. After a prolonged and at times emotional debate, that resolution was endorsed by a vote of 853 to 423.[161]

Other sections of the leadership's resolution made it clear that not only were the leaders fiercely opposed to the position on Quebec self-determination advanced by the Waffle and the Quebec NDP, but they were now even opposed to the whole approach to the Quebec question that the party had struggled so hard to develop during the 1960s. This too, they had concluded, was beyond the limits of acceptability for most English Canadians. Thus, "Towards a New Canada" declared,

> We have attempted to resolve these [constitutional] differences with phrases which have proven to be open to a dual interpretation, something which has created sharp difference within all political parties. These phrases, such as "two nations," "special status," "equal partnership," have often proved to be obstacles to agreement rather than aids. The time has come to find precise ways of stating the deep issues in order to bring to the fullest clarity the major differences.

The resolution offered no hint as to what the "precise ways" might be. It simply called for the NDP federal council to "establish machinery" that would define the assumptions and procedures for "a complete renegotiation of our constitutional arrangements."[162] In effect, it was calling a halt to the whole effort to find an accommodation of Quebec nationalism.

In the words of Charles Taylor, a leading figure in that effort, expressions such as "two nations" and "special status" had become "ping pong" words that meant different things in English Canada and Quebec, and that had come back to haunt the NDP.[163] To put it more concretely, the NDP's overtures to Quebec nationalism had not brought the expected electoral benefits in Quebec, and during the 1968 election they had become a liability in the rest of the country.[164]

The fact of the matter is that the reason "two nations" and "special status" had become a liability for the NDP was the new prominence of Pierre Trudeau and his message. Whereas the Quebec NDP, and Quebec in general, had been moving to a more radical position on Quebec–Canada relations, the leadership of the NDP and most of English Canada were stepping back. In both cases, the explanation is the same: when Pierre Trudeau became prime minister, the struggle to find in Canadian federalism an accommodation of the new Quebec nationalism, a struggle that had enlisted all three federal parties, had come to a full and irrevocable end. Now firmly established in power, Trudeau and his like-minded colleagues were free to pursue their new strategy for dealing with the Quebec question. In the process, the premises on which the Pearson government had struggled to develop its approach were definitively abandoned. Rather than seek to accommodate Quebec nationalism, "coming to terms with the Quiet Revolution" as Pearson put it in his memoirs, the Trudeau government tried to confront Quebec nationalism head on and to replace it with a new Canadian identity. By and large the federal government acted as if Quebec were simply a province like the others, and avoided policies that threatened to suggest otherwise.

We will see in the next chapter how the Trudeau government tried to apply its language policy on a pan-Canadian basis, minimizing concessions to regional differences in language use, and especially to the notion that in Quebec the Francophone majority might need special attention. The following chapter will consider why the Trudeau government rejected the concept of biculturalism, so carefully elaborated by the royal commission that Pearson had established, in favour of multiculturalism. Finally, we will see how, when it came to federalism and the constitution, the Trudeau government had no patience whatsoever for the Pearson government's notions of asymmetry and particular status.

Throughout the 1960s, Trudeau had insisted that the Pearson government's policy of accommodation could only intensify the national unity problem rather than ease it. His new confrontational approach promised to resolve the issue once and for all. Yet, as we shall see, 50 years later Canadians remain divided on the nature of their country.

Notes

1. "The just man must go to prison . . .," as reproduced in Pierre Elliott Trudeau, *Approaches to Politics* (Don Mills: Oxford University Press, 2015), 34.
2. Henry David Rempel, "The Practice and Theory of the Fragile State: Trudeau's Conception of Authority," *Journal of Canadian Studies* 10, no. 4 (Nov. 1975): 24–38.
3. This is the implication of the presentation of rights in "The right to protest" (Trudeau, *Approaches to Politics*, 80–3), and the rejection of plebiscites (ibid., 89).
4. Speech made by Pierre Trudeau at Sudbury, Ont., 5 June 1968, as quoted by Robert Vipond, "Citizenship and the Charter of Rights: Two Sides of Pierre Trudeau," *International Journal of Canadian Studies*, no. 14 (Fall 1996). Vipond argues that English Canadians have never accepted Trudeau's contention that individual rights should include language rights.
5. The proposal was contained in his submission to the Tremblay Commission. See Trudeau, *Federalism and the French Canadians* (Toronto: Macmillan, 1968), 53.
6. Ibid., 55. See also Peter C. Newman, *The Distemper of Our Times* (Toronto: McClelland & Stewart, 1968), 330.
7. Transcript of interview with Norman DePoe, 23 Jan. 1968, as quoted in Litt, *Trudeaumania* (Vancouver: UBC Press, 2016), 158.
8. See the chapters by Michael Higgins and John Turner in *The Hidden Pierre Elliott Trudeau: The Faith behind the Politics*, ed. John English, Richard Gwyn, and P. Whitney Lackenbauer (Toronto: Novalis. 2004).
9. John English, *Citizen of the World: The Life of Pierre Elliott Trudeau* (Toronto: Knopf Canada, 2006), 223. Also, see Max and Monique Nemni, *Trudeau Transformed: The Shaping of a Statesman, 1944–1965*, trans George Tombs (Toronto: McClelland & Stewart, 2011), 57.
10. G. Pelletier, *Years of Impatience*, 119 (as cited in Nemnis, *Trudeau Transformed*, 486).
11. Personalism is outlined, with stress on its communitarian dimension, by André Burelle, *Pierre Elliott Trudeau: l'intellectuel et le politique* (Montreal: Fides, 2005), 25–44. Burelle cites a number of passages from Trudeau's *Cité libre* texts that reflect the personalist communitarianism of Mounier and Maritain (ibid., 45–52). See also Mills, *Citizen Trudeau, 1944–1965: An Intellectual Biography* (Don Mills: Oxford University Press, 2016), 79–98. Trudeau's relationship with personalism is traced in Jacques Monet, "The Man's Formation in Faith," in English et al., *The Hidden Pierre Elliott Trudeau*, 87–94.

12. Trudeau, *Memoirs* (Toronto: McClelland & Stewart, 1993), 40.
13. The influence of personalism in 1950s Quebec is discussed in Jean-Philippe Warren, "Let the Jesuits and the Dominicans Quarrel: A French-Canadian Debate of the Fifties," in English et al., *The Hidden Pierre Elliott Trudeau*, 65–74. Trudeau was not himself involved with the JÉC, but addressed a JÉC event and was a close friend of JÉC leader, Gérard Pelletier. (Mills, *Citizen Trudeau*, 81.)
14. Stephen Clarkson and Christina McCall, *Trudeau and Our Times*, vol. 1 (Toronto: McClelland & Stewart, 1990), 55–6. Writing in the late 1990s, Trudeau declared:

    I was influenced . . . by my reading of Jacques Maritain and the so-called personalists. Personalism essentially said that the individual, not the state, must be supreme, with basic rights and freedoms, because the individual is the only moral entity, the only one who has significance. But, granted that, we should view the individual as a person involved in society and with responsibilities to it. . . . I found personalism a good way to distinguish my thinking from the self-centred individualism of *laissez-faire* liberalism (or modern-day neo-conservatism, for that matter) by bestowing it with a sense of duty to the community in which one is living. (Pierre Elliott Trudeau, *The Essential Trudeau*, ed. Ron Graham [Toronto: McClelland & Stewart, 1998] 5, emphasis in original.)

15. Burelle, *Trudeau*, 68. For their part, the Nemnis take great pains to dispute Burelle's linkage of Trudeau and Mounier. They tie Trudeau to Jacques Maritain alone, given Mounier's pro-Soviet sympathies, while making a case for Nicolas Berdyaev of whom Trudeau made no mention (Nemnis, *Trudeau Transformed*, 70–2 and 226–31). Yet Mills points out that in his later life Trudeau continued to refer to Mounier and that Trudeau himself was not without pro-Soviet sympathies at points in his early life. (Mills, *Citizen Trudeau*, 448 n. 56 and 450 n. 107).
16. See the account of the Asbestos Strike in Nemnis, *Trudeau Transformed*, 169–82.
17. See the account in ibid., 324–35.
18. English, *Citizen of the World*, 173.
19. Trudeau, *Memoirs*, 70.
20. English, *Citizen of the World*, 296 and 366, and Mills, *Citizen Trudeau*, 207.
21. Pierre Elliott Trudeau, "Economic Rights," *McGill Law Review* 8, no. 2 (1962): 122.
22. Ibid., 124. See also the account of Trudeau's writings in Mills, *Citizen Trudeau*, Chap. 6. Mills dismisses the argument of Clarkson and McCall that by the 1960s Trudeau had been converted to neo-liberal views through the influence of Albert Breton and others (ibid., 242–6). The 1962 publication date supports Mills's position. This is also the position of English, *Citizen of the World*, 380.
23. Mills, *Citizen Trudeau*, 294–5.
24. The ban was subsequently lifted (English, *Citizen of the World*, 270). This account of Trudeau's international views and initiatives draws upon Mills, *Citizen Trudeau*, Chap. 7. Mills effectively counters the Nemnis' claim that Trudeau had displayed no sympathies for the Soviet Union or Mao's China (ibid., 275).
25. English, *Citizen of the World*, 381.
26. "Although he had always been a reformer and a supporter of trade unionists and other social activists, his philosophy was liberal, left liberal," Ramsay Cook, *The Teeth of Time: Remembering Pierre Elliott Trudeau* (Montreal and Kingston: McGill-Queen's University Press, 2006), 97.
27. Wright, *Trudeaumania: The Rise to Power of Pierre Elliott Trudeau* (Toronto: Harper Collins, 2016), 32.
28. Mills, *Citizen Trudeau*, 438. Mills also states that when Trudeau joined the Liberals in 1965 he was a "socialist of social democratic sort," (246).
29. Nemnis, *Trudeau Transformed*, 286.
30. See the presentation in Burelle, *Pierre Elliott Trudeau*, 41–4.
31. Mills, *Citizen Trudeau*, 104.
32. Lord Acton and his ideas are presented ibid., 347–50.
33. Trudeau, *Federalism and the French Canadians*, 191 (emphasis in original).
34. Ibid. 192.
35. *Mémoire de la fédération des unions industrielles du Québec*, 7, as quoted in Nemnis, *Trudeau Transformed*, 334.
36. Pierre Elliott Trudeau, "De libro, tributo . . . et quibusdam aliis," *Cité libre*, Oct. 1954.

37. "Les octrois fédéraux aux universités," *Cité libre*, Feb. 1957.
38. Pierre Elliott Trudeau, "The Practice and Theory of Federalism," as reproduced in Trudeau, *Federalism and the French* Canadians, 137. Mills notes that by 1969 "Trudeau changed his mind on this issue" and proposed constitutionally entrenching a federal spending power. (Mills, *Citizen Trudeau*, 339.)
39. Mills traces the thinking along these lines of personalist theologian Joseph Thomas Delos, noting that this squared with Maritain but that Mounier's views were not so clear-cut. (Mills, *Citizen Trudeau*, 113, 344–6.)
40. Ibid.
41. My translation of "De la sorte, la doctrine sociale de l'Église, qui en d'autres pays ouvrait la voie large à la démocratisation des peuples, à l'émancipation des travailleurs et au progrès social, était invoquée au Canada français à l'appui de l'autoritarisme et de la xénophobie. Et, ce qui est plus grave, notre doctrine nous mettait dans l'impossibilité de résoudre nos problèmes. Car, du côté négatif, elle rejetait toute solution qui pût réussir chez nos 'ennemis': les Anglais, protestants, matérialistes, etc." Pierre Elliott Trudeau, ed., *La grève de l'amiante* (Montreal: Éditions du Jour, 1970), 21.
42. Pierre Elliott Trudeau, *Federalism and the French Canadians*, 106–7.
43. Pierre Elliott Trudeau, "La nouvelle trahison des clercs," *Cité libre*, Apr. 1962, as translated and reproduced in Trudeau, *Federalism and the French Canadians*, 180.
44. Casgrain, *A Woman*, 139, as cited by Mills, *Citizen Trudeau*, 471 n. 72.
45. English, *Citizen of the World* and *Just Watch Me: the Life of Pierre Elliott Trudeau, 1968–2000* (Toronto: Knopf, 2009); Mills, *Citizen Trudeau*; and Max and Monique Nemni, *Trudeau: fils du Québec, père du Canada* (Quebec: Éditions de l'Homme, 2006) and *Trudeau Transformed*.
46. English, *Citizen of the World*, 45.
47. My translation of "être homme d'État sera ma profession," Nemnis, *Trudeau: fils du Québec, père du Canada*, vol. 1, 393. This was also the case with his (unsuccessful) application for a Rhodes Scholarship. (Nemnis, *Trudeau*, vol. 1, 141, and English, *Citizen of the World*, 66.)
48. For his part, Robert Wright rejects Christina McCall's contention that Trudeau won the Liberal leadership through "cunning and charisma" by contending that "Almost nothing in the public record or Trudeau's private papers supports this claim. There was no grand design behind Pierre Trudeau's rise to power, nor any method, covert or otherwise, for achieving it." (Wright, *Trudeaumania*, 25.) It is hard to square Wright's statement with the evidence of such a long-standing political ambition.
49. English, *Citizen of the World*, 74–5.
50. My translation of "une communauté de foi, de génie, de sang, de langue," Nemnis, *Trudeau*, vol. 1, 285.
51. Ibid., 250–62.
52. English, *Citizen of the World*, 48–9.
53. Mills, *Citizen Trudeau*, 20.
54. Nemnis, *Trudeau*, vol. 1, Chap. 9; English, *Citizen of the World*, 76; Mills, *Citizen Trudeau*, 18, 24–25.
55. Nemnis, *Trudeau*, 78.
56. English, *Citizen of the World*, 49; Mills, *Citizen Trudeau*, 21.
57. Nemnis, *Trudeau*, vol. 1, 324–5.
58. Ibid., 338–44; English, *Citizen of the World*, 96.
59. Nino Ricci, *Pierre Elliott Trudeau* (Toronto: Penguin, 2009), 66–7.
60. My translation of "la Patrie qui renaîtra de la Révolution est catholique, française et laurentienne," Nemnis, *Trudeau*, vol. 1, 282. The group had as many as 500 supporters.
61. Nemnis, *Trudeau*, vol. 2, 295; English, *Citizen of the World*, 76. As English notes, "astonishingly" no journalist followed up on the question and response. René Matte, who posed the question, had himself been involved with a right-wing nationalist group in the early 1960s (*Journal de Québec*, 2 Mar. 2016).
62. Trudeau, *Memoirs*, 34. Trudeau contends that the speech "was, I believe, my only participation in the politics of that era." Nonetheless, during that time, Trudeau remained involved in activities of the *Bloc* (English, *Citizen of the World*, 117) as he had been with the Groupe LX. For that matter, much later, when he was prime minister and an essay he wrote in 1944 was to be translated and published, the text apparently was modified so as to remove

suggestion of nationalist leanings. (Cook, *The Teeth of Time*, 92, and English, *Citizen of the World*, 122.)

63. Actually, the contentions about Trudeau were first made, several years before the Nemnis' book, by Esther Delisle, *Essais sur l'imprégnation fasciste au Québec* (Montreal: Les Éditions Varia, 2002), 19–101. She has not displayed the same general sympathy for Trudeau. However, unlike the Nemnis, she did not have access to the Trudeau papers.
64. See English, *Citizen of the World*, 76, and Mills, *Citizen Trudeau*, 24.
65. English points to a claim by Jean Marchand, as reported by Gérard Pelletier, that such groups were "innumerable" at the time and that "the half-baked leaders of these little groups had no precise notion of what political action meant." (English, *Citizen of the World*, 101.)
66. Ramsay Cook, *The Teeth of Time*, 92. (Cook does acknowledge that on the basis of more recent research he recognized that Trudeau's transformation "was more radical and astonishing than I had realized or easily accepted," ibid.)
67. English, *Citizen of the World*, 101.
68. Trudeau, *Memoirs*, 17. On the other hand, Clarkson and McCall contend that, after the father's death, the mother and children "spoke English almost exclusively to one another." (Clarkson and McCall, *Trudeau and Our Times*, vol. 2, 35.)
69. Ibid., 18.
70. English, *Citizen of the World*, 102.
71. Ricci, *Pierre Elliott Trudeau*, 71.
72. Clarkson and McCall, *Trudeau and Our Times*, vol. 1, 38.
73. Nemnis, *Trudeau: fils du Québec, père du Canada*, 390.
74. Ibid., 200.
75. A British diplomat who lunched with Trudeau in 1984, just before he was to leave office, reported that Trudeau spoke "almost entirely about French Canada, French Canadians, the Jesuits, the Oblates and their respective methods of education, etc. It reminded us once more what a different world even Federal French Canadians inhabit, and how they still feel themselves an embattled minority." (Paul Waldie, "Files Show What U.K. Diplomats Really Thought of 1980s Canada, but Were Too Polite to Say," *Globe and Mail*, 23 Aug. 2016).
76. Apparently, Trudeau resisted these ideas initially. (Nemnis, *Trudeau Transformed*, 36.)
77. Ibid., 38.
78. Trudeau, *Memoirs*, 61.
79. English, *Citizen of the World*, 204.
80. Trudeau, *Memoirs*, 64. For their part, the Nemnis insist that the Ottawa stint was simply part of Trudeau's plan to prepare for political office. (Nemnis, *Trudeau Transformed*, 9.)
81. André Laurendeau, "Sur cent pages de Pierre Elliott Trudeau," *Le Devoir*, 6 Oct. 1956. (My translations of the following phrases: "est un Canadien français déçu des siens", "le blesse dans son être même", and "je crois qu'il a honte d'avoir de tels pères.") André Burelle cites Laurendeau's interpretation, in full agreement (Burelle, *Pierre Elliott Trudeau*, 71). The Nemnis acknowledge that Laurendeau's view "has gone down in history" but do not endorse it (Nemnis, *Trudeau Transformed*, 360).
82. My translation of "J'ai peur que l'antinationalisme de Pierre ne soit devenu un dogmatisme," Gérard Pelletier, *Les années d'impatience*, 135 (as quoted by Burelle, *Pierre Elliott Trudeau*, 71).
83. "Je suis plus sensibilisé que Pierre au nationalisme québécois. Bien sûr, je suis canadien. Mais, d'une certaine façon, je suis plus québécois que canadien." As quoted in Gérard Bergeron, *Notre miroir à deux faces* (Montreal: Québec/Amérique, 1985), 98 n. 73.
84. Nino Ricci writes of Trudeau's time at Harvard, "Much of his later intransigence toward Quebec nationalism likely went back to this time, when the scales fell from his eyes and he realized how blinded he had been by his own nationalism" (Ricci, *Pierre Elliott Trudeau*, 78).
85. To quote Michael Oliver: "Trudeau loathes, and has loathed since very early days in school, the S-nationalism [sociological nation] of French Canada. He did not believe it is possible to purge that kind of nationalism of the elements he most disliked—intolerance, narrowness, chauvinism." Oliver's translation of "Trudeau déteste, et a toujours détesté depuis ses premières années à l'école, le nationalisme du Canada français. Il ne pensait

pas qu'il fût possible de débarrasser cette sorte de nationalisme des éléments qu'il haïssait le plus—intolérance, étroitesse d'esprit, chauvinisme." See Michael Oliver, "Laurendeau et Trudeau: leurs opinions sur le Canada" in *L'engagement intellectuel: mélanges en l'honneur de Léon Dion*, ed. Raymond Hudon and Réjean Pelletier (Sainte-Foy: Presses de l'Université Laval, 1991), 351.

86. Trudeau, *Federalism and the French Canadians*, 204–12. Writing in the late 1990s, Trudeau declared that "I was delighted by the Quiet Revolution. Jean Lesage and his Liberals did a lot of progressive things in terms of reforming the election laws, the education system, and so on. But when they began talking about 'maîtres chez nous,' I sensed the return of *nationalism* under a new guise. It wasn't the same *nationalism* as Duplessis's, but I felt it was a mistaken direction nevertheless." (Trudeau, *The Essential Trudeau*, 105 [emphasis in original].)
87. Bergeron, *Notre miroir à deux faces*, 84.
88. Trudeau, *Federalism and the French Canadians*, 188. For a critique of this position see Oliver, "Laurendeau et Trudeau," 359.
89. Michel Vastel, *Trudeau: le Québécois* (Montreal: Éditions de l'Homme, 1989), 138.
90. André Laurendeau, *The Diary of André Laurendeau* (Toronto: Lorimer, 1991), 154.
91. "De son propre schéma personnel il aura fait l'extrapolation naturelle du modèle idéal du citoyen canadien." See Bergeron, *Notre miroir à deux faces*, 82.
92. Anthony Westell, "If Canada Doesn't Want Bilingualism, I Want Out," *Toronto Star*, 8 Feb. 1969.
93. Ramsay Cook, *The Maple Leaf Forever* (Toronto: Macmillan, 1971), 80.
94. Balthazar outlines the difference between Bourassa's thought and Trudeau's in Louis Balthazar, *Bilan du nationalisme au Québec* (Montreal: l'Hexagone, 1986), 90.
95. Clarkson and McCall, *Trudeau and Our Times*, 84.
96. In *Federalism and the French Canadians*, Trudeau makes a passing reference to Bourassa's relations with the Church hierarchy (109); credits the federal Liberal Party with preventing the rise of a federal nationalist party under Bourassa's leadership (119); acknowledges that Bourassa "humanized" the Canadian multinational state (165); and observes that, like Laurendeau, Bourassa was a target of separatists (172). On the other hand, many years later, in his campaign against the Meech Lake Accord, he started both his newspaper article and his address to the joint parliamentary committee by citing Bourassa on the need for Canadian patriotism. See Pierre Elliott Trudeau, "'Say Goodbye to the Dream' of One Canada," *Toronto Star*, 27 May 1987, and Special Joint Committee of the Senate and the House of Commons on the 1987 Constitutional Accord, *Minutes of Proceedings and Evidence*, 2nd session, 33rd Parliament, Issue no. 14, 27 Aug. 1987, 116.
97. Trudeau, *Federalism and the French Canadians*, 31.
98. Wright, *Trudeaumania*, 153.
99. Peter C. Newman, "Now There's a Third Viewpoint in the French–English Dialogue," *Toronto Star*, 2 Apr. 1966.
100. Don Peacock, *Journey to Power: The Story of a Canadian Election* (Toronto: Ryerson, 1968), 160.
101. See Vastel, *Trudeau*, 157, and Clarkson and McCall, *Trudeau and Our Times*, vol. 1, 106.
102. Speech to Quebec Liberal Convention, 28 Jan. 1968, reported in *Ottawa Citizen*, 29 Jan. 1968, as quoted in George Radwanski, *Trudeau* (Scarborough, Ont.: Macmillan-NAL, 1978), 286.
103. Jeremy Webber, *Reimagining Canada* (Montreal and Kingston: McGill-Queen's University Press, 1994), 60.
104. Peacock, *Journey to Power*, 277 and 294.
105. Claude Ryan, "Le choix du 25 juin," *Le Devoir*, 19 June 1968.
106. Wright, *Trudeaumania*, 172, and Litt, *Trudeaumania*, 170. According to Wright the petition contained 200 signatures; Litt refers to simply "over a hundred."
107. As quoted in Peacock, *Journey to Power*, 251.
108. Paul Gros d'Aillon, *Daniel Johnson: l'égalité avant l'indépendance* (Montreal: Stanké, 1979), 208–11; and Peacock, *Journey to Power*, 355–8.
109. Peacock, *Journey to Power*, 262.
110. Gérard Boismenu, "La pensée constitutionnelle de Jean Lesage," in *Jean Lesage et l'éveil d'une nation*, ed. Robert Comeau (Sillery, Quebec: Presses de l'Université du Québec, 1989), 96–104.

111. Richard Daignault, *Lesage* (Quebec City: Libre expression, 1981), 250–2. See also Jean-Louis Roy, *Le choix d'un pays: le débat constitutionnel Québec-Canada, 1960-1976* (Montreal: Leméac, 1978) 84.
112. Clarkson and McCall, *Trudeau and Our Times*, vol. 1, 99.
113. Dale Thomson, *Jean Lesage and the Quiet Revolution* (Toronto: Macmillan, 1984), 363; Anthony Westell, *Paradox: Trudeau as Prime Minister* (Scarborough, Ont.: Prentice-Hall, 1972).
114. Daignault, *Lesage*, 252. See also André Patry, "Témoignage," in Comeau, ed., *Jean Lesage et l'éveil d'une nation*, 138; and Thomson, *Jean Lesage and the Quiet Revolution*, 458.
115. Peacock, *Journey to Power*, 371.
116. Gordon Robertson, *Memoirs of a Very Civil Servant* (Toronto: University of Toronto Press, 2000), 236.
117. Wright, *Trudeaumania*, 128. John English refers to a meeting of the same three in Jan. 1968, during which Pearson tried to persuade Trudeau to run for the leadership (English, *The Life of Lester Pearson*, vol. 2, *The Worldly Years, 1949–1972* [Toronto: Knopf, 1992] 382).
118. Litt, *Trudeaumania*, 155.
119. Peacock, *Journey to Power*, 161–6, 195–201. Finally, a few days before the convention, Lamontagne declared for Trudeau, saying he shared Trudeau's opposition to the "extreme" form of special status favoured by Ryan. See "Le sénateur Lamontagne appuie Trudeau dont il dit partager 'en gros' les positions constitutionnelles," *Le Devoir*, 29 Mar. 1968.
120. Vastel, *Trudeau*, 168. Sullivan believes that support would have been much greater if Jean Marchand, the caucus leader, had acted more effectively. See Martin Sullivan, *Mandate '68* (Toronto: Doubleday, 1968), 305.
121. Correspondence from Jeffrey Simpson, Sept. 1995.
122. Cadieux said that Trudeau would not be his second choice either. See "Léo Cadieux donne son appui à Paul Hellyer," *Le Devoir*, 14 Mar. 1968.
123. Ibid.
124. See Donald V. Smiley, *Constitutional Adaptation and Canadian Federalism since 1945*, Documents of the Royal Commission on Bilingualism and Biculturalism, no. 4 (Ottawa: Queen's Printer, 1970), 135.
125. Wright, *Trudeaumania*, 179.
126. Ibid., 180.
127. "Trudeau est assuré de l'appui de 23 députés du Québec," *Le Devoir*, 20 Mar. 1968; and "Isabelle appuie plutôt Winters; Lessard, Hellyer," *Le Devoir*, 28 Mar. 1968.
128. "La course au leadership accentue les divisions dans le caucus du Québec," *Le Devoir*, 11 Apr. 1968.
129. Litt, *Trudeaumania*, 144, 156, and 364 (n. 14)
130. Sullivan, *Mandate '68*, 317–19, 340. Litt contends that Trudeau had the support of a "large majority of Quebec delegates" and credits "strong-arm tactics and the likelihood he would deliver them to power" (Litt, *Trudeaumania*, 217). Litt also refers to "intense pressure from power brokers in the Quebec wing to swing behind a French-Canadian candidate," (ibid., 144).
131. Wright, *Trudeaumania*, 98.
132. Donald V. Smiley, "The Case against the Canadian Charter of Human Rights," *Canadian Journal of Political Science* 2, no. 3 (Sept. 1969): 278.
133. H.D. Forbes, "Trudeau's Moral Vision," in *Rethinking the Constitution*, ed. A.A. Peacock (Toronto: Oxford University Press, 1996), 34.
134. Reg Whitaker, "Reason, Passion and Interest: Pierre Trudeau's Eternal Liberal Triangle," in *A Sovereign Idea*, ed. R. Whitaker. (Montreal and Kingston: McGill-Queen's University Press, 1992). 154.
135. John Robert Colombo, *Colombo's All-Time Great Canadian Quotations* (Toronto: Stoddart, 1994), 220. In 1977 he told the American Congress that the breakup of Canada would be nothing less than "a crime against humanism." See "Trudeau: Unity in Canada Won't Be Fractured," *Globe and Mail*, 23 Feb. 1977.
136. Litt, *Trudeaumania*, 192.
137. Ibid., 43.
138. The subtitle of Chap. 6 in Litt, *Trudeaumania*.
139. Litt, *Trudeaumania*, Chap. 3. See Tom Hawthorn's compendium of Centennial events across Canada (Tom Hawthorn, *The Year Canadians Lost Their Minds and Found Their Country* [Madeira Park, BC: Douglas & McIntyre, 2013]).

140. Litt, *Trudeaumania*, 128.
141. Newman, *Distemper of Our Times*, 461.
142. Richard Gwyn, *The Northern Magus* (Toronto: McClelland & Stewart, 1980), 71.
143. Claude Ryan, "Vieille tentation du Canada anglais," *Le Devoir*, 1 Feb. 1968.
144. "Faire du nationalisme la règle décidante des politiques et des priorités est un choix stérile et rétrograde. . . . Qu'il s'agisse du premier budget, en juin 1963, de l'honorable Walter Gordon, des règlements du Bureau des gouverneurs de la radio-diffusion sur le contenu canadien des programmes, de l'intolérance courante chez les 'White Anglo-Saxon Protestants', ou de la notion répandue selon laquelle 'l'État du Québec' serait l'arme économique du Canada français, on est en face du même problème." See Albert Breton et al., "Manifeste pour une politique fonctionnelle," *Cité libre*, May 1964, 16. In fact, they were quite explicit in their rejection of English-Canadian concern with American domination: "Nous ne sommes pas plus émus par les clameurs de certains milieux anglophones devant l'achat d'entreprises canadiennes par des intérêts financiers américains, que par l'adoption par la province de Québec de politiques économiques basées sur le slogan de 'Maîtres chez nous'." ("We are no more moved by the complaints from some Anglophone circles about the purchase of Canadian companies by American financial interests than by Quebec's adoption of economic policies based on the slogan 'Masters in our house.'")
145. "Il y a d'abord ce fait juridique et géographique: le Canada. . . . Vouloir le scinder . . . nous apparaît comme une véritable évasion en face des tâches réelles et importantes à accomplir. Vouloir l'intégrer à une autre entité géographique nous apparaît également comme une tâche futile à l'heure actuelle, même si un tel développement peut, en principe, sembler plus conforme à l'évolution du monde." (Ibid., 17.)
146. The quotation is from Vastel, *Trudeau*, 164. Vastel says that Gordon refused to support Trudeau. Sullivan, on the other hand, says he did (Sullivan, *Mandate '68*, 320), as do McCall and Clarkson, *Trudeau and Our Times*, vol. 2 87 and 453.
147. Wright, *Trudeaumania*, 183.
148. McCall and Clarkson, *Trudeau and Our Times*, 97–102.
149. J.L. Granatstein, *Canada 1957–1967* (Toronto: McClelland & Stewart, 1986), 362.
150. Newman, *The Distemper of Our Times*, 446.
151. English, *The Life of Lester Pearson*, 384.
152. Ibid.
153. Claude Lemelin, "Sharp: Ottawa devra faire preuve de souplesse sur la question constitutionnelle," *Le Devoir*, 23 Mar. 1968.
154. Wright, *Trudeaumania*, 188, 192, 204, and 210.
155. Peacock, *Journey to Power*, 356.
156. Anthony Westell, "PM Challenges Quebec Tories on Two Nations," *Globe and Mail*, 21 June 1968.
157. John Meisel, *Working Papers on Canadian Politics* (Montreal and Kingston: McGill-Queen's University Press, 1972), 34–6. On the basis of survey data, John Meisel shows that the Liberals would have received 64 per cent of the French-Canadian vote in Quebec in 1968. However, the data significantly inflate the Liberal vote, assigning them 68.5 per cent in Quebec as opposed to the actual 53.6 per cent (ibid., Table II, "Origin"). By my calculations, if non-French Canadians (who represented about 18 per cent of the electorate) had voted 75 per cent in favour of the Liberals, the French-Canadian Liberal vote would have been about 49 per cent.
158. This is confirmed by the various anecdotes and editorial statements which Peacock offers to document Trudeaumania. They are all drawn from outside Quebec. See Peacock, *Journey to Power*, 257–60.
159. Wright, *Trudeaumania*, 275.
160. Ronald Lebel, "PM Creating Great Division," *Globe and Mail*, 21 June 1968.
161. See André Lamoureux, *Le NPD et le Québec, 1958-1985* (Montreal: Les Éditions du Parc, 1985), 151–5, and Desmond Morton, *NDP: The Dream of Power* (Toronto: Hakkert, 1974), 126–7.
162. "Towards a New Canada: A New Canadian Constitution," in *New Democratic Policies, 1961–1976* (Ottawa: New Democratic Party, 1976), 92.
163. Desmond Morton, "The NDP and Quebec: A Sad Tale of Unrequited Love," *Saturday Night*, June 1972, 18.
164. Morton notes, "For the first time, NDP candidates began to be confronted with the [Quebec] issue in the rest of Canada." See Morton, *NDP*, 83.

Part II

Making a New Canada

Chapter 4

Official Bilingualism
Linguistic Equality from Sea to Sea

One of Pierre Elliott Trudeau's first acts, after the 1968 election confirmed his prime ministership, was to formulate and implement a language policy based on official bilingualism. The Official Languages Act, which was proclaimed in July 1969, establishes English and French as the official languages of Canada and provides a comprehensive framework for the federal government's use of French and English in its relations with citizens.

To be sure, public discussion of language policy didn't start with the arrival of Trudeau to power. It had been a central focus of public debate during the 1960s, including the many public sessions organized by the Royal Commission on Bilingualism and Biculturalism (B&B Commission). By the fall of 1968, the Commission had already produced two volumes of recommendations and provided the framework for the Official Languages Act. Moreover, the Pearson government had set general objectives for reform of the federal public service. In 1963, Maurice Lamontagne, president of the Privy Council, had committed the government to "perfect equality for the two official languages" in every department of the federal public service. In 1966, Pearson himself proclaimed a general policy under which public servants would be able to work in their own language and to apply "their respective cultural values." In effect, the government had committed itself to creating a public service that was not only bilingual but bicultural as well.[1]

Nonetheless, the federal government's language policy, and the means for achieving it, was effectively defined during the Trudeau years. Starting with the Official Languages Act, language policy was a top priority throughout Trudeau's tenure as prime minister. Indeed, over the period 1970–7 alone his government spent $1.4 billion on official languages.[2] Entrenchment of the educational rights of Francophone minorities was the central purpose of his drive to patriate the Canadian constitution with a bill of rights. For this reason, the federal government's language policy closely reflects the political world view that Trudeau brought to Ottawa. This can be seen in the fate of some of the B&B Commission's major recommendations, which were set simply aside.[3] Once in place, this policy, centred on official bilingualism, was generally followed by subsequent federal governments, even though it was resisted by most provincial governments and, manifestly, did not produce national unity in the way Trudeau had envisaged it.

The basic premises of a language policy, based on official bilingualism, flowed directly from the Trudeau political world view. First, the policy had to be centred on the individual, as opposed to any collectivity. "Only the individual is the possessor of rights."[4] Language rights involved the rights of individuals and their ability to choose one language over another. Thus, in 1990, Trudeau said of the Charter of Rights and Freedoms: "What we were seeking was for the individual himself to have the *right* to demand his choice of French or English in his relationships with the federal government, and the *right* to demand a French or English education for his children from a provincial government." By the same token, he was explicit that "language rights were assigned directly to individuals rather than collectivities."[5]

Understood this way, language rights are an extension of individual political and legal rights. They are necessary in the case of Canada, not because of any historical dualism, let alone bi-national past, but for purely pragmatic reasons: French-speakers are sufficiently numerous to break up the country. "In terms of *realpolitik*, French and English are equal in Canada because each of these linguistic groups has the power to break the country. And this power cannot yet be claimed by the Iroquois, the Eskimos, or the Ukrainians."[6] Moreover, conceiving language rights in terms of the individual leads directly to official bilingualism, and formal equality between English and French, so as to maximize the opportunity for individuals to choose between the two languages. This conception of language rights, which has a long tradition in the theoretical literature on language policy, is rooted in the personality principle: individuals have the right, as citizens, to use their language of choice anywhere in their country.[7]

Nonetheless, there is an opposing conception of language rights which claims that, unlike political and legal rights, they can be dealt with only in collective terms.[8] After all, languages are based on social networks and communities and cannot exist without them. Thus, to be at all meaningful, a language right must entail more than just the right to use a particular language with governments. The language in question must be a part of daily life, used in interaction with fellow speakers of it. In other words, language rights must be tied to ongoing linguistic communities. Beyond that, linguistic communities vary in relative social, economic, and political strength. In effect, languages are in competition and, with time, the stronger linguistic community may absorb the weaker one.[9] Language rights conceived in terms of individual rights do not address this competition. Instead language rights must take account of the legitimate needs for a linguistic community to survive, and even to flourish.

Arguments such as these lead to the territorial principle by which a language right can be exercised only in the parts of a country where a linguistic community is in place and to the argument that, within a given area, a single language should be pre-eminent and linguistic rights defined in terms of it. In a bilingual or multilingual country, equality between languages lies in the fact that each language has an area in which its community is dominant. In effect, each language trades majority rights in one region against minority rights in another. Needless to say, this line of argument has had a particular appeal to Quebec nationalists who contend that within the province of Quebec French should be pre-eminent, just as English is pre-eminent in the rest of the country. However, for his part Trudeau affirmed in 1990 that, during the constitutional negotiations while he was prime minister, "we rejected any proposal whose effect would have been to identify a linguistic collectivity (French Canadians) with the government of a province (Quebec)."[10]

Trudeau's political world view produced a second premise of federal language policy: language rights should be geared to nation-building and to persuading Quebec Francophones to identify with all of Canada rather than just Quebec. As Trudeau wrote in 1964,

> If certain language and educational rights were written into the constitution, along with other basic liberties, in such a way that *no* government—federal or provincial—could legislate against them, French Canadians would cease to feel confined to their Quebec ghetto, and the Spirit of Separatism would be laid [to rest] forever.[11]

On this basis, language rights should be uniform across the country; the personality principle should prevail. Moreover, given the central importance of nation-building, the same conception of language rights, with official bilingualism at its core, should prevail among provincial governments as well. Yet when Trudeau came to power, Canada's Francophones were far less present in some parts of the country than others. In all provinces but Quebec, Francophone minorities had faced strong assimilationist pressures. In some, the demographic presence of Francophones was so marginal as to make extremely tenuous notions of official bilingualism and equality between English and French. Nor were Francophones on an equal footing to Anglophones in economic terms. Even in the single province in which they formed the majority, Quebec, they were at a distinct economic disadvantage. Under these conditions, the territorial principle, with the pre-eminence of a single language, was bound to be compelling to many Francophones and to their political leaders.

Individualist assumptions and a commitment to nation-building shaped federal language policy in another fashion: an emphasis on personal bilingualism, which emerged as the quintessential Canadian experience. As Trudeau declared in 1988, "Bilingualism unites people; dualism divides them. Bilingualism means that you can speak to each other; duality means you can live in one language and the rest of Canada will live in another language."[12] Yet, here too, Canada's linguistic demography was an obstacle. While French-language training, especially French immersion, became remarkably popular for children if not adults in English-speaking Canada, in many parts of the country the Francophone communities were too small or lacked sufficient visibility to support French exchanges with Anglophones. For that matter, advocates of Francophone minorities sometimes saw French-immersion schools as a threat, siphoning students from their communities.

As the Trudeau government set about creating a new Canada, in which French and English would be equal and Quebec Francophones would see all of Canada as their country, the strategies it chose to pursue these ambitious objectives would closely shape the extent to which they could be attained. As it happened, the government chose strategies that minimized the chances of success.

Making Ottawa Bilingual

A central goal of Trudeau's language reform was to place French on an equal footing with English in the federal government's own institutions. Trudeau had experienced, and had been alienated by, the dominance of English and Anglophones during his unhappy years at the Privy Council Office between 1949 and 1951. He had come back to Ottawa determined to change all that.

Daunting as the objective of a bilingual federal government may have been, it clearly was a *sine qua non* of any strategy to deal with the Quebec question. Even the most nationalist of Quebec federalists agreed on that. After all, André Laurendeau, *Le Devoir* editor, who had deep family roots in Quebec's nationalist circles, had assumed leadership of a federal royal commission whose primary mandate was to establish bilingualism and biculturalism in federal institutions. Even if Quebec were to obtain special status, Ottawa would still be dealing with Quebec citizens in many areas. It needed to have the capacity to do so, and to be seen in Quebec to have that capacity.

For Trudeau, the objective of a bilingual federal government had another special importance. If he were to have any hope of reaching his consuming goal of making Quebec Francophones see the federal government as their *primary* government, Ottawa had to become truly bilingual. Quebeckers would have to be convinced that French was fully equal to English and that Francophones had finally assumed their rightful place.

Historical Role of French and Francophones

This would be a very tall order. Historically, the ideal of linguistic equality in Ottawa had never been acknowledged in more than the most symbolic of terms. Some parts of the federal government did have a certain bilingual public face, thanks to section 133 of the British North America Act. Both languages were used in the deliberations of Parliament and the Supreme Court. Laws, the record of parliamentary debates, and other important public documents were published in both languages. The internal operations of the government, however, were a different matter. Although Francophones usually had a share of cabinet seats that approximated their proportion of the Canadian population, they had never held portfolios with important economic responsibilities: finance, trade and commerce, or labour. Instead, they tended to predominate in such positions as postmaster general, secretary of state, minister of public works, and minister of justice.[13] For that matter, cabinet meetings were conducted almost exclusively in English.

As for the federal bureaucracy, it was essentially an English-language institution controlled by Anglophones. Francophones had always been under-represented in the upper levels of the federal civil service. This was true of the bureaucracy of the United Canadas;[14] Confederation did little to improve the situation. To make matters worse, after the First World War, the place of Francophones had been further weakened by the preferential status of war veterans and the establishment of the Civil Service Commission, whose recruiting practices tended to be oriented toward the English-language educational systems. As a result, the Francophone presence fell almost by half, from about 22 per cent in 1918 to 13 per cent in 1946.[15]

Moreover, most of the Francophones in the civil service had to work primarily in English. The assumption was that rationality and efficiency precluded the extensive use of French.[16] Thus, the status of French as a language of work was not seen as a legitimate policy concern. In fact, the federal government had no policy whatsoever on bilingualism in the public service until 1963.

For its part, the B&B Commission had seen as "inescapable" that "bilingualism becomes essential first in the institutions shared by all Canadians."[17] Thus, it called for English and French to be declared "the official languages of the Parliament of Canada, of the federal courts, of the federal government, and of the federal administration."[18] This would be embodied in a federal Official Languages Act.

Trudeau Governments

The first Trudeau government duly proposed an Official Languages Act, which largely followed the various recommendations of the Commission. It declared that "The English and French languages are the official languages of Canada for all purposes of the Parliament and Government of Canada." Beyond that, it called for notices, regulations, decisions, and similar materials to be published in both official languages; required departments, agencies, and Crown corporations to provide bilingual services in Ottawa-Hull, at its headquarters, in bilingual districts, and to the travelling public anywhere in Canada where demand warranted; stipulated the role of official languages in judicial proceedings; described the procedure for creating federal bilingual districts; and outlined the office, powers, and responsibilities of the commissioner of official languages.[19] The House adopted the bill unanimously, after a lengthy and at times divisive debate, but in the deliberate absence of a number of Conservative MPs. The Office of Official Languages was established in 1970, with Keith Spicer as its first commissioner.

In addition, Trudeau broke with historical patterns in naming his cabinets, appointing Francophones to the economic portfolios from which they had been absent. In his first cabinet after the 1968 election, Trudeau made Jean-Luc Pepin minister of industry, Jean-Pierre Côté minister of national revenue, and Jean Marchand minister of forestry and rural development. Jean Chrétien became minister of finance in 1977. By the same token, in appointing Jules Léger to replace Roland Michener as Governor General, and then replacing him by Ed Schreyer many years later, Trudeau further entrenched the alternation convention. However, the federal public service proved to be a far greater challenge. Indeed, the goal of a truly bilingual public service eluded the Trudeau government, due primarily to the strategy it chose to pursue.

The B&B Commission had placed great emphasis on reform of the public service but did so within the terms of its key concept of an "equal partnership" between English Canadians and French Canadians. For the Commission, a truly "bicultural" public service entailed "the coexistence and collaboration of the two cultures so that both can flourish and contribute to the overall objectives of government."[20] Equal partnership meant that Francophones must not only be present at all levels in the public service but they must be in a position both to work in their own language and to express their own culture. On this basis, the Commission had been highly critical of the Pearson government's reform efforts: "If we have not achieved a bicultural Public Service in Canada it is precisely because bilingualism in the Service has been individual and not institutional in character."[21] From the time it took office in 1963, the Pearson government had placed too great a reliance on French-language training, which produced very mediocre results. Pedagogy could be improved, but without the structural changes to the public service that it proposed, "students will only participate in a waste of time, energy, and money."[22] Moreover, "the French language cannot develop in direct competition with English, no matter how effective recruitment and language-training programmes may be."[23]

Accordingly, the Commission had called for radical new departures. First, for an "active and effective francophone participation at the highest levels," appointments to these positions should "be administered so as to ensure effectively balanced participation of anglophones and francophones at these levels."[24] Second, "French-language units" should be designated in all federal departments. In these units French would be the language of work, as it would be the language of communication with the rest of the public service. In this fashion, the public service could be made bilingual and bicultural without an enormous program of language training. In any event, the French-language units would give language-training graduates the opportunity to put their new linguistic skill to use.[25]

However more effective the Commission's preferred approaches might have been in achieving the goal of a bilingual civil service, they faced strong opposition. The *Globe and Mail* declared that, rather than seeking to bring Canadians together, the Commission's proposed French-language units seemed to call for a return to "The Two Solitudes" and, in doing so, tested the limits of English-Canadian support for bilingualism. The *Toronto Star* denounced the proposal for "French ghettos" in the public service.[26] Staff unions had reservations, fearing the impact on unilingual employees. Resistance to the idea of French-language units also came from Francophone civil servants who feared that without work experience in English their chances for mobility would be gravely handicapped. In other words, they presumed that English would continue to have pre-eminence in Ottawa no matter what reforms were introduced.[27]

Given hostile public opinion and resistance within the public service itself, Trudeau and his associates would have had to struggle very hard to bring about the reforms envisaged by the B&B Commission. By all indications, they were not prepared to do so. Notions of balancing appointments on a linguistic basis were hardly compatible with Trudeau's brand of liberalism nor was the segregation of workers according to first language. So the federal government carefully avoided any formal system of "balanced representation" at the top levels: instead, a number of positions were defined as "bilingual" and thus were open to all on the basis of skill in both languages. The B&B Commission's scheme of French-language units was not rigorously pursued.[28]

The Trudeau government did proclaim, in 1973, the right of public servants to work in their language of choice.[29] But it failed to adopt the strategies that the B&B Commission had proposed to reach this objective. Instead, opting for an individual-based approach rather than structural change, the Trudeau government followed the Pearson government's path of relying primarily upon language training to create a bilingual service—the approach that the B&B Commission had so firmly attacked. With the emphasis on language training, a very large number of positions were designated as bilingual. The number greatly exceeded the B&B Commission's assessment of what was necessary, given its alternative structural changes. In effect, the idea of French-language units was replaced by *bilingual* units. In fact, in response to pressure from staff unions the bilingual requirement was not rigorously applied to unilingual occupants of designated positions.[30]

As a result, the Trudeau government's efforts to reform the federal public service had mixed results. The public service became bilingual in the sense that a substantial proportion of positions formally required bilingualism: 30.3 per cent in 1995, although only 17.3 per cent of these positions required the top level of bilingualism.[31] Moreover, the proportion of Francophones in the public service grew from 21.5 per cent in 1961[32] to 28.0 per cent in 1995.[33] Most important, at the management level the proportion of Francophones rose to 20.6 per cent in 1980 and 22.9 per cent in 1993.[34] Thus, Francophones did secure a presence in even the upper levels of the public service that approximated their proportion of the Canadian population.[35] There was indeed substance to Trudeau's claim to have introduced "French Power" to Ottawa.

However, there was much less progress in making the public service a bilingual and bicultural institution, in which Francophones could work in their language and express their culture. As the commissioner of official languages declared in his 1990 report, "French still does not have its rightful place in the federal administration."[36] Virtually nothing had changed since a 1984 Treasury Board study which "showed that French was used only approximately 30 per cent of the time in bilingual regions. The prime minister himself deplored the fact in 1985 that language of work was often pure 'folklore.'"[37]

In short, without structural changes such as those proposed by the B&B Commission, the federal public service was doomed to remain a primarily English-language institution, albeit with a greatly increased number of Francophones.[38] Indeed, a 1973 Treasury Board review of bilingualism in the public service had warned that this failure to initiate structural reform would have "extremely important" consequences.[39] Some departments, such as Secretary of State, the Prime Minister's Office and the Privy Council Office, did develop a capacity in French. Nonetheless, by the end of the Trudeau era the federal public service had yet to become fully bilingual, let alone bicultural, despite the investment of enormous resources in language training.

Post-Trudeau Governments

The Trudeau government's choice among strategies was to prove fateful for the possibility of a truly bilingual federal government. Successor governments have largely remained with these strategies. As a result, while the public face of the federal government has been transformed the public service is still far from the bilingual ideal.

Leaders of national parties now are expected to be bilingual, as some leadership candidates have ruefully discovered. Stephen Harper is a prime example of an Anglophone prime minister who made his major public statements in both official languages, despite clearly feeling less confident in his French, which he only learned later in his career. (In an earlier role, as president of the National Citizens Coalition, Harper had even declared that "bilingualism is the god that failed"; as prime minister, he saw things differently.[40]) Indeed, bilingualism is expected of major cabinet ministers, along with Chief Justice and the Governor General. Francophones are much more visible in federal cabinets, assuming positions such as Finance and Trade and Commerce from which they had been absent in the distant past.

However, the Supreme Court remains an object of controversy. The B&B Commission recommended entrenchment, in a new version of the BNA Act's section 133, of the right to use either official language in federal courts. But it made no recommendation regarding the bilingual capacity of members of the bench.[41] When the act was revised in 1988, the Supreme Court was excluded from new bilingual requirements for judges and officers in federal courts.[42] For his part, Stephen Harper was responsible for nomination to the Court of a number of unilingual Anglophones. In response, the two opposition parties supported a bill requiring that all justices be able to understand presentations in either official language,[43] but the Harper government prevented passage of the bill. Nonetheless, Prime Minister Justin Trudeau has treated bilingualism as a necessary condition for appointments to the Court.

With respect to the public service, the part of the government to which the B&B Commission had devoted most of its attention, the results remain mixed, especially if measured against the Commission's conception of an "equal partnership." The presence of Francophones in the upper levels of the federal public service has grown steadily after the Trudeau era, reaching 31 per cent of public service executives in 2015–16.[44] (In effect, Francophones had become over-represented relative to the 22 per cent proportion of Francophones in the total Canadian population.) However, the ability of Francophones to use their language remains severely circumscribed.

The right to choose one's language of work in the federal public service was enshrined for the first time in the Official Languages Act when the act was revised in 1988 (as was a commitment to equal opportunity for Anglophones and Francophones to participate in the public service). A new preamble established the principle that employees of Parliament or the federal government "should have equal opportunities to use the official language of their choice."[45] To that end, a new section entitled "Language of Work" outlines how that right should be respected within the National Capital Region and "in any part or region of Canada, or in any place outside Canada, that is prescribed." The "prescribed" regions, which are limited to parts of Ontario and Quebec and the whole of New Brunswick, are contained in a list already set out in 1977.[46]

However, a 2002 Treasury Board Secretariat study found that in the National Capital Region Francophones used English 54 per cent of the time[47] and a 2004 study by the Office of the Commissioner of Official Languages found that, such was the prevalence of English, that sometimes Francophones used English even when speaking to fellow Francophones.[48] Indeed, a 2017 study conducted by two senior federal officials found that:

> English is the dominant language for most daily activities and Francophone employees do not consistently feel that they can work in the language of their choice . . . most written materials are prepared in

English and most meetings are conducted in English, particularly for the core items of discussion.[49]

While most senior positions in the National Capital Region and other bilingual regions now require bilingualism, Francophones still tend to deal with Anglophone superiors in English so as to ensure that they are fully understood.[50] For that matter, bilingualism is still not required for the position of deputy minister and English is still the working language in such key central agencies as the Treasury Board and the Privy Council Office.[51]

Making Canada Bilingual

The Trudeau regime's ambitions for language reform went far beyond establishing bilingualism in Ottawa, however central that objective may have been. The ultimate goal extended to the whole of Canada. Wherever they live, Canadians, as Canadians, were to be able to deal with the federal government in their own language, whether it be French or English. Moreover, in important areas such as education, they would be able to receive services in either language from provincial governments too. Within Trudeau's belief system, these objectives were a matter of allowing individuals to have freedom of choice. They also reflected a "nation-building" goal of enabling Quebec Francophones to see all of Canada as their homeland.

Historical Trends: The Marginalization of French

To make all of Canada home for the French language and Francophones, so that French Canada would stretch from coast to coast, would have been a tall order. Historically, French Canada had always been concentrated in Quebec, and the very presence of French in other parts of the country had been steadily receding ever since Confederation.

At Confederation, only one of the four original provinces had a Francophone majority. According to the 1871 census, 78 per cent of Quebec's population was of French descent;[52] French Canadians made up only 16 per cent of the population in New Brunswick,[53] 4.7 per cent in Ontario,[54] and 8.5 per cent in Nova Scotia.[55] The addition of more provinces to Confederation did not break this pattern. When Prince Edward Island joined in 1873 it was overwhelmingly Anglophone.[56] Initially, the incorporation of western Canada had offered the promise of a new Francophone base. When Manitoba became a province in 1870, English-speakers and French-speakers were about equal in numbers,[57] but by 1891, the Francophones had shrunk to 7.3 per cent.[58] In 1949, the last addition, Newfoundland, only reinforced the established pattern: according to the 1951 census, only 2321 individuals in Newfoundland had French as their mother tongue.[59]

By the time Pierre Trudeau assumed office in 1968, the linguistic structure of Canada was more rooted than ever in territorial division. The marginalization of Francophones in most provinces was dramatically revealed by the 1971 census, which for the first time supplemented its standard question on mother tongue with a question on the language Canadians normally used at home, a much more precise measure of the number of Francophones. In New Brunswick, 31.4 per cent gave French as their home language, but the proportions were far smaller in the other provinces. The next highest, Ontario, was only 4.6 per cent, followed by 4.0 per cent for Manitoba, 3.9 per cent for Prince Edward Island, and 3.5 per cent for Nova Scotia. In the remaining provinces the proportions with French as their home language were truly infinitesimal: 1.7 per cent in Saskatchewan, 1.4 per cent in Alberta, 0.5 per cent in British Columbia, and 0.4 per cent in Newfoundland.[60] Even in 1971, then, the idea of a French Canada that extended from sea to sea was unrealistic. In demographic terms, French Canada never had really stretched from coast to coast, and it was not at all clear that it could be *made* to do so.[61]

The steady decline in the French presence in most provinces had two causes. First, many provinces received large numbers of British immigrants; French immigrants were a rarity, even in Quebec. Immigrants of other origins tended to join the Anglophone populations, again even in Quebec where Anglophones were economically much stronger than the Francophone majority. Second, the Francophone minorities of most provinces lost ground through assimilation, especially as they left the relative isolation of rural communities to migrate to the major cities. In most cities, the overwhelming numerical superiority of Anglophone speakers, reinforced by control of the principal economic activities, ensured that assimilationist pressures of urban life would favour English. Thus, in every province but Quebec and New Brunswick, the majority of Canadians of French origin did not use French as their primary language at home.[62]

Canada's political institutions, of course, were themselves patterned on the assumption that French Canada was effectively concentrated in Quebec. For certain purposes federalism protected the position of Francophones in Quebec, making them an electoral majority. But, for the same purposes, it doomed Francophones elsewhere to political marginality. Nor did the terms of Confederation provide for offsetting measures. Historically, all governments but Quebec acted as if territorial unilingualism and the provision of public services in a single language were operative principles of Confederation. When Manitoba was created in 1870, English and French were given equal status in the new legislature but, in 1890, after the very rapid decline in the Francophone proportion of the province's population, the Manitoba government formally ended the official use of French in provincial institutions and abolished denominational schools, thus in effect eliminating publicly funded French-language education. The Ontario government passed Regulation 17 in 1912, requiring that English be the sole language of instruction after the third year of schooling.[63] Saskatchewan declared English to be the sole language of instruction in 1931. New Brunswick revoked Regulation 32 in the early 1930s, thus precluding French-language education in most of that province.[64] The pattern of provincial policy was clear.

For its part, the federal government had done little to counter this pattern. Typically, it did not call upon provincial governments to reverse their policies, nor was it very responsive to the entreaties of French-Canadian organizations such as the Conseil de la vie française en Amérique, which called upon Ottawa to use both official languages in its publications, to favour French-language radio in western Canada, and to project a bilingual image of the country. Ottawa even refused the Conseil's request to issue bilingual cheques throughout Canada; until 1962, it did so only in Quebec.[65] The Conseil's requests were heeded by the Quebec government, which in effect provided funds to the Conseil and to French-language organizations in other provinces. But with the rise of the new Quebec nationalism in the 1960s, Quebec government officials downgraded this support, focusing instead upon the state of French in Quebec.[66]

Under those circumstances, the Trudeau ideal of a pan-Canadian linguistic equality could not have been more ambitious. It sought to reverse the entrenched pattern of a century of Canadian history. Both demographic trends and political forces were stacked against it.

The B&B Commission

The B&B Commission had been very much concerned with the fate of the Francophone minorities and had struggled to develop a strategy through which the federal government, and the provinces, could provide needed support. Beyond seeking linguistic justice, the Commission saw the official-language minorities as important forces for Canadian political unity. In its *Preliminary Report*, the Commission had emphasized the symbolic importance of the Francophone minorities. It claimed that the bond that Quebec Francophones had formed with these minorities was an important force for national cohesion.[67]

Having commissioned studies of language policies in other countries, the Commission was closely familiar with the personality and territorial principles. Its sympathies clearly lay with the former and with the idea that government services should be available in French to Francophones throughout the country (in Quebec, they would be available in English to Anglophones). Application of the territorial principle, favouring the majority language in each part of the country, would have had the merit of guaranteeing priority for French in Quebec, but "it would lead to oppression of the official language minorities." Yet the Commission could not escape the fact that, in demographic terms, Francophones were simply not present in all parts of the country. Thus, it was forced to qualify its application of the personality principle, effectively recognizing territoriality although tying it to bilingualism rather than unilingualism as is typically the case: "We take as a guiding principle the recognition of both official languages, in law and practice, *wherever the minority is numerous enough to be viable as a group*" [emphasis added].[68] Thus, it recommended that the full provision of government services in official languages by the federal government, and the provinces, be limited to certain areas. Apparently inspired by the Finnish example, it proposed a scheme of "bilingual districts" in which the full range of government services—federal, provincial, and municipal—would be bilingual.[69] Federal and provincial governments would have to provide bilingual services directly through the offices they maintain in these districts, as opposed to relying upon communication with offices in their capitals. And all local governments in the district would need to provide bilingual services.

The Trudeau Government: Abandoning Bilingual Districts

For its part, the Trudeau government faithfully followed the Commission's recommendation and gave the notion of bilingual districts a central place in its Official Languages Act.[70] The act called for the creation of a Bilingual Districts Advisory Board to recommend where bilingual districts should be designated. Given provincial resistance to the idea of bilingual districts,[71] it would be a federal government creation rather than the federal–provincial body that the Commission had proposed but it would be required nonetheless to consult the provinces. As recommended by the Commission, the act set as the criterion for designation that at least 10 per cent of the area population have the minority mother tongue.[72]

Nonetheless, the proposed bilingual districts were never to be. In effect, they fell victim to the pressures, emerging in Francophone Quebec but also present in Anglophone Canada, for a different language regime based on territoriality and the pre-eminence of the majority language within a given region. In any event, to the extent that the bilingual districts placed territorial limits on bilingualism, they fell short of Trudeau's personal commitment to equality of languages, freedom of choice, and pan-Canadian nation-building.

Following the terms of the Official Languages Act, the government created two advisory boards to recommend which districts should be designated. The first board recommended the creation of 37 districts, involving all 10 provinces, but in doing so proposed that the whole provinces of Quebec and New Brunswick be declared bilingual districts.[73] (The B&B Commission had not gone that far in mapping out its proposal.[74]) In effect, committed to the personality principle, the Board stretched as far as possible the territorial limitations to linguistic equality.[75] For this reason, the recommendation was roundly rejected by Quebec Francophones seeking to protect French's position within the province. Even a member of the B&B Commission, Paul Lacoste, denounced the recommendation.[76] The broad-based opposition extended from labour unions to Quebec nationalists to the Montreal newspapers *La Presse*, which denounced the recommendation as absurd, and *Le Devoir*, which called upon Ottawa to defer any action until the Quebec government had settled on its own language policy.[77] Indeed, by the early 1970s, the Quebec government was under growing pressure to make French the only official language in Quebec, as the territorial principle would dictate. The Quebec government of Robert Bourassa had opposed the creation of any bilingual districts within its territory.[78]

The new Board embarked on a broad consultation, involving experts and stakeholders, as well as federal MPs and leaders of linguistic minorities and majorities. In the process, it consulted 800 people, twice the number of the first Board.[79] It also became acutely aware of sentiments in Quebec in favour of the pre-eminence of French and, as a result, became deeply divided over how to treat Montreal.[80] The Quebec government, in the form of Intergovernmental Affairs Minister François Cloutier, vigorously opposed the creation of bilingual districts in Quebec. In a private meeting with Board, Cloutier not only opposed federal bilingual districts in Quebec in general but reportedly went so far as to declare that making Montreal a bilingual district would cause a "general outcry" that would "put an end to Confederation." He was more restrained in public, presumably because of his government's commitment to federalism, simply stating that he hoped Ottawa would not create bilingual districts.[81]

Ultimately, the Board proposed 24 bilingual districts in nine provinces, largely paralleling the first Board's recommendations.[82] In the case of Quebec, the Board proposed that only parts of the province be designated, for a total of five bilingual districts.[83] Moreover, out of concern for Francophone opinion in Quebec, the Board decided by majority vote (5 to 4, with one abstention[84]) that Montreal should not be declared a bilingual district, even though English was the mother tongue of 21 per cent of the residents of the Montreal metropolitan census area.[85] The Board's report embraced the argument of Quebec nationalists that "if the public use of English increases in Montreal, the future of French in the metropolis and the province may well be more than a theoretical question"[86] and thus did not include Montreal among the five Quebec localities which it recommended be designated as bilingual districts.[87]

In effect, the second Board was declaring that the personality principle of linguistic equality, as proposed by the B&B Commission, was unable to meet the legitimate concerns of Quebec's Francophone majority. Falling into the territorial principle's logic, it declared that "in terms of long-term survival it is the French language which needs protection in Quebec rather than English"[88] and that it would be contrary to the Official Languages Act's objective of equality between French and English "if we were to make recommendations that were disadvantageous to the survival of French in the province which is its essential base."[89]

Such invocations of territoriality and the priority of the Francophone community in Quebec squarely contradicted the Trudeau vision of language rights, as well as the terms of the Official Languages Act if taken literally. Thus, when Minister Bud Drury tabled the report, in November 1975, he announced that, while the government would be proceeding with the creation of bilingual districts, it rejected outright the Board's recommendations for Quebec. Stating that the government would "review all Quebec areas, including Montreal and Sherbrooke" so as to apply the same "approach and principles" used with the other provinces, Drury declared that there would be one or more bilingual districts in Montreal and others across Quebec.[90] Nonetheless, a little over a year later, in December 1976, the federal cabinet decided to abandon the notion of bilingual districts altogether. A series of events, most notably the election of a Parti québécois government in November 1976, had convinced the Trudeau government that it could not run the risk of provoking nationalist sentiment in Quebec.[91] It had become clear that creation of bilingual districts would hinder the cause of Canadian unity rather than support it, as had been imagined by the B&B Commission, and presumably, the Trudeau government.[92] In September 1977, Robert Andras, Chair of the Treasury Board, announced that the government would not be establishing bilingual districts. In their place, it would simply rely on the set of administrative regions that the government already had adopted in 1977 to establish bilingual requirements within the public service.[93]

Thus, when the Official Languages Act was revised in 1988, the section on bilingual districts was removed. Instead, as with the Charter of Rights and Freedoms, the right of the public to receive services in either official language is extended broadly to wherever there is "significant demand" (in Canada *"or elsewhere,"* along with the National Capital Region) as well as where it is warranted by "the nature of the office" providing the service. The criteria for "significant demand" are left relatively vague: presence of linguistic minority members in an area and volume of communications in each language. Thus, the act no longer has a precise threshold, as with the 10 per cent criterion of the original act. Nor does the act, or the Charter, explicate "the nature of the office." Finally, the government is left free to act on its own; there is no longer a formal advisory committee proposing areas for designation.[94] As a result, in 1990 the federal government issued, in Kenneth McRae's words, "a highly complex web of administrative regulations to specify *where* and *what* offices would be required to offer bilingual services."[95] Reportedly, 94 per cent of Canada's minority-language populations are covered by these criteria.[96]

Beyond services to individuals, the Trudeau government went about pursuing bilingual services in ways that applied to the country as a whole. Thus, the 1960s and 1970s saw an expansion of Radio-Canada's television and radio services beyond Quebec with new stations in Vancouver, Edmonton, Saskatoon, Winnipeg, Toronto, Sudbury, and Windsor. At the same time, going well beyond the recommendations of the B&B Commission, the Trudeau government provided financial support directly to minority-language associations and organizations as part of a "social animation" strategy for which it established a new Social Action Branch.[97] By the same token, the Trudeau government reinforced financial support for minority-language education at the post-secondary level.[98]

Making Provinces Bilingual

Ottawa's Promotion of Official Bilingualism

The Trudeau government's campaign for linguistic equality on a pan-Canadian basis extended to provincial jurisdictions as well. Through a variety of techniques, it tried to persuade all the provinces to adopt official bilingualism. This can be seen clearly in the terms of the ill-fated Victoria Charter, the 1971 constitutional patriation package that died for want of Quebec's approval. For each element of official bilingualism, the government mustered the adhesion of as many provinces as it could, however demographically marginal their Francophone minorities. Thus, either language could be used in provincial legislatures, except in the three Prairie provinces. The statutes of all provinces were to be published in both languages, albeit with Ottawa providing a French-language translation where needed. French and English were to have equal status in the courts of Quebec, New Brunswick, and Newfoundland. Citizens could use either language to communicate with head offices of the governments of Ontario, Quebec, New Brunswick, Prince Edward Island, and Newfoundland. (Of course, Newfoundland, which appears under all headings, had the smallest proportion of minority-language speakers of any province.) A provision enabled all the recalcitrant provinces to "opt in" to each provision at a later point; clearly the hope was that they would be pressured to do so.[99]

In other cases, the federal government relied upon the various Francophone minority organizations, which received substantial federal funding, to lobby their provincial governments on behalf of official bilingualism. This practice was even formalized in a secretary of state *Grants and Contributions Manual, 1988*, which governed support for official minority-language communities. A list of the aims of activities that the secretary of state was prepared to support financially included "the passing and implementation of legislation recognizing the equal status of the two official languages."[100] In fact, the Fédération des communautés francophones et acadienne du Canada had long demanded that all provinces adopt official bilingualism.[101]

The B&B Commission commitment to official bilingualism at the provincial level had been more modest. It had called upon only two provinces, New Brunswick and Ontario, to adopt the Quebec model and to "recognize English and French as official languages and . . . accept the language regimes that such recognition entails"[102]—in effect, to become officially bilingual. Other provinces were to follow suit only should their official-language minority reach 10 per cent.

Otherwise, they should simply allow English and French in legislative debates and offer appropriate services in French for their Francophone minorities.[103]

New Brunswick: Official Bilingualism but Linguistic Communities

In the end, only a single province adopted official bilingualism: New Brunswick. But New Brunswick soon departed from the conception of language rights that Trudeau had championed. The New Brunswick Official Languages Act, adopted in 1969, was closely modelled on Ottawa's Official Languages Act. By the same token, in the Charter of Rights and Freedoms language rights for New Brunswick are set out in the same terms as for federal jurisdictions. However, in response to pressures from its Acadian community, the province subsequently shifted away from the individual-based approach to rights found in the Charter and its 1969 act, to one lodging rights in linguistic communities. Thus, An Act Recognizing the Equality of the Two Official Linguistic Communities in New Brunswick, passed in 1981, recognized the two official linguistic communities, granting them equal status and rights and entitling them to maintain separate institutions.[104] In 1993, this community-based conception of rights was entrenched through a constitutional amendment to the Charter of Rights and Freedoms, as it affected New Brunswick, bearing the statement that "the English linguistic community and the French linguistic community in New Brunswick have equality of status and equal rights and privileges, including the right to distinct educational institutions and such distinct cultural institutions as are necessary for the preservation and promotion of those communities."[105] This deviation from an individual-based approach to rights was rapidly denounced by a leading advocate of the Trudeau vision of Canada, Deborah Coyne:

> It is now proposed . . . to place linguistic freedom in New Brunswick in a different constitutional context. This would involve the constitutional partition of the province into two communities, each of which has equality of status, and the right to "distinct" institutions. This is linked to special legislative status for the New Brunswick government to "promote" these "distinct" institutions.[106]

Coyne threatened to challenge the measure in court but then abandoned the idea. Indeed, the amendment reportedly was opposed by Pierre Trudeau himself.[107]

Quebec: French as the Only Official Language

Meanwhile, Quebec, the province which had a long-established regime of official bilingualism and had been the model for both the B&B Commission and the federal government, formally abandoned linguistic equality and embraced the territorial principle. In 1974, the federalist government of Robert Bourassa adopted Bill 22, making French Quebec's sole official language. Upon election in 1976, the indépendantiste Parti québécois followed suit with Bill 101.

Pressure to legislate the pre-eminence of French within Quebec had been building steadily during the 1960s. First, a new demographic vulnerability faced Quebec. In the past, a high birth rate among Quebec Francophones had always compensated for the tendency of immigrants to integrate with Quebec's Anglophone population but with the 1960s the Francophone birth rate declined rapidly. This led to widespread concern among Quebec nationalists, supported by demographers' projections, that the Francophone proportion of the Quebec population would start falling from its historical level of 80 per cent and that Francophones could lose their predominance in Montreal.[108] Second, there had emerged during the 1950s a new Francophone middle class of salaried professionals focused on creating, disseminating, and applying knowledge, which they could best do in their first language, French. Often their professional mobility was blocked by the pre-eminence of English as a language of work in the upper levels of the Quebec economy.[109] During the 1960s, they had obtained work in the rapidly expanding provincial state and public sector but by the end of the 1960s such positions were no longer being created at the same rate. Increasingly, new middle-class Francophones had to look to the private sector for managerial opportunities. Confronted with the continued predominance of English in these positions, they called for intervention by the Quebec government to alter workplace language practices.

Thus, the Liberal government of Robert Bourassa, first elected in 1970, found itself confronted with growing Francophone concern over the twin issues of immigrant access to English-language schools and French as a working language. In 1972, the Gendron Commission, launched in 1969 by Bourassa's predecessor, Jean-Jacques Bertrand, to investigate the state of the French language in Quebec, delivered its report. Citing the central importance of "collective action . . . to affirm or consecrate the French fact in Quebec," the commission recommended that French alone be proclaimed the official language, while French and English would be declared "national" languages.[110] Although it did not make any recommendations about access to English-language schools, the commission proposed measures to make French the language of internal communication in the work world as well as to increase the proportion of Francophones in managerial positions.[111]

The Bourassa government responded in 1974 with its Bill 22, which made French alone the official language of Quebec and its governmental institutions; made access to English-language schools dependent upon children demonstrating a "sufficient knowledge" of English; and adopted a series of measures to induce private firms to "francize" their operations. The Parti québécois government's

Bill 101, passed in 1977, simply built upon the framework established by its federalist predecessors. Access to English-language schools was restricted on the basis of the parents' mother tongue (as measured by their language of education) rather than the child's knowledge of English. That is, a parent had to have been educated in English—and in Quebec. And private enterprises were to be obliged to pursue francization programs rather than simply urged to do so. To be sure, even Bill 101 assured Quebec Anglophones rights and services that exceeded those available to any of the Francophone minorities, with the possible exception of those in New Brunswick.[112]

The differences in language policy could not have been clearer. Ottawa had vigorously tried to establish a language regime inspired by the personality principle and by the ideals of linguistic equality and the protection of linguistic minorities. For Pierre Trudeau, only official bilingualism would do; Bill 22's departure from that formula made it totally unacceptable. Indeed, in an address to the Quebec wing of the federal Liberal Party in 1976, he branded the bill a "political stupidity."[113] Making French the only official language greatly complicated the federal government's efforts to persuade the rest of the country that there should be two official languages. Many years later, Trudeau even claimed that Bourassa's "taking a stand in opposition to the federal policy of bilingualism" led directly to the election of the Parti québécois in 1976.[114] By the same token, he was highly critical of Bill 101. Looking back in 1998, he wrote,

> Forcing people to do something is contrary to my nature. I believe in freedom of choice. Anyone who comes to Canada comes believing in a free country. Yet the first thing they're told is that their kids can't go to English schools. Even René Lévesque was ashamed of it, and my government only allowed Quebec to do it under the Charter as kind of temporary linguistic tariff, however much I disliked the spirit of it.[115]

While publicly denouncing both Bills 22 and Bill 101, Trudeau and his colleagues resisted pressure from Quebec's Anglophone community to use the federal disallowance power to invalidate each of the laws, if only because of the public backlash that such action would produce among Quebec Francophones.[116]

Quebec, on the other hand, was committed to a language regime based on territory and the language of the majority, even at the expense of minority rights. In fact, during the 1980s the Bourassa government opposed in court the demands by Francophone minorities outside Quebec to educational services under the Charter, for fear that a victory would hamper Quebec in its dealings with its Anglophone minority. It had recognized that only on the basis of French primacy could the Quebec state seek to reverse the historical inferiority of French in the Quebec economy, as well as to maintain the demographic strength of Francophones.

For its part, the B&B Commission had sought to reconcile economic intervention by the Quebec government with a regime of linguistic equality for Canada as a whole. After detailing at length the inferiority of French and Francophones in the Quebec economy, the Commission proposed that "in the private sector in Quebec, governments and industry adopt the objective that French become the principal language of work at all levels."[117] But this departure from the personality principle was not lost on one of the commissioners: Frank (F.R.) Scott, McGill law professor, pillar of the Montreal legal community, and mentor to Pierre Trudeau. In a spirited dissenting statement Scott declared, "It seems to me that, consciously or unconsciously, the other commission members have departed from the principles laid down in Book I of our *Report*, where we defined 'equal partnership' and rejected the territorial principle as being inappropriate for determining a language policy for Canada."[118]

In any event, the Trudeau government did not follow the Commission's lead and adopt measures of its own to enable French to become the principal language of work in Quebec. Thus, the federal government was rendered irrelevant to what had become the central language issue for Francophones in Quebec. The first commissioner of official languages, Keith Spicer, supported in his 1970 report, "within the Quebec sector of the federal administration, the often expressed will to make French Quebec's essential language of official, economic and social intercourse."[119] Indeed, there was substantial progress in making French the essential language of work in federal offices located in Quebec but less progress was made with federal Crown corporations. Nor did the federal government formally make working-language practices a criterion in awarding contracts to private enterprises, as the Quebec government did with its francization programs. In part, Ottawa was constrained by its commitment to official bilingualism and the welfare of linguistic minorities. But according to Gilles Lalande, co-secretary of the B&B Commission and deputy commissioner of official languages from 1980 to 1985, federal officials were also concerned that measures to strengthen French in Quebec might simply encourage Quebec nationalism (as the Trudeau orthodoxy would suggest). That is why federal authorities so consistently shied away from publicly acknowledging the need to consolidate the status of French in Quebec. Writing in 1987, Lalande called upon federal officials "to pay more attention to Quebec's desire—unequivocally expressed in three high-profile pieces of legislation (Bills 22, 63 and 101)—to make French the normal and usual language of work, education, communication, trade and commerce within its borders."[120]

To the extent the federal government did intervene in Quebec, it served to strengthen the position of the Anglophone minority rather than the Francophone majority. For instance, during the 1970s more than half of Ottawa's spending on minority-language and second-language education went to Quebec for its Anglophone minority.[121] In 1987–8, $2,220,000, 14 per cent of the Official Languages Communities program grants went to Quebec Anglophone groups.[122] In effect, during the Trudeau years Ottawa's language policy made no distinction between Quebec and the rest of Canada. In Quebec, as elsewhere, the focus was upon linguistic *minorities*. Indeed, when in 1988 the Mulroney government presented the draft of a revised Official Languages Act, the Quebec government (led by federalist Robert Bourassa) strongly objected to a provision which authorized Ottawa to support organizations promoting bilingualism, declaring that support for such organizations would contradict the objectives of Bill 101. Finally, Ottawa agreed to negotiate an agreement with Quebec to ease these concerns.[123]

Ontario: French as Official Language for Certain Purposes

As to the other provinces, none has adopted formal official bilingualism. Ontario, which has by far Canada's largest Francophone minority, has come closer than the rest.[124] In carefully staged incremental fashion, it has steadily raised the formal status of French in its institutions and expanded the range of government services to its Francophone minorities. Starting with authorization of French in the Ontario legislature in 1970, the province adopted a policy on French services in 1972 and created the Office of the Coordinator of French-Language Services in 1977. In 1984, the government approved the creation of a French-language TV Ontario network. Finally, the French Language Services Act, passed in 1986 under the Liberal government of David Peterson, declared that "the French language is recognized as an official language in the courts and in education,"[125] consolidating measures that had been adopted under the Conservatives. In addition, the law incorporates the B&B Commission's bilingual-districts scheme, designating 22 districts in which all ministries must provide French-language services (as they must at their head offices). Non-profit corporations may be designated under the act to have similar obligations. A French-Language Services Commissioner was established to oversee adherence to the act. Under the terms of the act, both languages may be used in legislative proceedings and are used in records of debates, and, since 1991, legislation is adopted in both languages. Nonetheless, Ontario has steadfastly avoided any declaration that French and English are official languages. Pierre Trudeau personally intervened with Premier Bill Davis, to no avail.[126] Even the Liberal governments of Dalton McGuinty and Kathleen Wynne failed to make the province *officially* bilingual.

During the 1980s, the three Prairie provinces were all forced by Supreme Court judgements to confront the issue of official bilingualism. In the case of Manitoba, a 1979 Supreme Court decision that the province was bound by the Manitoba Act of 1870 to pass acts in both official languages led the NDP government of Howard Pawley to propose that English and French be declared official languages (and that a number of statutes be translated into French and French-language services expanded). But the measure was abandoned in light of public protests and resistance by the Conservative opposition. In 1985, the Supreme Court reaffirmed the obligation to translate all past legislation into French. In 1990, a French-language services act was passed but there was no new attempt to make French an official language.

As for Saskatchewan and Alberta, the Supreme Court declared in 1988 (*R v. Mercure*) that they were still bound by the provision of the Northwest Territories Act, as amended in 1877, that all statutes be enacted and printed in both languages. However, the Court's judgement gave the provincial governments the option of repealing the provision and declaring all existing statutes valid even though they were enacted and printed in English only. Saskatchewan duly passed Bill 2, which affirmed the right to use English and French in the legislature and courts (in criminal cases), affirmed the validity (but not necessity) of enacting laws in both languages, and provided for the translation into French of statutes to be selected by cabinet.[127] For its part, Alberta passed Bill 60, which affirmed the right to use both languages in the legislature and in oral proceedings in certain courts but contained no undertaking to translate statutes nor allowed for the possibility of enacting laws in both languages.[128] In 2015, the Supreme Court affirmed in a split decision (6 to 3) in the *Caron* case that Alberta was not required to enact legislation and regulations in French as well as English.[129] In the remaining predominantly English-speaking provinces, there apparently has been no movement toward making French an official language in government institutions. Indeed, none of them recognizes the right to use French in legislative debates or in courts.[130]

In sum, among the provinces the Trudeau government's objective of official status for both French and English remains fully in place in a single instance, New Brunswick, and, even there, has evolved well away from the Trudeau individual-based ideal. Elsewhere, the principles of territoriality and pre-eminence of the majority language are in full rein, whether officially, in Quebec, or unofficially, elsewhere. The only exception is Ontario, which has by far the largest official-language minority in the country and has given French official status for specific purposes.

French-Language Services

With respect to French as a language of public services, as opposed to government institutions, most provinces have in fact adopted reforms. Change has occurred most dramatically in the case of elementary and secondary education. However, while initially framed in terms of Pierre Trudeau's notion of freedom of individual choice, support of Francophone minority education steadily shifted to more of a community-based model. In other areas as well Francophone leaders have, with some success, contended that French-language services should be tied to community structures.

Education

For the B&B Commission, French-language education for the Francophone minorities had been a major preoccupation. Indeed, the second volume of its report was devoted to minority-language education, along with second-language education which was much less of a priority. In formulating the Commission's recommendations, two commissioners had even proposed a constitutional requirement on the provinces to provide it. The notion was rejected by the majority, fearing it would provoke a crisis in Canadian federalism.[131] But the commissioners did agree on Ottawa providing the provinces with funds to support minority-language education. Beyond recommending that Ottawa cover "the additional costs in providing education in the official minority language," the Commission made a number of recommendations to the provinces as to how they should organize their offer of minority-language education. During the 1960s, some of the majority Anglophone provinces had started to provide access to French-language education for their minorities.[132]

For its part, the Trudeau government moved quickly on the matter, initiating discussions with the provinces during its first year in office. It initially sought to tie federal funding to constitutional entrenchment of language rights but was supported by only two provinces, New Brunswick and Ontario.[133] Abandoning this effort, Ottawa was finally able to announce, in September 1970, the Federal–Provincial Program of Cooperation for the Promotion of Bilingualism in Education. Ottawa was committed to providing $300 million to the provinces, over a four-year period. Closely reflecting the Trudeau government's views, the text of the agreement included among its objectives "to ensure that, insofar as it is feasible, Canadians have the opportunity to educate their children in the official language of their choice and that children have the opportunity to learn, as a second language, the other official language of their country."[134] The Ontario government protested this open access to its French-language education program.[135] Members of the Francophone minorities complained about the impact that the presence of Anglophone students would have on the French-language schools.[136] For its part, the new Bourassa government was preparing to limit the right to choose in Quebec.[137] Generally known as the Bilingualism in Education Program, it was renewed in 1974 for a five-year period but, significantly, without the commitment to parents being able to choose the language of instruction.[138] Over the period 1970–82, Ottawa provided the provinces with $789 million in funding for minority-language education.[139]

Finally, through adoption of the Charter of Rights and Freedoms in 1982, the Trudeau government did succeed in establishing a constitutional right to minority-language education, through section 23. Indeed, entrenchment of the right of Francophone minorities to education in their first language had been the driving purpose of the Charter. Moreover, although the right was restricted to members of the official-language minorities, it was indeed framed in individualist terms: the freedom of individuals to choose the language of instruction of their children. Nonetheless, thanks in part to representations from the Francophone minorities, judicial interpretations have had the effect over time of transforming what originally had been conceived as a right of individuals into a community-based right of official-language communities to maintain and control separate educational institutions.

Section 23 of the Charter declares that parents whose first language "learned and still understood" is the language of their province's official-language minority, or who have received primary school instruction anywhere in Canada in the language of that minority, have the right to publicly paid instruction in that language for their children.[140] However, the question soon arose among Francophone leaders as to whether section 23 involved the right not just to secure instruction in the minority language but to have that instruction provided within separate minority-language facilities and to have these facilities managed by minority-language parents. Indeed, during the negotiations leading up to adoption of the Charter, leaders of the Francophone minorities had expressed strong dissatisfaction with the proposed wording, declaring that it didn't guarantee the right of Francophone communities to separate schools.[141]

Most provincial governments (including Quebec, much to the consternation of the Francophone minorities) contended that the only requirement was that minority-language instruction be available; it need not be offered in separate facilities under minority-language parent control. Indeed, they claimed that the authors of section 23 had themselves declared this was not the case.[142] Nonetheless, in its 1990 decision in *Mahé v. Alberta*, the Supreme Court determined that, given sufficient numbers of eligible students, provincial governments did indeed have the obligation to provide instruction in separate facilities that are under some degree of management and control by minority-language parents. The Court stated that this need not entail separate school boards. However, through the combined effect of lobbying by Francophone leaders and subsequent decisions by lower courts, the right to "management and control" became understood as the right to such boards. All the provinces outside Quebec now not only recognize the notion of separate French-language schools but maintain Francophone school boards which, except in Manitoba, have exclusive authority for French-language schools.[143] In light of the *Mahé* decision, the federal government itself began offering financial support for the establishment of Francophone school governance just as its Court Challenges Program had financially supported the Francophones whose initiative had led to the *Mahé* decision itself.[144]

As well as insisting that French-language instruction be offered in separate schools controlled by the Francophone community, the Francophone minority leadership has contended that the same right should extend to the post-secondary level, as well as kindergarten. Here too there has been a strong movement in favour of purely Francophone institutions managed by the Francophone community. In fact, such institutions have existed for some time outside Quebec: four Francophone universities and six Francophone colleges. Recently, the issue was joined in Ontario, where virtually all French-language university studies are provided by bilingual, rather than distinctly Francophone, institutions.[145] While the University of Ottawa and Laurentian University, along with affiliated universities, provide French-language instruction to Eastern and Northern Ontario, the bilingual Glendon campus of York University is the only site of French-language university instruction in Southern Ontario, the primary area of growth in Ontario's Francophone population. Over recent years the Assemblée de la Francophonie de l'Ontario (the main organization of Ontario Francophones) campaigned strongly for the establishment of a Francophone university in Southern Ontario, as did a student group: le Regroupement étudiant franco-ontarien. For his part, the Ontario Commissioner for French Language Services firmly supported the cause.[146] For that matter, there have been periodic campaigns at the University of Ottawa, as well as Laurentian University, to place the Francophone section within a separate institution. In August 2017, the Ontario government committed to establishing such a university in Toronto, with its first class entering in the fall of 2020.[147]

In short, the model of a bilingual university, which embodies the Trudeau ideals of language equality, freedom of choice, and personal bilingualism, has been rejected by most of Ontario's Francophone leadership. Rather than being touted as the key to individual freedom and choice, let alone the means to improved relations between Francophones and Anglophones, bilingual institutions are seen as a menace to Francophones, leading to their assimilation.

Basing Support in Francophone Communities

The campaign of Francophone leaders to root public services, and indeed the conception of Francophone rights, in community structures was rewarded in the 1988 revision of the Official Languages Act. The preamble commits the federal government to "enhancing the vitality and supporting the development of English and French linguistic minority communities." A new section, Part VII, obliges "every federal institution" to pursue that objective.[148] The federal government's obligation to pursue this commitment was reinforced by a 2005 amendment to the act, pioneered by Franco-Ontarian senator Jean-Robert Gauthier, that rendered Part VII justiciable. Indeed since 1994, the federal department of Canadian Heritage has signed collaboration agreements with individual minority-language communities, enabling the communities to set their own priorities.[149]

By the same token, beginning in 2003, Ottawa has developed multi-year action plans or "roadmaps," following upon Part VII of the revised Official Languages Act which calls for the minister of Canadian Heritage to develop a co-ordinated federal approach to advancing the two official languages.[150] The "roadmaps" are developed through a broad consultation within the Francophone communities. Multi-year agreements are now in effect with almost all provinces.[151] Largely on a shared-cost basis, they support public services to official-language minorities in areas such as health care, social services, small business development, support for media, and legal services. Minority-language community development has been an important focus of these plans. In the current *Roadmap for Canada's Official Languages 2013–2018*, minority-language communities are one of three priorities, along with support for education and addressing the linguistic imbalance among immigrants. The document commits $1.124 billion in federal funding over the five-year period.[152]

Finally, the most dramatic instance of Francophone mobilization in favour of separate, community-based institutions is the campaign to preserve the (Francophone) Montfort Hospital in Ottawa, which had been slated for integration into the far larger and primarily English-language Ottawa General Hospital. While guarantees of minority-language service in the Charter of Rights and Freedoms are limited, at the provincial level, to the education sector alone (with the exception of New Brunswick), judicial action was successful nonetheless. While determining that Montfort was protected neither by the text of the Constitution Act, 1867, nor by the Charter, the Court declared that the hospital did receive the protection of an unwritten constitutional principle: the protection of minorities. The proposed restructuring of the health service delivery

> would greatly impair Montfort's role as an important linguistic, cultural and educational institution, vital to the minority francophone population of Ontario. This would be contrary to the fundamental constitutional principle of respect for and protection of minorities.[153]

The development of jurisprudence favouring a community-based notion of Francophone rights was the result of legal initiatives that were largely financed through the federally funded Court Challenges Program, that the Trudeau government had established in 1978. The Harper government sought twice to eliminate the Court Challenges Program; the Mulroney government had already eliminated but then reinstated it. Finally, in 2008 it established a new Language Rights Support Program in response to a legal challenge by the Fédération des communautés francophones et acadienne du Canada.[154] However, the future of the program is secure in the hands of the Justin Trudeau government.

In sum, Pierre Trudeau's government had relatively little success in its concerted effort to secure provincial adoption of its model of official bilingualism. In fact, only one province is now officially bilingual and even it has displaced the individual-based notion of rights that Trudeau had always advanced. Other provinces have openly resisted the notion of official bilingualism or, in the case of Quebec, have abandoned it outright. At the same time, all the English-speaking provinces have greatly expanded French-language services. Ontario has made French an official language in its courts and educational system. The

Charter of Rights and Freedoms has required the provinces to provide French-language services in education. Financial transfers from Ottawa have supported French-language services in other areas. Yet, here too, the individual-based notion of rights that the Charter's authors sought to put in place has been largely replaced by a community-based notion of rights that has been favoured by the Francophone minorities and supported by the courts.

Future of the Francophone Minorities

An important legal, political, and social structure is now in place to support the Francophone minorities. Clearly, it would not have come about without the determined leadership of Pierre Trudeau and his associates, even if his individual-based notion of language rights has been largely displaced. Moreover, successor governments have all respected the broad outline of Trudeau's legacy, maintaining and even reinforcing support for Francophone minorities. After all, it was with the Conservative government of Brian Mulroney that the Official Languages Act was revised and generally strengthened in 1988, with a new section devoted to the official-language minority communities. By the same token, the Harper government followed the Chrétien government's 2003 initiative of generating a comprehensive action plan for official languages and it developed, through broad consultations of official-language minority communities, two "road-maps" for official languages that maintained and even enhanced the funding levels of the 2003 Liberal plan.[155] The Francophone minorities' support structure is immeasurably stronger.

The question remains as to whether this structure is sufficient to secure the pan-Canadian presence of Francophone society that Trudeau had so earnestly envisaged. Arguably, the transition to a community-based conception of Francophone language rights has strengthened this possibility, just as the expansion of French-language services more than offsets what might have been gained through a wider adoption by the provinces of official bilingualism. Clearly, this comprehensive support structure has not been sufficient to date to reverse the historical demographic decline of the Francophone population outside Quebec. But perhaps it served to reduce the decline.

Still, the future of a Francophonie outside Quebec remains uncertain even if this support structure is now more squarely configured on a community basis.[156] On the one hand, the breadth of publicly funded support for the Francophonie is a strongly positive factor, as is the manifest commitment of Francophone leaders and associations to a strong Francophonie. On the other hand, the viability of Francophone society in most parts of Canada is threatened by such factors as the pervasiveness of English-language media in metropolitan settings, a low Francophone birth rate, the marginal place of Francophones among immigrants to Canada outside Quebec (2 per cent according to a 2011 study),[157] and the tendency of English

Table 4.1 Francophone Linguistic Retention Rate, 2011

French outside Quebec	1971	1981	1991	2001	2006	2016
Language spoken in the home	675,925	666,785	636,640	612,985	604,975	558,130
Mother tongue	926,400	923,605	976,415	980,270	975,390	947,040
Language ratio [Home language/Mother tongue (TRAL)]	0.73	0.72	0.65	0.63	0.62	0.59

Source: Data for 1971 through 2006 are taken from Rodrigue Landry, "Loi sur les langues officielles et démographie: comment les droits linguistiques peuvent-ils influencer la vitalité d'une minorité?" in Jedwab and Landry, *Life after Forty*, Table 1, p. 57. The data for 2016 are from Statistics Canada, "Language Highlight Tables, 2016 Census." (The 2016 data may not be fully comparable since they are based on "French" alone and exclude respondents using "French and English," "English and French and non-official language," and "French and non-official language.")

to dominate in marriages between Francophones and non-Francophones.[158] Table 4.1, comparing the numbers of individuals outside Quebec using French most often at home with the numbers having a French mother tongue, shows that over the decades the Francophone communities continued to lose a large share of their members through integration with the Anglophone majorities. Indeed, the rate of loss has increased over the decades. Thus, there is no indication that the language strategy of the Trudeau government served to arrest this phenomenon.

For that matter, a 2017 Statistics Canada study projects that by 2035 the proportion of the population outside Quebec whose mother tongue is French will have fallen to 2.7 per cent, from 3.8 per cent in 2011, and the proportion using French as their primary language at home will have fallen to 1.8 per cent from 2.4 per cent. The number with French as their mother tongue will have further declined, although the number of individuals with French as their home language will have grown.[159]

Making Canadians Bilingual

Beyond implanting bilingualism in Canada's political institutions, both national and provincial, and strengthening official-language minorities, especially Francophone ones, there was a final focus of the Trudeau government's language policy: making Canadians themselves bilingual.

The B&B Commission

For its part, the B&B Commission, especially its intellectual leader André Laurendeau, had not seen personal bilingualism as a priority. Instead, its focus had been on Canada's two linguistic communities, as distinct entities. It had declared that the health of these two communities, more specifically the French one, was of far greater urgency than the promotion of personal bilingualism.

And Canadian unity lay not in personal bilingualism but in creating an "equal partnership" between these two communities.

The Commission started from the premise that personal bilingualism is a relative term since very few individuals are truly bilingual: "We know that complete bilingualism—the equal command of two languages—is rare and perhaps impossible."[160] Even with this understanding, the Commission declared, bilingualism is not necessary on a widespread basis. If countries are bilingual it is because they contain two groups of people whose primary languages are different, not because their citizens are themselves bilingual. By the same token, the survival of a country's bilingualism depends upon the strength of each of these "unilingual nuclei—that is, two or more groups of persons who habitually live and work in one language, resorting to the other language only to communicate with fellow citizens of that language."[161] In fact, not only is widespread personal bilingualism not necessary, but promoting it could be counter-productive: "if everyone in a bilingual state becomes completely bilingual, one of the languages is rendered superfluous,"[162] and will disappear.

Thus, "the bilingual state is not intended as an instrument for the propagation of individual bilingualism."[163] Instead, a bilingual state must simply provide services to citizens in their own languages and ensure that members of the minority linguistic group are not disadvantaged. That may impose obligations upon the majority linguistic group "to guarantee survival and equality for the minority group."[164] To be sure, the Commission did propose that "the study of the second official language should be obligatory for all students in Canadian schools"[165] but it stressed that this experience would not produce fully bilingual students.[166] It was intended to create the *capacity* to become bilingual at a later stage in their lives. For that matter, unlike in the case of minority-language education, the Commission made no recommendation of federal funding support for second-language education.[167]

Pierre Trudeau and Personal Bilingualism

Nevertheless, personal bilingualism suited Trudeau's vision of a bilingual Canada. It accorded well with his belief in the pre-eminence of the individual and the importance of personal choice, as well as the need to implant a new pan-Canadian identity. Thus, his notion of a bilingual Canada was not that of the B&B Commission with two distinct linguistically defined societies.

Trudeau would disclaim any desire that *all* Canadians should become bilingual: "I never expect that the average Quebecer in Sainte-Tite-des-Caps will become perfectly bilingual, nor that the Anglophone in Calgary or Moose Jaw must know French. What we want is that the institutions be bilingual."[168] Trudeau's primary focus was on ensuring that *Francophones* could receive government services in their *own* language wherever they may be in Canada.

The ability of Anglophones to deal with Francophones in French, and vice versa, was at best a secondary objective.[169] But personal bilingualism accorded perfectly with his vision of national unity. To quote against his 1988 declaration, "Bilingualism unites people; dualism divides them. Bilingualism means that you can speak to each other; duality means you can live in one language and the rest of Canada will live in another language."[170] In addition, at least some Anglophone public servants would need to be bilingual if "the institutions," or governments, were to offer their services in French throughout the country.

For that matter, the ideal of personal bilingualism was central to Trudeau's public image. Trudeau's own example of seemingly perfect bilingualism affected how many Canadians, at least in English Canada, understood the ideal of a bilingual Canada. It was one in which Canadians would themselves embrace both languages. National unity would come by increasing the capacity of Canadians to deal with each other in both official languages. The lowering of language barriers would bring them together. This was a message that greatly appealed to many English Canadians: by becoming bilingual they could themselves take action to unite the Canadian nation. Or, if they didn't become bilingual, they could at least make certain that their children did.[171]

By the same token, if national unity could be achieved through expanding personal bilingualism then there would be no need to face the complexities of creating an "equal partnership" between Anglophone and Francophone communities, as the B&B Commission proposed, let alone the special arrangements that Quebec nationalists were seeking for their province. For many English-speaking Canadians this had a real appeal. Becoming bilingual would be the quintessential Canadian experience in which all Canadians, including Quebec Francophones, could share, as Canadians.

Trudeau Government and Personal Bilingualism

Here too the Trudeau government was trying to undo long-standing patterns. Historically, few Canadians had been bilingual. In 1961, only 12.2 per cent of Canadians said they could carry on a conversation in both English and French.[172] Moreover, reflecting the extent to which in all provinces but Quebec linguistic minorities have had little economic or political power, it is French Canadians who historically have been bilingual. In 1961, 70 per cent of bilingual Canadians had French as their mother tongue. In effect, they had to be bilingual to deal with the linguistic majority. Thus, reflecting the relative presence of the Francophones, bilingualism was spread unevenly across the country. It constituted 25.5 per cent of Quebec's residents and 19 per cent of New Brunswick's but less than 8 per cent of every other province's population.[173]

As already noted, the federal government included second-language education in the Bilingualism in Education Program of funding to the provinces that it announced in 1970. In Matthew Hayday's words, Secretary of State Pelletier "elevated second-language instruction to a level of importance greater than had been accorded by the commission."[174] At the same time, the program reflected the Trudeau government's view that, respecting the right of individuals to choose, majority-language parents should have full access to minority-language schools.[175]

The Trudeau government's emphasis on personal bilingualism and second-language education was further accentuated in 1976, as part of a reconfiguration of the government's official languages strategy. A disillusionment had set in with the language training program for federal public servants, given rising costs and disappointing results.[176] Instead, it was argued that the focus should be on children and youth, where second-language training is more likely to be successful. Trudeau stated publicly that he wished to shift to "greater support for teaching French in the schools—where it should be taught—rather than in crash programs for public servants."[177] This position was embodied in a comprehensive document, *A National Understanding*.[178]

Thus, over the period 1970–82, Ottawa provided the provinces with $304 million in funding for second-language education.[179] All provinces participated in this arrangement. Through this funding French-immersion programs emerged in a number of provinces. Indeed, all provinces had such programs by the end of the 1970s.[180]

At the same time, the federal government undertook to fund an organization that promoted second-language education, and especially French immersion: Canadian Parents for French (CPF). The secretary of state fully covered CPF's expenses for the first two years after its creation in 1977; in 1988–9 it was still covering 65 per cent of the CPF national office's expenses. For its part CPF actively lobbied both federal and provincial governments on behalf of bilingual education. In the early 1980s, it was influential in persuading Ottawa and the provinces to enter into a new multi-year agreement on funding for bilingual education.[181]

The combined effect of federal funding and promotion by CPF and other organizations resulted in a remarkable growth in French-language immersion enrolments. The number of Anglophone children registered in French-immersion programs soared from 37,835 in 1977–8 to 288,050 in 1990–1, involving 1592 schools and constituting over 7 per cent of all Anglophone students.[182] Outside Quebec, 6.8 per cent of schoolchildren were enrolled in immersion programs, as opposed to 2.1 per cent in 1980–1.[183] Primarily for this reason, bilingualism among Anglophones outside Quebec rose by 78 per cent between 1961 and 1981, reaching 5 per cent. In 1991, it stood at 6.4 per cent, as opposed to 3 per cent in 1971.[184]

Clearly, the Trudeau government's decision to make personal bilingualism a central objective of its language policy has left its mark. Indeed, successor governments have continued to provide provincial governments with funding to support second-language training.[185] The CPF's promotion of French immersion is now complemented by the work of other federally funded organizations such as French for the Future. As a result of all these efforts, bilingualism is no longer restricted primarily to Francophones; indeed, between 1961 and 2001 the proportion of bilinguals increased in every province.[186]

Nonetheless, the same trend did not continue into this century: excluding the province of Quebec (where personal bilingualism continued to grow) the proportion of the total population who claim personal bilingualism actually fell, going from 10.3 per cent in 2001 to 9.7 per cent in 2011 and 9.8 per cent in 2016.[187] Among young Anglophones 15 to 19 years of age living outside Quebec, personal bilingualism also fell, going from a peak of 15 per cent in 1996 to 12 per cent in 2006 and 11 per cent in 2011, while partially rebounding in 2016 to 13.5 per cent.[188] In part, the halt in the earlier trend toward personal bilingualism outside Quebec reflects the presence of recent immigrants, who are less likely to be bilingual in English and French (outside Quebec only 6 per cent in 2011) than the Canadian-born population (11 per cent in 2011). But it also reflects an overall decline in the study of French in schools outside Quebec. Whether due to curricular changes or other factors, the number of high school students taking regular French-as-a-second-language programs has declined dramatically (by 24 per cent from 1991 to 2010).

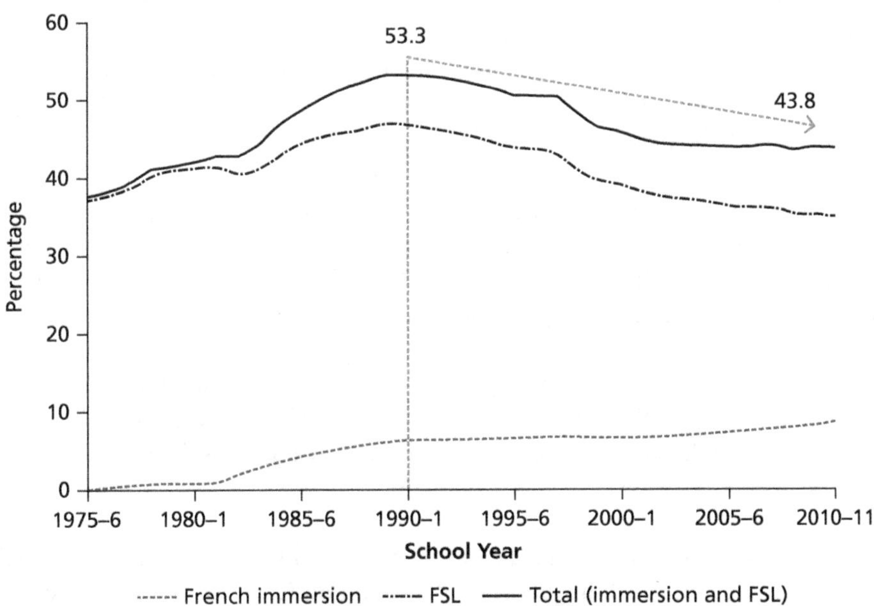

Figure 4.1 Continuous increase in French-immersion program registrations despite a decrease in French-as-a-second-language (FSL) instruction since 1991–2

Note: Data applies to elementary and secondary public school students in all provinces except Quebec.

Source: Jean-François and Jean-Pierre Corbeil, "The evolution of English–French bilingualism in Canada from 1961 to 2011," *Statistics Canada*, #75-006-X.

This trend is only partially offset by the continued growth in French-immersion students (28 per cent from 1991 to 2010). Thus, the future of personal bilingualism among Anglophones outside Quebec is heavily dependent upon the success of French immersion.[189]

While the popularity of French-immersion programs, especially among parents, is undeniable, some researchers have questioned the level of French-language capacity that graduates typically achieve.[190] Indeed, French-immersion graduates have typically experienced difficulty pursuing French-language university studies.[191] Beyond that, one can question the extent to which, especially outside Quebec, an acquired knowledge of French by Anglophones can actually lead to greater bilingual exchange. After all, in most parts of Canada the numbers of Francophones and thus the opportunities to use French are limited. In fact, in all provinces but New Brunswick (and Quebec), the number of Anglophone children in French-immersion programs is greater than the number of Francophone children in French-language schools.[192] That being said, some programs have been adopted to offset this difficulty. For instance, the federal government funds a program through which high school students can improve their second-language skills through exchange visits.[193] Similarly, the Association des collèges et universités de la francophonie canadienne (which groups together French-language and bilingual universities and colleges outside Quebec) offers a program through which its students can spend a period in a Quebec university or college, and Quebec students can spend a period in one of their institutions. Clearly, more such programs are sorely needed if French immersion is to be more than a classroom experience.

Be that as it may, personal bilingualism remains highly limited among Canadian Anglophones, reaching slightly more than 9 per cent in 2016. Among Francophones, bilingualism is much more substantial, reaching 46 per cent according to the 2016 Canadian census.[194] Still, Graham Fraser, the Official Languages Commissioner, is quite correct to state in his 2015 annual report,

> Canada is really two primarily unilingual language communities that live side by side. Some 90% of English-speaking Canadians do not speak French, while some 60% of French-speaking Canadians do not speak English.[195]

However, as we have seen, the B&B Commission viewed this as the normal state of affairs within a bilingual state. Indeed, if all Canadians were to become bilingual, French would become superfluous and, over time, would disappear.

Conclusions

In sum, the Trudeau government sought, with consuming determination, to put in place a comprehensive language policy for Canada. These efforts were to have a lasting impact since, by and large, successor federal governments have maintained, and even reinforced, the broad directions of policy that were set during the Trudeau era. The contours of the Trudeau government's language policy closely reflected the central beliefs and objectives that Trudeau himself brought to Ottawa: the centrality of the individual and freedom of choice, full equality of Canada's two primary languages, and the fullest possible application of the personality principle. To what extent have the various components of this policy been put into place and, to the degree they are in place, how far have they advanced their central objectives?

The Federal Government

The clearest area of success involves the federal government. Here the objective was to install official bilingualism and language equality within the government and in its relations with citizens. This objective was first legislated, through the Official Languages Act and then entrenched in the constitution, through the Charter of Rights and Freedoms. Beyond that, the federal government assumed a fully bilingual face: henceforth, public communications appear in both languages and Francophones are present in senior cabinet positions and, on an alternate basis, such key appointments as governor general. Personal bilingualism has become the norm for the prime ministership, as well as other senior political positions, although the Harper government did not always respect this norm when it came to appointments such as Supreme Court justices.

As to the federal public service, it now has a strong Francophone presence at the managerial level but it continues to function primarily in English alone. The right to select one's working language was enshrined in 1973 in Treasury Board regulations, as well as later in the revised Official Languages Act, but the opportunities to exercise such a right are highly circumscribed. As the B&B Commission had recognized, equality in working languages can come about only through structural changes. For whatever reason, Pierre Trudeau's government did not follow that path, nor have its successors. Nonetheless, the public face of the federal government is resolutely bilingual; to that extent the Trudeau nation-building purpose of language policy has been achieved.

With respect to citizens' relations with the federal government, the right to choose between official languages is clearly set out in the Charter and reaffirmed in the Official Languages Act. Nevertheless, this embodiment of the personality principle is limited by the provision "where there is significant demand."[196] Moreover, this provision itself falls short of the notion of "bilingual districts," as first formulated by the B&B Commission and then incorporated in the first version of the Official Languages Act. The "bilingual districts" would have offered citizens certainty as to where bilingual services are available and would have had a high "symbolic value that, arguably could have led provincial governments and municipalities to follow suit.[197] Nonetheless, the proposal was defeated by mobilization of support, most notably in Quebec, for the pre-eminence of the majority language. In any event, it is not entirely clear that the Trudeau government, and Trudeau himself, was committed to this proposal.

The Provinces

The Trudeau government was much less successful in its ambitions for the provinces. Indeed, its campaign to have all provinces adopt official bilingualism met with virtually total rejection: only New Brunswick complied. Quebec, under the federalist government of Robert Bourassa, opted for the territorial principle and French as the only official language. The other provinces, whether formally or informally, adopted the territorial principle, deferring to their English-language majority. While Ontario, with the country's largest Francophone minority, has recognized French as an official language in the courts and education, it has resisted adopting full official bilingualism, even under premiers who were themselves bilingual, such as David Peterson and Dalton McGuinty. In the end, with the exception of Quebec, the language regimes of the provinces reflect the relative demographic weakness of their linguistic minority. The only province where the two language groups at all approach parity, New Brunswick, does fall under the Charter's official bilingualism but it subsequently decided to recast language equality to one of communities, not individuals, much to the consternation of Pierre Trudeau himself.

As to services the provinces provide, the Trudeau government succeeded, through the Charter's section 23, in binding the provinces to offer education in both languages. To that extent, the Trudeau ideals of individual rights and freedom of choice have been constitutionally entrenched—in itself a signal accomplishment. However, the right to choose is limited to a small subset of citizens, members of official-language minorities, rather than to all citizens as the Trudeau government had originally envisaged in its transfers of funds to the provinces. Moreover, the initial conception of language rights has been transformed through jurisprudence that has had the effect of shifting section 23 away from the Trudeau model of individual rights toward recognition of a community's right to separate unilingual schools that it would itself manage. A tendency to tie language rights to communities, rather than individuals, also can be seen in the Montfort judgement, as well as in the addition to the Official Languages Act of a section on federal obligations to official-language minorities and the references to community development in successive official language roadmaps. In short, language rights, as developed in Canada, have moved steadily from Trudeau's concern with the individual, and freedom of choice to become focused on the collective needs of communities. Arguably, jurisprudence favouring minority-language communities' management of unilingual institutions supports a general right of these communities to institutional autonomy.[198]

However one might characterize the Trudeau government's success in achieving its objectives at both the federal and provincial levels, the question remains as to whether its successes have advanced the government's underlying nation-building goal: strengthening the Francophone presence throughout the country. Here the results are quite clear: the demographic decline of Francophones outside Quebec has continued unabated. Perhaps the decline would have been even greater without these policies but to date it has not been arrested, let alone reversed.

Personal Bilingualism

Finally, beyond transforming the language practices of governments, Trudeau's language policy had another focus: the promotion of personal bilingualism. Here, the long-term success record is most qualified. While personal bilingualism among Anglophones has grown over several decades, it remains at little more than 9 per cent. Outside Quebec, despite the commitment of both Ottawa and groups such as Canadian Parents for French, French-as-second-language enrolments are declining dramatically and French immersion still constitutes no more than 10 per cent of school enrolments. Overall, only 17.9 per cent of Canadians were bilingual in 2016.[199] In Canada, bilingualism remains a matter not of individuals but of two mainly unilingual communities.

Language Policy and Quebec Nationalism

While the language policy initiated by the Trudeau government may, with time, have a mixed record in terms of Pierre Trudeau's personal commitment to the primacy of the individual and personal choice, let alone personal bilingualism, where does it stand in terms of his other main purpose: creating a pan-Canadian national identity?

As we have seen, the federalist government of Robert Bourassa rejected official bilingualism in favour of making French the sole official language, through Bill 22. René Lévesque's PQ government reinforced Bill 22 through its own Bill 101. Arguably, by establishing the pre-eminence of French in Quebec, Bill 101 served the cause of Canadian federalism by eliminating one of the strongest grievances favouring Quebec independence. Indeed, Bill 101 remains the object of strong public support in Quebec. Yet the Trudeau government roundly denounced both Bill 22 and Bill 101, just as it ignored the B&B Commission's recommendation that the federal government collaborate with its Quebec counterpart to make French the primary working language in Quebec. The end result was to make the federal government appear opposed to reinforcing the French language in Quebec.

To be sure, the Trudeau government's language policy was designed to offer Quebec Francophones the promise of opportunities for the French language in the rest of Canada. While the provincial governments resisted official bilingualism they did agree, through the Charter of Rights and Freedoms, to recognize the right to French-language education across the country. Indeed, as we shall see, this was the primary purpose of the Charter within Trudeau's vision. Yet, by all indications, the primary focus of Quebec Francophones was upon the status of French within Quebec itself. This was the conclusion of Jean Marchand, member of the B&B Commission before entering federal politics with Trudeau and Gérard Pelletier:

> This is what I learned in the [B&B] Commission when we went around meeting the people. We visited a small place in the Lake St John area [in Quebec]. I'd say: "What's wrong?" And the people would say: "The manager of the mill or whatever it was has been here for ten years—and he has never learned to say either 'yes' or 'no' in French. We all had to learn English." The population in that area is 99.9 per cent French.
>
> So, for me, this was much more the cause of the trouble in Quebec than the fact that there was no bilingualism, say, at the Vancouver airport. Actually, at that time, nobody was travelling by airplane, or just a few people. I think that the main source of dispute or conflict or tension or friction—call it whatever you want—was Quebec itself and the federal institutions where there was surely no equality for all practical purposes.[200]

The basic irrelevance of pan-Canadian language rights to support for Quebec independence was confirmed in a 1977 survey in which Quebeckers were asked: "If French-speaking Canadians were treated as equals to English-speaking Canadians outside Quebec would this affect your attitude towards independence for Quebec?" Only 17 per cent said yes; 81 per cent said no.[201]

To be sure, the Trudeau government's campaign to implant language equality and official bilingualism across the country need not be justified solely in terms of defeating Quebec nationalism and support for independence. It can be readily justified in terms of equity and justice—including Pierre Trudeau's brand of liberalism, with its focus on the rights of the individual. But it was a concern for "national unity" that rallied many English Canadians to the cause.

Notes

1. This account of the Pearson initiatives is drawn from Royal Commission on Bilingualism and Biculturalism [hereinafter: B&B Commission], *Book III: The Work World*, 114–16. At the same time, the Commission notes that the commitment to "biculturalism" was not clearly defined and apparently did not entail creating culturally distinct environments.
2. Michael Behiels, *Canada's Francophone Minority Communities: Constitutional Renewal and the Winning of School Governance*

(Montreal and Kingston: McGill-Queen's University Press, 2004), 30.

3. For that matter, in his *Memoirs* Trudeau fails to acknowledge the Commission's work, simply stating that he set up a working group that, "following the general outlines provided by me," would prepare a draft of the Official Languages Act. He states "I already had an idea; all I had to do was to put it into effect," Trudeau, *Memoirs*, 123. In fact, a draft of the Official Languages Act had been prepared while Lester Pearson was prime minister, at his instigation (Daniel Bourgeois, *The Canadian Bilingual Districts: From Cornerstone to Tombstone* [Montreal and Kingston: McGill-Queen's University Press, 2006], 51). The Trudeau book does include a photo of the Commission's two co-presidents and a caption stating that they "did fine work in the 1960s" on the Commission (Trudeau, *Memoirs*, 123). Moreover, in his October 1968 statement to the House about the forthcoming official languages bill, Trudeau acknowledged the role of the Commission in stating that the bill would be implementing the Commission's recommendations. (Prime Minister's Office, *Statement by the Prime Minister in the House of Commons on the Resolution Preliminary to Introduction of the Official Languages Bill*, 17 Oct. 1968.)
4. Pierre Elliott Trudeau, "The Values of a Just Society" in *Towards a Just Society*, ed. Thomas S. Axworthy and Pierre Elliott Trudeau (Markham, Ont: Viking, 1990), 364.
5. Ibid., 368. Trudeau did acknowledge that in two other instances—Indigenous Peoples and Canada's multicultural heritage—the Charter does enshrine collective rights. (ibid., 365.)
6. Trudeau, *Federalism and the French Canadians*, 31.
7. The classic presentation of the competing principles of personality and territoriality is Kenneth D. McRae, "The Principle of Territoriality and the Principle of Personality in Multilingual States," *International Journal of the Sociology of Language* 4 (1975): 35–45.
8. Pierre Foucher, "The Official Languages Act of Canada," in *Life after Forty: Official Languages Policy in Canada/Après quarante ans: les politiques de langue officielle au Canada*, ed. Jack Jedwab and Rodrigue Landry (Kingston, Ont. School of Policy Studies, Queen's University, 2011), 97. Denise G. Réaume goes beyond the territorial principle to argue that language rights should be attached to communities (Denise G. Réaume, "Beyond Personality: The Territorial and Personal Principles of Language Policy Reconsidered," in *Language Rights and Political Theory*, ed. Will Kymlicka and Alan Patten [Oxford: Oxford University Press, 2003], 272–95).
9. Jean A. Laponce, *Languages and Their Territories* (Toronto: University of Toronto Press, 1987).
10. Trudeau, "Values of a Just Society", 368.
11. Pierre Elliott Trudeau, "We Need a Bill of Rights," *Maclean's*, 8 Feb. 1964 (as reproduced in Pierre Elliott Trudeau, *Against the Current: Selected Writings 1939–1996*, ed. Gérard Pelletier [Toronto: McClelland & Stewart, 1996], 216). The phrase "to rest" appears in the version of the text reproduced in Pierre Elliott Trudeau, *The Essential Trudeau*, ed. Ron Graham (Toronto: McClelland & Stewart, 1998), 79.
12. *Debates of the Senate*, 2nd session, 33rd Parliament, vol. 132, 30 Mar. 1988, 2993.
13. Frederick W. Gibson, ed., *Cabinet Formation and Bicultural Relations*, Studies of the Royal Commission on Bilingualism and Biculturalism, no. 6 (Ottawa: Queen's Printer, 1970), 165.
14. In 1863, French Canadians had held only about 35 per cent of positions on the headquarters staff of the United Canadas, "and these were obviously employed on less important tasks, for they received less that 20 percent of the total payroll." See Hodgetts, *Pioneer Public Service*, 57.
15. B&B Commission, *Book III: The Work World*, 101.
16. Ibid., 111.
17. The Commission declared, "No other part of the commission's terms of reference appears to us to be more urgent. If we wish 'to develop the Canadian Confederation on the basis of an equal partnership' between the two founding peoples, bilingualism becomes essential first in the institutions shared by all Canadians. This conclusion is inescapable." See B&B Commission, *Book I: The Official Languages* (Ottawa: Queen's Printer, 1967), 91.

18. Ibid., 91.
19. Official Languages Act, 1969, 1st session, 28th Parliament, C-120.
20. B&B Commission, *Book III: The Work World*, 263.
21. Ibid., 264.
22. Ibid., 178.
23. Ibid., 264.
24. Ibid., 272.
25. Ibid., 291.
26. "Back to the Solitudes," *Globe and Mail*, 18 Dec. 1969 and *Toronto Star*, 19 Dec. 1969. In the House, Opposition leader Robert Stanfield called on Prime Minister Trudeau to disown the French-language units proposal which "denie[d] any concept of effective bilingualism." (*Globe and Mail*, 19 Dec. 1969.) Outside the House he derided the creation of a "multitude of solitudes." (*Toronto Star*, 19 Dec. 1969.)
27. Helaina Gaspard, "Canada's Official Languages Policy and the Federal Public Service" in *State Traditions and Language Regimes*, ed. Linda Cardinal and Salma K. Sonntag (Montreal and Kingston: McGill-Queen's University Press, 2015), 197. See also Daniel Bourgeois, "La commission BB et la bureaucratie fédérale" *Mens* 14, no. 2-1 (2014): 37–8.
28. In the early 1970s, the federal government did designate, on an experimental basis, a number of entities to be French-language units but the overwhelming majority, 330 of 457, were in Quebec. (Commissioner of Official Languages, *Second Annual Report, 1971–72* [Ottawa: Information Canada, 1973], 22.) In Ottawa, those units accounted for only 5 per cent of the total number of positions (Commissioner of Official Languages, *Third Annual Report, 1972–73* [Ottawa: Information Canada, 1974], 27), and tended to be units that were already operating in French rather than the result of an effort to guarantee "equal partnership" throughout the public service as a whole. In 1975, the Treasury Board announced that as a result of this experiment it was prepared to adopt the scheme. But in response to protests from Anglophone civil servants and their union representatives, it accepted a series of qualifications that, in the opinion of the Commissioner of Official Languages, threatened to undermine the concept. (Commissioner of Official Languages, *Fifth Annual Report, 1975* [Ottawa: Information Canada, 1976], 15.) Three years later, the Treasury Board was still deliberating about where to locate the units. (Commissioner of Official Languages, *Annual Report 1978* [Ottawa: Supply and Services, 1979], 22.) In the end, the idea largely gave way to a scheme of designating regions in which, given the wide use of both English and French, employees can choose to work in either. (D'lberville Fortier, "Breaking Old Habits," *Language and Society*, no. 24 [Fall 1988]: 12. On the French-language units see Scott Reid, *Lament for a Notion* [Vancouver: Arsenal Pulp Press, 1993], Chap. 8). During the early 1970s, Keith Spicer, the first commissioner of official languages, defended the concept in each of his annual reports and attacked the government for foot dragging. See Commissioner of Official Languages, *First Annual Report, 1970–71* (Ottawa: Information Canada, 1971), 91; idem., *Second Annual Report, 1971–72*, 23–4; idem., *Third Annual Report, 1972–73*, 30; idem., *Fourth Annual Report, 1973–74*, 17; idem., *Fifth Annual Report, 1975*, 15–16. Many years later, Spicer acknowledged that the statutory basis for language of work, in the Official Languages Act, was "the Act's absolutely vague section 2 which spoke only of 'equal status, rights and privileges.'" Following Stephen Lewis's advice, he decided to "bluff" the idea of language of work into the provision. See Keith Spicer, "How the Linguistic World Looked in 1970," *Languages and Society*, Summer 1989, 12. In his last report he passed over French-language units in silence (Commissioner of Official Languages, *Sixth Annual Report, 1976* [Ottawa: Supply and Services, 1977]).
29. The provision, which was subject to certain conditions, was contained in Parliamentary Resolution on Official Languages in the Public Service passed in June 1973 (Marie-Ève Hudon, "Official Languages in the Public Service," Library of Parliament, 6 Mar. 2009, 1).
30. Gaspard, "Canada's Official Languages Policy," 200.
31. Commissioner of Official Languages, *Annual Report, 1995* (Ottawa: Supply and Services, 1996), Tables III.9 and III.11.

32. B&B Commission, *Book III: The Work World*, Table 49.
33. Commissioner of Official Languages, *Annual Report, 1995*, Table III.3.
34. Commissioner of Official Languages, *Annual Report, 1993* (Ottawa: Supply and Services Canada, 1994), Table III.7. Different measures give very different estimates for Francophone participation in senior levels in the 1960s. On the basis of income ($10,000 or more) the figure was 11 per cent in 1965, whereas the proportion in "management" positions in the same year was 19.9 per cent. See B&B Commission, *Book III: The Work World*, Fig. 9 and Table 50. Presumably the 1960s measure of "management" is not equivalent to that of the 1980s and 1990s.
35. See Sarra-Bournet's analysis of a sample of senior civil servants. His data even suggest that Francophones are over-represented, although this over-representation is restricted to Francophones from outside Quebec. See Michel Sarra-Bournet, "'French Power, Québec Power': La place des francophones québécois à Ottawa," in *Bilan québécois du fédéralisme canadien*, ed. François Rocher (Montreal: VLB, 1992), 220.
36. Commissioner of Official Languages, *Annual Report, 1990* (Ottawa: Supply and Services, 1991), x.
37. Ibid.
38. See the discussion in Sarra-Bournet, "French Power, Québec Power," 216–17.
39. Task Force on Bilingualism, *Module 22: Balanced Participation (Integrated Report), Ottawa*, 1973, 267 (as quoted in Gaspard, "Canada's Official Languages Policy," 196).
40. As quoted in Linda Cardinal, Heleina Gaspard, and Rémi Léger, "The Politics of Language Roadmaps in Canada: Understanding the Conservative Government's Approach to Official Languages," *Canadian Journal of Political Science* 48, no. 3, (Sept. 2015): 2. Harper's general views on language policy and his coming to terms with official bilingualism in the federal government are discussed in Graham Fraser, *Sorry I Don't Speak French: Confronting the Canadian Crisis That Won't Go Away* (Toronto: McClelland & Steweart, 2006), 274–80.
41. B&B Commission, *Book I: The Official Languages*, 149.
42. Canada, Official Languages Act, 1985, c. 31 (4th Supp.), 16(1).
43. Designed to amend the Supreme Court Act, Bill C-232 would have required that appointees to the Court understand French and English without the assistance of an interpreter. In 2017, the Justin Trudeau Liberals voted against a similar bill, Bill C-203, this time contending that the measure would require a constitutional amendment. Seventeen Liberal MPs did support the bill, which was proposed by an NDP MP, as was C-232.
44. Privy Council Office, "The Next Level: Normalizing a Culture of Inclusive Linguistic Duality in the Federal Public Service Workplace," 8.
45. Canada, Official Languages Act, 1985, c. 31 (4th Supp.), "Preamble."
46. Ibid., "Part V: Language of Work." The regions designated on the 1977 list include the National Capital Region, certain parts of Northern and Eastern Ontario, the Montreal region, some parts of the Eastern Townships, Western Quebec and of the Gaspé area, as well as New Brunswick (Commissioner of Official Languages, "Understanding Your Language Rights," 1 Sept. 2016).
47. Treasury Board Secretariat, *Attitudes Towards the Use of Both Official Languages within the Public Service of Canada, Ottawa, September 2002*, as cited in Office of the Commissioner of Official Languages, *Walking the Talk: Language of Work in the Federal Public Service of Canada*, Ottawa, 2004, 5.
48. Commissioner of Official Languages, *Walking the Talk*, 1. The Official Languages Commissioner's study was confirmed by retired senior civil servant Jim Mitchell who, in his own report, was highly critical of language training programs, contending that they "are not producing people who are truly functionally bilingual or have a continuing personal engagement with their second official language" (Paco Francoli, "Trudeau's Bilingual Dream Still Unfulfilled," *The Hill Times*, 7688 [20 Dec. 2004–9 Jan. 2005], 17.)
49. Privy Council Office, "The Next Level," 16.
50. Ibid.
51. Kathryn May, "Bilingualism is Stagnating in Federal Public Service, Says Report," *iPolitics*, 30 July 2017. May accessed the

review's preliminary findings and found that the use of French has actually declined in some parts of the federal public service.

52. Richard J. Joy, *Languages in Conflict* (Toronto: McClelland & Stewart, 1972), 91.
53. Richard J. Joy, *Canada's Official Languages: The Progress of Bilingualism* (Toronto: University of Toronto Press, 1992), 71.
54. Ibid., 93.
55. Joy, *Languages in Conflict*, 77.
56. According to the 1881 census, only 10 per cent of its population was of French descent. Ibid., 78.
57. Joy, *Canada's Official Languages*, 106.
58. Ibid., 107.
59. Ibid., 69.
60. Calculated from *Census of Canada, 1971*, vol. I, part 3 (cat. no. 92-726).
61. In fact, this bleak prognosis had already been clearly established in 1967 by Richard J. Joy in his *Languages in Conflict*. Originally published by the author himself, the book was published in 1972 by McClelland & Stewart.
62. *Census of Canada, 1971*, vol. I, part 3, Tables 2 and 26.
63. In 1927, the measure was pre-empted by a new policy allowing bilingual schools but remained a provincial statute until 1945.
64. See Donald J. Savoie, *The Politics of Language* (Kingston: Institute of Intergovernmental Relations, Queen's University, 1991), 7.
65. Marcel Martel, "Les relations entre le Québec et les francophones de l'Ontario: de la survivance aux *Dead Ducks*, 1937-1969," Ph.D. dissertation, History Department, York University, 1994, 125–8.
66. Ibid., 105, and Chap. 4.
67. "If, therefore, French-speaking Quebecers should decide to dissociate themselves from the fate of the French minorities, and particularly if they should adopt this attitude because they felt English-speaking Canada was not giving the minorities a chance to live, separatist tendencies might then be that much more encouraged." See B&B Commission, *Preliminary Report*, 119.
68. B&B Commission, *Book I: The Official Languages*, 86.
69. Ibid., 105–17.
70. Daniel Bourgeois contends that Trudeau was personally in favour of the proposal, recognizing that full linguistic equality could not be extended in all parts of the country. Daniel Bourgeois, *Canadian Bilingual Districts: From Cornerstone to Tombstone* (Montreal: McGill-Queen's Press, 2006), 56–7; and Daniel Bourgeois, "La prestation des services bilingues au Canada," in *Légifier en matière linguistique*, ed. Marcel Martel and Martin Pâquet (Quebec: Presses de l'Université Laval, 2008), 288, n. 32. In particular, he cites a passage in Trudeau, *Federalism and the French Canadians* (49). However, the passage in question speaks of committing entire provinces to language equality, on the basis of minority language presence, rather than particular regions within them. Nonetheless, Bourgeois demonstrates that Trudeau did defend the bilingual districts proposal at the February 1969 constitutional conference (Bourgeois, *Canadian Bilingual Districts*, 61).
71. Daniel Bourgeois, *Canadian Bilingual Districts*, 52 and 60.
72. Canada, *Official Languages Act*, 1969, c. 54, s. 1., 15(1) and 13(2)(b).
73. Canada, Recommendations of the Bilingual Districts *Advisory Board*, Mar. 1971 (Information Canada: 1971).
74. Report of Royal Commission, *Book I: The Official Languages*, 105–12. Also, see Bourgeois, *Canadian Bilingual Districts*, 42 and 85.
75. There were additional justifications, more of an administrative order, for the recommendation (see Bourgeois, *Canadian Bilingual Districts*, 85). There was no formal vote on the matter: the chair, Roger Duhamel, discerned a "consensus" and his conclusion was allowed to stand. Although the committee did not hold a regional session in Quebec, they were aware that the recommendation would provoke "separatists" but thought that it would be generally accepted (ibid., 85–6). In general, see Bourgeois's detailed account of the Board's deliberations in ibid., Chap. Three.
76. Ibid., 99.
77. Ibid., 98.
78. In an initial meeting, Quebec civil servants firmly opposed the creation of any bilingual districts in Quebec and claimed that this was the position of the government's elected leaders. Later, the cultural affairs minister wrote that his government could

not declare a position before the upcoming Victoria Charter. The Board's report was already set before the Victoria Conference took place. (Ibid., 80–2.)

79. Bourgeois, *Canadian Bilingual Districts*, 115.
80. See Kenneth D. McRae, "Bilingual Language Districts in Finland and Canada: Adventures in the Transplanting of an Institution" *Canadian Public Policy* 4, no. 3 (Summer 1978): 342, and Bourgeois, *Canadian Bilingual Districts*, Chap. 4.
81. Bourgeois, *Canadian Bilingual Districts*, 122.
82. British Columbia no longer qualified for a bilingual district given the 1971 census results. Canada, *Report of the Bilingual Districts Advisory Board*, October 1975 (Information Canada: 1975), 164.
83. Bourgeois, *Canadian Bilingual Districts*, 122.
84. The Board chair, Paul Fox, abstained (ibid., 142). In the end, eight of the ten members signed the report. Four, including the two who did not sign the report, submitted "minority statements." In these statements, three dissented from the Montreal recommendation.
85. The figure appears in *Bilingual Districts Advisory Board, 1975*, 105 no. 37. The B&B Commission had proposed both Îsle-de-Montréal and Îsle-Jésus as bilingual districts (B&B Commission, *Book I: The Official Languages*, 108).
86. Ibid., 73.
87. Ibid., 109.
88. Ibid., 35.
89. Ibid., 77.
90. Canada, House of Commons, *Debates*, 21 Nov. 1975, p. 9327–9, as cited in McRae, "Bilingual Language Districts," 348, and Bourgeois, *Canadian Bilingual Districts*, 160.
91. Conceivably, as Daniel Bourgeois argues in his exhaustive study of the whole question of bilingual districts, the federal cabinet might have been prepared to adopt a modified proposal in May of 1976 had it not been for a Treasury Board manoeuvre to substitute for bilingual districts its own existing scheme of bilingual administrative regions (ibid., 216–17). (Elsewhere, Bourgeois argues that the federal bureaucracy "sabotaged" the project [Bourgeois, "La commission BB et la bureaucratie fédérale," 13–51].) But even if the government had put the districts in place they would not have furthered national unity in the ways that their supporters had hoped. Instead, by the mid-1970s, given the growth of nationalist sentiment and opposition to bilingualism in Quebec, they would have had the opposite effect.
92. Bourgeois, *Canadian Bilingual Districts*, 215; and McRae, "Bilingual Language Districts in Finland and Canada," 348.
93. Bourgeois, *Canadian Bilingual Districts*, 196.
94. Canada, Official Languages Act, 1985, c. 31 (4th Supp.), Part IV. The pertinent section of the Charter of Rights and Freedoms is section 20.
95. Kenneth McRae, "Official Bilingualism: from the 1960s to the 1990s," in *Language in Canada*, ed. John Edwards (Cambridge: Cambridge University Press, 1998), 68. To further quote McRae, "this dense network of regulations savours more of bureaucratic complexity than of basic principles to appeal to the general public" (ibid., 69). The regulations appear in Treasury Board Secretariat, "Official Languages (Communications with and Services to the Public) Regulations," *Canada Gazette*, Part I, 23 Mar. 1991. The regulations employ a variety of criteria for "significant demand," including but not limited to, whether the minority-language populations constitute 5000 or 5 per cent of an area's population.
96. *Site for Language Management in Canada [SLMC]*, University of Ottawa. Nonetheless, in his 2015–16 annual report, the Official Languages Commissioner contended that the 5 per cent rule is too restrictive and that attention should be given to the vitality of an official language community (Commissioner of Official Languages, *Annual Report, 2015–16*).
97. Leslie A. Pal, *Interests of State: The Politics of Language, Multiculturalism and Feminism in Canada* (Montreal and Kingston: McGill-Queen's University Press, 1993), 102–3.
98. Matthew Hayday, *Bilingual Today, United Tomorrow: Official Languages in Education and Canadian Federalism* (Montreal and Kingston: McGill-Queen's University Press, 2005), 64–5.

99. *The Canadian Constitutional Charter, 1971*, Part II: Language Rights. See summaries in Simeon, *Federal–Provincial Diplomacy*, 118, and Smiley, *Canada in Question*, 76. Serge Joyal, a senator closely allied with Pierre Trudeau, contends with considerable exaggeration that through this text "the provinces of Ontario, Manitoba, Nova Scotia, New Brunswick, Prince Edward Island, and Newfoundland agreed to become officially bilingual" (Serge Joyal, "Foreword" in Michael D. Behiels, *Canada's Francophone Minority Communities: Constitutional Renewal and the Winning of School Governance* (Montreal and Kingston: McGill-Queen's University Press, 2004), x.
100. Pal, *Interests of State*, 134.
101. Behiels, *Canada's Francophone Minority Communities*, 32 and 70.
102. B&B Commission, *Book I: The Official Languages*, 97.
103. Ibid., 97–9.
104. Office of the Commissioner of Official Languages for New Brunswick, "History of Official Languages in New Brunswick." Peter Russell notes that the amendment serves to make New Brunswick an officially bicultural, as well as bilingual, province. (Peter Russell, *Constitutional Odyssey: Can Canadians Become a Sovereign People?* 3rd edn. [Toronto: University of Toronto Press, 2004], 249.)
105. Ibid.
106. Deborah Coyne, "Back-Door Constitutional Deal Rips Fabric of the Nation," *Toronto Star*, 6 Jan. 1993, A15. Coyne was also concerned that the amendment would assign the New Brunswick legislature a role in promoting the two communities, in a formulation similar to the distinct-society clause of the Meech Lake Accord which she, and Trudeau, had so vigorously opposed.
107. For his part, Justin Trudeau called for the dismantling of New Brunswick's separate school systems in 2007 but recanted his statement given a backlash among the province's Francophones (Riddell, "Explaining the Impact of Legal Mobilization and Judicial Decisions," 205).
108. These fears were given a certain authority by the publication of demographic projections. Most notably, in 1969 the province's leading demographer, Jacques Henripin, predicted that if current trends were to continue, by the year 2001 Francophones might constitute no more than 53 per cent of Montreal's population. To be precise, Henripin and two colleagues predicted that Francophones would be between 52.7 per cent and 60.0 per cent of Montreal's population and between 71.6 per cent and 79.2 per cent of Quebec's. See Hubert Charbonneau, Jacques Henripin, and Jacques Legaré, "L'avenir démographique des francophones au Québec et à Montréal en l'absence de politiques adéquates," *Revue de géographie de Montréal* 24 (1974): 199–202. Henripin later acknowledged that the estimate was erroneous owing to incomplete data. Indeed, the Francophone proportion increased rather than decreased, because of an unexpectedly large out-migration of Anglophones. See Jacques Henripin, "Population Trends and Policies in Quebec," in *Quebec: State and Society*, 2nd edn, ed. Alain Gagnon (Scarborough, Ont.: Nelson, 1993), 315.
109. These changes in French Quebec are detailed in McRoberts, *Quebec: Social Change and Political Crisis*, Chaps. 4 and 5.
110. *Rapport de la commission d'enquête sur la situation de la langue française et sur les droits linguistiques au Québec*, vol. 2, *Les droits linguistiques* (Quebec City, Dec. 1972), 67–8 (my translation).
111. Rapport de la commission d'enquête, vol. 1, *La langue de travail*.
112. Savoie, *The Politics of Language*, 16.
113. "Je n'en ai pas contre l'esprit de la loi mais contre la lettre, en certains endroits. . . . Une de mes critiques les plus fortes n'est même pas source d'injustice, c'est ce que j'appelle de la stupidité politique. . . . Si on avait dit la principale langue ou la langue de travail, la langue nationale. . . . Cela aurait grandement facilité les choses aux libéraux du reste du pays, à qui nous disons qu'il y a deux langues officielles, le français et l'anglais." "I have nothing against the spirit of the law but against the letter, in certain places. . . . One of my strongest criticisms is not even in terms of injustice but what I call political stupidity. . . . If they had said principal language or language of work, national language . . . that would have greatly helped things for Liberals in the rest of the

country, to whom we are saying that there are two languages, French and English." "Le discours de M. Trudeau: il faut qu'on se parle dans le blanc des yeux," *La Presse*, 8 Mar. 1976. (Apparently, this passage of the speech was originally given in English.) Trudeau did say that he would have accepted a designation of French as "the main language," "the language of work," or even "the national language." He even claimed to support "the spirit" of Bill 22. Also see Trudeau, *Memoirs*, 234, where he laments the fact that Bill 22 came at a time when "we had managed at Victoria to get the provinces to accept a measure of official bilingualism even at the provincial level."

114. Trudeau, "The Values of a Just Society," 366.
115. Trudeau, *The Essential Trudeau*, 138.
116. Trudeau claimed in 1998 that he had never considered disallowing Bill 22 (Pierre Elliott Trudeau, *The Essential Trudeau*, ed. Ron Graham [Toronto: McClelland & Stewart, 1998], 137). Garth Stevenson notes that nearly one-tenth of Quebec's residents had signed a petition against Bill 22. He suggests that, while Trudeau may have rejected the disallowance power as an anachronism, concern about the negative reaction of the province's Francophone majority would have led him to the same conclusion (Garth Stevenson, *Community Besieged: The Anglophone Minority and the Politics of Quebec* [Montreal and Kingston: McGill-Queen's University Press, 1999], 255). The English-language school boards' opposition to Bill 22 is described in Hayday, *Bilingual Today, United Tomorrow*, 91.
117. B&B Commission, *Book III: The Work World*, 559.
118. Ibid., 565. Scott noted that for Ontario and New Brunswick the Commission had proposed that task forces be created to determine what measures were necessary to put French on the same basis as English as a language of work. However, in the case of Quebec, the Commission set out rigid guidelines for such a task force: "So the principles differ depending on the provincial boundaries. This is a virtual acceptance of the territorial principle. My idea of 'equal partnership' is that it operates in similar fashion across Canada, wherever the minority is numerous enough to be viable as a group" (ibid).
119. Commissioner of Official Languages, *First Annual Report, 1970–71*, 4.
120. Gilles Lalande, "Back to the B and B," *Language and Society*, no. 19 (Apr. 1987): 24. Lalande did not himself refer to the "Trudeau orthodoxy."
121. Léon Dion, "The Impact of Demolinguistic Trends," 66. Between 1970 and 1978 the percentage was 58 per cent. See Federation of Francophones outside Quebec, *À la recherche du milliard* (Ottawa: 1981), as cited in Wilfrid B. Denis, "The Politics of Language," in *Race and Ethnic Relations in Canada*, ed. Peter S. Li (Toronto: Oxford University Press, 1990), 170. In the face of complaints from outside Quebec, the situation was altered somewhat. In 1989, of a total $225.7 million granted to the provinces and territories, 28 per cent went to the education of Quebec Anglophones, 35.8 per cent for Francophones outside Quebec, and 29.6 per cent to Anglophones outside Quebec. See Secretary of State, *Annual Report to Parliament, 1989–90*, 45, Fig. 4. See also the discussion in Denis, "The Politics of Language," 171. In 2014–15, Quebec's proportion of Canadian Heritage spending on official languages support had fallen to 23 per cent (calculated from Commission of Official Languages, *Annual Report, 2014–15*, Appendix 3).
122. Pal, *Interests of State*, Table 7.5.
123. Bernard Descôteaux, "Ottawa négociera avec le Québec sur la loi des langues," *Le Devoir*, 8 June 1988, and Bernard Descôteaux, "Ottawa et Québec s'entendent sur les langues officielles," *Le Devoir*, 18 Aug. 1988.
124. Initial discussions of Ontario's approach to the status of French took place in an advisory committee to Premier John Robarts (see Don Stevenson, "John Robarts' Advisory Committee on Confederation and Its Impact on Ontario's Language Policy," in Martel and Pâquet, *Légiférer en matière linguistique*, 183–9). The former co-ordinator of French-language services for the Ontario government, Don Stevenson, contends that with Bill 8 Ontario has for all intents and purposes become officially bilingual. See Don Stevenson, "What Is an Official Language?" unpublished

paper. To be sure, the formal declaration that English and French are official languages, as in New Brunswick, could be politically controversial, making this last step a very substantial one.

125. Ontario, *French Language Services Act*, 2nd session, 33rd Parliament, Bill 8 (1986).
126. Behiels, *Canada's Francophone Minority Communities*, 117. See also Chantal Hébert et Jean Lapierre, *Confessions post-référendaires* (Montreal: Les Éditions l'Homme, 2014), 212. Marcel Martel documents opposition to official bilingualism in letters written to Premier John Robarts in the 1960s (Marcel Martel, "Monsieur le premier ministre, je vous écris: les Ontariens et le bilinguisme, 1963-1971," unpublished paper).
127. Bill 2 does not require that records of legislative debates be kept in both languages; it left this matter for the legislative assembly to resolve. Also, the right to use French in courts is restricted to criminal cases.
128. The 1988 court decision followed upon (but was unrelated to) a dispute over the right to use French in the Alberta legislature. A Francophone legislator had demanded the right to do so, invoking the Northwest Territories Act, but his request was denied by the Speaker. Yet in the Saskatchewan legislature the occasional use of French (by non-Francophones) had apparently not been challenged. The Alberta dispute is recounted in Timothy J. Christian, "L'affaire Piquette," in *Language and the State*, ed. David Schneiderman (Cowansville, Que.: Yvon Blais, 1991), 107–21.
129. While recognizing duality and linguistic rights as elements of Canadian constitutionalism, the Court majority deferred to the principle of federalism. (Marie Vastel, "L'Alberta restera unilingue anglophone," *Le Devoir*, 21 Nov. 2015.)
130. Pierre Foucher, "Les droits linguistiques au Canada," in *Francophonie minoritaires au Canada: l'état des lieux*, ed. Joseph Yvon Thériault (Moncton: Éditions d'Acadie, 1999), 310.
131. Hayday, *Bilingual Today, United Tomorrow*, 40. The commissioners also agreed with parental choice of the language of instruction but had proposed that measures be adopted to ensure that minority-language education not be unduly affected by the presence of majority-language children (Hayday, *Bilingual Today, United Tomorrow*, 40, and B&B Commission, *Book II: Education*, 300 [recommendation 10]).
132. Hayday, *Bilingual Today*, 48–55.
133. Ibid., 56.
134. As quoted in ibid., 59. The importance of Trudeau's personal views to shaping federal policy is confirmed by ibid., 44.
135. Ibid., 59.
136. Ibid., 51 and 68.
137. Ibid., 90.
138. Ibid., 45 and 67.
139. Ibid., Table A1.
140. Section 23 declares that to exercise this right the parent must be a Canadian citizen whose mother tongue or language of instruction in Canada was English or French: "Citizens of Canada (a) whose first language learned and still understood is that of the English or French linguistic minority population of the province in which they reside, or (b) who have received their primary school instruction in Canada in English or French and reside in a province where the language in which they received that instruction is the language of the English or French linguistic minority population of the province have the right to have their children receive primary and secondary school instruction in that language in that province." (23 [1].) Parents also have this right if a child has already received education in that language. (23[2].) This right "(a) applies wherever in the province the number of children of citizens who have such a right is sufficient to warrant the provision to them out of public funds of minority-language instruction; and (b) includes, where the number of those children so warrants, the right to have them receive that instruction in minority-language educational facilities provided out of public funds." (23 [3a,b].)
141. Behiels, *Canada's Francophone Minority Communities*, 68–75. The organization representing the Francophone minorities, the Fédération des communautés francophones et acadienne du Canada, had struggled to no avail to secure the commitment of Trudeau and his government to "une série de *droits collectifs* qui permettront aux minorités officielles d'atteindre sur le plan social et culturel un statut égal à celui de la majorité," (FFHQ, *Pour ne plus être . . . sans pays*, as quoted by Behiels,

Canada's Francophone Minority Communities, 64 [Behiel's emphasis]). See also Troy Riddell, "Explaining the Impact of Legal Mobilization and Judicial Decisions: Official Minority Language Education Rights Outside Quebec," in *Contested Constitutionalism: Reflections on the Canadian Charter of Rights and Freedoms*, ed. James B. Kelly and Christopher P. Manfredi (Vancouver: UBC Press, 2009), 189.

142. Troy Q. Riddell, "Official Minority-Language Education Policy outside Quebec: The Impact of Section 23 of the Charter and Judicial Decisions," *Canadian Public Administration* 46, no. 1 (Spring): 37.
143. Foucher, "Les droits linguistiques," 316, and Riddell, "Official minority-language education policy outside Quebec," 34. See also Marcel Martel and Martin Pâquet, *Langue et politique au Canada et au Québec: une synthèse historique* (Montreal: Éditions du Boréal, 2010), 259–60.
144. Riddell, "Official Minority-Language Education Policy outside Quebec," 40. Riddell demonstrates that this development reflects both jurisprudence and the Francophone leadership's lobbying efforts, supported by federal funding (Riddell, "Explaining the Impact of Legal Mobilization and Judicial Decisions").
145. The one instance of a Francophone university institution is l'Université de Hearst, whose student population is quite small.
146. Commissariat aux services en français, Rapport d'enquête – *L'état de l'éducation: pas d'avenir sans accès postsecondaire en langue française dans le Centre-Sud-Ouest de l'Ontario*, 27 June 2012, ISBN 978-1-4435-9511-7.
147. Daniel Leblanc, "Feu vert à une université franco-ontarienne," *Le Droit*, 28 Aug. 2017.
148. Canada, Official Languages Act, 1988, Preamble and Part VII: Advancement of English and French.
149. Marie-Ève Hudon, "Official Languages in Canada: Federal Policy," Library of Parliament, 18 January 2016," 10.
150. Canada, Official Languages Act, 1988, Part VII. Kenneth McRae contends that this section of the act demonstrates how the federal government came to see in more expansive terms its language policy mandate (McRae, "Official Bilingualism," 79). By the same token, through section 82 the Act's "main operative sections" override all other laws or regulations than the Canadian Human Rights Act (ibid., 77).
151. Hudon, "Official Languages in Canada," 10.
152. Ibid., 16.
153. Ontario Court of Appeal, Lalonde v. Ontario Court of Appeal, "Commission de restructuration des services de santé," 7 December 2001 (Revised 8 Mar. 2002), p. 57, para 181. In discerning fundamental constitutional principles on which to base its decision, the Court was inspired by the approach that the Canadian Supreme Court had adopted in its judgement about Quebec's right to secession, to be discussed in Chapter 8.
154. See Hudon, "Official Languages in Canada," 2–3; and Graham Fraser, "Canadian Language Rights: Liberties, Claims and the National Conversation," in *Contested Constitutionalism: Reflections on the Canadian Charter of Rights and Freedoms*, ed. James B. Kelly and Christopher P. Manfredi (Vancouver: UBC Press, 2009), 183. While the Language Rights Support Program was less well funded, the Supreme Court has tended to absolve litigants of court costs (Emmanuelle Richez, "Francophone Minority Communities: The Last Constitutional Standard-Bearers of Trudeau's Language Regime," *International Journal of Canadian Studies*, no. 45–6, [2012]: para 14).
155. Cardinal, Gaspard, and Léger, "The Politics of Language Roadmaps," 12.
156. See the discussion in Rodrigue Landry, "Loi sur les langues officielles et démographie: comment les droits linguistiques peuvent-ils influencer la vitalité d'une minorité?" Jedwab and Landry, *Life after Forty*, 53–72.
157. Commissioner of Official Languages, *Annual Report, 2015–2016*, "Changes to immigration programs worry French-speaking communities."
158. See the discussion in Martel and Pâquet, *Langue et politique*, 263–6.
159. René Houle and Jean-Pierre Corbeil, *Language Projections for Canada, 2011 to 2036*, Catalogue no. 89-657-X2017001 (Ottawa: Statistics Canada, 2017), Tables 2.3 and 3.3. Under a "low immigration" scenario, one of three, the projections are slightly higher: 1.8 per cent and 2.8 per cent.

160. B&B Commission, *General Introduction*, xxviii.
161. B&B Commission, *Book I: The Official Languages*, 12.
162. Ibid.
163. Ibid.
164. Ibid., 14.
165. B&B Commission, *Book II: Education*, 302.
166. "Our concern . . . has not been to provide the opportunity to become highly proficient in all skills of the second official language. Rather, we wanted to ensure that all children should have an introduction to the language which would make it possible for them to further develop or re-acquire the skills after leaving school. The school is the place where the capacity for bilingualism can be established." (Ibid., 266.)
167. The Commission did recommend federal support for training centres to prepare second-language teachers. (Ibid., recommendations 41 and 42.)
168. Radawanski, *Trudeau*, 287.
169. Graham Fraser correctly argues that Trudeau didn't have a "bilingual dream" in which all Canadians would be bilingual. His concern was simply with whether Canadians could receive government services in their own language. (Fraser, *Sorry I Don't Speak French*, 90.) That being said, the development of bilingualism among young Anglophones did mesh well with his concern to build a strong national identity.
170. *Debates of the Senate*, 2nd session, 33rd Parliament, vol. 132, 30 Mar. 1988, 2993.
171. This English-Canadian attitude was seen in representations made to the B&B Commission during its cross-country hearings. In its *Preliminary Report* the Commission noted that English Canadians in such cities as London, Ontario, tended to concentrate on strategies for increased personal bilingualism, whereas Francophones in such places as Sherbrooke and Trois-Rivières expressed their discontent with the subordinate positions of the French language and of Francophones in the economy and society of Quebec, making few references to the Francophone minorities. See B&B Commission, *Preliminary Report*, 39.
172. Joy, *Canada's Official Languages*, 121.
173. B&B Commission, *Book I: The Official Languages*, 38.
174. Hayday, *Bilingual Today, United Tomorrow*, 45.
175. Ibid.
176. The ineffectiveness of the federal language training programs, and consequent dissatisfaction with them, is discussed in William F. Mackey, "Language Policies in Canada," in *Canadian Language Policies in Comparative Perspective*, ed. Michael A. Morris (Montreal and Kingston: McGill-Queen's University Press, 2010), 48. See also Fraser, *Sorry I Don't Speak French*, Chap. 5.
177. As quoted in Hayday, *Bilingual Today, United Tomorrow*, 107.
178. "In October of last year, the government announced in the Speech from the Throne its intention to shift the emphasis in its programs to achieve a better balance 'between money spent to introduce bilingualism in the public service and the money spent to enable more Canadians, particularly young people, to learn to communicate in both official languages.'" (Canada, *A National Understanding: The Official Languages of Canada* [Ottawa: Supply and Services Canada, 1977], 61.)
179. Ibid., Table A2
180. Matthew Hayday, "Finessing Federalism: The Development of Institutional and Popular Support for Official Languages," in *Life after Forty*, ed. Jedwab and Landry, 142.
181. Pal, *Interests of State*, 166–71. See also Hayday, *Bilingual Today, United Tomorrow*, 110–13.
182. Commissioner of Official Languages, *Annual Report, 1990*, Table D.I and p. 272.
183. Harrison and Marmen, *Languages in Canada*, Table 4.6.
184. Ibid., Table 4.4; and Commissioner of Official Languages, *Annual Report, 1992*, 16. The level of personal bilingualism also went up among Francophones during this period, reflecting the importance of English in the work world. Among Quebec Francophones, it went from 28.7 per cent in 1981 to 31.5 per cent in 1991; outside Quebec it went from 79.0 per cent to 81.1 per cent (Harrison and Marmen, *Languages in Canada*, Table 4.4). By 2011, 38 per cent of Quebec Francophones were bilingual, as were 87 per cent of Francophones outside Quebec. (Jean-François Lepage and Jean-Pierre Corbeil, "The Evolution of English–French Bilingualism

in Canada from 1961 to 2011," Statistics Canada, #75-006-X.)

185. Hayday, "Finessing Federalism," 145.

186. To be sure, there were qualifications to this success. The overall rise in personal bilingualism is based on simple self-declaration. One can always question the meaningfulness of respondents' claims to census takers that they have a working knowledge of another language.

187. Lepage and Corbeil, "The Evolution of English–French Bilingualism in Canada," and Statistics Canada, "English–French Bilingualism Reaches New Heights," *Census in Brief*, 31 Aug. 2017.

188. Statistics Canada, "English–French Bilingualism Reaches New Heights."

189. Data and analysis in this paragraph are taken from Lepage and Corbeil, "Evolution of English–French Bilingualism" and from Statistics Canada, "English–French Bilingualism Reaches New Heights." See also Matthew Hayday, *So They Want Us to Learn French: Promoting and Opposing Bilingualism in English-Speaking Canada* (Vancouver: UBC Press, 2015), 249–51.

190. Arthur Leblanc, *Bilingual Education: A Challenge for Canadian Universities in the '90s* (Winnipeg: Continuing Education Division, University of Manitoba, 1986), 52, as cited in Eric Waddell, "Implications of French Immersion," 427. See the discussion of the success of French immersion in *Language and Society*, no. 12 (1984): 44–60. Whereas in two articles education specialists are largely positive, in the third article Université de Montréal linguist and education professor Gilles Bibeau contends that the results of 20 years' experience suggest that "pure" immersion is "dépassé," since "it has not enabled children to become as bilingual as was hoped." He recommends simpler approaches that could be integrated with the education of most children. (Gilles Bibeau, "No Easy Road to Bilingualism," *Language and Society*, no. 12 [1984]: 47.) A critical evaluation is also offered by Marie-Claude Mosimann-Barbier, *Immersion et bilinguisme en Ontario* (Rouen: Université de Rouen, 1992). A positive assessment appears in Hayday, *So They Want Us to Learn French*.

191. For this reason, the University of Ottawa and the Glendon Campus of York University have developed special programs to ease the transition of French-immersion students to university study in French.

192. In 2013–14, there were 392,430 children in French-immersion programs (including Quebec) but only 155,590 in French minority-language schools. Commissioner of Official Languages, *Annual Report, 2014–15*, Appendix 6, Tables 11 and 13.

193. Maintained by the department of Canadian Heritage, the program is entitled "Expériences-Canada-Exchanges."

194. The exact figure for bilingualism among Anglophones is 9.2 per cent. Statistics Canada, "English–French Bilingualism Reaches New Heights."

195. Commissioner of Official Languages, *Annual Report, 2015–16*, "Letter to my Successor."

196. Canadian Charter of Rights and Freedoms, 20(1)a and Official Languages Act, 1985, 22(b).

197. Bourgeois, "La commission BB et la bureaucratie fédérale," 36.

198. See the discussion in Pierre Foucher, "Autonomie des communautés francophones minoritaires du Canada: le point de vue du droit," *Minorités linguistiques et société* no. 1 (2012): 90–114.

199. Privy Council Office, "The Next Level," 9.

200. As quoted in Peter Stursberg, *Lester Pearson and the Dream of Unity* (Toronto: Doubleday, 1978), 146. As Kenneth McRae commented, "in Quebec [federal language policies] ranged a federal authority proactive in favour of Anglophones against Quebec governments even more strongly proactive in defending what they saw as vital interests of their linguistically besieged Francophone majority. (McRae, " Official Bilingualism," 81.) 202.

201. Affirmative answers were apparently somewhat more frequent among Francophones (as opposed to Anglophones) while remaining a small minority. See "What Quebec Really Wants: English Consider Us Inferior, Quebec Feels," *Toronto Star*, 17 May 1977.

Chapter 5

Multiculturalism

Reining in Duality

In October 1971, Pierre Trudeau announced another element of Canada's new national identity: multiculturalism. Many Canadians associate multiculturalism as closely with Trudeau as they do bilingualism, if not more so. After all, he was the first head of government anywhere to adopt a policy of multiculturalism. And yet, before the day of the proclamation, he had never championed multiculturalism the way he had official bilingualism. Still, it assumed a central role in the national unity strategy he sought to implement.

Multiculturalism had not held a significant place in the many articles and speeches through which, before becoming prime minister, Trudeau had elaborated his political thought. Nor was it evoked in the various constitutional proposals he prepared, whether the 1967 presentation to the Canadian Bar Association, the 1968 constitutional conference, or, as we shall see, the failed Victoria Charter of 1971. Recognition of two official languages was front and centre in these proposals, but multiculturalism played no role. In his *Memoirs*, Trudeau refers with great pride to the Official Languages Act, treating it as his effective creation, yet makes no mention whatsoever of his multiculturalism proclamation.

In fact, multiculturalism did not fit readily within Trudeau's well-established political philosophy. Positing the primacy of the individual, Trudeau had always been suspicious of the political recognition of cultures or any other collective entity. Rights must be attached to individuals, he insisted, not collectivities; the state must be neutral in such matters. As we saw in the last chapter, when it came to recognizing *language* rights, which was a bit of a stretch given his premise of state neutrality, he had always been very careful to define them in terms of individuals and their freedom of choice. As we have seen, he had objected to any suggestion that Canada might be composed of "linguistic communities." Yet a major school of thought contends that language rights can be seen only in collective terms, since languages are the creations and possessions of communities rather than isolated individuals. The recognition of *cultures* raises the same problem. After all, as with languages, so cultures are created and transmitted by communities. It would be even more difficult to define the recognition of cultures in individual terms than it was to recognize languages. How, then, could Trudeau support a multicultural vision of Canada?

Biculturalism and the B&B Commission

Trudeau had clearly understood the danger in recognizing cultures when it came to the argument that Canada is *bicultural* and composed of *two* cultures that should be equally recognized and supported. While very much on side with the B&B Commission's focus on bilingualism, Trudeau always had been highly suspicious of the twin: "biculturalism." He said as much when he met with the commissioners, telling them to focus exclusively on the first part of their mandate.[1] When the Commission's *Preliminary Report* was released in 1965, he did not criticize the document publicly, since he was about to declare his intention to enter federal politics as a Liberal candidate, but he clearly had had a hand in preparing a *Cité libre* article that severely criticized the report.[2] Signed by five members of the Comité pour une politique fonctionnelle, of which Trudeau had been a member, the article recognized that bilingualism could be a valid objective in a modern state, as could equality between Anglophones and Francophones per se, but dismissed biculturalism and the notion of equality between citizens as members of one of two cultures. Indeed, it declared that the idea of equality between cultures

> is quite foreign to our legal thought and our political framework. . . . And what would be the meaning in practice of a Confederation that "develops according to the principle of equality between two *cultures*"? The idea of equality between peoples underlies the concept of national sovereignty, and it would have been interesting to see how the Commission intends to interpret its mandate without being led necessarily to propose the division of Canada into two national states.[3]

Yet, as we have seen, there was in fact a long tradition of thought in French Quebec that did presume that peoples could be equal within the same state. Far from being alien to Canadian thought, biculturalism or equality between peoples was central to most French Canadians' understanding of Canada. The B&B Commission's mandate, developed in close discussion with André Laurendeau, fell squarely within that tradition. It was instructed to "inquire into and report upon the existing state of bilingualism and biculturalism in Canada and to recommend what steps should be taken to develop the Canadian Confederation on the basis of an equal partnership between the two founding races."[4] To be sure, in an apparent recognition that some Canadians would feel excluded by this mandate, the Commission was to "tak[e] into account the contribution made by other ethnic groups to the cultural enrichment of Canada and the measures that should be taken to safeguard that contribution."[5] Nonetheless, the notion of cultural dualism was front and centre. And through the reference to "two founding races" it was presented in a way that placed it squarely within the vision of Canada that Henri Bourassa had articulated at the turn of the century and that had become the basis upon which most of French Quebec's political and intellectual classes understood Canada.

The continuity with the Bourassa tradition was no accident. As we saw, the idea of the Commission had originated with André Laurendeau, who was in many respects Bourassa's spiritual heir. Dualism was fundamental to his own vision of Canada; indeed, it was only on this basis that he would have been prepared to co-chair the Commission.[6] It is no surprise, then, that the interpretation of the Commission's terms of reference, which appears in the opening pages of the first volume of the Commission's report, offers an expansive understanding of "biculturalism." These famous "blue pages" were in fact written by Laurendeau himself. Even though Trudeau apparently professed never to have read the "blue pages," they do serve to confirm his apprehension about biculturalism and where it might lead.[7]

After surveying alternative definitions of culture, the Commission defines it broadly as "a way of being, thinking and feeling." Culture is "a driving force animating a significant group of individuals united by a common tongue, and sharing the same customs, habits, and experiences."[8] Therefore, it could only be Canada as a whole, rather than individual Canadians, that was bicultural: "Culture is to the group rather what personality is to the individual; it is rare for a person to have two personalities or two styles of living at the same time." Although cultures may not be water-tight compartments, neither should Canada's cultural duality be understood as a "*mixture* of the two cultures; each has its own existence."[9] Canada contained "two dominant cultures . . . embodied in distinct societies."[10] The Commission fully recognized the connotations of the term "distinct societies."[11] At the same time, the Commission tried to avoid any suggestion that these might be "closed" societies. Thus, it avoided the concept of "ethnicity," fearing that the term implied biological origin.[12] Similarly, the Commission strongly resisted the application of the term "ethnic" to non-British, non-French groups, even though the term "ethnic groups" was placed in the terms of reference for precisely that purpose. It did, however, recognize that if such individuals are "to participate fully in Canadian life," the two societies will have to welcome them and allow them "to preserve and enrich, if they so desire, the cultural values they prize."[13]

Having defined biculturalism in such broad terms, rooting it in distinct societies, the Commission was similarly bold in its definition of another term in its mandate: "equal partnership between the two founding peoples." It insisted that the equal partnership should apply not only to the two peoples, but to their languages and cultures as well.

It even called for *political* equality between the two peoples, conceiving it as a matter of "self-determination" or "the extent of the control each [society] has over its government or governments."[14] So as to make the point crystal clear, the Commission spelled out the various institutional arrangements this might entail: "a unitary or a federal system; special status for the province in which the minority group is concentrated; or again, for the same part of the country, the status of an associate state; or, finally, the status of an independent state." And it insisted that for the Commission to ignore the demand for autonomy that was so "deeply entrenched in Quebec . . . would very likely mean that Quebec would refuse to listen to us."[15] Similarly it argued that the concentration of Francophones in Quebec meant that "the place of Québécois in the French fact in Canada will in practice have to be recognized much more than it is today."[16] In short, Canadian dualism was one of two "distinct societies," historically rooted in two founding peoples that were organized on the basis of language and culture. And an equal partnership required that the two societies be politically and economically equal.

There was much for Trudeau to reject in such an understanding of biculturalism, and of Canada. It could not have been more diametrically opposed to his own political thought and vision of the country. As we shall see, Trudeau responded formally in Parliament to Book IV of the Commission's *Final Report*, on "The Cultural Contribution of the Other Ethnic Groups." But he did so in a manner designed to eliminate forever any discussion of biculturalism.

White Paper on Indian Policy

Soon after becoming prime minister, Trudeau applied his personal world view to a set of communities who had always seen themselves as a distinct nationality: Indigenous Peoples. Trudeau assumed a leading role in preparing his new government's White Paper on Indian Policy, as Indigenous Peoples were labelled in that era. Indeed, he claimed to have devoted more time to Indian policy, during his first year in office, than to any other issue.[17] The White Paper showed how the logic that had led to such a heated dismissal of biculturalism in 1965 was very much at work in the new Trudeau government.

Presented to Parliament in June of 1969, the White Paper on Indian Policy was clearly framed in terms of Pierre Trudeau's liberal individualism. Indigenous Peoples were to be seen, first and foremost, as citizens of the Canadian political community. As such, each "Indian" should possess all the rights and obligations held by every Canadian citizen—nothing less but nothing more: "To be an Indian must be to be free—free to develop Indian cultures in an environment of legal, social and economic equality with other Canadians."[18] Thus, the objective of government policy must be integration: "the full, free and non-discriminatory participation of the Indian people in Canadian society."[19] Just like any other group of citizens, Indigenous Canadians should not rely on special rights or arrangements. In fact, they have suffered from their historical separateness: "special treatment has made of the Indians a community disadvantaged and apart."[20] Therefore, as

Trudeau declared on another occasion, "we say we won't recognize aboriginal rights. We will recognize treaty rights . . . [but] perhaps the treaties shouldn't go on forever. It's inconceivable I think that in a given society one section of the society [could] have a treaty with the other section of the society. We must all be equal under the laws and we must not sign treaties among ourselves."[21] Finally, the White Paper was informed by Trudeau's conviction that policy should not be based on past injustices: "We can't recognize aboriginal rights because no society can be built on historical 'might-have-beens.'"[22]

On this basis, the White Paper proposed nothing less than the elimination of all arrangements that applied specifically to Indigenous Peoples, including repeal of the Indian Act, abolition of the department of Indian Affairs, elimination of Parliament's constitutional responsibility for Indigenous Peoples, transfer to the provinces of government services, and review of treaties to determine "how they can be equitably ended."[23] Thus, equality for Indigenous Canadians was to take precisely the same form as equality for all other Canadians: "non-discrimination" or equal status and services for people *as individuals*.[24] The reasoning was precisely the same as in his analysis of French Canada. In Trudeau's own words: as in "the case of the French in Canada . . . the way to be strong in Canada is not to be apart but to be equal to the English."[25] In short, Indigneous people "should become Canadians as all other Canadians."[26] In effect, through his deliberations Trudeau had simply developed his own rationale and strategy for what had always been the ultimate aim of federal policy: the assimilation of the Indigenous population into mainstream Canadian society.

While the government contended that the White Paper was a response to extensive consultation, it came as a total surprise to Indigenous leaders. For Harold Cardinal, leader of the Indian Association of Alberta, the paper constituted "a thinly disguised programme of extermination through assimilation."[27] His association issued a rebuttal, *Citizens Plus*, which became known as the "Red Paper." Indigenous organizations in other provinces joined in condemning the White Paper. For that matter, it repudiated directly the 1947 report of anthropologist Harry B. Hawthorn, which had been commissioned by the federal government under Lester Pearson. Documenting at length the deplorable living conditions of Indigenous People, the Hawthorn report had declared forthrightly that "integration or assimilation are not objectives which anyone else can properly hold for the Indian." Instead, "Indians should be regarded as 'citizens plus' . . . [who] possess certain additional rights as charter members of the Canadian community."[28]

Ultimately, Prime Minister Trudeau withdrew the White Paper, given the widespread resistance among Indigenous leaders, angrily declaring, "We'll keep them in the ghetto as long as they want."[29] Subsequently, impressed by the Supreme Court's judgement in the *Calder* case that the Nisga'a people in BC still held title to land, Trudeau did recognize the need to enter into negotiations with Indigenous communities regarding their historical titles. However, the government's clear purpose in the negotiations was to secure Indigenous agreement to the extinguishment of title.[30]

Mobilizing against Biculturalism

Given Trudeau's insistence on the primacy of the individual over any collectivity and the neutrality of the state, it followed logically that he would reject biculturalism. It was just as logical that he would reject any special arrangement for Indigenous people. How, then, could he embrace *multiculturalism*, which would imply the recognition of a multiplicity of cultures? In fact, unlike official bilingualism, multiculturalism came about through the efforts, not of Trudeau, but of others.

In particular, multiculturalism was the project of groups that felt excluded by the notion of "biculturalism" and by the deliberations of the B&B Commission. According to sociologist Raymond Breton,

> The Quebec independence movement and the royal commission heightened the status anxieties of many members of other ethnic groups. It increased their fear of being defined as second-class citizens, of having their culture and contributions to Canadian society devalued, and of being symbolically cheated or degraded while the status of another group was raised and glorified.[31]

Ethnic group leaders made their opposition known from the very moment that the B&B Commission was created; indeed, they were mobilized by the Royal Commission.[32] To be sure, just as the Commission's mandate included "the contribution of the other ethnic groups" so the Commission itself included among its 10 members two representatives of the "ethnic groups." In symmetrical fashion, they were each linked with different "dominant cultures." Paul Wyczynski, a Polish Canadian, was a professor of French literature at the University of Ottawa; J.B. Rudnyckyj, a Ukrainian Canadian, was chair of Slavic studies at the University of Manitoba. But to many, this was simply not enough. Thus, the appointment of the Commission was greeted with a complaint by John Diefenbaker, himself the first prime minister who claimed neither British nor French descent, that "very important ethnic groups in Canada will ask why it is they have no representation."[33] The NDP spokesman, Harold Winch, expressed the hope that the term "biculturalism" would not be construed so narrowly as to preclude consideration of "the various cultures of the other countries which go to make up what we call Canadianism."[34]

More pointed was the Senate speech of Ukrainian Canadian Paul Yuzyk, in March 1964. Apparently the first person to use the term "multiculturalism" in the Canadian Parliament,[35] Yuzyk declared that Canada had never been bicultural in the past, given both the Indigenous population and the ethnic pluralism of Britishers. And he cited the 1961 census figure of 30 per cent for a "third element" to show that Canada certainly was not bicultural then. Insisting on Canada's multicultural character, he proposed that British and French be treated as "senior partners," with full language rights, but that "third element ethnic or cultural groups" should have the status of "co-partners," entailing the right to have their languages and cultures offered as "optional subjects" at all levels of education, whenever numbers warrant.[36] Canadian Jewish leaders had also been quick to convey their unhappiness with the terms of the Commission's mandate, objecting in particular to the phrase "two founding races." For that reason, the Canadian Jewish Congress did not submit a brief to the Commission, while expressing in various other ways its concerns about the Commission and its activities.[37]

The Commission was obviously taken aback by this attack on biculturalism, especially when it started to convene formal meetings in the Prairie provinces, where Ukrainian-Canadian groups, in particular, were well prepared.[38] Indeed, the debate was joined within the Commission itself, as the Ukrainian-Canadian member argued vigorously that languages other than English and French should receive recognition. The first volume of the Commission's report, *The Official Languages*, which limited its recommendations to English and French, contained a lengthy dissenting statement by Rudnyckyj, echoing Yuzyk's demand by proposing that unofficial languages should have the status of "regional" language if they are spoken by more than 10 per cent of the population of an administrative unit. He did not, however, challenge the concept of biculturalism.[39]

The Commission felt obliged to prepare a full volume entitled *The Cultural Contribution of the Other Ethnic Groups*. There it proposed a series of initiatives such as anti-discrimination measures, equal access of all immigrants to citizenship, teaching of non-official languages in public schools, elimination of restrictions on non-official languages in private and public broadcasting, and support for organizations fostering "the arts and letters of cultural groups other than the British and French."[40]

However, despite the claims of some observers,[41] at no point did the Commission propose that the concept of biculturalism be abandoned for multiculturalism.[42] Even without Laurendeau's guiding hand, the Commission still maintained biculturalism as the basic framework for comprehending culture in Canada. While recognizing that some Canadians of non-British, non-French origin "consider Canada to be a country that is officially bilingual but fundamentally multi-cultural," the Commission rejected the notion. It countered that Canada's cultural diversity should be acknowledged, "keeping in mind that there are *two dominant cultures*, the French and British" [emphasis added].[43] Moreover, "those of other languages and cultures are more or less integrated" with Anglophone and Francophone communities and constitute a "third force" only in a statistical sense.[44] By the same token, the Commission declared, "[the immigrant to Canada] should know that Canada recognizes two official languages and that it possesses two predominant cultures that have produced two societies—Francophone and Anglophone—which form two distinct communities within an overall Canadian context."[45] In short, the Trudeau government adopted multiculturalism without the Commission's formal blessing.[46]

The federal government was undoubtedly under pressure from some non-British, non-French Canadians to substitute multiculturalism for biculturalism. Their proportion of the Canadian population had grown since the Second World War—from 20.0 per cent in 1941 to 25.8 per cent in 1961. It had been only 12.2 per cent at the turn of the century. Moreover, this segment of the population was more urban than in the past, and thus more visible to other Canadians.[47] It was also more skilled and better educated than in the past, and thus more apt to produce leaders able to express grievances on their behalf.[48]

It is not clear, however, that the mobilization of "third-force" groups was sufficiently broad-based to have alone induced the federal government's adoption of multiculturalism.[49] The mobilization of ethnic organizations was uneven, with little co-ordination among groups, and heavily dominated by Ukrainian-Canadian organizations.[50] Of the 55 briefs that were presented to the B&B Commission, supported by 14 ethnic groups, 32 came from Ukrainian-Canadian organizations.[51] Some of the other groups actually supported the Commission's positions, including Toronto's Italian-Canadian community leaders and the Trans-Canadian Alliance of German Canadians.[52] And two years after the multiculturalism policy was announced, a survey of members of 10 "minority ethnic groups" found that most of them still were not clearly aware of the policy.[53]

However, there was an additional reason for the Trudeau government to respond to these demands for recognition of multiculturalism: to protect its underlying goal of bilingualism. The call to make French an official language had met with resistance in areas, such as western Canada, where the Francophone presence was quite limited. The resistance was especially strong among parts of the population that had been offended by the notion of biculturalism. Granting multiculturalism could help to stave off opposition to the government's central project: a pan-Canadian official bilingualism.

Thus, there emerged a certain pressure within the government, and most notably the Liberal Party leadership, to adopt multiculturalism. In fact, the groups that felt excluded by biculturalism were well known for their support of the Liberal Party, with the exception of Ukrainian Canadians.[54] For that matter, several provincial governments supported a policy of multiculturalism: Alberta announced a multiculturalism policy in July 1971 and in September 1971, one month before Ottawa announced its policy, Ontario declared that it would convene an Ontario Heritage Conference in 1972.[55]

The actual proposal to proclaim a policy of multiculturalism emerged from the Cabinet Committee on Science, Culture and Information. In committee it had been framed by its advocates as a way of "developing the Canadian identity" and "a new concept of the presentation of Canadianism."[56] However, when it was brought to the full cabinet for discussion, Pierre Trudeau himself reportedly was most cautious, contending that the focus should be on self-help rather than government assistance.[57] In the end, he agreed to the proposal, apparently at the insistence of his political advisers.[58]

There is a final consideration that might well explain why Trudeau gave his accord to multiculturalism. He had his own reasons for doing so. Like multiculturalism's advocates, he too was opposed to biculturalism. We have seen how in the early days of the B&B Commission he had rejected biculturalism out of concern that, based on a dualistic understanding of Canada, it might serve to legitimize a special status for Quebec, if not independence. The various volumes of the Commission's report had fully confirmed his fears. Whatever reservations Trudeau might have had about multiculturalism, at least the adoption of it would preclude biculturalism, with all its potential implications. To quote Raymond Breton, himself a *Cité libre* colleague of Trudeau:

> Another incentive [for such a policy] was that multiculturalism turned out to be instrumental to the Trudeau government's political agenda. Indeed, the terms of the royal commission could be interpreted as lending support to the "two nations" view of Canada. A policy of cultural pluralism would help to undermine a notion that was seen as dangerously consistent with the Quebec independence movement.[59]

This interpretation was also offered by Bernard Ostry, who, as a senior civil servant, was in charge of the early implementation of the policy and worked closely with Trudeau and Pelletier.[60] From that perspective, the importance of multiculturalism was not so much what it offered as what it replaced: biculturalism. Still, multiculturalism had to be squared with Trudeau's individualist world view.

Substituting Multiculturalism for Biculturalism

Trudeau's proclamation of multiculturalism on 8 October 1971 took the form of a response to the B&B Commission's *Book IV: The Cultural Contribution of the Other Ethnic Groups*. Beyond his remarks to Parliament, Trudeau tabled a formal policy statement entitled "Federal Government's Response to Book IV." It outlined six new programs that the government planned to establish[61] and offered a general rationale for these initiatives.

Both the address and the policy statement made it clear that the Trudeau government was rejecting biculturalism in favour of multiculturalism. To cite the statement:

> The very name of the royal commission whose recommendations we now seek to implement tends to indicate that bilingualism and biculturalism

> are indivisible. But, biculturalism does not properly describe our society; multiculturalism is more accurate. [62]

Thus, the government would pursue "a policy of multiculturalism within a bilingual framework." Declaring that "although there are two official languages, there is no official culture,"[63] Trudeau committed his government to act in four areas:

> First, resources permitting, the government will seek to assist all Canadian cultural groups that have demonstrated a desire and effort to continue to develop a capacity to grow and contribute to Canada, and a clear need for assistance, *the small and weak groups no less than the strong and highly organized*.
>
> Second, the government will assist members of all cultural groups to overcome cultural barriers to full participation in Canadian society.
>
> Third, the government will promote creative encounters and interchange among all Canadian cultural groups in the interest of national unity.
>
> Fourth, the government will continue to assist immigrants to acquire at least one of Canada's official languages in order to become full participants in Canadian society [emphasis added].[64]

Putting his personal stamp on the new policy, Trudeau concluded his address by declaring that:

> I wish to emphasize the view of the government that a policy of multiculturalism within a bilingual framework is basically the conscious support of the individual freedom of choice. We are free to be ourselves.[65]

Taken at face value, Trudeau's claim that the new policy of multiculturalism is about "individual freedom of choice" seems a bit odd.[66] After all, normally one does not "choose" one's ethnicity, if ethnicity is understood in terms of ancestry or background; it is simply a "given," albeit a "socially constructed" one. Nor could one readily imagine an individual choosing to go from one ethnic group to another. The B&B Commission had talked of "freedom of choice," but this was in terms of the opportunity, especially for an immigrant, to choose within which of the societies, Anglophone or Francophone, he or she would be integrated.[67]

The policy statement that Trudeau tabled is not of much help in this regard since it does not even use the phrase "individual freedom of choice." Instead, its purpose is to defend the values of collective identity and, more precisely, cultural pluralism. Positing that "one of man's basic needs is a sense of belonging," it celebrates cultural pluralism as a barrier to the depersonalization and homogenization of "mass society."[68] Contending that "cultural pluralism is of the very essence of Canadian identity," it seeks to demonstrate that cultural and ethnic identities are fully compatible with "national allegiance" and that recognizing them does not "weaken the position of Canada's two official languages." The text acknowledges that "ethnic groups are certainly not the only way in which this need for belonging can be met," while insisting that "they have been an important one." Thus, it leaves open the possibility that the "sense of belonging" could be met by other types of entities, such as one of the two communities forming Canadian biculturalism or even Quebec's distinct society, let alone a Quebec nation. While the document text does note that "individuals in a democracy may choose not to be concerned about maintaining a strong sense of ethnic identity" and asserts that the government "does not plan on aiding individual groups to cut themselves off from the rest of society,"[69] the general line of argument clearly is not the most reliable for Trudeau's purposes.

To better understand the context for Trudeau's claim that the new policy is about "individual freedom of choice," we need to turn to Trudeau's address itself, where he personally selected the themes. Here, unlike the policy statement, there is no reference to the inherent value of pluralism in cultures and identities or to any presumed need of a "sense of belonging." There is the simple assertion that all groups have the same status: "there is no official culture, nor does any ethnic group take precedence over any other." But the real focus is indeed on the individual: the individual's freedom of choice and the need of individuals to express their own distinct identities.[70] The identity in question does appear to be an individual's *ethnic* identity (as opposed to a wholly personal one): the "freedom to be ourselves" is the freedom of individuals to express their ethnic identity. To that extent, the "freedom" proclaimed by Trudeau is quite limited, involving a specific collective identity. Still, there is the suggestion that freedom of choice is also the freedom to choose to be part of an ethnic group or to not be part of a group. Freedom of choice may in fact entail freedom *from* groups.[71]

Moreover, two of the new policy's four objectives could be readily understood in terms of individual freedom. Thus, evoking the commitment to assist immigrants to acquire at least one official language, Trudeau contends that "the individual's freedom would be hampered if he were locked for life within a particular cultural compartment by the accident of birth or language." Another policy objective fits perfectly: assisting "members of all cultural groups to overcome cultural barriers to full participation in Canadian society."

For good measure, Trudeau develops an additional line of argument for his new policy: the individual's need for confidence in his own identity.

> Such a policy should help break down discriminatory attitudes and cultural jealousies. National unity if it is to mean anything in the deeply

> personal sense, must be founded on confidence in one's own *individual* identity; out of this can grow respect for that of others and a willingness to share ideas, attitudes and assumptions. A vigorous policy of multiculturalism will help create this initial confidence. It can form the base of a society which is based on fair play for all [emphasis added].[72]

In this way, Trudeau's vision of multiculturalism can be seen as fundamentally about integration. In the words of political scientist H.D. Forbes, multicultural policy

> was designed from the start to promote "integration" (sharply distinguished from "assimilation," despite their similarity) by fighting prejudice and discrimination (or racism), thus making it possible for new and old Canadians to meet and mingle (and intermarry) on a footing of equality.[73]

Understood this way, multiculturalism would be the crucial step in creating "a new, distinctively Canadian national identity," based on "polyethnic pluralism," that would show the world how to transcend nationalism and the conflicts it inevitably engenders.[74] This falls squarely within Trudeau's long-standing political world view.

Indeed, especially in light of Trudeau's White Paper on Indian Policy, one might even question whether his particular notion of multiculturalism was just "integrative." With such an emphasis on the primacy of the individual and the free expression of individual identity, what is left for membership in a group? The model does indeed seem to view society as a mere aggregation of individuals and, to that extent, is quite "assimilative." Such phrases as "locked for life within a particular cultural compartment" seem to betray a rather negative view of ethnic groups or cultural communities, and their capacity to shackle individuals.

Arguably, Trudeau was outlining a commitment not to multiculturalism, as commonly understood with its emphasis on the value of cultural pluralism, but to a more conventional form of liberalism focused on individuals' equality of treatment and equality of opportunity. In David Miller's phraseology, this would be an "egalitarian liberalism," associated with such thinkers as John Rawls and Brian Barry, that "portrays a liberal society as one that treats its members as free and equal, but pays no attention to culture as such."[75] To that extent, Trudeau's address to Parliament was not at all the proclamation of a new Canadian multiculturalism. Rather than carving out a new multiculturalist vision of Canada, and of the role of the state, he was simply applying liberal ideals of equality to a culturally pluralist citizenry.

At the same time, the first of the primary objectives of Trudeau's new policy can only be seen as expressions of multiculturalism: assisting all Canadian cultural groups, "the small and weak groups no less than the strong and highly organized."

This is also true of the third objective, framed as it is in terms of groups: promoting "creative encounters and interchange among all Canadian cultural groups." For that matter, the specific programs outlined in the accompanying document go well beyond the B&B Commission's recommendations in providing for direct funding to cultural groups for such purposes as multicultural encounters, organizational meetings for new cultural groups, conferences and youth activities, and multicultural centres "where there is a demonstrated need and desire from the community for such a facility." Once again going beyond the B&B Commission, the government was to sponsor the preparation of histories of 20 cultural groups.[76]

It would be difficult to square financial support of ethnic groups with Pierre Trudeau's general individualism. In the case of language rights, Trudeau had been careful to frame them in terms of individual choice. If two languages were to be made official, and no others, it was justified on the pragmatic basis that the smaller language group, the Francophones, could break up the country. But the so-called cultural communities posed no such threat. In this case, the new policy clearly was responding to the demands of the multiculturalism advocates who precipitated it in the first place.[77] In any event, with its contradiction between "preservative" and "integrationist" objectives, the new policy of multiculturalism was not very coherent.[78]

To add to the confusion, Trudeau's speech to the House gave the impression that in adopting a policy of multiculturalism his government was acting on the recommendation of the B&B Commission. He led off by declaring that "the government has accepted all those recommendations . . . in Volume IV . . . directed to federal departments and agencies."[79] The policy statement claims that "the government accepts and endorses the recommendations and *spirit* of Book IV [emphasis added]."[80] Yet the term "multiculturalism" does not appear in any of the Commission's recommendations.[81] At no point did Trudeau acknowledge that the Commission had rejected the term "multiculturalism" and remained committed to biculturalism. Thus, it is not surprising that, over the years, so many commentators have assumed that the Commission had itself proposed the adoption of multiculturalism.

Moreover, Trudeau's presentation to the House took multiculturalism far from the preoccupation with cultural maintenance and relative status that had motivated its champions in the first place. The leaders of the various "ethnic" groups would hardly have been concerned about individuals being "locked for life" within a particular group. Nor, one suspects, would they have appreciated such phrases. However, apparently these were the terms upon which Trudeau was prepared to adopt multiculturalism, overcoming the caution he expressed in cabinet. As Michael Temelini has argued, it helped that multiculturalism's advocates were demanding not the juridical recognition of minority *rights*, which Trudeau would have had difficulty accepting, but the adoption of multiculturalism as public virtue and a way of life.[82] Moreover, as we shall see, Trudeau could always ignore the "preservative" elements as prime minister, once they had served their political purposes. The "integration" thrust of the policy could carry on, and be widely celebrated as his legacy of multiculturalism.

Whatever its internal logic or fidelity to the concerns of multiculturalism's proponents, Trudeau's proclamation of multiculturalism did serve his underlying purpose of displacing biculturalism and the conception of Canada that it entailed. The B&B Commission's Book IV gave him the opportunity to banish the Commission's guiding concept of biculturalism from the federal lexicon, securing the gratitude of a wide range of "ethnic groups" for doing so. Moreover, this was accomplished with finesse. Given his disingenuous claim to be adopting the B&B Commission's recommendations, and indeed the "spirit" behind them, such was the resulting confusion that both experts and public officials continue to state erroneously that the Commission had itself proposed multiculturalism.

Recognizing Multiculturalism in the Charter

There was a second initiative of the Trudeau government that formalized multiculturalism's centrality to its vision of Canada: the recognition of multiculturalism in the Charter of Rights and Freedoms. As with Trudeau's original proclamation of multiculturalism, it too came about through external political pressures.

There had been no reference to multiculturalism in the original text for a Charter that the Trudeau government proposed in the fall of 1980.[83] However, a special parliamentary committee, created to review the proposed text, recommended a number of additions, including a provision that the Charter be interpreted in a way consistent with "the preservation and enhancement of the multicultural heritage of Canadians." (It was responding to contentions from a variety of ethnocultural organizations[84] that reference to Canada's multiculturalism should appear in the Charter.[85]) Seeking to broaden support for its initiative, the Trudeau government duly adopted this and other recommendations.[86] Out of this process emerged section 27 of the Charter: "This Charter shall be interpreted in a manner consistent with the preservation and enhancement of the multicultural heritage of Canadians." It is an interpretive clause, intended to guide interpretation of the Charter as a whole. On this basis, its impact has been uncertain and a clear disappointment to the leaders of the established European-origin groups who had hoped that it would serve to buttress the "preservative" aspects of multiculturalism policy.[87]

Development of Multiculturalism Policy during the Trudeau Government

The adoption of multiculturalism was, first and foremost, a matter of proclaiming a particular vision of the country. In that sense, it was about "ideology." But, as was made clear by the policy statement that accompanied Trudeau's address, it was also about public policy. As David Miller has argued, the two aspects of multiculturalism, ideology and public policy, need to be clearly distinguished since their fates may be quite different.[88]

As to be expected, the first stage in policy development was significantly shaped by the groups that had so vigorously championed multiculturalism: largely white, second- and third-generation Canadians of non-British, non-French descent. For them, multiculturalism was all about the policy's first objective: the preservation and development of cultural groups. Even more, as Breton argues, it was about asserting their status in Canadian society, relative to the Charter groups.[89] During the tenure of the first minister of state for multiculturalism, Stanley Haidasz (himself a spokesperson for Polish Canadians),[90] several programs were established, including Canadian Identities (which focused on song and dance), Ethnic Group Liaison, Ethnic Press Analysis Service, Third-Language Teaching Aids, Immigration Orientation, and Multicultural Centres. Other government agencies established such units as the Canadian Centre for Folk Culture Studies, the Ethnic Canadian Program, and the National Ethnic Archives. But most financial resources were distributed through the Multicultural Projects Grants to groups and organizations "for such cultural activities as festivals, television programs, Saturday schools, literary clubs and art exhibits."[91] This program in particular gave rise to the popular complaint that multiculturalism had become heavily oriented toward the Liberal Party's electoral concerns. A charge that may well have had some basis in fact,[92] it was to persist.

By the mid-1970s, however, a shift away from cultural preservation was already beginning. In part, it came from a new minister of state for multiculturalism, John Munro, who shared public criticism that, through its emphasis on supporting folklore, the program was wasteful and tended to favour the better-organized groups. But it was also due to the emergence of new claimants for government programs: the leaders of racially defined groups and other "visible minorities." This new kind of leadership was itself a result of a change in immigration policy, going back to the mid-1960s, that broadened eligibility beyond the white, European categories that had tended to predominate among past immigrants. For these new immigrants, preservation of their cultural distinctiveness was far less important than the need to break down racial barriers to economic opportunity and social integration.

The older multicultural leaders bitterly resented the change in orientation. Indeed, the national chair of the Canadian Consultative Council on Multiculturalism denounced John Munro's plans so vehemently that Munro asked him to resign.[93] Nevertheless, by the 1980s, the program had been effectively reoriented to a focus on social issues, especially racism. In 1982, a Race Relations Unit was established; symposia were held on "race relations and the law" and "race relations in the media."[94] Greater emphasis was placed on promoting intercultural understanding. And the needs of immigrant women were identified as a particular concern.

For his part, Pierre Trudeau treated multicultural policy with indifference.[95] Indeed, he reportedly had nothing further to say about multiculturalism once he had made the 1971 proclamation.[96] Senior civil servants soon concluded that the program was not a priority and saw little incentive to pursue it.[97] Multiculturalism was assigned to junior ministers and given small and relatively weak administrative structures. As a result, there was little co-ordination among departments in the pursuit of multiculturalism nor did the principal central agencies of the federal government support the goals of the multiculturalism policy.[98] This general indifference is also seen in the meagre resources assigned to multiculturalism, especially when compared with official bilingualism. Daiva Stasiulis has calculated that in the first year of multiculturalism, 1971–2, the secretary of state spent over $78 million on bilingualism but only 2 per cent of that amount, or less than $2 million, on multiculturalism. Ten years later the gap remained: in 1981–2, close to $196 million was spent on bilingualism but only 7 per cent of that amount, or a little over $14 million on multiculturalism. In 1987–8, well after Trudeau's departure from the prime ministership, the ratio remained the same.[99]

The Fate of Trudeau's Vision of Multiculturalism

By the time Pierre Trudeau left the prime ministership, in June 1984, Canadian multiculturalism was already far removed from both the policy and the conception of Canada that he had proclaimed in 1971. These trends were largely confirmed by the successor governments. Multiculturalism has proven to be most flexible, if not chameleon-like,[100] both as policy and as ideology.

By 1984, multicultural policy was no longer geared to the established white European-origin populations whose leaders had brought it into being. Instead, it had become focused on recently arrived populations coming from elsewhere than Europe. In the process, it had become oriented primarily to the integration of immigrants, as opposed to the preservation of long-standing cultural communities, and to addressing the barriers that immigrants faced. To that extent, it was more in tune with Trudeau's own abiding concern with the individual and opportunities he (or she) enjoyed. However, especially with the new immigrant populations, the barriers to integration were no longer simply cultural or linguistic, they were largely based on race and thus much more difficult to transcend. Individuals faced discrimination *as members of a group*. Moreover, while the federal government's multicultural policy had become geared to race, it retained its original concern with ethnicity (as represented by the European ethnocultural organizations).[101] On both bases, then, it was concerned with the challenges and opportunities facing *groups*. As well, beyond an effort to ease these barriers to groups, multiculturalism had become a celebration of diversity among ethnically and racially defined groups. This direction was further cemented by the practice of subsequent governments to issue formal apologies to particular groups.

Thus, Pierre Trudeau's attempt to frame multiculturalism in terms of the individual and individual freedom of choice didn't really hold. As both policy and description of the country, Canadian multiculturalism followed its own group-based logic, as reinforced and shaped by the changing composition of the Canadian population.

Multiculturalism Post-Trudeau

These general trends in multiculturalism policy continued over the many successors to the Trudeau government. The total funds allocated to multiculturalism fell dramatically, going from a mid-1990s high of $27 million annually to $16 million in the next decade.[102] Funding specifically for the ethnocultural organizations of established European populations, the original focus of cultural preservation, virtually disappeared after a 1996–7 strategic review, falling from an average of $1.6 million in 1983–5 to just $55,000 in 2001.[103] On the other hand, funding for projects designed to combat racism became a priority, going from 9.6 per cent of the total budget over 1991 to 1993, to 30.2 per cent in 2001.[104]

This shift away from cultural preservation and toward racial issues can also be seen through a series of administrative changes in responsibility for multiculturalism. When a Department of Multiculturalism and Citizenship was established in 1991, its programs consisted of "Race Relations and Cross-Cultural Understanding," "Heritage Cultures and Languages," and "Community Support and Participation." However, two years later, partly in response to public criticism of cultural preservation funding, the programs were integrated with the Department of Canadian Heritage, where a secretary of state for multiculturalism was created. In 1997, the secretary of state for multiculturalism defined three objectives all of which were clearly "integrationist": social justice, civic participation, and identity (enabling people of all backgrounds to have a sense of belonging to Canada). At the same time, a Canadian Race Relations Foundation was created with a $24 million endowment. In 2008, when the Harper government transferred responsibility for multiculturalism to Citizenship and Immigration, the new priorities were, once again, firmly "integrationist": integration of new Canadians and cultural communities, support for at-risk youth of various cultural backgrounds, and promotion of inclusion and Canadian values. In the 2005 budget, the Harper government had announced a $56 million five-year commitment to Canada's Action Plan Against Racism.[105]

Canadian Multiculturalism Act

Finally, the shift away from cultural preservation can also been seen in the Canadian Multiculturalism Act, which the Mulroney government passed in 1988. Passage of the act, the first of its kind anywhere, was itself a significant event, especially given Trudeau's manifest indifference to multiculturalism. The Canadian Ethno-cultural Council, representing established European populations, had been lobbying for such an act since 1977. The Trudeau government did not see this as a priority,[106] but the Progressive Conservatives adopted the idea and, once they assumed power under Brian Mulroney, sought to bring it forward.[107] However, the emerging leadership representing "visible minorities" campaigned for a focus on racial barriers to participation in the Canadian economy and society. In 1987, a new parliamentary standing committee on multiculturalism proclaimed that multicultural policy had indeed evolved from cultural preservation to the promotion of equality.[108]

Thus, while the act mandates the federal government to recognize and enhance the development of "communities whose members share a common origin," it also calls upon the government to eliminate barriers to "the full and equitable participation [in Canadian society] of individuals and communities of all origins," to ensure that "all individuals receive equal treatment and equal protection under the law," and to assist Canadian "social, cultural, economic and political institutions . . . to be both respectful and inclusive of Canada's multicultural character."[109] Also, the act is careful to refer to Canadian diversity as "racial" as well as "cultural."[110] At the same time, the preamble makes a point of recognizing "the rights of the aboriginal peoples of Canada" and declaring that the status of the two official languages should not affect "any rights or privileges" of any other language (i.e., the non-official languages).[111]

Formal Apologies for Past Wrongs

On 22 September 1988, Prime Minister Brian Mulroney added a new dimension to multiculturalism's recognition of ethnic groups by issuing a formal apology for the Canadian government's past treatment of a specific group: Japanese Canadians, who had been interned during the Second World War. The Harper government continued this practice by issuing formal apologies to Chinese Canadians for a head tax and to Indigenous Canadians for treatment of their children in residential schools. Indeed, in 2006 it announced the creation of a Community Historical Recognition Program. These acts of apology by the Mulroney and Harper governments were part of an international trend involving the American, British, Australian, Japanese, and Italian governments, among others.[112]

Here too Pierre Trudeau had maintained a distinctive position: rejecting outright the notion of apologizing or offering redress for past acts of injustice. In 1984, on his last day in Parliament, Trudeau declared, "I do not see how I can apologize for some historical event to which we or these people in this House were not a party," and "I do not think it is the purpose of a government to right the past. I cannot rewrite history."[113] Stated in these terms, Trudeau's position clearly is of a piece with his brand of liberalism: individuals are responsible for their own actions but not for the actions of others. The Liberal governments of Jean Chrétien and Paul Martin resisted pressures to make such formal apologies,[114] presumably out of respect for Pierre Trudeau's views. However, during its first year in office, Justin Trudeau's government issued a formal apology for the Komagata Maru incident, in which a boat full of predominantly Sikh would-be immigrants was turned back to India. On 28 November 2017, Trudeau presented to the House an apology for the federal government's past discrimination against sexual minorities.[115]

Critiques of Canadian Multiculturalism

While Canadian multiculturalism has taken on a vastly different form than the one Trudeau originally sought to articulate, it appears to enjoy widespread public support. Opinion surveys suggest that about two-thirds of Canadians support multiculturalism, although about half of them do so conditionally.[116]

Nonetheless, from the 1980s onward, multicultural policy has engendered a number of critiques. Initially, as with Neil Bissoondath's best-seller book, *Selling Illusions: The Cult of Multiculturalism in Canada*,[117] the objections targeted the policy's preservationist objective, contending that it promoted separation of groups rather than their integration with Canadian society. But that argument lost force as the preservationist focus on European ethnocultural communities was phased out. Other critics contended that multiculturalism led to a cultural relativism: if there is to be no "official culture," then it is difficult to designate any set of values that characterize Canada. Thus, the most illiberal practices (such as genital mutilation) had to be tolerated. As Kymlicka has noted, this form of argument did lead to a decline in public support for multiculturalism in the early 1990s but support then rebounded, given multiculturalism's already extensive institutionalization, the evident commitment to liberal democracy of the major immigrant organizations, and the religious diversity of immigrant populations.[118] In 2005, public protests did lead the Ontario government to drop a proposal to allow the use, for family disputes, of faith-based tribunals, including ones based on Sharia law. A final concern, which has arisen in many countries, has to do with whether multiculturalism, and ethnic and racial diversity, might erode public support for welfare-state measures. If a sense of commonality is undermined by diversity or if immigrants draw disproportionately upon social assistance, the argument goes, citizens may be less inclined to support the state's social measures. Yet Keith Banting has demonstrated that, in the case of Canada, these dangers have been averted through a broadening of national identity, making multiculturalism a central part, as well as affording effective integration of immigrants and provision of social services on a universal basis.[119] Also, there has been concern that cultural enclaves harbour radicalism and threaten security. Yet the limited amount of terrorist activity in Canada does not fall within this profile.

A different line of criticism of multiculturalism contends that, as conceived, it does not go far enough. Accepting the logic of multiculturalism, critics argue that that it should be applied to language as well as culture and that the formula of "multiculturalism in a bilingual framework" is self-contradictory. Within this framework all cultures are to be equal yet the languages of only two of them have official status. Thus, the criticism: if the federal government is to support all cultures, however "weak and small," as it promised in 1971, how can it do so without supporting their languages? If multiculturalism is to be substituted for biculturalism, why not replace bilingualism with multilingualism?

On this basis, the federal government was drawn into supporting "non-official languages." The Trudeau government introduced a Cultural Enrichment Program, in 1977, to support supplementary heritage-language schools and, in 1991, the Mulroney government had Parliament approve an act to establish a Canadian Heritage Languages Institute in Edmonton.[120] Most provincial governments now maintain, with federal funding support, programs through which children of non-English and non-French origin can receive some training in their ancestral language. By 1989, there were 129,000 students studying 60 languages in supplementary schools. Some western Canadian provinces have gone further, allowing and even supporting not just the study of non-official languages, on a supplementary basis, but their use as actual languages of instruction.[121] This support for "non-official languages" has been resented by representatives of Francophone minorities, whose standing is closely tied to the dualist vision of Canada—with two official languages.[122]

For some academic commentators, supporting so-called non-official languages is not enough. Highly critical of the B&B Commission, Eve Haque contends that its privileging of only two languages as official languages reflects Canada's historical formation as a "white settler colony" and belies an intent to perpetuate "a racialized settler colonial narrative."[123] Yet the Commission had deliberately eschewed such terms as "race" and "ethnicity," even if the English version of its mandate had awkwardly used "race" as equivalent to the French "peuple." As we have seen, the "blue pages" extolled the model of Francophone and Anglophone societies in which individuals of all backgrounds might find a home and declared that the two societies must "accept newcomers much more readily than they have done in the past" and must "willingly allow other groups to preserve and enrich, if they so desire, the cultural values they prize."[124] Moreover, it is clear that in its deliberations the Commission was seized with addressing Quebec nationalism, and separatism, rather than ensuring the dominance of French- and English-speakers over any other language group. It is in those terms that most of the commissioners understood the Canadian crisis with which they were charged.[125]

Still, the question remains as to whether multiculturalism should also have led to a different language policy in which bilingualism, with its two official languages, is replaced by multilingualism. It is difficult to see how the status of "official language" could have been extended to all. As we have seen, simply making French a language in which the public is served by federal and provincial governments has been an enormous challenge. Making it a language in which the federal government itself functions has proven to be an insuperable challenge.

Even Commissioner Jaroslav (J.B.) Rudnyckyj, in his lengthy dissent, did not propose official status for any language other than English and French. Rather, while fully endorsing the Commission's recommendations for English and French as sole official languages, he called for applying a variant of the bilingual districts formula to "regional languages."[126] On this basis, Canada would still have been based on a "hierarchy" of languages.[127]

The fact remains that, then as now, Canada's linguistic demography has afforded clear supremacy to English and French. Together, the two official languages were understood by 98.7 per cent of the Canadian population in 1961[128] and 98.1 per cent in 2016.[129] In 1961, 58.5 per cent of the Canadian population had English as its mother tongue and 28.1 per cent had French; the next largest group (German mother tongue) represented only 3.1 per cent.[130] In the 2016 census, 58.1 per cent had English as mother tongue and 21.4 per cent had French;[131] the two next most frequent mother tongues, Mandarin and Cantonese, together represented only 3.5 per cent of Canadians.[132] While the Francophone proportion of the total population may be slipping, it is still by far the second most important language group; together French and English dominate Canada's linguistic demography. Yet the unequal symbolism and logical incoherence remain: two official languages amidst a multitude of cultures, all supposedly of equal status.

Even more challenging to multiculturalism is the fact that it takes no explicit account of Indigenous Peoples and the claim that they constitute "nations." Within multiculturalism, the various First Nations communities, as well as the Métis and Inuit peoples, simply constitute cultures of equal status with all the various other cultures, just like the French Canadians. Indeed, as we have seen, the purported "father" of multiculturalism, Pierre Trudeau, had no use for notions of special treatment or rights for Indigenous Peoples. By the same token, he would not have recognized any historical claims for Indigenous *languages*. He had argued that the French language warranted official status simply because its speakers, along with Anglophones, had "the power to break the country": "this power cannot yet be claimed by the Iroquois, the Eskimos, or the Ukrainians."[133]

For his part, Justin Trudeau has taken the position that Indigenous languages should indeed be recognized and supported; in December 2016, he announced his government's intention to introduce legislation to deal with the matter.[134] (For that matter, Nunavut's Official Languages Act of 2008 declares Inuktitut to be one of the territory's three official languages, along with English and French.) However, Justin Trudeau's commitment to Indigenous languages is framed in terms of his overall commitment to establish a "nation-to-nation" relationship with Indigenous Peoples. Implicitly, whether Justin Trudeau acknowledges it or not, the recognition of "nations" within Canada entails a very different understanding of Canada than does multiculturalism.

Multiculturalism and Canadian National Identity

An additional criticism of multiculturalism has been that, by stressing groups and group identities, it has undermined the bases of a distinct Canadian national identity. Rather than celebrating what Canadians have in common, multiculturalism has reinforced the divisions among them. Yet there is clear evidence that, to the contrary, multiculturalism has provided the underpinning for a new national identity that is able to mobilize substantial support, at least among English-speaking Canadians.

In fact, notwithstanding Trudeau's reservations about it, multiculturalism has become the central element of the new pan-Canadian identity that Trudeau had struggled to put in place. Within this new national identity, Canada is seen as a singular example of a country that has been able to accept differences in ethnicity, race, and religion and has learned how to avoid the conflicts that have plagued so many other countries. As we have seen, the decline of the British Empire had posed an existential challenge to English-speaking Canadians who had tended to see their country in terms of its historic British connection: it was no longer possible to see Canada as part of a hegemonic global English-speaking entity or simply to identify with Britain itself. Multiculturalism offered the prospect of a new collective identity, distinctive to Canada. Moreover, this new version of a Canadian identity responded to another long-standing concern of Anglophone Canadians, as opposed to Francophones: the need to differentiate themselves from Americans. The United States could be contrasted with Canada as wedded to "the melting pot" and prone to eruptions of anti-immigrant sentiment.[135] Thus, in a 2010 survey, 56 per cent of Canadian residents responded that multiculturalism was "very important" to Canadian national identity.[136] Similarly, a survey analysis by Richard Johnston et al. found that among white, native-born Canadians (excluding Quebec Francophones) "the very self-conception of the country has come to embrace the idea of a multicultural society which successive waves of immigrants have helped build. . . . In short, for this group, multiculturalism is now a part of Canadian nationalism."[137]

Given Pierre Trudeau's manifest purpose as prime minister, there is considerable irony that multiculturalism should emerge as the centrepiece of a new Canadian nationalism. After all, language rights, as entrenched through a charter, had always been his primary objective. He had displayed relative indifference to the notion of multiculturalism, adopting it only after being pressured to do so and reportedly never referring to it again. And, over the years, his various proposals for a charter had made no mention of it. The term became part of the Charter of Rights and Freedoms, in the form of an interpretative clause, only after multiculturalism's advocates complained about its absence from Trudeau's original draft. By the same token, back in the 1950s when he was a *citélibriste*, he had regularly proclaimed his opposition to nationalism in all its forms, including the Canadian variety.

Multiculturalism and Canadian Dualism

Finally, the most telling critique of Canadian multiculturalism is that it has not replaced biculturalism as Canada's underlying social and political reality. Despite Pierre Trudeau's fervent wish, duality has not been displaced as the basic premise by which Francophones understand Canada. Within Quebec, the predominant response to multiculturalism has been to reject it outright both as a description of Canadian society, since it reduces Francophones to being simply one of a multitude of ethnic groups, and as a framework for comprehending the complex forms of diversity in Quebec itself. In effect, with Anglophones embracing multiculturalism and Francophones rejecting it, the reaction to multiculturalism has been fundamentally bicultural.

Trudeau's proclamation of multiculturalism was denounced from the outset in Quebec.[138] Quebec premier Robert Bourassa wrote to Trudeau to protest the new policy, contending that it contradicted the B&B Commission's mandate and guiding principle: "the equality of the two founding peoples." The Quebec government, he declared, would not be adopting multiculturalism in its own jurisdictions, given its responsibility to ensure the persistence of the French language and culture in its territory and beyond.[139] The leaders of Quebec's opposition parties denounced the new policy as an attack on Canadian duality while dismissing it as an electoral ploy.[140] Claude Ryan, then editor of *Le Devoir*, insisted that multiculturalism directly contradicted the conception of Canada that the B&B Commission had presented in the "blue pages" of Book I, "which Trudeau claims never to have read," and which, Ryan insisted, the Commission maintained throughout its Book IV. The notion of separating language and culture was dear to Trudeau's heart but had been rejected by the Commission.[141] And a leading Quebec sociologist, Guy Rocher, declared,

> By separating bilingualism from biculturalism, the Trudeau government is betraying all the hopes French Canadians might have placed in bilingualism, as they conceived it—that is, clearly tied to its symbol and essential condition, biculturalism.[142]

Over the following years, Francophone intellectual and political élites continued to reject multiculturalism, associating it closely with Pierre Trudeau and his opposition to Canadian dualism.[143] At the same time, they began to articulate a different framework, distinct to Quebec, that became known as "interculturalism."

According to the advocates of interculturalism, multiculturalism views society as a simple juxtaposition of different cultural groups and engenders isolation among them, thus risking both the social cohesion needed to support a common welfare state and to ensure national security. Interculturalism, they claim, is better able to secure social cohesion since it distinguishes between the majority group and the various minority groups and seeks to create a dialogue between the two that can lead to the creation of a common identity.[144]

One might question whether multiculturalism and interculturalism are truly different as approaches. They do share a number of principles: rejection of assimilation, acceptance of cultural pluralism, respect for diversity, equality of citizens, and the notion of a common public culture.[145] Nor are they necessarily incompatible: one could imagine multiculturalism creating the conditions that would allow the interculturalist dialogue to take place.[146]

What is clear is that, in the case of Canada, multiculturalism and interculturalism have become closely linked to opposing political projects. Just as multiculturalism was adopted by the federal government as part of its national unity strategy, so it was perhaps inevitable that the Quebec government would seek to counter it with an opposing framework. However, this likelihood was surely enhanced by the provocative manner in which Trudeau introduced multiculturalism: substituting it for biculturalism, as conceived by the B&B Commission, along with the particular place of Quebec that flowed from that. As John English has noted, in presenting multiculturalism Trudeau "could not resist remarks that he surely knew would inflame many in Quebec."[147]

Whether its contradiction with multiculturalism is real or nominal, interculturalism has become the framework within which Quebeckers discuss how to deal with diversity within their society. Developed by both Liberal[148] and PQ governments during the 1970s, interculturalism was made official Quebec policy in 1981 with the proclamation by René Lévesque of an action plan: *Autant de façons d'être Québécois*. Explicitly dismissing multiculturalism as a model, the plan draws a distinction between Quebec's Francophones, who constitute the Quebec nation, and Quebec's various "cultural communities." To develop this relationship between the Francophone majority and the cultural communities, the Quebec government established a Council of Cultural Communities and Immigration in 1984. A 1990 white paper extended the Quebec nation to englobe all Quebec residents: *L'Énoncé de politique en matière d'immigration et d'intégration* eliminated the distinction between cultural communities and the Francophone majority. For their part, recent immigrants were to be bound by a "moral contract" governing their integration with Quebec society. Along with democratic participation and the role of French as the common public language, the "moral contract" stressed the intercultural objective of intercommunity exchanges.[149]

To be sure, the actual policies that the Quebec government has pursued in addressing diversity may have been more similar to Ottawa's own policies than is suggested by the competing policy frameworks, interculturalism versus multiculturalism. Once again, policy must be distinguished from ideology. The two governments were confronted with a common evolution of their clienteles. Thus, as Marie McAndrew and her colleagues have demonstrated, until at least the mid-1980s the Quebec ministry of immigration and cultural communities subsidized the "folklore" activities of various groups in the same way as did Ottawa. In the mid-1980s, the emphasis in Quebec's programs began to shift toward questions of racism, prejudice, and inequality, following by only a few years the reorientation of Ottawa's multiculturalism policy. As was the case with Ottawa, the reorientation was due to an increased presence of visible-minority immigrants. Subsequently, both governments felt obliged, by backlashes among the majority population, to distance themselves somewhat from the "cultural relativism" of their past policies.[150] Nonetheless, the fact that successive Quebec governments, both federalist and sovereigntist, have felt the need to develop a formal framework for policy that is distinct to Quebec, and in opposition to Ottawa's multiculturalism, and that public debates have taken place within that framework, clearly demonstrates the persistence of duality as a way of understanding Canada.

Debating Quebec's Fundamental Values

The 1990s and first decade of this century saw an increasingly intense debate among Quebeckers over what should be seen as the distinguishing values of the Quebec collectivity. Framed once again within the concept of interculturalism, the debate was shaped by Quebec's historical experience. Thus, the discussion initially focused on the French language as Quebec's defining value. The report of a general inquiry into the state of the French language in Quebec, issued in 2001, proposed that the French language should be viewed as the common heritage of all members of the Quebec nation. Indeed, it claimed, mastery of French constitutes the essential condition for participation in the public affairs of this nation and the exercise of citizenship. However, while French was generally assumed to be a defining Quebec value, it was not seen to be sufficient in itself.[151]

Thus, public debate soon shifted to another feature of Quebec's historical experience: the struggle from the 1960s onward to end the Church's hegemony and establish a truly "secular" society. (In fact, "secularism" does not fully convey the scope and central importance of *laicité*, the French term around which the debate was centred.) The discussion of secularism, as a defining principle, was prompted in part by ongoing developments within Quebec: the requests of religious groups, including but not limited to Islamic groups, for accommodation of distinctive needs to practise their religion. Some specific instances of religious accommodation were featured in the media, garnering public attention and considerable disapproval. Discussion of secularism and the appropriate limits to religious accommodations also was fuelled and shaped by debates taking place in France, where long-established Jacobin world views allowed no space for accommodation of cultural diversity.

In addition, there emerged a wide consensus among Quebec's political and intellectual élites that, along with secularism, gender equality was a fundamental principle of Quebec society. Yet there was no agreement as to how the two principles should be applied.

Faced with public objection to instances of specifically religious accommodation, in February 2007 the Liberal government of Jean Charest established a commission of inquiry, jointly chaired by two of Quebec's most eminent scholars, sociologist Gérard Bouchard and philosopher Charles Taylor. Entitled the "Consultation Commission on Accommodation Practices Related to Cultural Differences," it was mandated to examine practices of cultural accommodation in Quebec and elsewhere, conduct public consultations, and formulate recommendations for accommodation practices that would "conform to the values of Québec society as a pluralistic, democratic, egalitarian society."[152] The Commission held hearings and public sessions in 15 regions, as well as Montreal, and received and examined over 900 briefs. The public sessions provided televised occasions for citizens to express views, at time quite extreme, on not just reasonable accommodation but ethnic relations and immigration itself.

In their report, *Building the Future: A Time for Reconciliation*, the two commissioners declared that "the foundations of collective life in Québec are not in a critical situation."[153] Cultural accommodation was being practised widely but a few instances were misunderstood by the public due to erroneous media reports. Nonetheless, they contended, there was "an accommodation crisis" since public discussion of religious accommodation "spawned fears [among 'Quebecers of French-Canadian ancestry'] about the most valuable heritage of the Quiet Revolution, in particular gender equality and secularism."[154]

The commission co-chairs insisted that through interculturalism Quebec had developed an approach to cultural pluralism that is distinctive and, given Francophones' historical preoccupation with the survival of their language and culture, more appropriate to Quebec than multiculturalism. They argued that interculturalism is better able to promote social cohesion and maintain cultural continuity, contending that such issues are less salient in English Canada since the dominance of the majority language is assured. Indeed, they noted that almost all participants in the Commission's consultations favoured interculturalism over multiculturalism.[155] By the same token, they claimed that the interaction and negotiation among communities that interculturalism promotes can be transformative, shaping even the collective identity of the Quebec nation. Indeed, they observed, "a truly inclusive collective identity has been developing in Québec for several decades."[156] At the core of this "genuine Québec identity that all citizens can share"[157] is French as the common public language, a feeling of belonging to Québec society, along with common values, "a genuine national memory," and "the symbols and mechanisms of collective life."[158] As to secularism, they called for an "open secularism" that recognizes the need for the state to be neutral, and for the state and the Church to be autonomous, while also protecting freedom of conscience and religion and the moral equality of individuals.[159]

On this basis, the report recommended that the Quebec government issue both a formal commitment to interculturalism and a white paper that would outline the terms of "open secularism," as well as promote the proper application by citizens of cultural accommodation, support full integration of immigrants into the workforce and combat discrimination and racism. In particular, with respect to "open secularism," the report proposed that certain categories of public employees (judges, Crown prosecutors, police officers, prison guards, and the president and vice-president of the Quebec National Assembly) be prohibited from wearing religious symbols, that the crucifix be removed from the National Assembly, and that prayers no longer be offered at meetings of municipal councils.[160] Needless to say, these latter recommendations drew substantial public commentary and dissent. For its part, the Charest government was quick to reject removal of the crucifix from the National Assembly, nor did it follow up on most of the other recommendations, including production of a white paper on "open secularism" and a ban on religious symbols for certain public officials. In essence, the report was shelved.[161]

Five years later, however, the Parti québécois government of Pauline Marois decided that a much stricter understanding of *laicité* was in order and, in the fall of 2013, proposed the adoption of a Charter of Quebec Values. As it was presented in Bill 60, the Charter's preamble evoked two fundamental principles of Quebec society to justify its measures: "the religious neutrality and secular nature of the State" and "the value of equality between women and men."[162] (In fact, virtually all the Charter's provisions were framed in terms of the first principle.[163]) Under the Charter, the ban on religious dress and symbols (which are "by their nature conspicuous"[164]) was to be applied to *all* public employees. Moreover, the Charter required that any individual "must ordinarily have their face uncovered"[165] when receiving services from the Quebec state. Strict conditions were presented for any accommodation on religious grounds. At the same time, in an apparent concession to conservative Francophones, the Charter allowed the National Assembly to decide whether to retain a religious symbol (i.e., the crucifix) in its facility or to regulate "the wearing of religious symbols by its members."[166] It also afforded a transitional period to certain locally based public institutions such as municipal *arrondissements* or districts. Elected officials were to be exempted from the Charter's requirements.

The Charter faced deep opposition even within the Parti québécois. It was publicly denounced by former PQ premiers Jacques Parizeau (who stated that the Bouchard–Taylor recommendations on religious dress were sufficient), Lucien Bouchard, and Bernard Landry.[167] Bouchard and Taylor publicly opposed the

Charter,[168] as did the opposition parties. In any event, the PQ government had not put the measure in place before being defeated in the 2014 provincial election.

The two episodes—the Bouchard–Taylor Commission and the Charter of Quebec Values—demonstrated the existence of profound divisions within Quebec society over the meaning of secularism and the implications of female–male equality. Sociologist Danielle Juteau has shown that in each instance opposing sides included both feminists and recently arrived immigrants.[169] Yet the debates also demonstrated the existence of a clear consensus that secularism and gender equality are indeed fundamental principles of Quebec society, born of Quebec's historical experience and, in particular, its Quiet Revolution. Nor was there much dissent to the principle that French, and French alone, is the common public language of Quebec. Finally, and most important for our purposes, the debate was striking for its separateness from the rest of Canada. By and large, it was a debate among Quebeckers about Quebec and about questions that have been central to its historical experience. The debate itself was situated within a framework, interculturalism, that was seen as distinct from and superior to Canadian multiculturalism.[170] These assumptions have continued to shape how Quebeckers, at least Francophone Quebeckers, address the implications of Quebec's growing cultural diversity.

In the winter of 2017, the debate over cultural diversity was reignited when a Quebec Francophone attacked a Quebec City mosque, killing six worshippers and injuring another 25. Public discussion quickly focused on the extent to which Islamophobia is present in Francophone Quebec and the role which political leaders and media may have played in reinforcing it. Evidence emerged of specific groups that had been propagating hate against Muslims.[171] There was good reason to believe that Islamophobic sentiments had been given free rein on radio talk shows, specifically in the Quebec City area. Some political leaders, such as Jean-François Lisée, acknowledged that past statements on their part may have been ill-considered and contributed to public hostility against Muslims. By the same token, thousands of Quebeckers attended public gatherings to express grief over the killings and solidarity with Quebec's Muslim community. In the wake of the tragedy, Charles Taylor publicly disavowed the Bouchard–Taylor report's key recommendation that certain individuals occupying positions of authority, such as judges, police officers, and prison guards, be barred from wearing religious symbols. Instead, he contended, the focus should be on reconciliation with Quebec's Muslim community.[172]

Nonetheless, most of Quebec's political leadership continued to presume that some sort of state intervention was needed to address cultural diversity. In fact, a multi-party consensus had emerged in the National Assembly around precisely the recommendation of the Bouchard–Taylor Commission that Charles Taylor had decided to disavow. However, rather than adopting the measure, the Liberal government of Philippe Couillard followed a different tack. It introduced Bill 62,

"An Act to Foster Adherence to State Religious Neutrality,"[173] that simply required that public officials bare their faces and that individuals do the same while receiving public services. In effect, the Couillard government sought to define the issue at hand as one of maintaining civility rather than regulating the public display of religious dress. Unimpressed with this new approach, the two main opposition parties contended that, not only was the measure unworkable, but it did not come to terms with the issue of religious symbols and thus did not address the underlying need to ensure *laicité*. Insisting that the question be addressed directly they called for an outright ban on the wearing of religious symbols by various categories of public officials. Gérard Bouchard, who stood by his report's recommendation regarding positions of authority, publicly denounced the bill as neither viable nor necessary.[174] Other leaders, such as Montreal's mayor, expressed discomfort with the measure.[175] Nonetheless, the bill was duly passed by the National Assembly's Liberal majority. However, Quebec courts have suspended its application.

Whereas in Quebec public opinion was strongly in support of Bill 62 (70 per cent in favour of the underlying principle), this was not the case in the rest of the country (only 40 per cent were in favour).[176] Quebec remains the only province to have sought to regulate the dress of public servants or of citizens receiving public services. Commentators in Anglophone Canada were quick to see the bill as the reflection of a pervasive Islamophobia in Quebec. Yet as we have argued, the question of religious dress in public settings is tied directly to basic principles of *laicité* and gender equality that have a particular standing in Quebec.[177] Thus, even the Quebec Liberals, the only provincial party unabashedly committed to Canadian federalism, felt the necessity to act—albeit in an indirect manner. Clearly, the question of religious dress in public settings is viewed within the terms of a political culture that is distinctive to Quebec.

In sum, while multiculturalism may have provided the core element for a new Canadian national identity, it has not erased Canada's underlying duality. Quebec and Anglophone Canada have addressed the growth of cultural diversity in different terms. In effect, they have done so *biculturally*, just as the B&B Commission had understood the term. Thus, the impact of the new multicultural nationalism has been largely restricted to the Anglophone side of the duality. In their demonstration of how multiculturalism, as a value, is central to a new Canadian nationalism, Richard Johnston and his colleagues are careful to limit their argument to respondents outside Quebec.[178] Arguably, the appeal to Anglophone Canadians of this new Canadian nationalism, centred on multiculturalism, was reinforced by their apprehension or antipathy regarding Quebec nationalism. Portraying the latter as a distinctly *ethnic* nationalism helped to cement their attachment to a pan-Canadian national identity as inclusive and thus superior.[179] Thus, there was a readiness outside Quebec to see the 2017 Quebec City massacre as further evidence of the malevolence of Quebec nationalism.

When Pierre Trudeau first proclaimed Canadian multiculturalism, back in October of 1971, he was determined to situate it within his personal brand of liberalism, focused resolutely on the individual and suspicious of "collectivities" of any kind. Thus, he insisted, multiculturalism really was about the individual and freedom of choice. Multiculturalism was useful to him in his effort to discredit biculturalism's notion that Canada was composed of two linguistic and cultural communities. He wanted the support of the ethnocultural communities that had championed multiculturalism in the first place but did not attach much importance to their preservationist ambitions. Decades before, he had expanded his personal world view to embrace personalism, with its emphasis upon community, but there is little evidence of this in his presentation of multiculturalism. The policy statement which he tabled in Parliament did extol the importance of groups, drawing upon sociological theories of mass society to do so. But Trudeau did not choose to incorporate these notions in his remarks nor did he acknowledge the policy statement's premise that all individuals need a sense of belonging to a larger entity.[180] Nonetheless we have seen that, as developed by the federal government, Canadian multiculturalism has remained very much concerned with the fate of groups whether it be with visible minorities who are prevented from participating fully in Canadian society or with specific groups that deserve apologies for past wrongs. It could not be contained within the individualist notions that Trudeau had sought to impose on it.

As it happens, over recent decades liberal thinking has evolved substantially from the classical assumptions to which Trudeau was so wedded. Moreover, Canadian philosophers have played a central role in recasting liberalism to take proper account of the importance of community to all individuals. Charles Taylor, a life-long friend of Trudeau, has theorized about the conditions under which it could be acceptable within liberal values for a state to pursue the collective goals such as the linguistic and cultural survival of a community.[181] His notion of "deep diversity" between Quebeckers and other Canadians, as opposed to the "first-level" diversity among other Canadians, is not far removed from the biculturalist ideas that Trudeau tried so hard to discredit and displace.[182] The interculturalism that Taylor jointly expounded with Gérard Bouchard in their report posits an importance of groups that Trudeau had sought to drain from Canadian multiculturalism. By the same token, Will Kymlicka has developed a conception of "liberal multiculturalism" in which the state has the positive obligation to address the needs of immigrant populations, the long-established as well as recently arrived, through preservationist policies such as the ones of the 1971 proclamation for which Trudeau apparently had little interest.[183]

Nonetheless, these efforts to articulate a proper place for community within liberal thought led in directions that Trudeau would never have accepted. Kymlicka's theorization of "liberal multiculturalism" entailed the recognition of the distinctive autonomy needs of "national minorities," of which the Québécois are one.[184] And Taylor's defence of the liberal state's pursuit of collective goals extended to support for constitutional recognition of Quebec's National Assembly's responsibility to maintain Quebec cultural distinctiveness, as in the ill-fated Meech Lake Accord. Thus, Trudeau's apprehensions about the consequences of recognizing "collectivities" were well grounded. As we shall see, as prime minister and in later life Trudeau remained steadfast in his rejection of any recognition of Quebec as a national minority or "distinct society," however attenuated that may be. Indeed, this *idée fixe* was to dominate Canada's political life and constitutional deliberations for decades to come.

Notes

1. Michael Oliver, "Laurendeau et Trudeau: leurs opinions sur le Canada," in *L'engagement intellectuel: mélanges en l'honneur de Léon Dion*, ed. Raymond Hudon and Réjean Pelletier (Sainte-Foy: Presses de l'Université Laval, 1991), 341.
2. Le Comité pour une politique fonctionnelle, "Bizarre algèbre," *Cité libre* 15, no. 82 (Dec. 1965): 13–20. The signatories were Albert Breton, Claude Bruneau, Yvon Gauthier, Marc Lalonde, and Maurice Pinard. Trudeau had officially been a member of the group (see Clarkson and McCall, *Trudeau and Our Times*, vol. 1, 410) and as such had signed the group's "Manifeste pour une politique fonctionnelle" published in *Cité libre* in May 1964. Michael Oliver says that Jean Marchand persuaded Trudeau not to sign the document and that Trudeau later acknowledged to Laurendeau his "paternité partielle" of the article. (See Oliver, "Laurendeau et Trudeau," 342). Interestingly, another member of the committee, Raymond Breton, did not sign the 1965 document. Later a sociologist at the University of Toronto, Breton was to become a leader in the study of Francophone minorities and multiculturalism.
3. My translation of "elle est passablement étrangère à notre pensée juridique et à nos formes politiques. . . . Et que signifierait en pratique une Confédération qui 'se développe d'après le principe de l'égalité entre les deux *cultures*'? . . . l'idée d'égalité entre les peuples est à la base même du concept de souveraineté nationale, et on aurait aimé savoir comment la Commission entend interpréter son mandat, sans être amenée nécessairement à préconiser la division du Canada en deux États nationaux." (Comité, "Bizarre algèbre," 14.) To buttress their point that political science would allow no other conclusion, the authors quote statements by Max Weber and Robert McIvor suggesting that normally a nation secures its own state. Yet this was a partial and considerably outdated view of social science. For instance, at about the same time political scientists were beginning to write about the "consociational democracy" of smaller Western European democracies that showed how, through mutual vetoes and other devices, representatives of different cultures can enjoy equality within the institutions of a common state, and the state itself can be highly stable. See Robert A. Dahl, ed., *Political Oppositions in Western Democracies* (New Haven: Yale University Press, 1966); and Arend Lijphart, *The Politics of Accommodation: Pluralism and Democracy in the Netherlands* (Berkeley: University of California Press, 1968).
4. Royal Commission on Bilingualism and Biculturalism [hereinafter, B&B Commission], *Preliminary Report* (Ottawa: Queen's Printer, 1965), Appendix I.
5. To cite J.L. Granatstein, this provision was inserted in the original text of the mandate and was very much an "afterthought, along with the addition of two representatives of the ethnic communities to the

Commission: inclusion of ethnics smacked of nothing so much as tokenism" (J.L. Granatsein, *Canada: 1957–1967* [Toronto: McClelland and Stewart, 1968], 6).

6. Laurendeau had proposed the Commission in "Pour une enquête sur le bilinguisme," *Le Devoir*, 20 Jan. 1962. To be sure, as the Comité pour une politique fonctionnelle (see below) was to emphasize, Laurendeau's article had not mentioned biculturalism, referring only to bilingualism. Yet, as the "blue pages" attest, there can be no doubt that biculturalism was a central concept for Laurendeau. According to Donald Horton, it was after conversations with Laurendeau that Maurice Lamontagne proposed making biculturalism part of the projected commission's mandate. See Donald J. Horton, *André Laurendeau: French-Canadian Nationalist, 1912–1968* (Toronto: Oxford University Press, 1992), 250. Claude Ryan insists that Laurendeau would not have agreed to co-chair a commission devoted to language rights without considering the political context. See Claude Ryan, "Il a soulevé les vraies questions et refuté les réponses toutes faites," in *André Laurendeau: un intellectuel d'ici*, ed. Robert Comeau and Lucille Beaudry (Montreal: Presses de l'Université du Québec, 1990), 279.
7. Claude Ryan, "L'Aide aux groupes ethniques exige-t-elle l'abandon du biculturalisme?" *Le Devoir*, 9 Oct. 1971.
8. B&B Commission, *General Introduction* (Ottawa: Queen's Printer, 1967), xxxi.
9. Ibid.
10. Ibid., xxxiii.
11. Ibid. For the Commission, a society consisted of institutions and organizations that share "a rather large population" and extend over "quite a vast territory" where that population lives as "a homogenous group according to common standards and rules of conduct." And the Commission acknowledged that it is in precisely these terms that, in its *Preliminary Report*, it had recognized "the main elements of a distinct French-speaking society in Quebec." The Commission took pains to note that this French-speaking society was not restricted to Quebec alone since "elements of an autonomous society are taking shape elsewhere." But it saw Quebec as the heart of the Francophone side of Canadian duality.
12. To use ethnicity as a basic organizing principle of society would be objectionable on moral, as well as practical grounds, since it "would tend to create closed-membership groups with newcomers condemned to remain outsiders." Ibid., xxiii.
13. Ibid., xxv. And the Commission was clear that it was only as part of one society or the other that these individuals could participate in Canadian life; none of the various "ethnic" groups had a sufficiently comprehensive set of organizations and institutions to qualify as societies. See the analysis of the Commission's views in Michael Oliver, "The Impact of the Royal Commission on Bilingualism and Biculturalism on Constitutional Theory and Practice," *International Journal of Canadian Studies* 7–8 (Spring–Fall 1993): 320.
14. B&B Commission, *Book I*, xlv.
15. Ibid.
16. Ibid., xlvii.
17. Alan C. Cairns, *Citizens Plus: Aboriginal Peoples and the Canadian State* (Vancouver: UBC Press, 2000), 52.
18. Statement of the Government of Canada on Indian Policy, 1969, 1.
19. Ibid., 5.
20. Ibid., 1.
21. "Prime Minister Trudeau: Remarks on Aboriginal and Treaty Rights. Excerpts from a Speech Given August 8th, 1979, in Vancouver, British Columbia," Peter Cumming and Neil H. Mickenberg, *Native Rights in Canada*, 2nd edn (Toronto: Indian Eskimo Association of Canada, 1972), Appendix VI. See the commentary in John Borrows, *Recovering Canada: The Resurgence of Indigenous Law* (Toronto: University of Toronto Press, 2002), 102–3.
22. Sally M. Weaver, *Making Canadian Indian Policy: The Hidden Agenda 1968–1970* (Toronto: University of Toronto Press, 1981), 179.
23. Statement on Indian Policy, section 5 Claims and Treaties.
24. Weaver, *Making Canadian Indian Policy*, 166–8.
25. Ibid., 185.
26. "Prime Minister Trudeau: Remarks on Aboriginal and Treaty Rights."
27. "The White Paper, 1969," *Indigenousfoundations. Arts.ubc.ca*.
28. H.B. Hawthorn, *A Survey of the Contemporary Indians of Canada: Economic, Political,*

Educational Needs and Policies (Ottawa: Queen's Printer, 1968) vol. I, 13.

29. Naithan Lagace and Niigaanwewidam James Sinclair, "The White Paper, 1969," *The Canadian Encyclopedia* (Toronto: Historica Canada, 2015).
30. Peter H. Russell, *Canada's Odyssey: A Country Based on Incomplete Conquests* (Toronto: University of Toronto Press, 2017), 327–30.
31. Raymond Breton, "Multiculturalism and Canadian Nation-Building," in *The Politics of Gender: Ethnicity and Language in Canada*, Collected Research Studies of the Royal Commission on the Economic Union and Development Prospects for Canada, vol. 34, ed. Alan Cairns and Cynthia Williams (Toronto: University of Toronto Press, 1986), 44. Breton contends that "the concerns of the non-British, non-French segment of the society were not primarily with cultural maintenance." Instead, they reflected "status anxiety" (49).
32. Eve Haque, *Multiculturalism within a Bilingual Framework: Language, Race and Belonging in Canada* (Toronto: University of Toronto Press, 2012), Chap. 4, and Pal, *Interest of State*, 114. Because of this reaction, Gérard Pelletier regretted the Pearson government's charging the Commission with the very term "biculturalism" (Gérard Pelletier, *L'aventure au pouvoir: 1968-1975* [Montreal: Stanké, 1992], 63).
33. House of Commons, *Debates*, 22 July 1963, 2440.
34. Ibid., 2443.
35. Michael Temelini, "Multicultural Rights, Multicultural Virtues: A History of Multiculturalism in Canada," in *Multiculturalism and the Canadian Constitution*, ed. Stephen J. Tierney (Vancouver: UBC Press, 2008), 48.
36. Senate, *Debates*, 3 Mar. 1964, 51–8. Yuzyk's insistence on multiculturalism did not prevent him from ending his speech with the observation that "fundamentally we are a Christian . . . nation" (58).
37. John Jaworsky, "A Case Study of the Canadian Federal Government's Multiculturalism Policy," M.A. thesis, Political Science Dept., Carleton University, Sept. 1979, 49. See also Peter Stursberg, *Lester Pearson and the Dream of Unity* (Toronto: Doubleday, 1978), 141.
38. Jaworsky, "Federal Government's Multiculturalism Policy," 50. See also Horton, *André Laurendeau*, 225.
39. B&B Commission, *Book I: The Official Languages*, 155–69. An extended treatment of Rudnyckyj and critical assessment of his proposal appears in Roberto Perin, "Un adversaire du bilinguisme officiel à la Commission Laurendeau–Dunton," forthcoming in *Bulletin d'histoire politique*. See also Valérie Lapointe-Gagnon, "Penser et 'panser' les plaies du Canada: le moment Laurendeau-Dunton, 1963-1971," Doctoral thesis, Department of History, Laval University, 2013, 234–7.
40. B&B Commission, *Book IV: The Cultural Contribution of the Other Ethnic Groups* (Ottawa: Queen's Printer, 1970), 228–30.
41. Evelyn Kallen, "Multiculturalism: Ideology, Policy and Reality," *Journal of Canadian Studies* 17, no. 1 (Spring 1982), 53, and Richard Gwyn, *The Northern Magus* (Toronto: McClelland & Stewart, 1980), 231.
42. A member of the Commission, Paul Lacoste, declared, "Tout en étant très ouvert aux diverses cultures, il [Laurendeau] rejetait énergiquement la conception d'un Canada bilingue mais multiculturel." See Paul Lacoste, "André Laurendeau et la commission sur le bilinguisme et le biculturalisme," in *André Laurendeau*, ed. R. Comeau and L. Beaudry, 209.
43. B&B Commission, *Book IV: The Cultural Contribution*, 13. This is also the interpretation of Temelini, "Multicultural Rights, Multicultural Virtues," 54.
44. B&B Commission, *Book IV: The Cultural Contribution*, 10.
45. Ibid., 4.
46. As Temelini notes, while Trudeau claimed to be accepting the B&B recommendations in Volume 4, none of the 16 recommendations used the term "multiculturalism" (Temelini, "Multicultural Rights, Multicultural Virtues," 55). While the Commission did not formally abandon biculturalism for multiculturalism, Lapointe-Gagnon contends that the commissioners themselves were divided on the question during the Commission's later years. In the absence of a clear consensus around biculturalism, there was growing support for multiculturalism. She points, in particular, to the impact of both Rudnyckyj's interventions

and lobbying by Ukrainian organizations. (Lapointe-Gagnon, "Penser et 'panser' les plaies du Canada," 274–82.)

47. These data are taken from Breton, "Multiculturalism and Canadian Nation-Building," 34–5.
48. Bruno Ramirez and Sylvie Taschereau, "Les Minorités: le multiculturalisme appliqué," in Yves Bélanger, Dorval Brunelle, et al., *L'ère des Libéraux: le pouvoir fédéral de 1963 à 1984* (Sillery, Quebec: Presses de l'Université du Québec, 1988), 386.
49. This is the conclusion of Jaworsky, who cites "notable lack of effective coordination among representatives" of ethnic groups and "difficulty in demonstrating grass roots support." See Jaworsky, "Federal Government's Multiculturalism Policy," 56.
50. Kallen, "Multiculturalism," 55; and Jaworsky, "Federal Government's Multiculturalism Policy," 53. Raymond Breton has the same finding and states that "This does not suggest a widespread mobilization across groups" (Breton, "Multiculturalism and Canadian Nation-Building," 47).
51. Jaworsky, "Federal Government's Multiculturalism Policy," 55.
52. Ibid., 50–1.
53. Breton, "Multiculturalism and Canadian Nation-Building," 45–6.
54. English, *Just Watch Me*, 143.
55. Breton, "Multiculturalism and Canadian Nation-Building," 47.
56. Varun Uberoi, "Do Policies of Multiculturalism Change National Identities?" *The Political Quarterly* 79, no. 3 (July–Sept. 2008): 411; and Varun Uberoi, "Multiculturalism and the Canadian Charter of Rights and Freedoms," *Political Studies* 57 (2009): 809.
57. English, *Just Watch Me*, 144.
58. In the words of John English, Trudeau "agreed to recognize 'other' groups as his political advisers insisted he must," English, *Just Watch Me*, 146.
59. Breton, "Multiculturalism and Canadian Nation-Building," 47. Soon after the announcement of the policy, Ralph Heintzman offered a similar interpretation in "In the Bosom of a Single State," *Journal of Canadian Studies* 6, no. 4 (Nov. 1971): 63. Garth Stevenson has written, "As concept and symbol, multiculturalism may serve a number of purposes. For Trudeau, its primary purpose was to undermine and destroy the older ideological symbol of 'deux nations.'" Stevenson says that the very term "multiculturalism" was "invented by Prime Minister Trudeau." See Garth Stevenson, "Multiculturalism: As Canadian as Apple Pie," *Inroads*, no. 4 (1995): 74.
60. This is reported by Jaworsky on the basis of an interview with Ostry. In addition, Ostry recounted, Trudeau and Pelletier thought that multiculturalism might ease some of the opposition to official bilingualism. See Jaworsky, "Federal Government's Multiculturalism Policy," 59. This interpretation is also offered by Amy Nugent, "Demography, National Myths, and Political Origins: Perceiving Official Multiculturalism in Quebec," *Ethnic Studies* 38, no. 3 (2006): 31.
61. "Federal Government's Response to Book IV of the Report of the Royal Commission on Bilingualism and Biculturalism," House of Commons, *Debates*, Appendix, 8580–5. The document also details how the government is responding to each of the Commission's recommendations. Somewhat ingenuously, the document declares that "the government accepts and endorses the recommendations and *spirit* of Book IV" (ibid., 8580).
62. P.E. Trudeau, "Announcement of Implementation of Policy of Multiculturalism within Bilingual Framework," House of Commons, *Debates*, 8 Oct. 1971, 8581.
63. Ibid., 8546.
64. Ibid.
65. Ibid., 8545.
66. John English sees strengths and weaknesses in Trudeau's attitude and position on multiculturalism. The weaknesses are that "he shaped the statement in such a way that it was consistent with his carefully developed views on the role of an individual within society. In doing so, he could not resist remarks that he surely knew would inflame many in Quebec" (English, *Just Watch Me*, 146–7).
67. B&B Commission, *Book IV: The Cultural Contribution of the Other Ethnic Groups*, 5.
68. "Federal Government's Response," 8580. In effect, it draws upon the arguments of contemporary American sociologist William Kornhauser (William Kornhauser, *The Politics of Mass Society* [New York:

Free Press, 1959]). This is a surprising theoretical inspiration for Trudeau whose writings were situated primarily within British and American liberal philosophy. Perhaps he was not the sole author of the document.

69. "Federal Government's Response," 8581.
70. In a recent statement, Will Kymlicka insists that individual freedom has been part of Canadian multiculturalism from the outset and cites Trudeau's statements to that effect. In doing so, Kymlicka stresses the freedom of individuals to express a specifically ethnic identity: "multiculturalism from the start, has been understood in Canada as a policy of reducing the barriers and stigmas that limit the ability of individuals to freely explore and express their ethnic identities" (Will Kymlicka, "The Three Lives of Multiculturalism," in *Revisiting Multiculturalism in Canada*, ed. S. Guo and L. Wong [Rotterdam: Sense, 2015], 20).
71. Kallen notes that Trudeau's policy did not hold "the ideal model of cultural pluralism which assumes that every individual and group desires to maintain a distinctive ethnic identity and heritage" since it "gives recognition to the fact that some people will, inevitably, find greater human affinities *outside* their ethnic group than within it." See Kallen, "Multiculturalism," 53 (emphasis in original).
72. Ibid., 8545.
73. Hugh Donald Forbes, "Trudeau as the First Theorist of Canadian Multiculturalism" in Tierney, *Multiculturalism and the Canadian Constitution*, 40.
74. Forbes, "Trudeau as the First Theorist," 34. Contending that Trudeau "was the first and remains the most authoritative theorist of Canadian multiculturalism" (39), Forbes goes on to give Trudeau credit for a broad multicultural strategy that included anti-discrimination legislation, affirmative action, anti-hate legislation, and a non-discriminatory immigration policy. This may, in fact, be giving Trudeau too much credit. Anti-discriminatory legislation was becoming a norm before Trudeau assumed office and had already been adopted provincially. The shift to a new immigration policy was initiated under Pearson's leadership. While affirmative action proposals may have emerged within the Trudeau government, it remains to be seen whether they had his personal approval given his highly individualist beliefs. As we have seen, Trudeau avoided any notion of affirmative action in his efforts to create a bilingual federal public service.
75. David Miller, "The Life and Death of Multiculturalism," paper presented at Glendon College, York University, 19 Ap. 2016, 4.
76. "Federal Government's Response," 8582. The B&B Commission did call for "support for cultural and research organizations whose objectives are to foster the arts and letters of cultural groups" but not for funding of the general organizational activities of cultural groups nor did it call for the preparation of histories of ethnic groups (B&B Commission, *Book IV: The Cultural Contribution of the Other Ethnic Groups*, 228–30).
77. As Forbes notes, if these policy objectives had been limited to Canada's demography of 1971 they would have amounted to the rearrangement of status among European groups and, as such, would not have been of compelling interest. They have to be understood in terms of an immigration policy geared to a broad diversification of the Canadian population (Forbes, "Trudeau as the First Theorist," 39).
78. Will Kymlicka notes the incoherence of the proclamation: "We now know that there was no well-developed theory underlying the original policy. It was introduced in haste, largely as a way of deflecting opposition to the apparent privileging of French and English that was implicit in the introduction of official bilingualism. Multiculturalism was introduced without any real idea of what it would mean, or any long-term strategy for its implementation." (Will Kymlicka, *Finding Our Way: Rethinking Ethnocultural Relations in Canada* [Toronto: Oxford University Press, 1998], 42).
79. Trudeau, "Announcement of Implementation," 8545.
80. "Federal Government's Response," 8580 (emphasis added).
81. Temelini, "Multicultural Rights, Multicultural Virtues," 55.
82. Ibid., 50.
83. Uberoi notes that Trudeau's October 1980 statement on unilateral patriation included

the proposal that the Charter have a preamble. He contends that a draft preamble prepared by the federal government did contain a reference to Canada's multicultural nature. The Quebec government's objection to this reference to multiculturalism, wanting to substitute biculturalism, is one of the reasons that the federal government abandoned the effort to secure a preamble. It appears that, in any event, Trudeau was not firmly committed to the Charter having a preamble, preferring to define Canadian values through the Charter itself. Thus, the preamble of Bill C-60, the government's 1978 proposal, refers obliquely to Canada's diversity but doesn't actually use the term "multiculturalism." (Uberoi, "Multiculturalism and the Canadian Charter," 812 and 815.)

84. These organizations include the Canadian Ethnocultural Council, Canadian Consultative Council on Multiculturalism, the Ukrainian Canadian Committee, and the Chinese Canadian National Council for Equality (Pal, *Interests of State*, 205, and Uberoi, "Multiculturalism and the Canadian Charter," 815).
85. Uberoi shows that these groups were concerned that a reference to multiculturalism should appear in a proposed preamble as well as among the provisions of the Charter itself (Uberoi, "Multiculturalism and the Canadian Charter," 815).
86. Peter H. Russell, *Constitutional Odyssey: Can Canadians Become a Sovereign People?* 3rd edn (Toronto: University of Toronto Press, 2004), 111–15.
87. Jack Jedwab, "To Preserve and Enhance: Canadian Multiculturalism before and after the Charter," in *The Canadian Charter of Rights and Freedoms: Reflections on the Charter after Twenty Years*, ed. Joseph Eliot Magnet et al., (Markham: LexisNexis Canada, 2003), 309–44.
88. Miller, "Life and Death of Multiculturalism," 2–3.
89. Breton, "Multiculturalism and Canadian Nation-Building," 49.
90. The following account draws heavily from Pal, *Interests of State*, 136–40, and Breton, "Multiculturalism and Canadian Nation-Building," 51–3.
91. Breton, "Multiculturalism and Canadian Nation-Building," 52.
92. Pal, *Interests of State*, 136, and Jaworsky, "Federal Government's Multiculturalism Policy," 56.
93. Pal, *Interests of State*, 137.
94. Breton, "Multiculturalism and Canadian Nation-Building," 57.
95. As Manoly R. Lupul, a Ukrainian-Canadian scholar and activist, has written:

    Multiculturalism is not central to Trudeau's thinking, just as ethnicity is not central to his being. . . . In accepting multiculturalism as government policy, there is no reason to believe that he felt deeply about what he was doing. . . . Sheltered by his home and schooling even from Montreal's ethnic diversity, Trudeau never acquired first-hand knowledge of life in a multicultural society. . . . He is no ethnic; his bilingualism and biculturalism is not private and its reference point is not remote." (Manoly R. Lupul, "The Political Implementation of Multiculturalism," *Journal of Canadian Studies* 17, no. 1 [Spring 1982]: 96–7.)

96. Ibid., 98. Jaworsky comments, "Initially Trudeau and his advisors may have had an intellectual interest in the multiculturalism policy, hoping that it would provide a constructive alternative to the potentially divisive dichotomy posed by a policy of bilingualism and biculturalism. It appears, however, that they soon lost interest in the policy." See Jaworsky, "Federal Government's Multiculturalism Policy," 122.
97. Ibid., 124.
98. Ibid., 95–6.
99. Daiva K. Stasiulis, "The Symbolic Mosaic Reaffirmed: Multiculturalism Policy," in *How Ottawa Spends, 1988–89*, ed. Katherine A. Graham, (Ottawa: Carleton University Press, 1988), 95.
100. The phrase appears as a description of multicultural programming in Biles, "Canada's Multiculturalism Program," 12.
101. Kymlicka argues that concern with race was adopted "on top of" ethnicity, just as religion was adopted at a later point (Kymlicka, "Three Lives of Multiculturalism," 22).
102. Daiva Stasiulis and Yasmeen Abu-Laban, "Unequal Relations and the Struggle for Equality: Race and Ethnicity in Canadian politics," in *Canadian Politics in the 21st*

Century, ed. Michael Whittington and Glen Williams (Toronto: Thomson Nelson, 2008), 303.
103. McAndrew et al., "Heritage Languages to Institutional Change," 157–9. While responsibility for Heritage Languages apparently was left with Canadian Heritage in the 2008 reorganization, they do not seem to figure among Canadian Heritage's funding programs. See Canadian Heritage, "Funding Opportunities," 1 Sept. 2016.
104. McAndrew et al., "Heritage Languages to Institutional Change," Table 4.
105. This paragraph draws from Michael Dewing, "Canadian Multiculturalism," Library of Parliament, Canada, 2013 (#2009-20-E), 5–8. See also Yasmeen Abu-Laban, "Reform by Stealth: The Harper Conservatives and Canadian Multiculturalism," in Jedwab, *The Multiculturalism Question*, 149–72.
106. The Liberals did introduce a bill to Parliament in 1984 but too close to dissolution for the bill to be adopted.
107. Varon Uberoi, "Legislating Multiculturalism and Nationhood: The 1988 Canadian Multiculturalism Act," *Canadian Journal of Political Science* 49, no. 2 (June 2016): 267–87.
108. Pal, *Interests of State*, 138–9.
109. Canada, Canadian Multiculturalism Act, R.S.C., 1985, c. 24 (4th Supp.), 3(1).
110. "Multiculturalism reflects the cultural and racial diversity of Canadian society," Multiculturalism Act, 3(1)(a). The 1971 proclamation had referred to culture and ethnicity but not race.
111. Multiculturalism Act, Preamble.
112. Hector Mackenzie, "Does History Mean Always Having to Say You're Sorry?" *Canadian Issues*, Winter 2010, 47–50; and Mitch Miyagawa, "A Sorry State," *The Walrus*, Dec. 2009.
113. Canada, House of Commons, *Debates*, 32nd Parliament, 2nd Session, vol. 4 (1984), 5306–7, as quoted in John Biles, "The Government of Canada's Multiculturalism Program," in Jedwab, *The Multiculturalism Question*, 19.
114. Yasmeen Abu-Laban, "Reform by Stealth," in Jedwab, *The Multiculturalism Question*, 158.
115. The apology was made to "lesbian, gay, bisexual, transgender, queer, and two-spirit (LGBTQ2)" individuals who had been harmed by "federal legislation, policies and practice" ("Prime Minister Delivers Apology to LGBTQ2 Canadians," https://pm.gc.ca/eng/news. On 24 Nov. 2017, Trudeau announced an apology to former students of Newfoundland and Labrador residential schools. They had not been covered by the Harper government's apology for residential schools.
116. Randy Besca and Erin Tolley, "Does Everyone Cheer? The Politics of Immigration and Multiculturalism in Canada," paper presented to conference on "New Frontiers in Public Policy," Queen's University, 23 Sept. 2016.
117. Neil Bissoondath, *Selling Illusions: The Cult of Multiculturalism in Canada* (Toronto: Penguin, 1994).
118. Will Kymlicka, "The Canadian Model of Diversity" in Tierney, *Multiculturalism and the Canadian Constitution*, 72–4.
119. Keith Banting, "Is There a Progressive's Dilemma in Canada? Immigration, Multiculturalism and the Welfare State," *Canadian Journal of Political Science* 43, no. 4 (Dec. 2010): 809–13.
120. It is unclear whether the Institute actually was created.
121. Alberta allowed the use of non-official languages as the language of instruction in public schools in 1971. Saskatchewan did so in 1978, and Manitoba in 1979. By 1990, all three provincial governments were financially supporting bilingual programs in which Ukrainian or German is the language of instruction up to 100 per cent of the time in kindergarten and up to 50 per cent of the time thereafter. Alberta has other programs of instruction in English and another language—namely, Yiddish, Arabic, Polish, or Chinese. These data are drawn from Jim Cummins and Marcel Danesi, *Heritage Languages: The Development and Denial of Canada's Linguistic Resources* (Toronto: Our Schools/Our Selves Foundation, 1990), 26.
122. In 1978, the Fédération des francophones hors du Québec declared, "Another threat to the cultural identity and activity of Francophones outside Quebec is the concept of Canada as a bilingual but multicultural country. This federal policy, which has many followers among the provincial governments, pushes us too easily and subtly to the background, to the same level as any other ethnic minority." (The Federation of Francophones outside Quebec, *The Heirs of Lord Durham: Manifesto of a Vanishing People* [Toronto: Burns and MacEachern,

1978], 65, as quoted in Jaworsky, "Federal Government's Multiculturalism Policy," 86).

123. Haque contends that "The maintenance of these divisions [among English, French, Aboriginal, and 'Multicultural'] was a central concern of the B and B Commission, which sidelined the contesting subnational interests of 'other ethnic' and Indigenous groups in the larger project of establishing a new bicultural form of Canadian white-settler nationalism." Haque, *Multiculturalism in a Bilingual Framework*, 18. A similar argument is made in Thomas Ricento, "The Consequences of Official Bilingualism on the Status and Perception of Non-Official Languages in Canada," *Journal of Multilingual and Multicultural Development* 34, no. 5 (2013): 475–89.
124. B&B Commission, *Book I: The Official Languages*, xxv.
125. See Lapointe-Gagnon, "Penser et 'panser' les plaies du Canada," 22–3.
126. More precisely, Rudnyckyj proposed that non-official languages be recognized as "regional languages" when they constitute 10 per cent or more of an administrative unit's population and that services be provided within the units in that language. Canada, B&B Commission, *Book I: The Official Languages*, 168.
127. Rudnyckyj did recommend that the proposed Official Languages Act be dubbed simply Languages Act and that the proposed commissioner be the Commissioner of Languages in Canada (ibid., 169).
128. Calculated from Tables 8 and 9 in Canada, B&B Commission, *Book I: The Official Languages*.
129. Statistics Canada, "Update of the 2016 Census Language Data," 23 Aug. 2017, Table 1 ("neither English nor French" constituted 1.9 per cent).
130. B&B Commission, *Book I: The Official Languages*, Table 4.
131. Statistics Canada, "Update of the 2016 Census," Table 1.
132. Calculated from Statistics Canada, "Linguistic Diversity and Multilingualism in Canadian Homes," Table 1 (using 33,948,620 for total Canadian population, as calculated from ibid., Table 3).
133. Trudeau, *Federalism and the French Canadians*, 31.
134. Robert Everett-Green, "Trudeau Promises Aboriginal Language Bill, but Activists Say Whole System Needs Overhaul," *Globe and Mail*, 28 Dec. 2016.
135. Breton, "Multiculturalism and Canadian Nation-Building," 50.
136. This is greater than the response for hockey (47 per cent). (Irene Bloemraad, "Reimagining the Nation in a World of Migration: Legitimacy, Political Claims-Making, and Membership in Comparative Perspective," in *Fear, Anxiety and National Identity: Immigration and Belonging in North American and Europe*, ed. Nancy Foner and Patrick Simon [New York: Russell Sage Foundation, 2015], 59.)
137. Richard Johnston, Keith Banting, Will Kymlicka, and Stuart Soroka, "National Identity and Support for the Welfare State," *Canadian Journal of Political Science* 43, no. 2 (June 2010): 369. Another study found that, unlike in the United States, in Canada attachment to the country is positively associated with support for multiculturalism, as well as openness to immigration. The authors are careful to distinguish between Quebec Francophones, for whom the object of patriotism may be Quebec rather than Canada, and Canadians outside Quebec. The relationship holds for the latter. (Jack Citrin, Richard Johnston, and Matthew Wright, "Do Patriotism and Multiculturalism Collide? Competing Perspectives from Canada and the United States," *Canadian Journal of Political Science* 45, no. 3 [Sept. 2012]: 531–52.)
138. Ramirez and Taschereau, "Les minorités," 391.
139. The text of Bourassa's statement is reproduced in *Le Devoir*, 17 Nov. 1971, 2.
140. Jaworsky, "Federal Government's Multiculturalism Policy," 84.
141. Claude Ryan, "L'aide aux groupes ethniques exige-t-elle l'abandon du biculturalisme?" *Le Devoir*, 9 Oct. 1971.
142. Guy Rocher, "Multiculturalism: The Doubts of a Francophone," in *Multiculturalism as State Policy: Conference Report*, Second Canadian Conference on Multiculturalism, Canadian Consultative Council on Multiculturalism (Ottawa: Dept. of Supply and Services, 1976), 52.
143. See, for instance, Christian Dufour, *A Canadian Challenge / Le défi québécois* (Lantzville, BC, and Halifax, NS: Oolichan Books and IRPP, 1990), 79; and Louis Balthazar,

"Pour un multiculturalisme québécois," *Action nationale* 79 (Oct. 1989): 942–53.

144. Danielle Juteau, "La citoyenneté québécoise face au pluralisme," unpublished paper, n. 7; and Daniel Weinstock, "What Is Really at Stake in the Multiculturalism/Interculturalism Debate?" in Jedwab, *The Multicultural Question*, 188–90.
145. Geneviève Nootens, "Nationalism, Pluralism and Democratic Governance" in Jedwab, *The Multiculturalism Question*, 174.
146. Weinstock, "What Is Really at Stake?"
147. English, *Just Watch Me*, 146–7.
148. The Quebec Charter of Rights and Freedoms, adopted under the Bourassa government in 1975, refers specifically to the right of "persons belonging to ethnic minorities . . . to maintain and develop their own cultural interests with the other members of their group" (section 43). As Jedwab notes, section 27 of the Charter of Rights and Freedoms "makes no direct reference to ethnic groups" (Jedwab, "Canadian Multiculturalism," 331.)
149. In the wake of the defeated 1995 referendum on sovereignty, the Quebec government sought to integrate non-Francophones more effectively by developing the notion of a Quebec citizenship. However, the project fell into abeyance given resistance among the ethnocultural communities who felt that the notion of a common citizenship both marginalized them and was inspired by sovereigntist ambitions. Indeed, Danielle Juteau argues that the idea of a Quebec citizenship clashed with the pluralism that had marked the development during the 1980s and early 1990s of the notion of "cultural communities" and interculturalism. (Danielle Juteau, "La citoyenneté québécoise face au pluralisme," unpublished paper.
150. This account is drawn primarily from Marie McAndrew, "Multiculturalisme canadien et interculturalisme québécois: mythes et réalités," unpublished paper. See also Danielle Juteau, "The Canadian Experiment: Multiculturalism as Ideology and Policy," paper presented to Conference on Cultural Diversity in Europe, Berlin, 1990; Danielle Juteau, Marie McAndrew, and Linda Pietrantonio, "Multiculturalism à la Canadian and Intégration à la Québécoise: Transcending Their Limits," unpublished paper.
151. The report of the Larose commission on the French language is discussed in Juteau, "La citoyenneté québécoise," 13.
152. "The Order in Council establishing the Commission stipulated that it had a mandate to: a) take stock of accommodation practices in Québec; b) analyse the attendant issues bearing in mind the experience of other societies; c) conduct an extensive consultation on this topic; and d) formulate recommendations to the government to ensure that accommodation practices conform to Québec's values as a pluralistic, democratic, egalitarian society." Gérard Bouchard and Charles Taylor, *Building the Future: A Time for Reconciliation*, (Québec: Consultation Commission on Accommodation Practices Related to Cultural Differences, 2008), 34.
153. Ibid., 18.
154. Ibid.
155. Ibid., 121.
156. Ibid., 124.
157. Ibid.
158. Ibid., 124–7.
159. Ibid., 140.
160. Ibid., 266–83.
161. Reactions to the report are well summarized in Miriam Chiasson, "The Reasonable Accommodation Crisis," Centre for Human Rights and Legal Pluralism, McGill University, Aug. 2012. The relative failure to apply the report's recommendations is documented in Stéphane Baillargeon, "Dix ans après Bouchard-Taylor, tant reste à faire," *Le Devoir*, 4 Feb. 2017.
162. Québec, National Assembly, "Bill 60: Charter affirming the values of State secularism and religious neutrality and of equality between women and men, and providing a framework for accommodation requests," Québec Official Publisher, 2013.
163. The one reference to female–male equality appears in section 15, outlining the conditions for religious accommodation.
164. Ibid., section 5.
165. Ibid., section 7.
166. Ibid., section 39.
167. Radio-Canada.ca, "Pour ou contre la charte des valeurs?" 7 Nov. 2013.
168. "Charles Taylor et Gérard Bouchard dénoncent une charte nuisible," *Le Devoir*, 8 Nov. 2013.
169. Juteau, "La citoyenneté québécoise," 18 and 25.

170. As with the 1980s debates over constitutional patriation and the Meech Lake Accord, there is little evidence of collaboration between Quebec organizations and their counterparts outside Quebec. (Federal party leaders did publicly oppose Bill 60, as did the Canadian Civil Liberties Union and B'nai Brith Canada [Radio-Canada, "Pour ou contre la charte des valeurs"]).
171. Guillaume Piedboeuf, "L'extrême droite plus visible à Québec," *Le Soleil*, 1 Feb. 2017; and Isabelle Porter, "L'extrême droite de Québec sort de l'ombre," *Le Devoir*, 2 Feb. 2017.
172. Charles Taylor, "Neutralité de l'État: le temps de la reconciliation" *La Presse*, 14 Feb. 2017.
173. Quebec National Assembly, Bill 62: "An Act to foster adherence to State religious neutrality and, in particular, to provide a framework for requests for accommodations on religious grounds in certain bodies," 41st Legislature, 1st Session.
174. Lisa-Marie Gervais, "Gérard Bouchard juge la loi sur la neutralité religieuse peu utile and difficile à appliquer," *Le Devoir*, 20 Oct. 2017.
175. Jeanne Corriveau, "Coderre mal à l'aise à l'égard du projet de loi sur la neutralité religieuse," 8 Oct. 2017.
176. Respondents were asked to complete this sentence: "A woman visiting a government office in a 'niqab'—a veil worn by some Muslim women when they are out in public, covering all of the face except for the eyes—should be . . ." In the case of Quebec, the responses were as follows: 70 per cent marked "prohibited"; 23 per cent said "discouraged but tolerated"; and 8 per cent said "welcome." Outside Quebec, the responses were 40 per cent, 31 per cent, and 28 per cent, respectively. (Angus Reid and Daschi Kurl, "Religion, Multiculturalism and the Public Square," *Policy Options*, IRPP, 4 Dec. 2017, Figure 2.)
177. When asked "In Canada, organized religions qualify for special tax consideration. Would you say this . . . ," the majority of Quebec respondents answered, "is not reasonable—time to get rid of it" (55 per cent) as opposed to "is a reasonable policy—keep it in place" (45 per cent). In all other provinces, the majorities chose the latter option. (Reid and Daschi Kurl, "Religion, Multiculturalism and the Public Square," Figure 5.)
178. They note that "Canada is for many a multi-nation state, in which the Québécois see themselves and are increasingly seen by others as a distinct nation and the Aboriginal peoples define themselves as First Nations," (Johnston et al., "National Identity and Support for the Welfare State," 356).
179. Elke Winter, "A Canadian Anomaly? The Social Construction of Multicultural National Identity," in *Revisiting Multiculturalism in Canada*, ed. Cho and Wong, 51–68.
180. See note 68.
181. Charles Taylor, "The Politics of Recognition," in Charles Taylor, *Multiculturalism and The Politics of Recognition* (Princeton, N.J.: Princeton University Press, 1992), 51–61.
182. Taylor also includes Indigenous people within his conception of deep diversity (Charles Taylor, *Reconciling the Solitudes* [Montreal and Kingston: McGill-Queen's University Press, 1993], 182–3).
183. See Kymlicka's discussion of "polyethnic rights" in Will Kymlicka, *Multicultural Citizenship* (Oxford: Oxford University Press, 1995), 35–44 and 113–15.
184. Will Kymlicka, *Finding Our Way: Rethinking Ethnocultural Relations in Canada* (Toronto: Oxford University Press, 1998), Chap. 10.

Chapter 6

Federalism and the Constitution

Entrenching the Trudeau Vision

By putting in place the Official Languages Act, Pierre Trudeau addressed what he had long seen as a fundamental failing of Canadian political life. With his proclamation of multiculturalism, he repudiated any notion that Canada is a bicultural country. Both of these actions were shaped by the principles that Trudeau had championed for so many years: individualist liberalism and fierce opposition to nationalism, especially Quebec nationalism. A third, and far more daunting, challenge remained: transforming Canada's political institutions to reflect these same principles. Canadian federalism had to be reshaped, enlarging the role for the federal government as the government of all Canadians and normalizing the role of the Quebec government so as to be a province like the others. Even more challenging, Canada's constitution needed to be patriated, so that Canada could be fully sovereign and incorporate a charter of rights—especially language rights. This transformation of federalism and the constitution had to reflect Trudeau's individualist liberalism and, in particular, had to advance his goal of defeating Quebec nationalism. The struggle to achieve this objective was to guide, and even consume, his 16 years in power. By the end, Canada's political institutions were indeed transformed, even if Quebec nationalism was far from extinguished.

Trudeau's ambitions for both federalism and the constitution directly challenged assumptions that, as we have seen, had long dominated Francophone Quebec. The first assumption was that the role of the federal government should be restricted to the jurisdictions explicitly assigned to it by the BNA Act. Thus, even the Tremblay Report, not to mention the new Quebec nationalism of the 1960s, had dictated that much of Ottawa's post–Second World War edifice of social, cultural, and economic programs had to be dismantled as an improper intrusion in provincial jurisdiction. The second assumption was that Quebec was unique among the provinces, as the centre of Canada's Francophone collectivity. This basic premise had been a constant theme of Francophone thought from

Henri Bourassa's designation of Quebec as the "special inheritance" of all French Canadians to the Tremblay Commission's call for Quebec to be recognized as a "national" government to the Lesage government's schemes to grant Quebec new powers to meet its special responsibilities. Finally, it went without saying that Quebec and its government had to be party to any change in the constitutional framework. Canada was, after all, based on a compact, indeed a "double compact" of which Quebec was a senior party. So firmly embedded were these assumptions in Francophone Quebec that to challenge them was to run the risk of a powerful, even sovereigntist, response. Yet Pierre Trudeau was fully prepared to run the risk. Moreover, soon after assuming power as prime minister he found himself exceedingly well placed to do it.

Under the leadership of André Laurendeau, the Royal Commission on Bilingualism and Biculturalism had articulated an understanding of the country, and Quebec's place within it, that was fully congruent with these long-held assumptions. Laurendeau himself harboured ambitions for constitutional revision, focused on Quebec, that contradicted Trudeau's plans head on. There was no doubt in Laurendeau's mind that Canada's crisis could not be resolved on the basis of official bilingualism alone, however widespread it might be. There also had to be a redefinition of Quebec's position in the constitution: the "blue pages" of the first volume of the Commission's final report, with their broad treatment of "equal partnership" and "biculturalism" and their emphasis on Quebec as a "distinct society," give a clear sense of what he envisaged as necessary. Indeed, he had come to the conclusion that "a very special status" was needed for Quebec.[1] With this in mind, he had wanted the constitutional issues to be addressed in the first volume of the Commission's final report. Nonetheless, unable to overcome resistance to his plans among several other commissioners, led by Frank Scott, he had had to settle for the possibility that such discussions might be addressed in a final volume.[2] With Laurendeau's sudden death in June 1968, at age 56, that possibility disappeared.[3] Paul Lacoste, the first commission co-secretary who had become commissioner in 1965, took up the cause, contending that a final volume should deal with constitutional issues and, in particular, his notion of special status. But once again Scott and his supporters carried the day.[4] There was to be no additional volume. The Commission wound up its activities in January 1971. In a short letter to Prime Minister Trudeau announcing its closing the Commission underlined the importance of constitutional questions but acknowledged that the Commission not been able to come to a common position and therefore deferred the matter to the elected officials.[5] Needless to say, Trudeau was not displeased.[6]

As a result, there was no significant challenge in the federal arena to Trudeau's claim that his agenda of constitutional reform would satisfy the aspirations of Quebec Francophones. Certainly, the opposition parties were not going to claim otherwise; we have seen how they fell into line after the 1968 election. And in the Liberal government itself Trudeau's authority on the constitutional question was supreme. Indeed, as Mitchell Sharp recounts, the English-Canadian ministers deferred to Quebeckers on the question.[7] Dealing with Quebec and national unity was to become the preserve of Trudeau and his like-minded Quebeckers.

Implementing the Trudeau Strategy: 1968–1976

Building a Canadian Political Nationality

In Trudeau's strategy, it was essential that Canada not only be sovereign but also be seen to be sovereign. Quebec Francophones would not be able to think of themselves first and foremost as Canadians, rather than Québécois, unless the Canadian political community was formally defined so as to support such an identity. As we have seen, the St. Laurent government had started the process of giving form to a distinctly Canadian nationality in the late 1940s by passing the Canadian Citizenship Act and ending appeals to the Judicial Committee of the Privy Council. For its part, the Pearson government had replaced the Red Ensign with a new Canadian flag that bore no trace of the British connection. Logically, the ultimate goal in this process would have been to transform Canada formally from a monarchy to a republic. But despite Trudeau's personal discomfort in dealings with the Queen, he and his colleagues shrank from attempting this apparently for fear that the struggle would cost more than it was worth.[8]

There was the matter of "patriating" Canada's constitution, ending the symbolically embarrassing necessity of requesting the British Parliament to revise its British North America Act. Back in the 1920s, when Great Britain was preparing to grant full autonomy to what were then called "the White Dominions," Canada's federal and provincial governments had been unable to agree on an amending formula to the BNA Act. Thus, its essential constitutional document remained an act of the British Parliament. Countless efforts, over the decades, to resolve the matter had failed. While Trudeau was determined to achieve patriation, this meant contending with the provincial governments and their disparate agendas, including Quebec's, since it was presumed that patriation required the consent of all provincial governments. Nonetheless, the Trudeau government was free to make informal changes on its own. Thus, it reduced the visibility of royal symbols and discarded the term "dominion" to refer to the federal government or to Canada as a whole. Soon after assuming office Trudeau sought to have July 1 declared "Canada Day," replacing "Dominion Day."[9] The federal government became no less than "the Government of Canada," projecting a quasi-unitary image of the country. Similarly, the Trudeau government recast foreign and defence policy so as to put greater emphasis on Canada's "national" interests, such as the protection of its territory and the promotion of national unity.[10]

By the same token, the Trudeau government was concerned with developing a strong sense of Canadian identity to which all Canadians, including Quebec

Francophones, would adhere. It was on this basis that, in 1971, the Trudeau cabinet adopted its new policy of multiculturalism. In cabinet discussions ministers underlined "the importance and major significance of the policy as a new concept of the presentation of Canadianism" and contended that it would be a "unifying force to build a strong Canadian identity."[11]

Making Ottawa the National Government

According to Trudeau's analysis, Canadians would be more likely to identify with the federal government and Canada in general if they were to have a greater sense of personal connection with the federal government. This was especially the case in Quebec, where the federal government seemed to have become marginal to the lives of most Francophones, thanks to the Quiet Revolution and the new profile of the Quebec state.

This strategy led in several directions. First, a new emphasis was placed on making Canadians more familiar with the many benefits the federal government was indeed providing. For instance, Ottawa embarked on a major advertising campaign. Between 1970 and 1976, the federal government increased more than four-fold its spending on advertising; from the twelfth-largest advertiser in Canada, it became the largest.[12]

Second, there was an enhanced concern with the "visibility" to Canadians of federal activities. On this basis, a much harder look was taken at shared-cost programs, through which Ottawa provided the provinces with funds to carry out their own activities while adhering to federal priorities. After all, the provinces did not usually go out of their way to tell the recipients of provincial services that funding had come in part from Ottawa. Beyond that, shared-cost programs tied the federal government to provincial activities. One response was to set limits on federal contributions to the shared-cost programs, which Ottawa started to do in 1972.[13]

Another approach was to undertake federal initiatives independently. In effect, Ottawa tried to *make* the federal government more important in the lives of Canadians. In particular it attempted to create "new constituencies" for itself by funding groups that represented women, consumers, environmentalists, youth, and others.[14] The Trudeau government created its own urban affairs ministry despite the provincial governments' long-standing defence of municipalities as an exclusively provincial preserve, and began offering funds directly to municipalities.[15]

Even the Trudeau government's handling of the FLQ (Front de libération du Québec) crisis, in October 1970, may have reflected this determination to assert the role of the federal government in Quebec. According to one line of interpretation, the federal government was afraid the Quebec government might grant some of the demands of the FLQ kidnappers of British Trade Commissioner James Cross and Quebec cabinet minister Pierre Laporte. The Trudeau government's imposition of the War Measures Act served to place it fully in charge of the crisis. Another interpretation goes further, arguing that the War Measures Act and the stationing of Canadian soldiers in the streets of Montreal and elsewhere in Quebec were intended to intimidate not just the terrorists but all nationalists and separatists in Quebec. After all, among the more than 450 individuals detained under the powers of the act virtually all were associated in one way or another with the forces of Quebec nationalism.[16] For that matter, neither the imposition of the act nor the stationing of soldiers in Quebec was instrumental to locating the FLQ kidnappers. That was achieved through the powers normally available to police and other authorities.

In his *Memoirs* Trudeau discusses the October Crisis at great length, seeking to justify his government's actions. He notes that well before the kidnappings he had called upon the RCMP to

> gather information on the sources of financing for the *separatist* movement in Quebec, on *separatist* influence with the government of Quebec, the public service, *political parties*, universities, unions and professions, and on the political troubles in Quebec [emphasis added].[17]

While Trudeau insists that he was not encouraging the police to investigate "legitimate democratic opposition parties as such," let alone use illegal methods, this distinction is not evident in the text; the reference is to the sovereignty movement per se. As to the argument that the government was seeking to squelch pressures to negotiate with the FLQ, Trudeau relates that for him the deciding argument for imposing the War Measures Act was "a lot of irrational behaviour among people I had assumed to be more reasonable," namely a group of PQ leaders, labour leaders, and academics that had signed a call for the negotiation of "an exchange between hostages and political prisoners."[18] Such a recommendation for dealing with the crisis, however controversial, hardly constitutes the "apprehended insurrection" that was required to invoke the act. Whatever the merit of these arguments against the government's actions, they were supported not just by sovereigntists but by leading federalists. In the pages of *Le Devoir*, Claude Ryan vigorously protested Ottawa's subordination of the Quebec government.[19]

Clearly, the Trudeau government's imposition of the War Measures Act in peace time, the only such instance in Canadian history, is difficult to square with Pierre Trudeau's long-standing commitment to individual rights and civil liberties. It fits much more readily with his other core value: the urgent necessity to undermine Quebec nationalism.

Scaling Down Asymmetry

Beyond directly enhancing the role of Ottawa in Quebeckers' lives, the Trudeau government was also determined to eliminate the asymmetrical arrangements that the Quebec government had secured during the Pearson period. In some cases, as with such federally run programs as student allowances, the Quebec government replaced Ottawa as the provider of benefits, further marginalizing Ottawa in Quebec. Even in the case of shared-cost programs, which were still administered by the provincial governments, the symbolism of Quebec's ability to "opt out" was troubling. It gave concrete form to the claim of Quebec nationalists that Quebec was a province like no other.

A reaction against asymmetrical arrangements with Quebec was already being voiced in the Finance Department in the mid-1960s and had provided Finance with part of the rationale for the changes it wished to make to fiscal arrangements. Under a new scheme of tax abatements, post-secondary education in all provinces (including Quebec) was to be financed in precisely the same fashion. This process continued under the Trudeau government. In 1969, Ottawa announced that it was not formalizing the "contracting out" option in the Canada Assistance Plan. Instead the arrangements remained "transitional" and were regularly extended on that basis.[20] Quebec remained bound by the reporting obligations that went with that arrangement.

Elsewhere asymmetry, even on a "transitional" basis, simply disappeared. Under the Established Programs Financing Act, passed in 1977 but negotiated previously, federal transfers for health and post-secondary education were no longer linked to the costs of provincial programs: instead, they would be equal to a fixed proportion of Gross National Product. In the process, Ottawa rendered moot the framework for opting out that the Pearson government had established with its 1965 "interim arrangements." Under that scheme, Quebec (and any other province) could opt out of a host of designated shared-cost programs. Through the 1977 arrangements the programs were collapsed into block grants that went automatically to all provinces. So while the right to opt out had not been eliminated, in effect there was nothing left that Quebec, or any other province, might want to opt out of. By some readings, however, this strategy for eliminating Quebec's *de facto* special status had come with a very high price, for it undermined the federal government's capacity to influence social policy in *any* part of the country.[21] To that extent, the campaign to eliminate asymmetry ran at cross-purposes to the effort to heighten the importance of the federal government in citizens' lives.

Patriating and Revising the Constitution

In the end, though much could be accomplished by asserting the federal government's powers and redefining fiscal relations with the provinces, the Trudeau government's national unity strategy hinged on revising the constitution. By definition, the objective of making Canada fully sovereign, in form as well as fact, required that the constitution be patriated. Nor was federal action alone sufficient to accomplish Trudeau's goal of linguistic equality from sea to sea. If only to bring the provinces into line, language rights had to be constitutionally entrenched in a charter of rights. The trick was to focus constitutional revision on *these* matters.

In the 1960s, Trudeau had seen great risks in opening up the constitutional question. Just before entering federal politics in 1965, he had written, "We must not meddle with the constitution just yet."[22] Even after becoming justice minister he delayed addressing the question. But his hand and that of the Pearson government were forced by Ontario Premier John Robarts, who in 1967 convened an interprovincial conference grandly entitled "Confederation of Tomorrow."

To capture the initiative, the federal government organized a federal–provincial conference on the constitution, held in Ottawa in February 1968. There, as justice minister, Trudeau proposed a three-stage process.[23] First, there would be a discussion of the protection of human rights, of which he judged language rights to be central. Second, there would be an examination of "the central institutions of Canadian federalism"—Parliament, the Supreme Court, the federal public service, and the national capital—so as to make them more representative of "the federal character of the country." Only after those two stages had been completed would discussion turn to a third and final stage: the division of powers.[24]

Nonetheless, the provinces had other ideas. Thus, the conference discussed regional development as well as language rights. And on language rights, not all provinces shared Trudeau's views of what was needed. Most important, the Quebec government insisted that the priority should in fact be the division of powers rather than language rights; nor should language rights be imposed on any province. During subsequent federal–provincial conferences, the discussion ranged over the full set of constitutional matters, including Quebec's proposals for a bi-national constitution, and on to many non-constitutional matters, such as the state of the economy, regional development, and intergovernmental issues, which were of greater concern to many of the provincial governments. Ottawa even entered into discussions of the division of powers with proposals for limits on the spending power.[25]

With the April 1970 election to the Quebec government of Robert Bourassa's Liberal Party, which professed unqualified support for federalism, discussions became more intense and more focused. The result was the Victoria Charter, which emerged from a conference in Victoria in June 1971. Despite the wide-ranging discussions that had come to dominate the constitutional meetings, the Victoria Charter adhered quite closely to the priorities outlined by Trudeau at the February 1968 conference. Beyond patriation and an amending formula, the main feature of the Charter was the entrenchment of human rights—in effect, the first stage that Trudeau had identified. Included were political rights, such as freedom of expression and assembly, voting rights, and a limited set of legal rights. Also included were language rights, although, as we saw in Chapter Four, the obligations placed upon the provincial governments varied greatly among the provinces and did not extend to education rights.

On the other hand, with respect to Trudeau's second stage of constitutional discussions, the reform of central institutions, the Charter dealt only with the Supreme

Court, entrenching the long-established formula that three of nine judges are from the Quebec bar, ensuring that civil law cases would be heard primarily by Quebec judges, and affording provincial consultation about appointments to the Court. The Charter had relatively little to say about Trudeau's last stage of discussions, the division of powers. It did eliminate the powers of reservation and disallowance, which were already effectively defunct. More significantly, it expanded the areas of income security in which the federal government could act: family, youth, and occupational allowances would be added to the constitutional category of jurisdictions that are concurrent with provincial paramountcy.[26] (Such jurisdictions are held jointly by the two levels of government, but the provinces have prior rights.)

It was on income security that the battle was joined between Ottawa and Quebec City. The Quebec government had its own proposals for income security, submitting to provincial paramountcy policy areas where the federal government was already active, including unemployment insurance, family allowances, youth allowances, supplements to old-age pensions, and employment training. In the proposals being advanced by the Quebec government, unemployment insurance and guaranteed income supplements to old-age pensions would also be classified in the constitution as concurrent with provincial paramountcy. Moreover, Quebec's proposal spelled out just what provincial paramountcy would entail, in most cases requiring federal fiscal compensation.[27]

Quebec's proposals would have had major consequences, assuring it effective control over social policy. Underlying the Quebec government's proposals was its interest in establishing a comprehensive incomes policy, for which it would be responsible.[28] Still, Quebec's proposed constitutional scheme would have allowed Ottawa to play whatever role in the rest of Canada the other provincial governments accepted. In effect, Quebec was seeking a return of the kind of asymmetrical arrangement that the Pearson government had pioneered. Indeed, the terms of the proposal were largely compatible with those ad hoc arrangements.[29]

However, no matter what the possibilities might have been during the Pearson epoch, times had changed; not only was Trudeau opposed to particular status for Quebec in principle but his strategy for transforming the political allegiances of Québécois made it important for them to receive direct services and benefits from the federal government.[30] Indeed, the federal government was planning a comprehensive guaranteed income scheme of its own.[31] As a result, Quebec's aspirations for control of social policy had to be fiercely resisted.

In the words of a leading scholar of Canadian federalism, Donald V. Smiley, the Victoria Charter was "a very small constitutional package."[32] In effect, it was limited by the dictates of the Trudeau strategy. In particular, Quebec's proposals on social policy had to be rejected since they threatened the direct relations with individual Quebeckers that the Trudeau government was anxious to maintain and reinforce. Thus, while the Charter was generally acceptable to the other provinces, it was unacceptable to Quebec. At the conference, Premier Bourassa's position was equivocal, and some participants presumed that he was in fact favourable. However, upon returning to Quebec, Bourassa came under widespread pressure to reject the offer.

Opposition to the Charter in Quebec extended far beyond the Parti québécois and nationalist organizations such as the Société Saint-Jean-Baptiste to include the major unions, all four parties in the National Assembly,[33] the Quebec wing of the NDP,[34] prominent Quebec federalists such as Marcel Faribault and Gabriel Loubier, the new leader of the Union nationale,[35] and even the Montreal *Gazette*.[36] Leading the opposition in federalist ranks was Claude Ryan, who argued that the Charter "tends to consolidate the preponderance of the central government over the affairs of Canada and to reduce Quebec to the rank of a province like the others, without regard to its problems and priorities."[37] There is every reason to believe that in the Quebec cabinet the Charter was opposed by such leading figures as Claude Castonguay. Apparently, at the Victoria Conference, Castonguay had insisted that Quebec be given 10 days to make its decision.

Some prominent Quebeckers called on the Trudeau government to return to the bargaining table in an effort to resolve the social policy question. Trudeau made it clear, however, that the Charter had to be accepted as it was and that there was no room for further negotiation: "If there isn't agreement, then that is the end of the matter, for now, or for a while, I hope."[38]

Finally, after an all-night cabinet meeting, Bourassa conveyed to Trudeau his decision to reject the Charter.[39] Perhaps, through negotiation, this disagreement could have been resolved.[40] With some movement on Ottawa's part, Bourassa's position in Quebec might have been strengthened enough that he could have accepted the Charter; that had in any event been his inclination. The other provinces might have accepted additional changes regarding social policy if that would have resolved a question in which they had little interest. Of course, there can be no certainty that movement on social policy would have done the trick; some prominent Quebeckers were also dissatisfied with the Charter's amending formula.[41]

Whatever the possibility for resolving these questions, the Trudeau government made no further effort to get Quebec's consent on the constitutional question.[42] Nor did it take any other actions toward patriation. For three or four years, Trudeau acted as if Quebec's rejection of the Charter had in fact meant "the end of the matter." By 1974, however, he was beginning to suggest that patriation, even with a Charter, might be possible *without* provincial consent.[43] Finally, in a speech to the Quebec wing of the federal Liberal Party in March 1976, Trudeau threatened to proceed unilaterally with patriation, if necessary. In uncharacteristically colloquial French, he ridiculed the intellectuals and other nationalists who might object. Nor was he charitable toward Robert Bourassa, who was frustrating his constitutional plans.[44]

Constitutional impasses notwithstanding, the Trudeau government seemed confident that its overall national unity strategy was working. Certainly, no major figure at the federal level was prepared to say otherwise, and both opposition parties were deferring totally to the Trudeau government on this question. Moreover, Trudeau and his supporters could point to the overwhelming majorities of Quebec seats that his party won in the 1972 and 1974 general elections and to the defeat of the Parti québécois in the 1973 provincial election.[45] In fact, Trudeau even declared, in a widely quoted statement, "Separatism is dead."[46]

Nonetheless, despite the Parti québécois's miniscule presence in the National Assembly (6 of 110 seats after the 1973 election), the party's popular vote had risen from 23 per cent in the 1970 election to 30 per cent in 1973. The continuing impasse on the constitutional front, along with Trudeau's denunciation of the Bourassa government's position, gave added strength to the PQ's claim that Quebec's aspirations could never be met within the federal system. In its effort to counter the PQ's growing public support, the Bourassa Liberal government felt obliged to adopt the PQ's discourse in its own attempts to make the federal order more attractive to Quebeckers, using such expressions as "cultural sovereignty" and even referring to Quebec as "a French state within the Canadian common market." Such attempts to accommodate nationalist sentiments in the defence of federalism met with little sympathy in Ottawa, where they were the occasion for more scathing comments by Trudeau and his ministers. Yet they were a sign of a problem, namely that the Trudeau vision of Canada simply had little appeal to many Quebeckers.

Dealing with Setback: 1976–1980

By any reasonable standard, the election of the Parti québécois on 15 November 1976 was a serious setback for the Trudeau government and its national unity strategy. Although the PQ obtained only 41 per cent of the popular vote, it had the support of a majority of Francophones.[47] Votes for the PQ were not necessarily due to support for the party's option of sovereignty-association, since the PQ had said that this would be the object of a referendum. Indeed, surveys found that a number of PQ voters either did not support sovereignty-association or did not understand how great a change it would be.[48] Yet there could have been no doubt even among these voters that the PQ stood for the vigorous promotion of Quebec as a nation and as the first loyalty of Quebec Francophones. If nothing else, the PQ's electoral success demonstrated the failure of the federal government's campaign to convert Quebeckers to the Trudeau vision of Canada.

Opening to New Approaches on Federalism and Rights

Though the Trudeau government may not have read the election in precisely those terms, it did see the result as a setback. Moreover, it seemed to have been taken by surprise, and for a time appeared to be reassessing its strategy and considering options that it would previously have dismissed out of hand. Such was this apparent openness that some Quebec federalists were encouraged to believe that the

Trudeau orthodoxy could be transcended and federalist forces could finally come together in a common cause and with a common project. The rise of such hopes explains why so many Quebec federalists felt such a sense of betrayal when, in the early 1980s, the Trudeau government finally engineered a constitutional revision that fell fully within its orthodoxy.

The new tone was set by Trudeau himself in a speech to the Quebec City Chambre de commerce in January 1977, three months after the PQ election. Speaking from a text he had written himself, Trudeau began by contending that the PQ election in fact had positive aspects, notably that it would force a choice about the future of Quebec and Canada. The referendum would make it possible, indeed necessary, at last "to decide truly to be Canadian,"[49] something that Quebeckers and indeed all Canadians had never had to do. At the same time, implicitly recognizing that the prospect of such a choice would intensify the constitutional discussions, Trudeau declared that he was open to all possibilities: "If you want me to be flexible, I'll do it right now. I have a single condition for the constitution."[50] His condition was the entrenchment of rights. But, even there, he departed from his long-established position that rights could only be based upon individuals to evoke *collective* rights, even *collective language rights*:

> respect for the rights of men and women, respect for human rights, and *probably respect for the collective aspect of human rights. I am thinking of language,* I am thinking of the rights of regions to exist. Beginning from this condition, we can start from zero and write a new constitution. We haven't had a new one for 110 years; we can make one. I won't shrink from any challenge [emphasis added].[51]

As to the division of powers, Trudeau remarked that the premiers naturally wanted more power for themselves but also recognized that one could say as much of the federal leaders. In the end, he insisted, these are "politicians' quarrels."[52] All that should really count is "how people will be happier, better governed"[53]: "All that I ask, as long as I am here, is to establish functionally that such and such a power should be exercised at the federal level or at the provincial level in order for the Canadian collectivity to be better off."[54]

To be sure, in contending that Quebeckers would at last be forced to affirm their choice of being Canadian, Trudeau might be seen to deny that they might also maintain their identity as Quebeckers, at least as a primary allegiance. Nonetheless, his claim to be open to all manner of constitutional change, including a rethinking of the division of powers, and his explicit reference to collective linguistic rights seemed to be a major opening—especially to Quebec federalists, who were desperately hoping that a viable "renewed federalism" would emerge.

To spearhead the response to the new situation, Trudeau appointed Marc Lalonde to the new position of minister of federal–provincial relations in 1977.

Since Lalonde was a long-time close associate of Trudeau's, there is every reason to believe that his actions were based on regular communication with Trudeau and were fully in keeping with Trudeau's views of what should be done. Under Lalonde's leadership, several initiatives took form, each of which departed dramatically from Trudeau's past approach.

Pepin–Robarts: Drawing in Other Voices

In July 1977, the government established the Task Force on Canadian Unity, headed by five prominent Canadians, with a mandate, among other things, "to advise the Government on unity issues."[55] By reaching beyond its own confines and charging a group of high-profile Canadians with the unity question, the government seemed to be opening the door to approaches and proposals that departed from the path it had so rigorously been following.

The commissioners it appointed were virtually certain to produce just such ideas. One Quebec member, Solange Chaput-Rolland, was a well-known nationalist whose views on federalism and Canada were much closer to those of such federalists as Robert Bourassa and Claude Ryan than to those of Trudeau. One co-chair was former Ontario premier John Robarts, whose government in 1967 had held the "Confederation of Tomorrow" conference of which Trudeau had been so disapproving. Even more dramatic was the choice for the other co-chair: Jean-Luc Pepin, who had been closely associated with the Pearson government's notions of "co-operative federalism" and accommodation of Quebec nationalism. Indeed, during the 1960s, Pepin had come out squarely in favour of special status for Quebec and the two-nations idea of Canada.[56] Upon becoming prime minister, Trudeau had assigned Pepin a portfolio well removed from the national unity question: industry, trade, and commerce. After being defeated in the 1972 election, Pepin had left federal politics. With Pepin's appointment, Trudeau seemed to be signalling that his own views were up for serious re-examination.

Two years later the Pepin–Robarts Commission produced a report that fully met the expectations of radical departures. Basing its view of Canada on the twin concepts of dualism and regionalism, the report broke with Trudeau's notion of an essentially linguistic dualism by placing Quebec front and centre in its conception of dualism: "While we freely acknowledge that duality is many-sided, we would nevertheless insist that to confront the heart of the issue today is to address one main question, namely, the status of Quebec and its people in the Canada of tomorrow."[57] It based its proposals for a renewed federalism on the premise that "Quebec is distinctive and should, within a viable Canada, have the powers necessary to protect and develop its distinctive character; any political solution short of this would lead to the rupture of Canada."[58]

Presuming, as it did, that this meant that Quebec would have powers not necessarily desired by the other provinces, the Commission feared that a forthrightly asymmetrical federalism would be unacceptable in the rest of Canada.

Accordingly, it proposed "to allot to all the provinces powers in the areas needed by Quebec to maintain its distinctive culture and heritage."[59] The other provinces would not necessarily use these powers. In some cases, the powers would be declared concurrent, or shared, with provincial paramountcy; to displace Ottawa a provincial government would need to assert this paramountcy. (In effect, this was the approach embodied in the Bourassa government's proposal to the 1971 Victoria Conference.) In other cases, powers would be lodged with the provinces but could be delegated to the federal government.[60]

Nonetheless, the overall approach advocated by Pepin–Robarts started from the premise that Canadian federalism had to be restructured to accommodate the distinctiveness of Quebec, and that Quebec was bound to assume a role greater than the other provinces. In effect, it sought to resurrect the approach that the Pearson government had pioneered and that Trudeau had been so anxious to discard. Moreover, this approach stemmed from a conception of dualism that was centred on the Quebec question, as opposed to Trudeau's conception of a purely linguistic dualism based on the recognition of individual language rights.

In another section of its report the Commission went one step further: it sought to limit any imposition of the Trudeau type of linguistic equality to the federal government. Provincial governments would subscribe to certain rights for their official-language minorities but they would be free to define the status of the languages in whatever way they thought appropriate. In fact, on this basis, the Commission recommended that section 133 of the BNA Act should no longer apply to Quebec and that Manitoba should no longer be bound by the Manitoba Act of 1870. The Commission even went so far as effectively to endorse Bill 101: "We support the efforts of the Quebec provincial government and of the people of Quebec to ensure the predominance of the French language and culture in that province."[61] The rejection of the Trudeau orthodoxy could not have been more complete.

Nonetheless, in presenting the report to the House, Trudeau said his government accepts "the broad lines of the Task Force's analysis" and "endorses the basic principles which it believes should underlie the renewal of the Canadian federation."[62] The following day he did tell a press conference that the report was "dead wrong" in its language proposals;[63] he also made it clear over the next few days that he took exception to the report's emphasis on dualism and regionalism and its support for decentralization.[64] Still, Trudeau's formal statement to the House, with its broad acceptance of the report, may have encouraged Quebec federalists to believe that the Trudeau government would look to the report for guidance.

Cullen–Couture: Dealing with Quebec Differently

Beyond calling for advice on the unity question from a group of prominent Canadians that was bound to contradict the Trudeau orthodoxy, the government itself negotiated an agreement with the PQ government that seemed to signal a new willingness to recognize Quebec's claims for distinctive status. In February

1978, Ottawa and Quebec City signed a bilateral agreement on immigration, the Cullen–Couture Accord, named after the two ministers responsible.

Under Cullen–Couture, the Quebec government took effective control over the selection of a major category of immigrants to Quebec. Officials of the Quebec immigration department, normally based in Canadian immigration offices overseas and called "Immigration Officers" in the agreement, were given the power to choose among candidates for the status of independent immigrants who intended to settle in Quebec. The federal involvement would be restricted to such matters as health and security. The agreement also provided for Quebec to be involved in (but not to control) the choice of other categories of immigrants, and it committed the two governments to consult on areas of common interest concerning immigration and demographic planning.

In effect, the Accord was an attempt by the federal government to accommodate Quebec's wish to maintain the province's French character by choosing its own immigrants. Claiming that historically Ottawa had made no effort to attract Francophone immigrants, and that indeed the opposite had been the case, the Quebec government had established its own department of immigration in 1968.[65] No other province had involved itself directly in the selection of immigrants, at least in recent decades. Cullen–Couture was a direct response to Quebec's insistence that, given both the inability of the federal government to meet Quebec's distinctive needs and, as a consequence, the special responsibilities of the Quebec government to do so, it needed to have powers that in the rest of Canada were exercised by Ottawa. In effect, the Trudeau government seemed to be sanctioning a "special status" for Quebec.[66]

Cullen–Couture may have reflected the special circumstances of immigration, which is one of the few jurisdictions that the constitution explicitly designates as concurrent, that is, both a federal and a provincial responsibility. Even there, Ottawa had the advantage of federal paramountcy. Thus, the Trudeau government may have had no intention of generalizing this approach to other jurisdictions.

However, by entering into an agreement that was specific to Quebec, explicitly geared to reinforcement of Quebec's Francophone character, and creating responsibilities for Quebec that differed from those of the other provinces, the Trudeau government seemed to be demonstrating once again that it had recognized that a new flexible, asymmetrical approach to federalism and Quebec was needed, and that it was now prepared to pursue one.[67] After all, the Accord had been conceived and signed by Marc Lalonde, Trudeau's close and long-standing colleague.

A Time for Action: Revising the Constitution Comprehensively

In June of 1978, the Trudeau government came forward with its own proposals for constitutional change, entitled *A Time for Action*. Compared with the three-stage approach that Trudeau had announced in the 1960s upon becoming justice minister, or with the limited scope of the ill-fated Victoria Charter, the new proposals seemed to show a conversion to a much more comprehensive approach since they covered all areas of discussion, including the division of powers. For that reason, *A Time for Action* seemed to confirm the commitment made by Trudeau the previous year, in his Chamber of Commerce speech, that he was prepared to discuss all options.

In the document, the procedure for constitutional change was to be composed of two stages. A first stage, which was restricted to federal jurisdictions, and which the federal government was prepared to pursue unilaterally if necessary, was to consist of a declaration of the Canadian federation's fundamental objectives; a reform of federal-level institutions; and a charter of rights that, at first, would apply only at the federal level. The second stage was to address the division of powers and the amending formula. Patriation, then, would not take place until the federal government and the provinces had come to terms on the matters of much more concern to them, including Quebec.

A week later, Ottawa released Bill C-60, Constitutional Amendment Bill, which was to implement phase one. The bill outlined the transformation of the Senate into a House of the Federation, half of whose members were to be appointed by Parliament and half by the provincial legislatures. It would constitutionally entrench the Supreme Court while providing for the provinces to take part in the appointment of its members (through the House of the Federation) and enlarging its membership to 11 (with four from Quebec). At the same time, it would have codified into constitutional law the basic conventions of responsible government. A charter of rights and freedoms was initially to be binding on the federal government alone; it would apply to the provincial level only after a provincial legislature had formally adopted it. Finally, the bill contained a statement of "aims" that, though beginning with the assertion that "the people of Canada . . . declare and affirm . . . their expectation for a future in common," also recognized Quebec's uniqueness by asserting "a permanent national commitment to the endurance and self-fulfillment of the Canadian French-speaking society centred in but not limited to Quebec."[68]

As it happened, Bill C-60 and Ottawa's proposed unilateral first stage were stillborn. Early in 1979, the Supreme Court pronounced Bill C-60 to be unconstitutional since such matters as the Senate and the Supreme Court came under provincial as well as federal jurisdiction. In any event, at a federal–provincial conference in the fall of 1978, Trudeau had agreed to drop the distinction between two phases of constitutional discussion. Now, one agenda was to cover all items, including the division of powers. On this basis, negotiations proceeded on a comprehensive agenda that embraced a substantial degree of decentralization of powers: restriction of the federal spending and declaratory powers, and expansion of provincial jurisdiction over communications, fisheries, family law, and natural resources. Ultimately, at a constitutional conference in February 1979, the governments failed to agree.[69]

The openness on the part of Trudeau and his cabinet may have been the result of special circumstances, such as the Supreme Court ruling and an imminent federal election or even Trudeau's personal difficulties.[70] The fact remains, though, that here too the Trudeau government seemed to have abandoned its past approach to federalism and the Quebec question. Once again, Quebec federalists had reason to be encouraged. Although Trudeau had clearly not lost his antipathy to Quebec nationalism, apparently the shock of the PQ victory had forced him to recognize the continuing strength of Quebec nationalism and to re-examine his belief that with the right strategy Quebec nationalism could be eliminated and replaced with an allegiance to Canada.

The 1980 Quebec Referendum: Promising Change

The Lévesque government waited until its fourth year in office to announce the date of the referendum on Quebec sovereignty—20 May 1980. The delay seems to have been caused by tactical considerations, such as the hope that the referendum might have a better chance of winning once Trudeau had been replaced by a non-Quebecker, Joe Clark. Whatever the causes, the delay was probably a mistake, for with time the contradictions grew between the PQ's goal of sovereignty and its success in providing good government within the existing federal structure. Through such measures as Bill 101 and the Cullen–Couture Accord, some of the grievances which had fuelled popular support for sovereignty were being addressed, without sovereignty. The delay also allowed time for the Trudeau government to develop its new flexible approach to Quebec and the constitution.[71]

As far as the PQ government was concerned, the issue to be addressed in the referendum was not sovereignty per se, but sovereignty linked with a comprehensive economic association with the rest of Canada. That had been the party's position ever since it was founded in 1968, and it was faithfully reproduced, indeed considerably expanded, in the blueprint for sovereignty-association that the Lévesque government presented in the fall of 1979. It was called *Quebec–Canada: A New Deal* and sub-titled *The Quebec Government's Proposal for a New Partnership between Equals: Sovereignty-Association*.[72] As these lengthy titles indicated, the government intended to present the referendum question in terms of, not rupture or "separation," but continuity: redefining the relationship between Quebec and Canada as one of equals. In that way it hoped to tap into the ideal of a dualist Canada that had so long been the basis of the Francophone vision of the country. Moreover, the Lévesque government defined the purpose of the vote itself as not the actual endorsement of sovereignty-association but a mandate to the Quebec government to negotiate sovereignty-association with the federal government. Any agreement that emerged from these negotiations would have to be approved in a subsequent referendum.

These themes were developed systematically in the Lévesque government's campaign leading up to the referendum. A pamphlet sent to all voters by the Yes campaign declared: "Sovereignty-association is . . . neither the status quo, nor separatism. It is a realistic formula that will enable genuine change without the need to overturn everything or to begin from zero."[73] And in the National Assembly debate on the referendum question, Lévesque said, "We say that instead of this regime . . . that everyone admits is outdated, but without casting aside a long-standing tradition of coexistence that has created a whole network of exchanges, we now owe it to ourselves to enter into a new agreement between equals, with our neighbours and partners in the rest of Canada."[74]

By linking allegiance to Quebec with the ideal of equality with the rest of Canada, the PQ's option had a powerful appeal to the world view of most Quebec Francophones. Accordingly, the primary stratagem of the federalists became one of shifting the meaning of the referendum to more favourable ground, namely separation. For, as surveys regularly confirmed, most Quebec Francophones were very apprehensive about the economic consequences of sovereignty and needed to be assured that it would be linked to an economic association. Beyond that, many Francophones were not prepared to abandon the old idea of Canada, at least a dualist one.

Given the federal government's policies over the previous 12 years, especially before the 1976 Quebec election, federalist forces could hardly lay claim to the older Francophone vision of Canada, in which Quebec would have a distinct, even equal place. But they had no difficulty addressing the presumed economic consequences of sovereignty—and they did so with a vengeance. For that matter, the PQ was implicitly admitting that the economic consequences of sovereignty could be very serious since they were linking sovereignty to an economic association. If the federalists could focus the referendum on sovereignty or separation they would be in a strong position. The key was to show that the PQ's notion of an economic association was unrealistic and that sovereignty necessarily meant "separation."

Accordingly, federalist leaders insisted at every opportunity that the rest of Canada would never accept economic association with a sovereign Quebec. To support their case, they could point to statements by provincial premiers. The four western premiers declared that they would never negotiate sovereignty-association; two premiers, Allan Blakeney of Saskatchewan and Bill Davis of Ontario, said the same thing in speeches to the Montreal Board of Trade.[75]

Without access to Canadian markets, federalist leaders proclaimed, Quebec sovereignty could only result in horrendous economic costs for Quebec through loss of exports, withdrawal of firms, cancellation of investment plans, and so on. Beyond that, a sovereign Quebec state would not have the fiscal resources to maintain the social benefits to which Québécois were accustomed. Indeed, some prominent federalists claimed that under sovereignty-association there would be no old-age pensions.[76]

The federalist tactic appears to have worked as a way of building support for a No vote. Surveys indicate that for most voters the issue of the referendum was not sovereignty-association, let alone renewed federalism, as the Yes forces claimed, but the dissolution of Quebec's links with the rest of Canada. For many voters this meant the loss of economic and political ties; for others, the loss was one of identity as Canadians. Whereas at various points surveys showed that close to half of Quebeckers supported the mandate for sovereignty-association sought in the referendum question, an overwhelming majority rejected sovereignty without an economic association.[77] Federalist forces were thus able to establish ascendance well before the referendum took place. Although the slide in the Yes vote was due partly to PQ tactical errors during April, the most important factor was the federalist campaign about dangers of "separation." By late April, surveys suggested that the No vote was assured of victory.[78]

After joining the debate through the Speech from the Throne in mid-April, Prime Minister Trudeau intervened directly with three major speeches in Quebec.[79] The first, given in Montreal on 2 May, set the tone of his campaign. A Yes vote, he said, would lead to a deadlock since, rather than a vote for separation, it would provide only a mandate to negotiate sovereignty-association. The rest of Canada had made it clear that it was not interested in such a scheme. Thus, a Yes vote would lead to the humiliation of "the Quebec people." Demanding to know whether, in the case of a No vote, the Lévesque government was prepared to pursue a "renewed federalism," Trudeau insisted that federalists were very much committed to such a result:

> I know no one [among those who want to stay in Canada] who doesn't want to profit from this current upheaval to renew the constitution.
>
> Mr Ryan has proposed a Beige Paper. The governments of the other provinces, from Ontario to British Columbia, have presented reports. Our government, after establishing the Pepin–Robarts Commission, has proposed a formula called *A Time for Action*, a bill called C-60 which contained, by the way, a large number of proposals for a fundamental renewal.
>
> Those, then, who want to remain Canadian are ready to change it, are ready to improve federalism.[80]

So, from the outset, Trudeau linked a No vote with "renewal" of the federal system.

In his second speech, in Quebec City, Trudeau charged the PQ with cowardice in not asking "the real question" and in using a question "that puts our fate in the hands of others."[81] Joined on the stage by Jean Lesage, Trudeau evoked the courage of his Francophone predecessors, Wilfrid Laurier and Louis St. Laurent, and the greatness of Quebec premiers, including not only Jean Lesage but Maurice Duplessis, who had defended Quebeckers' rights. He insisted that "we went to Ottawa because that is how Quebeckers have always seen their place in Canada. They saw it by being proud to be Quebeckers, fighting here [Quebec City] to defend their rights, but also affirming their rights as Canadians by sending some of their best as representatives to Ottawa to affirm their place as Quebeckers within Canada."[82]

His third speech, given in Montreal six days before the referendum, took his argument about the possibilities of "renewed federalism" one step further. He was certain that with a No vote the changes needed would indeed take place:

> I know because I spoke to the [Liberal] MPs this morning, I know that I can make the most solemn commitment that following a No vote, we will start immediately the process of renewing the Constitution, and we will not stop until it is done. . . . We are putting ourselves on the line, we Quebec MPs, because we are telling Quebeckers to vote No, and we are saying to you in other provinces that we will not accept that you interpret a No vote as an indication that everything is fine, and everything can stay as it was before. We want change, we are putting our seats [in Parliament] on the line to have change.[83]

The referendum was, of course, a resounding victory for the No side and for Quebec remaining in the federal system. With only 40.4 per cent of the voters choosing Yes, the sovereigntists could not claim to have won a majority even of Francophone voters.[84]

By some accounts, Trudeau's statement was the turning point of the referendum campaign, delivering victory to the No side,[85] but that is far from certain. Surveys had been predicting a No victory well before Trudeau intervened in the campaign. Nor do the surveys suggest any surge in No support after Trudeau's three speeches.[86]

Whatever may have been its influence on the referendum, Trudeau's pledge of change was to shape the post-referendum political climate. To be sure, he had not been precise as to the form of change that he would seek.[87] Nonetheless, during the late 1970s, Trudeau and his government seemed to show a new willingness to accommodate Quebec's distinctive needs, including the Quebec government's demands for additional powers. It was reasonable to expect that such changes would be part of the constitutional renewal that he would now try to bring about. Certainly, during the referendum campaign he had said nothing to suggest otherwise. Consequently, the Quebec federalists who wanted such changes were free to believe that they would get them.

Seizing the Moment: 1980–1985

The Constitution Act, 1982

In a speech to the House of Commons the day after the referendum, Trudeau seemed to confirm that the constitution would indeed undergo a fundamental revision along the lines of his post-1976 statements and would satisfy the aspirations of Quebec. Declaring that the No vote must be interpreted as "massive support for change within the federal framework,"[88] he announced that his justice minister, Jean Chrétien, would immediately undertake a tour of the provincial governments to obtain their views on constitutional renewal.

He himself, Trudeau said, would place no conditions on constitutional discussions other than the ones he had stipulated in 1977 in his speech to the Quebec Chamber of Commerce. He outlined two conditions: "first, that Canada continues to be a true federation" and "that a charter of fundamental rights and freedoms be inserted in the constitution and that this charter extend to *the collective aspect of such rights as language*" [emphasis added]. Once again, then, he had professed a commitment to recognize *collective* language rights. Everything else, he insisted, was negotiable. To underline the point, he specifically referred to proposals that diverged from his own:

> The new constitution could include, if the people so wish, several provisions in our present organic laws, but it will also have to contain new elements reflecting the most innovative proposals emerging from our consultations or from the numerous analyses and considered opinions that have flowed in the last few years from the will to change of Canadians. I am referring, of course, to the many proposals made by the Canadian government since 1968, *but also to the Pepin–Robarts report*, to the policy papers issued by the governments of British Columbia, Ontario, Alberta, and by almost every province but Quebec, *to the constitutional proposals of the Liberal Party of Quebec*, many elements of which could orient the renewal of our constitutions if they were put forward by the political authorities of that province [emphasis added].[89]

Beyond that, at a September 1980 conference that he convened with the provinces, Trudeau presented a federal proposal that not only converged with Pepin–Robarts and the Beige Paper in its offer of decentralization and asymmetry in federal–provincial relations and reform of the Supreme Court and Senate, but proposed recognition in a preamble of "the distinct character of Quebec society, with its Francophone majority."[90]

Nonetheless, two years later a new constitution was adopted that falls far short of the broad range of proposals that Trudeau referred to. In fact, it contains little more than what, in 1968, Trudeau as justice minister had identified as the first stage of constitutional renewal: patriation and an amending formula coupled with a charter of rights. As for the subjects of the two subsequent stages, there is no reference to central institutions, and the only treatment of the division of powers is a section confirming provincial jurisdiction over certain natural resources. Even the limited measures of the Victoria Charter, such as elimination of the federal unilateral powers, do not appear.

Indeed, the contents are largely the same as the package Trudeau had presented in the fall of 1980 in the form of a resolution to Parliament. When he threatened to ask the British Parliament to act on the resolution, even without the consent of the provincial governments, eight provinces challenged in court his right to do so. Confronted with the Supreme Court's determination that such an action, though legal, would violate constitutional convention, the federal government had returned to negotiations with the provinces. But the outcome was not fundamentally different and faithfully reflected Trudeau's long-standing priorities and views.[91] In one significant respect, the act has less weight than did the original resolution: a notwithstanding clause allows for suspension of certain provisions of the Charter.[92]

The Constitution Act, 1982, has two main parts. It outlines an amending formula by which some items require the unanimous consent of Parliament and all the provincial legislatures but most require only the approval of Parliament and two-thirds of the provincial legislatures, representing 50 per cent of the population. Also, it outlines the terms of the Charter of Rights and Freedoms which, along with the standard political and legal freedoms, recognizes linguistic rights, mobility rights, and the right of individuals to equal treatment by the law irrespective of a variety of designated characteristics. Additional clauses declare that interpretation of the Charter must be consistent with "the preservation and enhancement of the multicultural heritage of Canadians" and cannot affect "any aboriginal treaty or other rights or freedoms that pertain to the aboriginal peoples of Canada." Also, the Charter's rights and freedoms are to be guaranteed equally to men and women. Under a "notwithstanding clause," Parliament or a provincial legislature may exclude a law from application of certain parts of the Charter. Beyond the amending procedure and Charter, the Constitution Act recognizes and affirms "the existing aboriginal and treaty rights of the aboriginal peoples of Canada." Finally, other provisions call for annual first ministers' conferences, declare a commitment to equalization of Canadians' well-being and reduction of regional disparities, and affirm the existing concurrent provincial power to regulate interprovincial trade in, and impose taxes upon, non-renewable resources, forestry products, and hydro-electrical energy.

So the package hardly embodies the openness to new ideas and approaches that Trudeau had proclaimed in his 1977 Chamber of Commerce speech and reiterated after the referendum. Nor does the package contain the recognition of *collective* language rights to which he had committed himself on both occasions. Indeed, Trudeau was later to pride himself on the fact that language rights had been recognized in exclusively individual terms: "Language rights were assigned directly to individuals rather than collectivities."[93]

A Response to Quebec?

It is difficult to see this document as a direct response to the ideas and proposals that had been circulating among the federalist milieu in Quebec. It falls far short of the outline of "renewed federalism" that the Lévesque government produced in the summer of 1980.[94] But it also falls short of two documents that Trudeau mentioned by name in his post-referendum speech to the House and that did enjoy widespread support in Quebec: the Pepin–Robarts Report, in which prominent Quebeckers had been major collaborators, and the Beige Paper, produced by the Quebec Liberal Party and bearing the clear imprint of party leader Claude Ryan.[95] Each of them envisaged major changes in the division of powers. In addition, both proposals contained provisions for changes in federal-level institutions.

Not only does the Constitution Act, 1982, fail to enhance the powers of the Quebec government or to reform central institutions, but under the Charter of Rights and Freedoms the powers of the Quebec government are reduced, directly affecting important Quebec laws. The provisions on language of education contradict Bill 101 by requiring public education in English to be available to all children whose parents were educated in English anywhere in Canada, as well as to any children who have already received (or have a sibling who has received) education in English in Canada.[96] The mobility provision, which guarantees access to employment in other provinces, jeopardized Quebec's law regulating its construction industry. Moreover, neither set of provisions is subject to the "notwithstanding clause."[97] Most significantly, unlike virtually all proposals for patriation, including that of the Trudeau government itself, the new amending formula did not grant Quebec a veto over all forms of constitutional change.[98]

Finally, beyond the content of the Constitution Act there is, of course, the manner in which it was brought into being. Simply put, the constitution was patriated without the approval of the Quebec government or National Assembly. In November 1980, 33 of the 42 members of the Liberal opposition had supported a government resolution that opposed the federal government's plans for unilateral action without the consent of the provinces, called upon the Canadian Parliament not to approve these plans since they would violate the very nature of Canadian federalism, and warned the British Parliament against adopting any modification to the BNA Act that did not have the consent of the provinces, "and, in particular, of Quebec."[99] On the day the House of Commons approved the constitutional patriation package to which the nine other provinces had agreed, Claude Ryan said he "deeply regretted that important decisions are being made in Ottawa without the consent of Quebec."[100] To express their displeasure with the procedure, if not the content of patriation, Ryan and most of the Liberal members boycotted the ceremonies.[101]

Indeed, the Quebec government appealed to the Supreme Court, arguing that such a move would be unconstitutional since the principle of duality gave

Quebec a veto. In presenting the case to the Court, Quebec counsel argued that beyond a "federal" aspect of duality, consisting of the two language groups and their constitutional protection (in effect the notion developed under the Trudeau regime), there is a "Quebec" aspect, which covers

> all the circumstances that have contributed to making Quebec a distinct society, since the foundation of Canada and long before, and the range of guarantees that were made to Quebec in 1867, as a province which the Task Force on Canadian Unity [Pepin–Robarts] has described as "the stronghold of the French-Canadian people" and the "living heart of the French presence in North America." These circumstances and these guarantees extend far beyond matters of language and culture alone: the protection of the British North America Act was extended to all aspects of Quebec society.[102]

In rejecting Quebec's claim, the Court was upholding a previous decision of the Quebec Court of Appeals; yet the Court's reasoning is far from persuasive.[103] Still, by the time the Court pronounced on the matter the Constitution Act, 1982, had already been proclaimed. The federal authorities had not felt obliged to hold up the proceedings until the Court rendered its judgement; British Prime Minister Thatcher had already rejected Quebec's request that the British Parliament not act until the judgement had come down.[104] To be sure, proclamation of the act did not end the matter since in its previous decision the Court had asserted its right and responsibility to adjudicate questions of convention. But in this case, a ruling that would have declared the new constitution to violate convention, to be in the words of Peter Hogg "an unconstitutional constitution,"[105] would have been exceedingly awkward. Perhaps this context shaped the Court's decision making. For Peter Russell, "it was a political response to a political challenge dressed up in judicial clothing."[106]

In any event, the Court's arguments did not impress a broad range of Quebec federalists for whom constitutional patriation without the approval of the Quebec National Assembly violated their basic understanding of Canada not only as a compact among provinces but as a dualistic compact between two founding peoples. Moreover, as the Quebec counsel had argued before the Supreme Court, this sense of dualism was profoundly rooted in Quebec and its cultural distinctiveness. Revision of the constitution without Quebec's consent violated both components of a "double compact" and was fundamentally unacceptable.[107]

The Trudeau government might have been on stronger ground if it had restricted itself simply to patriation and an amending formula, without a charter. There was a basic contradiction in arguing that Canada's self-respect required that the dependence on the British Parliament must be ended but using this connection to make a major change in the constitution just before patriation took place.

Why not "bring home" the constitution first and then have a charter adopted by Canadians, on their own, through their new amending procedure? (But, of course, Trudeau could not count on such an outcome.) Perhaps Quebec might have been led to agree to patriation on that basis. After all, as we shall see, in April 1981 it did agree with the seven other dissident provinces to a package composed simply of patriation and an amending formula.[108] Perhaps, then, patriation could have been accomplished with the consent of all the provinces, including Quebec, in the time-honoured Canadian fashion.[109] Quebec need not have been isolated. But, in that case, patriation would not have come tied to the charter of entrenched rights, especially *linguistic* rights, that Trudeau had so desperately sought.[110]

Ultimately, the question was one of the nature of Canada and Quebec's place in it. For all its efforts, the Trudeau government had not displaced the established French-Canadian view of these questions, even among leading federalists. As a result, rather than uniting the many Quebec Francophones who continued to support the Canadian federation, constitutional patriation served to divide them—with far-reaching consequences for all Canadians.

The Lévesque Government's Miscalculations

To a certain extent the outcome of the constitutional struggle was due to strategic errors on the part of the Lévesque government which, demoralized by its referendum failure, apparently had not developed a coherent strategy to counter Trudeau's initiatives.[111] Before the final stage of negotiations, the Lévesque government effectively abandoned Quebec's long-established demand that any patriated constitution both allow Quebec a veto over future constitutional change and give Quebec, with or without the other provinces, substantially enhanced powers. Quebec governments from Lesage to Johnson to Bertrand to Bourassa had always insisted that only under those conditions would they approve patriation. And this had been the PQ government's position in the summer of 1980.

Nonetheless, in April 1981, Lévesque joined the seven other dissident provinces in declaring that patriation would be acceptable if it simply provided an amending formula by which (1) most matters would require approval of two-thirds of the provinces, representing 50 per cent of the population; and (2) a province would be able to opt out, with compensation, from agreement among two-thirds of the provinces to transfer any provincial powers to the federal government. Ostensibly, Quebec's pact with the other dissident provinces stemmed from fear that if the Trudeau government were to seek patriation unilaterally the package would include a charter of rights. Thus, it was better to head off such a possibility by defining a basis upon which patriation would have the consent of the provinces. It may also have been that the Lévesque government was confident that Trudeau would never agree to such terms. Whatever the reasoning, this move had the effect of reducing Quebec's wishes to those of the other provinces, ensuring that any constitutional revision would ignore Quebec's own long-standing needs and aspirations.

By some accounts, Lévesque made a second mistake when, during the final negotiations, he agreed to (but later rejected) Trudeau's suggestion that the federal government's package be put to a referendum. In the process, he broke with the position that had been established with the other dissident provinces the previous April. The other premiers fiercely opposed Trudeau's referendum proposal, not the least because they feared they might lose any such contest. By seeming to break ranks with them, Lévesque ended the common front and ushered in the all-night negotiations between Ottawa and the other provinces that resulted in the compromise agreed to the next day—the basis of the Constitution Act, 1982.[112]

Whether Trudeau's referendum proposal and Lévesque's agreement to this alleged "trap" are alone responsible for this outcome is open to debate. When the other premiers went into the final negotiations, they were obviously uncomfortable with their formal alliance with the "separatist" PQ government; any pretext would have served their desire to be freed from it. Indeed, Lévesque may have accepted the Trudeau proposal because he was feeling a sense of estrangement from his ostensible allies.[113] In the end, the alliance between Quebec and the other premiers was an unnatural one since it had not been based upon any recognition of Quebec's particular goals.[114] Lévesque had simply "signed on" to a position that already had been defined by the English-Canadian premiers. That was his mistake.[115]

Having subscribed to this common position, the Lévesque government was in fact poorly placed to denounce the terms upon which Trudeau and the other groups had agreed. The deviation of the amending formula from the interprovincial agreement was minor; compensation for provinces that opt out of transfers of jurisdiction to the federal government would be limited to the areas of "education and culture."[116] The imposition of the Charter of Rights and Freedoms is, of course, a more substantial matter. But even there the direct impact on Quebec's jurisdictions had been somewhat minimized. In the case of Quebec, the provision regarding minority-language education would apply to immigrants only if the National Assembly should so decree; only application to Canadians would take effect immediately.[117] And the mobility rights would not apply as long as Quebec's unemployment rate was above the national average.[118] Most other provisions were subject to the notwithstanding clause. Indeed, as constitutional scholar Peter Russell has argued, perhaps Lévesque could have been brought on side at the October 1981 conference if greater effort had been made to do so—and to overcome his anger over being isolated by the nine other provinces.[119]

In the light of Quebec's historical demands, the primary failing of the Constitution Act, 1982, is that it neither gives Quebec a veto over constitutional change nor gives Quebec any new powers. Trudeau could correctly reply, as he was quick to do, that those goals had been abandoned by the PQ government. But these are debating points. In the end, the PQ's strategic errors may help to explain how it was possible to revise the constitution without taking account of Quebec's long-established demands, including those of most Quebec federalists. But they do not explain *why* it happened.

Keeping the Referendum Promise?

Through the patriation of 1982, the Trudeau government attained the ultimate goal in its national unity strategy: the entrenchment of language rights from coast to coast. Yet to secure this measure aimed at integrating Quebec Francophones with the rest of the country, it had had to incur the opposition of not just sovereigntists but also a good share of federalist opinion in Quebec. Indeed, Quebec federalists were to remain badly divided for years to come. Trudeau and his defenders could reply that the final constitutional package was totally consistent with the objectives he had declared years before, as indeed it was. However, that argument has not silenced his critics.

Among many Quebec federalists there was a lingering belief that Trudeau had in fact promised something quite different than the Constitution Act, something more in keeping with Quebec's established demands. In the one statement—his final referendum speech—in which Trudeau did make a promise, he in fact offered no specifics as to what he would try to deliver. He did not even promise to "renew" Canadian federalism; simply to renew the *constitution*. With the Charter he certainly did do that.

Yet Trudeau must have known the context in which he made his "promise," vague as it may have been. The very phrase "constitutional renewal" had acquired a specific meaning in the Quebec of 1980; therefore, it was reasonable for his audience to assume that it meant, among other things, a major enhancement of the powers of the Quebec government.[120] In fact, just before making the promise, in his final speech of the referendum campaign, Trudeau had explicitly linked constitutional change with a renewal *of federalism*: "If the answer to the referendum question is No, we have said that this No will be interpreted as a mandate to change the constitution, *to renew federalism*" [emphasis added].[121]

Moreover, through previous action the Trudeau government had created quite precise expectations of what a renewal of federalism would entail. It had appointed a task force of prominent Canadians, some of whom could have been expected to propose changes to Canadian federalism that would recognize Quebec's uniqueness. They did indeed make such proposals. Similarly, through Cullen–Couture, the federal government had entered into an asymmetrical arrangement that seemed to recognize Quebec's specific needs. And its own proposal, *A Time for Action*, had proposed that reform to central institutions and the division of powers be part of any constitutional change.

Defenders of the Trudeau government can respond that Trudeau and his cabinet had never actually endorsed the actual recommendations of the Pepin–Robarts task force and had largely ignored the report. As for *A Time for Action*, it was simply a proposal that was overtaken by events. But we have seen how in his first referendum speech, when he tried to show the extent to which Canada was headed for change, Trudeau had mentioned both the Pepin–Robarts task force (claiming credit for creating it) and *A Time for Action*, along with the Quebec Liberal Party's Beige Paper. It was in terms of these proposals that he depicted the pressures for a renewed federalism. Similarly, we saw how in his speech to the Chambre de commerce in 1977 Trudeau had declared a commitment to the entrenchment of *collective* linguistic rights—a concept he had always rejected in the past. For that matter, even *after* the referendum victory, Trudeau projected the same openness in his address to Parliament and in the position paper he presented to the September federal–provincial conference.

Over the following years Trudeau argued that there could have been no misunderstanding; his position on the nature of constitutional change had always been the one he defined in the late 1960s when the process of constitutional revision began: patriation with a veto for Quebec and a charter recognizing, among other things, language rights—precisely what was in the Constitution Act.[122] Yet these were not the notions he had evoked in the years following the 1976 PQ victory or even just after the referendum. Conceivably, he had evoked these notions in a deliberate effort to mislead Quebec voters. Yet the two post-referendum statements suggest that initially he had in fact intended to give effect to these ideas.[123]

In the last analysis, however, the debate over Trudeau's alleged "betrayal" points to something more profound. Given their own understanding of Quebec and its place in Canada, a wide spectrum of Quebec federalists conceived "constitutional renewal" in very different terms than did Trudeau. Indeed, there may have been a certain element of wishful thinking in their understanding of what the Trudeau government would do.

In short, the Constitution Act, 1982, was simply out of step with Quebec opinion. It was based upon an idea of Canada that most Quebec Francophones did not share, despite the best efforts of the federal government to bring them around to such an understanding. Thus, even if the Constitution Act kept the specific promise that Trudeau had made to Quebec, it could not possibly keep the larger promise of bringing Canadian unity.

A Response to English Canada?

If it is difficult to see the patriation package as a response to the predominant demands in Quebec, it is even more difficult to see it as a response to expectations and pressures in the rest of the country. Constitutional revision in general had never been a priority in English Canada. It was only the rise of constitutional discontent in Quebec that had placed it on the Canadian political agenda. With the clear-cut referendum result, many English Canadians saw no reason to pursue it any further.[124] If they felt embarrassed by the fact that the Canadian constitution was still an act of the British Parliament, presuming they were even aware of the fact, they were apparently quite prepared to live with it.[125]

As for the particular constitutional project that was so dear to the Trudeau government, an entrenched bill of rights, English-Canadian opinion was divided. Most of the English-Canadian premiers were firmly opposed to the concept, which they saw as a major and ill-advised departure from Canada's political traditions. At the first ministers' conference on the constitution in September 1980, Manitoba premier Sterling Lyon declared that "such a transfer of legislative authority [from Parliament] to courts would amount to a constitutional revolution entailing the relinquishment of the essential principle of Parliamentary democracy, the principle of Parliamentary supremacy." He urged his colleagues "to retain our own heritage, and reject experiments with concepts foreign to our tradition." The NDP premier of Saskatchewan, Allan Blakeney, put a social democratic gloss on the opposition, declaring that a charter would transfer power to the courts, giving "an advantage to the rich" and away from legislatures, which "were less of an advantage to the rich."[126] The premiers' opposition to entrenchment of rights extended even to the kind of right that, for Trudeau and his colleagues, was the heart of the proposed Charter: language rights. During discussions in the summer of 1980, only four provinces were prepared to support the recognition of minority-language rights.[127]

The premiers might have been accused of being self-serving in their opposition to the Charter, concerned simply with protecting their own power. Certainly, Trudeau and others were quick to charge them with precisely that. Yet, in their arguments against the notion of a charter, the premiers were drawing upon a tradition and body of thought with deep roots in English Canada. Thus, a good number of leading English-Canadian academics voiced opposition to the Trudeau project. Donald Smiley, who himself had long opposed an entrenched charter,[128] noted in 1981 that "there is no consensus about the matter and in legal and academic circles there is a continuing strain of anti-entrenchment argument." In fact, he ascribed such sentiment to "many of the more senior and respected members of the Canadian bar and bench."[129]

Nevertheless, there were also strong supporters of an entrenched charter. In 1960, John Diefenbaker had secured a Canadian Bill of Rights, a simple Act of Parliament that applied only to matters under Parliament's jurisdiction. For many years prominent legal scholars and civil liberties groups had been calling for an entrenched charter. Moreover, organizations representing specific categories of Canadians saw that a charter might protect or improve the position of their members.[130]

These areas of support were strongly in evidence when hearings were convened by a special parliamentary committee on the Trudeau government's constitutional resolution. Indeed, the government quickly decided to extend the televised hearings. Over 200 groups made presentations to the televised hearings; 900 individuals and groups made written submissions.[131] As a result, the committee heard from a wide spectrum of groups, including organizations of persons with disabilities, the Nation Action Committee on the Status of Women, the National Indian Brotherhood, the Canadian Civil Liberties Association, and the Canadian Association of Lesbians and Gay Men. Most of these groups actually argued for a stronger charter than the one being proposed.[132]

The Trudeau government was able to use these public expressions of support for a charter to challenge outright the legitimacy of the premiers' opposition. Claiming to speak for "the people" and defining its constitutional project as nothing less than a "people's package," the Trudeau government practised what Peter Russell has called a "new populist constitutionalism."[133] Indeed, the government was able to cite opinion surveys showing that a majority of Canadians supported a charter; apparently they had little knowledge of what would be in it.[134] Confronted with mobilization of support in favour of a charter, the premiers relented and agreed on condition that large sections of the Charter be subject to a notwithstanding clause.

Yet the public support that built up around the Charter does not, itself, *explain* the Trudeau government's actions. Rather than simply responding to pressures from English Canada, the Trudeau government activated these pressures by making an entrenched charter a distinct possibility.

The Trudeau government took quite a different position on other aspects of constitutional reform for which there was evidence of substantial support. First, with respect to the division of powers, most provincial governments had argued for significant modifications. Indeed, in February 1979, Trudeau had been prepared to discuss a long list of jurisdictional changes, most of them in the direction of the provinces. Yet, in the summer of 1980, he and his colleagues took quite a different position, rejecting many of the decentralizing items and adding new ones, such as eliminating provincial impediments to the economic union. At the September first ministers' conference, Trudeau summarily dismissed most of the items on a list that a coalition of premiers presented to him.[135] He had already decided to embark, alone if necessary, on a constitutional package in which there was no meaningful change to the division of powers.

Second, the provincial governments had expressed considerable interest in reform of the Senate and the Supreme Court. Some of the provincial governments had proposed that the Senate be converted to a body composed of representatives appointed by the provincial governments, modelled after the German *Bundesrat*.[136] At least one premier, Peter Lougheed of Alberta, was opposed to the concept.[137] On the other hand, there should have been no difficulty establishing a consensus on reform of the Supreme Court. This had, after all, been part of the Victoria Charter, to which all provinces but Quebec had agreed. But, unlike in the case of the Charter, the Trudeau government was not prepared to show leadership. In all likelihood, reform of central institutions fell victim to Ottawa's plans for unilateral action. The Supreme Court had already ruled, in its 1979 decision on Bill C-60, that the federal government could not unilaterally reform central institutions. Having not included this item in its agenda of unilateral action, Ottawa apparently was not prepared to see the item back on the table when it returned to negotiations with the provinces.

Clearly, the form and content of the Trudeau government's constitutional package was not a direct response to pressures from English Canada, any more than it was a direct response to the predominant pressures in Quebec. At the same time, the government was able to use the areas of English-Canadian support for one element of the package, the Charter, to mobilize opinion in favour of the project as a whole and against the opposition of provincial premiers and many others.

The Trudeau government also found support for its package by tapping a concern that was shared by a good many English Canadians: the need to respond to Quebec, especially in light of the promises that had been made during the referendum debate. Here, Trudeau and his cabinet were emphatic that their package was indeed such a response. Whereas they could readily dismiss the Lévesque government's opposition as the predictable response of a "separatist" government, the opposition of Quebec federalists, such as Claude Ryan and much of the Quebec Liberal Party, was a bit more difficult to dismiss. However, federal leaders described this position as misguided or, worse still, reflecting crypto-separatist tendencies. Or they dismissed the objection as a question of procedure rather than content. The Quebec people, Trudeau insisted, did not share the obsessions of their nationalist élite; they firmly supported the constitutional package and prized the pan-Canadian entrenchment of language rights that it offered. The argument carried some weight in English Canada. Once again, Trudeau had succeeded in interposing his own quite distinctive opinion of "what Quebec wants," and mobilizing English-Canadian support on that basis.

Finally, Indigenous leaders had also sought to shape the course of the patriation exercise. They were alarmed that patriation might threaten treaty rights that had been granted by the British Crown and, at the same time, wanted any new constitutional document to grant heightened recognition of Indigenous rights. Yet clearly their concerns were not a priority for the Trudeau government or, for that matter, the provinces. During the various negotiations among the federal and provincial governments, Indigenous leaders were limited to observer status. Indigenous leaders lobbied the British Parliament and initiated cases in British courts, contending that patriation could not take place without Indigenous consent, but their contention was rejected both in Parliament and in the courts. The package to which all first ministers but Quebec's agreed in November of 1981 included no recognition of Indigenous rights or treaty rights, given the rejection by a number of premiers to a draft provision to that effect. After intense lobbying by Indigenous leaders, the first ministers did agree to add a provision recognizing "*existing* aboriginal and treaty rights." However, most Indigenous leaders were dissatisfied with this formula.[138] In short, the end result cannot be seen as a faithful reflection of Indigenous concerns.

Entrenching the Trudeau Vision

In short, the final result closely matched long-established priorities and the vision of Trudeau himself; it is here that we must look for the primary explanation of the Constitution Act, 1982. Finding himself back in power in early 1980 and leading the federalist forces to a resounding referendum victory four months later, Trudeau saw a historic opportunity to achieve the central objectives of his national unity strategy. He no longer had to entertain new departures and approaches as he had appeared to do in the wake of the 1976 PQ victory.

Indeed, as Trudeau prepared this new constitutional initiative he was careful to choose officials who would share the ruthlessness that he could now exercise. This excluded advisers, such as André Burelle, who had joined Trudeau in the post-1976 period, encouraged by the new openness expressed in Trudeau's 1977 Chamber of Commerce speech. It also excluded Gordon Robertson, who not only had been deputy minister of federal–provincial relations in the post-1976 period but, as clerk of the Privy Council, had been closely involved with the negotiations leading up to the Victoria Charter. Several years later, Trudeau explained in these terms his choice of Michael Kirby over Robertson:

> Let's just say that in this last stage I felt one needed almost a putsch, a *coup de force*, and Gordon was too much of a gentleman for that. It was clearly going to be rough and Gordon Robertson wasn't the man: a mandarin, concerned with the common weal, afraid of irreparable damage to the fabric of society. So I made a different choice.[139]

Having witnessed, during his stint in the Privy Council Office, the halting and heavily qualified efforts of the St. Laurent government to formalize Canadian sovereignty, Trudeau was determined to resolve the matter once and for all by running the risks of unilateralism from which St. Laurent had shrunk.[140] He was equally determined to achieve his long-standing objective of entrenching linguistic equality. Thus, he was adamant that any charter must contain language rights. Indeed, he declared in Quebec City in the fall of 1980 that French-language rights were the whole purpose of the Charter and that the other rights had been added to avoid English-Canadian cries of "French power."[141] For the same reason, he rejected any qualification to the application of language rights, including the notwithstanding clause which he finally agreed to for less important parts of the Charter.[142]

National Unity through Pan-Canadian Nationalism

The Constitution Act, 1982, can best be understood as the imposition by the Trudeau government of its *own* conception of Canada. Where it could, the government mobilized support for its initiative, inserting provisions in the Charter of Rights and Freedoms that ensured the support of specific social groups, primarily in English Canada. But where necessary, Trudeau and his colleagues were more than prepared to defy those who opposed their initiative and the conception of Canada that underlay it. This meant defying much of public opinion in Quebec, federalist as well as sovereigntist.

To defend its course of action, the Trudeau government invoked its right, as the national government, to act on behalf of the Canadian nation. Indeed, a few weeks before the referendum, Trudeau had made abundantly clear how he saw the powers and responsibilities of the "national" government. He told the House that "We [the Members of Parliament] are the only group of men and women in this country who can speak for every Canadian. We are the only group, the only assembly in this country, which can speak for the whole nation, which can express the national will and the national interest." On this basis, Trudeau declared, it was appropriate that the Fathers of Confederation gave the federal government powers, including the reservation and disallowance powers, through which it might intervene against a province that was acting "contrary to the national interest." After all, "when there is a conflict of interest, not of laws, which will be judged by the courts, the citizens must be convinced that there is a national government which will speak for the national interest and will ensure that it does prevail."[143]

Such nationalist rhetoric was, of course, very much at odds with Trudeau's 1960s writings. There, Canada was presented not as a nation-state but as a "multinational state."[144] In fact, it was a "pact":

> Federalism is by its very essence a compromise and a pact. It is a compromise in the sense that when national consensus on *all* things is not desirable or cannot readily obtain, the area of consensus is reduced in order that consensus on *some* things be reached. It is a pact or quasi-treaty in the sense that the terms of that compromise cannot be changed unilaterally. That is not to say that the terms are fixed forever; but only that in changing them every effort must be made not to destroy the consensus on which the federated nation rests.[145]

Yet in those writings the celebration of Canadian federalism had always been driven by a more important theme, the need to defeat nationalism, especially Quebec nationalism.[146] Federalism was less an end in itself than a means of achieving a more important goal. And, as the Trudeau government demonstrated in the early 1980s, the values of federalism could be discarded if other more promising means should become available.

The threat of unilateral patriation and the subsequent patriation without Quebec's consent were not deviations from the Trudeau vision of Canada, born of the flush of referendum victory. They followed logically from that vision and the national unity strategy that had been pursued to put it in place. During the 1970s, this vision of Canada had already been evident in the substitution of multiculturalism for biculturalism and the attempt to apply a uniform language policy across the country. It had also been seen in the concerted efforts to assert the role of Ottawa as the "national government." As early as February 1976, Prime Minister Trudeau had declared that his government might seek patriation unilaterally if there should be no agreement among the provinces on a constitutional package.[147] With the 1980 referendum victory, the federal government felt it could act freely[148] and the underlying logic of its strategy was now revealed: *Quebec* nationalism was to be defeated by *Canadian* nationalism. For that matter, with the 1980s Trudeau's close collaborators included individuals, all Anglophone, who were themselves quite sympathetic to this Canadian nationalism.[149] Trudeau himself no longer had the counsel of the two fellow Quebeckers who had tempered his animosity to Quebec nationalism, Gérard Pelletier and Jean Marchand. In fact, there was virtually only one Francophone in his immediate entourage: André Burelle.[150]

To be sure, defenders of this approach would argue that this new Canadian nationalism was fundamentally different from Quebec nationalism. Rather than an "ethnic nationalism" it was a "civic nationalism," which rose above ethnicity and all other social divisions. Nonetheless it *was* nationalism and, moreover, it was one in which the nation consists of individuals who first and foremost are Canadian. As such, this Canadian nationalism directly contradicted the vision of a federal, dualist Canada with distinct societies and multiple identities, which had been so important to generations of Quebec Francophones.

The New Federal Unilateralism

The federal government's nationalism and its commitment to a unitary Canada can be seen in the way it dealt not just with the constitution but with the whole range of federal–provincial relations.[151] Thus, in November 1981, Trudeau explained why the federal government had revised its fiscal relations with the provinces so as to reserve funds for new national projects: "We have stopped the momentum that would have turned Canada into, in everything but name only, ten countries." The time had come, he declared, to "reassert in our national policies that Canada is one country which must be capable of moving with unity of spirit and purpose towards shared goals. If Canada is indeed to be a nation, there must be a national will which is something more than the lowest common denominator among the desires of the provincial governments."[152]

On this basis, the Trudeau government showed a new readiness to act unilaterally in areas where in the past it usually had sought the collaboration, even the consent, of the provinces. A striking case was the pricing of oil and gas, where the federal government simply announced new prices.[153] Similarly, in 1983, Ottawa made substantial changes and cuts to its fiscal transfers to the provinces without the usual amount of consultation.

At the same time, the Trudeau government showed a new determination to provide benefits and services directly to citizens in areas of clear provincial jurisdiction. After having agreed in 1978 to the provincial demand that it not directly fund municipalities, in 1981 it suddenly terminated the agreement and proceeded to establish new programs of direct funding of municipalities. Similarly, it altered the terms of its co-operation with provincial governments in regional development. Rather than co-fund common projects, Ottawa announced it would pursue "parallel" projects with the provinces. By delivering projects itself, Ottawa could be more certain of receiving public credit for them. And it established its own officials in each region to formulate new projects, as well as oversee their implementation.[154]

The importance of the Quebec question to the Trudeau government is seen from the number of unilateral federal measures related to Quebec. The federal government's Bill S-31, restricting provincial ownership in transportation enterprises, was triggered by apprehension over the use the Quebec government's Caisse de dépôt et placement, which invests pension and insurance funds, might make of its holdings in Canadian Pacific. Similarly, so as to satisfy Newfoundland's long-standing objections to the terms of its agreement with Hydro-Québec, Ottawa proposed in 1981 to expropriate a right of way through Quebec territory for transmission lines. And Ottawa twice unilaterally announced economic development projects in Quebec but not any other province.[155]

Finally, Ottawa undertook enormous advertising campaigns to ensure that citizens were aware of its activities.[156] Ottawa increasingly concentrated its funds in "advocacy" advertising in which it tried to win citizens over to its position in struggles with the provinces. Thus, the share of federal advertising funds used by the Canadian Unity Information Office rose from 4.5 per cent in 1978–9 to 25.3 per cent in 1980–1 and 21.1 per cent in 1981–2.[157]

Throughout these many measures the logic was that the key to national unity lay with the federal government's ability to rein in the provinces and assert its proper role as the "national" government of all Canadians. Not only that, but through such measures as the National Energy Program, it would defend the national interest against the American multinationals. In the 1960s, however, Trudeau had warned against trying to secure the cohesion of a multinational federation like Canada through appeals to nationalism rather than using reason to build a consensus:

> If my premises are correct, nationalism cannot provide the answer. Even if massive investments in flags, dignity, protectionism, and Canadian

> content of television managed to hold the country together for a few more years, separatism would remain a recurrent phenomenon. . . . If, for instance, it is going to remain *morally wrong* for Wall Street to assume control of Canada's economy, how will it become *morally right* for Bay Street to dominate Quebec's or—for that matter—Nova Scotia's? [emphasis in original][158]

As we shall see, the pan-Canadian nationalism of the final Trudeau administration did not prevent Quebec separatism from being "a recurrent phenomenon." Nor did it dissuade Quebec Francophones from giving their primary loyalty to Quebec. Indeed, such sentiments were to increase during the 1980s. The new Canadian nationalism may even have contributed to this directly, by provoking a reaction among Quebeckers. But the new Canadian nationalism engendered a recurrence of "separatism" in a more profound sense. By reinforcing English Canadians in their resistance to *any* recognition of the continuing Quebec identity within the Canadian federation, it left Quebec sovereignty as the only alternative.

Trying and Failing to Repair the Damage: The Meech Lake Accord

The departure of Pierre Trudeau from the political scene in the spring of 1984 opened the door to public debate about the need to repair the damage of 1982 and to obtain Quebec's consent to the constitution. Brian Mulroney's promise during the 1984 election campaign to tackle the issue appears to have contributed to his sweep of Quebec. René Lévesque rose to the challenge of defining the terms on which Quebec would sign, in the process triggering the departure of several cabinet colleagues. But since he left politics a few months later, it fell to the new Bourassa government to pick up the process. Given its clear commitment to Canadian federalism, it was much better placed to do so.

In Ontario a new premier, David Peterson, came to office in June 1985, convinced that the question had to be resolved. As long as Quebec was not a signatory to the constitution, and thus not a full participant in constitutional discussions, Canada was unable to address a host of pressing issues. Fully aware of Ontario's historical role as "broker" within Confederation, Peterson was prepared to make the case with the other premiers; indeed, two days after the election of the Bourassa government Peterson went to Montreal to meet with Bourassa.[159]

Not only were the leaders of relevant governments now committed to addressing the issue, but there appears to have been agreement among civil servants and academics concerned with intergovernmental relations that the question should be resolved. Many of the provincial officials who were veterans of the federal–provincial confrontations of the Trudeau era had never been converts to the Trudeau vision. Even among the federal mandarins there was apparently some sentiment that Quebec's absence carried real risks for the federation. The tone had been set by Gordon Robertson, the former clerk of the Privy Council and constitutional adviser whom Trudeau had passed over in his final constitutional battle. Just after the agreement of 5 November 1981 to constitutional revisions, Robertson had written, "It would be optimistic in the extreme to think that we can avoid a new crisis on the question of separation in a very few years."[160]

The initiative was taken by Robert Bourassa. From the outset, the "normalizing" of Quebec's place in Canada was a priority of his government. At the swearing-in of his new government, Bourassa broke with PQ practice and arranged for the Canadian flag to join the Quebec flag in the National Assembly, declaring, moreover, that the flag was there to stay.[161] Then, in March 1986, the Quebec minister of intergovernmental affairs, Gil Rémillard, announced that his government was abandoning the PQ government's practice of routinely invoking the notwithstanding clause of the Charter of Rights and Freedoms when passing legislation. Arguing that acceptance of the Charter was the logical position for federalists to take, Rémillard declared, "As for us, our principle is that we're federalists." At the same time, he was careful to reiterate that the Constitution Act as it stood was "unacceptable" to the Quebec government.[162]

The following May, at a special conference of academics, intergovernmental officials, and interested parties, Rémillard outlined the conditions under which the act could be acceptable to Quebec. There were five: a veto over constitutional change affecting Quebec, recognition of Quebec's status as a distinct society, limitation of the federal spending power, participation in Supreme Court nominations, and recognition of Quebec's existing powers related to immigration. In presenting these terms, Rémillard stressed that the election of his government "signifies a new era of federal–provincial and interprovincial relations. Faithful to our federalist government, we want to guarantee Quebec its rights as a distinct society and major partner in the Canadian federation."[163] Apparently, his presentation was well received by the audience; the five conditions he set out seemed to be "manageable."[164]

Collectively, the conditions were the most modest proposals for constitutional change that had come from any Quebec government in recent decades, including Bourassa's own proposals to the ill-fated Victoria Conference. In effect, they showed that the Bourassa government wanted to frame a set of proposals that might be acceptable to the rest of Canada, and thus resolve Quebec's anomalous constitutional status.[165] They also showed how little bargaining power the Bourassa government had. After the 1980 referendum, English Canadians had lost patience with the argument that Bourassa and other federalist premiers had used in the past: the need to head off the forces of Quebec sovereignty.

A tour of provincial capitals by Quebec officials found a general receptiveness to the proposals. In August, at their annual interprovincial conference, the premiers issued a communiqué announcing that their "top constitutional priority" was to begin federal–provincial discussions, based on Quebec's five proposals, to secure "Quebec's full and active participation in the Canadian federation."[166]

The federal government watched these developments with great interest. Indeed, before running in the 1985 Quebec election, Rémillard had been a special constitutional adviser to the Mulroney government.[167] Clearly, Prime Minister Mulroney welcomed a potential opportunity to make good on his election pledge to try to arrange for Quebec to accept the constitution. Such an effort, especially if it were successful, could only consolidate the PC's new electoral base in Quebec.

Yet electoral interests were not the only reason for the widespread responsiveness to Quebec's overtures. Even if the Mulroney government's motives could be reduced to electoral opportunism, itself a dubious proposition, Ontario premier David Peterson certainly had no reason to further the federal Tories' electoral ambitions. Nor could he necessarily expect the Ontario voters to reward him for his efforts. By the same token, electoral calculations would have had no significance to the intergovernmental relations experts and officials who had welcomed Rémillard's proposals. In short, the surge in discussions about securing Quebec's formal consent to the constitution was at least partly due to a belief among political leaders and public officials, outside Quebec as well as within, that the long-term interests of the Canadian federation required that action be taken.

After further tours of provincial capitals by both Quebec and federal officials, focused on the five-point proposal, Brian Mulroney wrote to the premiers identifying what he thought could be the basis of a consensus; his federal–provincial affairs minister, Senator Lowell Murray, sent proposals for the outstanding issues. On this basis, the first ministers met on 30 April at the prime minister's residence on Meech Lake. Their discussions resulted in the Meech Lake Accord, a package of constitutional revisions incorporating all of Quebec's five proposals and adding a sixth designed to placate the demand of Alberta premier Getty for Senate reform. Subsequently, on 13 June 1987, the first ministers agreed to a somewhat modified revision of the accord in legal language (generally known as the Langevin Accord).[168]

A Modest Set of Changes

Despite the many claims that the Meech Lake Accord would fundamentally change, even destroy, Canada, it was quite limited in scope, reflecting the modest nature of the Bourassa government's proposal which inspired it. Some of its provisions merely formalized practices and arrangements that already existed. Even where it did introduce new departures, they were quite carefully circumscribed.

The part that was to cause the greatest controversy was, of course, the "distinct-society clause." A purely interpretative clause, it stated that in interpreting the constitution the courts should do so in a way that is consistent with "the recognition that Quebec constitutes within Canada a distinct society."

Moreover, it affirmed that "the role of the legislature and Government of Quebec is to preserve and promote the distinct identity of Quebec."[169]

At the same time, this recognition of Quebec's uniqueness was carefully balanced by a preceding clause that referred to a Canadian linguistic duality that transcends Quebec's borders. This "duality clause" required the constitution to be interpreted in a manner consistent with "the recognition that the existence of French-speaking Canadians, centred in Quebec but also present elsewhere in Canada, and English-speaking Canadians, concentrated outside Quebec but also present in Quebec, constitutes a fundamental characteristic of Canada." Parliament and all the provincial legislatures were given the responsibility for preserving this "fundamental characteristic."[170]

So as to ensure that the clauses would be purely interpretative, a later provision declared that they were not to diminish the powers of either the federal government or the provincial governments.[171] On this basis, it is difficult to see how the distinct-society clause could have enabled Quebec to assume any jurisdictions exclusively held by the federal government. It is more likely that the distinct-society clause might have enabled the Quebec government to maintain measures within its existing jurisdictions that otherwise violated provisions of the Charter. Even then the Quebec government would have had to persuade the courts that the measure was, under the terms of section 1 of the Charter, "demonstrably justified in a free and democratic society." In the opinion of a leading English-Canadian constitutional authority, Peter Hogg, the section "should probably be seen as an affirmation of sociological facts with little legal significance."[172]

A second area of the Accord was immigration. The Accord would have had the effect of inserting in the constitution an agreement between the federal government and Quebec patterned after the Cullen–Couture Accord.[173] In effect, it would have "constitutionalized" the existing practice, providing Quebec with a guarantee of permanence that a simple intergovernmental agreement could not. In addition to the elements of Cullen–Couture, this constitutionalized Accord would have guaranteed Quebec a proportionate share of the total numbers for immigrants set by Ottawa each year and would have allowed Quebec to take responsibility for the integration of immigrants; Ottawa would have kept exclusive responsibility for awarding citizenship. The Accord also called for similar agreements to be negotiated with other provincial governments. Under the constitution, it should be borne in mind, immigration is concurrent or shared by both levels of government, but Ottawa has the power to override the provinces.

A third subject of the Accord was the federal government's use of its spending power within provincial jurisdictions.[174] If a province decided not to participate in a new shared-cost program established by Ottawa in an exclusive provincial jurisdiction, then it would have been entitled to "reasonable compensation" by the federal government. To do so, however, it would have had to maintain a "program or initiative" of its own that was "compatible with the national objectives."

By implication, these objectives would be set by the federal government. At the same time, Ottawa would have remained free to establish its own spending programs in jurisdictions that are exclusively provincial.

The Accord also dealt with the Supreme Court.[175] Beyond stipulating that three of the nine justices must be members of the Quebec bar, constitutionalizing a long-standing provision of the Supreme Court Act, the Accord specified that provincial governments would be allowed to draw up lists of candidates for appointment to the Court. The actual appointment would be made by the federal government, but it would be obliged to choose from such a list. In the case of the three Quebec justices, Ottawa would have been obliged to choose from a list submitted by Quebec. Otherwise, it could have chosen from whichever government's list it wished. And it can be assumed that, in the case of Quebec, if Ottawa was dissatisfied with the names submitted, it could have asked for a second list.

A similar procedure was to have been adopted for the Senate: in filling a Senate vacancy, Ottawa would choose from a list of names submitted by the government of the province in question. Like Supreme Court justices, senators would be appointed for life (to age 75, as they are now) rather than for fixed terms. The Senate arrangements were to be provisional, pending a thorough Senate reform.[176]

Finally, the Accord would have altered the amending formula so that amendments involving certain aspects of Parliament and the Supreme Court, as well as the creation of new provinces or the extension of existing ones, would require the support of all provinces. Also, "reasonable compensation" to provinces not agreeing to transfers of jurisdiction to the federal level would no longer have been restricted to matters involving education and culture.

Not only was the Accord modest in its scope, but every element had been under discussion for years in intergovernmental circles. Indeed, some of them fell considerably short of past proposals. Even the Trudeau government had made proposals along similar lines.[177]

Substantial Support in Quebec

Surprisingly perhaps, given its limitations, the Accord was quite well received in French Quebec. In a survey taken just after the Langevin version had been agreed to, 61 per cent of Quebec respondents said they approved of the agreement, and only 16 per cent said they disapproved.[178] The general satisfaction extended not only to such prominent federalists as Claude Ryan, who was now a member of Bourassa's cabinet, and Solange Chaput-Rolland,[179] who had been a member of the Pepin–Robarts Commission, but even people who had played key roles in the PQ government. Louis Bernard, who had been the senior civil servant under René Lévesque, and Jean-K. Samson, who had been a constitutional adviser to Lévesque, both served on a committee of the Bourassa government charged with preparing a legal version of the Accord. Even Lévesque himself had positive things to say about the Accord, citing the progress in immigration and declaring the Accord to be "neither very good nor catastrophic." Ultimately, he said he could not sign it until ambiguities in the text had been resolved.[180]

One reason the Accord was well received in Quebec may have been that its significance was interpreted very broadly. In an effort to persuade Quebeckers of the significance of the Accord, Bourassa had said that Meech would "enable us to consolidate what we already have and to make even further gains."[181] Intergovernmental Affairs Minister Gil Rémillard said that the Accord would enable Quebec to have an enhanced presence in international relations.[182]

Yet even without exaggeration of its concrete import, the Accord, especially its distinct-society clause, was very important in that it broke with the systematic rejection of Quebec's demands that had marked constitutional deliberations throughout the Trudeau era. It formally recognized the Quebec government's responsibility to protect and promote Quebec's distinctiveness, which was the essential claim of Quebec nationalists. In this, the Accord represented a clear break with the Trudeau era. In a sense, the distinct-society clause harked back to the preceding era, when Lester Pearson had tried to accommodate the new Quebec, proclaiming it to be a "nation within a nation." At the same time, Quebeckers could believe that agreement of all first ministers to Quebec's conditions for signing the constitution, minimal as they may have been, was an admission that the 1982 isolation of Quebec had been an error, indeed an injustice.

All this did not, of course, impress firmly committed indépendantistes. Jacques-Yvan Morin, a prominent member of Lévesque's cabinets, denounced the Accord as a "trap" because it did not give Quebec any additional powers.[183] Jacques Parizeau pronounced it a major setback to Quebec's traditional demands.[184] The Société Saint-Jean-Baptiste and the Mouvement national québécois tried to rally public opposition to the Accord. Then PQ leader Pierre-Marc Johnson called "the Meech Lake monster" a sell-out and, on that basis, rallied the party's national council behind him.[185]

These denunciations did not seem to have much resonance with the public. For Quebec Francophones who still saw themselves as members of the Canadian political community, even though their primary allegiance was to Quebec, the Meech Lake Accord and English Canada's apparent support for it meant that their vision of the country was recognized and accepted. No longer were they expected to conform to the Trudeau vision. They could be Canadians on their own terms. The Accord may have been only a minimal response to their aspirations, but it was nonetheless significant.

Growing Opposition in English Canada

On the other hand, however modest its terms, the Accord soon became the focus of intense opposition in English Canada. Moreover, this opposition was largely rooted in precisely the feature that had endeared it to Quebeckers: its contradiction of the Trudeau vision of Canada. At first, English Canadians had tended to support the Accord.[186] By April 1988, however, a Gallup poll found opinion evenly split among Anglophones: 26 per cent in favour, 27 per cent against, and 47 per cent undecided. By November of the following year, opinion was firmly against. In March of 1990, as time was running out for the Accord, Gallup found only 19 per cent of Anglophones in favour, with 51 per cent against and 30 per cent undecided.[187]

In part, English-Canadian opposition was due to the processes that had created the Accord—negotiations among first ministers behind closed doors. Those processes were denounced as undemocratic, and especially unacceptable when they affected the basic law of the country. Citizens had not been given the proper opportunity to express their views and participate in this revision of "their" constitution.

The fact of the matter is that Meech had been produced through the time-honoured practices of executive federalism, just like the Constitution Act, 1982. However, the Constitution Act had imposed a different set of rules for all subsequent revisions, including Meech: resolutions had to be approved not just by Parliament but by provincial legislatures. In effect, with Meech there were public debates in 10 different provincial legislatures, often with public hearings by special committees. Yet since the Accord had been negotiated among 11 first ministers, it would have been exceedingly difficult to modify the Accord in light of these debates.[188]

The determination of citizens and groups to express their views on Meech, usually hostile ones at that, also demonstrated another consequence of 1982. Thanks to the Charter, English Canadians had acquired a sense of "ownership" of the constitution. No longer concerned with just the jurisdictions of governments, the constitution now defined the relationship between citizens and their governments. For many English Canadians, it was indeed the "people's package" that the Trudeau government claimed it to be. Thus, it was all the more important that politicians should not be able to dispose of the constitution on their own.[189]

In the last analysis, however, English-Canadian opposition to Meech was an attempt to protect the Trudeau vision of Canada. As Alan Cairns asserts,

> The absence of support for the Trudeau vision of Canada among first ministers and in the leadership of the three national parties was not based on an accurate reading of the sentiments of Canadians. Pan-Canadianism, support of the Charter, belief in a leading role for the central government, and a deep uneasiness at the provincializing thrust of the Accord were generously represented, indeed probably predominant, among the groups and individuals that appeared before the Joint [Parliamentary] Committee [on the Meech Lake Accord] and in other fora outside Quebec.[190]

Several provisions of the Accord were attacked as threatening the federal government's role as the "national" government of all Canadians. In particular, a wide variety of organizations voiced concern that the federal spending power provisions would undermine Ottawa's ability to ensure that all Canadians, as Canadians, received health and social services. It would no longer be able to enforce "national standards" on the provinces; such new programs as a national day care system would be impossible.[191] By the same token, English-Canadian critics argued that the nomination provisions for the Senate and the Supreme Court would in effect turn control over to the provincial governments.[192]

Moreover, the debate over Meech soon became enmeshed in the struggle over the Mulroney government's proposed Canada–United States Free Trade Agreement. Opponents feared that it too would undermine the ability of the federal government to maintain national social services. With the adoption of the Free Trade Agreement, the bitterness among its opponents soon extended to the Meech Lake Accord as well. The connection was, of course, encouraged by the fact that, during the 1988 federal election, the large Quebec vote for the Progressive Conservatives had ensured that free trade would come into effect. (The massive PC vote in Alberta tended to be overlooked.) Through these processes, prominent figures in the English-Canadian left came to oppose Meech.[193]

Defence of a strong "national" government in Ottawa was a central tenet of the Trudeau vision, but was not exclusive to it. However, another line of attack on the Accord was intimately linked to the Trudeau vision: opposition to the distinct-society clause. Moreover, this clause was the most important focus of English-Canadian opposition to the Accord.

From the outset, English Canadians had been troubled by the distinct-society clause. A survey taken just after the Accord had been put in its final form, the Langevin version, found that among the specific provisions of the Accord, the distinct-society clause was the one to receive the least support of Canadians as a whole (46 per cent); 56 per cent of Canadians outside Quebec said they disapproved of it.[194] Similarly, in their analysis of a 1988 survey, Blais and Crête found that among Anglophones living outside Quebec only 28 per cent responded negatively to a simple question asking their opinion of the Accord, whereas 56 per cent responded negatively to a question that indicated that the Accord recognized Quebec's distinct character.[195]

The fact of the matter is that the distinct-society clause managed to offend each of the precepts of the Trudeau vision of Canada. For such opponents of Meech as Clyde Wells, who did not hesitate to acknowledge his intellectual debt to Trudeau,[196] the clause violated the principle of a "true" federation: the distinct-society clause "would not and should not create a special legislative status for one province different from that of the other nine provinces." Indeed, he warned, no such federation is likely to survive.[197]

For champions of multiculturalism, the Accord's distinct-society and duality clauses offended their idea of Canada. The parliamentary interventions of two Liberal MPs, Charles Caccia and Sergio Marchi, included statements that the Accord constituted "a rear-view mirror vision which may have been valid two generations ago, [an] outdated [definition of Canada] . . . primarily satisfied with only depicting our people's past and our country's history. . . . Millions of Canadians are left out who do not identify with either English or French. They have no place in the Accord, and they are outside the Constitution."[198]

For many critics, the distinct-society clause threatened the integrity of the Charter of Rights and Freedoms. Leading English-Canadian feminists feared that the distinct-society clause might lead to a downgrading of the hard-won equality provisions of the Charter. Law professor Kathleen Mahoney wrote,

> Since 1985, women have achieved remarkable advances largely due to Charter guarantees of equality before and under the law and the right to equal protection and equal benefit of the law without discrimination. . . . I suggest that the risks to women's rights in the 1987 Constitutional Accord are not slight. Rather, it is my opinion that the Accord, if passed, will likely diminish constitutional rights that Canadian women currently enjoy.[199]

Some English-Canadian feminists even argued that the distinct-society clause might lead to the oppression of Quebec women, by facilitating repressive and discriminatory measures by the Quebec government.[200] This latter line of attack earned a stern rebuke from Quebec feminists.[201]

As for the Trudeau ideal of Canadian bilingualism, groups such as Canadian Parents for French were quick to see in Meech a threat to national unity. In testimony to the joint parliamentary committee on Meech, the president of Canadian Parents for French attacked the Accord's duality clause for referring to simply the preservation of linguistic duality, unlike the distinct-society clause, which assigned the Quebec government the role of both preserving and promoting Quebec's identity.[202]

Pierre Trudeau: Reasserting His Vision

If in fact many English Canadians framed their opposition to the Meech Lake Accord in terms of the Trudeau vision, they of course had help from Trudeau himself.[203] After the Accord had been agreed upon at Meech Lake but before it was formalized at the Langevin session, Trudeau wrote an article virulently attacking the Accord. It was published in two major newspapers under the title "Say Goodbye to One Canada." This was an extraordinary act for a retired political leader.

In a polemical style that evoked Trudeau's earlier career as essayist and political activist, the article attacked each of the Accord's provisions, starting with the distinct-society and duality clauses:

> Those who never wanted a bilingual Canada—Quebec separatists and western separatists—get their wish right in the first paragraphs of the Accord, with recognition of "the existence of French-speaking Canada . . . and English-speaking Canada." Those Canadians who fought for a single Canada, bilingual and multicultural, can say goodbye to their dream: We are henceforth to have two Canadas, each defined in terms of its language.

Trudeau even attacked the motives and character of the Accord's federal and Quebec authors: "The provincialist politicians, whether they sit in Ottawa or in Quebec, are also perpetual losers; they don't have the stature or the vision to dominate the Canadian state, so they need a Quebec ghetto as their lair." In particular, he castigated that "weakling" Mulroney for caving into the premiers' demands and putting Canada on the "fast track" to sovereignty-association.[204] With these bitter personal attacks, the statement constituted nothing less than a diatribe.[205]

The influence of Trudeau's diatribe on English-Canadian opinion was seen in the much tougher position that Premier Peterson of Ontario adopted during the Langevin negotiations than he had in the first round of negotiations at Meech Lake.[206] In fact, apparently without acknowledging Trudeau's influence, Peterson and Manitoba premier Howard Pawley managed to have the phrasing modified in the duality clause that Trudeau had found particularly offensive: the terms "English-speaking Canada" and "French-speaking Canada" adopted at Meech Lake became "English-speaking Canadians" and "French-speaking Canadians."[207] Once again, Trudeau had succeeded in redefining Canadian dualism in purely individualist terms. Beyond that, the first ministers agreed to add a provision declaring that neither the duality clause nor the distinct-society clause could derogate from "the powers, rights or privileges" of the federal and provincial governments and legislatures.

Needless to say, Trudeau was not impressed with these modifications. He followed his newspaper article with dramatic multi-hour addresses to a joint parliamentary committee on the Meech Lake Accord and to the Senate. In the Senate presentation, where he condemned all the provisions of the Accord, he heaped particular scorn on the duality clause, even with its Langevin modifications. The problem was with the very notion of duality, however expressed. Declaring that "duality divides groups," Trudeau then proclaimed (despite the instances we have already noted):

> We did not use the expression "French-speaking Canadians" and "English-speaking Canadians" in any of our constitutions. We used the concept of bilingualism. Bilingualism unites people; dualism divides them.

> Bilingualism means you can speak to the other; duality means you can live in one language and the rest of Canada will live in another language, and we will all be good friends, which is what Mr Lévesque always wanted.[208]

As for the distinct-society clause, Trudeau believed that if it had any consequences at all, it would be harmful and if it did not, Quebeckers would feel they had been duped.[209] With the Meech Lake Accord and its emphasis on duality and Quebec's distinctiveness and its evisceration of the national government, "in vain, we would have dreamt the dream of one Canada."[210] Whatever the specific provisions of the Accord, and Trudeau had much to say about them, the underlying problem of the Accord was the vision of Canada on which it was based. Indeed, it was the one he had worked so hard to replace. Within the Trudeau vision of Canada, the Accord could only mean the destruction of the country itself.

Thanks to such aggressive leadership, English Canadians had, by the fall of 1988, turned against the Accord.[211] Many of them were to find their views confirmed in December 1988 when the Quebec government passed Bill 178, which reinstated, in a slightly modified form, the sign law that had been declared unconstitutional by the Supreme Court. By invoking the notwithstanding clause of the Charter, the Bourassa government was able to restore the provision of Bill 101 that required commercial signs to be in French only. In doing so, Bourassa was responding to strong pressure from Quebec Francophones. Francophones may have been divided about the necessity of the sign law, but with the Court decision the issue had become one of the integrity of Bill 101, and the ability of the Supreme Court to superimpose the Charter upon it. Thus, the Court's decision served to radicalize opinion on the sign law.[212] Under these circumstances, which directly affected an institution that was central to ensuring Francophone Quebec's cultural uniqueness, neither the Charter nor the Supreme Court had any authority for many Quebec Francophones. Accordingly, there was strong support among Quebec Francophones for Bourassa's use of the notwithstanding clause.[213] (The fact that two Quebec courts had already determined that the sign law violated Quebec's own charter was lost in the process.)

In the rest of Canada, on the other hand, Bill 178 provoked an outpouring of opposition. The notwithstanding clause may have been adopted in order to placate such English-Canadian leaders as Allan Blakeney but, over the following years, the Charter had become so deeply accepted in English Canada that the notwithstanding clause had ceased to be legitimate. Beyond that, Bill 178 was a direct attack on the ideal of a bilingual Canada that many English Canadians had adopted; Quebec seemed to be violating a contract into which it had entered with the rest of the country. Of course, this was not the first time that the Québécois had made it clear that they did not feel bound to accept official bilingualism at the Quebec provincial level. But this manifestation was perhaps the most dramatic, involving the actual suppression of the English language and any language other than French. Once again, Quebec seemed to be repudiating the Trudeau vision of Canada.

Yet rather than leading English-Canadian opinion to start questioning the viability of this vision, let alone the national unity strategy based on it, Bill 178 seemed instead to provoke sheer anger. The bill also provided a ready pretext for abandoning the Meech Lake Accord, on the assumption that the distinct-society clause would only facilitate greater outrages by Quebec. Manitoba premier Gary Filmon was quick to seize the opportunity and withdraw his support from the Accord, which was already widely opposed in Manitoba. On the other hand, whether Bill 178 actually turned English-Canadian opinion against the Accord is another matter. According to analysts Blais and Crête, a clear majority of English Canadians were already opposed to the Accord by the fall of 1988, before the episode began; the size of opposition did not significantly increase after that.[214]

Indigenous Resistance

For their part, Indigenous leaders saw nothing of value in the Meech Lake Accord, given its focus on Quebec's status and relationship with the rest of Canada. They had in fact been seeking, since the adoption of the Constitution Act in 1982, a more substantial recognition of Indigenous rights in the constitution. As required by the Constitution Act, in March of 1983 a conference was held of premiers, territorial heads, and Indigenous leaders that was devoted exclusively to Indigenous issues. The conference actually led to amendments that clarified the Act's guarantee of "existing aboriginal treaty rights."[215] An additional amendment required that two more constitutional conferences include discussion of Indigenous issues. Indeed, three such conferences took place. However, they ended in failure since government leaders would not agree to the Indigenous leaders' proposal of an "inherent right of self-government."[216] Thus, by the time the Meech Lake Accord emerged, most Indigenous leaders were frustrated with the whole process of constitutional negotiation. Some contended that in fact Indigenous interests could be advanced only through direct nation-to-nation relations with the federal government as opposed to participating in constitutional negotiations.

The Demise of Meech

In the end, of course, the Accord was not adopted. When the three-year time limit had expired, the legislatures of two provinces, Manitoba and Newfoundland, had still not approved it. This outcome was largely due to chance and personalities. Two of the original signatories to the Accord, the premiers of Manitoba and New Brunswick, were defeated before their legislatures had ratified the Accord. In the case of a third province, Newfoundland, ratification had been rescinded under the new premier, Clyde Wells. Yet those setbacks might have been overcome.

If Frank McKenna, the new premier of New Brunswick had quickly ratified the Accord, rather than delaying, pressure might have built upon the two other governments to ratify it. If Manitoba's projected ratification had not been delayed by the obstruction of one MLA, Elijah Harper, who reflected Indigenous disaffection from the whole process of constitutional negotiation, then the pressure on the remaining hold-out, Newfoundland, might have been irresistible. In short, with a somewhat different chain of events the Accord might have been saved.

Yet even if the Accord had passed, the battle was lost. The original purpose of the Meech Lake Accord had been to repair the damage of 1982 and "bring Quebec back into the Canadian family." The bitter public debate over Meech had only made matters worse. Indeed, in reaction to this debate, support for sovereignty began a marked climb, five months before the Accord finally collapsed.[217] Quebeckers were led to believe that the majority of English Canadians refused to recognize Quebec as a distinct entity within Canada; the polls showing enormous opposition to "distinct society" seemed to say as much. Rightly or wrongly, they took English-Canadian rejection of the Accord to be a rejection of Quebec.

For their part, many English Canadians were embittered by Quebec's repudiation of principles that they thought had become central to Canadian nationhood, some of which had in fact originated as ostensible concessions to Quebec.[218] The irony is that their opposition to the Accord and to Quebec was the result of a strategy that had been presented as a way to bring the country together: the Trudeau national unity strategy. Instead, it had left English Canadians and Quebec Francophones more deeply divided than ever before.

After the collapse of the Meech Lake Accord, most English Canadians remained convinced that the Accord should not have been ratified. Moreover, in a November 1990 survey, which asked who "best represented [their] view of Canada," close to 60 per cent displayed their commitment to the Trudeau vision by naming Clyde Wells, Jean Chrétien, or Trudeau himself. But among Quebec respondents, only 28 per cent chose one of those three; there is every reason to believe that among Francophones the percentage was considerably smaller.[219]

For many Quebec Francophones, the rejection of the Accord by English Canada was equivalent to rejection of Quebec itself. In the resulting wave of anger and humiliation, support for Quebec sovereignty soared to unprecedented heights. By November 1990, it had reached 64 per cent among Quebec residents, with only 30 per cent opposed.[220]

Canada had entered an acute crisis, far worse than any in the past. At the centre of the crisis was the difference between the Anglophone and Francophone idea of Canada, which, though hardly new, had never before been as clearly defined. The two visions of Canada were not only different, but mutually exclusive: Quebeckers persisted in an attachment to Quebec, as their prior allegiance. For many English Canadians, committed to the notion of Canada as a single political community, that was not only incomprehensible but unacceptable. After all, they had become imbued with a vision of Canada that had been designed specifically to exclude any distinctive place for Quebec. What is more, thanks to the Meech Lake debate, English Canadians and Quebec Francophones were now acutely aware that their ideas of Canada were diametrically opposed.

Confronted with such an overwhelming impasse, and keenly aware of how English-Canadian opinion had rallied against domination of constitutional matters by politicians, the first reaction of the federal government and most provincial governments was simply to abandon the whole question. Instead of taking action on its own, the Mulroney government appointed a special task force, composed of prominent Canadians and chaired by Keith Spicer, to ascertain the thoughts of citizens.[221]

For its part, the Bourassa government announced that, since the rest of the country had not honoured its commitment to the Meech Lake Accord, Quebec was simply withdrawing from any further constitutional talks. In a phrase pregnant with meaning, he told the National Assembly, "Quebec is today, and forever, a distinct society, free and capable of taking charge of its destiny and development."[222] He obviously felt a need to assuage the public's deep anger. Finally, on 4 September 1990, the government had a bill passed creating a special committee of the National Assembly on Quebec's political and constitutional future, popularly known as the Bélanger–Campeau Commission after its co-chairs Michel Bélanger and Jean Campeau. Soon afterward, in response to the nationalist sentiments sweeping post-Meech Quebec, the Quebec Liberal Party's constitutional committee produced a document, generally known as the Allaire Report, which called for a radical devolution of powers to Quebec.[223] Two months later, the Bélanger–Campeau Commission presented its report, which gave an overview of the constitutional impasse, outlined two options, a profoundly renewed federalism and sovereignty, and called for a referendum on sovereignty by October 1992.[224]

The Bourassa government acted on the recommendation but in a manner that gave it some of the room to manoeuvre it was so desperately seeking. In June 1991, the National Assembly passed Bill 150, which required the government to hold a referendum on sovereignty in June or October of 1992. The bill also established two special committees, one to study all issues related to Quebec sovereignty and one to evaluate whatever offers for a new constitutional arrangement might be made by the federal government. Finally, in affirming the sovereignty of the National Assembly over the wording of a referendum, it effectively reserved for the government the possibility of altering the wording of the referendum by amending the law should conditions warrant.[225]

If there was any doubt at the time, it is clear in retrospect that Robert Bourassa was, as ever, committed to Quebec's remaining within the federal system.[226] Given the state of public opinion immediately after the collapse of Meech he could have led Quebec out of Canada if he had wanted to. Yet he certainly could not ignore the public pressure for Quebec to respond to English Canada's rejection of Meech with a referendum of its own on Quebec's future. In 1991, support for sovereignty began to fall somewhat, but a majority vote for Quebec sovereignty was still a real possibility—unless the subject of the referendum could instead be a compelling offer of a new federation. The pressure on political leaders in the rest of Canada to produce such an offer could not have been greater. Yet, even then, the "offer" that eventually did emerge, otherwise known as the Charlottetown Accord, fell far short of expectations in Quebec, including the hopes of the Bourassa government.

Failing Again to Repair the Damage: The Charlottetown Accord

In the fall of 1991, more than a year after Meech collapsed, the Mulroney government took the initiative by presenting its proposals for constitutional renewal. The proposals were the subject of hearings by a joint parliamentary committee, the Beaudoin–Dobbie Committee whose report, published in March 1992, approved the government's proposals with some modifications. Unlike the Meech Lake Accord, the Mulroney proposals were highly comprehensive, covering most constitutional issues under discussion. They did not, however, address Quebec's jurisdictional demands, and Premier Bourassa felt compelled to reject them; he even declared that the report's discussion of the division of powers, "the key question," reflected an "overbearing federalism."[227]

Confronted with rejection of the Beaudoin–Dobbie Report not just in Quebec but in other quarters as well, the Mulroney government yielded to demands by provincial premiers, Indigenous leaders, and the heads of government of the two territories to be full partners in developing constitutional proposals. The ensuing "multilateral" negotiations involved the federal government, provincial governments, territorial leaders, and leaders of the four main Indigenous groups—but not the Quebec government. The Bourassa government persisted in the attitude it had adopted after the collapse of Meech: rather than participate in any more constitutional negotiations it would wait for the leaders of the rest of the country to formulate an offer they were prepared to support.

This new round of constitutional negotiations was confronted with two competing agendas. In Quebec, the continuing resentment at the rejection of Meech by English-Canadian public opinion fuelled a sense that to offset this "humiliation" any new constitutional package would have to go beyond Meech—it would have to be "Meech-plus." The Allaire Report had set the tone for these new expectations with its recommendations for a major devolution of powers to Quebec and exclusion of Quebec from the Charter and the Supreme Court. Bourassa had already denounced Beaudoin–Dobbie because it did not enhance Quebec's powers.

On the other hand, any new package had to be acceptable to the rest of Canada in a way that Meech manifestly was not. This meant addressing directly the needs and aspirations of other Canadians. Indeed, the new negotiations were widely touted as a "Canada Round," to be distinguished from the "Quebec Round" that had produced Meech. Any new package also had to be less offensive than Meech had been to the idea of Canada prevailing outside Quebec, in other words, to the Trudeau vision. The Meech debate had demonstrated that English Canadians were acutely sensitive to any differentiation between themselves and Quebec. It also had revealed a deep desire for the federal government to be able to fulfill its proper responsibilities as a "national" government.

English Canadians' attitudes regarding the constitutional question were also shaped by a greatly heightened sympathy for the demands of Indigenous Peoples. The crisis in Oka, Quebec, in the summer of 1990, triggered by a confrontation between Mohawks and the Quebec provincial police, had convinced many English Canadians that any constitutional revision would have to meet the demands of Indigenous Peoples. Indeed, a good number of English Canadians argued that Indigenous demands were far more urgent than Quebec's. The presence of Indigenous leaders in the new round of constitutional negotiations, for the first time in Canadian history, ensured that Indigenous concerns would be given a favourable hearing.

The July 7 Accord: English Canada's Constitutional Project

Despite the complexity of negotiations involving the federal government, nine provincial governments, two territories, and four Indigenous groups, an agreement was in fact reached on 7 July 1992. Although the Mulroney government's original proposals may have been the starting point, there were significant modifications and departures. The fact of an agreement was a surprise to many, not the least of whom was Prime Minister Mulroney.[228] But it was possible precisely because the Bourassa government was absent.[229] In effect, the agreement was English Canada's constitutional project. Indeed, there is good reason to believe that if a referendum on the Accord had been held in those provinces, it would have passed. By the same token, the Accord was a highly circumscribed response to Quebec's demands.[230]

The July 7 Accord did reiterate the Meech Lake Accord's distinct-society clause requiring that constitutional interpretation take account of Quebec's status as a "distinct society." This was a *sine qua non* of any post-Meech response to Quebec. Still, the framers of the Accord were keenly aware of how unpopular the clause was in English Canada. The Alberta minister of intergovernmental affairs had tried in vain to have the clause restricted to the Accord's preamble: "The reintroduction of these two words 'distinct society' in the proposal could have an explosive impact politically. . . . In the hands of Mr Trudeau or someone like that, it could destroy the whole process."[231]

Yet if the framers of the agreement were bound to include the clause, given expectations in Quebec, they at least could narrow its application. This time, then, it was to apply, not to the whole constitution, as with Meech, but only to the Charter. Beyond that, in an effort to weaken the recognition of Quebec as a "distinct society," they also inserted a reference to "distinct society" in a "Canada clause" that would "express fundamental Canadian values." There, "distinct society" was to appear as one of eight different "characteristics" that should guide the courts in interpreting the constitution. Needless to say, there was no response to the Allaire Report's demand that Quebec be excluded from the Supreme Court's jurisdiction.

As for the division of powers, the most important item on Quebec's agenda, Ottawa's prerogatives were carefully protected. By and large, any strengthening of provincial power was in areas already under provincial jurisdiction.[232] The reservation and disallowance powers would have been eliminated, but they had long been dormant.

The Accord addressed another of Quebec's demands by giving provincial governments the right to oblige the federal government to withdraw from training and labour market development activities. However, it gave the federal government the responsibility for setting national objectives, through negotiation with the provinces, that the provinces would be bound to respect.[233]

In the case of cultural affairs, another long-standing theme in Quebec's demands, the agreement called for a constitutional amendment specifying that "provinces should have exclusive jurisdiction over cultural matters within the provinces," but it was careful to stipulate that the proposed amendment would also recognize "the continuing responsibility of the federal government in Canadian cultural matters. The federal government should retain responsibility for national cultural institutions, including grants and contributions delivered by these institutions."[234] To be sure, the Accord did incorporate the spending power and immigration provisions of the Meech Lake Accord, along with its amending procedure.

At the same time, the July 7 Accord seriously addressed a number of matters that were on the agenda of English Canada. The "Canada clause" spelled out the many values that all Canadians held in common, including parliamentary democracy, federalism, equality of the provinces, and racial, ethnic, and gender equality. It proposed a statement of principles, not enforceable in courts, that would spell out basic social services and collective bargaining rights that all Canadians should enjoy while also supporting measures to strengthen the Canadian economic union. As with Meech, the Supreme Court's authority would be entrenched, and judges would be appointed by the federal government from names submitted by the provinces. In particular, the agreement addressed Indigenous concerns in an unprecedented manner, recognizing "an inherent right to self-government" for Indigenous Peoples and declaring Indigenous governments to be "one of three orders of government in Canada."

While maintaining the federal government's role as a "national" government, the agreement also sought to address the strong grievances of, in particular, western Canadians over the way the federal government functioned. The route was, of course, Senate reform. It was a matter about which the Trudeau government had been relatively indifferent. Yet the formula for reform—equality of the provinces—was fully consistent with the Trudeau vision. Indeed, Trudeau's disciple, Clyde Wells, had joined the western premiers in promoting the scheme for a triple-E Senate: equal, elected, and effective.[235]

In short, the July 7 agreement was faithful to the constitutional agendas prevailing outside Quebec. It respected the clearly stated desire of most English Canadians that the powers of the federal government not be fundamentally weakened. It embraced the project of constitutional change that had the most support in the rest of the country: the triple-E Senate. Finally, it effectively met the demand of Indigenous Peoples for self-government. At the same time, its response to Quebec's agenda went little beyond incorporating the elements of Meech; indeed, it sought to rein in Meech's recognition of Quebec's distinctiveness.

In the volatile atmosphere of post-Meech Quebec, that was not enough: only a substantial increase in the powers of the Quebec government would do. Not only did the July 7 Accord not grant such powers, but its project of a triple-E Senate would have reduced Quebec's Senate representation from 25 per cent to 10 per cent. At the same time, its provisions for Indigenous self-government led Quebec officials to fear that arrangements such as the James Bay Agreement might be endangered.

The Charlottetown Accord

As a result, prominent Quebec federalists rejected the July 7 Accord outright.[236] Even Francophone members of the Mulroney government denounced the agreement.[237] Reportedly, Bourassa had counted upon the "multilateral" negotiations failing, and officials in the Mulroney government had been drawing up a unilateral offer that would be satisfactory for Quebec.[238] Now, he was confronted with a fait accompli: English Canada had decided what kind of a constitution it wanted. Accordingly, Bourassa entered into a new round of negotiations in an effort to make the agreement satisfactory to Quebec, but, as the terms of the final agreement, the Charlottetown Accord, were to reveal, the most he could do was reduce the damage. The Accord remained devoid of any serious response to Quebec's agenda.

Instead of adding elements desired by Quebec, the main strategy for altering the July 7 Accord to accommodate Quebec was to dilute a major element of what was already there, the Senate reform so coveted by western Canada and, to a lesser extent, by the Atlantic provinces. For good measure, Quebec's (and Ontario's) representation in the House of Commons was expanded. In addition, the wording of the Indigenous self-government provisions was made satisfactory to Bourassa, if not to all members of the Quebec delegation.[239] Also, the ability of Quebec, or any other province, to veto changes to central institutions was strengthened.[240] But there was no significant expansion of the powers or general status of the Quebec government. Unlike the Senate reform agreed to on 7 July, the Charlottetown version fell far short of the triple-E model.[241]

As for the division of powers, Bourassa's efforts had little effect. His main proposal, which dealt with federal spending power, would have extended the provisions in the agreement, themselves derived from Meech, to any spending by Ottawa within a provincial jurisdiction, whether on a shared-cost or independent basis.[242] Presumably, it would have affected such wholly federal programs as family allowances and old-age pensions. The proposal was dismissed outright by the other first ministers, most of whom energetically defended the federal spending power. Moreover, none of them had any inclination to discuss new elements at that late stage, especially after the adjustments to the Senate and House, which, ostensibly, were concessions to Quebec. In effect, the deal was set.[243]

Essentially, Quebec had to settle for the treatment of the division of powers already contained in the July 7 agreement. Yet, as we have seen, this was of little significance, out of deference to English Canada's wish to maintain a strong federal government. The most substantial changes, the "six sisters," which had been drawn up by Ottawa, did not really correspond to Quebec's list. The measures regarding manpower and culture did address Quebec's concerns, but each had important qualifications that ensured a continued federal role. Beyond that, all that remained were the spending power, immigration, and amendment provisions drawn from the Meech Lake Accord,[244] plus the elimination of the long-defunct powers of reservation and disallowance.

The treatment of Quebec's status as a "distinct society" followed the same restrictive lines as in the July 7 Accord. Quebec's "distinct society" remained one of eight enumerated "fundamental characteristics" of Canada. In addition, the nature of Quebec's uniqueness was narrowed by the listing of its main elements: "Quebec constitutes within Canada a distinct society, which includes a French-speaking majority, a unique culture and a civil law tradition."[245] Finally, just to make certain that the Canada clause, including the "distinct society" reference, could not directly affect the division of powers, the Charlottetown Accord adopted Meech's provision that nothing in the clause could derogate from "the powers, rights or privileges" of Parliament and the government of Canada, or their provincial counterparts (while also referring to Indigenous governments and rights).[246]

The twin to the distinct-society clause, the "duality clause," also was modified to make it more acceptable outside Quebec and in line with the Trudeau vision. In response to pressure from the Francophone minorities, the wording was strengthened: "Canadians and their governments are committed to the vitality and development of official language minority communities throughout Canada."[247] Concerned about obligations to Quebec's Anglophone community that might stem from this wording, Quebec insisted that in the French version "committed" appear as *attachés* rather than the more equivalent *engagés*.[248]

In fact, the July 7 agreement and the Charlottetown Accord dealt with the division of powers and the status of Quebec within the same narrow limits as the federal government's constitutional proposals of October 1991 and the February 1992 report of the joint parliamentary committee (the Beaudoin–Dobbie Committee) established to assess those proposals. Premier Bourassa had denounced that package as nothing less than "an overbearing federalism." Six months later, despite Quebec's new participation in negotiations, nothing had changed. As Peter Russell concludes, "The division of powers, always the centre of attention for Quebecers engaged in the renewal of federalism, basically stood as in previous drafts."[249]

It could even be argued that Quebec's clearest "gain," to use one of Robert Bourassa's favourite terms, was not in the division of powers, but in representation in central institutions. Under the Charlottetown Accord, representation in the House of Commons was to be increased for Quebec from 75 to 93. In addition, Quebec was to be guaranteed, in perpetuity, 25 per cent of the seats of the House. Beyond that, a majority of Francophone senators in the new Senate was required on any matter that "materially affect[ed] the French language or culture in Canada." (To be sure, Francophone senators would not necessarily come from Quebec.) Although those changes were perhaps the most substantial of all the alterations to the July 7 agreement, representation in central institutions had not been a priority of the Quebec government. In fact, reduced representation might have been acceptable if traded off against enhanced powers for Quebec.[250] The Quebec government had not even asked for the guarantee of 25 per cent of seats in the House of Commons. Apparently, it was proposed by Saskatchewan premier Roy Romanow.[251]

There were, in fact, ways in which Quebec's demand for enhanced powers could have been met without a general weakening of the federal government. But this would have meant differentiating between Quebec and the rest of Canada—a cardinal sin in the Trudeau vision. Under schemes of asymmetry, any decentralization of powers could go to Quebec alone; Ottawa would continue to perform these functions in the rest of the country. In effect, English Canada could continue to have as strong a federal government as it wished. Asymmetrical federalism, as a basis for responding to Quebec's demands, had in fact been endorsed at the first of five public conferences organized by the federal government during the winter of 1992.[252]

Asymmetry does raise an institutional question that Pierre Trudeau used to pursue with relish: how could Quebec MPs vote on measures that, under asymmetry, did not apply to Quebec? How could they hold cabinet portfolios that involved programs that did not function in Quebec? The problem should not be exaggerated: after all, Quebec MPs have voted on laws dealing with the Canada Pension Plan, even though Quebec has its own Quebec Pension Plan, and three Quebec MPs (Monique Bégin, Marc Lalonde, and Benoît Bouchard) have even been responsible for these programs as ministers of health and welfare. In any event, at the time, various commentators, including Tom Kent, Lester Pearson's principal adviser, were suggesting ways in which this could be handled.[253]

There appears to have been no serious discussion of these possibilities. Apparently Federal Constitutional Affairs Minister Joe Clark simply canvassed his fellow politicians. Once they had told him that asymmetry would be unpopular in English Canada, they did not pursue it any further.[254]

In effect, the politicians were intimidated by English Canada's attachment to the principle of equality of the provinces, which was partly a legacy of the Trudeau era. As a consequence, however, the ministers had to try to handle Quebec's demands with devices that not only had no support in Quebec but were also deeply unpopular in English Canada. Rather than a trade-off between Quebec's demands for additional powers and western Canada's demands for a triple-E Senate, the result was a package that did not meet either demand and thus did not give either Quebec or the western and Atlantic provinces any reason to support it.

As to Indigenous issues, the Charlottetown Accord did contain the long-sought recognition that Indigenous Peoples held an "inherent right to self-government," while adding the phrase "within Canada" for good measure. On that basis, the Accord declared that Indigenous governments should constitute "one of three orders of government in Canada." A number of subsequent sections were devoted to stipulating the "Method of Exercise of the Right." For that matter, the Accord's preamble contained the statement that "the Aboriginal peoples of Canada, being the first peoples to govern this land, have the right to promote their languages, culture and traditions and to ensure the integrity of their societies, and their governments constitute one of three orders of government in Canada."[255]

The Referendum

Bourassa was determined that the referendum to which he was committed would deal not with sovereignty but with offers of a "renewed federalism." Thus, he consented to the only terms available. On 26 August 1992, all the parties signed what became known as the Charlottetown Accord. Recognizing that Quebec would be holding a referendum on the Accord, and facing considerable pressure in other parts of the country to hold one, the first ministers decided to hold a national referendum on 26 October 1992.

Despite the best efforts of its various authors, the Accord was rejected both in Quebec and in the rest of the country, although it did receive majorities in four provinces.[256] Once again, an attempt to revise the constitution, ostensibly designed to obtain Quebec's formal consent to the document, ended in a debacle. Unlike Meech, however, this package was rejected in Quebec too! Quebec had entered the negotiations seeking asymmetry in powers; instead it received asymmetry in the House of Commons, which was of little consequence to Québécois but of enormous consequence—all negative—to the rest of the country.

The Yes forces were plagued by a good number of problems: a poorly conceived advertising campaign; disputes among the three major parties and between them and citizen activists; the failure of some political leaders to campaign as vigorously for the cause as they might have; the inability or unwillingness of many voters to ignore their antipathy toward government leaders; and so on. But the primary explanation lies with the terms of the Accord itself.

From the outset, the Accord was attacked in Quebec for failing to address the essence of Quebec's demands: additional powers. Even federalists tended to think that Premier Bourassa could have done better. Jean Allaire, the author of the Quebec Liberal Party's constitutional position, denounced the Accord for not giving Quebec the additional powers it needed. He was joined in this by Mario Dumont, president of the Liberal Party youth wing. The two of them led a number of other Liberal dissidents in a "Réseau des libéraux pour le non."[257] Not surprisingly, support for the Accord among Quebec Francophones fell steadily over the course of the debate; at the outset the sides had been evenly divided.[258]

As for the rest of Canada, a major reason for the opposition in western Canada was the limited powers of the Senate. Supporters of the Accord could argue that the reformed Senate would have great influence since the members would be elected, relatively few in number, and, given their exclusion from the cabinet, could concentrate on their Senate tasks. And in a joint sitting the Senate might prevail if it remained cohesive and the government's majority in the House were narrow. But arguments like those were far too subtle for the average voter. And Quebec's expanded representation in the House could only be all the more galling to western Canadians, given the reductions in the Senate's powers.[259]

Surveys confirm that in western Canada, and everywhere else outside Quebec, Quebec's guarantee of 25 per cent of the seats in the House of Commons was enormously unpopular.[260] More generally, in every province other than Quebec, respondents gave "the concessions to Quebec" as the basis of their opposition far more often than any other factor.[261]

Another enormous liability of the Charlottetown Accord in English Canada was that it contained the provisions that had made Meech so unpopular in English Canada, most notably the distinct-society clause. However much it may have been limited and surrounded by a host of other "fundamental characteristics," the distinct-society clause was still there.[262]

Finally, the Accord's provisions on Indigenous issues did not secure the full support of Indigenous leaders, who were already disaffected with constitutional negotiations. In particular, they resented the stipulation that the inherent right to self-government applied "within Canada," as if there was any Indigenous intention to leave the country. For many, nation-to-nation treaties were the only acceptable way of handling relations with Canada. In fact, the No vote reached 60 per cent in polling stations located on reserves.[263]

Pierre Trudeau: Asserting His Vision Once Again

Once again, the Trudeau vision of Canada was offended; and, once again, to make certain that all Canadians saw this, Trudeau himself intervened with a major public speech. Beginning with an attack on the notion of collective rights, Trudeau contended that the Canada clause created a hierarchy of citizens. The distinct-society clause created "category number one, the first and most important one," enabling the National Assembly to act on the collective rights of the Francophone majority at the expense of other Quebeckers. The second category was Indigenous Peoples, whose governments would be empowered to use the notwithstanding clause, thus ensuring that the clause would remain part of the Charter in perpetuity. As for the "duality clause," he noted the weakness of the French *attaché* but declared that even the "committed" of the English version was meaningless. Proceeding through the rest of the Accord, he concluded with the thought that with a Yes vote Quebec's blackmail would continue and that "this mess deserves a big No."[264]

After Trudeau's speech, support for the Accord outside Quebec plummeted by a full 20 percentage points. Apparently, many of Trudeau's English-Canadian followers had supported the Accord in the mistaken belief that he did. After they learned otherwise, they changed their minds, and by the end of the campaign they were more likely to oppose the Accord than were voters who disliked Trudeau or were indifferent to him.[265]

The 1993 Federal Election

Like the collapse of Meech, the failure of the Charlottetown Accord left a profound mark on Canadian politics. Indeed, it closely shaped the results of the next federal election, one year later. The Liberals formed a majority government, led by Jean Chrétien, one of Trudeau's most faithful disciples. But for the first time in that century, the Liberals formed a government without a majority in Quebec, where they won only 19 of 75 seats and 33 per cent of the popular vote.

Instead, the Bloc québécois, under Lucien Bouchard, won 54 seats and 49.3 per cent of the popular vote. It had become the party of Quebec Francophones, winning the votes of about 60 per cent of them.[266] Officially committed to the goal of Quebec sovereignty, the Bloc had based its campaign on the failure of Canadian political institutions to accommodate Quebec's demands, and on Chrétien's personal involvement in both the 1982 patriation and the failure of Meech. By voting massively for the Bloc, Quebec Francophones could not have demonstrated more clearly their rejection of the Trudeau vision of Canada.[267]

In the rest of Canada, the Liberals received strong support in Ontario, winning all but one seat and 53 per cent of the popular vote. They also did well in the Atlantic provinces and Manitoba. Yet the vote in the west reflected both the continued impact of the Charlottetown debacle and the limits to English-Canadian support for the Trudeau vision. Building upon its successful campaign against the Accord, the Reform Party—a new right-wing formation—won overwhelming majorities in Alberta and British Columbia. Indeed its popular vote in the country as a whole was 18.7 per cent, well ahead of both the Bloc and the Progressive Conservatives. Although it shared some elements of the Trudeau vision, such as the absolute equality of the provinces, Reform had expressed clear opposition to official bilingualism and multiculturalism. Reformers also had decidedly mixed feelings about the Charter of Rights and Freedoms.[268]

In short, the election had produced a Parliament that closely reflected the divisions that the Trudeau strategy had created in the country.[269] With Jean Chrétien as prime minister, the government was deeply wedded to the Trudeau vision. The Bloc as Official Opposition, on the other hand, was formally committed to sovereignty, and much of its electoral support was based on continuing resentment of Trudeau's constitutional actions in 1982. Reform, the second-largest opposition party with 52 seats, was opposed to some of the federal government's most important measures, such as multiculturalism and official bilingualism. Yet it shared with the Trudeau vision of Canada a firm commitment to the equality of the provinces and a deep opposition to any recognition of Quebec's distinctiveness. That ensured that Reform could not offer a viable alternative approach to Canadian unity.

In sum, each of the two efforts to repair the damage of constitutional patriation without Quebec's consent ended in a debacle. In both cases, a large part of the reason was acceptance by English Canada, but continued rejection by Quebec, of the Trudeau vision of Canada that patriation had been intended to entrench.

The Meech Lake Accord may have represented the minimum conditions under which Quebec would have accepted the new constitution, but, especially with its distinct-society clause, it still violated the Trudeau vision. For that reason it was unacceptable to the overwhelming majority of English Canadians. So even if the Accord had passed, it could not have reconciled Quebec with the rest of Canada, as it was intended to do.

The Charlottetown Accord was designed to be less offensive to the Trudeau vision, attempting, for example, to rein in the scope of Quebec's distinctiveness with its distinct-society clause. But it did not give Quebec the additional powers that had become crucial in the radicalized opinion of post-Meech Quebec. Through asymmetry in government powers, the Accord might have satisfied Quebec without violating English Canadians' continued desire for a strong "national" government. But what might have been possible in the 1960s, when the Pearson government had pioneered asymmetry, was no longer possible after the Trudeau orthodoxy had made its inroads in English Canada. Instead of applying asymmetry to federal–provincial relations, the Charlottetown Accord applied it to representation in the House of Commons, guaranteeing Quebec 25 per cent of the seats and thereby ensuring that the Accord would be rejected in much of English Canada.

In each case, Trudeau himself intervened to make it absolutely clear to Canadians just how these accords violated the conception of Canada that he had struggled so hard to put in place. And in each case English-Canadian support for the proposed accord plummeted.

Those two episodes led directly to the election in 1993 of a Liberal government that depended on English Canada for its support and an Official Opposition that was committed to sovereignty. However, the most dramatic demonstration of the failure of the Trudeau strategy for national unity was yet to come, in a new referendum on Quebec sovereignty.

The Failure of the Trudeau Strategy

By the time he left the prime ministership, in June 1984, Pierre Elliott Trudeau had put in place all the basic elements of a comprehensive strategy for national unity. At the core of this strategy was (1) *language rights*: after just one year in office, he had adopted the Official Languages Act, establishing official bilingualism within federal institutions. Two years later, he proclaimed a policy of (2) *multiculturalism*, displacing biculturalism in favour of the equality of all cultures and, in particular, the primacy of individuals and freedom of choice. Through his 16 years of office, Trudeau affirmed and enhanced the role of the federal government as (3) *Canada's national government*: preserving and promoting its direct relationship with citizens, as when he rejected Quebec's social income proposals at Victoria, and undertaking unilateral initiatives, as with the National Energy Program. He promoted a (4) *uniform federalism*, as with eliminating fiscal arrangements that afforded a greater role to the Quebec government than the other provinces. Most important of all, he brought about a (5) *patriation of the constitution* coupled *with a charter of rights*. All these initiatives conformed with Trudeau's core beliefs of the primacy of the individual and opposition to Quebec nationalism.

With its five elements—official bilingualism, multiculturalism, strengthening of the "national" government, uniform federalism, and a charter—the Trudeau national unity strategy provided a coherent and comprehensive plan of action. Moreover, the Trudeau government pursued the strategy with a determination and a consistency that are rare in government. Trudeau and his colleagues may have had some second thoughts after the election of the PQ in 1976, but they more than made up for it in their final term in office.

In the end, the Trudeau government was remarkably successful in achieving its national unity objectives. The constitution was revised in the ways Trudeau had always wanted, and without the kind of changes he did not want. Language rights were entrenched in the Charter, indeed they had been its primary purpose, and, as such, they were protected from the Charter's notwithstanding clause.[270] Much of the asymmetry of Quebec's place in federal–provincial relations was eliminated. Moreover, under the new constitutional amending formula, Quebec's position was precisely the same as the other provinces. Multiculturalism was effectively established as a principle of federal politics, as well as in many provinces. The public face, if not the internal functioning, of the federal government was made bilingual.

To be sure, some initiatives evolved in ways that differed radically from Trudeau's intent. Rather than remaining bound by the concept of individual freedom of choice, Canada's language policies became linked, in various ways, to notions of collective rights. Language rights in the Charter have become framed in terms of linguistic communities, thanks to pressures from official-language minorities, as well as sympathetic jurisprudence. To varying degrees, provincial governments have deferred to their linguistic majorities, and the territorial principle, in establishing their own language policies. As for multiculturalism, Trudeau's effort to frame it in terms of individual freedom never really took hold; indeed, it was contradicted from the outset by "preservationist" provisions in the policy itself and the overt recognition of cultural communities and racially defined groups only grew over time. Even the Charter of Rights and Freedoms has a flagrant flaw in terms of Trudeau's world view: the notwithstanding clause. Many years later, Trudeau regretted that he had not approached the British Parliament unilaterally, rather than settle with the provinces, so as to secure the exact constitutional change he wanted.[271]

Still, whatever their limitations and subsequent evolution, these five measures put in place a new and quite coherent understanding of the nature of the country. Within this new conception, Canada is to be seen as composed of individual citizens, some of whom speak English while others speak French and a growing number speak both, who come from a multiplicity of ethnic and racial backgrounds. Sharing a common national government and bearing rights protected in a constitutionally entrenched charter, these citizens are the new locus of sovereignty. Thus, Canada is no longer a matter of communities, whether two nations or 10 provinces, and compacts among them. To the extent duality persists it applies to language alone but is to be established throughout Canada, from coast to coast. The various initiatives provided a ready basis for a new national identity, one which would lead Quebec Francophones to abandon their historical allegiance to Quebec and to identify first and foremost with the new Canadian political community, of which they are to be an integral part.

Subsequently, Trudeau had to return to public life to safeguard his legacy against what he saw as threats to his constitutional achievement. But his dramatic interventions against Meech and Charlottetown were remarkably successful, and a testimony to the power that his vision of the country held for some Canadians. Indeed, by securing the failure of these twin exercises in constitutional revision,

Trudeau ensured that over the following years there would be no serious constitutional discussions of any kind.

Yet, however coherent may have been Trudeau's national unity strategy and however successful he may have been in putting it in place, to what extent did he and his government actually succeed in creating national unity? This was a tall order. Trudeau and his colleagues would have had to persuade Canadians as a whole to their version of a Canadian national identity, eliminating all adherence to the historical understanding of the country, rooted in communities and compacts. Otherwise, if only part of the country were to adopt the new conception of Canada, and the rest were not, the result could only have been disunity on a grand scale. After all, the new conception of Canada had been designed in direct contradiction of the older one.

The Trudeau Strategy and Anglophone Canada

With respect to Canada's Anglophones, Trudeau assumed the prime ministership at a most propitious moment. In the late 1960s, many English-speaking Canadians were open to a new vision of the country. In fact, they were very much in need of one, given Canada's changed place in the world as well as the social and economic transformations it had undergone internally. Indeed, the desire for a new vision was such that many Anglophones embraced the very person who offered it and who even seemed to incarnate it. "Trudeaumania" was a distinctly English-Canadian phenomenon, responding to pressures and concerns that were themselves particular to English Canada.

Historically, as we have seen, most English Canadians rooted their notion of Canada in its connection to Great Britain. After all, United Empire Loyalists, who fled the American Revolution and remained loyal to the British monarchy, figured heavily in the settlement and subsequent leadership of the original colonies of British North America. Other immigrants came primarily from Great Britain itself. Thus, it was only natural to see Canada, in Sir John A. Macdonald's words, as "a British nation under the British flag and under British institutions."[272] Beyond the bonds of ancestry and political institutions, Canada was linked to Great Britain economically. Britain was the primary market for Canada's exports and the primary source of capital for its transportation and development projects.

Reinforcing this continuing attachment to Great Britain was apprehension about the United States. In part, there was fear that Canada might actually be incorporated into the United States. After all, American troops had invaded Quebec in the wake of the American Revolution. In the War of 1812, Canadian and British militia fought together to resist American annexation. Confederation itself had been sought, in part, to provide a stronger defence against possible invasion by the massive Union army that had been created to win the American Civil War. American politicians had even preached annexation of Canada as part of American "Manifest

Destiny." The British connection provided a secure defence against such American expansionism. Indeed, through the British Empire Canada was a privileged member of what was the world's largest empire. At the same time, Canada's subordination to Britain and the British Parliament bestowed upon it political institutions and traditions that clearly differentiated Canada from the United States.

Nonetheless, by the 1960s, it had become manifestly clear that the British connection no longer provided a solid basis for Canadian political and cultural identity. In 1931, Britain had already recognized the need of the "White Dominions" for greater autonomy by adopting the Statute of Westminster. Britain's economic decline, in the wake of the First World War onward, further weakened the bases of Canada's British connection: Canada could no longer rely on Britain to buy its exports or finance its development. At the same time, apprehension grew among English-Canadian intellectuals and opinion leaders that Canada was being drawn into the economic and cultural orbit of the United States, the postwar global superpower. Indeed, the 1960s saw a concerted reaction against American influence in Canada, whether it be the operations of American corporations or the presence of Americans in Canadian universities. The NDP's Waffle Movement, which had called for recognition of the Quebec nation, was fuelled primarily by the struggle against "American imperialism." More moderate forms of economic and cultural nationalism were articulated by Toronto-based figures such as Walter Gordon. As with "Trudeaumania," this anxiety about American influence was an essentially English-Canadian phenomenon, with little echo in Francophone Quebec where a separate language, a different history, and a strong sense of identity allowed the United States to be seen in more benign terms.

Within Canada itself social and economic change had prepared the way for a new vision of the country. During the first part of the twentieth century, immigration to Canada, especially western Canada, had broadened beyond Great Britain to other parts of Europe. As we have seen, Canadians of white European descent had led the movement against biculturalism and established notions of cultural duality. With the change of Canada's immigration policy to a point system, in 1967, immigration broadened to other parts of the world, leading to a more racially diverse population and the growth of visible minorities. This too reinforced the need for a new vision of Canada. In addition, Canada's political economy had been transformed by the emergence of energy resource industries in western Canada. Imbued with historical grievance against central Canadian economic domination, western Canadian politicians and economic élites had little patience for Quebec's claim to particular status and bicultural compacts, although they were also suspicious of Ottawa's pretentions to be Canada's "national government." Finally, by the 1960s, English-Canadian society was becoming more openly pluralist, with the feminist movement taking the lead in challenging received notions of social mores and societal roles.

The various elements of the Trudeau vision of Canada promised to resolve all these concerns and anxieties. By linking patriation to an entrenched charter of rights, proclaiming popular sovereignty, and affirming Ottawa's role as the "national government," the Trudeau vision offered a compelling alternative to older notions of Canada as a "British nation." (To be sure, the Trudeau government stopped short of outright republicanism, out of deference to lingering English-Canadian attachment to Britain and the monarchy.) Moreover, other terms of the Trudeau vision readily served to differentiate Canada from the United States: Canada had not just English but also French as an official language and, rather than being a "melting pot," it was a multicultural nation that respected and supported cultural diversity. While Trudeau's instinctive anti-nationalism initially inhibited any concerted attempt to offset American economic and cultural domination, much to the dismay of English-Canadian nationalists, with time the Trudeau government adopted limited protectionism by reviewing foreign corporate takeovers and requiring Canadian content in radio and television. The Trudeau vision of Canada not only offered a viable replacement for the British connection and a ready differentiation from the United States, but also vested Canada with a historic mission to show the world how cultural and ethnic divisions could be overcome and nationalism transcended. As he wrote in 1962, "Canadian federalism . . . could become a brilliant prototype for the moulding of tomorrow's civilization."[273] To be sure, this celebration of a Canadian "post-nation" state may itself be a form of nationalism but it had a strong appeal to English Canadians who were seeking a new and compelling purpose for their country.

At the same time, the various elements of Trudeau's national unity strategy responded directly to the social and economic changes that English Canada was experiencing. Multiculturalism was precisely what had been demanded by Canadians of non-British but European descent; it could readily be extended to accommodate the racially diverse waves of new immigrants. The adoption of a charter of rights had provided the perfect opportunity for a wide range of social entities, including feminists, multicultural advocates, Indigenous Peoples and official-language minorities, to secure formal recognition in the new Canada and, as "Charter Canadians,"[274] to become fierce defenders of Trudeau's constitutional legacy.

Affirmation of Ottawa as Canada's "national government" appealed to the many social groups that had been involved in the postwar construction of Canada's welfare state. Such policies as health care may have originated with specific provinces, but they ultimately reached most Canadians through the federal government. Thus, a 1987 survey found that, outside Quebec, overwhelming majorities preferred "a strong national government" to "strong provincial governments."[275] To be sure, some economic initiatives of this "national government," most notably the National Energy Program, were not well received in western Canada. However, Trudeau's insistence on the equality of all provinces, Quebec included, had a strong resonance with western Canadians—their provincial governments no longer accepted amending formulas that gave a veto to a particular province, whether Quebec or Ontario.

The final element of the new national identity, official bilingualism, may have been essential to Trudeau but clearly was a harder sell in English Canada. Traditionally, English Canadians had not seen language rights as a human right; support for the Charter did not necessarily extend to support of official bilingualism. Indeed, most provinces continued to give pre-eminent status to English, their majority language. Nonetheless, most English Canadians who did support the ideal of a bilingual Canada proved to be determined supporters of the Trudeau vision. For example, Canadian Parents for French, an organization that advocates French-immersion schooling, could be counted upon to defend the Trudeau legacy against the Meech Lake Accord.

In short, when Trudeau came on the political scene, many Anglophone Canadians were well disposed to see Canada in new and different terms given the transformations, both external and internal, that their country had undergone. While Trudeau's essential goal had been to incorporate Quebec within Canada, the vision of the country that he offered happened to respond directly to English-Canadian fears and ambitions. Moreover, on the basis of this vision, he presented a strategy that promised to resolve another English-Canadian fear: the break up of their country. Thus, he could mobilize widespread support for his distinctive strategy of national unity.

The Trudeau Strategy and Francophone Quebec

The various elements of the Trudeau government's strategy met with a very different response in Francophone Quebec. The constitutional entrenchment of French-language rights across Canada didn't affect Quebeckers' views on sovereignty as had been assumed; the status of French within Quebec remained the essential concern for 81 per cent of Quebeckers.[276] Nor did Quebeckers yield their attachment to the Quebec government: in the survey referred to above, 57 per cent of Quebec respondents preferred a "strong provincial government" over a "strong national government," in direct contradiction with the rest of the country.[277] Quebeckers continued to see Canada as a bicultural entity, refusing to view it in multicultural terms. As to the crowning achievement of the Trudeau strategy, patriation and the Charter of Rights and Freedoms, its appeal to Quebec Francophones was fatally compromised by the fact that it had been undertaken over Quebec's opposition: in a March 1982 survey, 55 per cent of Quebec respondents (61 per cent of Francophones) agreed that patriation should not have proceeded without the approval of the Quebec government—only 26 per cent agreed.[278]

As the rejection of each of the Trudeau government's initiatives would suggest, the national unity strategy failed to bring about the change in political identity among Quebeckers that it was designed to achieve. In fact, over the years that the Trudeau government pursued its strategy, the proportion of Quebec Francophones seeing themselves as "Québécois" grew steadily and the proportion calling

Table 6.1 Self-Identification of Quebec Francophones, 1970–90

	French Canadian	Québécois	Canadian	Others or Not Stated
1970	44%	21%	34%	1%
1977	51	31	18	A
1984	48	37	13	1
1988	39	49	11	1
1990	28	59	9	2

A = excluded from tabulation

Source: Reprinted with permission from Maurice Pinard, "The Dramatic Reemergence of the Quebec Independence Movement," *Journal of International Affairs* 45, no. 2 (Winter 1995): Table 3. Permission conveyed through Copyright Clearance Center, Inc.

themselves "Canadian" or "French Canadian" declined just as steadily. As Table 6.1 shows, by 1990, fully 59 per cent of survey respondents declared themselves to be "Québécois"—only 9 per cent declared that they were "Canadian."

It is difficult to see how the result could have been otherwise. The Trudeau strategy was attempting to displace an understanding of Canada that had been sustained by generations of Quebec's intellectual and political élites. Moreover, it was rooted in the sociological reality that Francophone society is indeed centred in Quebec. In comparison, the new vision of Canada and the appeal to Québécois's allegiances that the Trudeau government proffered could only have seemed artificial or "constructed." To be sure, the vision of a distinctly Quebec identity that neo-nationalists began creating in the 1960s was also a "construction" but it was based on an underlying sense of French-Canadian nationality with deep historical roots. The Trudeau alternative had no such roots. Any attempt to link it to the Canadian nationalism of Henri Bourassa, the most clearly "pan-Canadian" vision ever offered by a French-Canadian intellectual leader, was compromised by Trudeau's rejection of biculturalism and his dismissal of the centrality of Quebec to French Canada.

Conceivably, the Trudeau vision of Canada might have been more credible in Quebec if the language reforms that were the heart of the strategy had in fact created a Canada that was bilingual from coast to coast. But that was never a realistic goal. So there was no compelling reason for Québécois to abandon their historical assumption that Francophone society was centred in Quebec.

Without any real change to the linguistic structure of Canada, the elements of the Trudeau strategy that denied Quebec's uniqueness could only be provocative. This was especially the case, of course, with the rejection of constitutional demands from Quebec, culminating in patriation without Quebec's formal consent. In that respect, the Trudeau strategy not only failed to weaken identification with Quebec, but actually strengthened it. And by preventing any possibility of additional accommodation of this identity within Canadian political institutions, the Trudeau strategy actually strengthened the appeal of Quebec sovereignty.

In sum, while the Trudeau vision of Canada failed to take hold among Quebec Francophones, as the national unity strategy had envisaged, it did have a profound impact in the rest of the country. As we have seen, for their own reasons many Anglophone Canadians embraced the new national identity. However, since the new vision had been designed precisely to exclude any recognition of Quebec's specificity, its popularity among Anglophones made all the more difficult achievement of a semblance of national unity. This was dramatically demonstrated by English Canada's rejection of the Meech Lake Accord, following Pierre Trudeau's personal lead. That very success in preserving the Trudeau legacy produced a reaction in Quebec that the national unity strategy had been designed to prevent: a dramatic rise in support for Quebec sovereignty. A strategy to create national unity had produced precisely the opposite.

Notes

1. Valérie Lapointe-Gagnon, "Penser et 'panser' les plaies du Canada: le moment Laurendeau-Dunton, 1963-1971," Doctoral thesis, History Department, Laval University, 2013, 238 and 320.
2. Ibid., 256. The introductory "blue pages" of Book One, written by Laurendeau, constituted a sort of "consolation prize" for Laurendeau's failure to secure a discussion of constitutional questions in this first volume (ibid., 240). On the debate between Scott and Laurendeau at the Commission see Guy Laforest, *Trudeau et la fin d'un rêve canadien* (Sillery, Que. Septentrion, 1992), 96–104, and Graham Fraser, *Sorry, I Don't Speak French: Confronting the Canadian Crisis That Won't Go Away* (Toronto: McClelland & Stewart, 2006), Chap. 3.
3. Paul Lacoste, "André Laurendeau et la Commission sur le bilinguisme et le biculturalisme," in *André Laurendeau: un intellectuel d'ici*, ed. Robert Comeau and Lucille Beaudry (Sillery, Que.: Presses de l'Université du Québec, 1990), 207–13.
4. Lapointe-Gagnon, "Penser et 'panser' les plaies du Canada," 267–70.
5. Ibid., 272–3.
6. J.-P. Proulx, "L'Histoire d'un échec qui combla d'aise Pierre-Elliott Trudeau," *Le Devoir*, 5 Nov. 1988.
7. Mitchell Sharp relates

   > It wasn't that we were excluded from Liberal Party politics in Quebec. Rather, we realized that Quebeckers had to decide among themselves whether to stay or to leave and that our main contribution as English-speaking ministers was to give reality to Trudeau's contention that French-speaking Canadians from Quebec could play their full and appropriate part in the Government of Canada.

   See Mitchell Sharp, *Which Reminds Me . . . A Memoir* (Toronto: University of Toronto Press, 1994), 170.
8. According to Paul Martin, Trudeau was "touchy" about the monarchy but saw that trying to change it would raise national unity problems (Robert Bothwell and J.L. Granatstein, *Trudeau's World: Insiders Reflect on Foreign Policy, Trade, and Defence, 1968–84* [Vancouver: UBC Press, 2017], 326).
9. Raymond B. Blake and Bailey Antonishyn, "Pierre Trudeau, Citizenship, and Canada Day," in Matthew Hayday and Raymond B. Blake, *Celebrating Canada*, vol. 1 (Toronto: University of Toronto Press, 2016), 312. As the authors show, Trudeau encountered considerable resistance to his proposed Canada Day, which was not adopted until 1982. Nonetheless, he could move more rapidly to eliminate general usage of "dominion."
10. Bruce Thordarson, *Trudeau and Foreign Policy* (Toronto: Oxford University Press, 1972).
11. Cabinet documents as quoted in Varun Uberoi, "Multiculturalism and the Canadian Charter of Rights and Freedoms," *Political Studies* 37 (2009): 809.

12. Calculated from W.T. Stanbury, Gerald J. Gorn, and Charles B. Weinberg, "Federal Advertising Expenditures," in *How Ottawa Spends: The Liberals, the Opposition and Federal Priorities, 1983*, ed. G. Bruce Doern (Toronto: Lorimer, 1983), Table 6.2.
13. Richard Simeon and Ian Robinson, *State, Society and the Development of Canadian Federalism*, Collected Research Studies of the Royal Commission on the Economic Union and Development Prospects for Canada, vol. 71 (Toronto: University of Toronto Press, 1990), 287.
14. The term "new constituencies" appears in Donald V. Smiley, *Canada in Question*, 3rd edn (Toronto: McGraw-Hill Ryerson, 1980), 110. See also Leslie A. Pal, *Interests of State* (Montreal and Kingston: McGill-Queen's University Press, 1993), Chap. 5.
15. Anthony G.S. Careless, *Initiative and Response* (Montreal and Kingston: McGill-Queen's University Press, 1977), 196.
16. Trudeau acknowledges and regrets that "a number of innocent people were swept up in the police net" but insists that the lists were drawn up by the Quebec and Montreal police, with little RCMP input (Trudeau, *Memoirs*, 146).
17. Ibid., 130–1.
18. Ibid., 141. Trudeau also contends that he was under intense pressure from the Quebec government and Montreal authorities to invoke the act. However, others have claimed that this request was in fact orchestrated by Ottawa. See the discussion of this scenario, among others, in Marc Laurendeau, *Les Québécois violents* (Montreal: Boréal, 1974), 145–52. The contention that the extraordinary police powers were not necessary for the apprehension of the FLQ kidnappers appears in Ron Haggart and Aubrey E. Golden, *Rumours of War* (Toronto: New Press, 1971), 251–5.
19. Ryan's arguments can be found in Claude Ryan, "Les mesures de guerre: trois questions," *Le Devoir*, 17 Oct. 1970. The argument that the imposition of the War Measures Act was part of an effort to intimidate Quebec nationalists and separatists in general is given credence in Reg Whitaker, "Apprehended Insurrection? RCMP Intelligence and the October Crisis," *Queen's Quarterly* 100, no. 2 (Summer 1993): 401–5. See also Richard Gwyn, *The Northern Magus* (Toronto: McClelland & Stewart, 1980), 129–34. A critique of the Trudeau government's actions, claiming that they were an improper assertion of the federal government's authority, is made in Denis Smith, *Bleeding Hearts . . . Bleeding Country* (Edmonton: Hurtig, 1971). For an anthology of articles and speeches about the October Crisis see Guy Bouthillier and Édouard Cloutier, eds. *Trudeau's Darkest Hour: War Measures in Time of Peace, October 1970* (Montreal: Baraka Books, 2010).
20. Yves Vaillancourt, "Le Régime d'assistance publique du Canada: perspective québécoise," PhD thesis, Université de Montréal, political science, 1992, 239.
21. Simeon and Robinson, *State, Society and the Development of Canadian Federalism*, 201.
22. Pierre Elliott Trudeau, *Federalism and the French Canadians* (Toronto: Macmillan, 1968), 43.
23. The processes of constitutional discussions leading up to the Victoria Charter are recounted in Richard Simeon, *Federal–Provincial Diplomacy* (Toronto: University of Toronto Press, 1972), Chap. 5; and Smiley, *Canada in Question*, Chap. 3.
24. Smiley, *Canada in Question*, 42–3.
25. Pierre Elliott Trudeau, *Federal–Provincial Grants and the Spending Power of Parliament* (Ottawa: Queen's Printer, 1969), 38–48. The scheme is discussed in Smiley, *Canada in Question*, 86. As Smiley notes, under these schemes the citizens of a non-participating province rather than the government itself would be compensated by Ottawa.
26. The federal government would have been required to advise the provinces ahead of time of any proposed legislation in these areas. But, beyond that, the provision did not spell out the implications of provincial paramountcy. It simply said that such legislation could not "affect the operation of any law present or future of a Provincial Legislature in relation to any such matter."
27. In the cases of family allowances, manpower training, and old-age income supplements, a provincial government could, by exercising its paramountcy, displace federal measures while being entitled to fiscal compensation from Ottawa. In the remaining instances, youth allowances and unemployment insurance, any new federal program could not affect existing or future provincial measures. Conceivably, Ottawa's

blanket provision about not affecting the operation of provincial laws might have met this latter condition. But it certainly could not have met the former one.

28. Claude Castonguay, Quebec's minister of social welfare and former deputy minister of the same department, had already developed the plans for the scheme as co-chair of a provincial commission on social policy. He had been instrumental in preparing Quebec's pension fund proposals in 1964.
29. Arguably, two of the areas from which a provincial government might have been able to displace federal intervention, with compensation, namely, income supplements to the aged and manpower training, fell within the terms of the Pearson government's 1965 interim arrangements for contracting out. By the same token, youth allowances had been covered under a separate agreement of the Pearson government that allowed contracting out. As for the federal government's unemployment insurance program, it presumably would have been protected by the proposal's reference to "new" federal programs. This leaves family allowances as the only program not falling under the Pearson government's contracting out framework that would have been endangered by Quebec's proposal. This is based on Quebec's offer as reproduced in *Le Devoir*, 19 June 1971.
30. See Trudeau, *Memoirs*, 232, and Robertson, *Memoirs of a Very Civil Servant*, 283.
31. *Working Paper on Social Security for Canadians* (Ottawa: Information Canada, Apr. 1973).
32. Smiley, *Canada in Question*, 77.
33. According to the *Globe and Mail*, when Bourassa entered the National Assembly after having announced rejection of the Charter, he was "thunderously applauded by all four parties" (as cited by P.E. Bryden, "The Rise of Spectator Constitutionalism, 1967–81," Lois Harder and Steve Patten, eds., *Patriation and its Consequences: Constitution Making in Canada* [Vancouver: UBC Press, 2015], 101).
34. Simeon, *Federal–Provincial Diplomacy*, 120–1.
35. Claude Ryan, "Le dilemme de M. Bourassa," *Le Devoir*, 22 June 1971.
36. Not only would Quebec not gain significant powers but "an affirmative answer . . . would signify the acceptance in principle of a revised constitution that still fails to take account of the fact that Canada is, after all, a country composed of two distinct societies." ("If Quebec Says No to Victoria Charter," Montreal *Gazette*, 19 June 1971.)
37. In Ryan's opinion the Charter had been opposed by such a wide variety of groups in Quebec that its acceptance by the Quebec government could be a "tragic fraud" (Ryan, "Le dilemme de M. Bourassa").
38. Stanley McDowell, "Governments All Water Down Aims to Create Basis of New Constitution," *Globe and Mail*, 18 June 1971, as quoted in Simeon, *Federal–Provincial Diplomacy*, 121.
39. Peter H. Russell, *Constitutional Odyssey*, 3rd edn (Toronto: University of Toronto Press, 2004), 90. Claude Ryan concluded that in rejecting the Charter Bourassa had expressed the profound convictions of the whole Quebec people (*Le Devoir*, 25 June 1971, as paraphrased in Simeon, *Federal–Provincial Diplomacy*, 121). In his letter of rejection, Bourassa pointed to "uncertainty" in the provisions dealing with income security (Smiley, *Canada in Question*, 78), adding, "If this uncertainty were eliminated, our conclusion could be different." (Ibid.) Of course, rather than poor legal draftsmanship, the real problem was disagreement over how social policy should be handled.
40. Gordon Robertson suggests that Pearson, who was a "genius at achieving agreement where no one else could," might have been able to produce at agreement at Victoria. On this basis, the isolation of Quebec in 1981 might have been avoided. (Robertson, *Memoirs of a Very Civil Servant*, 294–5 and 379.)
41. In 1973, the Trudeau government did agree to allow Quebec and any other provincial government to determine, within limits, the levels of family allowances to be given to different categories of residents. This was simply an administrative agreement, with no constitutional backing.
42. In 1973, responding to objections from the Quebec government, Ottawa did agree to allow provincial governments to determine, within limits, the levels of family allowance benefits to be granted to their residents. Only one other province, Alberta, subsequently took advantage of this opportunity. See Donald V. Smiley, *The Federal Condition in Canada* (Toronto: McGraw-Hill Ryerson,

1987), 237; and Garth Stevenson, *Unfulfilled Union*, 3rd edn (Toronto: Gage, 1989), 169.
43. David Milne, *The Canadian Constitution* (Toronto: Lorimer, 1991), 60.
44. Marcel Pepin, "Si Québec ne collabore pas, Trudeau rapatriera tout seul la constitution," *La Presse*, 6 Mar. 1976. In an editorial, Claude Ryan suggested that Trudeau was driven by "a hunger for power that is totally incompatible with the spirit of federalism" ("un désir de puissance qui n'a rien de commun avec l'esprit fédéral"). See Claude Ryan, "Le rêve vain de M. Trudeau," *Le Devoir*, 8 Mar. 1976.
45. The reality was considerably more complex. The Trudeau Liberals' popular vote in Quebec had fallen to 49 per cent in 1972, returning to 54 per cent in 1974, just slightly above the 1968 level. Assuming that Liberal support in Quebec was higher among Anglophones than Francophones, Trudeau and the Liberals still would not have received a clear majority vote of Francophones. Nor is it certain that Trudeau's vision of Canada explained the support his party did receive in Quebec. At least part of it must have been due to the normal support of Quebec Francophones for one of "their own." This "native son" factor was demonstrated by Lemieux and Crête in their study of Quebec voting over the period 1930 to 1979: "An anglophone leader costs the Liberal party 6 percentage points in Quebec while a Francophone leader is worth, on average, an extra 2.7 percentage points." (Vincent Lemieux and Jean Crête, "Quebec" in *Canada at the Polls, 1979 and 1980*, ed. Howard R. Penniman [Washington, DC: American Enterprise Institute for Public Policy Research, 1981], 222.)
46. "Le séparatisme est mort, pense Trudeau," *Le Devoir*, 11 May 1976. (He based his claim on the fact that the PQ had linked sovereignty to a referendum rather than to the mere election of the party.)
47. This is demonstrated by data summarized in Kenneth McRoberts, *Quebec: Social Change and Political Crisis*, 3rd edn (Toronto: McClelland & Stewart, 1993), 327.
48. Ibid., 329.
49. My translation of "de choisir vraiment d'être Canadiens," *Pierre Elliott Trudeau à la Chambre de commerce de Québec, 28 janvier 1977* (Montreal: *La Presse*, 1977), 12.
50. My translation of "Si vous voulez que je me montre souple, je vais le faire tout de suite. Dans la constitution, à mon avis, il y a seulement un préalable" (ibid., 33).
51. My translation of "le respect des droits de l'homme et de la femme, le respect des droits humains, puis probablement le respect de l'aspect collectif de ces droits humains. Je pense à la langue, je pense aux droits des régions d'exister. À partir de ce préalable, on peut faire table rase, écrire une nouvelle constitution. Ça fait cent dix ans qu'on n'en a pas eu de nouvelle: on peut en faire une. Je ne refuse aucun défi! " (ibid., 33).
52. My translation of "des chicanes de politiciens" (ibid., 34).
53. My translation of "comment le peuple sera plus heureux, mieux gouverné" (ibid.).
54. My translation of "Tout ce que je demanderai, tant que je serai là, c'est d'établir fonctionnellement que tel ou tel niveau de pouvoir, par exemple, doit s'exercer au fédéral ou au provincial pour que la collectivité canadienne s'en trouve mieux" (ibid.).
55. The Task Force on Canadian Unity, *A Future Together: Observations and Recommendations* (Hull: Dept. of Supply and Services, 1979), 141. The Pepin–Robarts task force is discussed in David R. Cameron, "Not Spicer and Not the B&B: Reflections of an Insider on the Workings of the Pepin–Robarts Task Force on Canadian Unity," *International Journal of Canadian Studies* 7–8 (Spring–Fall 1993): 331–45; and David M. Thomas, "The Second Time Around: Pepin–Robarts Then and Now," paper presented to the Association for Canadian Studies in the United States, Seattle, 18–19 Nov. 1995.
56. See Chap. 2, note 32. According to Gordon Robertson, "[Trudeau's] thinking and that of Pepin were miles apart. . . . In establishing the task force [Trudeau] may have hoped for a miracle but I suspect he merely believed that something had to be done to respond to the PQ victory. . . . Whatever was good could be adopted; the rest could be ignored." (Robertson, *Memoirs of a Very Civil Servant*, 291.)
57. Task Force on Canadian Unity, *A Future Together*, 23.
58. Ibid., 87.
59. Ibid.

60. To be sure, the Commission did not spell out precisely which powers would need to be reassigned to the provinces. Moreover, its understanding of Quebec's distinctiveness and the powers the province therefore needed was a fairly traditional one focused upon a "distinctive culture and heritage." Would that lead, for instance, to the comprehensive control of incomes policy that Quebec sought at the Victoria Conference? For that matter, another section of the report proposed measures to strengthen the free flow of goods, capital, and workers within Canada (71). These might threaten some of the practices that the Quebec government had established during the 1960s and 1970s to exercise greater control over the Quebec economy.
61. Ibid., 51.
62. Canada, House of Commons, *Debates*, 4th session, 30th Parliament, 25 Jan. 1979, 2552.
63. Thomas, "The Second Time Around," 40.
64. Cameron, "Not Spicer and Not the B&B," 342.
65. See the account in Martin Paquet, "Le fleuve et la cité: représentations de l'immigration et esquisses d'une action de l'État québécois, 1945-1968," Ph.D. dissertation, History Department, Université Laval, Oct. 1994.
66. Indeed, the wording of the agreement departed clearly from Trudeau's established views regarding Quebec, with their emphasis on official bilingualism and linguistic equality. One passage of the agreement stated that immigration to Quebec "should contribute to the sociocultural enrichment of Quebec, taking into account its *French character*" (my translation of "doit contribuer à l'enrichissement socioculturel du Québec compte tenu de sa spécificité française," emphasis added [Quebec, Ministère de l'Immigration, *Accord entre le gouvernement du Canada et le gouvernement du Québec portant sur la collaboration en matière d'immigration et sur la sélection des ressortissants étrangers qui souhaitent s'établir au Québec à titre permanent ou temporaire*, Montreal, 1978]). Another passage recognized that the Quebec government intended to "take a position on the entry of foreign nationals in order to favour those who will be able to integrate rapidly into Quebec society." ("entend se prononcer sur la venue des ressortissants étrangers de manière à sélectionner ceux qui pourront s'intégrer rapidement à la société québécoise." [Ibid.])
67. To be sure, two previous agreements with the Bourassa government, one signed in 1971 and another in 1975, had already established procedures for Quebec officials to *participate* in the selection of immigrants. But only with Cullen–Couture did Quebec acquire the actual decision-making power. And the Trudeau government had granted this power to a government that had fallen into the hands of "separatists."

    After negotiating Cullen–Couture, the federal government was concerned about this apparent recognition of a special status for Quebec and actively encouraged other provincial governments to enter into bilateral agreements on immigration. Shortly after the agreement was signed, the federal immigration minister announced that negotiations were under way with five other provinces (as reported in *Canadian Annual Review, 1978* [Toronto: University of Toronto Press, 1980], 79). Ultimately, five provinces did sign agreements, but they were much more limited in scope than Cullen–Couture; none of them delegated the selection process or even involved locating provincial officers in Canadian immigration offices. These agreements are summarized in Kenneth McRoberts, "Unilateralism, Bilateralism and Multilateralism: Approaches to Canadian Federalism," in *Intergovernmental Relations*, Collected Research Studies of the Royal Commission on the Economic Union and Development Prospects for Canada, vol. 63, ed. Richard Simeon (Toronto: University of Toronto Press, 1985), 90.
68. The latter phrase, it might be noted, was very similar to the "duality clause" of the Meech Lake Accord that Trudeau was to criticize so severely 10 years later. Peter Russell notes that, as with Meech, these statements were placed not in a preamble to the constitution (which Meech critics found less objectionable), but in the opening substantive section. Russell, *Constitutional Odyssey*, 101. The proposals regarding the Senate and the Supreme Court also anticipate Meech. In his 1989 defence of Meech, Lowell Murray was

able to make these points with good effect. "Lowell Murray répond à Pierre Trudeau," *La Presse*, 5 Apr. 1989.

69. According to one observer, this round of constitutional negotiations was the closest that the first ministers ever came during the Trudeau era to a comprehensive agreement on constitutional reform, precisely because the Trudeau government was prepared to accept decentralization as the price of provincial agreement to the resolution of the constitutional question. (Russell, *Constitutional Odyssey*, 105.)
70. Ibid.
71. These questions are discussed in McRoberts, *Quebec: Social Change and Political Crisis*, Chap. 9.
72. *Quebec–Canada: A New Deal* (Quebec City: Éditeur officiel, 1979).
73. "La souveraineté-association, ce n'est . . . ni du statu quo, ni du séparatisme. C'est une formule réaliste qui permettra des changements véritables sans devoir tout bouleverser ni recommencer à zéro." Le Directeur général des élections du Québec, *Référendum: Oui-Non* (1980), 2, my translation.
74. "Nous disons . . . qu'au lieu de ce régime . . . dont tout le monde admet que tel quel il est dépassé . . . et sans renier pour autant une longue tradition de coexistence qui a créé tout un réseau d'échanges, nous nous devons d'arriver avec nos voisins et partenaires du reste du Canada à une nouvelle entente d'égal à égal." Assemblée nationale, *Journal des Débats*, 4th session, 31st legislature, 4 Mar. 1980, 4964, my translation.
75. McRoberts, *Quebec: Social Change and Political Crisis*, 312.
76. As reported by journalist Denise Bombardier ("Noir sur blanc," Radio-Canada, 17 May 1980). See also Gérald Bernier, "Les aspects économiques du débat: un dialogue de sourds," in En collaboration, *Québec: un pays incertain* (Montreal: Québec/Amérique, 1980), 123.
77. According to Maurice Pinard, in 1980, eight polls gave an average of 42 per cent in favour of sovereignty-association, 44 per cent against, and 14 per cent undecided. In the same year, nine polls gave an average of 24 per cent in favour of independence, 64 per cent against, and 12 per cent undecided. See Maurice Pinard, "The Dramatic Reemergence of the Quebec Independence Movement," *Journal of International Affairs* 45, no. 2 (Winter 1992): Tables 1 and 2.
78. Apparently, the referendum question had enjoyed majority support in June of 1979 and, after a slump in the fall of 1979, had rebounded following a National Assembly debate on the referendum question in March 1980. During April of 1980, however, the No side took the lead, and held it until the referendum. A CROP survey taken between 26 April and 8 May found a solid No lead: Yes, 39.6 per cent; No, 45.5 per cent; don't know or no response, 14.9 per cent, as reproduced in André Blais, "Le vote: ce que l'on en sait . . . ce que l'on n'en sait pas," in En collaboration, *Québec: un pays incertain*, Table 2. These figures underestimated the No lead. Most surveyors, including CROP, assumed that the non-responding category was in fact disproportionately inclined to vote No.
79. See the account of the three speeches in Laforest, *Trudeau et la fin d'un rêve canadien*, 42–8.
80. "Je n'en connais pas parmi eux qui ne veuillent pas profiter de ce tourbillon actuel pour renouveler la constitution. Monsieur Ryan a proposé un Livre beige. Les gouvernements des autres provinces, de l'Ontario à la Colombie, ont présenté plusieurs projets. Notre gouvernement, après avoir établi la Commission Pepin-Robarts, a proposé une formule qui s'appelait *Le Temps d'agir*, un bill, un projet de loi qui s'appelait le bill C-60 qui contenait, entre parenthèses, beaucoup de propositions pour un renouvellement fondamental. Ceux, donc, qui veulent rester Canadiens, sont prêts à le changer, sont prêts à améliorer le fédéralisme." See "Trudeau n'acceptera de négocier qu'après le 2e référendum," *La Presse*, 3 May 1980.
81. My translation of "met notre sort entre les mains des autres."
82. My translation of "Nous allions à Ottawa parce que c'est comme ça que les Québécois ont toujours vu leur place dans ce pays. Ils l'ont vue comme étant fiers d'être Québécois, se battant ici pour la défense de leurs droits, mais affirmant aussi leurs droits d'être Canadiens en envoyant parmi leurs meilleurs représentants à Ottawa pour affirmer la place des Québécois au sein du Canada."

83. My translation of "Je sais parce que je leur en ai parlé ce matin à ces députés, je sais que je peux prendre l'engagement le plus solennel qu'à la suite d'un NON, nous allons mettre en place immédiatement le mécanisme de renouvellement de la Constitution et nous n'arrêtons pas avant que ça soit fait . . . nous mettons notre tête en jeu, nous, députés québécois, parce que nous le disons aux Québécois de voter NON, et nous vous disons à vous des autres provinces que nous n'accepterons pas ensuite que ce NON soit interprété par vous comme une indication que tout va bien puis que tout peut rester comme c'était auparavant. Nous voulons du changement, nous mettons nos sièges en jeu pour avoir du changement." Prime Minister's Office, Transcription de l'allocution du Très Honorable Pierre Elliott Trudeau du centre Paul Sauvé, Montréal, Québec, le 14 mai 1980, 6–7.
84. McRoberts, *Quebec: Social Change and Political Crisis*, 327.
85. Clarkson and McCall write, "It was an inspired performance, probably the crucial act that secured the soft neo-federalist vote, directing it away from the Oui and towards the Non." See Stephen Clarkson and Christina McCall, *Trudeau and Our Times*, vol. 1 (Toronto: McClelland & Stewart, 1990), 239.
86. One firm, IQOP, conducted surveys just before and after Trudeau's 14 May speech. The result on 11 May was Yes, 37 per cent; No, 40 per cent; don't know or no response, 23 per cent. The 18 May survey actually indicated a slight surge for the PQ option: Yes, 40.4 per cent; No, 36.5 per cent; don't know or no response, 23.1 per cent. See André Blais, "Le vote: ce que l'on en sait . . . ce que l'on n'en sait pas," in En collaboration, *Québec: un pays incertain*, Table 2.
87. He had endorsed no proposals nor offered any propositions of his own; he had not even indicated the general direction that the change might take. The first stage of the federal government's *A Time for Action* had been rendered moot by the Supreme Court rejection of C-60; the second stage had not been spelled out in detail. As for the Pepin–Robarts Report, Trudeau had spoken favourably of it in general but criticized some of the proposals and then ignored it. Finally, he had avoided taking a position on a detailed outline of constitutional revision released by the Quebec Liberal Party in late 1979, *A New Canadian Federation* (commonly known as the "Beige Paper"). Apparently, he also had asked Claude Ryan not to refer to the Beige Paper during the referendum campaign. Claude Forget, who had been closely involved with the Beige Paper, has written that when Ryan was chosen party leader, Trudeau invited him to his residence in Ottawa. There Ryan agreed with Trudeau's suggestion that no mention should be made of the document during the referendum campaign. This had the effect of marginalizing both Ryan and the Beige Paper during the campaign and enabling Trudeau to take control of the constitutional question after the referendum had been won. See Claude E. Forget, "Référendum: les conséquences méconnues d'un vote négatif," *La Presse*, 29 Mar. 1995. Ryan, however, says there had never been any question of promoting the Beige Paper during the referendum campaign; he had said as much in his closing address to the Liberal convention that adopted the document. See Claude Ryan, "Référendum de 1980: Ryan en désaccord avec Forget," *La Presse*, 31 Mar. 1995.
88. House of Commons, *Debates*, 1st session, 32nd Parliament, 21 May 1980, 1263.
89. Ibid.
90. Burelle, *Pierre Elliott Trudeau*, 61–3, my translation. Still, there is a question as to whether the federal offer was made in good faith. At the time, there had been widespread suspicion that the Trudeau government was already contemplating a unilateral move. This was confirmed in a federal memo leaked the day before the September conference (See Clarkson and McCall, *Trudeau and Our Times*, vol. 1, 208–9.) At the conference itself, the premiers were most antagonistic to Trudeau and his colleagues; for his part, Trudeau dismissed out of hand a "Château Consensus" proposal that they put together. As Peter Russell notes, the meeting was "one of the most acrimonious on record." (Russell, *Constitutional Odyssey*, 110.) On the October 1980 meeting see also Ron Graham, *The Last Act: Pierre Trudeau – The Gang of Eight and the Fight for Canada* (Toronto: Penguin Canada, 2012), 61–7.
91. The basic components are the same, but they did undergo some modification. In the case of the amending formula, a referendum mechanism was dropped, and Ontario and

Quebec lost their automatic vetoes. (Ottawa had in fact allowed for agreement on an alternative scheme within two years. See Milne, *The Canadian Constitution*, 100.) In the case of the Charter, the notwithstanding clause was added, application of mobility rights was qualified, and clauses dealing with Indigenous Peoples, multiculturalism, and gender were added. The final version still does not deal with central institutions, and the division of powers is ignored except for a section, added to the final version, affirming provincial jurisdiction over non-renewable natural resources, forestry resources, and electrical energy. See the discussion in McWhinney, *Canada and the Constitution*, 94–100; the texts of the original resolution and the final version appear in Appendices A and E. It should be noted that some of the modifications had already been inserted in the revised version of Ottawa's initial resolution. See Milne, *The Canadian Constitution*, 109—12.

92. Section 33, which allows legislatures to exempt law from certain provisions of the Charter, does not extend to Trudeau's central goal of language rights. Apparently, he accepted this provision with great reluctance (Barry K. Strayer, "The Evolution of the Charter," Harder and Patten, *Patriation and its Consequences*, 90).
93. Pierre Elliott Trudeau, "The Values of a Just Society," in *Towards a Just Society*, ed. Thomas S. Axworthy and Pierre Elliott Trudeau (Markham, Ont.: Viking, 1990), 368.
94. Under this scheme patriation must be linked to a substantial revision of the division of powers, any constitutional declaration of principles must contain a recognition of Quebec's distinctiveness, there must be no entrenchment of language rights (at least with respect to Quebec), and the Supreme Court should be reorganized to give Quebec justices equality on a constitutional bench or "near equality" in the Court as a whole. The Quebec government's position was reproduced in a two-page advertisement in *La Presse*, 21 Aug. 1980.
95. Under the Beige Paper all provinces were to receive exclusive jurisdiction over such matters as job training, family law, social insurance (including unemployment insurance), and health and social services. (In effect, the change exceeded the Bourassa government's proposals to the Victoria Conference.) The provinces would be given exclusive jurisdiction over offshore resources (although this would be subject to the federal emergency power). They were to be allowed access to any means of taxation and were to be assigned the residual power. As we have seen, the Pepin–Robarts Report had also envisaged a transfer of jurisdictions to the provinces but with the provision whereby provincial governments would not necessarily exercise them, with the result that Quebec could well emerge with a *de facto* special status. Both proposals also abolished the reservation, disallowance, and declaratory powers of the federal government. Both reports called for a new upper chamber, whose members would be chosen exclusively by the provincial governments and that would have such powers as a suspensive veto over federal legislation in concurrent jurisdictions, a permanent veto over bills involving spending and emergency powers, and the power to approve appointments to key federal agencies and the Supreme Court. In this upper chamber, Quebec would be entitled to 25 per cent of the voting seats under the Quebec Liberal Party's proposal and 20 per cent under the task force's proposal. As for the Supreme Court, Pepin–Robarts would have established a "near equality" in the number of justices from Quebec and the rest of the country; the Beige Paper would have established a "constitutional" bench on which half of the justices would be from Quebec. See Task Force, *A Future Together*, and Le Comité constitutionnel du Parti libéral du Québec, *Une nouvelle fédération canadienne* (Montreal: Parti libéral du Québec, 1980). As McWhinney documents, some Quebec intellectuals did criticize the Beige Paper for not stressing enough the uniqueness of Quebec. See McWhinney, *Canada and the Constitution*, 30–7.
96. Constitution Act, 1982, s. 23. This provision clearly contradicts Bill 101's "Quebec clause," which restricts access to English-language schools to children whose parents have themselves been educated in English in Quebec or who have a sibling who has been educated in English in Quebec. But it even contradicts the Quebec clause to the extent that it covers children who have received, or have a sibling who has received, education

in English anywhere in Canada—whatever the status of the parent. At the same time, a special provision in the Charter prevents the language-of-education provisions from applying to children of any Canadian whose first language is English until this is authorized by the Quebec government or the National Assembly.

97. Constitution Act, 1982, s. 6. This provision is inoperable so long as a province's employment is below the national average.

98. The Fulton–Favreau formula and the Victoria Charter had both given Quebec a veto over all forms of constitutional change. The Quebec Liberal Party's *A New Canadian Federation* adopted the Victoria Charter formula. In the federal government's own proposed resolution of October 1980, all amendments would have to be approved by the Quebec National Assembly. In the case of the Pepin–Robarts Report, Quebec representatives on the Council of the Federation would not have a veto over constitutional amendments (only a majority would be necessary), but a proposed amendment would have to be ratified by a majority of Quebec electors voting in a Canada-wide referendum.

99. Bernard Descôteaux, "L'Assemblée adopte la motion Lévesque sans l'appui du PLQ," *Le Devoir*, 22 Nov. 1980. The PQ government had in fact sought a commitment to unanimous support from the Liberal opposition, but the Liberals were divided on the matter. In particular, some Anglophone members voted against the measure. Jean-Pierre Proulx, "Servir deux maîtres," *Le Devoir*, 24 Nov. 1980.

100. My translation of "regrettait profondément que des décisions importantes soient prises à Ottawa sans le consentement du Québec." See Jean-Claude Picard, "La tristesse à l'Assemblée nationale," *Le Devoir*, 3 Dec. 1981. The Liberals refused to support a PQ resolution, passed on 1 Dec. 1981, condemning the agreement and invoking Quebec's right to veto it. Ryan attacked the Lévesque government for sacrificing the veto in the first place and called on the government to pursue further negotiations with Ottawa.

101. Ryan said, "The absence of a person like myself will serve as a reminder that there are still important issues to resolve: this agreement [on the constitution] was arrived at without Quebec's consent," as quoted in McWhinney, *Canada and the Constitution*, 137.

102. "Re: Objection to a resolution to amend the constitution" [1982], 2 S.C.R., 813.

103. To reach its decision, the Court imposed a standard for the existence of conventions that was far more exacting than the one it had used in a previous case. (See Andrew Petter, "Maître chez Who? The Quebec Veto Reference," *Supreme Court Law* 6 [1984]: 387–99; and G.J. Brandt, "The Quebec Veto Reference: A Constitutional Postscript," *University of Western Ontario Law Review* 21, no. 1 [1983]: 163–71.) Whereas Petter is highly critical of this use of a more exacting standard in the Quebec case, Brandt defends it; he argues that, confronted by the "crisis" raised by the patriation case, namely a deadlock between governments, the Court was quite correct in inferring acceptance from conduct. The situation required the Court to involve itself in "the creation of convention." Now that the crisis had passed, it was proper for the Court to retreat to a more traditional judicial approach. The latter argument exaggerates the exceptional aspects of the crisis behind the first reference and ignores the profound crisis behind the second.

Several months earlier, in ruling on the Trudeau government's plans for unilateral patriation over the opposition of eight provinces, the Supreme Court had defined a three-fold test for the existence of a convention: the past behaviour of governments; attitudes of politicians; and the existence of a supporting principle. In doing so, it was drawing on the work of leading British legal scholar, Ivor Jennings. On this basis, it had ruled that the Trudeau government had violated a convention that "a substantial degree" of consent among provincial governments was necessary for constitutional amendments that directly affected provincial jurisdiction. In the Quebec decision, the Court interpreted the second standard, politicians' attitudes, in a much more exacting manner. In effect, only explicit statements of attitudes would do; attitudes could not be inferred from behaviour. So the Court was able to argue that a Quebec veto did not exist, even though two previous attempts at constitutional revision had been abandoned when Quebec objected: the

Fulton–Favreau formula of 1964 and the Victoria Charter of 1971. Critics argue that these actions (or non-actions) speak for themselves. (See Donald V. Smiley, "A Dangerous Deed: The Constitution Act, 1982," in *And No One Cheered*, ed. Keith Banting and Richard Simeon [Toronto: Methuen, 1983], 77; and Andrew Petter, "Maître chez Who?") Indeed, in its previous decision the Court had viewed them as significant evidence for the "substantial degree of provincial consent" convention ("Re: Resolution to amend the constitution" [1981], 1 S.C.R., 893–4). For that matter, the Court's insistence on explicit statement of an attitude seemed to contradict the statement of Ivor Jennings that "convention implies some form of agreement, whether expressed or implied. . ." The court ruled that the assertion "must be qualified"; though conventions may not be "reduced to writing," they must at least be the object of "utterance" (ibid., 817).

104. McWhinney, *Canada and the Constitution*, 126.
105. As quoted in Petter, "Maître chez Who?" 390.
106. Russell, *Constitutional Odyssey*, 129.
107. In a 1995 study, Claude Ryan harks back to George C.F. Stanley's elaboration of a bicultural compact and maintains that if the Court had given due regard to Stanley's arguments it could not possibly have rejected Quebec's claims to a veto (Claude Ryan, *Regards sur le fédéralisme canadien* [Montreal: Boréal, 1995], 194). Trudeau had said repeatedly that Quebec's consent was not necessary since patriation had the support of all but four of the Quebec members of the House of Commons and had a majority of votes even if the Quebec MPs' votes were combined with the National Assembly vote on a 1 Dec. resolution (*Debates of the Senate*, 2nd session, 33rd Parliament, 30 Mar. 1988, 2996). Ryan called that claim "a distortion of history" (Ryan, *Regards sur le fédéralisme canadien*, 137).
108. Against the widespread contention that Lévesque would have rejected any proposal developed at the November 1981 conference, Peter Russell makes a compelling case that the dynamics of the meeting, with exclusion of Quebec from the overnight negotiations among the Gang of Eight, precluded Lévesque from doing so. With greater time, and a serious effort, Lévesque might have been brought on side. (Peter Russell, "Patriation and the Law of Unintended Consequences," in Harder and Patten, *Patriation and Its Consequences*, 234.)
109. Apparently, Trudeau did propose simply patriation with an amending formula (the Victoria Charter formula) to the premiers over a dinner in April 1975. However, it became clear subsequently that Quebec, Alberta, and BC were opposed. (Robertson, *Memoirs of a Very Civil Servant*, 284.) Nonetheless, those same provinces did agree to such a package (with a different amending formula) in April 1981.
110. As Ron Graham notes, "If constitutional reform had meant nothing more than patriation and an amending formula, it's unlikely that Pierre Trudeau would have wasted so much time and political capital trying to get them. . . . What spurred the fight was Trudeau's decision to yoke the federal government's Resolution to a Charter of Rights and Freedoms." (Graham, *The Last Act*, 81).
111. Laforest and Readman make this argument, drawing upon Pierre Godin's biography of René Lévesque (Guy Laforest and Rosalie Readman, "Plus de détresse que d'enchantement: les négociations constitutionnelles de novembre 1981 vues du Québec," in *Le nouvel ordre constitutionnel canadien: du rapatriement de 1982 à nos jours*, ed. François Rocher and Benoît Pelletier [Quebec: Presses de l'Université du Québec, 2013], 70). See also Burelle, *Pierre Elliott Trudeau*, 85.
112. Over the years Trudeau placed great stock in the contention that Lévesque betrayed the other dissident premiers by initially agreeing to a referendum. On this basis, Trudeau could blame Quebec for isolation. See, for instance, Pierre Elliott Trudeau, "J'accuse Lucien Bouchard!," *La Presse*, 3 Feb. 1996.
113. Indeed, at the opening of the conference Allan Blakeney submitted an elaborate proposal, backed by a lengthy document, that was a departure from the Gang of Eight agreement. This confirmed Lévesque's apprehension that Blakeney, and the other premiers, were abandoning him. (Clarkson and McCall, *Trudeau and Our Times*, vol. 1, 377, and Graham, *The Last Act*, 112.)
114. Ibid., 111.
115. For that matter, Trudeau's referendum offer was itself questionable since the procedures

developed by federal officials (in haste, after Trudeau made the proposal) required that the federal government's resolution, without any modification, first be presented to the British Parliament. (See Graham, *The Last Act*, 137–8, and, for a slightly different reading of the procedures but the same general conclusion, Jean-François Lisée, "Constitution 1982 et 1992: aux sources de l'échec," in Rocher and Readman, *Nouvel ordre constitutionnel*, 88–9.) For his part, Justice Minister Jean Chrétien had always seen the referendum idea as simply a "strategic threat," as did Bill Davis and Richard Hatfield (Graham, *The Last Act*, 161–2).

116. Though not part of the original agreement among Trudeau and the nine premiers, this was later added by the federal government.
117. This provision had not been part of the agreement among Trudeau and the nine premiers. It emerged from a subsequent attempt by the federal government to obtain Quebec's consent. See *Canadian Annual Review, 1981* (Toronto: University of Toronto Press, 1984), 74–6.
118. The qualification to mobility rights had been added to placate Newfoundland Premier Brian Peckford.
119. See note 108.
120. Laforest, *Trudeau et la fin d'un rêve canadien*, 44–8.
121. "Si la réponse à la question référendaire est Non, nous avons tous dit que ce Non sera interprété comme un mandat pour changer la Constitution, pour renouveler le fédéralisme." Transcript of the address by the Right Honorable Pierre Elliott Trudeau, 14 May 1980, 6.
122. "L'accord constitutionnel de 1982 n'a pas été un marché de dupes pour le Québec," *La Presse*, 10 Mar. 1989. For his part, Ramsay Cook argues that there could have been no confusion about Trudeau's intentions for "anyone who made an effort to understand his fundamental ideas and had attentively watched his efforts to reform the constitution since 1965" since "he had repeated his goals ad nauseum for all to hear" (Cook, *The Teeth of Time*, 139). Yet not all members of the Quebec public would have made that effort. Moreover, there is the disjunction between his long-standing positions and the statements and initiatives he took in the wake of the 1976 PQ victory. Indeed, in his biography of Trudeau, Nino Ricci contends that Trudeau's statement of what he had promised "can't help but sound disingenuous" and that if he "had offered these things [patriation with a charter and amending formula] from the stage—the very ones that he had always been fighting for, Trudeau said in his defense, but also the ones Quebec had always rejected—the referendum would surely have been lost." (Nino Ricci, *Pierre Elliott Trudeau* [Toronto: Penguin Canada, 2009], 162) For Gordon Robertson, Trudeau's original deputy minister for federal–provincial relations, it is obvious that Trudeau misled Quebec voters in his Paul Sauvé address. He writes that Trudeau then charged them "with 'misunderstanding' what he had said. They should have known that he did not mean what he obviously intended them to think he meant." (Robertson, *Memoirs of a Very Civil Servant*, 377)
123. Burelle insists on the latter interpretation. It was only after the failure of the September 1980 conference, which Trudeau attributed to the Lévesque government's machinations among the other premiers, that Trudeau's position hardened and his intense opposition to Quebec nationalism prevailed. Burelle affirms that until that point Trudeau's intellectual commitment to personalism (his "reason") had held his individualism and anti-nationalism (his "passion") in check (Burelle, *Pierre Elliott Trudeau*, 68). Thus, the discourse he adopted after the 1976 PQ victory is an authentic expression of personalism rather than simply a ploy to build support for a No referendum vote. Still, we have seen instances before 1976, most notably his presentation of multiculturalism, where personalist references would have been most appropriate but were absent.
124. Milne, *The Canadian Constitution*, 70; and Clarkson and McCall, *Trudeau and Our Times*, vol. 1, 280.
125. To be sure, among constitutional scholars there had developed over the decades a school of "constitutional nationalism" that did see patriation as an important objective. Many English-Canadian scholars were especially dissatisfied with the "provincialist" rulings of the Judicial Committee of the Privy Council. (Eric M. Adams, "Constitutional Nationalism," Harder and Patten,

Patriation and its Consequences, 49–71.) For their part, French-Canadian scholars tended not to share this dissatisfaction and to be apprehensive about any termination of appeals to the JCPC. Whether these concerns had filtered beyond scholarly circles to the larger public, as Adams contends, is a debatable question. In any event, appeals to the JCPC had been ended in 1949.

126. In the first quotation, Lyon was quoting from a paper by Carleton University professor G.P. Browne. All these quotations are taken from Milne, *The Canadian Constitution*, 89–91.
127. Ibid., 76.
128. Donald V. Smiley, "The Case against the Canadian Charter of Human Rights," *Canadian Journal of Political Science* 2, no. 3 (Sept. 1969): 278–91.
129. Donald V. Smiley, *The Canadian Charter of Rights and Freedoms, 1981* (Toronto: Ontario Economic Council, 1981), 14–5.
130. Cynthia Williams, "The Changing Nature of Citizen Rights," in *Constitutionalism, Citizenship and Society in Canada*, Collected Research Studies of the Royal Commission on the Economic Union and Development Prospects for Canada, vol. 33, ed. Alan Cairns and Cynthia Williams (Toronto: University of Toronto Press, 1985), 111–23.
131. Lois Harder and Steve Patten, "Looking Back on Patriation and Its Consequences," Harder and Patten, *Patriation and its Consequences*, 12.
132. The list of groups is drawn from Russell, *Constitutional Odyssey*, 114. See also Milne, *The Canadian Constitution*, 107; Williams, "Changing Nature of Citizen Rights"; and Rainer Knopff and F.L. Morton, "Nation-Building and the Canadian Charter of Rights and Freedoms," in Cairns and Williams, *Constitutionalism, Citizenship and Society in Canada*, 150–7.
133. Russell, *Constitutional Odyssey*, 113.
134. Ibid., 116.
135. Milne, *The Canadian Constitution*, 95.
136. See the discussion of the proposals of the Ontario Advisory Committee on Confederation and the BC government in McWhinney, *Quebec and the Constitution*, Chap. 7.
137. Ibid., 90.
138. Peter H. Russell, *Canada's Odyssey* (Toronto: University of Toronto Press, 2017), 226, 386–7, and John Borrows, *Freedom and Indigenous Constitutionalism* (Toronto: University of Toronto Press, 2016), 114–22. Borrows underlines divisions among Indigenous leaders over the notion of participating in the patriation process, as opposed to seeking a nation-to-nation relationship with the Canadian state.
139. Quoted in Clarkson and McCall, *Trudeau and Our Times*, vol. 1, 280–1.
140. Ibid., 249–53.
141. "Des provinces ont prié Ottawa de leur imposer le respect du français," *Le Devoir*, 23 Oct. 1980.
142. Milne recounts how in the final negotiations Trudeau "lashed out" at the proposal by the eight dissident premiers that minority-language educational rights be subject to a provincial opting-in clause, accusing them of being "duped" by the PQ. See Milne, *The Canadian Constitution*, 165. As for the notwithstanding clause, language rights are one of the few provisions to which it does not apply.
143. Canada, House of Commons, *Debates*, 1st session, 32nd Parliament, 15 Apr. 1980, 32–3.
144. Pierre Elliott Trudeau, *Federalism and the French Canadians* (Toronto: Macmillan, 1968), 165.
145. Ibid., 191.
146. Ibid., 151–81.
147. P.E. Bryden, "The Rise of Spectator Constitutionalism, 1967–81," in Harder and Patten, *Patriation and Its Consequences*, 102.
148. Sheppard and Valpy recount: "The referendum win, where Ottawa believed it had stepped in and rescued the situation from the foundering provincial Liberals, produced an enormous sense of self-confidence in the Trudeau government at the outset of its mandate. . . . They were almost drunk with a new sense of power and accomplishment." See Robert Sheppard and Michael Valpy, *The National Deal* (Toronto: Fleet Books, 1982), 40.
149. Examples would be Jim Coutts, Trudeau's principal secretary; Tom Axworthy, his chief of staff; and Michael Kirby, in charge of federal–provincial relations.
150. See Burelle, *Pierre Elliott Trudeau*, 79. In fact, after his disavowal of this nationalist *virage*, Burelle was removed from responsibility for constitutional matters (ibid.). To be sure, Marc Lalonde played a critical role as energy minister.

151. The nationalism of the last Trudeau administration is analyzed in David Milne, *Tug of War* (Toronto: Lorimer, 1986), 200–18.
152. Ian Mulgrew, "Provinces Using Federal Money but Ottawa is Not Credited: PM," *Globe and Mail*, 25 Nov. 1981.
153. Whereas throughout the 1970s the Trudeau government had followed a practice of negotiated bilateral agreements with the producer provinces—Alberta, Saskatchewan, and British Columbia—on 28 Oct. 1980 Ottawa simply announced what the new prices would be. In fact, its National Energy Program entailed a number of other measures that the producing provinces saw as unwarranted intrusions into their jurisdictions and prerogatives. This discussion draws on McRoberts, "Unilateralism, Bilateralism and Multilateralism," 98–9.
154. Ibid., 104–5.
155. Ibid., 102–3.
156. To quote Secretary of State Gerald Regan: "I cannot overstate the importance of good communication by the federal government as fundamental to the survival of a strong Canada. Put starkly, unless Canadians know the worth of national government, they will not care enough to continue to have a national government." As quoted in Stanbury, Gorn, and Weinberg, "Federal Advertising Expenditures," 135.
157. Ibid., 145.
158. Trudeau, *Federalism and the French Canadians*, 202.
159. Patrick J. Monahan, *Meech Lake: The Inside Story* (Toronto: University of Toronto Press, 1991), 47.
160. As quoted in Robert Sheppard and Michael Valpy, *The National Deal* (Toronto: Fleet Books, 1982), 317–18.
161. Monahan, *Meech Lake*, 46.
162. My translation of "Nous, notre principe, c'est que nous sommes fédéralistes." "Pas une adhésion à la Constitution," *Le Devoir*, 7 Mar. 1986. The price paid by the government for this decision was the resignation of its special constitutional adviser, Léon Dion, who considered it a strategic error to make this gesture independently of any agreement on a revised constitution. See Gilles Lesage, "Opposé à l'adhésion à la charte canadienne, Léon Dion quitte le gouvernement Bourassa," *Le Devoir*, 17 Mar. 1986.
163. From the text of Rémillard's address as reproduced in Peter M. Leslie, *Rebuilding the Relationship: Quebec and Its Confederation Partners* (Kingston: Institute of Intergovernmental Relations, Queen's University, 1987), 47.
164. Ibid., 37. At the same time, Leslie acknowledges that the conference tended to draw people who were sympathetic to the underlying premise that Quebec's constitutional status needed to be resolved. See ibid., 9.
165. Indeed, the reaction to the proposals among those attending the conference was uniformly positive. See ibid., 57.
166. Monahan, *Meech Lake*, 61.
167. Ibid., 45.
168. These processes are detailed in ibid., Chaps. 4 and 5.
169. Constitutional Amendment, 1987, s. 2(1b) and s. 2(3) as reproduced in Peter W. Hogg, *Meech Lake Constitutional Accord Annotated* (Toronto: Carswell, 1988), Appendix IV.
170. Ibid., s. 2(1a) and s. 2(2).
171. Ibid., s. 2(4).
172. Hogg, *Meech Lake*, 12. This judgement may be excessively narrow; see Jeremy Webber, *Reimagining Canada* (Montreal and Kingston: McGill-Queen's University Press, 1994), 128.
173. Constitutional Amendment, 1987, s. 95, and 1987 Constitutional Accord, s. 2 (as reproduced in Hogg, *Meech Lake*, Appendix II). Quebec would have been allowed to exceed by 5 per cent its proportionate share of immigrants. Agreements with a number of other provinces would also have been constitutionalized.
174. Constitutional Amendment, 1987, s. 106A.
175. Ibid., s. 101.
176. Ibid., s. 25.
177. Constitutional recognition that Quebec formed a "distinct society" had been proposed by the Macdonald Commission in 1985, although as part of the constitution's preamble. ("At the outset, what is required in principle is a statement in the preamble of the Constitution which might be worded along the following lines: 'Recognizing the distinctive character of Quebec society as the principal though not exclusive centre of Canadian Francophones, and accepting as fundamental the duality of the Canadian federation . . .'" Royal Commission on the Economic Union and Development Prospects for Canada, *Report*, vol. III [Ottawa: Supply and Services, Canada, 1985], 333.) (As we saw, the phrase itself had originated

in the 1960s with the Royal Commission on Bilingualism and Biculturalism.) In an "Open Letter to the People of Quebec" signed by Pierre Trudeau on 11 July 1980, in the midst of public debate over a preamble to the constitution, Trudeau had insisted on the existence of "two principal linguistic and cultural communities . . . with the French community having its focus and centre of gravity in Quebec." Acknowledging that the preamble he had submitted to the premiers "can be improved," Trudeau declared, "All I ask is that any changes in its wording reflect even more accurately the existence of two principal linguistic *and cultural* communities in Canada, *with the French community having its focus and centre of gravity in Quebec*, but at the same time extending across the country" [emphasis added]. (Prime Minister's Office, "An Open Letter to the People of Quebec," Translation, 11 July 1980, 2). This does not square with Trudeau's claim to the Senate that "We did not use the expression 'French-speaking Canadians' and 'English-speaking Canadians' in any of our constitutions." See Trudeau, "Who Speaks for Canada? Defining and Sustaining a National Vision," in Michael D. Behiels, ed., *The Meech Lake Primer* (Ottawa: University of Ottawa Press, 1989), 84. At a minimum, he had expressed an openness to terminology that went considerably further than the phrases he found so objectionable in Meech. As we saw, Bill C-60, which the Trudeau government had introduced in 1978, referred to "the Canadian French-speaking society centred in but not limited to Quebec." (Of course, the Trudeau government had never proposed to recognize Quebec as a "distinct society.") The immigration provisions effectively formalized a practice established during the Trudeau era, while adding provisions regarding integration of immigrants and shares of total immigrants. The provision limiting the federal spending power fell considerably short of the proposals of the Pepin–Robarts Commission and the Beige Paper and even the Trudeau government's own 1969 proposal. The use of the federal spending power would have required approval by a two-thirds majority of the new provincially appointed upper chamber under both Pepin–Robarts and under the Beige Paper. To be sure, as Trudeau pointed out in his Senate presentation on Meech, the 1969 federal proposal provided for direct distribution of funds to *citizens* rather than the governments of opting-out provinces (Pierre Elliott Trudeau, "Who Speaks for Canada?" 77). Provincial participation in the selection of Supreme Court justices had been an element of the Victoria Charter. (In his Senate presentation, Trudeau insisted the Victoria procedure, by which disputes would be submitted to an electoral college, was different. See Trudeau, "Who Speaks for Canada?" 78.) Under Pepin–Robarts, Quebec would have had near equality (5 of 11) in the number of justices; under the Beige Paper it would have had equality on a special constitutional bench. The procedure for Senate appointments was quite in line with previous proposals: under Trudeau's Bill C-60, half the senators would have been named independently by provincial legislatures; under both Pepin–Robarts and the Beige Paper, members of the upper body would have been appointed wholly by provincial governments and would have acted as their delegates. As for the extension of the provincial veto of amendments, it affected only four categories of changes.

178. "Voice of the People," *Maclean's*, 15 June 1987.
179. Chaput-Rolland said, "[The agreement] largely exceeds our hopes." See "Il n'y a pas de monstre au lac Meech," *Le Devoir*, 8 May 1987. Claude Ryan issued a spirited defence of the agreement in response to Pierre Trudeau's attack. See Bernard Descôteaux, "L'accord du lac Meech permettra au Québec de faire des gains importants et incontestables," *Le Devoir*, 30 May 1987.
180. Robert Lévesque, "Lévesque fait bande à part," *Le Devoir*, 4 May 1987.
181. Milne, *The Canadian Constitution*, 214.
182. "L'accord du lac Meech confirmera le statut du Québec dans les relations internationales," *Le Devoir*, 10 June 1987. Rémillard did not argue that the distinct-society clause, per se, gave new powers to Quebec. Rather he contended that with the distinct-society clause the courts might be more sympathetic to Quebec's arguments about the international role that derived from Quebec's jurisdiction over education and culture.

183. Jacques-Yvan Morin, "Nous sommes devant un nouveau piège," *Le Devoir*, 20 May 1987.
184. Pierre O'Neill, "Parizeau incite Bourassa à ne pas signer l'accord du lac Meech," *Le Devoir*, 15 May 1987.
185. Pierre O'Neill, "Le lac Meach *[sic]* a rallié les péquistes de toutes tendances," *Le Devoir*, 4 May 1987. Indeed, Max Nemni argues that the Accord was opposed by the majority of constitutional experts, groups, and associations that presented briefs to the Bourassa government between April and June 1987. See Max Nemni, "Le 'dés' accord du Lac Meech et . . .," in *Le Québec et la restructuration du Canada, 1980-1992*, ed. Louis Balthazar et al. (Sillery, Quebec: Septentrion, 1991), 188–9. Yet, in a book which is highly critical of Meech and sympathetic to the sovereigntist cause, Pierre Fournier ruefully acknowledges that during the early days of Meech these criticisms had little popular impact and that nationalist critics were "crying in the desert." See Pierre Fournier, *A Meech Lake Post-Mortem* (Montreal and Kingston: McGill-Queen's University Press, 1991), 34.
186. In a survey conducted on 3 and 4 June 1987, approval of the Accord ranged from 57 per cent in Atlantic Canada to 46 per cent in Ontario and 47 per cent in the West. The survey is reported in "Voice of the People," *Maclean's*, 15 June 1987, 13. The proportions disapproving of Meech in that survey were: Atlantic Canada, 18 per cent; Ontario, 33 per cent; the West, 32 per cent.
187. André Blais and Jean Crête, "Pourquoi l'opinion publique au Canada anglais a-t-elle rejeté l'Accord du Lac Meech?" in *L'engagement intellectuel: mélanges en l'honneur de Léon Dion*, ed. Raymond Hudon and Réjean Pelletier (Sainte-Foy: Presses de l'Université Laval, 1991), 386. Immediately after the collapse of Meech, only 30 per cent of Anglophones felt that the Accord should have been ratified: among Anglophones the most popular politician was Newfoundland premier Clyde Wells, the Accord's fiercest adversary (ibid.).
188. Monahan, *Meech Lake*, 32–6. See also Richard Simeon, "Why Did the Meech Lake Accord Fail?" in *Canada: The State of the Federation 1990*, ed. Ronald L. Watts and Douglas M. Brown (Kingston: Institute of Intergovernmental Relations, Queen's University, 1990), 30.
189. Alan C. Cairns, *Charter versus Federalism* (Montreal and Kingston: McGill-Queen's University Press, 1992), 62–95.
190. Alan C. Cairns, "Citizens (Outsiders) and Governments (Insiders) in Constitution-Making: The Case of Meech Lake," *Canadian Public Policy*, 14, supplement (Sept. 1988): S135.
191. Deborah Coyne, "The Meech Lake Accord and the Spending Power Proposals: Fundamentally Flawed," in *Meech Lake Primer*, ed. M. Behiels, 245–71.
192. Deborah Coyne, "Beyond the Meech Lake Accord," in *Language and the State: The Law and Politics of Identity*, ed. David Schneiderman (Cowansville, Que.: Yvon Blais, 1991), 445 and 449.
193 Serge Denis, *Le long malentendu: le Québec vu par les intellectuels progressistes au Canada anglais, 1970-1991* (Montreal: Boréal, 1992), Chap. 6; and Philip Resnick, *Letter to a Québécois Friend* (Montreal and Kingston: McGill-Queen's University Press, 1990), 64–5.
194. "Voice of the People," *Maclean's*, 15 June 1987, 12.
195. Blais and Crête, "Pourquoi l'opinion publique," 389.
196. "If somebody says it [Wells's position on the distinct-society clause] resembles Mr Trudeau's thinking, believe me, I take it as a great compliment." (Clyde Wells quoted in Glen Allen, "Grit Stands Fast," *Maclean's*, 20 Nov. 1989, 25.)
197. As quoted in Jeffrey Simpson, *Fault Lines: Struggling for a Canadian Vision* (Toronto: HarperCollins, 1993), 165.
198. Alan Cairns, "Political Science, Ethnicity, and the Canadian Constitution," in *Federalism and Political Community: Essays in Honour of Donald Smiley*, ed. David Shugarman and Reg Whitaker, (Peterborough, Ont.: Broadview, 1989), 124.
199. Kathleen Mahoney, "Women's Rights," in *Meech Lake and Canada: Perspectives from the West*, ed. Roger Gibbins (Edmonton: Academic, 1988), 159.
200. See the discussion in Barbara Roberts, "Smooth Sailing or Storm Warning? Canadian and Québec Women's Groups and the Meech Lake Accord," *Feminist Perspectives féministes*, no. 12a, CRIAW, n.d., 12ff.
201. In testimony before the joint parliamentary committee on the Meech Lake Accord, Francine C. McKenzie, president of the

Conseil du statut de la femme du Québec, declared:

> There is no doubt that the concept [of distinct society] covers basic elements such as the aim of ensuring equality between men and women, which is already recognized in Quebec. Over the past 25 years Quebec policies have reflected this principle to such an extent that it can be said that they are an inherent part of the distinct society of Quebec. Thus it would be most odd if the recognition of this distinct society were to be seen as justifying fears of legislation undermining the rights already obtained by Quebec women as part of such society. (Special Joint Committee of the Senate and the House of Commons on the 1987 Constitutional Accord, *Minutes of Proceedings and Evidence*, 2nd session, 33rd Parliament, 31 Aug. 1987, issue 15, 82.)

202. "The limitation of the constitutional obligations on the Anglophone provinces to no more than preserve the linguistic character of Canada, while recognizing Quebec as a distinct society, could eventually result in a linguistic curtain being drawn around Quebec creating not a distinct society but a ghetto, ripe for the fostering of events that might again lead towards separation. . . . Emphasis on the promotion of French outside Quebec, on the other hand, would likely result in a greater outreach to Quebec by other Canadians, Francophone and non-Francophone, asking her to share with them their rich cultural heritage" (Ibid., 4 Aug. 1987, issue 4, 43).
203. Guy Laforest analyzes at length Trudeau's part in turning English-Canadian opinion against Meech, through both his speeches and his influence on various opinion leaders. See Laforest, *Trudeau et la fin d'un rêve canadien*, Chap. 5. See also David M. Thomas, "Edmund Burke's Ghost, an Abeyance Exhumed, and Pierre Trudeau's Undertaking," paper presented to the Canadian Political Science Association, June 1995.
204. Pierre Elliott Trudeau, "'Say Goodbye to the Dream' of One Canada," *Toronto Star*, 27 May 1987.
205. To quote Gordon Robertson, "it was a purely political and highly emotional attack, skilfully designed to excite all the suspicions that could so easily be aroused about the most inflammatory subject in Canada." (Robertson, *Memoirs of a Very Civil Servant*, 338.)
206. Pierre Fournier, *Autopsie du lac Meech* (Montreal: VLB, 1990), 90.
207. Monahan, *Meech Lake*, 125.
208. Senate *Debates*, 2993.
209. Ibid., 2996–7.
210. Ibid., 2997.
211. Blais and Crête, "Pourqoui l'opinion publique," Tables 1 and 4.
212. Jean-H. Guay, Richard Nadeau, and Édouard Cloutier, "La Crise linguistique au Québec: une étude du mouvement de l'opinion publique engendré par le jugement de la Cour suprême sur l'affichage commercial," paper presented at the annual meeting of the Canadian Political Science Association, May 1990. In their survey of university students, the authors found support for a proposal on commercial signs that was framed explicitly in terms of collective rights: "Dans le domaine de la langue d'affichage, les droits collectifs de la majorité francophone doivent avoir la priorité sur les droits individuels." ("With regard to the language of signs, the collective rights of the Francophone majority should have priority over individual rights.") Before the Supreme Court judgement on the issue, 46 per cent of the sample supported this proposition; afterward, 57 per cent did (ibid., 17).
213. For instance, a survey in January 1989 found that 69 per cent of Francophone respondents agreed that "le gouvernement du Québec a raison de restreindre le droit d'afficher en anglais ou dans une autre langue pour assurer la protection du français." ("The Quebec government is justified in restricting the right to post signs in English or another language in order to protect French.") Twenty-six per cent disagreed. Among non-Francophones the percentages were 15 per cent and 81 per cent, respectively. See Louis Falardeau, "Francophones et anglophones sont insatisfaits de la loi 178," *La Presse*, 21 Jan. 1989.
214. Blais and Crête, "Pourquoi l'opinion publique," 394.
215. The amendments entailed the addition of subsections to section 35 (2 and 3) which stipulated that "land claim agreements" are indeed "treaties" and that "the Aboriginal and treaty rights" applied equally to males and females. See Russell, *Canada's Odyssey*, 392–3.
216. Ibid. The history of negotiations over an Indigenous "inherent right to self-

government" is traced in Russell Diabo, "When Moving Past the *Indian Act* Means Something Worse," *Policy Options politiques*, 22 Sept. 2017.

217. Richard Nadeau, "Le virage souverainiste des Québécois, 1980-1990," *Recherches sociographiques* 23, no. 1 (Jan.–Apr. 1992): 24.

218. Of course, a good number of other English Canadians were opposed to Meech and its distinct-society clause from sheer animosity toward Quebec and its language rather than from any allegiance to the Trudeau vision. In at least some cases, the outrage over the suppression of English-language rights in Quebec was not matched by any particular concern with French-language rights outside Quebec. The Association for the Preservation of English Canada, for example, considered Canada to be an exclusively English-language country. The problem with Meech was not the particular way it recognized the French language, but with the very notion of recognition of French in any form. But the principled opposition of Clyde Wells and others to the Accord made it easier for these groups to express their basic animosity to Quebec and the French language. See Simpson, *Fault Lines*, 173.

219. Results of an Environics survey cited in Simpson, *Fault Lines*, 171.

220. "Portrait des Québécois," *L'Actualité*, Jan. 1991, 13–16. Maurice Pinard, in his list of surveys using the terms "independence" or "sovereignty," reports 56 per cent for Nov.–Dec. 1990. See Pinard, "The Dramatic Reemergence," 480. To be sure, he and others report a decline in support for sovereignty at the beginning of 1991.

221. After extensive public meetings, it duly reported back that the citizens were deeply frustrated with the actions of their elected leaders on constitutional questions, and indeed on most matters. In particular, it said, they were displeased with official bilingualism; the commissioners called for an independent review to clear the air. It also found citizens discontented with multiculturalism, another element of the Trudeau vision. The report proposed that funding for programs of cultural preservation be eliminated and that heritage courses be restricted to young immigrant children. But the Commission offered no concrete directions as to how the constitutional question should be addressed. (Citizens' Forum on Canada's Future, *Report to the People and Government of Canada* [Ottawa: Supply and Services Canada, 1991], 126 and 129.)

222. "Le Québec est aujourd'hui et pour toujours une société distincte, libre d'assumer son destin et son développement." As quoted in Rapport du Comité constitutionnel du Parti libéral du Québec, *Un Québec libre de ses choix*, 28 Jan. 1991.

223. The report did not specify (presumably it was indifferent) whether a similar devolution was to take place in the rest of the country. At the same time, it was crystal clear in its rejection of the most visible manifestation of the Trudeau vision of Canada, the Charter of Rights and Freedoms with the Supreme Court of Canada as its ultimate interpreter. The report proposed that the Supreme Court no longer have jurisdiction over Quebec: the possibility of appealing cases, including Charter cases, beyond Quebec's own courts would be eliminated outright. Ibid., 47–9. The provision concerning appeals from Quebec courts reads: "Les décisions des tribunaux supérieurs du Québec ne feront plus l'objet d'appels auprès de la Cour suprême du Canada mais plutôt auprès d'une nouvelle instance ultime complètement québécoise" (49). ("Decisions of Quebec superior courts will no longer be subject to appeal to the Canadian Supreme Court but rather to a new body of final appeal that will be totally Québécois.") There is no suggestion that this elimination of appeals would be restricted to cases involving Quebec law, as opposed to federal law.

Moreover, Quebec's own Charter of Human Rights and Freedoms would become part of a new Quebec constitution. Finally, the report proposed that a referendum be held by the autumn of 1992 either to approve an agreement with the rest of Canada based on the proposal, if there was one, or to approve Quebec sovereignty, to be coupled with an offer to the rest of Canada of economic association. (Comité constitutionnel, *Un Québec libre de ses choix*, 57.)

The Allaire Report represented a radical shift from the Liberal Party's 1980 Beige Paper. Reflecting the nationalist mood of the party, it was adopted at a

Liberal convention as official party policy, with only slight modification (an amendment specified that the Charter of Rights and Freedoms would continue to apply in Quebec [see Pierre O'Neill, "Bourassa choisit d'abord le Canada," *Le Devoir,* 11 Mar. 1991]). Still, in an attempt to limit the damage, Bourassa closed the convention with the declaration that the party in fact has "chosen Canada," and that "our first choice must be to develop Quebec within Canada, in a federal structure" (ibid.).

224. *Rapport de la Commission sur l'avenir politique et constitutionnel du Québec,* Mar. 1991.
225. See the analysis in François Rocher, "Le dossier constitutionnel: l'année des consultations et des valse-hésitations," in *L'année politique au Québec, 1991,* ed. Denis Monière (Montreal: Québec/Amérique, 1992), 91.
226. Jean-François Lisée tries to show that at the height of the crisis Bourassa hid his intentions from nationalists so as to buy time. See Lisée, *Le tricheur* (Montreal: Boréal, 1994).
227. My translation. See Michel Venne, "Robert Bourassa flaire un 'fédéralisme dominateur'," *Le Devoir,* 4 Mar. 1992.
228. Apparently, Mulroney was counting on the talks to fail; that would allow him to draw up unilaterally a package of revisions in close collaboration with Bourassa. Just before the final agreement was reached, he had in fact instructed his constitutional affairs minister Joe Clark to terminate the proceedings. See Jean-François Lisée, *Le naufrageur* (Montreal: Boréal, 1994), 249.
229. Various participants in the multilateral talks did speak to Quebec officials to determine the acceptability of various proposals, but the process was very haphazard and it produced confused, even contradictory, interpretations of Quebec's position, especially as it bore upon the idea of a triple-E Senate.
230. The following discussion of the July 7 agreement and the Charlottetown Accord draws upon my "Disagreeing on Fundamentals: English Canada and Quebec," in *The Charlottetown Accord, the Referendum, and the Future of Canada,* ed. Kenneth McRoberts and Patrick J. Monahan (Toronto: University of Toronto Press, 1993), 249–63.
231. Jim Horsman, as quoted in Lisée, *Le naufrageur,* 219 (my translation from Lisée's French rendition of Horsman's words).
232. Perhaps the clearest enhancement of provincial power was in the "six sisters": urban affairs, tourism, recreation, housing, mining, and forestry. There, the provinces could oblige the federal government to withdraw completely. Yet not only are these all areas of exclusive provincial jurisdiction, but they are areas in which federal activity was in any event minimal.
233. "There should be a constitutional provision for an ongoing federal role in the establishment of national policy objectives for the national aspects of labour market development. National labour market objectives would be established through a process which could be set out in the Constitution including the obligation for presentation to Parliament for debate." (Canada, *Status Report: The Multilateral Meetings on the Constitution* [Final Version, 16 July 1992], s. 28).
234. Ibid., s. 29.
235. The Senate was to be composed of an equal number of elected representatives (eight) from each province, plus two from each territory and an undetermined number of Indigenous representatives. Moreover, it had a clear promise of being "effective," since a simple majority could veto bills "that involve[d] fundamental tax policy changes directly related to natural resources"; on most other bills, 60 per cent could force reconciliation and, if needed, a joint sitting of the House and Senate; 70 per cent could veto a bill outright (ibid., s. 12).
236. Claude Castonguay declared that the Accord reflected "a vision which is that of anglophone Canada, based on equality of the provinces; an increased control by small provinces of central institutions and, despite appearances, a reinforcement of central power." Since the division of powers was essentially "unchanged," Castonguay concluded, "In my opinion, it's a regression." ("une vision qui est celle du Canada anglophone, fondée sur l'égalité des provinces; un contrôle accru des petites provinces sur le pouvoir central et, malgré les apparences, un raffermissement du pouvoir central. . . . À mon avis, on a régressé.") (As quoted in Lisée, *Le naufrageur,* 263.)
237. Ibid., 4.
238. Ibid., 247.
239. See the account in ibid., 342–55.

240. Russell, *Constitutional Odyssey*, 217.
241. Representation would indeed have been "equal," with the same number (six) of representatives from each province, plus an indeterminate number of Indigenous representatives. But it would not necessarily have been elected: to placate Premier Bourassa, provincial legislatures had the option of appointing the representatives. And in terms of the powers it would wield, the Senate was much less likely to be "effective." Although the Senate could still veto, by a majority vote, bills taxing natural resources, it could no longer veto (by 70 per cent) most other measures, as in the July 7 agreement. Bills rejected in the Senate would go to joint sittings, where senators would be outnumbered by MPs five to one. To add insult to injury, in the House, central Canadian representation was to be increased by 36 seats, from 59 per cent to 62.3 per cent. (Canada, *Draft Legal Text, October 9, 1992* [best-efforts text based on the Charlottetown Accord], 3–13.)
242. The proposal specified that in all provincial jurisdictions (1) Ottawa could use its spending power only upon agreement with provincial governments; (2) existing arrangements for the use of this power could be renegotiated should a province wish; and (3) in the absence of an agreement, all provinces would be entitled to federal withdrawal with compensation if they undertook to introduce a measure compatible with national objectives defined at a first ministers' conference. This is based upon a text reproduced in Lisée, *Le naufrageur*, 363.
243. In the end, only two minor additions were made to accommodate Quebec's objections to the division of powers: a commitment to establish a general framework to guide the use of the federal spending power and a commitment to negotiate an agreement to co-ordinate and harmonize the regulation of telecommunications. The discussions of the division of powers are related in Lisée, *Le naufrageur*, 369–82.
244. See Jacques Fremont's analysis of how the Charlottetown Accord falls short of Quebec's minimal demands regarding the division of powers, in Jacques Fremont, "The Charlottetown Accord and the End of the Exclusiveness of Provincial Jurisdictions," in *The Charlottetown Accord, the Referendum, and the Future of Canada*, ed. McRoberts and Monahan, 93–101.
245. *Draft Legal Text*, s. 2(1c). In effect, the delineation was based upon a traditional conception of Quebec's distinctiveness: French-language majority, distinct culture, and the civil code; there was no reference to the distinctive economic and social institutions of contemporary Quebec.
246. Ibid., s. 2(3). In their comparison of the July 7 and Charlottetown texts, Brown and Young point out that, unlike the July 7 text, Charlottetown does not link "distinct society" specifically to the Charter; it appears only in the Canada clause and thus applies to the Accord as a whole. See Robert Young and Douglas Brown, "Overview," in *Canada: The State of the Federation 1992*, ed. Douglas Brown and Robert Young (Kingston: Institute of Intergovernmental Relations, Queen's University, 1992), 16. However, any gain this might represent for Quebec is very much circumscribed by the more restrictive terms of the clause itself.
247. Ibid., s. 2(1d).
248. Lisée, *Le naufrageur*, 394.
249. Russell, *Constitutional Odyssey*, 217.
250. Documents prepared by top Quebec civil servants suggest that Senate reform might have been acceptable to Quebec if it had been accompanied by additional powers for the Quebec government: "Owing to its distinct character, Quebec would have difficulty accepting a Senate reform in which its representation was significantly reduced. Such a reduction of Quebec's Senate representation might be justified hypothetically only by granting a particular status that would revise the division of powers to Quebec's liking." My translation of: "En raison de son caractère distinct, le Québec peut difficilement accepter une réforme du Sénat où sa représentation serait sensiblement amoindrie. Seule l'obtention d'un statut particulier—réformant au gré du Québec le partage des pouvoirs—pourrait hypothétiquement justifier une diminution sensible de sa représentation au Sénat." See Jean-François Lisée, "Dossiers secrets de Bourassa," *L'Actualité*, 1 Nov. 1992, 64.)
251. Susan Delacourt, *United We Fall* (Toronto: Penguin, 1994), 174; and Lisée, *Le naufrageur*, 319.

252. "The majority feeling about the evolution of Canadian Division of Powers appeared to be that Canada should support Québec by accepting the need for the government of that province to exercise a wider range of provincial powers, but in a constitution flexible enough to allow for the desire for citizens in other provinces for a federal government able both to maintain national standards and to address diversity and regional disparities." (Atlantic Provinces Economic Council, Renewal of Canada: Division of Powers, *Conference Report*, Halifax, 17–19 Jan. 1992, 12.)

Indeed, "the term [asymmetry] was used recurrently, especially (but not exclusively) when discussion turned to the implications of Quebec's possible assumption of powers that would remain in federal hands for the rest of Canada. There was a belief that diversity needs to be allowed regardless of whether asymmetry is the result." (Ibid., 10.)

While there apparently was clear agreement on Quebec assuming an asymmetrical status, the conference report did not take a definitive position on just how that was to be accomplished and whether it was to be reserved to Quebec alone. (Compare ibid., 16, 21, and 22. See also David Milne, "Innovative Constitutional Processes," in *Canada: The State of the Federation 1992*, ed. Douglas Brown and Robert Young [Kingston: Institute of Intergovernmental Relations, 1992], 45 and n. 21.)

In general, the preferred mechanism for bringing about an asymmetrical status for Quebec was concurrence with provincial paramountcy, or shared jurisdiction but with a provincial option to override Ottawa. (Atlantic Provinces Economic Council, *Conference Report*, 16.)

253. Tom Kent, "Recasting Federalism," *Policy Options* 12, no. 3 (Apr. 1992): 3–6. See also Reg Whitaker, "The Dog That Never Barked: Who Killed Asymmetrical Federalism?" in McRoberts and Monahan, *The Charlottetown Accord*, Chap. 8. For instance, Quebec MPs might simply not vote on such measures, which would not be considered questions of confidence. Moreover, as some commentators pointed out, on this basis the grievances of the west against central Canadian domination would receive at least some response. Without Quebec MPs voting, MPs from the western and Atlantic provinces would have a majority. In that case a triple-E Senate might not even be necessary. (See, for instance, Gordon Laxer, "Distinct Status for Québec: A Benefit to English Canada," *Constitutional Forum constitutionnel* 3, no. 3 [Winter 1992]: 60.)

254. Delacourt, *United We Fall*, 133–6, 402–3; and Lisée, *Le naufrageur*, 216–25.

255. Passages are from "Consensus Report on the Constitution Charlottetown, August 28, 1992, Full Text," McRoberts and Monahan, *The Charlottetown Accord*, Appendix.

256. In Quebec, among valid votes 56.7 per cent were No and 43.3 per cent were Yes; in addition, 2.2 per cent of the ballots were spoiled—far more than in any other province. Outside Quebec, 54.3 per cent voted No. and 45.7 per cent Yes. About two-thirds of Quebec Francophones voted No according to André Blais, "The Quebec Referendum: Quebeckers Say No," in McRoberts and Monahan, *The Charlottetown Accord*, 203. The proposition was approved in only Newfoundland, Prince Edward Island, New Brunswick, and Ontario (where it won with only 50.1 per cent of votes).

257. The voters' doubts were confirmed when the transcripts of a cellular telephone conversation between two prominent Quebec officials, closely involved in the negotiations, were made public. The negotiators expressed their regret that Bourassa had "caved in" to the English-Canadian premiers and their disbelief that he would have agreed to the Accord. One of them, who had been deputy minister for Quebec's relations with the rest of Canada, called the Accord "a national disgrace. . . . Monsieur Bourassa should have taken a plane right away and left. What a humiliation!" (Michel Venne, "Il fallait pas accepter ça," *Le Devoir*, 1 Oct. 1992 [my translation]). At the same time, survey analysis also confirms that Quebec voters were unimpressed by the provision guaranteeing 25 per cent of seats in the House of Commons (Richard Johnston and André Blais, as cited by Lisée, *Le naufrageur*, 593).

258. According to Andre Blais's analysis of survey results: "In our Quebec sample, 43 per cent said that in their view Quebec was a loser in the agreement, while only 26 per cent perceived Quebec to be a winner. Even among

those opposed to sovereignty, 29 per cent had come to the conclusion that Quebec had lost. This perception had a powerful impact on the vote of non-sovereigntists." (André Blais, "The Quebec Referendum: Quebeckers Say No," 203.)

259. In fact, even some experts were not impressed. Professor David Elton, of the University of Lethbridge, one of the originators of the concept of the triple-E Senate, campaigned against the Accord. His critical evaluation is contained in "The Charlottetown Accord Senate: Effective or Emasculated?" in McRoberts and Monahan, *Charlottetown Accord*, Chap. 2. This assessment was shared by Professor Roger Gibbins, of the University of Calgary, who declared the Accord to be nothing less than a "humiliation." In Gibbins's words, "it is bitterly ironic that the new agreement on Senate reform will strengthen central Canadian dominance, and more specifically Quebec's dominance, of the national political process." See Roger Gibbins, "Something Not So Funny Happened on the Way to Senate Reform," *Canada Watch* 1, no. 2 (Sept. 1992): 22.

Some survey analyses suggest that the Senate issue had little direct influence on the average western Canadian voter, as opposed to opinion leaders, although this may reflect indifference to the stripped-down reform contained in the Accord rather than indifference to the issue itself. (Richard Johnston, André Blais, Elisabeth Gidengil, and Neil Nevitte, "The People and the Charlottetown Accord," in *Canada: The State of the Federation 1993*, ed. Ronald L. Watts and Douglas M. Brown [Kingston: Institute of Intergovernmental Relations, Queen's University, 1993], 27). Even so, the fact remains that the Senate issue had an enormous indirect effect on the western Canadian vote since it was the deficiencies of the Accord's Senate proposal that virtually forced the Reform Party to declare itself against the Accord.

260. LeDuc and Pammet, "Attitudes and Behaviour in the 1992 Constitutional Referendum," 27; and Russell, *Constitutional Odyssey*, 226. Whereas LeDuc and Pammet find that opposition to the measure was not a "significant" factor in western Canada, the data cited by Russell suggest otherwise.

261. The results of an Angus Reid poll cited in Canada West Foundation, *Canada 2000: Towards a New Canada*, Jan. 1993, 4.

262. According to LeDuc and Pammet, the distinct-society clause was the element of the agreement that had the greatest impact on voting. See LeDuc and Pammet, "Attitudes and Behaviour in the 1992 Constitutional Referendum," 27.

263. See Russell, *Canada's Odyssey*, 418.

264. Pierre Elliott Trudeau, *A Mess That Deserves a Big "No"* (Toronto: Robert Davies, 1992), 33.

With such a resounding popular rejection of the Charlottetown Accord, there was a temptation among commentators and analysts to conclude that the whole question was beyond repair and that the constitution simply cannot be revised so as to obtain Quebec's consent. Both the minimalist approach of Meech and the comprehensive approach of Charlottetown ended in disaster. The question remains, however, whether a different approach might have had a better chance. Granted that Meech was not enough to win the support of English Canada and a "Canada Round" was necessary, might the Charlottetown Accord have been successful if in fact it had responded directly to what the different parts of Canada were demanding?

As we have seen, Quebec's wish for more powers could have been accommodated without wholesale decentralization. Such asymmetry might have been acceptable to other parts of Canada if it clearly benefited them, for example, by restricting voting by Quebec MPs, or if it had been coupled with a meaningful Senate reform. By the same token, with a real devolution of powers, Quebeckers might even have been ready to forgo the distinct-society clause. To be sure, the leaders of English Canada would have had a "hard" sell in some parts of the country, but at least they could have pointed to concrete benefits.

Of course, one question that still remains: the "Trudeau factor." Asymmetry in powers would have evoked only too clearly the "special status" that Trudeau had campaigned against for so long. Many English Canadians might well have agreed with him that it offended their idea of Canada just as much as did recognition of Quebec as a "distinct society." To that extent, the kind of accommodation that had been possible years before, under the leadership of Lester Pearson and others, may no longer have been available.

265. Johnston et al., "The People and the Charlottetown Accord," 30. Allan Gregg recorded a similar reaction according to Lisée, *Le naufrageur,* 589. On the other hand, LeDuc and Pammet argue that Trudeau had no net effect on the vote. See LeDuc and Pammet, "Attitudes and Behaviour in the 1992 Constitutional Referendum," 23.
266. Alain Noël, "The Bloc Québécois as Official Opposition," in *Canada: The State of the Federation 1994*, ed. Douglas M. Brown and Janet Hiebert (Kingston: Institute of Intergovernmental Relations, Queen's University, 1994), 22.
267. Noël argues that the Bloc vote was based largely upon identification with Quebec, as opposed to economic protest: "Most Quebeckers voted quite naturally for the party that best represented their vision of themselves and the country" (ibid., 23–4). Similarly, Blais and his colleagues conclude that the Bloc's success was due to the support of sovereigntists and of non-sovereigntists who were motivated primarily by identification with Quebec. See André Blais et al., "L'Élection fédérale de 1993: le comportement électoral des québécois," *Revue québécoise de science politique*, no. 27 (Spring, 1995): 46.
268. Thérèse Arseneau, "The Reform Party of Canada: Past, Present and Future," in *Canada: The State of the Federation 1994*, ed. Brown and Hiebert, 37–57.
269. Further magnifying the impact of the Bloc's and Reform's attacks on the Trudeau vision was the functioning of the electoral system. Not only did it inflate Quebec's share of seats in the House, with the result that the Bloc formed the Official Opposition, but it discriminated heavily against the Progressive Conservatives, whose popular vote of 16 per cent was rewarded with only two seats in the House!
270. Clarkson and McCall say of the Charter that its "bitter core—the minority-language education rights that were to be imposed on Quebec for anglophones and on the other provinces where numbers warranted for Francophones—was to be coated with layer upon layer of sweetener. . . . With all these favourable aspects of the package diverting attention, the 'constitutionalization' of the official languages law and the entrenchment of minority-language education rights would be camouflaged." See Stephen Clarkson and Christina McCall, *Trudeau and Our Times*, vol. 1 (Toronto: McClelland & Stewart, 1990), 292–3.
271. Graham, *The Last Act*, 259.
272. P.B. Waite, *The Life and Times of Confederation, 1864–1867* (Toronto: University of Toronto Press, 1962), 22.
273. Trudeau, "New Treason of the Intellectuals" in Trudeau, *Federalism and the French Canadians*, 179.
274. The term was first developed in Alan C. Cairns, "Reflections on the Political Purposes of the Charter: The First Decade," in *Reconfigurations*, ed. Douglas E. Williams (Toronto: McClelland & Stewart, 1995), 194–214.
275. By region, the proportions opting for "a strong national government" were: British Columbia, 67.8 per cent; the Prairies, 64.2 per cent; Ontario, 75.4 per cent; and the Atlantic provinces, 66.9 per cent ("Meech Lake Accord Gains General Support, Polls Show," *Toronto Star*, 1 June 1987).
276. In a 1977 survey, Quebec respondents were asked: "If French-speaking Canadians were treated as equals to English-speaking Canadians outside Quebec would this affect your attitude towards independence for Quebec?" Only 17 per cent said yes; 81 per cent said no. Affirmative responses were apparently somewhat more frequent among Francophones (as opposed to Anglophones) while remaining a small minority. See "What Quebec *Really* Wants: English Consider Us Inferior, Quebec Feels," *Toronto Star*, 17 May 1977.
277. "Meech Lake Accord Gains General Support, Polls Show," *Toronto Star*, 1 June 1987.
278. Jacques Bouchard and Pierre Vennat, "Lévesque n'a pas la majorité pour réaliser son projet de souveraineté-association," *La Presse*, 30 Mar. 1982.

Part III

Struggling with the Trudeau Legacy

Chapter 7

The 1995 Quebec Referendum

Making Sovereignty a Real Possibility

On 30 October 1995, the Quebec government held a second referendum on Quebec sovereignty, 15 years after the failed first one. The Parti québécois had come into power under a confirmed separatist, Jacques Parizeau, and was determined to lead Quebeckers toward independence. Yet in many ways the referendum and the debate which preceded it were dominated by an event that had taken place years before: the collapse of the Meech Lake Accord, defeated by the Trudeau vision of Canada and by Trudeau himself. As much as a debate about the merits of sovereignty, the 1995 referendum was a debate about the implications of that event. In rejecting the Accord, English Canada had repudiated the dualist vision through which Quebec Francophones had historically supported Canada. Thus, in the immediate aftermath of Meech's collapse, a majority of Quebeckers opted for Quebec sovereignty, for the very first time. Yet in the fall of 1994, when Parizeau and his colleagues turned to defining the terms of Quebec sovereignty, they were confronted with the fact that most Quebeckers still wanted to maintain a relationship with the rest of Canada, based on dualism. It was only by promising such a relationship that the Yes could come remarkably close to winning the referendum. And it was only by promising to recognize Quebec's distinctiveness, breaking with the Trudeau orthodoxy, that the No forces could be victorious.

Prelude to the Referendum

Reacting to Meech

The collapse of the Meech Lake Accord provoked a deep and intense reaction in Francophone Quebec. After all, the Accord had been designed to secure Quebec's adhesion to the Canadian constitution, rectifying its 1982 dissent. With its distinct-society clause in particular, the Accord reaffirmed Quebeckers' historical understanding of their place in Canada. At the same time, it was widely perceived by most Quebeckers to be a very modest package, constituting the minimal conditions under which Quebec might become a party to the new constitution. And yet it was rejected by the clear majority of English Canadians. Indeed, never before had the rest of Canada been so clear and firm in its rejection of Quebec's demands. The essential condition of Quebec Francophones' historical support for Canada, the ability and legitimacy of the Quebec government to protect their interests, had been placed in question.

The reaction to Meech's collapse was swift. On Quebec's Fête nationale, two days before the final deadline for approval of the Accord, 500,000 Quebeckers joined a massive demonstration of solidarity on the streets of Montreal.[1] Premier Robert Bourassa attempted to assuage public anger by declaring that the Quebec government was withdrawing from any further constitutional talks since the rest of the country had not honoured its commitment to the Accord. In a phrase pregnant with meaning, he told the National Assembly, "Quebec is today, and forever, a distinct society, free and capable of taking charge of its destiny and development."[2] The Bourassa government secured unanimous approval in the National Assembly for a bill to create a special committee on Quebec's political and constitutional future that became popularly known as the Bélanger–Campeau Commission, after its co-chairs Michel Bélanger and Jean Campeau.

Within the general public, support for Quebec independence had already been on the rise before the Accord collapse. But in the wake of the collapse, it reached unprecedented heights: 56 per cent of survey respondents supported Quebec independence with only 36 per cent opposed. Support for sovereignty with an economic association reached 65 per cent, with 28 per cent opposed.[3] Clearly, the demise of Meech had placed in open question Quebeckers' support for the Canadian political order.[4]

The Gathering Forces for Sovereignty

Public anger over Meech's demise and growth in support for independence confirmed the Parti québécois in its essential goal of Quebec sovereignty. Its commitment to Quebec independence had already been sharpened through the accession of Jacques Parizeau to the party's leadership in 1988. A central figure in the Quebec government from the Quiet Revolution onward, Parizeau held a deep belief in the capacity of the Quebec state for positive intervention and, on that basis, had long championed full sovereignty for Quebec. He had had little patience for René Lévesque's notions of a comprehensive Quebec–Canada union, let alone Lévesque's readiness to pursue the "beau risque" of a renewed federalism. Upon assuming leadership of the PQ, Parizeau had been able to mobilize the party members around his more rigid vision of Quebec sovereignty.[5] For the PQ, the collapse of Meech, and the demonstration that Canadian federalism could not be renewed to accommodate Quebec, meant that the path to independence was clearer than ever.

More surprising was the radicalization of views within the Liberal Party, ostensibly committed to Quebec remaining within Canadian federalism. In January 1991, the party's constitutional committee produced a document, generally known as the Allaire Report, which called for a radical devolution of powers to Quebec. Twenty-two jurisdictions that were exclusively federal or shared with the provinces would become exclusively provincial; Ottawa would be restricted to defence, customs, the currency, equalization, and management of the federal debt.[6] The report did not state whether a similar devolution was to take place in the rest of the country (presumably it was indifferent). At the same time, it was crystal clear in its rejection of the most visible manifestation of the Trudeau vision of Canada, the Charter of Rights and Freedoms with the Supreme Court of Canada as its ultimate interpreter. The report proposed that the Supreme Court no longer have jurisdiction over Quebec: the possibility of appealing cases, including Charter cases, beyond Quebec's own courts would be eliminated outright.[7] Moreover, Quebec's own Charter of Human Rights and Freedoms would become part of a new Quebec constitution. Finally, the report proposed that a referendum be held by the autumn of 1992 either to approve an agreement with the rest of Canada based on the proposal, if there were one, or to approve Quebec sovereignty, to be coupled with an offer to the rest of Canada of economic association.[8]

The Allaire Report represented a radical shift from the Liberal Party's past documents, such the 1980 Beige Paper. Reflecting the new nationalist mood of the party, it was adopted at a Liberal convention as official party policy with one main modification: an amendment specified that the Charter of Rights and Freedoms would continue to apply in Quebec.[9] Attempting to limit the damage, Bourassa closed the convention by declaring that the party in fact has "chosen Canada," and that "our first choice must be to develop Quebec within Canada, in a federal structure."[10]

Bourassa Government: Waiting for "a Renewed Federalism"

In March 1991, the Bélanger–Campeau Commission presented its report. After reviewing the constitutional impasse, the report outlined two options, a profoundly renewed federalism and sovereignty, and called for a referendum on sovereignty by October 1992.[11] The Bourassa government acted on the recommendation but in a manner that gave it some room to manoeuvre. In June 1991, the National Assembly passed Bill 150, which required the government to hold a referendum on sovereignty in June or October of 1992. The bill also established two special committees, one to study all issues related to Quebec sovereignty and one to evaluate whatever offers for a new constitutional arrangement might be made by the federal government. Finally, in affirming the exclusive responsibility of the National Assembly for the wording of a referendum, it effectively reserved for the government the possibility of altering the wording of the referendum by amending the law should conditions warrant.[12]

If there was any doubt at the time, it is clear in retrospect that Robert Bourassa was, as ever, committed to Quebec's remaining within the federal system.[13] Given the state of public opinion immediately after the collapse of Meech he could have led Quebec out of Canada if he had so wanted.[14] Yet he certainly could not ignore the public pressure for Quebec to respond to English Canada's rejection of Meech by holding a referendum of its own on Quebec's future. In 1991, support for sovereignty began to fall somewhat, but a majority vote for Quebec sovereignty was still a real possibility—unless the subject of the referendum could instead be a compelling offer of a new federation. The pressure on political leaders in the rest of Canada to produce such an offer could not have been greater. Yet, even then, the "offer" that eventually did emerge, the Charlottetown Accord, fell far short of expectations in Quebec, as well as the hopes of the Bourassa government. Thus, while the referendum on Quebec's future dealt with the Charlottetown Accord, rather than sovereignty, it was duly defeated.

The Parizeau Government: Going for Sovereignty

The September 1994 election of the Parti québécois and assumption of the premiership by Jacques Parizeau put an end to any search for a renewed federalism: the Quebec government was now committed to independence. Parizeau and his colleagues were determined to move quickly and firmly on their essential objective, thus avoiding the mistakes of the first PQ government, under René Lévesque. The Lévesque government had sought to dispel public doubts about sovereignty by moving slowly, providing good government in the meantime, and linking sovereignty to a comprehensive economic association with the rest of Canada. The long delay in holding the first referendum probably worked against the PQ's option, allowing time for the federalists to organize their counter-offensive, for tensions to develop between the PQ government and party members, and so on. The delay also gave economic and political élites outside Quebec a chance to reject publicly the very idea of association, thus undermining the credibility of sovereignty. Instead, the Parizeau government was committed to hold a referendum within six months of assuming power and to define sovereignty simply, without extensive links with Canada.

This bold commitment to sovereignty apparently robbed the Parti québécois of some potential support in the September 1994 election.[15] It emerged with only 44.7 per cent of the popular vote, although that gave them 77 of the 125 seats. The Liberals, under the firmly federalist leadership of Daniel Johnson, won almost as many votes, 44.4 per cent, but received only 47 seats. The bulk of the remaining votes (6.5 per cent) were won by the Action démocratique du Québec (ADQ), led by Mario Dumont. Dumont, the only ADQ candidate to be elected, had left the Liberal Party in protest over Bourassa's consent to the Charlottetown Accord and now advocated a new Quebec–Canada partnership that fell well short of the PQ's version of sovereignty.[16]

Nonetheless, the new Parizeau government proceeded with its declared strategy. Three months after securing office, on 6 December 1994, it released the draft of a bill to be placed before the National Assembly. The proposed law was to come into force one year after a successful referendum unless the Assembly approved an earlier date. Beginning with the declaration that "Quebec is a sovereign country," it defined sovereignty as the exclusive power to pass laws, collect taxes, and sign agreements with other states. Other provisions of the bill affirmed that, as a sovereign state, Quebec would keep its existing boundaries, use the Canadian dollar as its currency, grant Quebec citizenship to all Canadian citizens living in Quebec while allowing them to retain Canadian citizenship, apply for membership in the United Nations and other international organizations, and apply existing Canadian laws in its territory unless they were repealed or amended by the National Assembly. In addition, it would adopt a new constitution that would guarantee "the English-speaking community that its identity and institutions will be preserved" and recognize "the right of aboriginal nations to self-government" while, in both cases, remaining "consistent with the territorial integrity of Quebec." The draft bill authorized the government to conclude, "with the Government of Canada, an agreement the purpose of which is to maintain an economic association between Quebec and Canada," but it did not give any indication of the scope or terms of such an agreement.[17]

In short, under the Parizeau government's definition of sovereignty, Quebec was to assume all the powers normally held by a sovereign state. Moreover, according to the terms of the draft bill, sovereignty could be secured unilaterally, given a successful referendum. At the same time, it was not at all clear what kind of economic association Quebec would offer to the rest of Canada.

The government showed that it intended to move quickly to hold its referendum. The draft bill was to be circulated to all households in Quebec. A series of consultations were to be held in 16 regions of Quebec as well as among young people and senior citizens. The results of these consultations were to be presented to a special committee of the National Assembly, which would decide on the final version of the bill to be presented to the Assembly. These various stages were to be completed in a matter of months. By all indications, the government intended to hold the referendum in May or June of 1995, assuming it was in a position to win.

Apparently, the Parizeau government believed that by acting so resolutely and defining sovereignty so clearly it could inspire Quebeckers to have a new confidence in sovereignty, and in themselves, and could persuade them to forget their apprehensions over sovereignty. Surveys continued to show, however, that only about 40 per cent of Quebec residents would support sovereignty without an economic association; about 55 per cent would support sovereignty if it were combined with an economic association.[18] In a January 1995 survey, 73 per cent agreed that economic association with Canada would be essential to the success of a sovereign Quebec.[19] This public unease with sovereignty was confirmed in the various regional consultations, where most participants wanted to discuss, not the government's sovereignty plans, but their grievances against the government over a whole host of routine matters.

As long as sovereignty continued to be defined as it had been by the Parizeau government, the federalist forces had the upper hand. After so many constitutional disasters, the federalists would have had difficulty promising any type of "constitutional renewal," as Trudeau had in 1980. Nor, with the major scaling down of the federal government then under way, could they stress the concrete benefits of federalism as they had in 1980. But they could still count on mobilizing the public's fear of the economic costs of sovereignty. That tactic had been enough to ensure a federalist victory in 1980. Indeed, the federal government was sufficiently confident of victory that it saw no need even to attempt any accommodation of Quebec's distinct identity. Nor, unlike the Trudeau government in 1980, did it see any need to develop a "Plan B" strategy for responding to a Yes vote, should it somehow happen.[20]

A Quebec–Canada Partnership: Keeping the Link to Canada

For precisely these reasons, Bloc québécois leader Lucien Bouchard tried to redefine the sovereigntist option. In early April 1995, he declared that sovereignty should be coupled with a proposal to Canada of a political partnership, inspired by the European Community.[21] Bouchard's position was strengthened several days later when the Commission nationale sur l'avenir du Québec, which the Parizeau government had established, presented its final report. Presided by Monique Vézina, a former Progressive Conservative cabinet minister, and containing the heads of 16 consultation committees, the Commission reported on its public consultations. While declaring that sovereignty is the only option that responds to the collective aspirations of Quebeckers, the report also proposed that "once acquired, sovereignty will, for Quebec, mean a new departure to a partnership with Canada which would not exclude, eventually, a form of political union."[22] Given similar sentiments among some of his closest associates, such as Bernard Landry,[23] Parizeau's hand was forced. On 12 June 1995, he signed an agreement with Bouchard and ADQ leader Mario Dumont by which, after a successful referendum, the Quebec government was committed to propose to Canada "a treaty on a new economic and political Partnership."[24] By the same token, on 7 October Parizeau announced that Lucien Bouchard would be in charge of negotiations with the rest of Canada, following a Yes vote.[25]

The tripartite agreement stipulated that, beyond addressing matters related to sovereignty, such as dividing federal assets and managing the common debt, the projected treaty "will ensure that the Partnership is capable of taking action" regarding a customs union; free flow of goods, individuals, services, and capital; monetary policy; labour mobility; and citizenship. In addition, "nothing will prevent the two member States from reaching agreement in any other area of common interest," such as trade, international representation, defence, and environmental protection, among others.

By the same token, the treaty would "create the joint political institutions required to administer the new Economic and Political Partnership," namely (1) a Partnership Council with decision-making power over implementation of the treaty, in which Quebec and Canada would each have a veto; (2) a parliamentary assembly, composed of parliamentarians appointed by the Canadian Parliament (75 per cent) and the Quebec National Assembly (25 per cent), which would be limited to making recommendations; and (3) a tribunal to resolve any disputes relating to the treaty.

In effect, the agreement outlined a large number of areas in which there *might* be collaboration, without actually committing Quebec to any of them. And it called for the creation of three institutions that are commonplace in international relations. Indeed, counterparts to all three already existed between Canada and the United States. The Partnership Council and tribunal would have been similar to the Free Trade Commission and dispute settlement mechanism found in NAFTA (North American Free Trade Agreement). As for the parliamentary assembly, a Canada–United States Inter-Parliamentary Group had met annually since 1958.[26]

Not only was it unclear what would be the scope of any economic collaboration under the Quebec–Canada Partnership, but the agreement did not make the partnership a condition for Quebec sovereignty. The Quebec government was simply to present the proposal of partnership to Canada. The negotiations were not to continue for more than one year, unless the National Assembly decided otherwise. "In the event that negotiations prove to be fruitless," the National Assembly would be in a position to declare Quebec's sovereignty.[27] Nevertheless, by outlining the potential terms of an "Economic and Political Partnership," involving not just economic association but such common political institutions as a parliamentary assembly, the 12 June agreement at least gave a concrete meaning to the notion of a relationship between Quebec and Canada, one based upon dualism.

Clearly, many Quebeckers saw the promise of a continuing relationship with the rest of Canada as a necessary condition for voting Yes. Indeed, many Yes supporters professed a continuing attachment to Canada. In a survey taken just a month before the referendum, 67 per cent of Quebeckers claimed to be "deeply attached to Canada" and 34 per cent of those planning to vote Yes said they were attached to Canada.[28] By the same token, in a survey taken four months after the referendum, in which 54.3 per cent said they would vote Yes in a new referendum, 78.1 per cent agreed that "we should be proud of what francophones and anglophones have accomplished together in Canada" and 85.5 per cent agreed that "Canada is a country where it is good to live."[29]

Heading into the referendum, a number of voters may have been confused as to the precise institutional arrangements that would come with sovereignty. In one survey, 22 per cent of respondents intending to vote Yes thought that under sovereignty Quebec would continue to be a province of Canada.[30] It also appears that some Yes voters hoped that a Yes vote would precipitate a "renewal" of federalism by giving Quebec new bargaining power within Canada, although they must have recognized that sovereignty was at least a possible outcome. Finally, the surveys show that most Yes voters firmly expected that, if it were to occur, sovereignty would be linked to an economic and political partnership with Canada.[31]

To be sure, some Yes voters obviously wanted total sovereignty, and nothing else. They would have voted in favour of the Parizeau government's original proposition. But many Yes voters apparently were rejecting, not Canada per se, but a particular idea of Canada, and corresponding institutions, that denied their own conception of Quebec and its place in Canada.

Yet if some Yes voters may have been uncertain as to the precise arrangements to be created through a Yes vote, and some even preferred that the result be a "renewed federalism," most of them must have expected it would result in Quebec sovereignty. That was certainly the import of the two documents that the referendum question referred to—the National Assembly bill and the partnership agreement. Indeed, during the final week of the campaign Prime Minister Chrétien warned the voters that a Yes vote would lead to sovereignty. In his televised "Address to the Nation" he declared, "A Yes vote means the destruction of the economic and political union we already enjoy."[32]

The Referendum

The Question

In September 1995, the National Assembly was presented with a modified version of the Parizeau government's original bill.[33] It was to be adopted if the Yes prevailed in the referendum. Set for 30 October 1995, the referendum was to ask the question "Do you agree that Quebec should become sovereign, after having made a formal offer to Canada for a new Economic and Political Partnership, within the scope of the Bill respecting the Future of Quebec and of the agreement signed on 12 June 1995?"

In effect, the question made the *proposal* of partnership a condition for Quebec sovereignty, but did not require that the proposal be *accepted*. Moreover, there was no requirement, as there had been in the 1980 referendum, to hold a second referendum after its negotiations with the rest of Canada. However, sovereigntist leaders insisted that, if the rest of Canada were confronted with a clear Yes vote, it would have no choice but to agree to such an arrangement.[34]

The Campaign for Yes

The contention that the rest of Canada would necessarily agree to a partnership seems to have reassured a certain number of voters. Indeed, that is apparently why support for a Yes vote increased over the summer of 1995.[35] After remaining stable in September, the Yes support began to climb again in late September and early October. This second increase roughly corresponded with the announcement that, after a successful referendum, Bouchard would head the team that would negotiate a partnership with Canada.[36] The announcement gave further credibility to the notion that sovereignty would be coupled with an economic and political association (it also served to make Bouchard the effective leader of the Yes campaign). These assurances effectively dispelled many Quebeckers' fears about the economic consequences of sovereignty. Indeed, a survey of Quebeckers during the last week of the campaign found that half of Francophone respondents believed that with sovereignty there would be *no* short-term economic costs. Moreover, 55 per cent believed that over the long term Quebec's economic state would actually improve, and of these, half believed that it would be greatly improved.[37]

Once the voters were free to base their decision on considerations other than the economic consequences, the whole dynamic of the referendum was changed. In particular, those who felt a strong identity with Quebec could respond to the sovereigntist contention that allegiance to Quebec necessarily required a Yes vote. Beyond that, Lucien Bouchard could make this argument with particular effectiveness because he had left the Mulroney government and founded the Bloc québécois in protest against proposals to weaken the recognition of Quebec's identity in the Meech Lake Accord.

Quebeckers apparently made their final decision primarily on the basis of how they defined their identity. Just as in the past, support for sovereignty was greatest among those who defined themselves, first and foremost, as Quebeckers.

The Campaign for No

In principle, the leader of the No campaign was Daniel Johnson, leader of the Quebec Liberal Party, who was president of the No committee established under the Quebec referendum law. In practice, however, the campaign was directed from Ottawa, by Prime Minister Jean Chrétien.[38] Inevitably, then, the No campaign was confined by the national unity strategy that had been developed by Pierre Trudeau and had guided his many years in office. Jean Chrétien was closely associated personally with this strategy. As justice minister in the early 1980s, he had been directly involved in the events leading to patriation and a Charter without Quebec's formal consent. His selection as Liberal leader, over Paul Martin who had supported Meech, met with Trudeau's clear approval. Indeed, during the campaign sovereigntist leaders personally attacked Chrétien, implying that he had been a "traitor" to Quebec.[39] Thus, federalist forces were singularly ill-placed to respond to questions of identity. While primary identification with Quebec might be compatible with federalism in principle, it was not compatible with the Trudeau vision of Canadian federalism.[40]

For most of the campaign, then, the federalist forces continued to stress the economic costs of sovereignty. Despite entreaties from Quebec federalists, especially Liberal leader Daniel Johnson, Chrétien and his cabinet refused to endorse proposals to accommodate Quebec identity, whether by amending the constitution or by modifying federal–provincial relations. The federalist leaders did, however, apparently agree that their cause could only be damaged if Trudeau himself intervened; he was sidelined throughout the campaign, much to his annoyance.[41]

At the same time, the campaign featured efforts by Canadians outside Quebec to express affection for Quebec and to mobilize Quebeckers around Canadian national unity. Most provincial legislatures passed resolutions to that effect. In addition, individual Quebeckers were contacted personally by members of the Francophone minority communities and by participants in the French-immersion schooling movement.[42] The most dramatic initiative was a rally, days before the referendum, in downtown Montreal of Canadians from across the country, numbering as many as 150,000. In support of the event, Air Canada had offered reduced fares to participants, as did Canadian Airlines and Via Rail, and bus rides were organized from Toronto, Ottawa, and Windsor. The initiative had come from Brian Tobin and other federal cabinet ministers from outside Quebec, who had grown increasingly anxious about the possibility of a Yes vote. Tobin saw it as an opportunity for Canadians "to show Quebeckers that they *do* care."[43] However, the idea had been vigorously opposed by the Quebec members of the federal government, fearing that the presence of large numbers of non-Quebeckers appealing to Canadian unity would simply produce a backlash.[44] Quebec Liberal leader Daniel Johnson had even lobbied companies against offering reduced fares or other support for participation in the event.[45]

In the end, the Montreal rally served to weaken rather than strengthen the No vote. As Quebec federalists had feared, some Quebeckers saw the event as an intrusion by non-Quebeckers into their proper concern. Beyond that, there were allegations that the discounted fares and other expenditures were in violation of the Quebec law regulating spending during the referendum campaign. Surveys showed that the No vote actually declined in the wake of the rally.[46]

As the campaign entered its last week, panic began to set in among the No forces. Surveys showed that the federalist strategy was not working and that support for a Yes vote had continued to grow. Confronted with the distinct possibility of defeat, the Ottawa federalists finally heeded the fervent pleas of federalist forces in Quebec and moved beyond their national unity orthodoxy.[47] In a dramatic speech, five days before the vote, Chrétien effectively recognized the constitutional demands of Quebec federalists. Insisting that with a No vote all means of securing change would remain open, including constitutional ones, he responded directly to the demand for a Quebec veto: "Any change in the constitutional powers of Quebec will be made only with the consent of Quebeckers." He even acknowledged Quebec's claim to be a "distinct society," effectively repudiating Pierre Trudeau's deeply held position. Chrétien stated that during the campaign he had been listening to his "fellow Quebeckers"

> saying that they want to see this country change and evolve towards their aspirations. They want to see Quebec recognized as a distinct society within Canada by virtue of its language, culture, and institutions. I've said it before and I'll say it again. I agree. I have supported that position in the past, I support it today and I will support it in the future, whatever the circumstances.[48]

It was not clear precisely how these commitments to a Quebec veto and recognition of a distinct society were to be met. Chrétien did not explicitly advocate placing the distinct-society clause in the constitution; at most, he was saying that he would agree to it. The fact of the matter is that despite his claim to have always supported recognition of Quebec as a distinct society, Chrétien had publicly opposed the Meech Lake Accord, in part because of its distinct-society clause.[49] But this last-minute recognition of Quebec's distinctiveness apparently did shore up support for a No vote.[50]

At the same time, in making such a statement Chrétien tacitly acknowledged that the Trudeau national unity strategy had failed.[51] Only by directly recognizing Quebec's distinctiveness could he hope to improve the chances of a No victory. Indeed, other parts of Chrétien's speech also appealed directly to Quebec nationalism and were quite out of character with his normal discourse. He even adopted a phrase he credited to Jean Lesage: "Canada my country; Quebec my fatherland."[52]

The Referendum Vote

The turnout for the referendum was extraordinarily high—93.52 per cent of the Quebec electorate. The result was extraordinarily close—49.42 per cent voted Yes; 50.58 per cent voted No. Indeed, the No won by only 54,288 votes. Moreover, the results might easily have been the reverse. Over the weeks prior to the vote, surveys had placed the Yes vote at as high as 56 per cent.[53]

Whereas the Quebec electorate as a whole was almost evenly divided, the two primary linguistic groups were not. Nearly 60 per cent of Francophones voted Yes; about 95 per cent of non-Francophones voted No. The proportion of Francophone votes for the Yes seems to have been fairly consistent across the province. Where there were large differences among regions, they mainly reflected differences in the proportions of Francophone and non-Francophone voters. According to sociologist Pierre Drouilly, the Francophone Yes vote was higher in eastern Montreal (66.7 per cent) and the northeastern periphery of Montreal (65.2 per cent) than in the province as a whole. West Montreal was the only section of Montreal where the Francophone Yes vote was lower (52.6 per cent) than in the province as a whole. In Quebec City and in urban and rural areas of the rest of Quebec, the proportions of Francophones voting Yes were 57.0 per cent, 59.5 per cent, and 56.9 per cent, respectively.[54]

A third component of Quebec's population—Indigenous people—was largely missing from the referendum results. Three Quebec Indigenous communities had in fact held referendums of their own several days before the Quebec government's referendum. Not surprisingly, given the long-standing opposition of Indigenous leaders to Quebec sovereignty, all three referendums massively rejected the government's proposition. The Cree voted No by 96 per cent, the Inuit by 95 per cent, and even the Francophone Montagnais by 99 per cent.[55]

After the referendum, it was alleged that the official result of the government referendum was not fully accurate. Supporters of the No vote claimed that a significant number of No ballots had been improperly rejected by scrutineers who were themselves supporters of a Yes vote.[56] Some No supporters also alleged that election officials had intimidated non-Francophones, who were probably No voters, and had hindered non-residents in exercising their right to vote.[57] For their part, Yes supporters countered with charges that a leading federalist organization had encouraged non-residents to declare fraudulently that they intended to return to Quebec, so that they could vote in the referendum.[58] For that matter, in 2006 Quebec's electoral office determined that during the referendum campaign the federal government's department of Canadian Heritage had funnelled close to $10.5 million directly to two pro-No organizations so as to escape the provisions of Quebec's referendum law. But there is no way of determining whether use of the funds had actually swayed voters to the No side.[59]

While it appears that the No side did indeed secure a majority of the legal votes in the referendum, it was only a razor-thin majority involving about 55,000 voters. Indeed, survey results over the days just before the vote suggest that the majority could just as easily have been for a Yes. The result was to have a profound effect on both Quebec and English Canada.

The Referendum's Aftermath

Within Quebec: Contradictory Processes

In Quebec, the referendum was followed by quite contradictory processes. The first was the replacement of the Parti québécois leader. Apparently, Jacques Parizeau had planned ahead of time to resign in the event of a No vote,[60] but his departure was hastened by the adverse public reaction to his referendum night speech, blaming "money and the ethnic vote" for the defeat. His comments evoked a narrow ethnic nationalism that contradicted the PQ's official policy and was rejected by many Quebec Francophones within the party, as well as outside it. Parizeau's logical successor was Lucien Bouchard, architect of the partnership commitment that had brought the sovereigntists so close to victory.

Despite a widely held assumption that Bouchard would move quickly to call a new referendum, given the near victory of the Yes forces, he saw no advantage in doing so.[61] Instead, as party leader and Quebec premier, Bouchard sought to draw attention away from the sovereignty question toward issues confronting Quebec as a province within Canada, such as its mounting public deficit. He declared that the next referendum would take place only after a provincial election, which would be called as late as possible so as to allow time to address Quebec's public finances.[62] Such a stance could be justified within a sovereigntist strategy: Quebec would be better placed to assume sovereignty if its financial house was in order. More generally, he argued that the next referendum would have to await the emergence, or creation, of "winning conditions"; Quebec could not afford to lose yet another referendum. This position also recognized that, for the time being, Quebec voters were weary of the whole question.

If the Bouchard government seemed determined to declare a moratorium on the sovereignty question, forces outside the Parti québécois kept the question front and centre. First, the shock of the close referendum result produced among Quebec's Anglophone and allophone population a new determination to oppose not only sovereignty, but Quebec nationalism itself. With the loss of confidence in Quebec's established federalist leadership, new leaders emerged who favoured more radical strategies. In an attempt to stave off the effects of any future referendum victory for sovereignty, some groups advocated that parts of Quebec should remain in Canada if the majority of residents wished them to. Anglophone groups also began to mobilize in favour of English-language rights, not only demanding that their rights under Bill 101 be fully respected but challenging outright the notion that Quebec should be defined as a primarily French-speaking society. The campaigns in favour of partition and English-language rights alarmed Daniel Johnson and other Quebec federalists, who were anxious to retain Francophone support for federalism, but both ideas were publicly endorsed by Prime Minister Chrétien.[63] Once again, the federalists were badly divided, and at the heart of the division was the disagreement over the nature of Quebec and its Francophone character.

By embracing the principle of partition, the new Anglophone spokespersons were adopting a position that had long been proclaimed by Quebec's Indigenous leaders. Over the years Indigenous leaders had invoked legal arguments to support their position that Indigenous Peoples should be able to decide whether the territory they inhabit would become part of a sovereign Quebec or remain part of Canada: most of these territories had not become part of Quebec until after

Confederation, the states that had previously claimed them (Britain and France) did not have a strong argument for doing so, and the federal government has a fiduciary relationship with Indigenous Peoples under the constitution.[64] Indeed, Indigenous leaders argued that as distinct nations they have a clearer right to self-determination than do Quebeckers. Just like the partitionist claims of Quebec Anglophones, so those of Indigenous Peoples were rejected, not only by sovereigntist leaders but also by the leader of Quebec's federalists, Daniel Johnson.[65] Nevertheless, the combined opposition from Indigenous and Anglophone groups helped to keep the question of sovereignty at the centre of public debate.

In short, the referendum had made Quebec sovereignty a distinct possibility. As a consequence, it set in motion forces within Quebec that favoured a continuing, and acrimonious, debate over the very idea of sovereignty, however keen the Quebec government was to divert discussion to other subjects. There could be no avoiding the fact that with the referendum Quebec had crossed a threshold.

Outside Quebec: No More Threats of Quebec Independence

In the rest of Canada, there also was a hardening of position on Quebec and on Quebec sovereignty. The result of the referendum had been totally unexpected, and the shock was profound. Having long assumed that the No forces would win by a wide margin, Canadians were now confronted with the fact that the Yes side had almost won, and might in fact do so in a near-future referendum that was widely expected.

Moreover, most English Canadians had great difficulty understanding what could have impelled so many Quebec Francophones to take such a radical step. After all, since the late 1960s, the federal government had been led by Quebeckers, with a few very brief exceptions. The federal government had pursued with energy, and at great expense, the national unity strategy proposed by the first of those prime ministers from Quebec, Pierre Trudeau. In particular, official bilingualism had become the norm at the federal level, transforming the face of federal institutions not only in Ottawa but throughout the country. Provincial governments had been persuaded, to varying degrees, to offer French-language services to minorities that often made up only tiny proportions of provincial populations. After all this, Quebeckers were still so dissatisfied that they were prepared to leave the country!

Indeed, many English Canadians had resented such measures, which had been justified as necessary to national unity. The Reform Party had made inroads in English-Canadian public opinion with its arguments that official bilingualism, as well as multiculturalism, constituted improper uses of public resources. Arguing that the promotion of minority languages and the preservation of cultures should be private matters, Reform was calling for many of the Trudeau government's reforms to be reversed.

The fact that all these ostensible "concessions" to Quebec had been framed in such a way as to deny Quebec's uniqueness was lost on most English Canadians. Nor could they fathom the argument that patriation with a Charter entrenching language rights was a "humiliation" of Quebec. After all, patriation had been engineered by a Quebecker.

Beyond incomprehension as to its causes, the referendum also produced anger over its near consequences. In effect, through their Yes vote Quebeckers were threatening the survival of Canada. By declaring a desire to leave Canada, they ceased to be fellow citizens; they had become "foreigners." And as foreigners, they had even less claim to any further generosity or magnanimity on the part of Canadians.[66]

Perhaps an informed leadership might have been able to make this situation intelligible to English Canadians and to organize the type of response that was needed, but the Chrétien government was ill-equipped to offer such leadership. Chrétien and his cabinet were too firmly linked to the national unity strategy that had produced this state of affairs to be ready and able to enlist English Canadians in a different strategy focused on accommodating the aspirations of Quebeckers.[67]

As political and intellectual élites outside Quebec struggled to respond to the new state of affairs, they soon settled on a "two-track" strategy.[68] One form of response, which became known as "Plan A," was somehow to make Canada more attractive to Quebeckers so as to prevent the occurrence of another referendum on sovereignty—or at least to ensure that it would be defeated. The other, "Plan B," was to prepare for the possibility that, despite such efforts, Quebeckers might still vote for sovereignty. This meant defining negotiating positions, if indeed there was to be negotiation, and imagining the possibility of a Canada without Quebec. Given the intellectual and psychological hurdles to framing a response based on the first plan, plus continuing anger against Quebec over the closeness of the referendum vote, it was perhaps inevitable that energies would tend to focus on the second.

As we shall see in the next chapter, the Chrétien government did put in place some elements of a "Plan A," such as seeking to win Quebeckers' favour through appealing to Canadian patriotism and raising the federal government's visibility within Quebec society. But these initiatives were largely ineffective or even counter-productive. The Chrétien government even departed outright from the Trudeau national unity orthodoxy in trying to repair the damage of Quebec's isolation during the 1982 constitutional patriation and seeking to secure constitutional recognition of Quebec as a "distinct society." Yet the provincial premiers and the general public outside Quebec had little patience for such notions—nor did the Chrétien government have much credibility in pursuing them. Beyond post-referendum fatigue and anger, there was the simple fact that many Anglophone Canadians had long been converted to the vision of their country that Pierre Trudeau had so tirelessly promoted. By design, as the Meech debacle had so clearly demonstrated, that vision left no room for recognizing Quebec's distinctiveness.

Rather than "Plan A," Anglophone Canada had much more appetite for a "Plan B" to ensure that there would never be another referendum or at least, if it were to happen, it could not lead to Quebec independence. Ever since the arrival of Pierre Trudeau to the prime ministership, Anglophone leaders in the federal government and within Canada more generally had deferred to Trudeau and his Quebec colleagues to take care of the Quebec question. After the "near-death" experience of the 1995 referendum, they were determined to do so no longer. The Montreal national unity rally, counter-productive as it may well have been, reflected this determination of English Canadians to become directly involved in the Quebec question. However, rather than rethinking the Trudeau strategy and devising a new one that might accommodate Quebec's aspirations, their predominant stance, having come so close to "losing the country," was to try to put an end to the Quebec question one and for all.

Thus, public debate in the English-Canadian media tended to concentrate on possible responses to any future Yes vote. From the outset, prominent columnists in English Canada called for a hard line on all the questions surrounding sovereignty.[69] Another tack was to insist that the rest of Canada, as such, had no institutional coherence. Thus, there was no basis for negotiating a new partnership with Quebec or even the very accession of Quebec to sovereignty.[70] Nor, given English Canadians' likely trauma over a Yes vote and the imminent break, would there be a readiness to enter into negotiations. A spate of "analyses" tried to show that Quebec's accession to sovereignty inevitably would entail violence and chaos.[71] A November 1996 survey found that 63 per cent of Canadians outside Quebec agreed that the federal government "should emphasize the tough conditions Quebec would have to meet if it were to leave Canada"; only 13 per cent agreed that Ottawa "should focus on giving Quebec some of the changes it wants." (As to be expected, most Quebeckers saw things differently: only 17 per cent supported an emphasis on "tough conditions" with 45 per cent supporting a focus on changes to accommodate Quebec.[72])

The Chrétien government echoed these sentiments by emphasizing the costs and difficulties of Quebec sovereignty. For instance, it adopted a "hard" position on the boundaries of any sovereign Quebec. In his previous profession as university professor, the new minister of intergovernmental affairs, Stéphane Dion, had written that Quebec should not expect to keep its present boundaries; upon becoming minister, he confirmed that this was still his opinion. Chrétien quickly affirmed that this was his position as well.[73] Several days later, Indian Affairs Minister Ron Irwin said that Indigenous territory in Quebec does not belong to the province and would not belong to Quebec if it were to become sovereign.[74] The prime minister also declared that in any future referendum the threshold for a victory must be more than 50 per cent.[75] At one point, Chrétien even said that Quebec would not be "allowed" to hold another referendum on sovereignty; it was not clear how this would be enforced.[76] The ostensible leader of federalist forces in Quebec, Daniel Johnson, publicly dissociated himself from such opinions on partition and the threshold for a referendum victory, calling them "totally off base."[77]

Supreme Court Reference on Quebec's Secession

By the same token, in September 1996 the federal government announced that it was submitting to the Supreme Court a reference on the legality of Quebec's accession to sovereignty.[78] In explaining the reasons for the reference, Justice Minister Allan Rock went to great lengths to insist that the federal government was not suggesting that Quebec could not become sovereign: "The leading political figures of all our provinces and the Canadian public have long agreed that the country cannot be held together against the clear will of Quebecers. This government agrees with that." It was only insisting that sovereignty must be obtained under the rule of law; change should take place in an orderly process within the legal framework.[79]

Accordingly, the government's Supreme Court reference posed three questions:

1. Under the Constitution of Canada, can the National Assembly, legislature or government of Quebec effect the secession of Quebec from Canada unilaterally?
2. Does international law give the National Assembly, legislature or government of Quebec the right to effect the secession of Quebec from Canada unilaterally? In this regard, is there a right to self-determination under international law that would give the National Assembly, legislature or government of Quebec the right to effect the secession of Quebec from Canada unilaterally?
3. In the event of a conflict between domestic and international law on the right of the National Assembly, legislature or government of Quebec to effect the secession of Quebec from Canada unilaterally, which would take precedence in Canada?

The reference had been the strongly opposed by federalist leaders in Quebec. Daniel Johnson had protested the measure publicly, declaring that "the federal government should be concerned about exercising leadership to change Canada and to improve Canadian federalism. I would prefer that it focus its attention on other things instead of going to the Supreme Court."[80] Indeed, most Quebec members of the Chrétien cabinet reportedly were also against the initiative,[81] as was Progressive Conservative leader Jean Charest. At a much later point, when the Court's judgement was imminent, Claude Ryan and Daniel Johnson both declared publicly that the reference never should have been submitted since the issue was political in nature.[82]

Indeed, it is difficult to see, in purely legal terms, why a ruling by the Supreme Court was needed. It was clear enough that Quebec could not exempt itself from the Canadian constitution simply by declaring as much. For this to come about, the Constitution Act would need to be appropriately amended; the act provided procedures for doing this. To be sure, the Quebec government did contend, at one point, that Quebec was not bound by the Canadian constitution since it did not give its consent to the 1982 revision. However, the Supreme Court had already ruled on this matter in 1982, when it declared that Quebec did not possess a veto over constitutional change.[83] Rather than *Canadian* law, the case for a unilateral declaration of independence was based essentially upon *international* law: as a distinct people, Quebec possessed a right to self-determination that extended to independence. But the Canadian Supreme Court was poorly placed to adjudicate questions of international law.[84]

However, the reference could serve other purposes. A Supreme Court judgement declaring Quebec sovereignty to be illegal might ease public anxieties, especially in English Canada, that another referendum could take place soon and Quebec use it to declare independence outright. For that matter, it might deter some Quebeckers from voting Yes in a referendum on sovereignty, especially if their goal was simply to secure a renewed federalism. It could also be used by the federal government to insist that a Yes vote must be larger than simply 50 per cent plus 1.[85] Thus, rather than an attempt to clarify a legal point the reference can better be seen as a *political* act.

The Chrétien government's expectation in posing the reference questions was obvious from the manner in which the questions had been framed: it was looking for a simple response from the Court that "No, Canadian law does not allow for a unilateral declaration of independence" and "No, international law does not either." Even if somehow its response to the second question were positive, the Court could be relied upon to declare that Canadian law had precedence.

However, while the Court did provide the expected answers, it had a great deal more to say. In a unanimous decision endorsed by all nine justices, the Court did declare that a unilateral declaration of independence would not be legal under Canadian law: "the secession of Quebec cannot be accomplished . . . unilaterally, that is to say without principled negotiations, and be considered a lawful act."[86] Nonetheless, it went on to argue that the favourable expression of a "clear" majority in response to a "clear question" on sovereignty could not be ignored:

> A clear majority vote in Quebec on a clear question in favour of secession would confer democratic legitimacy on the secession initiative which all of the other participants in Confederation would have to recognize.[87]

Indeed, the rest of the country would have a constitutional obligation to enter into good faith negotiations with Quebec regarding the terms under which sovereignty is to come about.[88]

The Court rooted its argument in four principles that it contended were at the heart of Canada's constitutional structure: federalism, democracy, respect for minorities, and the rule of law. While it is not evident what would be the outcome of any negotiations over the terms of Quebec's secession, the constitutional obligation to enter into such negotiations, based on the four principles of Canadian constitutionalism was clear, in the Court's view. Indeed, rejection of negotiations would add legitimacy to the secessionist demands.

The Court was silent on some issues. It did not specify precisely what would constitute a "clear majority" in a referendum. Moreover, by stating that "we refer to a 'clear' majority as a qualitative evaluation,"[89] the Court extended the criteria beyond the size of a majority to include the *manner* in which a referendum is conducted. Nor did the Court specify what would be a "clear question." Also, the Court did not indicate who would be the parties to these negotiations with the Quebec government. Would it be simply the federal government and the other provinces? Would Indigenous leaders or representatives of the two northern territories need to be participants as well?[90] Finally, the Court did not specify which amending formula of the Constitution Act, 1982, would apply.[91] It left all these matters to political leaders, claiming that it lacked the information needed to resolve them.[92] Beyond that, it posited a constitutional obligation to enter into good faith negotiations without addressing the possibility that such negotiations fail.

Nevertheless, the judgement did provide a coherent framework, rooted in the constitution, for achieving secession on a lawful basis. In the process, it recognized that in fact a province *could* secede. Indeed, it stated that nothing in the Canadian constitution precludes modifying it to allow for a secession. Moreover, it stated that should Quebec face "unreasonable intransigence on the part of other participants at the federal or provincial level,"[93] when seeking to initiate negotiations on the basis of the Canadian constitutional principles, Quebec would then be more likely to secure international recognition.

As to international law, the Court contended that the right of peoples to self-determination is confined to three specific circumstances: colonial rule, alien oppression, or denial of "meaningful access to government."[94] Dismissing outright any notion that the first two conditions might apply to Quebec, the Court detailed how, by holding a variety of positions in the federal government, Quebeckers clearly have had access to government. Satisfied that none of the three conditions prevailed, the Court avoided pronouncing on whether, in fact, Quebeckers constitute "a people."

In sum, while rejecting any claim that Quebec has a right to self-determination under international law, the Court provided an alternative route for Quebec secession through its interpretation of Canadian constitutionalism. Quebec secession would have to be secured in a manner that is consistent with the basic principles of Canadian constitutionalism. But, by these same principles, the rest of Canada would be bound to enter into good faith negotiations to bring this about.

The fact of the matter is that the Court was very much a trailblazer with its judgement on Quebec secession. Indeed, the Court was the first court in a constitutional democracy anywhere to have tackled the question.[95] Very few states recognize this possibility in their written constitutions. In fact, some constitutions, such as Spain's, explicitly prohibit it, declaring that their countries are "indivisible."[96]

The Court's judgement can be seen also as innovative with respect to the philosophical treatments of the right to self-determination, even if it does not refer explicitly to the literature where they appear. As with international law, theories of the right to secession typically restrict the right to specific circumstances such as suspension of basic rights or a threat to cultural survival while also presuming the absence of any means of self-government or recognition of minority rights. It is generally assumed that Quebec does not qualify under the latter count.[97] However, the Court's judgement falls quite readily within a different approach that grounds the argument for self-determination in democratic ideals. In the words of philosopher Daniel Philpott, "self-determination is a basic right, rooted in liberal democratic theory, available to any group the majority of whose members desire it."[98] Here too, however, there are conditions. Philpott insists on the presence of certain qualities: liberal democratic values and norms at least as strong as the existing state, majority preference for self-determination, protection of minority rights, and distributive justice.[99] To be sure, unlike such "plebiscitary" theories of democracy and secession, the Court did not posit an *absolute* right to secede. Instead, on the basis of Canada's constitutional principles, it proposed a right to initiate negotiations with the rest of Canada on the terms of secession. These negotiations might fail due not to ill will but to the intractability of the matters to be resolved.

In submitting its reference, the federal government had not been asking the Court to delineate a path through which Quebec could lawfully secede. It received one nonetheless. At the same time, the judgement had a salutary effect more generally in Canada, helping to attenuate the growing confrontation between public opinion in Quebec and in the rest of the country.[100] Indeed, the federal and Quebec governments both expressed satisfaction with the judgement. Jean Chrétien focused on the Court's affirmation of the rule of law whereas Lucien Bouchard cited its emphasis on the need to respect a democratic decision in favour of sovereignty.[101] Beyond that, elements of the judgement may have addressed the sense of grievance that many Quebeckers felt over Quebec's place in the Canadian constitutional order, given both its isolation in 1982 and the rejection of the Meech Lake Accord. First, the judgement clearly affirmed federalism as a fundamental constitutional principle.

Indeed, in its presentation of the four constitutional principles it chose to start with federalism. Second, in its presentation of the federal principle, the Court outlined how, in the case of Quebec, federalism has allowed the Francophone majority to pursue collective goals and to "exercise the considerable provincial powers . . . in such a way as to promote their language and culture." In effect, it echoed the Meech Lake Accord's notion that the Quebec legislature had the role of promoting a "distinct society."[102] With this emphasis on the accommodation of Quebec's specificity within Canadian federalism, the Court was giving new legitimacy to the vision of Canada that had been lost during the Trudeau years.

Nevertheless, the Chrétien government soon saw a need to assert more firmly the role that Ottawa would play in any future referendum on Quebec sovereignty.[103] Accordingly, on 15 March 2000, the House of Commons passed the Clarity Act and, after protracted debate, the Senate followed suit. Under the terms of the act, once a referendum question on sovereignty has been released by a provincial government (in all likelihood, Quebec), the House of Commons would determine whether the question "would result in a clear expression of the will of the population of a province" on whether the province should become "an independent state."[104] In doing so, it is to exclude any question that asks for merely a mandate to negotiate[105] or that envisages other possibilities in addition to secession, such as economic or political arrangements with Canada, that would "obscure" the expression of popular will.[106] Arguably, these restrictions on the content of the referendum question conflict with the call for negotiations that marked the Court's judgement on the secession reference. Such negotiations might well entail consideration of "economic or political arrangements" that fall short of outright secession.[107]

The act also stipulates that, after a referendum has taken place, the House of Commons would determine whether the result represents "a clear expression of a will by a clear majority of the population of that province" taking into account the size of the majority and the percentage of eligible voters who participated.[108] In addition, the act specifies particular considerations that would have to be addressed in the negotiations that would follow upon a Yes vote, including "any changes to the borders of the province," the position of Indigenous Peoples, and "the protection of minority rights."[109] In short, through implying that a "clear majority" should constitute more than a simple majority of 50 per cent plus 1 and setting out an agenda for subsequent negotiations, the effect of the act is to raise substantially the bar that would have to be met for Quebec to accede, in a lawful manner, to sovereignty. For that matter, whereas the House is to pronounce on the acceptability of the question *before* the referendum, its decision as to what constitutes a "clear majority" is reserved until *after* the referendum has taken place. Normally, full and transparent democratic procedure would call for setting "the rules of the game" before a vote is held.

For its part, the Bouchard government responded with its own act, which was passed by the National Assembly on 7 December 2000.[110] Invoking "the principle of equal rights and self-determination of peoples" which is held by "the Quebec people," the act asserts the "inalienable right" of the Quebec people "to decide the political regime and legal status of Quebec."[111] Responding directly to the Clarity Act, it declares in particular that "50 per cent of the valid votes cast plus one" constitutes a majority in a Quebec referendum and that "the territory of Québec and its boundaries cannot be altered except with the consent of the National Assembly."[112] Nor does it acknowledge the Supreme Court's notion of a constitutional obligation to enter into good faith negotiations with the rest of Canada.[113]

It remains unclear whether the Clarity Act responded to a real need. No formal machinery is needed to determine the acceptability of a referendum question; during the 1995 referendum campaign Prime Minister Chrétien made it well known that the federal government found the question to be unclear. By the same token, through imposing criteria for assessing the "clarity" of a referendum question or a majority vote, let alone items to be included in any negotiation, the act seeks to bind the hands of future parliaments despite the principle of parliamentary sovereignty. Since the circumstances of any future referendum on Quebec sovereignty are bound to be different than those of 1995, it would have been wiser, and more in keeping with parliamentary tradition, to leave free the hands of any future Parliament. In any event, as a simple Act of Parliament the Clarity Act could be revised or replaced by any future Parliament to suit its particular purposes. For that matter, it could even be argued that the act is unconstitutional given its restrictions on the content of a referendum question, its arrogation to the House of Commons of responsibility to determine the clarity of the question and its evocation of an enhanced majority.[114]

The Clarity Act did have the effect of easing concern, especially in English Canada, that a new referendum on Quebec sovereignty would take place soon and might well lead to Quebec independence. The act seemed to make this possibility much more remote. At the same time, by providing such assurance the act further weakened public interest in the other component of the "two-track" strategy, the so-called Plan A to build Quebeckers' attachment to Canada. For many outside Quebec, the Quebec question simply had lost its urgency.

In sum, secession became a real option, winning the support of a majority of Quebeckers, only in reaction to English Canada's repudiation of the Meech Lake Accord and the dualist understanding of Canada which it embodied. By eliminating dualism but failing to implant a different understanding among Quebeckers of their place in Canada, the Trudeau national unity strategy had left secession as the only credible option. Still, especially after their initial reaction to Meech's collapse had begun to subside and a sovereignty referendum was deferred by the Bourassa government, the majority of Quebeckers would support sovereignty only if it were coupled with a continuing economic and political relationship with the rest of Canada, based on dualism. Even then, when sovereignty was defined on that basis and a referendum finally was held, it did not secure a majority vote.

Nonetheless, in the wake of the referendum Canadian public debate focused on the form of sovereignty that Quebeckers had never really supported: sovereignty without any continuing relationship with Canada. The Supreme Court brought much-needed perspective to the debate, drawing upon Canada's constitutional principles to show how secession could be achieved legally. The Chrétien government's Clarity Act sought to define the Court's pre-condition for secession, "a clear majority on a clear question," in ways that would reduce the likelihood that Quebeckers would ever support secession.

As it happens, Canada has been an innovator in actually allowing a referendum on independence. It is one of the few countries to do so. With each of the two Quebec referendums, critics complained that the questions were too ambiguous to provide a clear expression of support for secession. But few argued against the very notion of a referendum on independence. Beyond that, as we have seen, Canada's Supreme Court rendered a judgement that should the population of a province declare its desire for secession, through a clear majority on a clear question, the rest of the country would have *a constitutional obligation* to enter into negotiations on the terms of such a secession. Moreover, it grounded its decision in Canada's basic constitutional principles. The Clarity Act may well be too rigid in defining the terms of such a referendum, but it does constitute recognition that under certain conditions secession can take place.

Yet this was all beside the point. Full secession had never been the goal of most Quebeckers, and the best efforts of Jacques Parizeau and his colleagues could not make it so. For that matter, Parizeau's own rejection of a comprehensive association with Canada, and proclivity for a unilateral declaration of independence, was itself a departure from what had been the Parti québécois's historical position from its foundation under René Lévesque, who advocated linking Quebec sovereignty to a "New Canadian Union." By focusing the Yes campaign on the notion of a Quebec–Canada Partnership, Bouchard was realigning the party with that tradition.

The 1995 Quebec referendum was the ultimate proof that the Trudeau national unity strategy had failed. Not only had it failed to supplant the identification with Quebec that was crucial to generating a Yes vote, but sovereigntist leaders were able to use the results of the strategy, most notably the Constitution Act, 1982, and the collapse of Meech, as proof to Quebeckers that their identity could not be recognized within the Canadian federation. By forcing Quebeckers to choose between Quebec and Canada, the federalist campaign had in fact made them more likely to vote Yes. A majority Yes vote may have been averted only by a last-minute disavowal of the Trudeau vision of Canada and the constitution.

Yet the continued influence of the Trudeau vision in the rest of Canada prevented English Canada from attempting to respond to the referendum result by accommodating the grievances that had produced it. Instead, energy was spent debating how the rest of Canada should respond to a new referendum with a Yes majority. In a sense, the Trudeau strategy had the perverse effect that many English Canadians could more easily imagine recognizing Quebec's distinctiveness *outside* Canada than within it.

Notes

1. L. Ian MacDonald, *From Bourassa to Bourassa: Wilderness to Restoration*, 2nd edn (Montreal and Kingston: McGill-Queen's University Press, 2002), 321.
2. "Le Québec est aujourd'hui et pour toujours une société distincte, libre d'assumer son destin et son développement." As quoted in Rapport du Comité constitutionnel du Parti libéral du Québec, *Un Québec libre de ses choix*, 28 Jan. 1991.
3. Robert Bernier, Vincent Lemieux, and Maurice Pinard, *Un combat inachevé* (Quebec: Presses de l'Université du Québec, 1997), Appendix, Tables A and D. These figures are based on a sample that includes Quebec Anglophones.
4. Ibid., 78–83.
5. Ibid., 76–7.
6. Comité constitutionnel, *Un Québec libre de ses choix*, 45.
7. Ibid., 47–9. The provision concerning appeals from Quebec courts reads: "Les décisions des tribunaux supérieurs du Québec ne feront plus l'objet d'appels auprès de la Cour suprême du Canada mais plutôt auprès d'une nouvelle instance ultime complètement québécoise" (49). ("Decisions of Quebec superior courts will no longer be subject to appeal to the Canadian Supreme Court but rather to a new body of final appeal that will be totally Québécois.") There is no suggestion that this elimination of appeals would be restricted to cases involving Quebec law, as opposed to federal law.
8. Comité constitutionnel, *Un Québec libre de ses choix*, 57.
9. See Pierre O'Neill, "Bourassa choisit d'abord le Canada," *Le Devoir*, 11 Mar. 1991. Amendments were also adopted to reassure the Anglophone minority and to clarify that only the Senate in its current form would be abolished.
10. Ibid.
11. *Rapport de la Commission sur l'avenir politique et constitutionnel du Québec*, Mar. 1991.
12. See the analysis in François Rocher, "Le dossier constitutionnel: l'année des consultations et des valse-hésitations," in *L'année politique au Québec*, 1991, ed. Denis Monière (Montreal: Québec/Amérique, 1992), 91.
13. Jean-François Lisée tries to show that at the height of the crisis Bourassa hid his intentions from nationalists so as to buy time. See Lisée, *Le tricheur* (Montreal: Boréal, 1994).
14. Chantal Hébert also argues that, in the wake of Meech, Bourassa could have secured a majority for sovereignty if he had wished. She offers an additional factor to explain why he did not pursue independence: his discovery that he had cancer. (Hébert, *Confessions post-référendaires*, 259.)
15. See the analysis of the election in François Rocher, "Les aléas de la stratégie pré-référendaire: chronique d'une mort annoncée," in *Canada: The State of the Federation* 1995, ed. Douglas M. Brown and Jonathan W. Rose (Kingston: Institute of Intergovernmental Relations, Queen's University, 1995), 19–45.
16. The ADQ proposed a Quebec–Canada union, similar to the European Union, in which Quebec and Canada would hold most government functions but would have a common elected parliament responsible for a limited set of jurisdictions. The party program did not specify whether Quebec would be formally sovereign. See Action démocratique du Québec, *Québec–Canada: A New Partnership*, n.d.

17. Quebec National Assembly, An Act Respecting the Sovereignty of Quebec, 1st session, 35th Legislature, Bill 1 (Quebec City: Éditeur officiel, 1994).
18. Rocher, "Les aléas de la stratégie," 31.
19. Jean Paré, "Noui au Canada; Non à Ottawa," *L'Actualité*, 15 Mar. 1995, 56.
20. Robert Wright, *The Night Canada Stood Still: How the 1995 Quebec Referendum Nearly Cost Us Our Country* (Toronto: Harper Collins, 2014), 113, and Hébert, *Confessions post-référendaires*, 139 and 203. Hébert contends that Chrétien was personally fearful that any documents outlining a potential response to a Yes outcome might somehow be leaked into the public domain.
21. Pierre O'Neill, "Bouchard entraîne le Bloc dans son 'virage'," *Le Devoir*, 10 Apr. 1995.
22. "une fois acquise, la souveraineté sera, pour le Québec, le signal d'un nouveau départ dans un partenariat avec le Canada qui n'exclurait pas éventuellement une forme d'union politique." Québec, Commission nationale sur l'avenir du Québec, 81.
23. Wright, *Canada Stood Still*, 111.
24. "L'Entente tripartite du 12 juin," as reproduced in Guy Lachapelle, Pierre P. Tremblay, and John E. Trent, eds, *L'impact référendaire* (Sainte-Foy: Presses de l'Université du Québec, 1995), 405–9. The negotiations leading to the agreement are recounted in Michel Vastel, *Lucien Bouchard: en attendant la suite* (Outremont: Lanctôt, 1996), 210–11. Chantal Hébert notes that Bouchard had in fact sought that any agreement with the rest of Canada would have to be ratified in a second referendum; Parizeau did not agree to that. (Chantal Hébert and Jean Lapierre, *Confessions post-référendaires*, 34.)
25. In fact, despite his appointment as negotiator-in-chief, Bouchard was marginalized from pre-referendum strategy discussions of strategy and was not aware of documents that had been prepared. Parizeau would have kept for himself control of any post-referendum negotiations by appointing the other members of the negotiating team (Hébert and Lapierre, *Confessions post-référendaires*, 58–9).
26. Robert Howse, "Sovereignty . . . But Where's the Association?" *Canada Watch* 3, no. 7 (May/June 1995): 97–102. Reportedly, PQ leaders saw the proposal as entailing no more than what already existed under US–Canada free trade (Vastel, *Lucien Bouchard*, 210).
27. "L'Entente tripartite du 12 juin." For his part, Parizeau feared that negotiation of a comprehensive economic and political association would work against accession to Quebec sovereignty: either it would be rejected outright by the rest of Canada or negotiations would be prolonged and unsuccessful. Thus, he envisaged the negotiations being restricted to the minimum of items and counted on the possibility of a unilateral declaration of independence. Bouchard and Mario Dumont were fearful that Parizeau would rush to a unilateral declaration. (Hébert and Lapierre, *Confessions post-référendaires*, 54–62.)
28. Michel Venne, "67 p. cent des Québécois sont profondément attachés au Canada," *Le Devoir*, 3 Oct. 1996.
29. Richard Mackie, "Poll Finds Quebeckers Proud of Canada," *Globe and Mail*, 24 Feb. 1996.
30. Venne, "67 p. cent des Québécois."
31. It is less clear what they understood such a partnership to entail. At least one study suggests that some understood partnership to be simply a free trade agreement. (Lemieux, "Le référendum de 1995," 66; and Vincent Lemieux and Robert Bernier, "Voters' Questions in the 1995 Québec Referendum," paper presented to the Canadian Political Science Association, St Catharines, Ont. June 1996, 3.)
32. "Chrétien: Why Destroy Canada?" *Globe and Mail*, 26 Oct. 1996.
33. The text of the bill appeared in *Le Devoir*, 8 Sept. 1995. There were two main changes from the 1994 version. First, Quebec's accession to sovereignty was no longer to be automatic in one year; it would depend upon a proclamation by the National Assembly. Second, any such proclamation "must be preceded by a formal offer of economic and political partnership with Canada."
34. Jean Dion, "Le Canada 'suppliera' Québec de négocier, affirme Bouchard," *Le Devoir*, 28 Sept. 1995.
35. Harold D. Clarke and Allan Kornberg, "Choosing Canada? The 1995 Quebec Sovereignty Referendum," paper delivered to the Canadian Political Science Association, June 1996, 5.

36. Several analysts believe that Bouchard's appointment was not directly responsible for this new increase in Yes support, which apparently had begun before the announcement was made. They argue that the increase may instead have been due to especially aggressive statements by leaders in the No campaign. Claude Garcia, head of an insurance company, had told a meeting of No leaders, "We must not just win on 30 October, we must crush them"; Laurent Beaudoin, head of Bombardier, had announced that his firm might move its factories if Quebec became sovereign. (See Pierre O'Neill, "L'UQAM se dissocie des propos de Garcia," *Le Devoir*, 27 Sept. 1995; and Michel Laliberté and Jean Dion, "Les patrons pour le NON ripostent," *Le Devoir*, 4 Oct. 1995. The survey data are presented by Édouard Cloutier, "The Quebec Referendum: From Polls to Ballots," *Canada Watch* 4, no. 2 [Nov./Dec. 1995]: 37–9; and Pierre Drouilly, "La progression du OUI dans les sondages," *La Presse*, 21 Oct. 1996.) There was a further surge in Yes support later when Finance Minister Paul Martin warned that up to one million jobs would be threatened by sovereignty; this represented a third of Quebec's total workforce (Cloutier, "The Quebec Referendum," 39).

    Nonetheless, if this argument is valid, the surges in Yes support would still have been made possible by the partnership proposal. It appears that once they were convinced that sovereignty would be coupled with an economic association, some Quebeckers considered the comments by Paul Martin and others as hollow threats—and were alienated by them. (André Blais, "Pourquoi le oui a-t-il fait des gains pendant la campagne référendaire?" in *Quebec–Canada: Challenges and Opportunities*, ed. John E. Trent, Robert A. Young, and Guy Lachapelle [Ottawa: University of Ottawa Press, 1996], 71–6.) Blais insists that it is incorrect to suggest that the Yes side gained support because the Québécois stopped worrying about the economic consequences of sovereignty. They simply changed their assessment of these consequences. On the impact of Bouchard's joining the campaign, as future negotiator-in-chief, see Hébert and Lapierre, *Confessions post-référendaires*, 30, and Wright, *Canada Stood Still*, 186. Reinforcing Bouchard's campaign efforts was the Partenaires pour la souveraineté, which brought together Quebec unions, the Société Saint-Jean-Baptiste, and 10 other organizations.
37. Personal communication from André Blais, 27 Sept. 1996.
38. Hébert and Lapierre, *Confessions post-référendaires*, 103.
39. For example, at a Yes rally during the last week of the campaign, Bouchard criticized at length Chrétien's involvement in patriation without Quebec's consent. While avoiding the word "traitor," he displayed a newspaper headline that read, "Lévesque trahi par ses alliés." See Jean Dion, "Bouchard," *Le Devoir*, 26 Oct. 1995.
40. To cite Vincent Lemieux, a leading political scientist who was himself associated with the Quebec Liberal Party: "L'aspect le plus déterminant des positionnements dans l'espace identitaire fut sans doute l'incapacité du camp fédéraliste et de Jean Chrétien, en particulier, de convaincre les non-croyants qu'ils pouvaient demeurer canadiens sans restreindre pour autant leur identité québécoise, c'est-à-dire que l'identification à la nation québécoise n'était pas incompatible avec l'identification à la nation canadienne." ("The most critical aspect of positioning with respect to identity was undoubtedly the inability of the federalist camp and of Jean Chrétien, in particular, to convince the non-believers [not clearly committed to either federalism or sovereignty] that they could remain Canadian without having to limit their identification with Quebec, in other words that identification with the Quebec nation is not incompatible with identification with the Canadian nation.") Vincent Lemieux, "Le Référendum de 1995: quelques pistes d'explication," in Trent et al., *Québec–Canada*, 67.
41. Jean Dion, "Trudeau accuse Lucien Bouchard d'avoir menti aux Québécois," *Le Devoir*, 7 Nov. 1995.
42. Wright, *Canada Stood Still*, 221.
43. Brian Tobin, *All in Good Time* (Toronto: Penguin, 2002), 146, as cited in Wright, *Canada Stood Still*, 331. This general account of the Montreal rally draws from Chap. 12 of Wright, *Canada Stood Still*.
44. Hébert and Lapierre, *Confessions post-référendaires*, 80.
45. Ibid., 104.

46. See Wright, *Canada Stood Still*, 234, and Winsor, "Poll Disputes No Rally's Success."
47. Wright, *Canada Stood Still*, 200–1.
48. "Tout changement des compétences constitutionnelles du Québec ne se fera qu'avec le consentement des Québécois"; "J'ai appuyé cette position dans le passé, je l'appuie aujourd'hui et je l'appuierai dans l'avenir, en toute circonstance." See Jean Dion, "Aucun moyen n'est exclu pour assurer le changement, dit Chrétien," *Le Devoir*, 25 Oct. 1995. Statements also drawn from Richard Mackie and Rhéal Séguin, "Chrétien, Bouchard to Address Nation," *Globe and Mail*, 25 Oct. 1995.
49. Robert Wright contends that Chrétien had been prepared to accept a distinct-society clause as long as it was in a preamble rather than the body of the constitutional text, as was the case with the Meech Lake Accord (Wright, *Canada Stood Still*, 8).
50. After Chrétien's speech, the No side was ahead for the first time since early October, according to one survey. See Hugh Winsor, "Poll Disputes No Rally's Success," *Globe and Mail*, 11 Nov. 1995.
51. Indeed, this was the conclusion of Lucienne Robillard, federal cabinet minister and representative on the No campaign committee and Jean Charest, leader of the Progressive Conservatives (Hébert and Lapierre, *Confessions post-référendaires*, 87). Robert Wright calls it "a thinly veiled mea culpa" (Wright, *Canada Stood Still*, 12.)
52. My translation of "Le Canada mon pays, le Québec ma patrie." See Dion, "Aucun moyen n'est exclu."
53. Hébert and Lapierre, *Confessions post-référendaires*, 31.
54. Pierre Drouilly, "An Exemplary Referendum," *Canada Watch* 4, no. 2 (Nov./Dec. 1995): 25–7.
55. See the account of the Cree referendum in Grand Chief Matthew Coon Come, "Dishonourable Conduct: The Crown in Right of Canada and Quebec, and the James Bay Cree," *Constitutional Forum constitutionnel* 7, no 2/3 (Winter/Spring 1996): 81–3. See also Wright, *Canada Stood Still*, 210–11.
56. However, the Quebec director of elections, Pierre-F. Côté, concluded on the basis of a special inquiry by Judge Alan Gold, that only 31 of the 22,342 referendum scrutineers appeared to have acted improperly; charges were laid against all 31 but they were all acquitted (Norman Delisle, "La fin ne justifie pas les moyens," *Le Devoir*, 11 May 1996, and Wright, *Canada Stood Still*, 268).
57. Marie-Claude Lorde, "Vote hors Québec: le directeur des élections durement critiqué," *La Presse*, 26 Oct. 1996.
58. Another set of allegations had to do with expenditures for the 27 October rally that were not channelled through the official No organization, as required under the Quebec referendum law. Airlines had made tickets available at reduced fares and corporations and associations provided funds to rent buses and other means of transportation. Declaring that such actions "infringed, in a certain sense, on democracy in general in Quebec," the director of elections laid charges against 18 individuals, nine of them outside the province. (See Delisle, "La fin ne justifie pas les moyens.") Still, as we have seen, the rally may have served to reduce rather than increase the No vote.
59. The investigation is recounted in Wright, *Canada Stood Still*, 268.
60. He announced as much in an interview recorded before the results were known (Hébert, *Confessions post-référendaires*, 65).
61. Beyond a post-referendum exhaustion felt by most Quebeckers, and especially by him, Bouchard believed that the particular conditions that produced the close result had passed and that time was needed for new ones to be established. (Hébert, *Confessions post-référendaires*, 29.)
62. Pierre O'Neill, "Pas d'élections avant longtemps," *Le Devoir*, 17 Jan. 1996.
63. Chrétien did not simply support the demand that merchants give English the full visibility allowed by Bill 101. He criticized the law itself, stating that he did not like certain restrictions in it and did not like its "language police." See Jean Chartier, "Affichage: Chrétien approuve le boycottage anglophone," *Le Devoir*, 2 Aug. 1996. For his endorsement of the principle of partition, see Ross Howard, "Quebec Divisible, Chrétien Says," *Globe and Mail*, 30 Jan. 1996.
64. See Grand Council of the Crees, *Sovereign Injustice: Forcible Inclusion of the James Bay Crees and Crees Territory into a Sovereign Quebec* (Nemaska, Que., 1995). See also Mary Ellen Turpel, "Does the Road to Quebec Sovereignty Run through

Aboriginal Territory?" in *Negotiating with a Sovereign Quebec*, ed. Daniel Drache and Roberto Perin (Toronto: Lorimer, 1992), 93–106; and Kent McNeil, "Aboriginal Nations and Quebec's Boundaries: Canada Couldn't Give What It Didn't Have," in ibid., 107–23.

65. While he was premier, Daniel Johnson declared that "the position of all those elected to the Quebec legislature, the premier, the government and obviously the opposition is to defend everywhere and forever the territorial integrity of Quebec" (Montreal *Gazette*, 19 May 1994, as quoted in Robert A. Young, *The Secession of Quebec and the Future of Canada* [Montreal and Kingston: McGill-Queen's University Press, 1995], 214).
66. Alan C. Cairns, "Looking Back from the Future," in Trent et al., *Québec–Canada*, 77–9.
67. Chantal Hébert suggests that the Chrétien Liberals were loath to undertake the devolution of powers that would have been required to renew federalism along the lines demanded by Quebec (Hébert, *Confessions post-référendaires*, 133.)
68. Alan C. Cairns, "The Legacy of the Referendum: Who Are We Now?" *Constitutional Forum constitutionnel* 7, no. 2/3 (Winter/Spring 1996): 35–9; Reg Whitaker, "Thinking about the Unthinkable: Planning for a Possible Secession," ibid., 58–64; and Jeff Rose, "Beginning to Think about the Next Referendum," occasional paper, Faculty of Law, University of Toronto, 21 Nov. 1995.
69. Andrew Coyne, "Making Offers to Quebec Is Part of the Problem, Not the Solution," *Globe and Mail*, 29 Jan. 1996; and Diane Francis, "Children Suffer While Their Parents Bicker," *Maclean's*, 14 Oct. 1996, 9. See also Diane Francis, *Fighting for Canada* (Toronto: Key Porter, 1996).
70. See Alan C. Cairns, "The Quebec Secession Reference: The Constitutional Obligation to Negotiate," *Constitutional Forum constitutionnel* 10, no. 1 (1998): 26.
71. Robert Lecker, "The Writing's on the Wall," *Saturday Night*, July–Aug. 1996, 15–51.
72. Hugh Winsor and Edward Greenspon, "Hard Line on Separatism Popular Outside Quebec," *Globe and Mail*, 16 Nov. 1996. The survey also showed that only 34 per cent of Canadians outside Quebec would "support recognizing Quebec as a distinct society in the constitution if it meant that Quebec would stay in Canada"; 52 per cent were opposed.
73. Ross Howard, "Quebec Divisible, Chrétien Says," *Globe and Mail*, 30 Jan. 1996. Apparently, Chrétien had wanted to raise the boundaries issue during the 1995 referendum campaign but yielded to objections from Johnson's strategists. (Eddie Goldenberg, *The Way It Works: Inside Ottawa* [Toronto, McClelland & Stewart, 2006], 202.)
74. Jean Dion, "Les territoires autochtones n'appartiennent pas au Québec, dit Irwin," *Le Devoir*, 14 Feb. 1996. Irwin's position was denounced by Robert Bourassa, as well as by the Bouchard government. See Manon Cornellier, "Bourassa contredit Irwin," *Le Devoir*, 15 Feb. 1996.
75. Ross Howard, "Slim Vote Can't Split Canada, PM Says," *Globe and Mail*, 31 Jan. 1996.
76. Hugh Winsor and Tu Thanh Ha, "Chrétien Signals New Resolve on Quebec," *Globe and Mail*, 12 Dec. 1995; and Jean Dion, "Chrétien refuse de définir ses 'pouvoirs'," *Le Devoir*, 13 Dec. 1995.
77. "C'est absolument à côté de la track" (Pierre O'Neill, "Les discours des ténors fédéraux irritent Johnson," *Le Devoir*, 2 Feb. 1996). The idea of partition was also dismissed by Liberal constitution critic Jean-Marc Fournier; see "L'intégrité du territoire fait consensus à Québec," *Le Devoir*, 23 Jan. 1996.
78. Ottawa had entered into a court action to support the claim of Guy Bertrand, indépendantiste turned federalist, that Quebec would continue to be bound by the constitution after a Yes vote, implying in turn that Quebec could become sovereign only if the constitution were duly amended to that effect. However, after the Quebec government had decided not to contest Bertrand's action any further, the federal government decided to act on its own and submit a reference. Subsequently, Bertrand declared that he was once again firmly committed to Quebec independence and published a book criticizing the PQ's leadership but supportive of the cause.
79. Statement to the House of Commons on 26 Sept. 1996, as reproduced in "Rock: Does the Law Permit Quebec's Unilateral Secession?" *Globe and Mail*, 27 Sept. 1996.

80. Rhéal Séguin, "Federalists Split Over Call for Court Ruling," *Globe and Mail*, 28 Sept. 1996. See also "Chrétien devrait s'attacher à améliorer le fédéralisme," *La Presse*, 28 Sept. 1996. Claude Ryan had similar comments after Ottawa's initial decision to enter the Bertrand case. See Manon Cornellier, "Le plan B: une vision électoraliste, déplore Ryan," *La Presse*, 21 May 1996. In late February 1996, Daniel Johnson had said that sovereignty was a political matter; it was not appropriate to make sovereignty a legal question. See Jean Dion, "Le plan B refait surface," *Le Devoir*, 27 Feb. 1996.
81. This would, of course, exclude Stéphane Dion and the Prime Minister. See Chantal Hébert, "Droit de sécession: Ottawa s'adresse à la Cour Suprême," *La Presse*, 25 Sept. 1996.
82. Robert A. Young, *The Struggle for Quebec* (Montreal and Kingston: McGill-Queen's University Press, 1999), 146.
83. Moreover, in tacit recognition that Quebec was bound by the constitution, the Quebec government had, over several years in the 1980s, used a blanket invocation of the notwithstanding clause to exempt itself from the Charter of Rights and Freedoms.
84. During the 1995 referendum debate, the Parizeau government was committed, in principle, to securing sovereignty on an orderly basis rather than through a unilateral declaration. Even if Canada should refuse to discuss the "partnership" proposal, the Quebec government would still seek to reach an agreement with Canada regarding the conditions of Quebec's accession to sovereignty. For instance, Parizeau had always recognized that before becoming sovereign Quebec would want to reach an agreement on the division of assets and the debt. This is indicated in Bill 1 (s. 25) and the 12 June agreement. In the speech that he had prepared to deliver in the event of a Yes vote, Parizeau stressed the finality of the referendum result but also insisted that Quebec's accession to sovereignty would not be proclaimed immediately; up to a year could pass. This would give needed time both for Quebec to prepare itself for sovereignty and to negotiate a partnership offer with Canada. (Jacques Parizeau, "Si le Québec avait dit Oui," *Le Devoir*, 22 Feb. 1996.) Arguably, there was a consensus among all parties, including the general public, that negotiations should be part of any process leading to Quebec secession (Yuk Radmilovic, "Strategic Legitimacy Cultivation as the Supreme Court of Canada: Quebec Secession Reference and Beyond," *Canadian Journal of Political Science* 43, no. 4 [Dec. 2010], 854).

    That being said, there has been speculation that with a successful referendum Parizeau would have moved quickly to declare independence without any prior agreement with Canada. Journalist Benoit Aubin claimed that the Parizeau government had in fact planned to do so (Benoit Aubin, *Chroniques de mauvaise humeur* [Montreal: Boréal, 1996], 215–18). Parizeau's collaborators claimed that the planned speech proves that he did not intend to move precipitously (Michel Venne, "Qu'aurait dit Parizeau si le OUI l'avait emporté?" *Le Devoir*, 18 Feb. 1996). However, more recently, Chantal Hébert established through her interview with Parizeau that he expected to move quite quickly to a unilateral declaration of independence (UDI), the rest of Canada failing to enter into negotiations (Chantal Hébert, *The Morning After: The 1995 Quebec Referendum and the Day That Almost Was* [Toronto: Alfred A. Knopf Canada, 2014], 45). Indeed, her interviews with Chrétien and other federal figures confirm that they would not have entered into negotiations upon a Yes vote (ibid., 62, 133, 247; see also Goldenberg, *The Way It Works*, 220). Apparently, Bouchard and Dumont were both very concerned that, should the leadership of the rest of Canada refuse to negotiate, Parizeau would move quickly to a UDI (ibid., 20, 34). Still, it is unlikely such a declaration would have been based upon Canadian law as opposed to international law—or that a ruling by the Supreme Court would have deterred the Parizeau government from making it. Parizeau's proclivity toward a UDI and Chrétien's refusal to recognize a Yes vote are also discussed in Wright, *Canada Stood Still*, 274–5.
85. Young, *Struggle for Quebec*, 109. See also Nathalie Des Rosiers, "Secession: From Québec Veto to Québec Secession: The Evolution of the Supreme Court of Canada on Québec–Canada Disputes," *Canadian Journal of Law and Jurisprudence* (2000): 13, n. 10.

86. 1998 (2) S.C.R., "Reference regarding the Secession of Quebec," para 104.
87. Ibid., para 220.
88. Ibid., para 221.
89. Ibid., para 87. The court did not raise the quantitative aspect of a "clear majority" (Dave Guénette and Alain-G. Gagnon, "Du référendum à la sécession—le processus québécois d'accession à la souveraineté et ses enseignements en matière d'autodétermination" *Revista catalana de dret públic*, no. 54 [June 2017]: 113).
90. See Alan C. Cairns, "The Quebec Secession Reference."
91. Donna Greschner, "The Quebec Secession Reference: Goodbye to Part V?" *Constitution Forum constitutionnel* 10, no. 1 (1998): 19–25, and Patrick J. Monahan, *Constitutional Law* (Concord: Irwin Law, 1997), 197–200.
92. S.C.R. "Secession of Quebec," para 100.
93. Ibid., para 103.
94. Ibid., para 138.
95. Russell, *Constitutional Odyssey*, 245.
96. The Spanish constitution declares "the Constitution is based on the indissoluble unity of the Spanish Nation, the common and indivisible country of all Spaniards" (Presidencia del Gobierno, *Spanish Constitution*, 1978, art. 2). Spain's Constitutional Court recently cited this provision to declare illegal any attempt by Catalonia to hold a referendum on secession.
97. For example, see Allen Buchanan, *Secession: The Morality of Political Divorce from Fort Sumter to Lithuania and Quebec* (Boulder: Westview Press, 1991), 61–4 and 153; and Alan Patten, *Equal Recognition: The Moral Foundations of Minority Rights* (Princeton: Princeton University Press, 2014), Chap. 7. See also the general discussion in Margaret Moore's introduction to her edited volume *National Self-Determination and Secession* (Oxford: Oxford University Press, 1998).
98. Daniel Philpott, "Self-Determination in Practice," in *National Self-Determination and Secession*, ed. Moore, 3.
99. Ibid.
100. In Des Rosiers's terms, the reference had a therapeutic effect (Des Rosiers, "From Québec Veto to Québec Secession," para 49, and Stephen Tierney, "The Constitutional Accommodation of National Minorities in the United Kingdom and Canada" in *The Conditions of Diversity in Multinational Democracies*, ed. Alain-G. Gagnon, Montserrat Guibernau, and François Rocher [Montreal: Institute for Research on Public Policy, 2003], 182.)
101. Lucien Bouchard declared that the judgement "added to the credibility of the sovereignty project" ("ajout[ait] à la credibilité du projet souverainiste"), as quoted in Marie-Claude Ducas, "La souveraineté est renforcée", *Le Devoir*, 22 Aug. 1998. For his part, Jean Chrétien declared that the judgement was "an important reminder of some basic elements of democratic life and civil order," as quoted in Brenda Branswell and Bruce Wallace, "Supreme Court Rules on UDI," *Maclean's*, 31 Aug. 1998.
102. See Des Rosiers, "From Québec Veto to Québec Secession," para 42. That being said, the Court failed to identify dualism as a distinct constitutional principle, instead placing linguistic duality within the more general category of minority rights (Claude Ryan, "Consequences of the Quebec Secession Reference," C.D. Howe Institute Commentary, no. 139 [Apr. 2000], 3.) The distinct role of the Quebec government could have been more clearly identified if dualism had been set as a fundamental principle. The failure to identify dualism as a general principle may reflect the need to develop a text acceptable to all nine justices. (Gregory Millard, "The Secession Reference and National Reconciliation: A Critical View," *Canadian Journal of Law & Society* 14, no. 2 [Fall, 1999]: 14 and n. 41).
103. Apparently, the initiative was originally conceived by Jean Chrétien. It was strongly supported by Stéphane Dion but initially resisted by cabinet colleagues who feared it would produce a backlash in Quebec. In particular, Paul Martin contended that the law was not necessary and favoured a prime ministerial declaration (Goldenberg, *The Way It Works*, 249–253).
104. S.C. 2000, c. 26 Clarity Act, s. 1(4). In making this determination, the House would take account of views expressed by political parties in provincial legislatures, including the province in question, and of statements of provincial governments, Senate, and "the representatives of the Aboriginal peoples of Canada," especially from the province in question (Clarity Act, s. 1[5]).

105. "a referendum question that merely focuses on a mandate to negotiate without soliciting a direct expression of the will of the population of that province on whether the province should cease to be part of Canada" (Clarity Act, s. 1[4][a]).
106. "that envisages other possibilities in addition to the secession of the province from Canada, such as economic or political arrangements with Canada, that obscure a direct expression of the will of the population of that province on whether the province should cease to be part of Canada" (Clarity Act, s. 1[4][b]).
107. Patrick Taillon, "De la clarté à l'arbitraire: le contrôle de la question et des résultats référendaires par le parlement canadien," *Revista d'estudis autonòmics i federals*, 20 Oct. 2014, 25–8.
108. Clarity Act, s. 2(1). With respect to a "clear majority," a simple majority (or 50 per cent plus 1) has been the established criterion in Canada for all direct consultations of voters. (See Claude Ryan ["Consequences of the Quebec Secession Reference," 11]. Ryan does acknowledge the possibility of requiring a simple majority of all registered to vote [ibid., 12].) The simple majority rule was followed in the 1949 referendum through which Newfoundland became a Canadian province and was generally recognized in the Quebec referendums of 1980 and 1995 (see also Taillon, "De la clarté à l'arbitraire," 28–36). The United Kingdom, the source of Canada's parliamentary tradition, followed the simple majority rule in recent referendums on Scottish independence and on withdrawal from the European Union.
109. Clarity Act, s. 3(2).
110. R.S.Q., chapter E-20.2, "An Act Respecting the Exercise of the Fundamental Rights and Prerogatives of the Québec People and the Québec State."
111. Ibid., 1.
112. Ibid., 4 and 9.
113. Guénette and Gagnon, "Du référendum à la sécesssion," 112.
114. Taillon, "De la clarté à l'arbitraire," 13–59; and François Rocher and Nadia Verrelli, "Questioning Constitutional Democracy in Canada," in *The Conditions of Diversity*, 220–2, 227–233.

Chapter 8

Failing to Break the Impasse

The Persisting Quebec Identity

Over the more than 20 years that have followed the 1995 referendum, the debate about Quebec and its relationship to Canada has remained frozen in two polar opposites: the Trudeau vision versus full independence. Both of them were defined many decades before—in the 1960s. It was in direct response to the full independence championed by the Ralliement pour l'indépendance nationale and other early separatists that Pierre Elliot Trudeau conceived his vision of Canada. In fact, he assumed that for all Quebec nationalists full secession was the ultimate objective, whether they realized it or not. Thus, in his view, the 1960s attempts of Lester Pearson and others to accommodate Quebec nationalists were doomed to fail and, worse still, would only legitimize and reinforce the separatist drive. Moreover, he was fully confident that, presented with a choice between secession and his vision of Canada, Quebeckers would choose the latter. Indeed, it was on the basis of this argument that he had won the Liberal Party leadership and become prime minister.

In the end, however, neither option could attract majority support in Quebec. Continuing to resist the Trudeau vision of Canada, Quebec Francophones persisted in identifying primarily with Quebec. Indeed, their proclivity to identify with Quebec only grew during the post-referendum years, even if much of the rest of Canada had become deeply attached to the Trudeau vision of the country. Yet most Quebeckers also continued to reject full independence for Quebec. Thus, during the 1995 referendum campaign each side was forced to diverge from its polar option: the Yes camp embracing a new Canadian partnership and the No side calling for recognition of Quebec as a "distinct society." Even then, neither side clearly prevailed in the final vote.

Persisting to Identify with Quebec

Over the last two decades, most Quebec Francophones have continued to identify first and foremost with Quebec, as opposed to Canada as a whole. Thus, in a 2014 survey 63 per cent of Quebec Francophones stated that they identified primarily with Quebec—either with Quebec first, over Canada, (44.8 per cent) or exclusively with Quebec (18.2 per cent). Another 27.8 per cent declared that they identified equally with Canada and Quebec; only 9.3 per cent declared that they identified exclusively or first with Canada.[1] Similarly, in a 2016 survey, only 37 per cent of Quebeckers (non-Francophones included) agreed that they have "a deep emotional attachment to Canada" and that they "love the country and what it stands for." In this, Quebeckers differed dramatically from respondents in the rest of Canada, as demonstrated in Figure 8.1: in all regions but Quebec overwhelming majorities agreed with the statement.[2] By the same token, Quebeckers were much more likely than other Canadians to opt instead for a conditional attachment to Canada, dependent on Canada providing "a good standard of living."[3]

Still, over the post-referendum years most Quebeckers also remained opposed to Quebec independence. Indeed, as Figure 8.2 demonstrates, support for Quebec independence has fallen over time.[4]

It would be difficult to credit the Trudeau national unity strategy with this relatively low level of support for Quebec independence. After all, that strategy had been based upon leading Quebeckers to identify with Canada as whole. But identification with Quebec did not necessarily entail support for independence. Thus, the 2016 survey which found that most Quebeckers denied any "deep attachment to Canada" also found that most Quebeckers overwhelmingly rejected Quebec independence: 75 per cent agreed that "ultimately, Quebec should stay in Canada" and 64 per cent agreed that "the issue of Quebec sovereignty is settled, and Quebec will remain in Canada."[5]

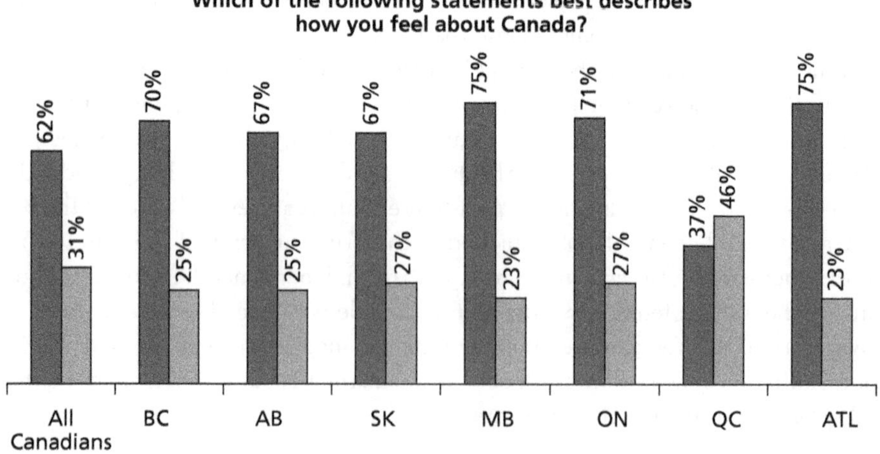

Figure 8.1 Emotional versus conditional attachment to Canada by province/region
Source: Angus Reid Institute, "What Makes Us Canadians? A Study of Values, Beliefs, Priorities and Identity," 3 Oct. 2016, 5.

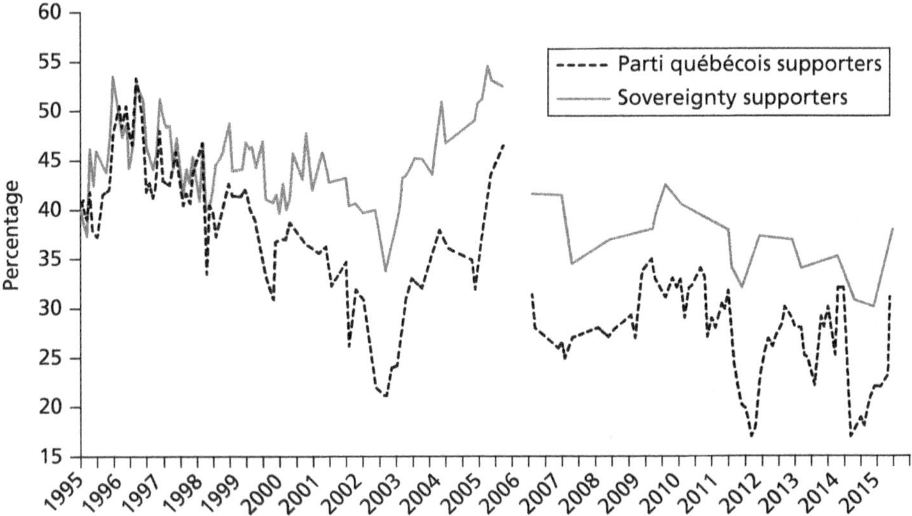

Figure 8.2 Yes to sovereignty and support for Parti québécois by survey dates, 1995 to 2015, for Quebec

Source: Simon Langlois, "L'appui à la souveraineté du Québec de 1995 à aujourd'hui," *Colloque sur la démocratie référendaire*, Université Laval, 30 Oct. 2015 (from Power Point supplied by Simon Langlois, reprinted with his permission). It should be noted that up to 2005 figures represent responses to questions that evoke an association with Canada; with 2005 and after the questions include no such reference.

In short, as long as the debate was defined in terms of the two polar opposites of the Trudeau vision of Canada and Quebec secession it could only lead to an impasse. Both options explicitly rejected the dualist vision of Canada that most Quebec Francophones continued to hold. Thus, over the two decades following the referendum all federal governments, as well as Quebec governments committed to federalism, broke with the Trudeau orthodoxy by adopting one form or another of dualism. However, all these initiatives failed to resolve the impasse. Typically, they were defeated by the Trudeau vision's continued hold on English-speaking Canada, and its continued rejection in Quebec.

Jean Chrétien Government

In the wake of the referendum, the federal government of Jean Chrétien sought to accommodate Quebec's sense of distinctiveness, making good on Chrétien's desperate overture during the last days of the referendum campaign. Thus, despite Chrétien's personal association with the Trudeau vision, his government sought to enlist the provinces in approving two formal constitutional changes: recognition that Quebec represents a "distinct society" and guarantee of a Quebec veto over constitutional change. Yet there was little readiness among the provincial premiers to follow suit. The tone was set by Ontario's Mike Harris, newly arrived in office, who made it clear in a tense meeting with Jean Chrétien that he was focused exclusively on his "Common Sense" agenda for Ontario and would not enter into new constitutional discussions.[6]

As a result, the Chrétien government had to settle for initiatives on the part of the Canadian Parliament alone, in the form of resolutions. On 11 December 1995, the House of Commons passed a "Resolution Respecting the Recognition of Quebec as a Distinct Society." Under the resolution the House recognized "that Quebec is a distinct society within Canada"; defined Quebec's distinctiveness in the traditional terms of language, culture, and civil law; undertook "to be guided by this reality"; and encouraged "the legislative and executive branches of [the federal] government to take note of this recognition and be guided in their conduct accordingly."[7] The practical effect of the resolution was not at all evident.[8] At the same time, given the commitment of most provincial governments to the absolute equality of the provinces, no provincial legislature adopted similar resolutions. The best the provinces could manage was the "Calgary Declaration" of September 1997, by which the provincial (excluding Quebec) and territorial governments both affirmed "the equality of status" of the provinces and recognized "the unique character of Quebec society," defining this uniqueness in traditional terms.[9] The Declaration had no practical effect and was soon forgotten.

As to the matter of a Quebec veto, the Chrétien government sought to guarantee one by requiring that, in the case of constitutional changes not requiring the approval of all provinces, federal governments would introduce to the House only changes that had the prior approval of Quebec's legislature, along with a sub-set of other provincial legislatures. Initially, it sought to limit the other legislatures to those specified by the ill-fated Victoria Charter amending formula: Ontario, and two or more provinces from Atlantic Canada and western Canada that contain 50 per cent of the population of their respective regions. However, after howls of protest from British Columbia, Ottawa agreed to afford a veto to BC as well. After heated debates in both the House and the Senate, a bill to this effect became law on 2 February 1996.[10] The procedure governing constitutional amendments remains an Act of Parliament which can be revoked or modified by future Parliaments, although it could be politically difficult to do so.[11]

With the appointment of Stéphane Dion as intergovernmental affairs minister in late January of 1996, the Chrétien government tried once again to persuade English Canada to support constitutional entrenchment of a distinct-society clause.[12] But public opinion outside Quebec remained opposed[13] and the Chrétien government still failed to get the support of enough premiers.[14]

With respect to the actual conduct of federal–provincial relations, as opposed to the formal constitutional framework, the Chrétien government did undertake some significant steps, acknowledging in its February 1996 Throne Speech that "the referendum result gave a clear message that Quebeckers want change in the federation."[15] It declared that any new shared-cost programs in exclusively provincial jurisdictions would need the consent of a majority of provinces and then would allow provinces to opt out with compensation if they established equivalent programs.[16] The government also announced that it was ready to withdraw from several areas, most notably labour market training which had been a long-time concern of Quebec in particular[17] and promised to "work in partnership [with the provinces]" in other areas.[18] This new flexibility resulted in 1998 in a formal agreement with the Quebec government: the Canada–Quebec Labour Market Development Agreement.[19] In addition, a new federal National Child Benefit program effectively allowed Quebec, and the other provinces, to dispose of improved federal transfers as it wished.[20]

However, as 1996 progressed, the Chrétien government turned away from accommodation of Quebec's distinctiveness to initiatives that fell squarely within the established Trudeau national unity strategy: trying to lead Quebeckers to identify more fully with Canada, and with the federal government itself.[21] Thus, the government established a Canada Information Office, with a budget of $20 million, which was designed to promote Canadian identity and hence Canadian unity—and to counter the "lies" propagated by separatists.[22] Coupled with this initiative was a program to make Canadian flags available to citizens free of charge but the program had little impact in Quebec: as of August 1996 only 8.3 per cent of the requests had come from Quebec.[23]

Finally, a campaign was initiated to raise the federal government's "visibility" in Quebec. At the centre of this effort was a program to sponsor community events. Administered by the federal department of public works with an annual budget of $50 million, the "sponsorship" program became notorious for the misuse of public funds for partisan and personal gain and ultimately was the focus of a commission of inquiry. In this fashion, the "sponsorship" program seriously hurt, rather than helped, the federalist cause in Quebec.[24]

Not only were these attempts to instil directly among Quebeckers a greater attachment to Canada unsuccessful, but Quebec's estrangement from the rest of Canada was confirmed by its absence from the Social Union Framework that Ottawa and the nine other provinces signed in 1999. Entitled a "Framework to Improve the Social Union for Canadians," the agreement enshrined the right of Canadians to social programs, wherever they may be in the country. While the refusal of the Quebec government to sign the agreement might be explained in terms of its control by Lucien Bouchard and the Parti québécois, the fact of the matter is that the agreement also was rejected by the opposition Liberals, under Jean Charest, as well as Mario Dumont's Action démocratique, as an affront to Quebec's jurisdictions, especially by its sanction of the federal spending power.[25]

In effect, after initial attempts to accommodate Quebec's distinctiveness, which were largely resisted in the rest of Canada, the Chrétien government found itself focusing on the polar options which Quebeckers had already rejected.

In line with the Trudeau strategy, it resorted to efforts to lead Quebeckers to attach themselves directly to Canada—which proved to be counter-productive. And, as we saw in the previous chapter, it became increasingly focused on a "Plan B" effort to demonstrate the obstacles to full independence—an option which Quebeckers had in any event rejected.

Paul Martin Government

For its part, the Paul Martin government made a much more sustained effort to break through the federal orthodoxy and openly recognize Quebec's distinctiveness. Rather than seeking constitutional change, Martin and his colleagues sought to accommodate Quebec through asymmetry in their dealings with the provincial governments, restoring one of the key strategies of the 1960s Pearson government. During the late 1980s, Paul Martin had already departed from the Trudeau national unity strategy by supporting the Meech Lake Accord, with its distinct-society clause. Indeed, his support of the Accord had been a central focus of debate in his unsuccessful competition with Jean Chrétien for the Liberal Party leadership. It was only natural that when Martin finally did secure the Liberal leadership and the prime ministership, in late 2003, he would depart from the Trudeau orthodoxy when it came to dealing with Quebec. Thus, under his leadership the federal government entered into arrangements that clearly differentiated Quebec from the other provinces. Asymmetrical federalism became the new approach to the Quebec question, and the Martin government made a point of saying so. It was well received by the Quebec government, now led by Jean Charest who was seeking to establish credibility among Quebeckers.[26]

In September 2004, the federal government entered into an agreement on health care with the Quebec government that explicitly embraced "asymmetrical federalism": "that is, flexible federalism that notably allows for the existence of specific agreements and arrangements adapted to Quebec's specificity." On this basis, Quebec was authorized to establish its own wait time reduction plan and to use federal funding "to implement its own plan for renewing Quebec's health system."[27] By the same token, in 2005 the Martin government signed with the Charest government an agreement on parental insurance, a long-time objective of the Quebec government which Jean Chrétien had fiercely opposed.[28] Under the parental insurance agreement Quebec, unlike the other provinces, would receive funds for its child care program without being accountable to any Canada-wide standards. To be sure, neither agreement afforded Quebec any additional formal powers; they were simply administrative agreements rather than permanent constitutional changes.[29] Nonetheless, in practice they did allow Quebec to exercise a degree of autonomy that was greater than that of the other provinces and that was explicitly justified by Quebec's specificity.[30]

However well received it was in Quebec, this resurrection of the Pearsonian approach to Quebec violated directly the Trudeau vision of the Canadian nation. Indeed, adherents to that vision were quick to denounce this heresy, contending that Prime Minister Trudeau would never have accepted such arrangements with Quebec. In an article entitled "Quebec's Final Victory" pollster Allan Gregg bewailed asymmetrical federalism and Martin's capitulation to Charest on health care, declaring that he was "awaiting the next side-deal that will push Quebec ever closer to full independence."[31] He lamented the absence of Pierre Trudeau's readiness to "impose his iron will" on the provinces.

At the same time, the Martin government vigorously dissociated itself from an initiative of the Chrétien government that had been quite consistent with the Trudeau strategy: the "sponsorship" program designed to raise the federal government's visibility in Quebec by funding community events. The program's funds had been largely awarded in contracts to private advertising firms, averaging $40 million annually between 1996 and 2002. In the final two years of the Chrétien government, it had become public knowledge that the funds had not been rigorously managed. Indeed, Auditor General Sheila Fraser declared that "senior public servants broke just about every rule in the book" in awarding the contracts and initiated an audit of the program as whole. Her February 2004 report established that little or no work had been performed for more than $100 million of these funds.

Declaring himself to be "mad as hell," Martin sought to distance himself from the scandal. Cancelling the program, Martin declared that the government would sue individuals and corporations that had over-billed the government, and appointed Justice John Gomery to conduct a review of the apparent misuse of funds. Gomery determined that "the Sponsorship Program [had been used] for purposes other than national unity or federal visibility."[32] In fact, there had been "a complex web of financial transactions among Public Works and Government Services Canada (PWGSC), Crown Corporations, and communication agencies, involving kickbacks and illegal contributions to a political party"[33]—the Liberal Party in Quebec. A close friend of Jean Chrétien, Jacques Corriveau, had been "the central figure in an elaborate kickback scheme by which he enriched himself personally and provided funds and benefits" to the Liberal Party's Quebec headquarters.[34]

As it happened, Paul Martin's attack on the "sponsorship" program did not reverse the slide in Liberal support in Quebec that revelations about the program had already engendered.[35] Indeed, Martin's public denunciations of the program may have reinforced the slide: in the 2006 federal election the Liberals secured only 13 of the 75 seats in Quebec.[36] Nationally, the Conservatives won power with Stephen Harper as leader. For its part, the Liberals remained a marginal force in Quebec for the next two decades. More importantly, the revelations about such a massive misuse of public funds clearly affected Quebeckers' confidence in the federal government itself, undermining any favourable impact of

Martin's asymmetrical initiatives. Finally, the fact that funds intended to promote national unity could be so readily diverted to partisan purposes and personal gain demonstrated the weakness of federalist forces in Quebec and the failure of the Trudeau strategy to nourish and reinforce them.

Liberals in Opposition

After their loss of power, the Liberals continued to be haunted by the Trudeau orthodoxy and the need to break out of it. During the fall of 2006, as they went about choosing a successor to Paul Martin, they became bitterly divided over the Quebec question. In his policy platform, leadership candidate Michael Ignatieff declared outright that Quebec (along with Indigenous Peoples) should be recognized as a nation, and that this recognition should be incorporated in the Canadian constitution. He contended that "Quebeckers . . . have come to understand themselves as a nation, with a language, culture and territory that marks them out as a separate people."[37] None of the other candidates agreed. For his part, Justin Trudeau, son of Pierre Trudeau, decried such thinking, contending that Quebec nationalism is an outmoded "idea from the nineteenth century" that "has nothing to do with the country that we should be building." Jean Chrétien echoed agreement.[38] Adherents of the Trudeau national vision, such as Senator Serge Joyal and former Supreme Court Justice Claire L'Heureux-Dubé, were quick to denounce the proposal as a return to isolationism that diminishes the greatness of Canada and leads to division.[39] Nonetheless, at a Montreal meeting in late October, the Quebec wing of the federal Liberal Party adopted a resolution to the effect that recognition of the Quebec nation be "officialized."[40] (The resolution was withdrawn from the subsequent leadership convention, saving the Liberals from a searing debate, thanks to a House of Commons resolution to be discussed below.)

Ultimately, Stéphane Dion defeated Ignatieff to become the party leader. For his part, Dion was not as firmly opposed as Trudeau had been to constitutional recognition of Quebec's specificity. After all, upon becoming minister of intergovernmental affairs he had tried, unsuccessfully, to persuade the provincial premiers to support constitutionalizing a distinct-society clause. However, he largely avoided the question during his short period as party leader. Finally assuming the party leadership in 2008, after the Liberal electoral defeat, Ignatieff did not raise anew the notion of constitutionalizing Quebec's national status during his three-year tenure.[41]

Stephen Harper Government

Stephen Harper, first leader of the new Conservative Party that was formed through the merger of the Progressive Conservatives and the Canadian Alliance in 2003, and ultimately prime minister of Canada for nine years, brought to bear a political world view that differed radically from that of most of Canada's postwar political leadership, including Pierre Trudeau and such acolytes as Jean Chrétien, let alone Paul Martin or Lester Pearson. At the core of this world view was a deeply set distrust of the ability of any government to pursue collective goals for a society or to solve social problems. Coupled with this conservative (or "neo-liberal") hostility to the state in general was Harper's personal immersion in the political culture of Alberta, with its own aversion to governmental intervention, whether provincial or federal.

At the age of 19, Harper left his native Toronto to settle in Alberta where, after first holding a position in a multinational (Imperial Oil), he pursued graduate studies in economics at the University of Calgary. The "Calgary School" of economists and political scientists, inspired by the views of Friedrich Hayek and other anti-state thinkers, confirmed Harper in his belief that the federal government had vastly exceeded its proper role. At the same time, Harper came to share his adoptive province's historical grievances against Pierre Trudeau and his actions as prime minister. Front and centre was rejection of the National Energy Program and its treatment of Alberta,[42] but not far behind was dismissal of Trudeau's language policies, as noted in Chapter 4. In a 2001 op-ed piece, Harper declared bilingualism, understood in Trudeau's pan-Canadian terms, to be "the god that failed."[43] Given these various beliefs, Harper was the prime mover behind the "Alberta Agenda," an open letter to Alberta premier Ralph Klein which called upon him to reclaim provincial jurisdictions so as "to build firewalls around Alberta, to limit the extent to which an aggressive and hostile federal government can encroach upon legitimate provincial jurisdiction."[44]

Thus, as Conservative leader and then prime minister, Stephen Harper sought no less than to implant a new vision of the Canadian nation, inspired by neo-liberal goals of reducing the role of government, reining in Ottawa's excesses, and freeing the private sector. In the process, the Liberal Party would be destroyed and the NDP would be left to compete with the Conservatives along a more conventional right–left terrain. While Harper shared Pierre Trudeau's insistence on the absolute equality of the provinces, opposed the Meech Lake Accord, and had anticipated the Clarity Act through a 1996 private member's bill,[45] there was little place in his vision of the country for such Trudeau-era preoccupations as making Ottawa a truly "national" government or promoting multiculturalism, let alone creating a "just society." Indeed, Trudeau's signal achievements of patriation and the Charter of Rights and Freedoms were no longer to be held sacred within this new understanding of Canada. In fact, as prime minister Harper and his colleagues sought to place the British connection in a new more positive light, restoring the prominence of the monarchy and celebrating Canada's military tradition as Great Britain's key partner, whether in the War of 1812 or in the two world wars. As for the Charter, it had led to rampant intrusions by the courts on individual freedoms promoted by the "court party" of special interests.

A Vision of Open Federalism and Accommodation of Quebec

Within his neo-liberal premises, Stephen Harper developed a new vision of Canadian federalism that differed radically from the Trudeau orthodoxy. Well before the 2006 election brought the Conservatives to power, Harper had proclaimed his party's commitment to an "open federalism."[46] Central to that vision was the establishment of a classical federalism in which each level of government confined itself to its own set of powers and jurisdictions. The heavy federal involvement in provincial jurisdictions which had characterized Liberal governments from the Second World War onward, drawing upon Ottawa's superior fiscal capacity, would come to an end. Indeed, the "fiscal imbalance" between Ottawa and the provinces would be terminated and the federal government's spending power would be bound by a new charter that would put an end to "a federalism of domination, a paternalist federalism which is a serious menace to the future of our federation."[47] By the same token, with this federal withdrawal to its own jurisdictions each level of government would be able to operate quite independently of the other. There would no longer be need for the heavy machinery of federal–provincial relations that the Liberals had put in place, including the first ministers' conference that had so frequently been the occasion of bitter federal–provincial confrontation.

Within this vision of "open federalism," Harper fashioned an approach to Quebec that departed directly from the Trudeau orthodoxy. As with all the provincial governments, Quebec would have effective control of its jurisdictions, free from federal intervention. But, beyond full provincial autonomy, Harper's "open federalism" allowed a certain accommodation of Quebec's distinctive concerns. (After all, Harper had concluded that his party needed a strong contingent of Quebec MPs if it was to form a government.[48]) Thus, Harper declared that his "open federalism" would recognize "the special cultural and institutional responsibilities of the Quebec government."[49] On this basis, his government would invite Quebec to participate in the United Nations Educational, Scientific, and Cultural Organization (UNESCO), a goal of the Charest government.

Initially, this vision of a new "open federalism" was well received in Quebec. Quebec commentators and academics welcomed it as a breath of fresh air.[50] Indeed, the new approach may well explain the Conservatives' relative success in Quebec during the 2006 election, winning 10 ridings and 24.6 per cent of the popular vote, after having won no seats and 8.8 per cent in 2004. Without the breakthrough in Quebec, the Conservatives likely would not have been able to form a minority government.

Moreover, during their first term in office the Harper Conservatives took some significant steps to recast Canadian federalism. In particular, they addressed the widely held complaint of a "fiscal imbalance" between Ottawa and the provinces. The notion of a "fiscal imbalance" had been a long-standing contention of the Quebec government, going back to the Tremblay Commission of the early

1950s.[51] In 2001, the Quebec government of Lucien Bouchard had established a Commission on Fiscal Imbalance, led by former Liberal revenue minister Yves Séguin, whose 2002 report called upon the federal government to cede fully the goods and services tax (GST) to the provinces, reform the equalization program, and forgo the "spending power" through which Ottawa had long acted within provincial jurisdictions.[52] Jean Charest took up the cause upon assuming office in 2003. For its part, the Harper government directly responded to this campaign, recognizing the legitimacy of the complaints. Thus, it reduced the federal GST, leaving greater "tax room" to the provinces; augmented and extended on a long-term basis the federal contribution to ongoing transfer programs that the Martin government had initiated; and redesigned and enhanced the system of equalization payments to the provinces. By the same token, the Harper government established no new federal programs in areas of provincial jurisdiction.[53]

At the same time, in recognition of Quebec's specificity the Harper government did indeed arrange the Quebec government's participation in UNESCO, announcing in May 2006 that a permanent representative of the Quebec government would be included in the Canadian delegation. To be sure, the Quebec representative would fall under the authority of the delegation's head, appointed by the federal government, who alone would continue to represent Canada. In effect, the Quebec representative was to be a "lobbyist" within the Canadian delegation.[54] As such, the arrangement falls far short of the status that the Mulroney government had afforded Quebec within the Agence de la Francophonie, allowing it to participate directly in discussions that bear on co-operation and development.[55] Nonetheless, the Harper initiative represented the first arrangement of any kind for a Quebec presence in UNESCO.

Accommodation of Quebec's specificity was also facilitated by the Harper government's practice of "one-off federalism" through which it entered into individual bilateral agreements with each province rather than reaching a single multilateral agreement with all provinces. As David McGrane argues, this practice came naturally for a government which, given its neo-liberalism, was not seeking to apply a pan-Canadian vision of public policy and instead was pursuing a national unity strategy of "disengagement." At the same time, the agreements with Quebec allowed it considerably greater autonomy than did the agreements with the other provinces.[56] Nonetheless, thanks to the basic secrecy of "one-off federalism," these particular arrangements did not violate the English-Canadian public's commitment to the principle of equality of the provinces.[57]

"A Québécois Nation within a United Canada"

Most dramatically, the Harper government was responsible for a House of Commons resolution that declared that the Québécois constitute a nation. The initiative stemmed indirectly from the federal Liberal Party's campaign to find a successor to Paul Martin. As we have seen, Michael Ignatieff had triggered a bitter debate within the party by proposing constitutional recognition that Quebec constitutes a nation. The Bloc québécois, for its part, sought to capitalize on this development to stir further division among federalist forces and introduced to the House a resolution declaring that "Quebeckers form a nation." The Harper government decided to turn the Bloc initiative to its own advantage by rendering the Bloc's text acceptable within its own federalist terms. In particular, it added the phrase "within a united Canada." Thus, the resolution became: "That this House recognize that the Québécois form a nation within a united Canada." Even with this revision, which had been negotiated with Stéphane Dion among others, the resolution was opposed by 15 Liberal MPs (of the 103-member Liberal caucus). In addition, several Conservative MPs absented themselves from the vote and a minister resigned from the Harper cabinet over the issue.[58] Nonetheless, most Conservative MPs voted in favour, as did all NDP MPs, and the resolution passed on 27 November 2006 by a majority of 266 to 16. The Quebec National Assembly in turn unanimously approved a motion, introduced by the Charest government, celebrating the Commons resolution.

Clearly, the Harper government had found a dramatic way to break with the Trudeau vision of Quebec's place in Canada, incurring the bitter dissent of many of the vision's adherents. In the process, it had burnished its credentials as a "national unity" party of its own by blunting an initiative of the secessionist Bloc. Nonetheless, as formulated by the Harper Conservatives, the resolution bore a fundamental ambiguity about the nature of the Quebec nation. The original Bloc resolution had in its French-language version referred to "les Québécoises et les Québécois" forming a nation, using the term "Quebeckers" in the English-language version. The Harper resolution also referred to "les Québécoises et les Québécois" in French but in English referred to not "Quebeckers" but "Québécois," thus declaring that: "The Québécois form a nation."[59] Was the intent to limit the idea of a Quebec nation to just a part of the Quebec population: to French-speakers or even just to French-speakers of French-Canadian descent? In other words, was the Quebec nation to be defined ethnically rather than as a "civic" nation composed of all residents of Quebec, as had become the favoured formulation of Quebec's political leadership, federalist or sovereigntist?[60] As a result, the resolution constituted an incomplete, or at least highly ambiguous, recognition of the Quebec nation. In any event, as a mere resolution of the House of Commons it had little practical impact. It certainly fell far short of the constitutional recognition that Ignatieff had originally proposed. Nonetheless, whatever its shortcomings, the resolution served well the Harper Conservatives' purpose of repudiating the Trudeau legacy. Surprisingly perhaps, it generated relatively little public opposition.[61]

Despite these efforts to accommodate Quebec's "national" specificity, the 2008 election was a disappointment for the Harper Conservatives. They won only 10 seats in Quebec, the same number as in 2006; their share of the Quebec popular vote actually dropped from 24.6 per cent to 21.7 per cent. Apparently, the resistance of Quebec voters can best be explained by concerns other than Quebec's status within Canada: Quebeckers maintained quite distinctive preferences on public policy. On issues such as gun control, child care, the environment, and military intervention in Afghanistan, Quebeckers didn't share the positions held by the Harper government.[62] During the campaign itself, the Conservatives' proposals to strengthen sentences for young offenders apparently further alienated Quebeckers, as did the Harper government's close collaboration with the United States.[63] Moreover, the working relationship between the Harper government and Jean Charest's Quebec government had dissolved in 2007, when Charest decided to use the greatly enhanced equalization payments, resulting from the Harper government's "fiscal imbalance" initiative, to finance an income tax cut.[64] Nor did Tory fortunes in Quebec improve with the 2011 federal election: they lost five seats and their popular vote fell to 16.5 per cent. Nonetheless, thanks to gains elsewhere in the country, especially in Ontario, the Harper Conservatives won their first majority government. In the process, they demonstrated that, contrary to Harper's earlier assumption, Quebec was not at all essential to electoral victory.

With the failure of the Harper Conservatives' Quebec electoral strategy, there were no further efforts to accommodate Quebec's distinctiveness. Indeed, the Harper government's "open federalism" gave way to unilateral tendencies, as with announcement of the terms of future federal transfers to the provinces or attempts to secure Supreme Court confirmation of federal authority to reform the Canadian Senate and to establish a national securities commission. By the same token, the Harper government failed to follow through on its pledge for a legislative restriction on the use of the federal spending power. (In any event, a proposal it had drafted would have been judged inadequate by the Charest government.[65])

The NDP: Embracing Quebec's Specificity

With the assumption of the federal NDP's leadership by Jack Layton in 2005, the party set about embracing Quebec's distinctiveness much more openly. Born and raised in Quebec, Layton was personally committed to reversing the party's historical electoral weakness in the province.[66]

The new strategy was dramatically confirmed in 2005 with the adoption by the Quebec section of the NDP's General Council of a statement entitled "Québec's Voice and a Choice for a Different Canada" and subsequently known as the Sherbrooke Declaration. Underlining the necessity for the NDP to make electoral inroads in Quebec and denouncing the Liberal "lack of vision" that had led to the sponsorship scandal, the Declaration forthrightly declares that "fully understood and recognized, Quebec nationalism can be a strength for Canada, not a threat" and that "the national character of Quebec" can be recognized within

Canada. Indeed, "the NDP understands Canada's status as a 'multinational' country," with the consequent obligation to deal with "the realities of Quebec as with those of the Aboriginal communities."[67] In short, the Trudeau vision of Canada was fully rejected.

On this basis, the Sherbrooke Declaration reiterates the NDP's long-standing support for an asymmetrical federalism under which Quebec has the "specific powers and room for manoeuvring" that it needs to meet its distinctive challenges.[68] It laments the fact that the 1999 Social Union Framework Agreement did not have the signature of the Quebec government: "An agreement to which Québec does not consent is not at an agreement at all: it's a disagreement."[69] At the same time, it goes on to address the even more controversial question of Quebec's right to self-determination. Affirming that "the NDP recognizes Quebec's right to self-determination, which implies the right of the people of Quebec to decide freely its own political and constitutional future," the Declaration is careful to state that this right need not entail sovereignty: "the right to self-determination can be exercised within Canada."[70] Nonetheless, with respect to sovereignty the text addresses the "political" process by which it might be attained: "to legally formalize this process is not useful or necessary." With that, it effectively rejects the Clarity Act. Indeed, the Declaration directly contradicts the act by proclaiming outright that "the NDP would recognize a majority decision (50 per cent plus 1) of the Quebec people in the event of a referendum on the political status of Quebec." By the same token, recognizing the right of the Quebec National Assembly to set the referendum question, it stipulates that the federal government should respond to the results "in the spirit of the Supreme Court ruling [Quebec secession reference] and under international law."[71]

As would be expected, most public discussion of the Sherbrooke Declaration focused on its provisions regarding Quebec's accession to sovereignty. Not only were they widely denounced in English-speaking Canada but they provoked debate within the NDP itself. Roy Romanow publicly rejected the proposed threshold as insufficient and defended the Clarity Act as "a great act of political vision and courage and determination."[72] For that matter, back in 2000 most NDP MPs had voted in favour of the act, despite the request of the party's federal council that they oppose it.[73] Nor, in 2013, was there full support for an NDP MP's private member's bill, designed to replace the Clarity Act, that both reiterated the 50 per cent plus 1 threshold and sought to clarify the nature of a "clear question."[74] Nonetheless, the Sherbrooke Declaration, especially its commitment to Quebec self-determination, served to transform the NDP's image in Quebec.[75]

Reflecting the NDP's new priority on a Quebec electoral breakthrough, the Sherbrooke Declaration's open embrace of Quebec nationalism was reinforced by the allocation of greater resources to the party's Quebec operation and greater visibility in Quebec to leader Jack Layton, as well as by Layton's personal popularity there.[76] This effort was finally rewarded in 2011 with the stunning election of no less than 59 NDP candidates, and an equally remarkable Quebec popular vote of 43 per cent. The NDP's Quebec caucus had gone from a single member (Thomas Mulcair, who won a by-election in 2007) to constitute more than half of the 103-member NDP caucus. Facilitating this Orange Wave (*Vague orange*) was the surprising collapse of the Bloc québécois, a sovereigntist party created in 1991 under Lucien Bouchard, in the wake of the Meech Lake Accord's defeat. Entering the 2011 election with 47 seats, the Bloc lost all but four, and fell to 23.4 per cent of the popular vote. Clearly, the NDP, with its opening to Quebec, generated a public excitement that had long left the Bloc.[77] Despite this, however, the NDP was unable to sustain its breakthrough. In the 2015 federal election, it fell to only 16 seats in Quebec, with a popular vote of 25.4 per cent. In part, this result reflected the loss of Jack Layton, who was highly popular in Quebec but died shortly after the 2011 election. For its part, the Bloc won 10 seats but fell in popular vote (19.3 per cent).

The 2015 Federal Election

In 2015, it was the Liberals, led by new leader Justin Trudeau, who scored a breakthrough in Quebec, securing 40 seats and a popular vote of 35.7 per cent. The party had finally returned from an exile in political wilderness dating back to 2005 when backlash against the sponsorship scandal had reduced it to 13 seats—the Liberals hadn't secured more than 14 seats ever since. While it might be tempting to explain the Liberal success in terms of the national unity vision of the father, Pierre Elliott Trudeau, there is little evidence to support this. Justin Trudeau did not make this the theme of his campaign. Nor, as we have seen, is there evidence that Quebeckers had undergone a much belated conversion to that vision. More plausible is the notion that Liberal support, still limited to a third of Quebeckers, surged on the basis of antipathy to the Harper Conservatives, who had long ago ceased to appeal to Quebec's distinctiveness and whose policies in any event met with disfavour in Quebec. The Liberals could more credibly offer to replace the Harper Conservatives than could the NDP, which had never formed a federal government.

In sum, for one reason or another, during the first two post-referendum decades all three major federal parties openly broke with the Trudeau orthodoxy but failed in their attempts to put in place a new relationship between Quebec and the federal government. The Chrétien government's effort to constitutionalize Quebec's distinctiveness lacked credibility with provincial leaders and was soon displaced by a "Plan B" focus on the costs of Quebec sovereignty. The Martin government's forthright embrace of asymmetry was well received in Quebec but the scandals of its predecessor's sponsorship program, which the Martin government greatly publicized, served to alienate Quebeckers from the federal government, as well as the Liberal Party. The Harper government's deliberate appeal to

Quebec's distinctiveness never bore fruit given the dissonance between its policy agenda and Quebec's political culture. Finally, the NDP's opening to Quebec, well received as it was initially, was soon overwhelmed by the desire in Quebec, as well as the rest of the country, to defeat the Harper Conservatives by installing the most credible alternative—a rehabilitated Liberal Party. By the same token, as we shall now see, efforts by successive Quebec governments to install a new relationship between Quebec and the rest of the country also failed.

Lucien Bouchard: Waiting for "Winning Conditions"

In the immediate wake of the 1995 referendum, Jacques Parizeau resigned as Quebec premier, whether it was his original intention or his response to the widespread condemnation of his "money and the ethnic vote" explanation of the referendum defeat. As the new premier, Lucien Bouchard was charged with handling the affairs of the province while, at the same time, seeking to build the conditions for success ("winning conditions" in his words) in a new referendum.

As we have seen, Bouchard's own notion of Quebec sovereignty entailed a comprehensive partnership with the rest of Canada. Indeed, his conversion to the goal of sovereignty had come about with the unravelling of the Meech Lake Accord and, with it, the prospect of Quebec's recognition within the Canadian federation. During the referendum campaign he had been alarmed by Parizeau's intention to secure full sovereignty through a post-referendum unilateral declaration. Nonetheless, his notions of a Quebec–Canada partnership had little credibility, given their total rejection in the rest of Canada. Moreover, as leader of the sovereignty cause, Bouchard had to respond to initiatives of the Chrétien government that were squarely focused on the conditions of accession to full sovereignty. Premier Bouchard could welcome the result of Ottawa's reference to the Supreme Court on the legality of secession, given the Court's recognition of a constitutional obligation on the rest of Canada to enter into negotiations after a successful referendum. However, the Clarity Act was a different matter, implying as it did that, even with a referendum question that met Ottawa's approval, a 50 per cent plus 1 majority could be insufficient and that the boundaries of a sovereign Quebec could be up for negotiation. As we have seen, the Bouchard government responded with a measure of its own, upholding the right of Quebec to determine its future. Nonetheless, Quebec public opinion was not moved by the question to the extent that the Bouchard government had hoped. The Supreme Court judgement may itself have eased the Quebec public's concern to protect its right to self-determination.

At the same time, beyond protecting Quebec's ability to secure full independence, which was not his personal option in any event, Premier Bouchard had to go about managing the affairs of his province. In doing so, he was led to adopt initiatives that could only undercut public support for sovereignty and the very possibility of "winning conditions." In particular, he and his government became focused on consolidating the province's public finances. Yet the Bouchard government ran the risk of alienating the social democratic part of its constituency—public sector workers, citizens' groups, and other social forces still committed to state intervention—who would be critical to the success of any future referendum. Bouchard and his colleagues did manage to secure re-election in 1998; the Liberal campaign had been weakened by the failure of its new leader, former federal politician Jean Charest, to outline a plan for securing Quebec's recognition within the Canadian federal order. Nonetheless, after five years as premier, Bouchard was still unable to produce the conditions for success of a new referendum; he resigned in frustration. Nor was his successor, Bernard Landry, able to produce "winning conditions" during his short tenure before defeat by the Charest Liberals in March 2001.

Jean Charest Government: Giving Federalism a New Chance

Although he had built his political career in Ottawa and had become leader of the Progressive Conservatives, Jean Charest succumbed in 1998 to pressure from federalist leaders to assume leadership of the Quebec Liberal Party and to work from within Quebec to defeat the forces of Quebec sovereignty. Thus, when he finally won the premiership in 2003 Charest was confronted with the challenge of securing recognition of Quebec's distinctiveness within the federal order. As it happened, a blueprint for achieving that objective was already available thanks to a special Liberal Party committee, chaired by Liberal legislator Benoît Pelletier, which in 2001 had produced a report entitled *A Project for Quebec: Affirmation, Autonomy and Leadership*.[78] Moreover, Pelletier assumed the position of minister of Canadian intergovernmental affairs in the new Charest government. Forthrightly advocating federalism as the system within which Quebec can best achieve its objectives, the report calls for two orders of change: "a rediscovery of the true meaning of federalism" and formal constitutional change. The first order of change entails establishing a federalism that is based upon three pillars: asymmetry, collaboration, and balance.

The Charest government met with some success in each of the three pillars of a new federalism. In terms of asymmetry in federal–provincial relations, the Charest government had a willing partner in both the Martin and Harper governments. As we have seen, Paul Martin was not at all bound by the Trudeau orthodoxy and thus was quite prepared to embrace asymmetry as the formula for accommodating Quebec's distinctiveness. Several agreements were signed to that effect. In turn, the Harper government not only entered into asymmetrical agreements with Quebec on social policy but, meeting a specific recommendation of the Pelletier Report, afforded the Quebec government a presence within the Canadian delegation to UNESCO.[79] By the same token, in terms of the Pelletier Report's concern with "balance," the Harper government did respond to the Charest government's contention that it should eliminate the "fiscal imbalance" that affected Quebec and all the other provinces. Finally, with respect to intergovernmental collaboration, the Pelletier Report had proposed the creation of a council of the federation. The Council of the Federation was duly established in 2003 but fell far short of the Pelletier Report's proposal: the Council has no federal government participation, contains representation of the territories as well as the provinces, and makes decisions by consensus as opposed to any system of regional vetoes.[80]

Nonetheless, whatever success the Charest government had in pursuing the Pelletier Report's recommendations for recovering the "true meaning of federalism," there remained the report's second order of change: formal constitutional revision. Indeed the report made a large number of recommendations for constitutional change, centred on Quebec's distinctiveness and replicating the failed Meech Lake Accord: recognition of Quebec's specificity and the role of the National Assembly; provision of a Quebec veto; provincial nominations to the Supreme Court and guarantee of three justices from Quebec; restriction of the federal spending power; Senate reform; and constitutionalization of administrative agreements, including the current federal–provincial agreement on immigration.[81] Here, the Charest government made no headway whatsoever. Public opinion outside Quebec remained hostile to any renewal of constitutional discussions. Nor were the Martin or Harper governments prepared to enter into such an enterprise, however open they were to accommodating Quebec through ad hoc arrangements. Indeed, throughout his tenure in office Charest made little effort to press publicly the case for constitutional change, recognizing that conditions were not favourable.[82]

Pauline Marois Government

In the 2012 Quebec election, the Parti québécois regained power with a minority government led by Pauline Marois. However, while committed in principle to Quebec sovereignty the Marois government did little directly to advance the cause during its two-year tenure. Knowing that there was limited support from the Quebec public for sovereignty, or even for a new referendum, the PQ government instead concentrated on pursuing objectives within the existing political order, as a provincial government. Toward the end of its time in office it became focused, as we saw in Chapter 5, on its *Charter of Quebec Values*. Seeing this measure as a means to secure a majority government, the Marois government called an election for April 2014, so as to have a mandate to put its Charter in place. However, the strategy was upended by the Quebec public's continued aversion to a new referendum on sovereignty. The nomination of Pierre Karl Péladeau, leading Quebec businessman and lifelong secessionist, as a PQ candidate brought to the forefront the party's commitment to sovereignty, especially after Péladeau publicly confirmed his commitment to the cause. Thus, the election instead resulted in a massive PQ defeat and the formation of a Liberal majority government under Philippe Couillard.

In sum, over the two decades following the 1995 referendum, successive Quebec governments broke openly with the Trudeau vision of Canada but failed to put in place their own formulas for recognizing Quebec's distinctiveness. While the Charest government made progress in securing ad hoc arrangements with Ottawa, it deferred seeking constitutional accommodation of Quebec's distinctiveness. By the same token, two PQ governments were manifestly unable to overcome the Quebec public's resistance to even considering the alternative of Quebec independence.

Justin Trudeau Government: Avoiding the Question

One might have anticipated that upon his assumption of the prime ministership in November 2015, Justin Trudeau would have reaffirmed his father's vision of national unity. Yet in his election night address he made no mention of his father. Instead, he referred to another prime minister, also a Liberal Francophone from Quebec—Wilfrid Laurier—and embraced Laurier's notion of "sunny ways."[83] While in fact Laurier's own search for compromise and national unity may have led him to abandon the interests of Prairie Francophones,[84] the association with Laurier fitted well with Trudeau's effort to project his own vision of a new optimistic non-confrontational approach to public life geared to "bringing people of all different perspectives together."[85] At the same time, Justin Trudeau departed fully from his father's vision when it came to Indigenous Peoples, declaring that "a renewed nation-to-nation relationship . . . that respects rights and honours treaties must be the basis for how we work to close the gap and walk forward together."[86]

With respect to Quebec, however, Trudeau expressed no need for any national recognition or closing of a gap, although promising that collaboration with the provinces would be the first principle of his government's actions. Instead, he simply observed that "Quebec has truly returned to the Government of Canada" and told his fellow Quebeckers that "we have chosen to re-engage in the governance of a country that reflects our values and our ambitions."[87] For that matter, a few days later Trudeau declared explicitly that he saw no need to reopen the constitution "even to include Quebec." While recognizing that past constitutional developments had produced a sense of exclusion in Quebec, he insisted that it was not up to him to defend the actions of past prime ministers, including those of his father.[88]

In effect, Trudeau was seeking to transcend the confrontations over national unity that had dominated his father's public career. He would usher in a new "sunny ways" era based upon a more positive and hopeful vision of public life than that of his Conservative predecessor. In this, Trudeau had the advantage of his relative youthfulness; the transition to a new era of politics would be brought about by a new generation of political leaders who could themselves appeal to youthful voters.

Over its first two years in office, his government generally followed the "sunny ways" vision Justin Trudeau staked out on election night. Relations with Indigenous Peoples did indeed become a priority of the new government as it undertook to implement the recommendations of the Truth and Reconciliation Commission and establish nation-to-nation relationships with Indigenous Peoples, to invest in First Nations infrastructure, and to install an inquiry on murdered and missing Indigenous women and girls. In June 2016, the Trudeau government established a Federal, Provincial, Territorial, and Indigenous Forum.[89] Moreover, the federal government did engage more directly with the provinces, reinstating the first ministers' conferences that Stephen Harper had avoided. After intensive bargaining all but two provinces—Saskatchewan and Manitoba—agreed with Ottawa to a pan-Canadian climate-change strategy,[90] and all provinces but Manitoba signed on to a health care agreement.[91] To be sure, some premiers complained of federal "strong arming"; Ottawa forced recalcitrant provinces on board by first signing bilateral agreements with provinces that were more favourably disposed. But when it came to Quebec, the Justin Trudeau government respected the province's demand for asymmetry. In the case of health care, Quebec could claim that its agreement with Ottawa maintained the asymmetrical arrangements that had been established in 2004 with the Paul Martin government.[92] As to child care, where Quebec already had its own program in place, Ottawa undertook to provide transfers even though the province did not sign a multilateral agreement on a national child care program.[93] Still, with regard to the constitution, there was no serious discussion of formal constitutional change, whether it focused on Quebec or on any other question.

Philippe Couillard Government: Raising the Constitutional Issue, without Success

At the same time, Justin Trudeau's effort to escape the national unity struggles of the past was greatly aided by the fact that the Quebec government, which had been at the centre of those debates, was not itself raising the national question. Premier Couillard made it clear early in his mandate that Quebec's adhesion to the constitution was not a priority, even if it might be desirable as part of Canada's 150th anniversary celebrations in 2017.[94] Nor, during the first three years of its time in office, did the Couillard government take any major initiative on that front, whether to produce a document outlining a federalist vision of Quebec's place in Canada, comparable to the Pelletier Report of the Charest government or the Beige Paper of Claude Ryan's Liberal leadership, or to call for an expansion of Quebec's autonomy, as with Robert Bourassa's notion of "cultural sovereignty." Indeed, the Couillard government was the first federalist government since the Godbout administration of the early 1940s not to advocate a distinctive vision of Quebec's role in the federal order.

Nonetheless, in June of 2017 the Couillard government finally did issue a comprehensive vision of Quebec's place in Canada, close to 200 pages in length, entitled *Quebecers: Our Way of Being Canadian. A Policy for Quebec's Affirmation and for Canadian Relations*.[95] The report presents Quebec as the primary, indeed "national" identity of Quebeckers while insisting that in fact most Quebeckers also identify with Canada.[96] While arguing that Quebeckers have played a central role in the creation and development of Canada, the document traces Quebeckers' historical struggle for autonomous political institutions and the more recent emergence of a distinct Quebec identity. On this basis, the 1982 patriation over Quebec's dissent is presented as a denial of Quebec's historical place in Canada, leading Quebeckers to see themselves as "exiles within their own country."[97]

In terms of constitutional change, the document evokes the Meech Lake Accord, as did the Pelletier Report.[98] Indeed, it details each of five key elements of the Meech Lake Accord and tries to show how, during the post-referendum years, they already have been recognized by the federal Parliament or the Supreme Court or federal–provincial agreements.[99] Nor does it evoke any other constitutional changes. However, it does go beyond Meech (and the Pelletier Report) by referring to Quebec not just as a "distinct society" but as a "nation"—a term that is even more problematic to Canadians outside Quebec. Moreover, the text explains that the Quebec nation is not restricted just to Francophones but includes all residents of Quebec including Anglophones and First Nations.[100] By the same token, it insists that the Canadian federation has always been plurinational and was formed as a pact between two founding peoples, recognizing that Indigenous Peoples must be seen as a third partner.[101] While the document is resolutely federalist—'The Government of Québec considers that federalism is still the most suitable political system for Canada's situation'[102]—there could not be a clearer repudiation of Pierre Trudeau's conception of Canada and the Canadian federation.

In presenting the report, Couillard and his intergovernmental affairs minister tried to avoid any replication of the bitter debate surrounding Meech. The proposals were being offered to the rest of Canada not as an ultimatum but as an invitation to dialogue. There would be no "knife to the throat," to cite a famous phrase from the Meech debates. Moreover, this dialogue with Canada outside Quebec would be very broadly based to include not just the federal, provincial, and territorial governments but Indigenous Peoples, Francophones outside Quebec, and civil society. Indeed, it would entail a dialogue and rapprochement among citizens. Initiated by this "affirmation of Quebec and proactive Canadian relations," discussion would turn to the constitution only when a consensus had been created. Constitutional change "should be seen as the end-point rather than the starting-point of the dialogue."[103]

Nonetheless, confronted for the first time as prime minister by nationalist proposals from a federalist Quebec government, Prime Minister Justin Trudeau wasted no time rejecting them out of hand. Even before the document had been released, he simply declared "We are not opening the constitution."[104] Couillard was left to state that "Canada constitutes more than the person occupying the Canadian prime ministership" and to suggest that the document at least be read.[105] A few days later, Trudeau expanded on his initial comment. Without confirming whether he had in fact read the document, Trudeau declared that Canadians, including Quebeckers, have other priorities—economic growth, job creation, stabilization of pensions, and the environment—from which constitutional debate would be a distraction.[106] The new Conservative leader, Andrew Scheer, echoed Trudeau's sentiment. At the federal level, only the NDP leader, Tom Mulcair, welcomed the Couillard initiative.[107]

Trudeau's dismissive comments accorded well with general reaction outside Quebec. None of the provincial governments expressed interest in opening the discussion, except for Saskatchewan premier Brad Wall who saw an opportunity to attack Canada's equalization system and its excessive payments to Quebec.[108] More generally, media commentary dismissed the idea of renewing discussion of Quebec's place in Canada, evoking the long and bitter debate around the Meech Lake Accord and contending that it would necessarily lead to discussion of a host of other questions.[109] The Quebec question was only one of many outstanding issues and could not be addressed in isolation. The primary exception to this reaction was among some Indigenous leaders who saw the opening of constitutional discussions as an opportunity to pursue their own agenda. Indeed, the Couillard document declares a readiness of the Quebec government to work with Indigenous leaders to secure national recognition of both Quebec and First Nations.[110]

In issuing such a document after more than three years of relative silence, the Couillard government may have been concerned primarily with public opinion within Quebec itself, seeking to demonstrate its credentials as defender of Quebec's interests or to embarrass its federalist adversary, the Coalition avenir Québec. But to the extent the government was seeking to engage opinion outside Quebec, it had limited chance of success. While some Indigenous leaders saw an opportunity, most Anglophone Canadians saw no reason to enter into a new round of constitutional debate, with all its challenges and risk of failure, precisely because there was no longer a "knife to the throat": support for Quebec independence had dropped substantially.

Support for Quebec Independence: At a Low Ebb

As we have seen, the post-referendum years saw a steady decline among Quebeckers in support for independence, as well as for its standard-bearer the Parti québécois. Indeed, as of January 2017, only 33 per cent of Quebeckers stated that they would vote Yes in a referendum on sovereignty; 67 per cent declared that they would vote No.[111] Yet, as we have also seen, throughout these years Quebeckers continued to identify primarily with Quebec, as opposed to Canada as a whole. Thus, the weakness of support for independence cannot be explained in terms of any belated success of the Trudeau national unity strategy: Quebeckers remained largely impervious to the Trudeau vision of the country.

Quebeckers' persistent rejection of independence can be better explained in terms other than any primary attachment to Canada. First, there was the experience of the 1995 referendum itself. Profoundly divisive within Quebec society, it clearly provoked an enduring aversion among Quebeckers to repeating such a painful experience. In a 2014 survey, 64 per cent of Quebeckers opposed a new referendum on Quebec sovereignty.[112]

Second, the post-referendum years have seen less of the confrontation between Ottawa and the Quebec government that marked earlier decades, as with Pierre Trudeau's attacks on not just the Lévesque government but on the federalist Bourassa government's positions on language policy, the division of powers, and the terms of constitutional renewal. While during the late 1990s, there were marked tensions between the Chrétien government and the PQ government of Lucien Bouchard, the following years were relatively harmonious, exception made for the short-lived Marois premiership. Both the Martin and Harper governments made major efforts to come to terms with Quebec.[113] The Charest government, fully committed to federalism, was a generally willing partner. By the same token, neither the Charest government nor, during its first three years in office, the Couillard government pressed the case for securing Quebec's signature to the constitution, thus avoiding any backlash in English-speaking Canada. In short, there was less reason for Quebeckers to rally around "their" government and to see independence as necessary to protect the collective interests of their province.

Finally, the decline in the number of Quebeckers committed to independence can be understood in terms of a transition between political generations. The cause of Quebec independence had been the project of the particular generation of Quebeckers that entered political life in the 1960s and 1970s and saw Quebec independence as the logical next step in the general processes of secularization, public sector expansion, and affirmation of the French language that had marked those years. With the collapse of Meech, and the deep anger that induced among Quebec Francophones, support for independence may have spread more broadly among Quebeckers. But it remained the project of a core "political generation."

In the post-referendum decades, that generation became less central to Quebec's political life.

Quebeckers who entered political life in the years after the 1995 referendum faced a very different social and political reality than their elders had faced upon their entry into politics. The conditions of the 1960s and 1970s which had led the earlier generation to embrace independence with such enthusiasm were no longer present. The upper levels of the Quebec economy were no longer dominated by the English language, and by Anglophones, thanks to the expansion of public enterprises linked to the Quebec state, such as Hydro-Québec, and the emergence of Francophone-controlled and -managed private corporations, fostered by the Quebec government. A complex of fully secular institutions had assumed responsibility for education, health, and social services, thanks to the reforms of the Quiet Revolution. In the process, the historical inferiority of Francophone to Anglophone incomes in Quebec had been eliminated.[114] The French language had been enshrined as Quebec's sole official language, thanks to Bill 22 and Bill 101, and immigrants to Quebec were obliged to send their children to French-language schools, thanks to Bill 101.

Thus, Quebec independence would not have had the same meaning for young Quebeckers that it did for their elders. The social and economic conditions which had favoured independence had been largely eliminated. Moreover, with the rise of neo-liberalism in Quebec as elsewhere, the role of the Quebec government was put in question.[115] Without the promise of an active, interventionist state, independence itself could have had less appeal. Thus, while as likely as their elders to identify first and foremost with Quebec, the post-referendum generation does not do so with the same intensity.[116] In addition, as youth, its members may hold more leftist social views than do members of the older generation and, reflecting Quebec's changed demographic composition, may be more attuned to social diversity.[117] In short, the post-referendum generation of Quebeckers has its own political world view, reflective of its distinctive experience. Quebec independence, and the national question, are not front and centre. Thus, studies show that support for independence is substantially lower within the generation of Quebec Francophones who came of political age during the 1990s and 2000s.[118]

Even among the older generation of Quebec Francophones, the bearers of the cause of independence, support for the project may have been attenuated by the easing of the social and economic conditions that drew them to independence in the first place. As well, dissatisfaction with the Parti québécois's actions in power, such as the Bouchard government's focus on reducing public spending, may also have induced disenchantment with the cause.[119]

The phenomenon of political generations is also clearly evident in the fate of independence's historical vehicle itself, the Parti québécois. Political scientist Vincent Lemieux has demonstrated that the Parti québécois is one of a series of generational parties that have marked Quebec's political history. Born of dissatisfaction with the government party in place and offering a new direction, these generational parties draw, in particular, upon young voters. Over a period of 30 to 40 years, they pass through maturity and then decline.[120] Thus, the Parti québécois, formed in 1968, reached its highest popular vote in 1981 and has been in steady decline ever since.[121] In particular, it has had growing difficulty recruiting younger voters. A 2017 internal study of the PQ concluded that the party has become "a party that is frozen, conservative and aging, looking like a 'social club'."[122] It also found that Quebec youth have no interest in the issue of religious symbols, the focus of the Marois government's *Charter of Quebec Values*. Indeed, in February 2017, the PQ's national youth committee rejected outright the notion of banning religious symbols among public sector employees.[123]

The PQ's attempts to correct its long-term decline have, if anything, served to accelerate the decline. After the PQ's 2014 defeat, due in large part to Pierre Karl Péladeau's introduction of the Quebec independence issue into the campaign, Péladeau succeeded Marois as PQ leader. However, PQ support continued to decline and, in May 2016, Péladeau resigned the leadership. His successor, long-time PQ official and strategist Jean-François Lisée, declared that should a PQ government be elected under his leadership it would defer any referendum on sovereignty to a second term in office. In effect, even with a PQ return to power the referendum would be put off until at least 2023. There could not be a clearer recognition that the Parti québécois, the historical vehicle of Quebec sovereignty, is unable to mobilize Quebeckers around independence. At the same time, by forgoing any possibility over the short term of a new referendum on Quebec independence the PQ also freed Quebec politics from its historical division between indépendantiste and federalist parties. This has allowed the Coalition avenir Québec (CAQ) to emerge as a compelling alternative to the Quebec Liberal Party and take first place among Quebec parties in pre-election surveys. The PQ can no longer assume that disaffection with the Couillard government will necessarily be to its benefit and lead to the PQ's inevitable return to power.[124]

For that matter, the Parti québécois has been challenged in its historical role of the essential party of Quebec independence. The Option nationale, founded in 2011, articulated a more resolute commitment to sovereignty but was unable to win a seat in either 2012 or 2014. However, Québec solidaire, founded in 2006, won three seats and 7.6 per cent of the popular vote in 2014. It combines sovereignty with both a commitment to social justice and a resolutely pluralist vision of Quebec society. At a May 2017 Québec solidaire conference, delegates rejected a proposal to collaborate with the Parti québécois in the 2018 provincial election, with some accusing the PQ of xenophobia and racism.[125] Among Quebec's political generations, the youngest one provides the greatest support for these two parties—and the least for the PQ.[126] In May of 2017, a leader of the 2012 student mobilization against the Charest government, Gabriel Nadeau-Dubois, was elected to a senior position in Québec solidaire and to a seat in the Quebec National Assembly. His political ascension, and a concomitant surge in support for Québec solidaire,[127] raises the possibility that a new vision of Quebec sovereignty, based squarely on progressive reform and an inclusive nationalism, might take hold among young Quebeckers and might even be the basis of a new political generation. In December 2017, Option nationale was merged with Québec solidaire, reinforcing the latter's status as an indépendantiste alternative to the PQ. Among Quebeckers, support for the PQ fell steadily over the fall of 2017, reaching 20 per cent in December of that year (23 per cent among Francophones) and placing it third among Quebec's parties. In December, support for Québec solidaire stood at 12 per cent (among all Quebeckers and among Francophones alone).[128]

The decline of the independence movement has had an even more dramatic impact on the PQ's counterpart at the federal level: the Bloc québécois has lost its primary raison d'être of promoting Quebec independence. Gone are the glory days of the 1993 federal election when, under leader Lucien Bouchard, it won 54 seats and became the House of Commons' Official Opposition. The Bloc did recover briefly in the wake of the sponsorship scandal, returning to 54 seats in 2004, but since then its standing has fallen significantly with each election. In the 2011 election, which gave the NDP its breakthrough in Quebec, the Bloc won only four seats—leader Gilles Duceppe even lost his own seat. In the 2015 election, the party secured 10 seats but recorded its lowest popular vote ever: 19.3 per cent of the Quebec vote. By December 2017, according to a survey, support for the Bloc had fallen to only 18 per cent of Quebeckers; the Justin Trudeau Liberals stood at 47 per cent.[129]

In sum, a complex of factors can best explain the post-referendum decline in support for Quebec independence and, in particular, its relative inability to mobilize young Quebeckers. The Parti québécois and the Bloc québécois are both testimony to the descent of the independence cause. But if Quebeckers have resisted the goal of independence, so too have they resisted the appeal to switch their primary identity from Quebec to Canada as a whole, as the Trudeau national unity strategy had been designed to achieve. Yet the very success of that national unity strategy outside Quebec, institutionalizing a conception of Canada that allowed no place for Quebec's distinctiveness, effectively undermined the efforts of federal governments, under Paul Martin and Stephen Harper, to implement a new vision of Quebec's place in Canada just as it prevented the Charest government from seeking constitutional recognition of such a vision. The short shrift that public opinion outside Quebec gave to the Coulliard government's belated initiative confirms that whatever opportunities for reconciliation might have existed before the 1995 referendum have been foreclosed.

Notes

1. François Rocher and Benoît Pelletier, eds., *Le nouvel ordre constitutionnel canadien: du rapatriement de 1982 à nos jours* (Quebec: Presses de l'Université du Québec, 2013), Table 8A.17. See also Éric Bélanger and Chris Chhim, "National Identity and Support for Sovereignty in Quebec," in *Quebec Questions: Quebec Studies for the Twenty-First Century*, ed. Stéphan Gervais, Christopher Kirkey, and Jarrett Rudy (Don Mills: Oxford University Press, 2016), 334.
2. In the country as a whole, including Quebec, 62 per cent of Canadians were in agreement (Angus Reid Institute, "What Makes Us Canadians? A Study of Values, Beliefs, Priorities and Identity," 3 Oct. 2016, 5). Recent survey analyses confirm the same pattern for young Quebeckers. A 2014 study found that 56 per cent of "Generation Y" Quebeckers identified primarily with Quebec. (Valérie-Anne Mahéo and Éric Bélanger, "Is the Parti Québécois Bound to Disappear? A Study of the Generational Dynamics of Electoral Behaviour in Contemporary Quebec," paper presented at a conference on "The State of Democratic Citizenship in Canada," Centre for the Study of Democratic Citizenship, Montreal, Sept. 23–24, 2016 and Annual Meeting of the American Political Science Association, Philadelphia, Sept. 1–4, 2016, Table 1. See also the discussion of the study in Alain Nöel, "The Land Where We First Loved," *Policy Options*, 7 Oct. 2016.) Indeed, youth are more likely (66 per cent) than older Quebeckers (55 per cent) to declare that they are "above all Québécois," according to a 2015 study (Alec Castonguay, "L'attachement au Canada grimpe ches les jeunes," *Le Devoir*, 23 Nov. 2014). At the same time, Quebec youth may be more likely to profess a secondary attachment to Canada, now that they are no longer as pressured by Ottawa to identify with Canada as a whole. Whereas in the 2015 study 79 per cent of young Quebeckers agreed that being Canadian was part of their identity, in a 1992 survey only 66 per cent of young Quebeckers had been in agreement (ibid.). In 2014, 68 per cent of Quebec youth agreed that being Canadian was part of their identity (Katia Gagnon, "Les jeunes et la souveraineté: la génération 'Non'," *La Presse*, 2 June 2014). Finally, young Quebeckers may be less intense in general in their attachments: the Mahéo/Bélanger study found that young Quebeckers were much less likely than older Quebeckers to adopt the strongest option: "very attached to Quebec," however they were also less likely to see themselves as "very attached to Canada" (Nöel, "The Land Where We First Loved").
3. A similar pattern appears in a 2017 study comparing respondents in Quebec and Ontario. In particular, 73 per cent of Ontarians declared that they were strongly attached to Canada whereas only 38 per cent of Quebeckers did so. 58 per cent of Quebeckers declared that they were strongly attached to their province, but only 41 per cent of Ontarians stated the same. (Andrew Parkin, Erich Hartmann, and Kiran Alwani, *Portraits 2017: A Fresh Look at Public Opinion and Federalism* [Toronto: Mowat Centre, 2017], 9.)
4. See Simon Langlois, "L'appui à la souveraineté du Québec de 1995 à aujourd'hui," *Colloque sur la démocratie référendaire*, Université Laval, 30 Oct. 2015; and Simon Langlois, "L'appui à l'indépendance du Québec en déclin," *Regards sur la société*, 17 Nov. 2015. See also Bélanger and Chhim, "National Identity and Support for Sovereignty," 341.
5. Angus Reid, "What Makes Us Canadian?" 7.
6. Eddie Goldenberg, *The Way It Works: Inside Ottawa* (Toronto: McClelland & Stewart, 2006), 222. According to Chantal Hébert, Harris was also concerned about anti-French sentiments within his party's electoral base and the possibility that Reform might capitalize on them. For that matter, Chrétien had not consulted Harris before making his Verdun speech commitments. (See Hébert, *The Morning After*, Chap. 14.)
7. House of Commons, *Journals*, 1st session, 35th Parliament, no. 273, 11 Dec. 1995, 2232.
8. Under the Meech Lake Accord, as well as Charlottetown, recognition of Quebec's distinctiveness had involved a clause guiding the courts' interpretation of the constitution. The requirement that the federal

government should take account of Quebec's distinctiveness in its own activities is quite a different matter. Apparently, there is no evidence that subsequent federal governments have taken this resolution into account.

9. "In Canada's federal system, where respect for diversity and equality underlies unity, the unique character of Quebec society, including its French speaking majority, its culture and its tradition of civil law, is fundamental to the well being of Canada. Consequently, the legislature and Government of Quebec have a role to protect and develop the unique character of Quebec society within Canada." ("The Calgary Declaration," Ted Glenn, Research Officer Ontario Legislative Library Legislative Research Service). The text stipulated that should constitutional amendment grant additional powers to a province, the same powers must be afforded to all provinces. Both the Parliamentary resolution and the Calgary Declaration are discussed in Russell, *Constitutional Odyssey*, 238.
10. An Act Respecting Constitutional Amendments, *Statutes of Canada 1996*, 1st session, 35th Parliament, Bill C-110.
11. At the same time, some experts have argued that the measure is itself unconstitutional, since it has the effect of altering the operation of the amending formula from its original authors' intentions (F.L. Morton, "Why Chretien's Proposal Won't Wash in the West," *Globe and Mail*, 30 Nov. 1995). In any event, the matter remains moot since no federal government has actually introduced a constitutional amendment to the House. See the discussion of this measure in Russell, *Constitutional Odyssey*, 238–9.
12. Stéphane Dion, "The Constitution Must Recognize Quebec's 'Special Distinction'," *Globe and Mail*, 26 Jan. 1996.
13. In a March 1996 survey, 55 per cent of respondents outside Quebec opposed constitutional recognition of Quebec as a "distinct society"; 43 per cent were in favour. See Hugh Winsor, "Quebeckers Prefer Canada 2–1, Poll Says," *Globe and Mail*, 26 Mar. 1996.
14. Chantal Hébert notes that in the post-referendum period public opinion would have opposed any attempt by Romanow "to give Chrétien more wiggle room than [Preston] Manning" did (Hébert, *The Morning After*, 197). At a conference in June 1996, the first ministers' collective inability or unreadiness to address the constitutional question led to almost farcical behaviour. The prime minister believed that he and the premiers were bound by a constitutional obligation to discuss the functioning of the amending formula adopted in 1982. Even though Premier Bouchard absented himself from this part of the proceedings, it was over in a matter of seconds. Indeed, there was some confusion as to whether it had even take place (Michel Venne, "Chrétien se libère de l'échéance de 1997," *Le Devoir*, 23 June 1996). Such was the determination to avoid the constitutional question, however urgent it may have seemed in Quebec to do so. In vain had Quebec Liberal leader Daniel Johnson gone to Ottawa to persuade the English-Canadian premiers to frame a constitutional response to Quebec.
15. Prime Minister's Office, "Speech from the Throne: 27 Feb. 1996."
16. This measure is in fact stronger than the spending-power provision of the Meech Lake Accord.
17. The speech listed "such areas as labour market training, forestry, mining, and recreation." (Prime Minister's Office, "Speech from the Throne: 27 Feb. 1996.") In late May, the Chrétien government detailed its proposal for job training. Calling its scheme one of "partnership," it offered to withdraw from job training within a maximum of three years while making funds available to the provincial governments for them to assume the responsibility. The federal government would negotiate the terms with each province and enter into bilateral agreements with the provinces. Bouchard called the move a "step in the right direction" and gave his government credit for helping to produce it. ("Chrétien fait des ouvertures," *Le Devoir*, 31 May 1996.) On the other hand, according to Eddie Goldenberg, the transfer was vehemently opposed by Liberal Ontario MPs who valued announcing training grants to their electors. Negotiations moved quickly with Quebec but, in deference to the Ontario MPs, dragged on for years with the Ontario government. (Goldenberg, *The Way It Works*, 137–8.)

18. "focussing on such priorities as food inspection, environmental management, social housing, tourism, and freshwater fish habitat" (Prime Minister's Office, "Speech from the Throne: 27 Feb. 1996").
19. Alain Nöel, *Asymmetry at Work: Quebec's Distinct Implementation of Programs for the Unemployed* (Toronto: Mowat Centre for Policy Innovation, 2011), 4 and 10.
20. Ibid., 8.
21. Apparently, this constituted the third element, along with providing good government and transferring certain powers to the provinces, of a strategy developed by a national unity cabinet committee headed by Marcel Massé (Goldenberg, *The Way It Works*, 237–8).
22. Jean Dion, "Un bureau d'information vantera les vertus du Canada," *Le Devoir*, 10 July 1996.
23. Hugh Winsor, "Ottawa Caught Short by Flag Fever," *Globe and Mail*, 29 Aug. 1996. On the resistance of Quebeckers to a "flag war" see Chantal Hébert, *The Morning After*, 111.
24. For his part, Goldenberg sees this damage as the result of the Gomery Report's "incendiary language" and media sensationalism. He contends that the instances of fraud were made possible by erroneously assigning the role of political minister for Quebec to the minister of public works (Goldenberg, *The Way It Works*, 238–41).
25. *The Canadian Social Union without Quebec: Eight Critical Analyses* (Montreal: Institute for Research on Public Policy, 2000), 1.
26. Peter Graefe and Rachel Laforest, "La grande séduction: Wooing Quebec," in *How Ottawa Spends, 2007–8: The Harper Conservatives: Climate of Change*," ed. G. Bruce Doern (Montreal and Kingston: McGill-Queen's University Press, 2007), 51.
27. Health Canada, "Health Care System: Asymmetrical Federalism that respects Quebec's Jurisdiction," 15 Sept. 2004. The agreement is discussed in F. Leslie Seidle and Gina Bishop, "Public Opinion on Asymmetrical Federalism: Growing Openness or Continuing Ambiguity?" Asymmetry Series 2005, Institute of Intergovernmental Relations, Queen's University. Nonetheless, following a growing trend in intergovernmental relations, the agreement was never signed. It was simply announced separately by each of the two parties. In this case, Ottawa was able to avoid a formal commitment to this new, and controversial, embrace of asymmetry. (Alain Nöel, "Déblocages?" *Options politiques*, Nov. 2004, 48).
28. Nöel, *Asymmetry at Work*, 5.
29. Moreover, as political scientists François Rocher and Philippe Cousineau-Morin note, the programs in question fall in areas that reflect federal objectives and are the subject of arrangements with all the provinces (François Rocher and Philippe Cousineau-Morin, "Fédéralisme asymétrique et reconnaissance des nations internes au Canada," in Michel Seymour and Guy Laforest, *Le fédéralisme multinational: un modèle viable?* [Brussels: Peter Lang, 2011], 290).
30. Together, the labour market agreement of 1999, which the Harper government renewed in 2009, the 2005 parental insurance agreement, the 1998 National Child Benefit and the Harper government's adaptations of the federal Working Income Tax Benefit resulted in a significant degree of asymmetry that allowed the Quebec government to develop its own distinctive approach to labour market and income support (Nöel, *Asymmetry at Work*, 2).
31. Allan Gregg, "Quebec's Final Victory," *The Walrus*, Feb. 2005, 50–61. Nöel documents how "many scholars outside Quebec" were fearful of the loss of national standards and accountability that came with this new flexibility (Nöel, *Asymmetry at Work*, 6).
32. Commission of Inquiry into the Sponsorship Program and Advertising Activities, *Who is Responsible? Fact Finding Report*, 1 Nov. 2005, Major Findings, 6.
33. Ibid., 6.
34. Ibid., 286. See CBC News Online, "Gomery Report: Liberals' Worst Fears," 1 Nov. 2005, and Stephen Azzi, "Commission of Inquiry into the Sponsorship Program and Advertising Agencies," *Canadian Encyclopedia*, 3 July 2014.
35. In 2004, the Liberal percentage of Quebec votes fell from 44.2 per cent in 2000 to 28 per cent, largely due to the sponsorship scandal.
36. Nonetheless, in 2006 the Liberal percentage of votes in Quebec remained stable at 28.1 per cent.

37. As quoted in Donald G. Lenihan, "Reconstituting the 'Nation': What Ignatieff Really Needs to Recognize about Quebec," *Options*, Nov. 2006.
38. Sean Gordon, "Sounding Like his Father, Justin Trudeau Takes Aim at Michael Ignatieff's Idea of Quebec as a 'Nation'," *Toronto Star*, 27 Oct. 2006. Jean Chrétien also opposed the proposal (ibid.).
39. Claire L'Heureux-Dubé, "Débat au Parti libéral – Le Québec nation? Il y a, c'est certain, une meilleure avenue!" *Le Devoir*, 13 Nov. 2006.
40. Sujit Choudhri, "Bills of Rights as Instruments of Nation Building," in *Contested Constitutionalism*, ed. James B. Kelly and Christopher P. Manfredi (Vancouver: UBC Press, 2009), 234, and Juliet O'Neill, "Author of Grit Quebec Nation Resolution Victim of Good Intention," *CanWest News*, 9 Nov. 2006.
41. Joan Bryden, "Ignatieff Rules Out Quebec Nation in Constitution," *Canadian Press*, 18 Dec. 2008.
42. William Johnson, *Stephen Harper and the Future of Canada* (Toronto: McClelland & Stewart, 2007), 20.
43. John Ibbitson, *Stephen Harper* (Toronto: McClelland & Stewart, 2015), 125. In 1987, Harper was also very critical of the Mulroney revision of the Official Languages Act, contending that it went even further in promoting the two official languages than had Trudeau himself (Johnson, *Stephen Harper*, 96).
44. Stephen Harper et al., "The Alberta Agenda," *Policy Options*, http://policyoptions.irpp.org/magazines/western-alienation/the-alberta-agenda.
45. See Johnson, *Stephen Harper*, Chap. 3. On Harper's 1996 bill, C-341, Johnson contends that it went much further than the Clarity Act and was superior for that reason (ibid., 254–7 and 276–8).
46. See Christopher Dunn "Harper without Jeers, Trudeau without Cheers: Assessing 10 Years of Intergovernmental Relations," Institute of Research on Public Policy, *Insight*, Sept. 2016, no. 8, 3.
47. "un fédéralisme dominateur, un fédéralisme paternaliste, qui est une menace sérieuse pour l'avenir de notre fédération" (Conservative Party, "Harper annonce le programme conservateur pour le Québec," 19 Dec. 2005).
48. Ibbitson, *Stephen Harper*, 199.
49. "Nous reconnaîtrons . . . des responsabilités culturelles et institutionnelles spéciales du gouvernement du Québec" (Conservative Party, "Harper annonce le programme conservateur pour le Québec," 19 Dec. 2005).
50. Éric Montpetit, *Le fédéralisme d'ouverture: la recherche d'une légitimité canadienne au Québec* (Quebec: Septentrion, 2007) and Réjean Pelletier, "Les relations fédérales-provinciales sous le gouvernement Harper," in *Le fédéralisme selon Harper: la place du Québec dans le Canada conservateur*, ed. Julian Castro-Rea and Frédéric Boily (Quebec: Presses de l'Université Laval, 2014), 135.
51. Hubert Rioux Ouimet, "Quebec and Canadian Fiscal Federalism: From Tremblay to Séguin and Beyond," *Canadian Journal of Political Science* 47, no. 1 [Mar. 2014]: 47–69.
52. Alain Nöel, "Balance and Imbalance in the Division of Financial Resources," in *Contemporary Canadian Federalism: Foundations, Traditions, Institutions*, ed. Alain-G. Gagnon (Toronto: University of Toronto Press, 2009), 292–3.
53. See Dunn, "Harper without Jeers," 4–5, and Pelletier, "Les relations fédérales-provinciales sous le gouvernement Harper," 135. Nöel points out that, focused upon transfers, the Harper reforms failed to address the underlying fiscal gap between the federal and provincial governments (Nöel, "Balance and Imbalance," 294).
54. "Lobbyist" is Réjean Pelletier's term (Pelletier, "Relations fédérales-provinciales sous le gouvernement Harper," 124); others refer to a "foldaway seat" (Jean-François Caron and Guy Laforest, "Canada and Multinational Federalism: From the Spirit of 1982 to Stephen Harper's Open Federalism," *Nationalism and Ethnic Politics* 15 [2009]: 48).
55. See the discussions in Pelletier, "Relations fédérales-provinciales sous le gouvernement Harper," 124–5, and Rocher and Morin, "Fédéralisme asymétrique et reconnaissance des nations internes au Canada," 292.
56. David McGrane, "One-Off Federalism" in *How Ottawa Spends: 2013–2014*, ed. Christopher Stoney and G. Bruce Doern (Montreal and Kingston: McGill-Queen's University Press, 2013).

57. McGrane contends that the provincial governments themselves tended to accept this distinctive treatment of Quebec (ibid., 121).
58. John Ibbitson argues that Harper would never have supported such a resolution in his Reform Party days but was acting partly on "political calculation." Harper's insistence that all caucus members give their accord led to the resignation of his intergovernmental affairs minister, Michael Chong, who abstained from voting (Ibbitson, *Stephen Harper*, 248–51).
59. "That this House recognize that the Québécois form a nation within a united Canada." / "Que cette Chambre reconnaisse que les Québécoises et les Québécois forment une nation au sein d'un Canada uni." House of Commons, *Official Report (Hansard)*, 24 Nov. 2006, 39th Parliament, 1st Session, Volume 141, Number 086.
60. See the discussions in Richard Fidler, "A Québécois Nation: Harper Fuels an Important Debate," *The Bullet: Socialist Project*, E-bulletin no. 40, 18 Dec. 2006, and Guy Laforest, "Stephen Harper, Michael Ignatieff and the Recognition That (Québec-the Québécois-Quebeckers) Form a Nation/Within a United Canada," paper presented to Canadian Political Science Association, 31 May–2 June 2016, 16–24.
61. David Cameron contends that in recognizing Quebec as a nation, the resolution "went further than granting special status to Quebec or recognizing it as a distinct society" and that the lack of public reaction to it confirmed that post-referendum Canada had returned to "normal politics" (David Cameron, "Quebec and the Canadian Federation," in *Canadian Federalism: Performance, Effectiveness and Legitimacy*, ed. Herman Bakvis and Grace Skogstad [Don Mills: Oxford University Press, 2012], 52).
62. Graefe and Laforest, "La grande séduction," 55–6.
63. Graefe and Laforest note that the close relationship between the Harper government and the George H.W. Bush administration was unpopular in Quebec (ibid., 56).
64. According to John Ibbitson , the Harper–Charest relationship "chilled instantly. Neither would lend a hand to help the other in elections to come, which didn't help Tory ambitions in Quebec." (Ibbitson, *Stephen Harper*, 266.)
65. Pelletier, "Relations fédérales-provinciales," 127. Rather than seeking to accommodate Quebec's specificity further, the Harper government undertook a series of unilateral measures which, in some cases, were strongly opposed by Quebec (ibid., 125–30).
66. Lynda Erickson and David Laycock, "The NDP and Quebec" in *Reviving Social Democracy: The Near Death and Surprising Rise of the Federal NDP*, ed. David Laycock and Lynda Erickson (Vancouver: UBC Press, 2015), 68.
67. Quebec Section of the NDP General Council, "Québec's Voice and a Choice for a Different Canada," 2005, 1–2.
68. Ibid., 5.
69. Ibid., 6.
70. Ibid., 7.
71. Ibid., 8.
72. Joan Bryden, "Roy Romanow on 'Unity Bill': 50-Plus-One Not Sufficient to Break Up Country," *Canadian Press*, 4 Apr. 2014.
73. Erickson and Laycock, "The NDP and Quebec," 69.
74. Introduced by MP Craig Scott, the bill was framed in terms of "constitutional change" as opposed to Quebec sovereignty per se. It called for the federal government to endorse any question set by Quebec that it finds to "clearly set out the constitutional change being sought" through a referendum and to appeal to Quebec courts if it finds that the question does not do so. In addition, the bill itself set out two questions on Quebec sovereignty that would meet this test of clarity. Should a clear question secure "a majority of valid votes," Ottawa would be bound to enter into negotiations with the Quebec government. (House of Commons of Canada, Bill C-470, An Act Respecting Democratic Constitutional Change, 2013.)
75. Erickson and Laycock, "The NDP and Quebec," 69.
76. Thus, in the 2011 federal election the NDP was able to spend $3 million in Quebec, three times its expenditure during the 2008 election campaign (Erickson and Laycock, "The NDP and Quebec," 72).
77. François Rocher, "The Orange Wave: A (Re) Canadianization of the Quebec Electorate?" in *Canada: The State of the Federation, the Changing Federal Environment: Rebalancing Roles?* Institute of Intergovernmental

Relations, Queen's University, ed. Nadia Verrelli (Montreal and Kingston: McGill-Queen's University Press, 2014), 71–3.

78. Parti liberal du Québec, *Un projet pour le Québec: affirmation, autonomie et leadership*, Rapport final (Montreal: Parti libéral du Québec, 2001).
79. Ibid., 116–17.
80. The history and functioning of the Council are analyzed in Emmet Collins, "Coming into Its Own? Canada's Council of the Federation, 2003–16," IRPP *Insight*, no. 15, Mar. 2017.
81. Parti liberal, *Un projet pour le Québec*, 147–60. The main recommendation of constitutional change that does not replicate the Meech Lake Accord is to entrench the principle of "convivialité fédérale" (ibid., 160).
82. Canadian Press, "Charest Wants Quebec Recognized as Nation Under Constitution, Some Day," 14 Aug. 2011.
83. Justin Trudeau, "We Beat Fear with Hope." 20 Oct. 2015. Retrieved from http://www.macleans.ca/politics/ottawa/justin-trudeau-for-the-record-we-beat-fear-with-hope/ (my translation of extracts that are in French).
84. In the 1890s, Laurier chose not to intervene in the struggle over French-language Catholic schools in Manitoba, signing an agreement to that effect with the Manitoba premier in 1896, and in 1905 brought about the creation of Alberta and Saskatchewan without any guarantees for French-language rights.
85. Trudeau, "We Beat Fear with Hope."
86. Ibid.
87. Ibid.
88. Radio-Canada.ca, "Trudeau ne voit aucune raison de rouvrir la Constitution," 17 Dec. 2015.
89. See Dunn, "Harper without Jeers, Trudeau without Cheers," 16.
90. While the Saskatchewan premier was adamantly opposed to the agreement, Manitoba's stated that he agreed to the substance but was awaiting negotiations with Ottawa on health care (Mia Rabson, "Pallister Holds Out on Carbon Pricing Deal," *Winnipeg Free Press*, 19 Dec. 2016).
91. The Manitoba premier's recalcitrance is analyzed in Paul Thomas, "Let's Make a Deal: Time for Pallister's Health-Care Troublemaking to End," CBC *News*, 3 Apr. 2017. Manitoba finally signed on in August 2017 (Elisha Dacey and Laura Glowacki, "Manitoba Final Province to Sign Health-Care Pact with Feds," CBC *News Manitoba*, posted 21 Aug 2017).
92. While insisting that it maintained the right to set its own priorities, the Couillard government proclaimed priorities that were identical to the ones Ottawa had wanted for the other provinces (Hélène Buzzetti, "Le Québec signe à son tour une entente sur les transferts en santé," *Le Devoir*, 11 Mar. 2017). See also Gloria Galloway, "Health Accord Nearly Sealed as Ontario, Quebec, Alberta Reach Deals," *Globe and Mail*, 10 Mar. 2017.
93. Michelle Zilio, "Ottawa Signs Child-Care Deal Targeting Families in Need," *Globe and Mail*, 12 June 2017; and Hélène Buzzetti, "Québec obtiendra 88 millions par année pour offrir un soutien direct aux familles," *Le Devoir*, 13 June 2017.
94. Bertrand Marotte, "Signing Constitution Not on Quebec Premier's Agenda," *Globe and Mail*, 7 Sept. 2014. Also Ontario Radio-Canada, "Plaidoyer de Philippe Couillard pour un fédéralisme coopératif," 11 May 2015.
95. Official translation of: *Québécois: notre façon d'être Canadiens. Politique d'affirmation du Québec et de relations canadiennes*, Gouvernement du Québec, 2017.
96. "une allégeance Québécoise à laquelle s'additionne une appartenance canadienne représente la réalité identitaire d'une vaste majorité de Québécois, réalité dont les racines plongent jusqu'au cœur de l'histoire de notre nation," *Notre façon d'être Canadiens*, 131.
97. *Notre façon d'être Canadiens*, 47.
98. Of these five components of Meech: "Si le contexte politique et constitutionnel a beaucoup changé depuis leur formulation, elles demeurent une illustration concrète des garanties constitutionnelles qui doivent découler d'une reconnaissance adéquate de la Nation québécoise." (Ibid., 125.)
99. Ibid., 43–67. These are the elements that responded to the five conditions that the Bourassa government had set for signing the Canadian constitution. The other key element of Meech, Senate reform, is omitted in this presentation.
100. Ibid., 97.

101. Ibid., 101.
102. Government of Quebec, *Our Way of Being Canadian: Policy on Québec Affirmation and Canadian Relations*, 2017 [official translation of *Québécois: notre façon d'être Canadiens*], 84.
103. Ibid., 141.
104. Janyce McGregor, "'We Are Not Opening the Constitution': Trudeau Pans Quebec's Plans," CBC *News*, 1 June 2017.
105. My translation of "le Canada ne se résume pas à la personne du premier ministre du Canada." (Radio-Canada.ca, "Couillard veut relancer le dialogue entre les peuples fondateurs," 1 June 2017.)
106. Jöel-Denis Bellavance, "Le débat constitutionnel est une distraction, selon Trudeau," *La Presse*, 5 June 2017; and Mélanie Marquis, "Non à un débat sémantique sur la Constitution, dit Trudeau," *La Presse*, 6 June 2017.
107. Mulcair declared "I think that Philippe Couillard is showing himself to be a bridge builder, and Justin Trudeau is slamming the door on that for his own partisan, petty political gain rather than looking at the long game for the country. Using Quebec as a whipping boy is a very old strategy, and Trudeau son is trying to emulate Trudeau *père* [father], and frankly it's unbecoming a prime minister of Canada whose No. 1 job is keeping the country together." (McGregor, "We Are Not Opening the Constitution.")
108. Marco Bélair-Cirino et al., "Couillard, entre idéalisme et réalisme constitutionnel," *Le Devoir*, 2 June 2017.
109. See, for instance, Andrew Coyne, "Meech Lake, Again? How About We Just Don't," *National Post*, 2 June 2017; and "Globe Editorial: Reopen the Constitution? No Thank You," *Globe and Mail*, 1 June 2017. Conversely, see Konrad Yakabuski, "Quebec Is Right to Reopen a Constitutional Discussion," *Globe and Mail*, 2 June 2017.
110. "Quebec will support the aboriginal nations to ensure that their place is recognized." (Official translation of: *Québécois: notre façon d'être Canadiens*, 121) and "It is possible and even advisable for Canada to provide suitable recognition for the Quebec nation and the aboriginal nations without calling into question its unity or its ability to develop." (ibid., 89). Apparently, Couillard had already met with Indigenous leaders to discuss such a strategy (Les Perreaux, "Some Indigenous Groups Embrace Quebec's Proposal to Reopen Constitution," *Globe and Mail*, 4 June 2017).
111. CROP, "Politique au Québec: perceptions des québécois," Jan. 2017, "Intentions de vote référendaire—après répartition" The question: "Si un référendum avait lieu aujourd'hui vous demandant si vous voulez que le Québec devienne un pays souverain, voteriez-vous Oui ou voteriez-vous Non?"
112. Denis Lessard, "Sondage: l'idée d'un référendum n'a pas la cote" *La Presse*, 18 Mar. 2014. 58 per cent of respondents agreed that the sovereignty question is "depassée."
113. Writing in 2015, Ibbitson contended that "under the Conservatives there have been fewer major federal–provincial disputes than at any time since Louis St. Laurent was prime minister." (Ibbitson, *Stephen Harper*, 272.)
114. Jean-Herman Guay, "Sovereignty at an Impasse: The Highs and Lows of Quebec Nationalism," IRPP *Insight*, no. 18 (Oct. 2017): 19. See also Marc V. Levine, *The Reconquest of Montreal: Language Policy and Social Change in a Bilingual Society* (Philadelphia: Temple University Press, 1990), especially Chap. 7.
115. Guay, "Sovereignty at an Impasse," 21.
116. See note 2.
117. Mahéo and Bélanger, "Is the Parti Québécois Bound to Disappear?" 6–8 and Table 1.
118. This is the Generation Y of Mahéo and Bélanger, (ibid.). See also Guay, "Sovereignty at an Impasse," Figure 1.
119. Guay, "Sovereignty at an Impasse," 16. See the steady decline in support for sovereignty among members of Generation X in Guay, Figure 1.
120. Vincent Lemieux, *Les partis générationnels au Québec: passé, présent, avenir* (Quebec: Presses de l'Université Laval, 2011), Chap. 3.
121. Ibid., Chap. 7.
122. My translation of "un parti figé, conservateur et vieillissant aux allures de 'club social'" (Marco Bélair-Cirino, "Le PQ, 'un parti figé, conservateur et vieillissant,' selon St-Pierre Plamondon," *Le Devoir*, 9 Feb. 2017).
123. Vicky Fragasso-Marquis, "Les jeunes péquistes refusent de revenir à la charte des valeurs," *Le Devoir*, 20 Feb. 2017. The resistance of Generation Y to the *Charte* is confirmed in Mahéo and Bélanger, 13.

124. Chantal Hébert, "Parti Québécois the Author of Its Own Misfortune," *Toronto Star*, 1 Nov. 2017.
125. Marco Bélair-Cirino, "Pour Manon Massé, 'le Parti québécois n'est pas raciste'," *Le Devoir*, 30 May 2017.
126. Mahéo and Bélanger, 10.
127. With the arrival of Nadeau-Dubois, support for Québec-solidaire surged from 9 per cent in January 2017 to 14 per cent in March 2017, primarily at the expense of the Parti québécois. The party had received 8 per cent of the popular vote in the 2014 election. By the same token, over the five days following Nadeau-Dubois's announcement of his electoral candidacy, 4000 new members joined Québec solidaire. (Stéphane Baillargeon, "Québec solidaire gruge des appuis au Parti québécois," *Le Devoir*, 18 Mar. 2017.)
128. Léger/*Le Devoir*, "La politique provinciale au Québec," 2 Dec. 2017, http://leger360.com/admin/upload/publi_pdf/La_politique_provinciale_au_Quebec_20171202.pdf
129. Ibid.

Chapter 9

Conclusions

A National Unity Strategy

Pierre Elliott Trudeau was remarkably successful in putting in place the elements of a national unity strategy. The central components of the strategy had been clearly defined well before he assumed office through articles, books, and countless speeches and interviews. Once he became prime minister, he moved quickly and systematically to implement the strategy. Through his 16 years in office, national unity, as he envisaged it, remained his central preoccupation and retained priority over other prime ministerial responsibilities. Nor did he ever waver from his strategy and the long-held beliefs that underlay it. Indeed, after retirement he returned to public life to combat his successor's deviation from what he had put in place.

This single-minded pursuit of a coherent, overarching strategy is unusual for political leaders in Canada, or anywhere else, and is testimony to Trudeau's determination and skills. Whether the strategy actually produced national unity, however, is an entirely different matter. We have argued that in fact the strategy had the opposite effect, leaving Quebeckers and other Canadians further apart than ever before. Be that as it may, the strategy and the various measures that composed it left an indelible mark on Canada and continue to shape Canadian politics in fundamental ways.

The Charter

Pierre Trudeau's greatest single achievement, unquestionably, is the Charter of Rights and Freedoms. The Charter has transformed Canadian politics, affording a new importance to the judiciary and expanding and guaranteeing rights in many directions. Moreover, there is good reason to believe that the Charter would not have come about without Trudeau's determination. Certainly, language rights would not have been front and centre in any charter that somehow emerged under a different prime minister. But it is quite possible that no charter at all would have been created without Trudeau at the helm. After all, back when it was being debated legal circles were divided over the very notion of a charter; it was opposed by most provincial premiers, not just Quebec's. Trudeau could readily have secured the premiers' unanimous consent to patriation alone, without a charter. But, following the terms of his strategy, he insisted that patriation must be tied to a charter even if that meant ignoring Quebec's objections. Gordon Robertson, the distinguished public servant who served four different prime ministers, makes it clear in his memoirs that only Trudeau would have done that.[1]

Bilingualism

The new legal and political status of the French language was also central to the Trudeau legacy. Of course, Trudeau did not initiate Ottawa's concern with language policy. Well before Trudeau assumed power, the Pearson government had already acted to strengthen the role of French in the federal public service. In 1967, the B&B Commission had outlined a detailed plan for official bilingualism, providing the basic elements of what became, early in Trudeau's tenure, the Official Languages Act. However, reflecting his individualist world view, Trudeau put his personal imprint on federal language policy and took it in a distinctive direction. It was Trudeau who pressured all the provincial governments to commit constitutionally to official bilingualism, going well beyond the recommendations of the B&B Commission. And it was Trudeau who promoted personal bilingualism and encouraged many Anglophone Canadians to develop a capacity in French, here too with measures that greatly exceeded the B&B Commission's recommendations. To be sure, over time language rights have taken more of a group-based direction than Trudeau had in mind. As well, the federal public service has not become fully bilingual and the Commission's key proposal of bilingual districts has been permanently shelved. But no prime minister could have been more committed to the cause of bilingualism, or better able to personify it. Thus, since Trudeau's time in office it has been generally accepted that the prime minister, if not all the members of cabinet, must be proficient in both official languages.

Multiculturalism

By proclaiming Canadian multiculturalism early in his first government, Trudeau upended a widespread understanding that had emerged over the 1960s that Canada is bicultural. By all appearances, Trudeau had no personal commitment to the concept of multiculturalism and Ottawa's multicultural policy soon strayed far from his personal individualism. Thus, it is ironic that multiculturalism should be so closely associated with him and have become a central value, perhaps *the* central value, of the new national identity he articulated. But, once again, a fundamental change in Canadian politics might not have come about without Trudeau. While multiculturalism was promoted by groups who felt excluded by biculturalism, Trudeau had his own reasons to proclaim it. He was the first head of government anywhere to do so.

Uniform Federalism

Here too, Trudeau destroyed a general consensus that had developed during the 1960s: the acceptance of asymmetrical federalism, under which Quebec assumes a greater role than the other provinces given its special responsibilities. Under Lester Pearson, the Liberals had repeatedly allowed Quebec to "opt out" of federal and federal–provincial programs. The NDP was formally committed to it and Progressive Conservative leader Robert Stanfield had given his blessing. Yet Trudeau put an end to the practice that he had so frequently decried before assuming office. As it happened, some senior public servants had already been voicing their opposition to "opting out." With Trudeau's ascension to the prime ministership these views became policy. Years later, when the Meech Lake Accord threatened to constitutionalize a role that was distinct to Quebec, Trudeau's dramatic public intervention made the difference in undermining the agreement.

Strong National Government

Trudeau may not have been the first prime minister to call the federal government a "national government," but he greatly reinforced the idea. During the Trudeau era the federal government's public face was cleared of virtually all vestiges of Canada's historical relationship to Great Britain and the monarchy. During the patriation debates, he proclaimed that the federal government is the only government to represent all Canadians and, as such, deserves to have the constitutional power to overturn provincial legislation. He was quick to dismiss Joe Clark's notion of Canada as "a community of communities" and to assert Ottawa's right to protect the national interest through the National Energy Program. While the Harper government's "open federalism" entailed decentralization and correction of "the fiscal imbalance," the continued popularity of such measures as the Canada Health Act speaks to public support for Ottawa. Indeed, once again with the exception of Quebec, Canadians generally support the federal government over their respective provincial governments.[2]

Together, these five elements provided the basis for a new national identity for Canada. In practice, some of them have strayed from the individualist assumptions on which Trudeau had tried to base them. The Charter's language rights have, through jurisprudence, become group rights. Multicultural policy has become concerned with the status and needs of groups, extending even to formal apologies to groups for past state transgressions—a notion that Trudeau had always opposed. Nonetheless, these five measures were all closely associated with Trudeau and became the substance of a powerful Canadian nationalism.

A New Canadian Nationalism

Ironically, this new national identity did not find favour with the population for whom the national unity strategy had been conceived: the Francophones of Quebec. Instead, it took hold primarily outside Quebec, building upon the nationalist sentiments that had emerged in English-speaking Canada in the 1960s. It is ironic as well, given Trudeau's personal rejection of nationalism, that his initiatives should have given rise to a new and powerful form of nationalism. To be sure, the new Canadian nationalism is not an *ethnic* nationalism, at least in content. Indeed, with its emphasis on internal diversity, it has often portrayed Canada as "post-national." It is nationalism nonetheless—the nationalism of the "non-nation." By the same token, the implementation of Trudeau's national unity strategy was in fact an exercise in nation-building—and the development and deployment of a state nationalism.

As Paul Litt demonstrates in his book *Trudeaumania*, this new Canadian nationalism was born of the specific conditions of English Canada in the 1960s. The manifest decline of Great Britain and the postwar dominance of the United States had intensified English Canadians' search for an authentically Canadian identity. Exalted by the Centennial celebrations and Expo 67's success, they were at the same time alarmed by the threat of Quebec secession. The proverbial right man at the right time, Pierre Trudeau offered a strategy for not only saving the Canadian nation but taking it to new heights. These circumstances produced nothing less than "the birth of a nation."[3]

During the 1970s, the Trudeau government systematically put in place the elements of a state nationalism. Indeed, seeing the term "dominion" as a signifier of subordination to Great Britain, Trudeau eliminated its use in the federal government. With his intervention in the 1980 referendum campaign, he burnished his credentials as defender of the Canadian nation. Capitalizing on the referendum victory, the Trudeau government embarked on a campaign to make the Canadian nation whole by taking ownership of its constitution from Great Britain and entrenching the rights of Canadians in a charter. As we have seen, this ultimate venture in nationalism was led by a team that included few Quebec Francophones but was closely tied to Canadian nationalists in the rest of the country.[4] At the same time, the struggle to tie patriation to a charter involved the mobilization of a variety of rights-based groups, almost exclusively from English-speaking Canada. A few years later, these same groups were mobilized again, largely by Trudeau's own intervention, to attack the Meech Lake Accord over concessions to Quebec that they thought would weaken the Canadian nation.

In sum, Trudeau's success in putting in place the elements of his national unity strategy involved much more than personal will and determination. Nor was it simply a matter of personal charisma, "Trudeaumania," or superior logic and debating skills. A "great man" theory of history is not needed to comprehend Trudeau's remarkable success in establishing his new conception of the country. Instead, the explanation lies with social forces already in play, primarily outside Quebec, and Trudeau's ability to draw upon them. "Old stock" English Canadians in search of a national identity rallied around his vision for the country, making it a nationalist project, as did the growing immigrant populations. Rights-based groups, largely outside Quebec, could be counted on to support and defend Trudeau's constitutional objectives, as they did during the patriation struggle and the Meech Lake debacle. Of course, he did not have the same opportunities in Quebec.

Also favouring implementation of Trudeau's national unity strategy was the generally positive attitude to state initiatives that characterized the times. As elsewhere, the post war years had been marked by a widespread consensus, rooted in Keynesianism and an implicit collaboration between capital and labour, that the state had a responsibility to provide for a society as a whole and in fact had the ability to do so. In the 1950s, the federal government had used these notions to justify a massive expansion in its economic and social role so as to create a welfare state. This favourable disposition to state intervention persisted into the Trudeau era, at least in the early years, and facilitated efforts to build and strengthen the Canadian nation. Of course, the Quebec government could draw upon the same notions to support its own nation-building project.

Assessing the Strategy's Success

The question remains: to what extent did the national unity strategy actually achieve its objective? On the face of it, there is little room for argument. Not only was the cause of independence defeated in two referendums, but in contemporary Quebec support for independence has fallen to its lowest level in decades. As we saw in Chapter 8 (Figure 8.2) the results of opinion surveys suggest that a third referendum would be soundly defeated were it to take place. Indeed, Jean-François Lisée secured the Parti québécois leadership in part by proposing that the next referendum not take place during the first term of a new PQ government but would have to await the one after that. Nonetheless, can the Trudeau national unity strategy be properly credited with this state of affairs?

Defeating the Independence Movement

First, does the Trudeau vision explain why only 40 per cent of Quebeckers voted Yes in the 1980 referendum? Some analysts point to Pierre Trudeau's three dramatic addresses during the campaign, contending that they turned the tide by mobilizing support for the No side. Yet we have seen that survey analyses do not confirm that the speeches had a major impact on public opinion in Quebec. For that matter, the import of Trudeau's third and most important speech was simply to promise that a No victory would lead to change. He did not reiterate his personal vision of what the changes might be. Perhaps if he had done so, confirming his opposition to any reinforcement of Quebec's status, his speech would indeed have had an impact: a negative one.

Second, it would be difficult to explain the razor-thin No victory of the 1995 referendum in terms of Trudeau and his vision of Canada. On the decision of the No side organizers, Pierre Trudeau was totally absent from the debate. He did not speak at the massive Pro-Canada rally, nor was he even invited to attend it. By the same token, Jean Chrétien, Trudeau's close associate in the patriation exercise, felt obliged during the final days of the campaign to declare empathy for the distinct-society clause which, during the Meech Lake debate, both he and Trudeau had so vigorously attacked.

The fact of the matter is that the Yes side almost won the referendum precisely because of the Trudeau national unity strategy and its impact. As we have seen, it was the Meech Lake Accord's reinforcement of Quebec's status, especially through the distinct-society clause, that propelled Trudeau's personal intervention and the mobilization of his vision's supporters. The subsequent dramatic rise in support for Quebec independence was in direct response to the rest of Canada's rejection of the Accord. The rejection of such a modest package was widely seen in Quebec as confirmation that no accommodation of Quebec's concerns was possible. Under these conditions, a referendum on Quebec independence would surely have passed if Premier Bourassa had wished to call one. Simply put, rather than securing national unity the Trudeau strategy almost precipitated the break up of the country. Rather than the solution to separatism, it became a catalyst for it.

Finally, we have seen that the current low level of support for Quebec sovereignty cannot be explained in terms of some belated effect of the national unity strategy. The explanation lies more with changes in Quebec itself. While it was important to give the federal government a bilingual face, actions taken by the Quebec government have been far more important in attenuating separatism. Beginning with the Quiet Revolution about which Trudeau had been so diffident, the Quebec government has effectively eased many of the grievances that led to the emergence and growth of the independence movement. The expansion of the Quebec public sector and growth of Francophone-led businesses have helped to eliminate the historical gap in income and general well-being between Quebec's Francophones and Anglophones. Quebec's language laws, Bills 22 and 101, which Trudeau had so bitterly denounced, have also supported this transformation. At the same time, these laws have provided Quebec Francophones with a certain linguistic security: the pre-eminence of French as Quebec's official language and primary language of work, and the integration of immigrant children with the Francophone majority by means of French-language schooling.

By the 1980s, these various measures were having their impact, restructuring Quebec society. The indépendantiste surge of the 1990s, produced by the Meech Lake Accord's collapse, simply concealed the effects of these long-term trends. Thus, young Quebec Francophones who entered political age in this new social and economic reality have not been drawn to Quebec independence in the same fashion as their elders. While identifying with Quebec, this political generation is less likely to see the need for independence.

Further contributing to the decline in support for Quebec independence has been the fact that recent federal governments have deliberately avoided confrontation with the Quebec government, openly breaking with the Trudeau orthodoxy to do so. It has become a given in the conduct of federal–provincial relations, although not in Canada's formal constitutional structure, that Quebec should exercise a greater degree of autonomy than the other provinces. To a certain extent, then, both Quebec society and Canadian federalism have completed processes of adjustment that were initiated in the 1960s but were disrupted or obscured during the Pierre Trudeau era. The result has been to weaken greatly the case for Quebec independence. Conversely, recent indications that French is in fact losing ground as the language of work in Quebec point to a potential revival in indépendantiste sentiment.[5]

One might try to defend the Trudeau national unity strategy by contending that at least it allowed the transformation of Quebec society to occur. In the end, the Trudeau government did not disallow Bill 22 or Bill 101, despite the clamour of Quebec's Anglophone leaders that it do so. Yet by denouncing these measures, Trudeau and his colleagues placed in question their legitimacy and impeded the processes of restructuring. Nor did the Trudeau government play the positive role it might have assumed if it had followed the B&B Commission's recommendation to use its powers to advance the role of French as the language of work in Quebec. With its focus on establishing bilingualism on a pan-Canadian basis, the national unity strategy was effectively beside the point. Indeed, the strategy as a whole served to prolong Canada's national unity crisis by impeding needed processes of adjustment that were rooted in Canadian federalism and the transformation of Quebec society by the Quebec government.

Transforming Identities

At the heart of the Trudeau national unity strategy was the transformation of identities: the cause of Quebec independence would be beaten by leading Quebeckers to identify with all of Canada and not with their province. In Jeremy Webber's words, Trudeau:

> would often tell Quebecers [that] they had to choose between two alternative—and not complementary—objects of allegiance: Quebec or Canada.Although Trudeau's administration preached respect for provincial jurisdiction, when it came to allegiance he used the language of a unitary state.[6]

Clearly, this transformation did not take place. Unlike Canadians in every other province, Quebec Francophones continue to identify first and foremost with their province, and their provincial government, rather than with Canada as a whole.

In Quebec, Trudeau's efforts simply could not connect with the forces of change as they had done in the rest of the country. Instead, Trudeau became their adversary. Quebec Francophones did not feel the need for a new national identity that had led so many English Canadians to rally around Trudeau's vision of Canada, and around Trudeau himself. They already had a national identity—defined a century before as "French Canada" and, with the 1960s and the Quiet Revolution, redefined as simply "Quebec." With the Quiet Revolution, the Quebec government had begun to articulate a distinctly Quebec nationalism, directly countering Ottawa's Canadian nationalism. In fact, many of the same social groups that in the rest of the country had rallied around Trudeau's constitutional vision were, in the case of Quebec, thoroughly integrated with Quebec society and had few linkages with their counterparts outside the province. This was so clearly revealed during the Meech debate, when Quebec feminist leaders dismissed outright the attacks of English-Canadian feminists on the distinct-society clause. Thus, in the case of Quebec, the Trudeau government's nation-building efforts attracted few supporters and, typically, were seen as provocations.

Sustaining the Quebec Identity

The Quebec identity continues to be sustained and reinforced by a complex of structures and networks that is distinct to Quebec, largely because of language, and ranges from media and the cultural industry to voluntary associations and labour unions. The Francophone section of Canada's bifurcated public broadcaster, Société Radio-Canada, is based in Montreal; most of its audience is located in Quebec. Most of Canada's privately owned French-language broadcasting is located in Quebec and geared to the Quebec audience. Thus, the television programs most popular among Quebeckers are produced mainly within Quebec itself—and are unknown outside the province. The cultural industries as a whole are segregated, with the Francophone complex operating almost exclusively in Quebec. Even voluntary associations follow the same general structure with a "national" organization, which may or not be bilingual, serving Canada outside Quebec paralleled by an autonomous or independent organization serving Quebec, essentially in French. Thus, the Canadian Council on Social Development is paralleled by the Conseil québécois de développement social. There may be little conflict between the parallel organizations as they assume their respective responsibilities.[7] Yet the prevalence of such arrangements speaks to the distinctiveness, and separateness, of Francophone Quebec.

Much of Quebec's economy is in the hands of "Quebec Inc," a complex of Francophone-owned enterprises that emerged from the Quiet Revolution and often work closely with the Quebec government and its state enterprises. With time, these enterprises have become more active in other parts of Canada, most notably Ontario, as they move on to global markets. They have remained, nonetheless, French-language organizations centred in Quebec. Labour organizations are also distinctive to the province. The Quebec-based Confédération des syndicats nationaux has always been independent of the Canadian Labour Congress. The predecessor of the Fédération des travailleurs et travailleuses du Québec did join the CLC, but withdrew after years of acrimony.

Most important of all, the Quebec provincial government, renamed "l'État du Québec," plays a central role in the lives of all Quebeckers. Ever since the Quiet Revolution, if not before, it has assumed the role of a *national* state—the provincial legislature became *l'Assemblée nationale*—and articulated a distinctively Quebec nationalism. Pierre Trudeau had proposed that, through official bilingualism and support for Francophone minorities, Quebec's Francophones could be led to identify with Francophones throughout Canada and, if only on that basis, with Canada as whole. After all, until the middle of the twentieth century Quebec's Francophones had indeed been linked to Francophones elsewhere in Canada through common institutions, largely tied to the Church, which gave form to "French Canada." But these linkages were lost with the Quiet Revolution; the nation became Quebec. As the role of the provincial government expanded, displacing the Church in the process, it became more and more important that only in Quebec was a government accountable to a Francophone majority and that only there could French be installed as the sole official language. The fact that no other province than New Brunswick gave full official status to French only reinforced the point. Nor did it help that over the years the demographic presence of Francophones continued to decline in most provinces other than Quebec, despite the sustained effort of Ottawa and some provincial governments to reverse the trend. The long-standing "territorialization" of Canada's two official languages, with French concentrated more and more in Quebec and English outside Quebec, continued unabated.[8] Quebec remained home to nine out of ten Francophones. Reconstituting French Canada under these conditions was an enormous challenge.

The rest of Canada has itself tacitly recognized Quebec's separateness. The celebrated phrase "Two Solitudes" remains as apt as ever, even if the names of the "solitudes" have changed: "English Canada" and "French Canada" are now "Canada" and "Quebec." In much of the country, the term "Canada" is really intended to denote English-speaking Canada or Canada outside Quebec.[9] For that matter, within Francophone Quebec, "Canada" has also become shorthand for English Canada or Canada outside Quebec.

As the persistence of the "Two Solitudes" so clearly demonstrates, the fundamental problem with Trudeau's vision for Canada was the individualist premises upon which it was based. Confounding Trudeau's political world view, in politics as elsewhere, was the continuing importance of communities and their collective identities. This is most dramatically demonstrated by the persistence of identification with Quebec as the primary identity for Quebec Francophones. Outside Quebec, the official-language minorities succeeded in transferring Charter language rights to their communities, even though these provisions of the Charter were deliberately framed in terms of individuals and their ability to choose between official languages. Trudeau may have insisted that Canadian multiculturalism was all about the individual, but the advocates of multiculturalism were able to secure policies geared to groups and to their cultural preservation. As for Indigenous Peoples, their leaders quickly recognized that the individualist assumptions of the White Paper left no space for them—and could only lead to the destruction of their communities.

Given Trudeau's fervent rejection of nationalism as a threat to the individual, it is ironic that his vision of Canada was embraced by so many in the name of another collective identity—the Canadian nation. Indeed, there always was a tension between Trudeau's individualism and his effort to create a new national identity for Canadians. Within this form of Canadian nationalism, as it became mobilized around Trudeau, there was no room for other national identities. Thus, it was unthinkable that the Canadian constitution recognize Quebec's specificity: the Meech Lake attempt to recognize Quebec as a distinct society was heresy and could only lead to disaster.[10] Nor, for that matter, could the constitution openly recognize First Nations, leading to Indigenous protests over the terms of patriation.

Remedying Constitutional Failure

As a result, Canada's Constitution Act remains incomplete, lacking Quebec's formal adhesion. This fundamental shortcoming of Canada's central constitutional document represents the most glaring failure of a strategy designed to produce national unity, and of the individualist premises upon which it was based. Moreover, there appears to be little hope that this failure can be remedied; the constitution is generally regarded as beyond repair.

All post-Trudeau federal governments have openly broken with the Trudeau orthodoxy to enter into asymmetrical administrative agreements with Quebec. However, after the half-hearted effort of the Chrétien government, no federal government has attempted to secure an accommodation of Quebec in the constitution. While distinct arrangements for Quebec may have become the norm in the practice of federal–provincial relations, stating as much in the constitution is widely viewed as impossible, given the affront to Canadian nationalism.

The obstacles facing a renewal of constitutional discussions cannot be dismissed. The history of failures to reach and maintain an agreement would be sufficient to frighten off most political leaders. Beyond that, the very requirements for constitutional change have become most daunting. Given the precedent of the Charlottetown Accord, any agreement that meets the formal amending procedure would also have to be approved by public referendum. Nor can it be presumed that, as with Meech, the Quebec question can be dealt with in isolation. A host of other issues would also be on the table. Thus, it was not surprising that virtually all government leaders outside Quebec rejected, or simply ignored, Premier Couillard's invitation to discuss his government's document.[11]

Given these obstacles, it might be tempting simply to dismiss the constitutional issue as of no real consequence. According to Prime Minister Justin Trudeau, the whole question of securing Quebec's signature is simply one of semantics and a distraction from real priorities of Canadians, including Quebeckers.[12] Yet the constitution is of fundamental importance in any country. It explicitly or implicitly declares a country's purpose and objectives, establishes the rule of law, sets out the procedures by which laws are made, and delineates who are citizens of the country. A constitutional document is especially important in a federal system where it sets out the responsibilities of the member governments, each of which is sovereign in its domain. It constitutes a pact among the various parts of a political community setting out the terms under which they commit morally to share it. The fact that Quebec is legally bound by the Constitution Act, even if the Quebec government did not sign it, is surely beside the point. Much more is at stake than mere "semantics."

Beyond the inherent importance of securing Quebec's formal signature to Canada's constitution, there are other issues that cannot be addressed until Quebec is party to the Constitution Act. As it stands, the act does not recognize Indigenous Peoples as nations.[13] Repeated efforts by Indigenous and government leaders to come to terms on constitutionalizing an "inherent right to self-government" have ended in abject failure. Progress has been made in other areas, such as the creation of Nunavut, the deliberations of a Truth and Reconciliation Commission on residential schools, and even potential implementation of the United Nations Declaration on the Rights of Indigenous Peoples, which Canada at one time had voted against.[14] Upon becoming prime minister, Justin Trudeau called for a "renewed, nation-to-nation relationship with Indigenous Peoples" and, to that end, his government is developing a new "legal framework" to support Indigenous self-government.[15] But such a legal framework would not have constitutional status. The formal constitutional treatment of Indigenous Peoples remains frozen and surely will remain frozen unless Quebec has been led to sign on to the Constitution Act. By the same token, the Supreme Court has ruled that the Canadian Senate can be reformed only through constitutional amendment. It rejected the Harper government's attempt to establish unilaterally a procedure for electing senators rather than appointing them. There are other issues about the Senate that remain unresolved. What proportion of senators should come from each province or region? What should be the terms of office?

These have been critical issues to many Canadians, especially in the West. Here too securing Quebec's constitutional signature is a pre-condition to meaningful action. Yet it is difficult to see how resolution of the status of Indigenous Peoples and their rights, or reform of the Senate, can be accomplished without the constitutional accommodation of Quebec.

Finally, Quebec's absence from the Constitution Act constitutes one of the strongest arguments for advocates of Quebec independence, contending that there is no place in Canada for Quebec. While support for independence may be currently low in Quebec, the contemporary importance of secession movements in such settings as Scotland and Catalonia suggests that even in Quebec new circumstances could put independence back on the political agenda.

Clearly, Canada's constitutional impasse can be broken only through a different approach to the Quebec question, and so many other questions.

Understanding Canada Differently

A new approach to the Quebec question could begin with taking a fresh look at Canada as a whole, and at the purposes of Canadian federalism. The fact of the matter is that Canada is not a nation-state—it is much more complex than that. Rather than constituting a single, homogenous nation, Canada contains a host of "internal nations." Quebec is one. Indigenous Peoples collectively represent many more. Even Acadians, based primarily in New Brunswick, can claim national status. Yet even if Canada is not literally a single nation-state, the vast majority of Canadians, primarily English-speaking, do understand Canada on this basis. For them, all of Canada is the nation and Ottawa is the national state. But to comprehend Canada exclusively in those terms, as did Pierre Trudeau's conception of national unity, is to reject the primary identities and aspirations of a substantial part of the Canadian population. It is a recipe for protracted conflict and frustration.

Nor is it helpful simply to deny the existence of all these nationalisms—Canadian, Quebec, and Indigenous—by portraying Canada as "post-national," as if it has somehow transcended its internal nationalisms let alone transcended the nationalism of the Canadian state.[16] These various nationalist forces within Canada are too powerful to be ignored. At the same time, despite Justin Trudeau's claim that "There is no core identity, no mainstream in Canada," his father was able to entrench within Canada's political institutions, and its constitution, a quite coherent conception of a Canadian identity, which has become the basis of a strong state nationalism: the nationalism of the "non-nation."

Beyond viewing Canada as a multinational entity, a different approach would see federalism in much broader terms. It would recognize that an essential and legitimate purpose of Canadian federalism is to accommodate and support Canada's "internal nations." This would not mean adopting a *new* understanding of Canadian federalism. Instead, it would simply entail retrieving the historical and understanding of federalism. The fact of the matter is that, at its creation in 1867, Canadian federalism was deliberately designed to recognize and accommodate cultural or national differences, as well as purely regional or territorial ones,[17] and was the first federation anywhere to be so designed. In fact, Canada was the first federation to be based upon *both* types of division, cultural or national *and* territorial—and probably remains the only one anywhere.[18] This tension between the national and territorial dimensions of Canadian federalism is at the heart of so much of Canada's historical and contemporary conflict.

For the Maritime colonies, federalism was the means to offset their distance from the new government in Ottawa. As provinces were developed in western Canada, their primary rationale was also to offset the impact of vast distance and geography, as well as competing economic interests. But for Quebec, federalism was about protecting cultural, even national, distinctiveness. It allowed for a jurisdiction where Francophones were in the majority, and could protect their cultural distinctiveness from the Anglophone majority that would dominate the central government. As we saw in the first chapter, it was only on this basis that a bare majority of the French-Canadian members of the United Canadas' legislature were ready to agree to a common political order and it was on this basis that the new order was presented to the Quebec public: "we form a state within a state" and receive "the formal recognition of our national independence." It also was for this reason that the new federation was misrepresented as a "Confederation."

This cultural or national dimension of Canadian federalism has been lost—buried by a vision of Canada in which federalism is exclusively about territory and thus all provinces must be equal. Within this vision of Canadian federalism, as the Meech Lake debacle so clearly demonstrated, the Quebec government can no longer claim formal responsibility for protecting and fostering a "distinct society," even though it has been doing precisely that for 150 years. Tentative and carefully couched as it might be, the Couillard government's proposal for securing Quebec's formal adherence to the constitution is properly hinged on recognizing Quebec as a nation. As such, it harks back to the historical understanding of Canadian federalism—an understanding that must be retrieved.

Canada's historical experience has provided fertile ground for scholars to theorize a distinctive approach to federalism. Canadian scholars, both Francophone and Anglophone, have acquired an international reputation for their efforts to imagine how the federal principle might be applied in a multinational setting.[19] The academic literature even refers to a "Canada School of Multinational Federalism."[20] Multinational federalism is seen as a way to accommodate not only the Quebec nation but Indigenous Peoples as well. Some aspects of this approach have even made their way into public debate.

At the core of a multinational federation is formal constitutional *recognition* of the federation's "internal nations." In the case of the Quebec nation this means recognition of its full population and territory, as the Couillard government has recently proposed, and not just of Quebec Francophones, as the Harper government's resolution seems to imply. Beyond recognition, such a federation would afford *autonomy* to its various nations. In some cases, as with Nunavut, this may mean the creation of a new, discrete territorial unit. In other cases, it may mean the creation of distinctly Indigenous governments that operate in conjunction with federal and provincial governments over the same territory, as with the Charlottetown Accord's proposal for a third level of government devoted to First Nations. With respect to the Acadian nation, the answer may lie with providing autonomy within a province, as with the 1992 New Brunswick constitutional amendment that incurred Pierre Trudeau's disdain by recognizing that the province is composed of two communities: Francophone and Anglophone. Beyond granting autonomy, in one form or another, a multinational federation would bestow *legitimacy* on an internal nation's use of autonomy to maintain and reinforce its national distinctiveness, just as the distinct-society clause of the ill-fated Meech Lake Accord sought to do. Within this understanding of nationhood, the legitimate use of Indigenous Peoples' autonomy would not be limited just to maintaining traditional practices but would encompass the pursuit of contemporary national objectives as well.[21] Finally, a multinational federation inevitably would feature a substantial degree of *asymmetry* between nations and other units or among nations, as with the First Nations which vary enormously in size and resources.

Critics have been too quick to presume that formal recognition of "internal nations," especially Quebec, would lead to secession. Recognizing Quebec as a nation need not mean ending any role for the federal government in Quebec. We have seen how most Quebec Francophones maintain a secondary identification with Canada. However, while it was essential to give Ottawa a bilingual face so that Quebec Francophones could see it as a government that could meet some of their needs, that reform was never sufficient in itself. It could not have served as an *alternative* to recognizing Quebec's national character.

Of course, recognizing multinationalism as a central dimension of Canadian federalism need not preclude respecting the territorial dimension. For most Canadians, their respective province does not constitute an "internal nation." They look to their provincial government to offset Canada's vast distances and to serve regional economic interests, rather than to be their "national" government. Thus, Canadian federalism cannot be modelled on a *purely* multinational basis. It must accommodate both principles, territory and multinationalism, with all the tensions and contradictions that come from that. The genius of Canadian federalism lies in its complexity.

As we have seen, important opportunities were lost in the past to formalize the national dimension of Canadian federalism. Perhaps the passage of time will allow for new opportunities. Indeed, both Canadian public opinion and the federal government led by Justin Trudeau have been recently moving to a fuller and more open recognition of past and ongoing oppression of Indigenous Peoples. Recognition of this basic fact, and the international shame it brings to Canada, might be sufficient to force new constitutional discussions.

If these discussions do happen, they will necessarily have to address the Quebec question as well, and thus come fully to terms with Canada's underlying multinational reality. Justin Trudeau's professed determination to establish a "nation-to-nation" relationship with Indigenous Peoples is in direct contradiction with his refusal to deal with the Quebec question. It is not at all clear that he can address one question without addressing the other—unlike his father who was resolute in rejecting both of them. In the past, especially when Quebec independence was under discussion, advocates of Indigenous Peoples and the Quebec nation were at loggerheads. Perhaps in the future they can be allies. Quebec premier Couillard said as much when, after releasing his call for constitutional recognition of the Quebec nation, he proposed that the right to self-determination be recognized for both First Nations and Quebec.[22]

As recent history has shown, Canada is uniquely complex and cannot be made to fit a single formula, least of all one based on an individualist liberalism. Thus, Canadian federalism and the constitution cannot be just about territory and geography but must also accommodate differences in national identities, since confounding any nationalism of the country as a whole are the nationalisms of "internal nations," of both Quebec and Indigenous Peoples. By the same token, Canada's linguistic dualism represents not just the ability of individuals to choose between English and French in receiving public services but the existence of two communities, one that functions essentially in English and the other in French, centred in different parts of the country. That too must be accommodated within Canada's federalism and its constitution. Finally, there is the need to recognize Indigenous languages and communities, indeed Indigenous nations, not because of any danger of secession but as a matter of simple justice. Only through recognizing these different dimensions of complexity, and confronting its underlying multinationalism, can Canada overcome the impact of a national unity strategy that was designed to impose a new, one-dimensional conception of the country.

Notes

1. This is the implication of Robertson's comment, in a chapter entitled "The Trudeau Power Play, 1980–1982," that "No one who had worked with Mackenzie King, Louis St. Laurent and Lester Pearson could believe that a power play, however successful in the short term, was the way to solve a constitutional problem." (Gordon Robertson, *Memoirs of a Very Civil Servant: Mackenzie King to Pierre Trudeau* [Toronto: University of Toronto Press, 2000], 350.)

2. This was confirmed in a survey taken in the wake of the Trudeau era (see Chap. 6 of this volume, note 275).
3. Litt, *Trudeaumania* (Vancouver: UBC Press, 2016), 43.
4. Chap. 6 of this volume, notes 149 and 150.
5. Mylène Crête, "Recul du français comme langue de travail principale au Québec," *Le Devoir*, 29 Nov. 2017.
6. Jeremy Webber, *Reimagining Canada: Language, Culture, Community, and the Canadian Constitution* (Montreal and Kingston: McGill-Queen's University Press, 1994), 60.
7. David Cameron and Richard Simeon, eds., *Language Matters: How Canadian Voluntary Associations Manage French and English* (Vancouver: UBC Press, 2009).
8. Kenneth McRoberts, "Les politiques de la langue au Canada: un combat contre la territorialisation," in *La politique de Babel: du monolinguisme d'État au plurilinguisme des peuples*, ed. Denis Lacorne and Tony Judt (Paris: Éditions Karthala, 2009).
9. This was readily demonstrated in 2004 when the CBC staged a competition to select "The Greatest Canadian." No collaboration was arranged with Radio-Canada; the search for the greatest Canadian was limited to Anglophone audiences. Not surprisingly then, with one exception—Pierre Trudeau—the 10 leading choices for "Greatest Canadian" were themselves all Anglophone and had made their careers fully outside Quebec: (1) Tommy Douglas, (2) Terry Fox, (3) Pierre Trudeau, (4) Sir Frederick Banting, (5) David Suzuki, (6) Lester Pearson, (7) Don Cherry (8), Sir John A. Macdonald, (9) Alexander Graham Bell, and (10) Wayne Gretzky. Similarly, the Giller Prize in Canadian fiction is limited to works published in English. (Now called the Scotiabank Giller Prize, the prize is awarded to "the author of the best Canadian novel or collection of short stories published in English, either originally, or in translation." https://scotiabankgillerprize.ca/about/submissions/)
10. Litt, *Trudeaumania*, 337.
11. A November 2017 internal study by the Quebec Ministère du Conseil exécutif found that seven of the thirteen heads of provincial governments and territories had not even reacted to the document and that media attention had occurred primarily within Quebec itself rather than in the rest of Canada. It found that outside Quebec it is mainly in universities that the document had been the focus of debate and discussion. The account in Marie-Michèle Sioui, "Constitution: le ROC reste sourd aux appels de Couillard," *Le Devoir*, 4 Jan. 2018, produced a spirited response by Minister Jean-Marc Fournier, detailing the extent to which the document had been discussed in universities and think tanks outside Quebec (Jean-Marc Fournier, "L'écho à la politique d'affirmation du Québec: la relation Québec-Canada ne se résume pas qu'à celle de deux solitudes," *Le Devoir*, 6 Jan. 2018). The discussion at one such occasion, a conference at an Ontario university, is presented as largely desultory and negative by Alain Nöel, "Résignés, notre façon d'être fédéralistes," *Policy Options politiques*, 9 June 2017. More recent discussions, featuring Minister Fournier, have been more positive including a Sept. 2017 conference at the Glendon campus of York University and reportedly other Ontario events.
12. Jöel-Denis Bellavance, "Le débat constitutionnel est une distraction, selon Trudeau," *La Presse*, 5 June 2017, and Mélanie Marquis, "Non à un débat sémantique sur la Constitution, dit Trudeau," *La Presse*, 6 June 2017.
13. Veldon Coburn, "Indigenous Peoples and the Constitutional Conversation," *Policy Options politiques*, 9 June 2017.
14. Russell, *Canada's Odyssey*, 428–40. While it is officially committed to implementing the UN declaration, the federal government shows signs of bureaucratic resistance (Stefan Labbé, "Why the UN's Declaration on Indigenous Rights Has Been Slow to Implement in Canada," *Open Canada*, 21 July 2017).
15. Justin Trudeau reportedly seeks, through this new legal framework, to "give new life to Section 35 of the Constitution Act." (John Paul Tasker, "Trudeau Promises New Legal Framework to Indigenous People," *CBC News*, 14 Feb. 2018.) Yet it is difficult to see how this "new life" can be achieved without addressing directly the inadequacies of the constitutional text.
16. Charles Foran, "The Canadian Experiment: Is This the World's First 'Postnational' Country?" *The Guardian*, 4 Jan. 2017.
17. The Swiss confederation is sometimes cited as the first federation to be based

on cultural divisions. However, as noted by Will Kymlicka, it was based entirely on cantons that were ethnically and linguistically Germanic (Will Kymlicka, *Finding Our Way*, [Toronto: Oxford University Press, 1998] 206, n. 17).

18. Contemporary Spain might be seen as also incorporating both territorial and cultural/national division but it does not qualify as a federation. In "Canada and the Multinational State," I try to show that all federations other than Canada are based exclusively on territorial or cultural divisions (Kenneth McRoberts, "Canada and the Multinational State," *Canadian Journal of Political Science*, 34: 4 [Dec. 2001]: 701). See the discussion of multinational federations in Will Kymlicka, *Politics in the Vernacular: Nationalism, Multiculturalism and Citizenship* (New York: Oxford University Press, 2001), Chap. 5.

19. See, for instance, Will Kymlicka, *Finding Our Way*, and Michel Seymour and Guy Laforest, eds. *Le fédéralisme multinational: un modèle viable?* (Brussels: Peter Lang, 2011).

20. Eric Woods, "Beyond Multination Federations: Reflections on Nations and Nationalism in Canada," *Ethnicities* 12, no. 3 (June 2012): 270–92, and Robert Schertzer and Eric Taylor Woods, "Beyond multinational Canada," *Commonwealth and Comparative Studies* 49, no. 2, 2011, 196–222. To be sure, these authors are highly critical of the "Canada School."

21. Critical analyses of the Supreme Court's jurisprudence of section 35, contending that it focuses unduly on traditional Indigenous practice, appear in John Borrows, *Freedom and Indigenous Constitutionalism* (Toronto: University of Toronto Press, 2016), Chap. 4, and Dimitrios Panagos *Uncertain Accommodation: Aboriginal Identity and Group Rights in the Supreme Court of Canada* (Vancouver: UBC Press, 2016).

22. Marie-Michèle Sioui, "Couillard se dit favorable à l'auto-détermination des Premières Nations," *Le Devoir*, 28 June 2017.

Bibliography

Chapter One

Ajzenstat, J. 1988. *The Political Thought of Lord Durham.* Montreal and Kingston: McGill-Queen's University Press.

Arès, R. 1967. *Dossier sur le pacte fédératif de 1867.* Montreal: Bellarmin.

Behiels, M. 1985. *Prelude to Quebec's Quiet Revolution: Liberalism Versus Neo-nationalism, 1945–1960.* Montreal and Kingston: McGill-Queen's University Press.

Bernard, J.-P. 1971. *Les rouges.* Montreal: Presses de l'Université du Québec.

Bissell, C. 1982. *Massey Report and Canadian Culture,* 1982 John Porter Memorial Lecture. Ottawa: Carleton University.

Black, E.R. 1975. *Divided Loyalties: Canadian Concepts of Federalism.* Montreal and Kingston: McGill-Queen's University Press.

Bonenfant, J.-C. 1969. *La naissance de la Confédération.* Montreal: Leméac.

Bourassa, H. 1901. *Grande Bretagne et Canada.* Montreal: Imprimerie du Pionnier.

———. 1902. *Le patriotisme canadien-français: ce qu'il est, ce qu'il doit être.* Montreal: Cie de pub. de la Revue canadienne.

———. 1912. *Pour la justice.* Montreal: Imprimerie du Devoir.

———. 1915. *La langue française au Canada.* Montreal: Imprimerie du Devoir.

———. 1970. "Réponse amicale à la Vérité," as translated and reproduced in J. Levitt (ed.), *Henri Bourassa on Imperialism and Biculturalism, 1900–1918.* Toronto: Copp Clark.

Brossard, R., and H.F. Angus. 1937. "The Working of Confederation," *Canadian Journal of Economics and Political Science* 3, no. 3: 335–54.

Brunet, M. 1964. *La présence anglaise et les canadiens.* Montreal: Beauchemin.

Canada. 1867. British North America Act.

———. House of Commons, *Debates.* Various years.

Cartwright, R. 1955. "Reminiscences: Toronto, 1912." In Hodgetts, *Pioneer Public Service.* Toronto: University of Toronto Press.

Coleman, W.D. 1984. *The Independence Movement in Quebec, 1945–1980.* Toronto: University of Toronto Press.

Cook, R. 1969. *Provincial Autonomy, Minority Rights and the Compact Theory, 1867–1921.* Studies of the Royal Commission on Bilingualism and Biculturalism, no. 4. Ottawa: Queen's Printer.

Cook, R., with J.T. Saywell and J.C. Ricker. 1963. *Canada: A Modern Study.* Toronto: Clarke Irwin.

Craig, G.M. (ed.). 1963. *Lord Durham's Report.* Carleton Library no. 1. Toronto: McClelland & Stewart.

Creighton, D. 1964. *The Road to Confederation.* Toronto: Macmillan.

———. 1970. *Canada's First Century.* Toronto: Macmillan.

De Celles, A. 1907. *Cartier et son temps.* Montreal: Beauchemin.

Drolet J. 1974. "Henri Bourassa: une analyse de sa pensée." In F. Dumont, et al., *Idéologies au Canada français, 1900–1929.* Quebec City: Presses de l'Université Laval.

Falardeau, J.-C. 1960. "Les Canadiens français et leur idéologie." In M. Wade (ed.), *Canadian Dualism.* Toronto: University of Toronto Press.

Hamelin, J., and L. Beaudoin. 1972. "Les cabinets provinciaux, 1867–1967." In R. Desrosiers (ed.), *Le personnel politique québécois.* Montreal: Boréal.

Hodgetts, J.E. 1955. *Pioneer Public Service.* Toronto: University of Toronto Press.

Kelly, S. 1995. "Les imaginaires canadiens du 19e siècle." Thèse de doctorat, Département de sociologie, l'Université de Montréal.

Lacoursière, J., and C. Bouchard. 1972. *Notre histoire Québec–Canada.* Montreal: Éditions Format.

Linteau, P.-A., R. Durocher, and J.-C. Robert. 1979. *Histoire du Québec contemporain: de la Confédération à la crise.* Montreal: Boréal.

Litt, P. 1991. "The Massey Commission, Americanization, and Canadian Nationalism." *Queen's Quarterly* 98, no. 2 (Summer): 375–87.

Loranger, T.J.J. 1884. *Letters upon the Interpretation of the Federal Constitution known as the British North America Act,* (1867). Quebec City.

McRoberts, K. 1993. *Quebec: Social Change and Political Crisis,* 3rd edn with postscript. Toronto: McClelland & Stewart.

Morton, W.L. 1970. "The Cabinet of 1867." In F.W Gibson (ed.), *Cabinet Formation and Bicultural Relations*. Studies of the Royal Commission on Bilingualism and Biculturalism, no. 6. Ottawa: Queen's Printer.

Oliver, M. 1991. *The Passionate Debate: The Social and Political Ideas of Quebec Nationalism, 1920–1945*. Montreal: Véhicule.

Ormsby, W. 1969. *The Emergence of the Federal Concept in Canada, 1839–1845*. Toronto: University of Toronto Press.

Paquin, S. 1999. *L'invention d'un mythe: le pacte entre deux peuples fondateurs*. Montreal: VLB Éditeur.

Pickersgill, J.W. 1975. *My Years with Louis St. Laurent: A Political Memoir.* Toronto: University of Toronto Press.

Pope, J. 1930. *Memoirs of the Right Honourable Sir John Alexander Macdonald*. Toronto: Musson.

Quebec. 1956. *Rapport de la commission royale d'enquête sur les problèmes constitutionnels*, 5 vols.

———. 1956. *Report of the Royal Commission of Inquiry on Constitutional Problems*, vol. 1.

Regenstreif, P. 1969. "Note on the 'Alternation' of French and English Leaders in the Liberal Party of Canada." *Canadian Journal of Political Science* 2 (Mar.): 118–22.

Resnick, P. 1990. *The Masks of Proteus*. Montreal and Kingston: McGill-Queen's University Press.

Romney, P. 1999. *Getting It Wrong: How Canadians Forgot Their Past and Imperilled Confederation*. Toronto: University of Toronto Press.

Royal Commission on Bilingualism and Biculturalism. 1967. *Book I: The Official Languages*. Ottawa: Queen's Printer.

Russell, P.H. 2004. *Constitutional Odyssey: Can Canadians Become a Sovereign People?* 3rd edn. Toronto: University of Toronto Press.

Ryerson, S.B. 1968. *Unequal Union: Confederation and the Roots of Conflict in the Canadas, 1815–1873*. Toronto: Progress.

Silver, A.I. 1982. *The French-Canadian Idea of Confederation, 1864–1900*. Toronto: University of Toronto Press.

Simeon, R., and I. Robinson. 1990. *State, Society and the Development of Canadian Federalism*. Collected Research Studies of the Royal Commission on the Economic Union and Development Prospects for Canada, vol. 71. Toronto: University of Toronto Press.

Smiley, D.V. 1967. *The Canadian Political Nationality*. Toronto: Methuen.

———. 1970. *Constitutional Adaptation and Canadian Federalism since 1945*. Documents of the Royal Commission on Bilingualism and Biculturalism, no. 4. Ottawa: Queen's Printer.

———. 1977. "French–English Relations in Canada and Consociational Democracy." In M.J. Esman (ed.), *Ethnic Conflict in the Western World*. Ithaca: Cornell University Press.

———. 1980. *Canada in Question: Federalism in the Eighties*, 3rd edn. Toronto: McGraw-Hill Ryerson.

Stanley, G.F.C. 1956. "Act or Pact: Another Look at Confederation." *Proceedings of the Canadian Historical Association*.

Staples, J. 1974. "Consociationalism at Provincial Level: The Erosion of Dualism in Manitoba." In K. McRae (ed.), *Consociational Democracy: Political Accommodation in Segmented Societies*. Toronto: McClelland & Stewart.

Stevenson, G. 1989. *Unfulfilled Union: Canadian Federalism and National Unity*, 3rd edn. Toronto: Gage.

Thomson, D.C. 1967. *Louis St. Laurent: Canadian*. Toronto: Macmillan.

———. 1970 "The Cabinet of 1948." In Gibson (ed.), *Cabinet Formation and Bicultural Relations*, Studies of the Royal Commission on Bilingualism and Biculturalism, no. 6. Ottawa: Queen's Printer.

Verney, D.V. 1986. *Three Civilizations, Two Cultures, One State: Canada's Political Traditions*. Durham, NC: Duke University Press.

Vipond, R.C. 1991, *Liberty and Community: Canadian Federalism and the Failure of the Constitution*. Albany, NY: State University of New York Press.

Waite, P.B. 1962. *The Life and Times of Confederation, 1864–1867: Politics, Newspapers and the Union of British North America*. Toronto: University of Toronto Press.

———. 1963. *The Confederation Debates in the Province of Canada, 1865*. Carleton Library, no. 2. Toronto: McClelland & Stewart.

Zemans, J. 1995. "The Essential Role of National Cultural Institutions." In McRoberts, (ed.) *Beyond Quebec: Taking Stock of Canada*. Montreal and Kingston: McGill-Queen's University Press.

Chapter Two

Behiels, M. 1985. *Prelude to Quebec's Quiet Revolution: Liberalism Versus Neo-nationalism, 1945–1960*. Montreal and Kingston: McGill-Queen's University Press.

Black, E.R. 1975. *Divided Loyalties: Canadian Concepts of Federalism*. Montreal and Kingston: McGill-Queen's University Press.

Boismenu, G. 1989. "La pensée constitutionnelle de Jean Lesage." In R. Comeau (ed.), *Jean Lesage et l'éveil d'une nation*. Sillery, QC: Presses de l'Université du Québec.

Camp, D. 1968. "Reflections on the Montmorency Conference." *Queen's Quarterly* 76, no. 2 (Summer): 185–99.

Canada. House of Commons, *Debates*. Various years.

Canadian Annual Review. Toronto: University of Toronto Press. Various issues.

Canadian Dimension. 1967. "The NDP Federal Convention—1967," Sept.–Oct.: 4, 37–8.

Careless, A.G.S. 1977. *Initiative and Response: The Adaptation of Canadian Federalism to Regional Economic Development*. Montreal and Kingston: McGill-Queen's University Press.

Champion, C.P. 2010. *The Strange Demise of British Canada: The Liberals and Canadian Nationalism, 1964–1968*. Montreal and Kingston: McGill-Queen's University Press.

Clarkson, S., and C. McCall. 1990. *Trudeau and Our Times*, vol. 1, *The Magnificent Obsession*. Toronto: McClelland & Stewart.

Cohen, A. 2008. *Lester B. Pearson*. Toronto: Penguin,

Coleman, W.D. 1984. *The Independence Movement in Quebec, 1945–1980*. Toronto: University of Toronto Press.

Le Devoir. 1967. "Stanfield: gare aux mots." 1 Sept.

Diefenbaker, J.G. 1976. *One Canada, vol. 2: The Years of Achievement, 1957–1962*. Toronto: Macmillan.

Dion, L. 1975. *Nationalismes et politique au Québec*. Montreal: Hurtubise HMH.

English, J. 1992. *The Life of Lester Pearson, vol. 2, The Worldly Years, 1949–1972*. Toronto: Knopf Canada.

Forsey, E. 1962. "Canada: Two Nations or One?" *Canadian Journal of Economics and Political Science* 28, no. 4 (Nov.): 485–501.

Graefe, P. 1996. "From Coherence to Confusion: The CCF–NDP Confronts Federalism." Major research paper, M.A. Program in Political Science, York University.

Graham, G., and S. Chaput-Rolland. 1965. *Dear Enemies: A Dialogue on French and English Canada*. New York: Devin-Adair Co.

Granatstein, J.L. 1986. *Canada 1957–1967: The Years of Uncertainty and Innovation*. Toronto: McClelland & Stewart.

Grant, G. 1965. *Lament for a Nation*. Toronto: McClelland & Stewart.

Guindon, H. 1988. *Quebec Society: Tradition, Modernity, and Nationhood*. Toronto: University of Toronto Press.

Horowitz, G. 1965. "The Future of English Canada." *Canadian Dimension*, July–Aug., 12 and 25.

Howard, F. 1967. "Davis Assures Quebec Areas of Agreement Remain Ontario's Goal." *Globe and Mail*, 8 Aug.

Igartua, J. 2006. *The Other Quiet Revolution: National Identities in English Canada, 1945–71*. Vancouver: UBC Press.

Johnson, D. 1965. *Egalité ou indépendance*. Montreal: Editions de l'Homme.

Kent, T. 1988. *A Public Purpose: An Experience of Liberal Opposition and Canadian Government*. Montreal and Kingston: McGill-Queen's University Press.

Laforest, G. 1992. *Trudeau et la fin d'un rêve canadien*. Sillery, QC: Septentrion.

Lamoureux, A. 1985. *Le NPD et le Québec, 1958–1985*. Montreal: Les Éditions du Parc.

Lapointe-Gagnon, V. 2014. "Les origines intellectuelles de la commission Laurendeau–Dunton: de la présence d'une volonté de dialogue entre les deux peoples fondateurs du Canada au lendemain de la Seconde Guerre mondiale, 1945–1965," *Mens* 14, no. 2-1: 146–54.

La Terreur, M. 1973. *Les tribulations des conservateurs au Québec de Bennett à Diefenbaker*. Quebec City: Presses de l'Université Laval.

Laurendeau, A. 1962. "Pour une enquête sur le bilinguisme." *Le Devoir*, 20 Jan.

LePan, D. 1966. "The Old Ontario Strand in the Canada of Today," *Queen's Quarterly* 73.

Lévesque, R. 1968. *An Option for Quebec*. Toronto: McClelland & Stewart.

Levitt, K. 1970. *Silent Surrender: The Multinational Corporation in Canada*. Toronto: Macmillan.

Lumsden, Ian (ed.). 1970. *Close the 49th Parallel*. Toronto: University of Toronto Press.

Maclean's. 1990. "Cross-Canada Checkup." 12 Nov., 18–19.

McCall, C. and S. Clarkson. 1994. *Trudeau and Our Times, vol. 2, The Heroic Delusion*. Toronto: McClelland & Stewart.

McRoberts, K. 1985. "Unilateralism, Bilateralism and Multilateralism: Approaches to

Canadian Federalism." In R. Simeon (ed.), *Intergovernmental Relations*. Collected Research Studies of the Royal Commission on the Economic Union and Development Prospects for Canada, vol. 63. Toronto: University of Toronto Press.

———. 1993. *Quebec: Social Change and Political Crisis*, 3rd edn with postscript. Toronto: McClelland & Stewart.

———. 1996. "La Thèse tradition-modernité: l'historique québécois." In Mikhael Elbaz, Andrée Fortin, and Guy Laforest (eds), *Les Frontières de l'identité: modernité et post-modernisme au Québec*. Sainte-Foy: Presses de l'Université Laval.

Morton, D. 1974. *NDP: The Dream of Power*. Toronto: Hakkert.

———. 1986. *The New Democrats, 1961–1986: The Politics of Change*. Toronto: Copp Clark Pitman.

Newman, P.C. 1963. *Renegade in Power: The Diefenbaker Years*. Toronto: McClelland & Stewart.

———. 1968. *The Distemper of Our Times: Canadian Politics in Transition, 1963–1968*. Toronto: McClelland & Stewart.

Oliver, M. 1991. "Laurendeau et Trudeau: leurs opinions sur le Canada." In R. Hudon and R. Pelletier (eds), *L'engagement intellectuel: mélanges en l'honneur de Léon Dion*. Sainte-Foy: Presses de l'Université Laval.

———. 1996. Private communication, 9 June.

Oliver, M., and C. Taylor. 1991. "Quebec." In Heaps (ed.), *Our Canada*. Toronto: James Lorimer

Peacock, D. 1968. *Journey to Power: The Story of a Canadian Election*. Toronto: Ryerson.

Pearson, L.B. 1975. *Mike: The Memoirs of the Right Honourable Lester B. Pearson*, ed. J.A. Munro and A.I. Inglis. Toronto: University of Toronto Press.

Pepin, J.-L. 1964. "Co-operative Federalism," *Canadian Forum* (Dec.): 207.

Pinard, M. 1992. "The Dramatic Reemergence of the Quebec Independence Movement." *Journal of International Affairs* 45, no. 2 (Winter): 472–95.

Progressive Conservative Policy Advisory Conference of the Centennial Convention. n.d. Report on the Montmorency Conference, Courville, Quebec, 7–10 Aug, 1967.

Radawanski, G. 1978. *Trudeau*. Scarborough, ON: Macmillan–NAL.

Resnick, P. 1977. *The Land of Cain: Class and Nationalism in English Canada, 1945–1975*. Vancouver: New Star.

Robertson, G. 2000. *Memoirs of a Very Civil Servant*. Toronto: University of Toronto Press.

Roy, J.-L. 1976. *La marche des Quebecois: le temps des ruptures*, 1945–1960. Montreal: Leméac.

———. 1978. *Le choix d'un pays: le débat constitutionnel Québec–Canada, 1960–1976*. Montreal: Leméac.

Royal Commission on Bilingualism and Biculturalism. 1965. *Preliminary Report*. Ottawa: Queen's Printer.

Ryan, C. 1967. "Le Congrès conservateur de Toronto." *Le Devoir*, 7 Sept.

Sharp, M. 1994. *Which Reminds Me… A Memoir*. Toronto: University of Toronto Press.

Simeon, R. 1972. *Federal–Provincial Diplomacy: The Making of Recent Policy in Canada*. Toronto: University of Toronto Press.

Simeon, R., and I. Robinson. 1990. *State, Society and the Development of Canadian Federalism*. Collected Research Studies of the Royal Commission on the Economic Union and Development Prospects for Canada, vol. 71. Toronto: University of Toronto Press.

Smart, P. 1990. "The Waffle and Quebec," *Studies in Political Economy* 32 (Summer): 195–201.

Smiley, D.V. 1970. *Constitutional Adaptation and Canadian Federalism Since 1945*. Documents of the Royal Commission on Bilingualism and Biculturalism, no. 4. Ottawa: Queen's Printer.

Socialist History Project. 1969. *The Waffle Manifesto: For an Independent Socialist Canada*.

Stursberg, P. 1975. *Diefenbaker: Leadership Gained, 1956–62*. Toronto: University of Toronto Press.

———. 1978. *Lester Pearson and the Dream of Unity*. Toronto: Doubleday.

Sullivan, M. 1968. *Mandate '68*. Toronto: Doubleday.

Thomson, D.C. 1984, *Jean Lesage and the Quiet Revolution*. Toronto: Macmillan.

Vaillancourt Y. 1992. "Le Régime d'assistance publique du Canada: perspective québécoise." Thèse de doctorat en science politique, l'Université de Montréal.

———. 1993. "Quebec and the Federal Government: The Struggle Over Opting Out." In D. Glenday and A. Duffy (eds), *Canadian Society: Understanding and Surviving in the 1990s*. Toronto: McClelland & Stewart.

Vineberg, M. 1968. "The Progressive Conservative Leadership Convention of 1967." M.A.

thesis, Dept. of Economics and Political Science, McGill University.
Wade, M. (ed.). 1960. *La dualité Canadienne: essais sur les relations entre Canadiens français et Canadiens anglais/Canadian Dualism: Studies of French–English Relations*. Quebec: Laval University Press and Toronto: University of Toronto Press.
Westell, A. 1967. "Diefenbaker Won't Continue; Tories Back 2-Nation Plan." *Globe and Mail*, 8 Sept.
———. 1972. *Paradox: Trudeau as Prime Minister*. Scarborough, ON: Prentice-Hall.
Whitehorn, A. 1992. *Canadian Socialism: Essays on the CCF–NDP*. Toronto: Oxford University Press.
Wright, R. 2016. *Trudeaumania: The Rise to Power of Pierre Elliott Trudeau*. Toronto: Harper Collins.

Chapter Three

d'Aillon, P.G. 1979. *Daniel Johnson: l'égalité avant l'indépendance*. Montreal: Stanké.
Balthazar, L. 1986. *Bilan du nationalisme au Québec*. Montreal: l'Hexagone.
Bergeron, G. 1985. *Notre miroir à deux faces*. Montreal: Québec/Amérique.
Boismenu, G. 1989. "La pensée constitutionnelle de Jean Lesage." In R. Comeau (ed.), *Jean Lesage et l'éveil d'une nation*. Sillery, QC: Presses de l'Université du Québec.
Breton, A., et al. 1964. "Manifeste pour une politique fonctionnelle." *Cité libre*, May: 11–17.
Burelle, A. 2005. *Pierre Elliott Trudeau: l'intellectuel et le politique*. Montreal: Fides.
Cité libre. 1967. "Les octrois fédéraux aux universités." Feb.
Clarkson, S., and C. McCall. 1990. *Trudeau and Our Times*, vol. 1, *The Magnificent Obsession*. Toronto: McClelland & Stewart.
Colombo, J.R. 1994. *Colombo's All-Time Great Canadian Quotations*. Toronto: Stoddart.
Cook, R. 1971. *The Maple Leaf Forever: Essays on Nationalism and Politics in Canada*. Toronto: Macmillan.
———. 2006. *The Teeth of Time: Remembering Pierre Elliott Trudeau*. Montreal and Kingston: McGill-Queen's University Press.
Daignault, R. 1981. *Lesage*. Quebec, QC: Libre expression.
Delisle, E. 2002. *Essais sur l'imprégnation fasciste au Québec*. Montreal: Les Éditions Varia.
Le Devoir. 1968. "Léo Cadieux donne son appui à Paul Hellyer." 14 Mar.
———. 1968. "Trudeau est assuré de l'appui de 23 députés du Québec." 20 Mar.
———. 1968. "Isabelle appuie plutôt Winters; Lessard, Hellyer." 28 Mar.
———. 1968. "Le sénateur Lamontagne appuie Trudeau dont il dit partager 'en gros' les positions constitutionnelles." 29 Mar.
———. 1968. "La course au leadership accentue les divisions dans le caucus du Québec." 11 Apr.
English, J. 1992. *The Life of Lester Pearson, vol. 2, The Worldly Years, 1949–1972*. Toronto: Knopf Canada.
———. 2006. *Citizen of the World: The Life of Pierre Elliott Trudeau, 1919–1968*. Toronto: Knopf Canada.
———. 2009. *Just Watch Me: The Life of Pierre Elliott Trudeau, 1968–2000*. Toronto: Knopf Canada.
English, J., R. Gwyn, and P. Whitney Lackenbauer (eds). 2004. *The Hidden Pierre Elliott Trudeau: The Faith behind the Politics*. Toronto: Novalis.
Forbes, H.D. 1996. "Trudeau's Moral Vision." In A. A. Peacock (ed.), *Rethinking the Constitution: Perspectives on Canadian Constitutional Reform, Interpretation, and Theory*. Toronto: Oxford University Press.
Globe and Mail. 1977. "Trudeau: Unity in Canada Won't Be Fractured." 23 Feb.
Granatstein, J.L. 1986. *Canada 1957–1967: The Years of Uncertainty and Innovation*. Toronto: McClelland & Stewart.
Gwyn, R. 1980. *The Northern Magus*. Toronto: McClelland & Stewart.
Hawthorn, T. 2013. *The Year Canadians Lost Their Minds and Found Their Country*. Madeira Park, BC: Douglas & McIntyre.
Lamoureux, A. 1985. *Le NPD et le Québec, 1958–1985*. *Journal du Québec*. 2016. 2 Mar. Montreal: Les Éditions du Parc.
Laurendeau, A. 1956. "Sur cent pages de Pierre Elliott Trudeau." *Le Devoir*, 6 Oct.
———. 1991. *The Diary of André Laurendeau: Written During the Royal Commission on Bilingualism and Biculturalism, 1964–1967*. Toronto: Lorimer.

Lebel, R. 1968. "PM Creating Great Division." *Globe and Mail*, 21 June.

Lemelin, C. 1968. "Sharp: Ottawa devra faire preuve de souplesse sur la question constitutionnelle." *Le Devoir*, 23 Mar.

Litt, P. 2016. *Trudeaumania*. Vancouver: UBC Press

McCall, C, and S. Clarkson. 1994. *Trudeau and Our Times, vol. 2, The Heroic Delusion*. Toronto: McClelland & Stewart.

Meisel, J. 1972. *Working Papers on Canadian Politics*. Montreal and Kingston: McGill-Queen's University Press.

Mills, A. 2016. *Citizen Trudeau, 1944–1965: An Intellectual Biography*. Don Mills, ON: Oxford University Press.

Monet, J. 2004. "The Man's Formation in Faith." In English, Gwyn, and Lackenbauer (eds), *The Hidden Pierre Elliott Trudeau: The Faith Behind the Politics*. Toronto: Novalis.

Morton, D. 1972. "The NDP and Quebec: A Sad Tale of Unrequited Love." *Saturday Night*, June, 17–20.

———. 1974. *NDP: The Dream of Power*. Toronto: Hakkert.

Nemni, M., and M. Nemni. 2006. *Trudeau: fils du Québec, père du Canada, vol. 1*. Quebec: Éditions de l'Homme.

———. 2011. *Trudeau Transformed: The Shaping of a Statesman, 1944–1965*, trans George Tombs. Toronto: McClelland & Stewart.

New Democratic Party. 1976. "Towards a New Canada: A New Canadian Constitution." In *New Democratic Policies, 1961–1976*. Ottawa: New Democratic Party.

Newman, P.C. 1966. "Now There's a Third Viewpoint in the French–English Dialogue." *Toronto Star*, 2 Apr.

———. 1968. *The Distemper of Our Times: Canadian Politics in Transition, 1963–1968*. Toronto: McClelland & Stewart.

Oliver, M. 1991. "Laurendeau et Trudeau: leurs opinions sur le Canada." In R. Hudon and R. Pelletier (eds), *L'engagement intellectuel: mélanges en l'honneur de Léon Dion*. Sainte-Foy: Presses de l'Université Laval.

Patry, A. 1989. "Témoignage." In R. Comeau (ed.), *Jean Lesage et l'éveil d'une nation*. Sillery, QC: Presses de l'Université du Québec.

Peacock, D. 1968. *Journey to Power: The Story of a Canadian Election*. Toronto: Ryerson.

Radwanski, G. 1978. *Trudeau*. Scarborough, ON: Macmillan-NAL.

Rempel, H.D. 1975. "The Practice and Theory of the Fragile State: Trudeau's Conception of Authority," *Journal of Canadian Studies* 10, no. 4 (Nov.): 24–38.

Ricci, N. 2009. *Pierre Elliott Trudeau*. Toronto: Penguin.

Robertson, G. 2000. *Memoirs of a Very Civil Servant*. Toronto: University of Toronto Press.

Roy, J.-L. 1978. *Le choix d'un pays: le débat constitutionnel Québec–Canada, 1960–1976*. Montreal: Leméac.

Ryan, C. 1968. "Vieille tentation du Canada anglais." *Le Devoir*, 1 Feb.

———. 1968. "Le choix du 25 juin." *Le Devoir*, 19 June.

Smiley, D.V. 1969. "The Case against the Canadian Charter of Human Rights." *Canadian Journal of Political Science* 2, no. 3 (Sept.): 278–91.

———. 1970. *Constitutional Adaptation and Canadian Federalism Since 1945*. Documents of the Royal Commission on Bilingualism and Biculturalism, no. 4. Ottawa: Queen's Printer.

Sullivan, M. 1968. *Mandate '68*. Toronto: Doubleday.

Thomson, D.C. 1984. *Jean Lesage and the Quiet Revolution*. Toronto: Macmillan.

Trudeau, P.E. 1954. "De libro, tributo . . . et quibusdam aliis," *Cité libre*. Oct.

———. 1957. "Les octrois fédéraux aux universités," *Cité libre*, February.

———. 1962. "Economic Rights," *McGill Law Journal* 8, no. 2, 1–5.

———. 1962. "La nouvelle trahison des clercs," *Cité libre*, Apr., 1962, as translated and reproduced in Trudeau, *Federalism and the French Canadians*. Toronto: Macmillan.

———. 1968. *Federalism and the French Canadians*. Toronto: Macmillan.

———. 1968. Speech at Sudbury, ON, 5 June 1968. Quoted in "Citizenship and the Charter of Rights: Two Sides of Pierre Trudeau," by R. Vipond, *International Journal of Canadian Studies*, no. 14 (Fall 1996).

———. 1987. "'Say Goodbye to the Dream' of One Canada." *Toronto Star*, 27 May.

———. 1987. Special Joint Committee of the Senate and the House of Commons on the 1987 Constitutional Accord, *Minutes of Proceedings and Evidence*, 2nd session, 33rd Parliament, issue no. 14 (27 Aug.): 116–58.

———. 1993. *Memoirs*. Toronto: McClelland & Stewart.

———. 1998. *The Essential Trudeau*. Edited by Ron Graham. Toronto: McClelland & Stewart.

———. 2015. *Approaches to Politics*. Don Mills: Oxford University Press

Trudeau, P.E. (ed.). 1970. *La grève de l'amiante*. Montreal: Éditions du Jour.

Vastel, M. 1989. *Trudeau: le Québécois*. Montreal: Éditions de l'Homme.

Vipond, R. 1996. "Citizenship and the Charter of Rights: Two Sides of Pierre Trudeau," *International Journal of Canadian Studies*, no. 14 (Fall): 189–92.

Waldie, P. 2016. "Files Show What U.K. Diplomats Really Thought of 1980s Canada." *Globe and Mail*, 23 Aug.

Warren, J.-P. 2004. "Let the Jesuits and the Dominicans Quarrel: a French-Canadian Debate of the Fifties." In English, Gwyn, and Lackenbauer (eds), *The Hidden Pierre Elliott Trudeau: The Faith Behind the Politics*. Toronto: Novalis.

Webber, J. 1994. *Reimagining Canada: Language, Culture, Community and the Canadian Constitution*. Montreal and Kingston: McGill-Queen's University Press.

Westell, A. 1968. "PM challenges Quebec Tories on Two Nations." *Globe and Mail*, 21 June.

———. 1969. "If Canada Doesn't Want Bilingualism, I Want Out." *Toronto Star*, 8 Feb.

———. 1972. *Paradox: Trudeau as Prime Minister*. Scarborough, ON: Prentice-Hall.

Whitaker, R. 1992. "Reason, Passion and Interest: Pierre Trudeau's Eternal Liberal Triangle." In R. Whitaker (ed.), *A Sovereign Idea*. Montreal and Kingston: McGill-Queen's University Press.

Wright, R. 2016. *Trudeaumania: The Rise to Power of Pierre Elliott Trudeau*. Toronto: Harper Collins.

Chapter Four

Behiels. M. 2004. *Canada's Francophone Minority Communities: Constitutional Renewal and the Winning of School Governance*. Montreal and Kingston: McGill-Queen's University Press.

Bibeau, G. 1984. "No Easy Road to Bilingualism." *Language and Society* no. 12 (Winter): 44–7.

Bourgeois, D. 2006. *The Canadian Bilingual Districts: From Cornerstone to Tombstone*. Montreal and Kingston: McGill-Queen's Press.

———. 2008. "La prestation des services bilingues au Canada." In Martel and Pâquet (eds), *Légiférer en matière linguistique*. Quebec, QC: Presses de l'Université Laval.

———. 2014. "La commission BB et la bureaucratie fédérale" *Mens* 14, no. 2-1: 37–8.

Bouthillier, G., and É. Cloutier (eds). 2010. *Trudeau's Darkest Hour: War Measures in Time of Peace, October 1970*. Montreal: Baraka Books.

Canada. 1969. Official Languages Act, 1st session, 28th Parliament, C-120.

———. 1971. *Canadian Constitutional Charter* (Victoria Charter).

———. 1971. *Recommendations of the Bilingual Districts Advisory Board*, Mar. 1971. Information Canada.

———. 1975. *Report of the Bilingual Districts Advisory Board*, Oct. 1975. Information Canada.

———. 1977. *A National Understanding*. Ottawa: Supply and Services Canada.

———. 1982. *Charter of Rights and Freedoms*. Constitution Act, Sections 1 to 34.

———. 1985. Official Languages Act, c. 31 (4th Supp.), 16(1).

———. 1988. *Debates* of the Senate, 2nd session, 33rd Parliament, 1986–87–88, 30 Mar: 2982–3023.

———. 1988. Official Languages Act, amended, 2nd session, 33rd Parliament, C-72.

———. 2015. Heritage Canada, *Official Languages Annual Report*, 2014–15.

———. Privy Council Office. 2017. "The Next Level: Normalizing a Culture of Inclusive Linguistic Duality in the Federal Public Service Workplace" https://www.canada.ca/en/privy-council/corporate/clerk/publications/next-level.html

———. House of Commons, *Debates*. Various years.

———. Senate, *Debates*. Various years.

Cardinal, L., H. Gaspard, and R. Léger. 2015. "The Politics of Language Roadmaps in Canada: Understanding the Conservative Government's Approach to Official Languages," *Canadian Journal of Political Science* 48, no. 3 (Sept. 2015): 577–99.

Charbonneau, H., J. Henripin, and J. Legaré. 1974. "L'avenir démographique des francophones au Québec et à Montréal en l'absence de politiques adéquates." *Revue de géographie de Montréal* 24: 199–202.

Christian, T. J. 1991. "L'affaire Piquette." In D. Schneiderman, *Language and the State*. Cowansville, QC: Yvon Blais.

Commissariat aux services en français. 2012. *Rapport d'enquête – L'état de l'éducation: pas d'avenir sans accès postsecondaire en langue française dans le Centre-Sud-Ouest de l'Ontario,* 27 June.

Commissioner of Official Languages. *Annual Reports*. Ottawa: Information Canada or Supply and Services. Various years.

———. 2004. *Walking the Talk: Language of Work in the Federal Public Service of Canada*. Ottawa.

———. 2016. *Understanding Your Language Rights*. Ottawa.

Coyne, D. 1993. "Back-Door Constitutional Deal Rips Fabric of the Nation." *Toronto Star,* 6 Jan.

Descôteaux, B. 1988. "Ottawa négociera avec le Québec sur la loi des langues." *Le Devoir,* 8 June.

———. 1988. "Ottawa et Québec s'entendent' sur les langues officielles." *Le Devoir,* 18 Aug.

Denis, W.B. 1990. "The Politics of Language." In Peter S. Li (ed.), *Race and Ethnic Relations in Canada*. Toronto: Oxford University Press.

Dion, L. 1989. "The Impact of Demolinguistic Trends on Canadian Institutions." In *Demolinguistic Trends and the Evolution of Canadian Institutions*, special issue of *Canadian Issues* of the Association of Canadian Studies: 57–71.

Federation of Francophones outside Quebec. 1981. *A la recherche du milliard* (Ottawa), as cited in Wilfrid B. Denis, "The Politics of Language." In Li, *Race and Ethnic Relations in Canada*. Toronto: Oxford University Press, 1990.

Fortier, D. 1988. "Breaking Old Habits." *Language and Society* no. 24 (Fall): 12–13.

Foucher, P. 1999. "Les droits linguistiques au Canada." In Thériault (ed.), *Francophonie minoritaires au Canada: L'état des lieux*. Moncton: Éditions d'Acadie.

———. 2011. "The Official Languages Act of Canada." In Jedwab and Landry (eds), *Life after Forty/Après quarante ans: Official Languages Policy in Canada/ les politiques de langue officielle au Canada*. Kingston: School of Policy Studies, Queen's University.

———. 2012. "Autonomie des communautés francophones minoritaires du Canada: le point de vue du droit." *Minorités linguistiques et société*, no. 1: 90–114.

Francoli, P. 2005. "Trudeau's Bilingual Dream Still Unfulfilled," *The Hill Times*, 20 Dec.–9 Jan.

Fraser, G. 2006. *Sorry I Don't Speak French: Confronting the Canadian Crisis That Won't Go Away*. Toronto: McClelland & Stewart.

———. 2009. "Canadian Language Rights: Liberties, Claims and the National Conversation." In Kelly and Manfredi (eds), *Contested Constitutionalism: Reflections on the Canadian Charter of Rights and Freedoms*. Vancouver: UBC Press.

Gaspard, H. 2015. "Canada's Official Languages Policy and the Federal Public Service." In Cardinal and Sonntag (eds), *State Traditions and Language Regimes*. Montreal and Kingston: McGill-Queen's University Press.

Gibson, F.W. (ed.). 1970. *Cabinet Formation and Bicultural Relations*. Studies of the Royal Commission on Bilingualism and Biculturalism, no. 6. Ottawa: Queen's Printer.

Globe and Mail. 1969. "Back to the Solitudes." 18 Dec.

Harrison, B.R., and L. Marmen. 1994. *Languages in Canada*. Scarborough, ON.: Prentice-Hall. Published jointly with Statistics Canada.

Hayday, M. 2005. *Bilingual Today, United Tomorrow: Official Languages in Education and Canadian Federalism*. Montreal and Kingston: McGill-Queen's University Press.

———. 2011. "Finessing Federalism: The Development of Institutional and Popular Support for Official Languages." In Jedwab and Landry (eds), *Life after Forty: Official Languages Policy in Canada*. Montreal and Kingston: McGill-Queen's University Press.

———. 2015. *So They Want Us to Learn French: Promoting and Opposing Bilingualism in English-Speaking Canada*. Vancouver: UBC Press.

Hébert, C., and J. Lapierre. 2014. *The Morning After: The 1995 Quebec Referendum and the Day that Almost Was*. Toronto: Alfred A. Knopf Canada.

———. 2014. *Confessions post-référendaires.* Montreal: Les Éditions l'Homme.

Henripin, J. 1993. "Population Trends and Policies in Quebec." In A. Gagnon (ed.), *Quebec: State and Society.* 2nd edn. Scarborough, ON: Nelson.

Hodgetts, J.E. 1955. *Pioneer Public Service.* Toronto: University of Toronto Press.

Houle, R., and J. Corbeil. 2017. *Language Projections for Canada, 2011 to 2036,* Catalogue no. 89-657-X2017001. Ottawa: Statistics Canada.

Hudon, M. 2009. "Official Languages in the Public Service," Library of Parliament, 6 Mar.

———. 2016. Official Languages in Canada: Federal Policy," Library of Parliament, 18 Jan.

Joy, R.J. 1972. *Languages in Conflict: The Canadian Experience.* Toronto: McClelland & Stewart.

———. 1992. *Canada's Official Languages: The Progress of Bilingualism.* Toronto: University of Toronto Press.

Joyal, S. 2004. "Foreword." In M.D. Behiels, *Canada's Francophone Minority Communities: Constitutional Renewal and the Winning of School Governance.* Montreal and Kingston: McGill-Queen's University Press.

La Presse. 1976. "Le discours de M. Trudeau: il faut qu'on se parle dans le blanc des yeux." 8 Mar.

Landry, R. 2011. "*Loi sur les langues officielles et démographie*: comment les droits linguistiques peuvent-ils influencer la vitalité d'une minorité?" In Jedwab and Landry (eds), *Life after Forty.* Montreal and Kingston: McGill-Queen's University Press.

Lalande, G. 1987. "Back to the B and B." *Language and Society* no. 19 (Apr.): 22–4.

Laponce, J.A. 1987. *Languages and Their Territories.* Toronto: University of Toronto Press.

Leblanc, A. 1986. *Bilingual Education: A Challenge for Canadian Universities in the '90s.* Winnipeg: Continuing Education Division, University of Manitoba.

Leblanc, D. 2017. "Feu vert à une université franco-ontarienne," *Le Droit*, 28 Aug.

Lepage, J., and J. Corbeil. 2016. "The Evolution of English–French Bilingualism in Canada from 1961 to 2011," Statistics Canada, #75-006-X.

McRae, K. 1975. "The Principle of Territoriality and the Principle of Personality in Multilingual States." *International Journal of the Sociology of Language* 4: 35–45.

———. 1978. "Bilingual Language Districts in Finland and Canada: Adventures in the Transplanting of an Institution." *Canadian Public Policy* 4, no. 3 (Summer): 331–51.

———. 1998 "Official Bilingualism: From the 1960s to the 1990s." In J. Edwards (ed.), *Language in Canada.* Cambridge: Cambridge University Press.

McRoberts, K. 1993. *Quebec: Social Change and Political Crisis,* 3rd edn with postscript. Toronto: McClelland & Stewart.

Mackey, W.F. 2010. "Language Policies in Canada." In Morris (ed.), *Canadian Language Policies in Comparative Perspective.* Montreal and Kingston: McGill-Queen's University Press.

Martel, M. 1994. "Les relations entre le Québec et les francophones de l'Ontario: de la survivance aux *Dead Ducks*, 1937–1969." Ph.D. dissertation, History Department, York University.

———. n.d. "Monsieur le premier ministre, je vous écris: les Ontariens et le bilinguisme, 1963–1971." Unpublished paper.

———, and M. Pâquet. 2010. *Langue et politique au Canada et au Québec: une synthèse historique.* Montreal: Éditions du Boréal.

Martel, M., and M. Pâquet (eds). 2008. *Légifier en matière linguistique.* Quebec: Presses de l'Université Laval.

May, K. 2017. "Bilingualism is Stagnating in Federal Public Service, Says Report," *iPolitics*, 30 July.

Mosimann-Barbier, M.-C. 1992. *Immersion et bilinguisme en Ontario.* Rouen: l'Université de Rouen.

New Brunswick. n.d. Office of the Commissioner of Official Languages for New Brunswick, "History of Official Languages in New Brunswick." http://officiallanguages.nb.ca/publications-links-other/history-official-languages

Ontario. 1986. *An Act to Provide French Language Services in the Government of Ontario,* 2nd session, 33rd Parliament, Bill 8.

Ontario Court of Appeal. 2002. "Lalonde v. Commission de restructuration des services de santé," 7 Dec. 2001 (Revised 8 Mar. 2002).

Pal, L.A. 1993. *Interests of State: The Politics of Language, Multiculturalism and Feminism in Canada.* Montreal and Kingston: McGill-Queen's University Press.

Prime Minister's Office. 1968. *Statement by the Prime Minister in the House of Commons on the Resolution Preliminary to Introduction of the Official Languages Bill,* 17 Oct.

Quebec 1972. *Rapport de la commission d'enquête sur la situation de la langue française et sur les droits linguistiques au Québec*, vol. 1, *La langue de travail;* vol. 2, *Les droits linguistiques*. Quebec City.

Radwanski, G. 1978. *Trudeau*. Scarborough, ON: Macmillan–NAL.

Réaume, D.G. 2003. "Beyond Personality: The Territorial and Personal Principles of Language Policy Reconsidered." In Kymlicka and Patten (eds), *Language Rights and Political Theory*. Oxford: Oxford University Press.

Reid, S. 1993. *Lament for a Notion: The Life and Death of Canada's Bilingual Dream*. Vancouver: Arsenal Pulp.

Richez, E. 2012. "Francophone Minority Communities: The Last Constitutional Standard-Bearers of Trudeau's Language Regime," *International Journal of Canadian Studies*, no. 45–46: 35–53.

Riddell, T. 2003. "Official Minority-Language Education Policy outside Quebec: The Impact of Section 23 of the Charter and Judicial Decisions," *Canadian Public Administration* 46, no. 1 (Spring): 37.

———, 2009. "Explaining the Impact of Legal Mobilization and Judicial Decisions: Official Minority-Language Education Rights Outside Quebec." In Kelly and Manfredi (eds), *Contested Constitutionalism: Reflections on the Canadian Charter of Rights and Freedoms*. Vancouver: UBC Press.

Royal Commission on Bilingualism and Biculturalism. 1965. *Preliminary Report*. Ottawa: Queen's Printer.

———. 1967. *General Introduction*. Ottawa: Queen's Printer.

———. 1967. *Book I: The Official Languages*. Ottawa: Queen's Printer.

———. 1968. *Book II: Education*. Ottawa: Queen's Printer.

———. 1969. *Book III: The Work World*. Ottawa: Queen's Printer.

Russell, P.H. 2004. *Constitutional Odyssey: Can Canadians Become a Sovereign People?* 3rd edn. Toronto: University of Toronto Press.

Sarra-Bournet, M. 1992. "'French Power, Québec Power': la place des francophones québécois à Ottawa." In F. Rocher (ed.), *Bilan québécois du fédéralisme canadien*. Montreal: VLB.

Savoie, D.J. 1991. *The Politics of Language*. Kingston: Institute of Intergovernmental Relations, Queen's University.

Schneiderman, D. (ed.). 1991, *Language and the State: The Law and Politics of Identity*. Cowansville, QC: Yvon Blais.

Secretary of State. 1990. *Annual Report to Parliament, 1989–1990: Official Languages*. Ottawa.

Simeon, R. 1972. *Federal–Provincial Diplomacy: The Making of Recent Policy in Canada*. Toronto: University of Toronto Press.

Smiley, D.V. 1980. *Canada in Question: Federalism in the Eighties*, 3rd edn. Toronto: McGraw-Hill Ryerson.

Spicer, K. 1989. "How the Linguistic World Looked in 1970." *Languages and Society*, Special Edition (Summer): R-10–R-12.

Statistics Canada. 1971. *Census of Canada*.

———. 2017. "English–French Bilingualism Reaches New Heights." *Census in Brief*, 31 Aug.

Stevenson, D. 2008. "John Robarts' Advisory Committee on Confederation and Its Impact on Ontario's Language Policy." In Martel and Pâquet (eds), *Légiférer en matière linguistique*. Quebec, QC: Presses de l'Université Laval.

———. n.d. "What Is an Official Language?," unpublished paper.

Stevenson, G. 1999. *Community Besieged: The Anglophone Minority and the Politics of Quebec*. Montreal and Kingston: McGill-Queen's University Press.

———. 1977. "What Quebec Really Wants: English Consider Us Inferior, Quebec Feels." 17 May.

Treasury Board Secretariat. 1991. "Official Languages (Communications with and Services to the Public) Regulations," *Canada Gazette*, Part I, 23 Mar.

Trudeau, P.E. 1964. "We Need a Bill of Rights," *Maclean's*, 8 Feb. (as reproduced in Pierre Elliott Trudeau, *Against the Current: Selected Writings 1939–1996*, ed. Gérard Pelletier. Toronto: McClelland & Stewart, 216–7.

———. 1968. *Federalism and the French Canadians*. Toronto: Macmillan.

———. 1971. "Announcement of Implementation of Policy of Multiculturalism within Bilingual Framework," House of Commons, *Debates*, 8 Oct. 1971, 8545–48, Appendix, 8580–85.

———. 1990. "The Values of a Just Society." In T.S. Axworthy and P.E. Trudeau (eds), *Towards a Just Society: The Trudeau Years*. Markham, ON: Viking.

———. 1993. *Memoirs*. Toronto: McClelland & Stewart.

———. 1996. *Against the Current: Selected Writings 1939–1996*. Edited by Gérard Pelletier. Toronto: McClelland & Stewart.

———. 1998. *The Essential Trudeau*. Edited by Ron Graham. Toronto: McClelland & Stewart.

Vastel, M. 2015. "L'Alberta restera unilingue anglophone." *Le Devoir,* 21 Nov.

Waddell, E. 1991. "Some Thoughts on the Implications of French Immersion for English Canada," in D. Schneiderman, *Language and the State*, 423–32. Cowansville, QC: Editions Yvon Blais Inc.

Chapter Five

Abu-Laban, Y. 2014. "Reform by Stealth: The Harper Conservatives and Canadian Multiculturalism." In Jedwab (ed.), *The Multiculturalism Question: Debating Identity in 21st Century Canada*. Montreal and Kingston: McGill-Queen's University Press.

Baillargeon, S. 2017. "Dix ans après Bouchard–Taylor, tant reste à faire." *Le Devoir,* 4 Feb.

Balthazar, L. 1989. "Pour un multiculturalisme québécois." *Action nationale* 79 (Oct.): 942–53.

Banting, K. 2010. "Is There a Progressive's Dilemma in Canada? Immigration, Multiculturalism and the Welfare State," *Canadian Journal of Political Science* 43, no. 4 (Dec): 797–820.

Besca, R., and E. Tolley. 2016. "Does Everyone Cheer? The Politics of Immigration and Multiculturalism in Canada." Paper presented to conference on "New Frontiers in Public Policy," Queen's University, 23 Sept.

Biles, J. 2014. "The Government of Canada's Multiculturalism Program." In Jedwab (ed.), *The Multiculturalism Question: Debating Identity in 21st Century Canada*. Montreal and Kingston: McGill-Queen's University Press.

Bissoondath, N. 1994. *Selling Illusions: The Cult of Multiculturalism in Canada*. Toronto: Penguin.

Bloemraad, I. 2015. "Reimagining the Nation in a World of Migration: Legitimacy, Political Claims-Making and Membership in Comparative Perspective." In Foner and Simon (eds), *Fear and Anxiety over National Identity*. New York: Russell Sage Foundation Press.

Borrows, J. 2002. *Recovering Canada: The Resurgence of Indigenous Law*. Toronto: University of Toronto Press.

Bouchard, G., and C. Taylor. 2008. *Building the Future: A Time for Reconciliation*. Quebec, QC: Consultation Commission on Accommodation Practices Related to Cultural Differences.

Breton, A., et al. 1964. "Manifeste pour une politique fonctionnelle." *Cité libre*, May: 11–17.

Breton, R. 1986. "Multiculturalism and Canadian Nation-Building." In A. Cairns and C. Williams (eds), *The Politics of Gender, Ethnicity and Language in Canada*. Collected Research Studies of the Royal Commission on the Economic Union and Development Prospects for Canada, vol. 34. Toronto: University of Toronto Press.

Cairns, A.C. 2000. *Citizens Plus: Aboriginal Peoples and the Canadian State*. Vancouver: UBC Press.

Canada. 1969. *Statement of the Government of Canada on Indian Policy (The White Paper)*.

———. 1985. "Canadian Multiculturalism Act", R.S.C., 1985, c. 24 (4th Supp.).

———. Prime Minister's Office. 2017. *Prime Minister Delivers Apology to LGBTQ2 Canadians,* 28 Nov.

———. House of Commons, *Debates*. Various years.

———. Senate, *Debates*. Various years.

Chiasson, M. 2012. "The Reasonable Accommodation Crisis," Centre for Human Rights and Legal Pluralism, McGill University, Aug.

Citrin, J., R. Johnston, and M. Wright. 2012. "Do Patriotism and Multiculturalism Collide? Competing Perspectives from Canada and the United States," *Canadian Journal of Political Science* 45, no. 3 (Sept.): 531–52.

Clarkson, S., and C. McCall. 1990. *Trudeau and Our Times*, vol. 1, *The Magnificent Obsession*. Toronto: McClelland & Stewart.

Comité pour une politique fonctionelle. 1965. "Bizarre algèbre." *Cité libre* 15, no. 82 (Dec): 13–20.

Corriveau, J. 2017. "Coderre mal à l'aise à l'égard du projet de loi sur la neutralité religieuse," 8 Oct.

Cummins, J., and M. Danesi. 1990. *Heritage Languages: The Development and Denial of Canada's Linguistic Resources*. Toronto: Our Schools/Our Selves Foundation.

Dahl, R.A. (ed.). 1966. *Political Oppositions in Western Democracies*. New Haven: Yale University Press.

Dewing, M. 2013. "Canadian Multiculturalism." Library of Parliament, Canada (#2009-20-E).

Dufour, C. 1990. *A Canadian Challenge/Le défis québécois*. Lantzville, BC and Halifax: Oolichan Books and IRRP.

English, J. 2009. *Just Watch Me: The Life of Pierre Elliott Trudeau, 1968–2000*. Toronto: Knopf Canada.

Everett-Green, R. 2016. "Trudeau Promises Aboriginal Language Bill, but Activists Say Whole System Needs Overhaul." *Globe and Mail*, 28 Dec.

Federation of Francophones outside Quebec. 1978. *The Heirs of Lord Durham: Manifesto of a Vanishing People* (Toronto: Burns and MacEachern), as quoted in "Federal Government's Multiculturalism Policy" by J. Jaworsky, M.A. thesis, Department of Political Science, Carleton University.

Forbes, H.D. 2008. "Trudeau as the First Theorist of Canadian Multiculturalism." In Tierney (ed.), *Multiculturalism and the Canadian Constitution*. Vancouver: UBC Press.

Gervias, L. 2017. "Gérard Bouchard juge la loi sur la neutralité religieuse peu utile and difficile à appliquer." *Le Devoir*, 20 Oct.

Granatstein, J.L. 1968. *Canada 1957–1967: The Years of Uncertainty and Innovation*. Toronto: McClelland & Stewart.

Gwyn, R. 1980. *The Northern Magus*. Toronto: McClelland & Stewart.

Hawthorn, H.B. 1968. *A Survey of the Contemporary Indians of Canada: Economic, Political Educational Needs and Policies. Ottawa:* Queen's Printer. Vol I.

Hawthorn, T. 2013. *The Year Canadians Lost Their Minds and Found Their Country*. Madeira Park, BC: Douglas & McIntyre.

Haque, E. 2012. *Multiculturalism within a Bilingual Framework Language, Race and Belonging in Canada*. Toronto: University of Toronto Press.

Heintzman, R. 1971. "In the Bosom of a Single State." *Journal of Canadian Studies* 6, no. 4 (Nov.): 1–2, 63–4.

Horton, D.J. 1992. *André Laurendeau: French-Canadian Nationalist, 1912–1968*. Toronto: Oxford University Press.

Jaworsky, J. 1979. "A Case Study of the Canadian Federal Government's Multiculturalism Policy." M.A. thesis, Department of Political Science, Carleton University.

Jedwab, J. 2003. "To Preserve and Enhance: Canadian Multiculturalism before and after the Charter." In Magnet et al. (eds), *The Canadian Charter of Rights and Freedoms: Reflection on the Charter after Twenty Years*. Markham: LexisNexis Canada.

——— (ed.). 2014. *The Multiculturalism Question: Debating Identity in 21st Century Canada*. Montreal and Kingston: McGill-Queen's University Press.

Johnston, R., et al. 2010. "National Identity and Support for the Welfare State." *Canadian Journal of Political Science* 43, no. 2 (June): 349–77.

Juteau, D. 1990. "The Canadian Experiment: Multiculturalism as Ideology and Policy." Paper presented to Conference on Cultural Diversity in Europe, Berlin.

———. n.d. "La citoyenneté québécoise face au pluralisme." Unpublished paper.

———, M. McAndrew, and L. Pietrantonio. n.d. "Multiculturalism à la Canadian and Intégration à la Québécoise: Transcending Their Limits." Unpublished paper.

Kallen, E. 1982. "Multiculturalism: Ideology, Policy and Reality." *Journal of Canadian Studies* 17, no. 1 (Spring): 51–63.

Kornhauser, W. 1959. *The Politics of Mass Society*. New York: Free Press.

Kymlicka, W. 1995. *Multicultural Citizenship*. Oxford: Oxford University Press.

———. 1998. *Finding Our Way: Rethinking Ethnocultural Relations in Canada*. Toronto: Oxford University Press.

———. 2008. "The Canadian Model of Diversity." In Tierney (ed.), *Multiculturalism and the Canadian Constitution*. Vancouver: UBC Press.

———. 2015. "The Three Lives of Multiculturalism." In Guo and Wong (eds), *Revisiting Multiculturalism in Canada*. Rotterdam: Sense Publishers.

Lacoste, P. 1990. "André Laurendeau et la commission sur le bilinguisme et le biculturalisme." In R. Comeau and L. Beaudry (eds), *André Laurendeau: un intellectuel d'ici*. Sillery, QC: Presses de l'Université du Québec.

Lagace, N., and N.J. Sinclair. 2015. "The White Paper, 1969." *The Canadian Encyclopedia*. Retrieved from https://www.thecanadianencyclopedia.ca/en/article/the-white-paper-1969/.

Lapointe-Gagnon, V. 2013. "Penser et 'panser' les plaies du Canada: le moment Laurendeau–Dunton, 1963-1971," Doctoral thesis, History Department, Laval University.

Laurendeau, A. 1962. "Pour une enquête sur le bilinguisme." *Le Devoir*, 20 Jan.

Le Devoir. 1971. Bourassa's statement, as reproduced in *Le Devoir*, 17 Nov.

———. 2013. "Charles Taylor et Gérard Bouchard dénoncent une charte nuisible." 8 Nov.

Lijphart, A. 1968. *The Politics of Accommodation: Pluralism and Democracy in the Netherlands*. Berkeley: University of California Press.

Lupul, M.R. 1982. "The Political Implementation of Multiculturalism." *Journal of Canadian Studies* 17, no. 1 (Spring): 96–7.

McAndrew, M., D. Helly, C. Terrier, and J. Young. 2008. "From Heritage Languages to Institutional Change: An Analysis of the Nature of Organizations and Projects Funded by the Canadian Multiculturalism Program (1983–2002)." *Canadian Ethnic Studies Journal* 40, no. 3: 149–69.

McAndrew, M. n.d. "Multiculturalisme canadien et interculturalisme québécois: mythes et réalités." Unpublished paper.

Mackenzie, H. 2010. "Does History Mean Always Having to Say You're Sorry? *Canadian Issues* (Winter): 47–50.

Miller, D. 2016. "The Life and Death of Multiculturalism." Paper presented at Glendon College, York University, 19 Apr.

Miyagawa, M. 2009. "A Sorry State," *The Walrus*, Dec.

National Assembly of Quebec. 2013. Charter Affirming the Values of State Secularism and Religious Neutrality and of Equality Between Women and Men, and Providing a Framework for Accommodation Requests, 1st session, 40th Legislature, Bill n°60.

———. 2017. An Act to Foster Adherence to State Religious Neutrality and, in Particular, to Provide a Framework for Requests for Accommodations on Religious Grounds in Certain Bodies, 1st session, 41st Legislature, Bill n°62.

Nootens, G. 2014. "Nationalism, Pluralism, and the Democratic Governance of Diversity." In Jedwab (ed.), *The Multiculturalism Question: Debating Identity in 21st Century Canada*. Montreal and Kingston: McGill-Queen's University Press.

Nugent, A. 2006. "Demography, National Myths, and Political Origins: Perceiving Official Multiculturalism in Quebec." *Ethnic Studies* 38, no. 3.

Oliver, M. 1991. "Laurendeau et Trudeau: leurs opinions sur le Canada." In R. Hudon and R. Pelletier (eds), *L'engagement intellectuel: mélanges en l'honneur de Léon Dion*. Sainte-Foy: Presses de l'Université Laval.

———. 1993. "The Impact of the Royal Commission on Bilingualism and Biculturalism on Constitutional Theory and Practice." *International Journal of Canadian Studies* 7–8 (Spring–Fall): 315–32.

Pal, L.A. 1993. *Interests of State: The Politics of Language, Multiculturalism and Feminism in Canada*. Montreal and Kingston: McGill-Queen's University Press.

Pelletier, G. 1992. L'aventure au pouvoir: 1968–1975. Montreal: Stanké.

Perin, R. n.d. "Un adversaire du bilinguisme officiel à la Commission Laurendeau–Dunton." *Bulletin d'Histoire politique (forthcoming)*.

Piedboeuf, G. 2017. "L'extrême droite plus visible à Québec," *Le Soleil*, 1 Feb.

Porter, I. 2017 "L'extrême droite de Québec sort de l'ombre." *Le Devoir*, 2 Feb.

Quebec. 2013. National Assembly, "Bill 60: Charter affirming the values of State secularism and religious neutrality and of equality between women and men, and providing a framework for accommodation requests," Québec Official Publisher, 2013.

Radio-Canada.ca. 2013. "Pour ou contre la charte des valeurs?" 7 Nov.

Ramirez, B., and S. Taschereau. 1988. "Les minorités: le multiculturalisme appliqué." In Y. Bélanger, et al., *L'Ère des libéraux: le pouvoir fédéral de 1963 à 1984*. Sillery, QC: Presses de l'Université du Québec.

Reid, A., and D. Kurl. 2017. "Religion, Multiculturalism and the Public Square." *Policy Options*, IRPP, 4 Dec.

Ricento, T. 2013. "The Consequences of Official Bilingualism on the Status and Perception of Non-official Languages in Canada." *Journal of Multilingual and Multicultural Development* 34, no. 5: 475–89.

Rocher, G. 1976. "Multiculturalism: The Doubts of a Francophone." In Second Canadian Conference on Multiculturalism, Canadian Consultative Council on Multiculturalism (ed.), *Multiculturalism as State*

Policy: Conference Report. Ottawa: Dept. of Supply and Services.

Royal Commission on Bilingualism and Biculturalism. 1965. *Preliminary Report*. Ottawa: Queen's Printer.

———. 1967. *General Introduction*. Ottawa: Queen's Printer.

———. 1967. *Book I: The Official Languages*. Ottawa: Queen's Printer.

———. 1970. *Book IV: The Cultural Contribution of the Other Ethnic Groups*. Ottawa: Queen's Printer.

Russell, P. H. 2004. *Constitutional Odyssey: Can Canadians Become a Sovereign People?* 3rd edn. Toronto: University of Toronto Press.

———. 2017. *Canada's Odyssey: A Country Based on Incomplete Conquests*. Toronto: University of Toronto Press.

Ryan, C. 1971. "L'aide aux groupes ethniques exige-t-elle l'abandon du biculturalisme?" *Le Devoir*, 9 Oct.

———. 1990. "Il a soulevé les vraies questions et refuté les réponses toutes faites," in *André Laurendeau: un intellectuel d'ici*, ed. Robert Comeau and Lucille Beaudry. Montreal: Presses de l'Université du Québec.

Stasiulis, D.K. 1988. "The Symbolic Mosaic Reaffirmed: Multiculturalism Policy." In K.A. Graham (ed.), *How Ottawa Spends, 1988–89*. Ottawa: Carleton University Press.

Stasiulis, D.K., and Y. Abu-Laban. 2008. "Unequal Relations and the Struggle for Equality: Race and Ethnicity in Canadian Politics." In Whittington and Williams (eds), *Canadian Politics in the 21st Century*. Toronto: Thomson Nelson.

Statistics Canada. 2017. "Linguistic Diversity and Multilingualism in Canadian Homes." *Census in Brief*, 2 Aug.

———. 2017. "Update of the 2016 Census Language Data," 23 August.

Stevenson, G. 1995. "Multiculturalism: As Canadian as Apple Pie." *Inroads* 4: 72–87.

Stursberg, P. 1978. *Lester Pearson and the Dream of Unity*. Toronto: Doubleday.

Taylor, C. 1992. "The Politics of Recognition." In Taylor (ed.), *Multiculturalism and "The Politics of Recognition."* Princeton, NJ: Princeton University Press.

———. 1993. *Reconciling the Solitudes: Essays on Canadian Federalism and Nationalism*. Montreal and Kingston: McGill-Queen's University Press.

———. 2017. "Neutralité de l'État: le temps de la reconciliation." *La Presse*, 14 Feb.

Temelini, M. 2008. "Multicultural Rights, Multicultural Virtues: A History of Multiculturalism in Canada." In Tierney (ed.), *Multiculturalism and the Canadian Constitution*. Vancouver, UBC Press.

Trudeau, P.E. 1968. *Federalism and the French Canadians*. Toronto: Macmillan.

———. 1971. "Announcement of Implementation of Policy of Multiculturalism within Bilingual Framework," (including "Federal Government's Response to Book IV of the Report of the Royal Commission on Bilingualism and Biculturalism") House of Commons, *Debates*, x, 8580–5. *Debates*, 8 Oct., 8580-5.

———. 1980. "Remarks on Aboriginal and Treaty Rights. Excerpts from a Speech Given August 8th, 1979, in Vancouver, British Columbia." In Cumming and Mickenberg (eds), *Native Rights in Canada*. 2nd edn. Toronto: Indian Eskimo Association of Canada.

Uberoi, V. 2008. "Do Policies of Multiculturalism Change National Identities?" *The Political Quarterly* 79, no 3 (July–Sept.): 404–17.

———. 2009. "Multiculturalism and the Canadian Charter of Rights and Freedoms." *Political Studies* 57, no. 12: 805–27.

———. 2016. "Legislating Multiculturalism and Nationhood: The 1988 Canadian Multiculturalism Act." *Canadian Journal of Political Science* 49, no. 2 (June): 267–87.

Weaver, S.M. 1981. *Making Canadian Indian Policy: The Hidden Agenda 1968–1970*. Toronto: University of Toronto Press.

Weinstock, D. 2014. "What Is Really at Stake in the Multiculturalism/Interculturalism Debate?" In J. Jedwab (ed.), *The Multiculturalism Question: Debating Identity in 21st Century Canada*. Montreal and Kingston: McGill-Queen's University Press.

Winter, E. 2015. "A Canadian Anomaly? The Social Construction of Multicultural National Identity." In Cho and Wong (eds), *Revisiting Multiculturalism in Canada*. Rotterdam: Sense Publishers.

Chapter Six

L'Actualité. 1991. "Portrait des Québécois." 13–16 Jan.

Adams, E.M. 2015. "Constitutional Nationalism: Politics, Law, and Culture on the Road to Patriation." In Harder and Patten (eds),

Patriation and Its Consequences: Constitution Making in Canada. Vancouver: UBC Press.

Allen, G. 1989. "Grit Stands Fast." *Maclean's*, 20 Nov., 25.

Arsenau, T. 1994. "The Reform Party of Canada: Past, Present and Future." In D. Brown and J. Hiebert (eds), *Canada: The State of the Federation 1994*. Kingston: Institute of Intergovernmental Relations, Queen's University.

Atlantic Provinces Economic Council. 1992. *Renewal of Canada: Division of Powers: Conference Report*. Halifax, 17–19 Jan.

Bernier, G. 1980. "Les aspects économiques du débat: un dialogue de sourds," in collaboration, *Québec: un pays incertain*. Montreal: Québec/Amérique.

Blais, A. 1980. "Le vote: ce que l'on en sait . . . ce que l'on n'en sait pas." In En Collaboration, *Québec: un pays incertain*, 157–82.

———. 1993. "The Quebec Referendum: Quebeckers Say No." In McRoberts and Monahan (eds), *The Charlottetown Accord, the Referendum, and the Future of Canada*, 200–7.

Blais, A., and J. Crête. 1991. "Pourquoi l'opinion publique au Canada anglais a-t-elle rejeté l'Accord du Lac Meech?" In R. Hudon and R. Pelletier (eds), *L'engagement intellectuel: mélanges en l'honneur de Léon Dion*. Sainte-Foy, QC: Presses de l'Université Laval.

Blais, A., et al. 1995. "L'élection fédérale de 1993: le comportement électoral des québécois." *Revue québécoise de science politique* 27 (Spring): 15–47.

Blake, R.B., and B. Antonishyn. 2016. "Pierre Trudeau, Citizenship, and Canada Day." In Hayday and Blake, *Celebrating Canada*, vol 1. Toronto: University of Toronto Press.

Bombardier, D. 1980. "Noir sur blanc." Radio-Canada, 17 May.

Borrows, J. 2016. *Freedom and Indigenous Constitutionalism*. Toronto: University of Toronto Press.

Bothwell, R., and J. L. Granatstein. 2017. *Trudeau's World: Insiders Reflect on Foreign Policy, Trade, and Defence, 1968–84*. Vancouver: UBC Press.

Bouchard, J., and P. Vennat. 1982. "Lévesque n'a pas la majorité pour réaliser son projet de souveraineté-association." *La Presse*, 30 Mar.

Bouthillier, G., and É. Cloutier (eds). 2010. *Trudeau's Darkest Hour: War Measures in Time of Peace, October 1970*. Montreal: Baraka Books.

Brandt, G.J. 1983. "The Quebec Veto Reference: A Constitutional Postscript." *University of Western Ontario Law Review* 21, no. 1: 163–71.

Bryden, P.J. 2015. "The Rise of Spectator Constitutionalism, 1967–81." In L. Harder and S. Patten (eds), *Patriation and Its Consequences: Constitution Making in Canada*. Vancouver: UBC Press.

Burelle, A. 2005. *Pierre Elliott Trudeau: l'intellectuel et le politique*. Montreal: Fides.

Cairns, A.C. 1988. "Citizens (Outsiders) and Governments (Insiders) in Constitution-Making: The Case of Meech Lake." *Canadian Public Policy* 14, supplement (Sept.): SI21–45.

———. 1989. "Political Science, Ethnicity, and the Canadian Constitution." In D.P. Shugarman and R. Whitaker (eds), *Federalism and Political Community: Essays in Honour of Donald Smiley*. Peterborough, ON: Broadview.

———. 1992. *Charter versus Federalism: The Dilemmas of Constitutional Reform*. Montreal and Kingston: McGill-Queen's University Press.

———. 1995. "Reflections on the Political Purposes of the Charter: The First Decade." In Douglas E. Williams (ed.), *Reconfigurations: Canadian Citizenship and Constitutional Change*. Toronto: McClelland &Stewart.

Cameron, D.R. 1993. "Not Spicer and Not the B&B: Reflections of an Insider on the Workings of the Pepin–Robarts Task Force on Canadian Unity." *International Journal of Canadian Studies* 7–8 (Spring–Fall): 331–45.

Canada. 1973. Department of Health and Welfare, *Working Paper on Social Security for Canadians*. Ottawa: Information Canada.

———. 1979. Task Force on Canadian Unity. *A Future Together: Observations and Recommendations*. Hull: Dept. of Supply and Services.

———. 1982. Constitution Act, 1982.

———. 1980. Prime Minister's Office. *Transcription de l'allocution du Très Honorable Pierre Elliott Trudeau du centre Paul Sauvé*, Montréal, Québec, 14 May.

———. 1987. Special Joint Committee of the Senate and House of Commons on the 1987 Constitutional Accord, *Minutes of Proceedings and Evidence*. Various issues.

———. 1988. *Debates* of the Senate, 2nd session, 33rd Parliament, 1986–87–88, 30 Mar: 2982–3023.

———. 1992a. *Consensus Report on the Constitution: Charlottetown, August 28, 1992.*

———. 1992b. *Status Report: The Multilateral Meetings on the Constitution*, Final Version, 16 July.

———. 1992c. Draft Legal Text, October 9, 1992. [Chartottetown Accord].

———. House of Commons, *Debates*. Various years.

Canada West Foundation. 1993. *Canada 2000: Towards a New Canada*. Jan.

Canadian Annual Review. Toronto: University of Toronto Press. Various issues.

Careless, A.G.S. 1977. *Initiative and Response: The Adaptation of Canadian Federalism to Regional Economic Development*. Montreal and Kingston: McGill-Queen's University Press.

Chaput-Rolland, S. 1987. "Il n'y a pas de monstre au lac Meech." *Le Devoir*, 8 May.

Citizens' Forum on Canada's Future. 1991. *Report to the People and Government of Canada*. Ottawa: Supply and Services Canada.

Clarkson, S., and C. McCall. 1990. *Trudeau and Our Times*, vol. 1, *The Magnificent Obsession*. Toronto: McClelland & Stewart.

Comité constitutionnel du Parti libéral du Québec. 1980. *Une nouvelle fédération canadienne*. Montreal: le Parti libéral du Québec.

———. 1991. *Un Québec libre de ses choix*. 28 Jan.

Cook, R. 2006. *The Teeth of Time: Remembering Pierre Elliott Trudeau*. Montreal and Kingston: McGill-Queen's University Press.

Coyne, D. 1989. "The Meech Lake Accord and the Spending Power Proposals: Fundamentally Flawed." In M. Behiels (ed.), *Meech Lake Primer*. Ottawa: University of Ottawa Press.

———. 1991. "Beyond the Meech Lake Accord." In D. Schneiderman (ed.), *Language and the State*. Cowansville, QC: Yvon Blais.

Delacourt, S. 1994. *United We Fall: In Search of a New Canada*. Toronto: Penguin.

Denis, S. 1992. *Le long malentendu: le Québec vu par les intellectuels progressistes au Canada anglais, 1970–1991*. Montreal: Boréal.

Descôteaux, B. 1980. "L'Assemblée adopte la motion Lévesque sans l'appui du PLQ." *Le Devoir*, 22 Nov.

———. 1987. "L'accord du lac Meech permettra au Québec de faire des gains importants et incontestables." *Le Devoir*, 30 May.

Le Devoir. 1971. Quebec's offer, as reproduced in *Le Devoir*, 19 June.

———. 1976. "Le séparatisme est mort, pense Trudeau." 11 May.

———. 1980. "Des provinces ont prié Ottawa de leur imposer le respect du français." 23 Oct.

———. 1987. "L'accord du lac Meech confirmera le statut du Québec dans les relations internationales." *Le Devoir*, 10 Jun.

Diabo, R. 2017. "When Moving Past the Indian Act Means Something Worse." *Policy Options politiques*, 22 Sept.

Elton, D. 1993. "The Charlottetown Accord Senate: Effective or Emasculated?" In McRoberts and Monahan (eds), *The Charlottetown Accord, the Referendum, and the Future of Canada*.

Falardeau, L. 1989. "Francophones et anglophones sont insatisfaits de la loi 178." *La Presse*, 21 Jan.

Forget, C.E. 1995. "Référendum: les conséquences méconnues d'un vote négatif." *La Presse*, 29 Mar.

Fournier, P. 1990. *Autopsie du lac Meech: la souveraineté est-elle inévitable?*, Montreal: VLB.

———. 1991. *A Meech Lake Post-Mortem: Is Quebec Sovereignty Inevitable?* Montreal and Kingston: McGill-Queen's University Press.

Fraser, G. 2006. *Sorry I Don't Speak French: Confronting the Canadian Crisis That Won't Go Away*. Toronto: McClelland & Stewart.

Fremont, J. 1993. "The Charlottetown Accord and the End of the Exclusiveness of Provincial Jurisdictions." In McRoberts and Monahan (eds), *The Charlottetown Accord, the Referendum, and the Future of Canada*.

Gibbins, R. 1992. "Something Not So Funny Happened on the Way to Senate Reform." *Canada Watch* 1, no. 2 (Sept): 22–3.

Graham, R. 2012. *The Last Act: Pierre Trudeau, The Gang of Eight, and the Fight for Canada*. Toronto: Penguin Canada.

Guay, J.-H., R. Nadeau, and E. Cloutier. 1990. "La crise linguistique au Québec: une étude du mouvement de l'opinion publique engendré par le jugement de la Cour suprême sur l'affichage commercial." Paper presented at the annual meeting of the Canadian Political Science Association, May.

Gwyn, R. 1980. *The Northern Magus*. Toronto: McClelland & Stewart.

Haggart, R., and A.E. Golden. 1971. *Rumours of War*. Toronto: New Press.

Harder, L., and S. Patten. 2015. "Looking Back on Patriation and Its Consequences."

In Harder and Patten (eds), *Patriation and Its Consequences: Constitution Making in Canada*. Vancouver: UBC Press.

Harder, L., and S. Patten (eds). 2015. *Patriation and Its Consequences: Constitution Making in Canada*. Vancouver: UBC Press.

Hogg, P.W. 1988. *Meech Lake Constitutional Accord Annotated*. Toronto: Carswell.

Johnston, R., et al. 1993. "The People and the Charlottetown Accord." In R.L. Watts and D.M. Brown (eds), *Canada: The State of the Federation 1993*. Kingston: Institute of Intergovernmental Relations, Queen's University.

Kent, T. 1992. "Recasting Federalism." *Policy Options* 12, no. 3 (Apr.): 3–6.

Knopf, R., and F.L. Morton. 1985. "Nation-Building and the Canadian Charter of Rights and Freedoms." In A. Cairns and C. Williams (eds), *Constitutionalism, Citizenship and Society in Canada*. Collected Research Studies of the Royal Commission on the Economic Union and Development Prospects for Canada, vol. 33. Toronto: University of Toronto Press.

Lacoste, P. 1990. "André Laurendeau et la Commission sur le bilinguisme et le biculturalisme." In R. Comeau and L. Beaudry (eds), *André Laurendeau: un intellectuel d'ici*. Sillery, QC: Presses de l'Université du Québec.

Laforest, G. 1992. *Trudeau et la fin d'un rêve canadien*. Sillery, QC: Septentrion.

———, and R. Readman. 2013. "Plus de déstresse que d'enchantement: les négociations constitutionnelles de novembre 1981 vues du Québec." In Rocher and Pelletier (eds), *Le nouvel ordre constitutionnel canadien: du rapatriement de 1982 à nos jours*. Quebec: Presses de l'Université du Québec.

Lapointe–Gagnon, V. 2013. "Penser et 'panser' les plaies du Canada: le moment Laurendeau-Dunton, 1963–1971," Doctoral thesis, History Department, Laval University.

Laurendeau, M. 1974. *Les Québécois violents: un ouvrage sur les causes et la rentabilité de la violence d'inspiration politique au Québec*. Montreal: Boréal.

Laxer, G. 1992. "Distinct Status for Quebec: A Benefit to English Canada." *Constitutional Forum constitutionnel* 3, no. 3 (Winter): 62–6.

Leduc, L., and J.H. Pammet. 1995. "Attitudes and Behaviour in the 1992 Constitutional Referendum." *Canadian Journal of Political Science* 28, no. 1 (Mar.): 3–33.

Lemieux, V., and J. Crête. 1981. "Quebec." In H. Penniman (ed.), *Canada at the Polls, 1979 and 1980*. Washington, DC: American Enterprise Institute for Public Policy Research.

Lesage, G. 1986. "Opposé à l'adhésion à la charte canadienne, Léon Dion quitte le gouvernement Bourassa." *Le Devoir*, 17 Mar.

Leslie, P.M. 1987. *Rebuilding the Relationship: Quebec and Its Confederation Partners*. Kingston: Institute of Intergovernmental Relations, Queen's University.

Lévesque, Robert. 1987. "Lévesque fait bande à part." *Le Devoir*, 4 May.

Lisée, J.-F. 1992. "Dossiers secrets de Bourassa." *L'Actualité*, 1 Nov.

———. 1994. *Le tricheur: Robert Bourassa et les Québécois, 1990–1991*. Montreal: Boréal.

———. 1994. *Le naufrageur: Robert Bourassa et les Québécois, 1991–1992*. Montreal: Boréal.

———. 2013. "Constitution 1982 et 1992: aux sources de l'échec." In Rocher and Pelletier (eds), *Le nouvel ordre constitutionnel canadien: du rapatriement de 1982 à nos jours*. Quebec: Presses de l'Université du Québec.

Maclean's. 1987. "Voice of the People." 15 June, 12–13.

McRoberts, K. 1985. "Unilateralism, Bilateralism and Multilateralism: Approaches to Canadian Federalism." In R. Simeon (ed.), *Intergovernmental Relations*. Collected Research Studies of the Royal Commission on the Economic Union and Development Prospects for Canada, vol. 63. Toronto: University of Toronto Press.

———. 1993. "Disagreeing on Fundamentals: English Canada and Quebec." In McRoberts and Monahan (eds), *The Charlottetown Accord, the Referendum, and the Future of Canada*.

———. 1993. *Quebec: Social Change and Political Crisis*, 3rd edn with postscript. Toronto: McClelland & Stewart.

———, and P.J. Monahan (eds). 1993. *The Charlottetown Accord, the Referendum, and the Future of Canada*. Toronto: University of Toronto Press.

McWhinney, E. 1979. *Quebec and the Constitution, 1960–1978*. Toronto: University of Toronto Press.

———. 1982. *Canada and the Constitution, 1979–1982: Patriation and the Charter*

of Rights. Toronto: University of Toronto Press.
Mahoney, K. 1988. "Women's Rights." In R. Gibbins (ed.), *Meech Lake and Canada: Perspectives from the West*. Edmonton: Academic.
Milne, D. 1986. *Tug of War: Ottawa and the Provinces under Trudeau and Mulroney*. Toronto: Lorimer.
———. 1991. *The Canadian Constitution*. Toronto: Lorimer.
———. 1992. "Innovative Constitutional Processes." In D. Brown and R. Young, *Canada: State of the Federation, 1992*. Kingston: Institute of Intergovernmental Relations, Queen's University.
Monahan, P.J. 1991. *Meech Lake: The Inside Story*. Toronto: University of Toronto Press.
Montreal *Gazette*. 1971. "If Quebec Says No to Victoria Charter." 19 June.
Morin, J.-Y. 1987. "Nous sommes devant un nouveau piège." *Le Devoir*, 20 May.
Mulgrew, I. 1981. "Provinces Using Federal Money but Ottawa Is Not Credited: PM." *Globe and Mail*, 25 Nov.
Murray, L. 1989. "Lowell Murray répond à Pierre Trudeau." *La Presse*, 5 Apr.
Nadeau, R. 1992. "Le virage souverainiste des Québécois, 1980–1990." *Recherches sociographiques* 23, no. 1 (Jan.–Apr.): 9–28.
Nemni, M. 1991. "Le 'dés' accord du Lac Meech et la construction de l'imaginaire symbolique des Québécois." In L. Balthazar, G. Laforest, and V. Lemieux (eds), *Le Québec et la restructuration du Canada, 1980–1992: enjeux et perspectives*. Sillery, QC: Septentrion.
Noël, A. 1994. "The Bloc Québécois as Official Opposition." In D.M. Brown and J. Hiebert (eds), *Canada: The State of the Federation 1994*. Kingston: Institute of Intergovernmental Relations, Queen's University.
O'Neill, P. 1987. "Le lac Meach *[sic]* a rallié les péquistes de toutes tendances." *Le Devoir*, 4 May.
———. 1987. "Parizeau incite Bourassa à ne pas signer l'accord du lac Meech." *Le Devoir*, 15 May.
———. 1991. "Bourassa choisit d'abord le Canada." *Le Devoir*, 11 Mar.
Pal, L.A. 1993. *Interests of State: The Politics of Language, Multiculturalism and Feminism in Canada*. Montreal and Kingston: McGill-Queen's University Press.
Paquet, M. 1994. "Le fleuve et la cité: représentations de l'immigration et esquisses d'une action de l'État québécois, 1945–1968." Ph.D. dissertation, History Department, l'Université Laval.
Pepin, M. 1976. "Si Québec ne collabore pas, Trudeau rapatriera tout seul la constitution." *La Presse*, 6 Mar.
Petter, A. 1984. "Maître chez Who? The Quebec Veto Reference." *Supreme Court Law* 6: 387–99.
Picard, J.-C. 1981. "La tristesse à l'Assemblée nationale." *Le Devoir*, 3 Dec.
Pinard, M. 1992. "The Dramatic Reemergence of the Quebec Independence Movement." *Journal of International Affairs* 45, no. 2 (Winter): 472–95.
La Presse. 1977. "Pierre Elliott Trudeau à la Chambre de commerce de Québec." 28 Jan.
———. 1980. "Trudeau n'acceptera de négocier qu'après le 2e référendum." 3 May.
———. 1980. Two-page advertisement. 21 Aug.
———. 1989. "L'accord constitutionnel de 1982 n'a pas été un marché de dupes pour le Québec." 10 Mar.
———. 1980. *An Open Letter to the People of Quebec*. Translation, 11 July.
Proulx, J.-P. 1980. "Servir deux maîtres." *Le Devoir*, 24 Nov.
———. 1988. "L'Histoire d'un échec qui combla d'aise Pierre Elliott Trudeau." *Le Devoir*, 5 Nov.
Quebec. 1978. *Accord entre le gouvernement du Canada et le gouvernement du Québec portant sur la collaboration en matière d'immigration et sur la sélection des ressortissants étrangers qui souhaitent s'établir au Québec à titre permanent ou temporaire*. Ministère de l'Immigration, Montreal.
———. 1979. National Assembly. *Quebec–Canada: A New Deal*. *Quebec City*: Editeur officiel.
———. 1980. Directeur général des élections du Québec. *Référendum: Oui–Non*.
———. 1980. *Journal des Débats*, 4th session, 31st Legislature.
———. 1991. *Rapport de la Commission sur l'avenir politique et constitutionnel du Québec*. Quebec: Secrétariat de la Commission.
Resnick, P. 1990. *Letter to a Québécois Friend*. Montreal and Kingston: McGill-Queen's University Press.
Ricci, N. 2009. *Pierre Elliott Trudeau*. Toronto: Penguin.
Roberts, B. 1988. "Smooth Sailing or Storm Warning? Canada and Quebec Women's Groups and the Meech Lake Accord."

Feminist Perspectives féministes 12a, CRIAW.

Robertson, G. 2000. *Memoirs of a Very Civil Servant*. Toronto: University of Toronto Press.

Rocher, F. 1992. "Le Dossier constitutionnel: l'année des consultations et des valse-hesitations." In D. Moniere (ed.), *L'année politique au Québec, 1991*. Montreal: Québec/Amérique.

Royal Commission on the Economic Union and Development Prospects for Canada. 1985. *Report*, vol. III. Ottawa: Supply and Services Canada.

Russell, P.H. 2004. *Constitutional Odyssey: Can Canadians Become a Sovereign People*? 3rd edn. Toronto: University of Toronto Press.

———. 2015. "Patriation and the Law of Unintended Consequences," in L. Harder and S. Patten (eds), *Patriation and its Consequences*. Vancouver: University of British Columbia Press.

———. 2017. *Canada's Odyssey: A Country Based on Incomplete Conquests*. Toronto: University of Toronto Press.

Ryan, C. 1970. "Les mesures de guerre: trois questions." *Le Devoir*, 17 Oct.

———. 1971. "Le dilemme de M. Bourassa." *Le Devoir*, 22 June.

———. 1976. "Le rêve vain de M. Trudeau." *Le Devoir*, 8 Mar.

———. 1995. "Référendum de 1980: Ryan en désaccord avec Forget," *La Presse*, 31 Mar. 1995

———.1995. *Regards sur le fédéralisme canadien*. Montreal: Boréal.

Sharp, M. 1994. *Which Reminds Me . . . A Memoir*. Toronto: University of Toronto Press.

Sheppard, R., and M. Valpy. 1982. *The National Deal: The Fight for a Canadian Constitution*. Toronto: Fleet Books.

Simeon, R. 1972. *Federal–Provincial Diplomacy: The Making of Recent Policy in Canada*. Toronto: University of Toronto Press.

———. 1990. "Why Did the Meech Lake Accord Fail?" In R.L. Watts and D.M. Brown (eds), *Canada: The State of the Federation 1990*. Kingston: Institute of Intergovernmental Relations, Queen's University.

Simeon, R., and I. Robinson. 1990. *State, Society and the Development of Canadian Federalism*. Collected Research Studies of the Royal Commission on the Economic Union and Development Prospects for Canada, vol. 71. Toronto: University of Toronto Press.

Simpson, J. 1993. *Fault Lines: Struggling for a Canadian Vision*. Toronto: Harper Collins.

Smiley, D.V. 1969. "The Case against the Canadian Charter of Human Rights." *Canadian Journal of Political Science* 2, no. 3 (Sept.): 278–91.

———. 1980. *Canada in Question: Federalism in the Eighties*, 3rd edn. Toronto: McGraw-Hill Ryerson.

———. 1981. *The Canadian Charter of Rights and Freedoms*, Toronto: Ontario Economic Council.

———. 1983. "A Dangerous Deed: The Constitution Act, 1982." In K. Banting and R. Simeon (eds), *And No One Cheered: Federalism, Democracy and the Constitution Act*. Toronto: Methuen.

———. 1987. *The Federal Condition in Canada*. Toronto: McGraw-Hill Ryerson.

Smith, D. 1971. *Bleeding Hearts . . . Bleeding Country: Canada and the Quebec Crisis*. Edmonton: Hurtig.

Stanbury, W.T., G.J. Gorn, and C.B. Weinberg. 1983. "Federal Advertising Expenditures." In G.B. Doern (ed.), *How Ottawa Spends: The Liberals, the Opposition and Federal Priorities, 1983*. Toronto: Lorimer.

Stevenson, G. 1989. *Unfulfilled Union: Canadian Federalism and National Unity*, 3rd edn. Toronto: Gage.

Strayer, B.K. 2015. "The Evolution of the Charter." In Harder and Patten (eds), *Patriation and Its Consequences: Constitution Making in Canada*. Vancouver: UBC Press.

Supreme Court of Canada. 1981. Re: Resolution to amend the Constitution. 1 S.C.R.

———. 1982. Re: Objection to a Resolution to amend the Constitution. 2 S.C.R.

Thomas, D.M. 1995. "The Second Time Around: Pepin-Robarts Then and Now." Paper presented to the Association for Canadian Studies in the United States, Seattle, 18–19 Nov.

Thordarson, B. 1972. *Trudeau and Foreign Policy*. Toronto: Oxford University Press.

Trudeau, P.E. 1968. *Federalism and the French Canadians*. Toronto: Macmillan.

———. 1969. *Federal–Provincial Grants and the Spending Power of Parliament*. Ottawa: Queen's Printer.

———. 1977. *Pierre Elliott Trudeau à la Chambre de commerce de Québec*, Montreal: *La Presse*, 28 Jan.

———. 1987. "'Say Goodbye to the Dream' of One Canada." *Toronto Star*, 27 May.

———. 1990. "The Values of a Just Society." In T.S. Axworthy and P.E. Trudeau (eds), *Towards a Just Society: The Trudeau Years.* Markham, ON: Viking.

———. 1992. "A Mess That Deserves a Big No." Toronto: Robert Davies.

———. 1993. *Memoirs.* Toronto: McClelland & Stewart.

———. 1996. "J'accuse Lucien Bouchard!" *La Presse*, 3 Feb.

Toronto Star. 1987. "Meech Lake Accord Gains General Support, Polls Show." 1 June.

———. 1977. "What Quebec *Really* Wants: English Consider Us Inferior, Quebec Feels." 17 May.

Uberoi, V. 2009. "Multiculturalism and the Canadian Charter of Rights and Freedoms." *Political Studies* 57, no. 12, 805–27.

Vaillancourt Y. 1992. "Le Régime d'assistance publique du Canada: perspective québécoise." Thèse de doctorat en science politique, l'Université de Montréal.

Venne, M. 1992. "Robert Bourassa flaire un 'fédéralisme dominateur'," *Le Devoir*, 4 Mar.

———. 1992. "Il fallait pas accepter ça." *Le Devoir*, 1 Oct.

Waite, P.B. 1962. *The Life and Times of Confederation, 1864–1867: Politics, Newspapers and the Union of British North America.* Toronto: University of Toronto Press.

Webber, J. 1994. *Reimagining Canada: Language, Culture, Community and the Canadian Constitution.* Montreal and Kingston: McGill-Queen's University Press.

Whitaker, R. 1993. "The Dog That Never Barked: Who Killed Asymmetrical Federalism?" In McRoberts and Monahan (eds), *The Charlottetown Accord, the Referendum, and the Future of Canada.*

———. 1993. "Apprehended Insurrection? RCMP Intelligence and the October Crisis," *Queen's Quarterly* 100, no. 2 (Summer).

Williams, C. 1985. "The Changing Nature of Citizen Rights." In A. Cairns and C. Williams (eds), *Constitutionalism, Citizenship and Society in Canada.* Collected Research Studies of the Royal Commission on the Economic Union and Development Prospects for Canada, vol. 33. Toronto: University of Toronto Press.

Young, R., and D. Brown. 1992. "Overview." In D. Brown and R. Young (eds), *Canada: The State of the Federation 1992.* Kingston: Institute of Intergovernmental Relations, Queen's University.

Chapter Seven

Action démocratique du Québec. n.d. Québec-Canada: A New Partnership.

Aubin, B. 1996. *Chroniques de mauvaise humeur.* Montreal: Boréal.

Bernier, R., et al. 1997. *Un combat inachevé.* Quebec: Presses de l'Université du Québec.

Blais, A. 1996. "Pourquoi le oui a-t-il fait des gains pendant la campagne référendaire?" In Trent, Young, and Lachapelle (eds), *Québec–Canada: Challenges and Opportunities.*

Branswell, B., and B. Wallace. 1998. "Supreme Court Rules on UDI," *Maclean's*, 31 Aug.

Buchanan, A. 1991. *Secession: The Morality of Political Divorce from Fort Sumter to Lithuania and Quebec.* Boulder: Westview Press.

Canada. 2000. Clarity Act, 2nd session, 36th Parliament, C-20.

Cairns, A. 1996. "The Legacy of the Referendum: Who Are We Now?" *Constitutional Forum constitutionnel* 7, nos 2 and 3 (Winter–Spring): 35–9.

———. 1996. "Looking Back from the Future." In J.E. Trent, et al. *Québec–Canada.*

———. 1998. "The Quebec Secession Reference: The Constitutional Obligation to Negotiate." *Constitutional Forum constitutionnel* 10, no. 1: 26–30.

Chartier, J. 1996. "Affichage: Chrétien approuve le boycottage anglophone." *Le Devoir*, 2 Aug.

Clarke, H.D., and A. Kornberg. 1996. "Choosing Canada? The 1995 Quebec Sovereignty Referendum." Paper delivered to the Canadian Political Science Association, June 1996.

Cloutier, É. 1995. "The Quebec Referendum: From Polls to Ballots." *Canada Watch* 4, no. 2 (Nov./Dec.): 37–9.

Comité constitutionnel du Parti libéral du Québec. 1991. *Un Québec libre de ses choix.* 28 Jan.

Coon Come, M. 1996. "Dishonourable Conduct: The Crown in Right of Canada and Quebec, and the James Bay Cree," *Constitutional Forum constitutionnel* 7, no.2/3 (Winter/Spring).

Cornellier, M. 1996. "Bourassa contredit Irwin." *Le Devoir*, 15 Feb.

———. 1996. "Le plan B: une vision électoraliste, déplore Ryan," *La Presse*, 21 May.

Coyne, A. 1996. "Making Offers to Quebec Is Part of the Problem, Not the Solution." *Globe and Mail*, 29 Jan.

Delisle, N. 1996. "La fin ne justifie pas les moyens." *Le Devoir,* 11 May.

Des Rosiers, N. 2000. "From Québec Veto to Québec Secession: The Evolution of the Supreme Court of Canada on Québec–Canada Disputes." *Canadian Journal of Law and Jurisprudence* 13, no.2 (July 2000): 171–83.

Dion, J. 1995. "Le Canada 'suppliera' Québec de négocier, affirme Bouchard." *Le Devoir,* 28 Sept.

———. 1995. "Aucun moyen n'est exclu pour assurer le changement, dit Chrétien." *Le Devoir,* 25 Oct.

———. 1995. "Trudeau accuse Lucien Bouchard d'avoir menti aux Québécois." *Le Devoir,* 7 Nov.

———. 1995. "Chrétien refuse de définir ses 'pouvoirs'." *Le Devoir,* 13 Dec.

———. 1996. "Les territoires autochtones n'appartiennent pas au Québec, dit Irwin." *Le Devoir,* 14 Feb.

———. 1996. "Le plan B refait surface." *Le Devoir,* 27 Feb.

Drouilly, P. 1996. "La Progression du oui dans les sondages." *La Presse,* 21 Oct.

———. 1995. "An Exemplary Referendum." *Canada Watch* 4, no.2 (Nov./Dec.).

Ducas, M.-C. 1998. "La souveraineté est renforcée." *Le Devoir,* 22 Aug.

Fournier, J.-M. 1996. "L'intégrité du territoire fait consensus à Québec." *Le Devoir,* 23 Jan.

Francis, D. 1996. "Children Suffer While Their Parents Bicker." *Maclean's,* 14 Oct.

———. 1996. *Fighting for Canada.* Toronto: Key Porter.

Globe and Mail. 1996. "Rock: Does the Law Permit Quebec's Unilateral Secession?" 27 Sept.

———. 1996. "Chrétien: Why Destroy Canada?" 26 Oct.

Goldenberg, E. 2006. *The Way It Works: Inside Ottawa.* Toronto: McClelland & Stewart.

Grand Council of the Crees. 1995. *Sovereign Injustice: Forcible Inclusion of the James Bay and Crees Territory into a Sovereign Quebec.* Nemaska, QC.

Greschner, D. 1998. "The Quebec Secession Reference: Goodbye to Part V?" *Constitution Forum constitutionnel* 10, no 1: 19–25

Guénette, D., and A.G. Gagnon. 2017. "Du référendum à la sécession—le processus québécois d'accession à la souveraineté et ses enseignements en matière d'autodétermination." *Revista catalana de dret públic,* no 54. June.

Hébert, C. 1996. "Droit de sécession: Ottawa s'adresse à la Cour suprême." *La Presse,* 25 Sept.

Hébert, C., and J. Lapierre. 2014. *The Morning After: The 1995 Quebec Referendum and the Day That Almost Was.* Toronto: Alfred A. Knopf Canada.

———. 2014. *Confessions post-référendaires.* Montreal: Les Éditions l'homme.

Howard, R. 1996. "Quebec Divisible, Chrétien Says." *Globe and Mail,* 30 Jan.

———. 1996. "Slim Vote Can't Split Canada, PM Says." *Globe and Mail,* 31 Jan.

Howse, R. 1995. "Sovereignty . . . But Where's the Association?" *Canada Watch* 3, no. 7 (May/June): 97–102.

Lachapelle, G., P.P. Tremblay, and J.E. Trent (eds). 1995. *L'impact référendaire.* Sainte-Foy: Presses de l'Université du Québec.

Laliberté, M., and J. Dion. 1995. "Les patrons pour le NON ripostent," *Le Devoir,* 4 Oct.

Lecker, R. 1996. "The Writing's on the Wall." *Saturday Night,* July–Aug., 15–51.

Lemieux, V. 1996. "Le référendum de 1995: quelques pistes d'explication." In Trent, et al., *Québec–Canada.*

———, and R. Bernier. 1996. "Voters' Questions in the 1995 Québec Referendum." Paper presented to the Canadian Political Science Association, June.

Lisée, J.-F. 1994. *Le tricheur: Robert Bourassa et les Québécois, 1990–1991.* Montreal: Boréal.

Lorde, M.-C. 1996. "Vote hors Québec: le directeur des élections durement critiqué." *La Presse,* 26 Oct.

MacDonald, L.I. 2002. *From Bourassa to Bourassa: Wilderness to Restoration.* 2nd edn. Montreal and Kingston: McGill-Queen's University Press.

McNeil, K. 1992. "Aboriginal Nations and Quebec's Boundaries: Canada Couldn't Give What It Didn't Have." In D. Drache and R. Perin (eds), *Negotiating with a Sovereign Quebec.* Toronto: Lorimer.

Mackie, R. 1996. "Poll Finds Quebeckers Proud of Canada." *Globe and Mail,* 24 Feb.

Mackie, R., and R. Séguin. 1995. "Chrétien, Bouchard to Address Nation." *Globe and Mail,* 25 Oct.

Millard, G. 1999. "The Secession Reference and National Reconciliation: A Critical

View." *Canadian Journal of Law & Society* 14, no. 2 (Fall): 1–19.

Monahan, P.J. 1997. *Constitutional Law.* Concord: Irwin Law.

Moore, M. (ed.). 1998. *National Self-Determination and Secession.* Oxford: Oxford University Press.

O'Neill, P. 1991. "Bourassa choisit d'abord le Canada." *Le Devoir,* 11 Mar.

———. 1995. "Bouchard entraîne le Bloc dans son 'virage'." *Le Devoir,* 10 Apr.

———. 1995. "L'UQAM se dissocie des propos de Garcia." *Le Devoir,* 27 Sept.

———. 1996. "Pas d'élections avant longtemps." *Le Devoir,* 17 Jan.

———. 1996. "Les discours des ténors fédéraux irritent Johnson." *Le Devoir,* 2 Feb.

Paré, J. 1995. "Noui au Canada; Non à Ottawa." *L'Actualité,* 15 Mar.

Parizeau, J. 1996. "Si le Québec avait dit Oui." *Le Devoir,* 22 Feb.

Parti libéral du Québec. 1991. *Un Québec libre de ses choix.* Rapport du Comité constitutionnel. 28 Jan.

Patten, A. 2014. *Equal Recognition: The Moral Foundations of Minority Rights.* Princeton: Princeton University Press.

Philpott, P. 1998. "Self-Determination in Practice." In Moore (ed.), *National Self-Determination and Secession.* Oxford: Oxford University Press.

La Presse. 1996. "Chrétien devrait s'attacher à améliorer le fédéralisme." 28 Sept.

Quebec. 1991. *Rapport de la Commission sur l'avenir politique et constitutionnel du Québec.* Quebec City: Secrétariat de la Commission.

———. National Assembly. 1994. An Act Respecting the Sovereignty of Quebec, 1st session, 35th Legislature, Bill. *Journal des débats.* Various years.

———. 2000. An Act Respecting the Exercise of the Fundamental Rights and Prerogatives of the Québec People and the Québec State, 1st session, 36th Legislature, Bill no. 99.

Radmilovic, Y. 2010. "Strategic Legitimacy Cultivation as the Supreme Court of Canada: Quebec Secession Reference and Beyond." *Canadian Journal of Political Science* 43, no. 4 (Dec.).

Rocher, F. 1992. "Le Dossier constitutionnel: l'année des consultations et des valse-hesitations." In D. Moniere (ed.), *L'année politique au Québec, 1991.* Montreal: Québec/Amérique.

———. 1995. "Les aléas de la stratégie pré-référendaire: chronique d'une mort annoncée." In D.M. Brown and J.W. Rose (eds), *Canada: The State of the Federation 1995.* Kingston: Institute of Intergovernmental Relations, Queen's University.

Rocher, F., and N. Verrelli. 2003. "Questioning Constitutional Democracy in Canada." In Gagnon (eds.), *The Conditions of Diversity in Multinational Democracies.* Montreal: Institute for Research on Public Policy.

Rose, J. 1995. "Beginning to Think about the Next Referendum." Occasional paper, Faculty of Law, University of Toronto, 21 Nov.

Russell, P.H. 2004. *Constitutional Odyssey: Can Canadians Become a Sovereign People?* 3rd edn. Toronto: University of Toronto Press.

Ryan, C. 2000. "Consequences of the Quebec Secession Reference," *C.D. Howe Institute Commentary,* no. 139, Apr.

Séguin, R. 1996. "Federalists Split Over Call for Court Ruling." *Globe and Mail,* 28 Sept.

Spain. 1978. *Spanish Constitution.*

Supreme Court of Canada. 1998. Re: Secession of Quebec. 2 S.C.R. 217.

Taillon, P. 2014. "De la clarté à l'arbitraire: le contrôle de la question et des résultats référendaires par le parlement canadien." *Revista d'Estudis Autonòmics i Federals* 20 (Oct.): 13–59.

Tierney, S. 2003. "The Constitutional Accommodation of National Minorities in the United Kingdom and Canada." In A.-G. Gagnon, M. Guibernau, and F. Rocher (eds), *The Conditions of Diversity in Multinational Democracies.* Montreal: Institute for Research on Public Policy.

Tobin, B. 2002. *All in Good Time.* Toronto: Penguin.

Turpel, M.E. 1992. "Does the Road to Quebec Sovereignty Run through Aboriginal Territory?" In D. Drache and R. Perin (eds), *Negotiating with a Sovereign Quebec.* Toronto: Lorimer.

Vastel, M. 1996. *Lucien Bouchard: en attendant la suite.* Outremont: Lanctôt.

Venne, M. 1996. "Qu'aurait dit Parizeau si le OUI l'avait emporté?" *Le Devoir,* 18 Feb.

———. 1996. "67 p. cent des Québécois sont profondément attachés au Canada." *Le Devoir,* 3 Oct.

Whitaker, R. 1996. "Thinking about the Unthinkable: Planning for a Possible Secession." *Constitutional Forum constitutionnel* 7, nos 2 and 3 (Winter–Spring): 58–64.
Winsor, H. 1995. "Poll Disputes No Rally's Success." *Globe and Mail,* 11 Nov.
Winsor, H., and E. Greenspon. 1996. "Hard Line on Separatism Popular Outside Quebec." *Globe and Mail,* 16 Nov.
———, and T.T. Ha. 1995. "Chrétien Signals New Resolve on Quebec." *Globe and Mail,* 12 Dec.
Wright, R. 2014. *The Night Canada Stood Still: How the 1995 Quebec Referendum Nearly Cost Us Our Country.* Toronto: Harper Collins.
Young, R. 1995. *The Secession of Quebec and the Future of Canada.* Montreal and Kingston: McGill-Queen's University Press.
———. 1999. *The Struggle for Quebec.* Montreal and Kingston: McGill-Queen's University Press.

Chapter Eight

Angus Reid Institute. 2016. "What Makes Us Canadians? A Study of Values, Beliefs, Priorities and Identity." 3 Oct.
Azzi, S. 2014. "Commission of Inquiry into the Sponsorship Program and Advertising Agencies." *Canadian Encyclopedia,* 3 July.
Baillargeon, S. 2017 "Québec solidaire gruge des appuis au Parti québécois." *Le Devoir,* 18 Mar.
Bélair-Cirino, M., et al. 2017. "Le PQ, 'un parti figé, conservateur et vieillissant,' selon St-Pierre Plamondon." *Le Devoir,* 9 Feb.
———. 2017. "Pour Manon Massé, "Le Parti québécois n'est pas raciste." *Le Devoir,* 30 May.
———. 2017. "Couillard, entre idéalisme et réalisme constitutionnel." *Le Devoir,* 2 June.
Bélanger, É. and C. Chhim. 2016. "National Identity and Support for Sovereignty in Quebec." In Gervais, Kirkey, and Rudy (eds), *Quebec Questions: Quebec Studies for the Twenty-First Century.* Don Mills, ON: Oxford University Press.
Bellavance, J-D. 2017. "Le débat constitutionnel est une distraction, selon Trudeau." *La Presse,* 5 June.
Bryden, J. 2008. "Ignatieff Rules Out Quebec Nation in Constitution." *Canadian Press,* 18 Dec.
———. 2014. "Roy Romanow on 'Unity Bill': 50-Plus-One Not Sufficient to Break Up Country." *Canadian Press,* 4 Apr.
Buzzetti, H. 2017. "Le Québec signe à son tour une entente sur les transferts en santé." *Le Devoir,* 11 Mar.
———. 2017. "Québec obtiendra 88 millions par année pour offrir un soutien direct aux familles." *Le Devoir,* 13 June.
Canada, Prime Minister's Office. 1996. *Speech from the Throne,* 27 Feb.
———. House of Commons. 1995. "Resolution Respecting the Recognition of Quebec as a Distinct Society. *Journals,* 1st session, 35th Parliament, no. 273, 11 Dec., 2232.
———. 1996. "An Act Respecting Constitutional Amendments." *Statutes of Canada 1996,* 1st session, 35th Parliament, C-110.
———. 2006. "Québécois as Nation resolution." *Official Report (Hansard),* 24 Nov., 39th Parliament, 1st Session, Vol. 141, No.086.
———. 2013. "An Act Respecting Democratic Constitutional Change," Bill C-470.
Canadian Press. 2011. "Charest Wants Quebec Recognized as Nation." 14 Aug.
Cameron, D.R. 2012. "Quebec and the Canadian Federation." In Bakvis and Skogstad (eds), *Canadian Federalism: Performance, Effectiveness and Legitimacy.* Don Mills, ON: Oxford University Press.
Caron, J., and G. Laforest. 2009. "Canada and Multinational Federalism: From the Spirit of 1982 to Stephen Harper's Open Federalism." *Nationalism and Ethnic Politics* 15, no. 1: 27–55.
Castonguay, A. 2014. "L'attachement au Canada grimpe chez les jeunes." *Le Devoir,* 23 Nov.
CBC News Online. 2005. "Gomery Report: Liberals' Worst Fears." 1 Nov.
Choudhri, S. 2009. "Bills of Rights as Instruments of Nation Building." In Kelly and Manfredi (eds), *Contested Constitutionalism.* Vancouver: UBC Press.
Collins, E. 2017. "Coming into Its Own? Canada's Council of the Federation, 2003–16." *IRPP Insight,* no. 15 (Mar.): 1–20.
Commission of Inquiry into the Sponsorship Program and Advertising Activities. 2005. *Who Is Responsible? Fact Finding Report,* 1 Nov.
Conservative Party. 2005. "Harper annonce le programme conservateur pour le Québec." 19 Dec.

Coyne, A. 2017. "Globe Editorial: Reopen the Constitution? No Thank You." *Globe and Mail*, 1 June.

———. 2017. "Meech Lake, Again? How About We Just Don't," *National Post*, 2 June.

CROP. 2017. "Politique au Québec: Perceptions des Québécois." Jan. 2017. Montreal: CROP.

Dacey, E. and L. Glowacki. 2017. "Manitoba Final Province to Sign Health-Care Pact with Feds." *CBC News*, 21 Aug.

Le Devoir. 1996. "Chrétien fait des ouvertures." 31 May.

Dion, J. 1996. "Un Bureau d'information vantera les vertus du Canada." *Le Devoir*, 10 July.

Dion, S. 1996. "The Constitution Must Recognize Quebec's 'Special Distinction'." *Globe and Mail*, 26 Jan.

Dunn, C. 2016. "Harper without Jeers, Trudeau without Cheers: Assessing 10 Years of Intergovernmental Relations." Institute of Research on Public Policy, *Insight*, no. 8 (Sept.): 3.

Erickson, L., and D. Laycock. 2015. "The NDP and Quebec." In Laycock and Erickson (eds), *Reviving Social Democracy: The Near Death and Surprising Rise of the Federal NDP*. Vancouver: UBC Press.

Fidler, R. 2006. "A 'Québécois Nation': Harper Fuels an Important Debate." *The Bullet: Socialist Project*, E-bulletin, no. 40, 18 Dec.

Fragasso-Marquis, V. 2017. "Les jeunes péquistes refusent de revenir à la charte des valeurs." *Le Devoir*, 20 Feb.

Gagnon, A., and H. Segal (eds). 2000. *The Canadian Social Union without Quebec: 8 Critical Analyses*. Montreal: Institute for Research on Public Policy.

Gagnon, K. 2014. "Les jeunes et la souveraineté: la génération 'Non'," *La Presse*, 2 June.

Galloway, G. 2017. "Health Accord Nearly Sealed as Ontario, Quebec, Alberta Reach Deals." *Globe & Mail*, 10 Mar.

Goldenberg, E. 2006. *The Way It Works: Inside Ottawa*. Toronto: McClelland & Stewart.

Gordon, S. 2006. "Sounding Like his Father, Justin Trudeau Takes Aim at Michael Ignatieff's Idea of Quebec as a 'Nation'." *Toronto Star*, 27 Oct.

Graefe, P., and R. Laforest. 2007. "Le Grande Seduction: Wooing Quebec." In Doern (ed.), *How Ottawa Spends, 2007–8: The Harper Conservatives: Climate of Change*. Montreal and Kingston: McGill-Queen's University Press.

Gregg, A. 2005. "Quebec's Final Victory." *The Walrus*, Feb.: 50–61.

Guay, J.-H. 2017. "Sovereignty at an Impasse: The Highs and Lows of Quebec Nationalism." *IRPP Insight*, no. 18, Oct.

Harper, S. et al. 2001. "The Alberta agenda." Available at: *http://policyoptions.irpp.org/magazines/western-alienation/the-alberta-agenda*.

Health Canada. 2004. "Health Care System: Asymmetrical Federalism that Respects Quebec's Jurisdiction." 15 Sept.

Hébert, C. 2017. "Parti québécois the author of its own misfortune." *Toronto Star*, 1 Nov.

Hébert, C., and J. Lapierre. 2014. *The Morning After: The 1995 Quebec Referendum and the Day That Almost Was*. Toronto: Alfred A. Knopf Canada.

L'Heureux-Dubé, C. 2006. "Débat au Parti libéral: Le Québec nation? Il y a, c'est certain, une meilleure avenue!" *Le Devoir*, 13 Nov.

Ibbitson, J. 2015. *Stephen Harper*. Toronto: McClelland & Stewart.

Johnson, W. 2007. *Stephen Harper and the Future of Canada*. Toronto: McClelland & Stewart.

Laforest, G. 2016. "Stephen Harper, Michael Ignatieff and the Recognition that (Québec-the Québécois-Quebeckers) Form a Nation/Within a United Canada." Paper presented to the Canadian Political Science Association, 31 May–2 June, 16–24.

Langlois, S. 2015. "L'appui à la souveraineté du Québec de 1995 à aujourd'hui." *Colloque: La démocratie référendaire*. Université Laval. 30 Oct.

———. 2015. "L'appui à l'indépendance du Québec en déclin." *Regards sur la société*, 17 Nov.

Léger/*Le Devoir*. 2017. "La politique provinciale au Québec," 2 Dec. Available at https://www.ledevoir.com/documents/pdf/sondage_polqc052018.pdf.

———. 2017. "La politique fédérale au Québec," 2 Dec. Available at: http://leger360.com/admin/upload/publi_pdf/La%20politique%20f%C3%A9d%C3%A9rale%20au%20Qu%C3%A9bec_Ao%C3%BBt%202017-%20FR%20FED.pdf.

Lemieux, V. 2011. *Les partis générationnels au Québec: passé, présent, avenir*. Quebec: Presses de l'Université Laval.

Lenihan, D.G. 2006. "Reconstituting the 'Nation': What Ignatieff Really Needs to Recognize about Quebec." *Options*, Nov.

Lessard, D. 2014. "Sondage: l'idée d'un référendum n'a pas la cote." *La Presse*, 18 Mar.

Levine, M.V. 1990. *The Reconquest of Montreal: Language Policy and Social Change in a Bilingual Society*. Philadelphia: Temple University Press.

McGrane, D. 2013. "One-Off Federalism." In C. Stoney and G.B. Doern (eds), *How Ottawa Spends: 2013–2014*. Montreal and Kingston: McGill-Queen's University Press.

McGregor, J. 2017. "'We Are Not Opening the Constitution': Trudeau Pans Quebec's Plans." *CBC News*, 1 June.

Mahéo, V.-A., and É. Bélanger. 2016. "Is the Parti Québécois Bound to Disappear? A Study of the Generational Dynamics of Electoral Behaviour in Contemporary Quebec." Paper for presentation to conference on "The State of Democratic Citizenship in Canada," Centre for the Study of Democratic Citizenship, Montreal, 23–24 Sept., and Annual Meeting of the American Political Science Association, Philadelphia, 1–4 Sept.

Marotte, B. 2014. "Signing Constitution Not on Quebec Premier's Agenda." *Globe and Mail*, 7 Sept.

Marquis, M. 2017. "Non à un débat sémantique sur la Constitution, dit Trudeau." *La Presse*, 6 June.

Montpetit, É. 2007. *Le fédéralisme d'ouverture: la recherche d'une légitimité canadienne au Québec*. Quebec: Septentrion.

Morton, F.L. 1995. "Why Chretien's Proposal Won't Wash in the West." *Globe and Mail*, 30 Nov.

New Democratic Party. 2005. Quebec Section of the NDP General Council. "Québec's Voice and a Choice for a Different Canada."

Noël, A. 2004. "Déblocages?" *Options politiques*, Nov.

———. 2009. "Balance and Imbalance in the Division of Financial Resources." In Gagnon (ed.), *Contemporary Canadian Federalism: Foundations, Traditions, Institutions*. Toronto: University of Toronto Press.

———. 2011. *Asymmetry at Work: Quebec's Distinct Implementation of Programs for the Unemployed*. Toronto: Mowat Centre for Policy Innovation.

———. 2016. "The Land Where We First Loved." *Policy Options*, 7 Oct.

O'Neill, J. 2006. "Author of Grit Quebec Nation Resolution Victim of Good Intention." *CanWest News*, 9 Nov.

O'Neill, P. 1998. "The Calgary Declaration." Ted Glenn, Research Officer, Ontario Legislative Library. Legislative Research Service.

Ontario Radio-Canada. 2015 "Plaidoyer de Philippe Couillard pour un fédéralisme coopératif." 11 May.

Parkin, A., E. Hartmann, and K. Alwani. 2017. *Portraits 2017: A Fresh Look at Public Opinion and Federalism*. Toronto: Mowat Centre.

Parti libéral du Québec. 2001. *Un projet pour le Québec: affirmation, autonomie et leadership*, Rapport final. Montreal: Parti libéral du Québec.

Pelletier, R. 2014. "Les relations fédérales–provinciales sous le gouvernement Harper." In Castro-Rea and Boily (eds), *Le fédéralisme selon Harper: la place du Québec dans le Canada conservateur*. Quebec: Presses de l'Université Laval.

Perreaux, L. 2017. "Some Indigenous groups embrace Quebec's proposal to reopen Constitution." *Globe and Mail*, 4 June.

Quebec, Government of Quebec. 2017. *Our Way of Being Canadian: Policy on Québec Affirmation and Canadian Relations, [official translation of Québécois: notre façon d'être Canadiens]*. https://www.sqrc.gouv.qc.ca/documents/relations-canadiennes/politique-affirmation-en.pdf.

Rabson, M. 2016. "Pallister Holds Out on Carbon Pricing Deal." *Winnipeg Free Press*, 19 Dec.

Radio-Canada.ca. 2015. "Trudeau ne voit aucune raison de rouvrir la Constitution." 17 Dec.

———. 2017. "Couillard veut relancer le dialogue entre les peoples fondateurs." 1 June.

Rocher, F., and P. Cousineau-Morin. 2011. "Fédéralisme asymétrique et reconnaissance des nations internes au Canada." In Seymour and Laforest (eds), *Le fédéralisme multinational: un modèle viable?* Brussels: Peter Lang.

Rioux Ouimet, H. 2014. "Quebec and Canadian Fiscal Federalism: From Tremblay to Séguin and Beyond." *Canadian Journal of Political Science* 47, no. 1 (Mar.): 47–69.

Rocher, F. 2014. "The Orange Wave: A (Re)Canadianization of the Quebec

Electorate?" In Verrelli (ed.), *Canada: The State of the Federation, the Changing Federal Environment: Rebalancing Roles?* Institute of Intergovernmental Relations, Queen's University. Montreal and Kingston: McGill-Queen's University Press.

Rocher, F., and P. Cousineau-Morin. 2011. "Fédéralisme asymétrique et reconnaissance des nations internes au Canada." In Seymour and Laforest (eds), *Le fédéralisme multinational: un modèle viable?* Brussels: Peter Lang.

Rocher, F., and B. Pelletier (eds). 2013. *Le nouvel ordre constitutionnel canadien: du rapatriement de 1982 à nos jours*. Quebec: Presses de l'Université du Québec.

Russell, P.H. 2004. *Constitutional Odyssey: Can Canadians Become a Sovereign People?* 3rd edn. Toronto: University of Toronto Press.

Seidle, F.L., and G. Bishop. 2005. "Public Opinion on Asymmetrical Federalism: Growing Openness or Continuing Ambiguity?" Asymmetry Series 2005, Institute of Intergovernmental Relations, Queen's University.

Thomas, P. 2017. "Let's Make a Deal: Time for Pallister's Health-Care Troublemaking to End." *CBC News*, 3 Apr.

Trudeau, J. 2015. "We Beat Fear with Hope." 20 Oct. Retrieved from http://www.macleans.ca/politics/ottawa/justin-trudeau-for-the-record-we-beat-fear-with-hope/.

Venne, M. 1996. "Chrétien se libère de l'échéance de 1997." *Le Devoir*, 23 June.

Winsor, H. 1996. "Quebeckers Prefer Canada 2–1, Poll Says." *Globe and Mail*, 26 Mar.

———. 1996. "Ottawa Caught Short by Flag Fever." *Globe and Mail*, 29 Aug.

Yakabuski, K. 2017. "Quebec is Right to Reopen a Constitutional Discussion." *Globe and Mail*, 2 June.

Zilio, M. 2017. "Ottawa Signs Child-Care Deal Targeting Families in Need." *Globe and Mail*, 12 June.

Chapter Nine

Bellavance, J.-D. 2017. "Le débat constitutionnel est une distraction, selon Trudeau." *La Presse*, 5 June.

Borrows, J. 2002. *Recovering Canada: The Resurgence of Indigenous Law*. Toronto: University of Toronto Press.

———. 2016. *Freedom and Indigenous Constitutionalism*. Toronto: University of Toronto Press.

Cameron, D., and R. Simeon (eds). 2009. *Language Matters: How Canadian Voluntary Associations Manage French and English*. Vancouver: UBC Press.

Coburn, V. 2017. "Indigenous Peoples and the Constitutional Conversation." *Policy Options politiques*, 9 June.

Crête, M. 2017. "Recul du français comme langue de travail principale au Québec." *Le Devoir*, 29 Nov.

Foran, C. 2017. "The Canadian Experiment: Is This the World's First 'Postnational' Country?" *The Guardian*, 4 Jan.

Fournier, J.-M. 2018. "L'écho à la politique d'affirmation du Québec: la relation Québec–Canada ne se résume pas qu'à celle de deux solitudes." *Le Devoir*, 6 Jan.

Kymlicka, W. 1998. *Finding Our Way: Rethinking Ethnocultural Relations in Canada*. Toronto: Oxford University Press.

———. 2001. *Politics in the Vernacular: Nationalism, Multiculturalism and Citizenship*. New York: Oxford University Press.

Labbé, S. 2017. "Why the UN's Declaration on Indigenous Rights Has Been Slow to Implement in Canada." *Open Canada*, 21 July.

Litt, P. 2016. *Trudeaumania*. Vancouver: UBC Press.

McRoberts, K. 2001. "Canada and the Multinational State." *Canadian Journal of Political Science* 34, no. 4 (Dec.): 683–713.

———. 2009. "Les politiques de la langue au Canada: un combat contre la territorialisation." In Lacorne and Judt (eds), *La politique de Babel: du monolinguisme d'Etat au plurilinguisme des peuples*. Paris: Karthala.

Marquis, M. 2017. "Non à un débat sémantique sur la Constitution, dit Trudeau." *La Presse*, 6 June.

Noël, A. 2017. Résignés, notre façon d'être fédéralistes." *Policy Options politiques*, 9 June.

Panagos, Dimitrios. 2016. *Uncertain Accommodation: Aboriginal Identity and Group Rights in the Supreme Court of Canada*. Vancouver: UBC Press.

Robertson, G. 2000. *Memoirs of a Very Civil Servant: Mackenzie King to Pierre Trudea*. Toronto: University of Toronto Press.

Russell, P.H. 2017. *Canada's Odyssey: A Country Based on Incomplete Conquests*. Toronto: University of Toronto Press.

Schertzer, R., and E. Taylor Woods. 2011. "Beyond multinational Canada,"

Commonwealth and Comparative Politics, 49, No. 2: 192–222.

Seymour, M., and G. Laforest (eds). 2011. *Le fédéralisme multinational: un modèle viable?* Brussels: Peter Lang.

Sioui, M.-M. 2017. "Couillard se dit favorable à l'auto-détermination des Premières Nations." *Le Devoir*, 28 June.

———. 2018. "Constitution: le ROC reste sourd aux appels de Couillard." *Le Devoir*, 4 Jan.

Tasker, J.P. 2018. "Trudeau Promises New Legal Framework to Indigenous People." *CBC News*, 14 Feb.

Webber, J. 1994. *Reimagining Canada: Language, Culture, Community and the Canadian Constitution*. Montreal and Kingston: McGill-Queen's University Press.

Woods, E. 2012. "Beyond Multination Federations: Reflections on Nations and Nationalism in Canada." *Ethnicities* 12, no. 3 (June), 270–92.

Index